TAKING SIDES

Clashing Views in

Death and Dying

TAKING SIDES

Clashing Views in

Death and Dying

Selected, Edited, and with Introductions by

William J. Buckley
Seattle University

and

Karen S. Feldt
Seattle University

Mc Graw Hill   *Connect Learn Succeed*™

TAKING SIDES: CLASHING VIEWS IN DEATH AND DYING

Published by McGraw-Hill, a business unit of The McGraw-Hill Companies, Inc., 1221 Avenue of the Americas, New York, NY 10020. Copyright © 2013 by The McGraw-Hill Companies, Inc. All rights reserved. Printed in the United States of America. No part of this publication may be reproduced or distributed in any form or by any means, or stored in a database or retrieval system, without the prior written consent of The McGraw-Hill Companies, Inc., including, but not limited to, in any network or other electronic storage or transmission, or broadcast for distance learning.

Some ancillaries, including electronic and print components, may not be available to customers outside the United States.

Taking Sides® is a registered trademark of the McGraw-Hill Companies, Inc.
Taking Sides is published by the **Contemporary Learning Series** group within the McGraw-Hill Higher Education division.

1 2 3 4 5 6 7 8 9 0 DOC/DOC 1 0 9 8 7 6 5 4 3 2

MHID: 0-07-805039-1
ISBN: 978-0-07-805039-8
ISSN: 2164-9944 (print)
ISSN: 2164-9952 (online)

Managing Editor: *Larry Loeppke*
Sr Developmental Editor: *Dave Welsh*
Senior Permissions Coordinator: *Shirley Lanners*
Senior Marketing Communications Specialist: *Mary Klein*
Project Manager: *Erin Melloy*
Design Coordinator: *Brenda A. Rolwes*
Cover Graphics: *Rick D. Noel*
Buyer: *Nicole Baumgartner*
Media Project Manager: *Sridevi Palani*

Compositor: MPS Limited
Cover Images: © PhotoLink/PhotoDisc/Getty Images RF

Editors/Academic Advisory Board

Members of the Academic Advisory Board are instrumental in the final selection of articles for each edition of TAKING SIDES. Their review of articles for content, level, and appropriateness provides critical direction to the editors and staff. We think that you will find their careful consideration well reflected in this volume.

TAKING SIDES: Clashing Views in DEATH AND DYING

EDITORS

William J. Buckley
Seattle University

Karen S. Feldt
Seattle University

ACADEMIC ADVISORY BOARD MEMBERS

Editors/Academic Advisory Board continued

Preface

Crucial end-of-life decisions that are personally meaningful and publicly debated are examined in this new volume. *Taking Sides: Clashing Views in Death and Dying* features 18 closed-end (Yes–No) questions organized to challenge readers in debates about the critical issues and decisions related to death and dying. The text highlights important articles and some cutting-edge research that have been specially selected to provide point-counterpoint readings. The introductions provide insight into the controversial topics related to dying, and the questions for critical thinking are established at the end of each issue to assist readers in understanding and discussing critical areas. This work reaches across issues, professions, and cultures. It provides a look at death and dying from clinical, ethical, legal, and policy perspectives.

Our focus on practical questions creates a text that is of special interest to those in general studies in humanities and social sciences, as well as pre-professional and professional programs. These include law, nursing, medicine, anthropology, sociology, political science, liberal studies, theology, and religious studies. The selected topics are designed to help readers understand that the challenges and possibilities for good humane dying are also a matter of justice. We approach some of the difficult questions: Does Depression Make End-of-Life Decisions Untrustworthy? (Issue 1); Does Too Much Treatment Result in an Inhumane Dying? (Issue 7); Does a Dying Person with Severe Pain Have a Right to Effective Pain Management? (Issue 5); Should Pain Be Alleviated if It Hastens Death? (Issue 6); Can Legal Suicide Really Safeguard Against Abuse? (Issue 11); When is someone dead? (Issue 13: Is Brain Death Dead Enough?); Is It Better to Die in Hospice Than Hospitals (Issue 14); Is Dying Improved by Belonging to a Religious Community Rather Than Simply Being a Spiritual Person? (Issue 16). The Internet reference page that begins each unit offers relevant Internet site addresses (URLs) that provide connections to organizations, documentaries, and resources that should help to further engage the student discussions.

A Word to the Instructor This publication adds to a series currently composed of more than 50 titles in many disciplines under multiple editions (Taking Sides). As a new edition, we encourage instructors to use the *Instructor's Manual with Test Questions* (multiple choice and essay), which is available through the publisher. In addition, we encourage instructors who have access to online library resources, to examine the resource articles listed in the reference list. There is a general guidebook available through the publisher called *Using Taking Sides in the Classroom*, which discusses methods and techniques for instruction of the opposing points of view. The online version of *Using Taking Sides in the Classroom* is also available. These approaches and resources can help enhance students' grasp of the depth and breadth of the debate in these critical areas.

Acknowledgments   We would like to extend our appreciation to the faculty colleagues who assisted with advice on the manuscript: Kathleen B., Jim B., Dan S., Ed P., Carol T., Linda G., Kathryn T., Charles P., Lisa C., Stanley H., James G., William S., and Rosalie, B., and to student research assistants who helped with literature searches and final review of the references: Molly Mullen, Maria Hanelin, Lisa Wheeler, Jacqueline Hermer, and Joy Lee.

Finally, we would like to thank our families: Mary Beth, Grace, my students and those whose dying has taught me so much about living together. We would also like to thank Ruth, Philip, Jordan, and all of those patients and families who have taught me about death and dying.

William J. Buckley
Seattle University

Karen Feldt
Seattle University

Contents in Brief

Contents

Benjamin Brody, a psychiatry resident physician, offers a discussion of cases he was called to evaluate for decisional capacity because of concerns about depression impairing decisional capacity. He demonstrates that each case must be uniquely approached and that in some cases depression can impair decisions related to end-of-life care. The National Ethics Committee of the Veterans Health Administration warns against using a single diagnosis as a criterion for the lack of decisional capacity. Instead they provide guidelines on what persons should be able to understand about their specific treatment in order to have decisional capacity.

University of Michigan physicians Silveira, Kim, and Langa found that if older adults had advance directives, the end-of-life care that they received was strongly associated with their previously stated preferences. In their study, about 25 percent of older adults were decisionally incapacitated at the end of life and required a surrogate decision-maker. The study found that those who had advance directives (AD) received care that was consistent with their previously expressed preferences. Professor of geriatric ethics in the Netherlands C. M. P. M. Hertogh argues that despite their history in enabling "prospective autonomy," many problems emerge for ADs. These include low frequency, low compliance, low adherence, changing preferences, unstable health, and a "disability paradox" that people change their minds as their health changes. To resolve potential conflicts between prior values of a competent person and best interests of one later incapacitated, he suggests patients shift instead to an ongoing dialogue between doctor and patient.

Kathryn L. Tucker, the Director of Legal Affairs for the Compassion and Choices in Seattle, discusses the case of Lester Tomlinson, an 85-year-old patient dying of cancer whose family was successful in reaching an agreement after a lawsuit against the hospital and health providers for inadequate pain treatment. Brushwood (2004) and Johnson (2004) qualify Tucker's claims. Rodney Syme argues that it is surprising that under current laws more physicians are not prosecuted for homicide when delivering high doses of pain medications at the end of life. He identifies a need for a defense for medical homicide based on the necessity to relieve pain.

Richard A. Mularski, a physician from the Center for Health Research at Kaiser Permanente Northwest, and colleagues from around the country discuss palliative care and end-of-life care in the intensive care unit. They identify that the intent of pain medications in this setting is the relief of pain and suffering, even if the possibility exists that these treatments will hasten death. Charles L. Sprung, MD, JD, a physician, lawyer, and professor at Haddasah University Hospital, in Jerusalem, writes with colleagues from around the world about their concerns with treatments and medications in the ICU that actively shorten the dying process. They raise concerns about the lack of distinction between alleviating suffering and active euthanasia and that inappropriately large doses of pain medications may be given to hasten death "in the guise" of relieving pain and suffering.

In the Afterword of her book, medical journalist Shannon Brownlee offers a poignant story of an elderly man with an implanted small battery-powered electrical impulse generator to correct an irregular heartbeat (called an implanted cardiac defibrillator or ICD). She raises serious concerns about whether we can sustain a "do everything" approach in health care, and what this means for end of life care. Amanda Bennett, an executive editor with Bloomberg News, and Charles Babcock, editor-at-large for *InformationWeek*, write about Mrs. Bennett's experience of the last years of her husband's life. She balances the discussion of the costs of his care with the value of his last years of life, the important family events and experiences that made it worth it to go through expensive treatments.

Allen Sandler, an associate professor for special education, offers a case that demonstrates that nutrition and hydration were inappropriately viewed as futile treatment in a person with disabilities who was not truly terminal. He argues that persons with disabilities must have access to the same life-sustaining treatment as provided to those without a disability, including feeding tubes, and that decisions about futility must be carefully considered. David Orentlicher, professor of law, and Christopher Callahan, a physician, present the historical underpinnings of feeding tubes and how laws have allowed withholding or withdrawing feeding tubes in persons with serious or terminal illnesses. They provide evidence that allowing refusals of tube feedings has not led to the slippery slope of requiring tube feeding removals as once feared. Rather, there continues to be an overuse of feeding tubes in persons with terminal diseases.

According to Nathan Goldstein, Associate Professor of Geriatrics and Palliative Medicine at Mount Sinai Hospital in New York, and colleagues, physicians viewed deactivating implanted cardiac defibrillators (ICD) differently than withdrawal of other life-sustaining treatments; physicians also expressed discomfort in approaching this discussion with patients or family members. Daniel P. Sulmasy, a Franciscan friar, ethicist, and physician at the University of Chicago Medical Center, discusses the ethics of withdrawing futile treatments, and establishes the difference between forgoing a life-sustaining treatment (such as deactivating an ICD) and the intent implied in the word "killing."

UNIT 4 ASSISTED SUICIDE 251

Katrina Hedberg, the Oregon State Epidemiologist, Public Health Division, and colleagues discuss the characteristics of persons who have taken action under the Oregon Death with Dignity Act. These authors found that most of the dying patients who requested medications to end their lives felt a strong need for autonomy and control. Susan Wolf, the McKnight Presidential Professor of Law, Medicine & Public Policy at the University of Minnesota, discusses her long-standing opposition to physician-assisted suicide and reflects on how her father's death challenged that view.

Ronald Lindsay, a lawyer and CEO of the Center for Inquiry, reviews the first decade of the Oregon Death with Dignity Act and identifies that key ethical and legal concerns raised by opponents are addressed with legal protections put into place. Cofounder of the Hastings Research Center, Daniel Callahan argues that advocates for physician-assisted suicide describe what they do in confusing terms and prescribe regulations without adequate public scrutiny.

Margaret Battin, a philosopher and ethicist from the University of Utah, argues that clinical practices of palliative sedation and euthanasia are conceptually alike yet different in ways that generate public debates concerning distinctions between misuses and abuses of palliative sedation. The National Ethics Committee of the Veterans Health Administration outlines guidelines for palliative sedation as an approach of last resort for dying patients with intolerable symptoms.

UNIT 5   DETERMINING DEFINITIONS OF DEATH   353

Eun-Kyoung Choi and colleagues at the Charles Warren Fairbanks Center for Medical Ethics in Indianapolis review the current definitions and call for national standard for brain death that would eliminate uncertainty across hospitals, states, and jurisdictions. Kristin Zeiler, a medical ethicist, argues that the definitions of whole brain death as the irreversible cessation of "all" functions of the brain is limiting, because it doesn't embrace other biological possibilities of death. She discusses the need to link death definitions with operational criteria and the specific tests that can measure those criteria when someone has died.

Maryjo Prince-Paul of the Francis Payne Bolton School of Nursing at Case Western discusses the hospice model of care and the criteria that need to be met to enroll in hospice. David Crippen, a physician in the Department of Critical Care at the University of Pittsburgh Medical Center, presents a roundtable discussion with physicians around the world who have very different views about how to approach the care of a dying patient who is using an expensive intensive care resource at the end of life.

In a National Bureau of Economic Research paper, researchers Samuel Marshall and Jonathan Skinner of the Department of Economics at Dartmouth College and Kathleen McGarry of the Department of Economics at UCLA discuss the out-of-pocket costs for hospital and nursing home care at the end of life and how these can be a drain on households even though elders have some subsidized medical care through Medicare. Li-Wei Chao and José A. Pagán of the University of Pennsylvania and Beth J. Soldo of the University of Texas Pan Am identify that older adults were more likely to want expensive end-of-life treatments if they were subsidized by Medicare, but less likely to want treatments if survival chances were poor or their spouse would be impoverished by their care.

Robert Kastenbaum, Professor Emeritus of Gerontology and Communications at University of Arizona at Tempe, discusses the historic and current reasons why the rituals of funerals are important to those who mourn. Nicholas Köhler, a writer/journalist with *Maclean's,* a national news magazine in Canada, discusses inadequacies in Kübler-Ross's five stages of grieving as protective bereavement, and relates newer research by George Bonanno that indicates how individuals have unique grieving processes that include elements of constructive resilience.

Correlation Guide

The *Taking Sides* series presents current issues in a debate-style format designed to stimulate student interest and develop critical thinking skills. Each issue is thoughtfully framed with an issue summary, an issue introduction, and a section on exploring the issue. The pro and con essays—selected for their liveliness and substance—represent the arguments of leading scholars and commentators in their fields.

Taking Sides: Clashing Views in Death and Dying is an easy-to-use reader that presents issues on important topics such as *assisted suicide, cost of care, coping, and ethical decisions*. For more information on *Taking Sides* and other *McGraw-Hill Contemporary Learning Series* titles, visit www.mhhe.com/cls.

This convenient guide matches the issues in **Taking Sides: Clashing Views in Death and Dying** with the corresponding chapters in our best-selling McGraw-Hill Death and Dying textbook by DeSpelder/Strickland.

Taking Sides: Clashing Views in Death and Dying	The Last Dance: Encountering Death and Dying, 9/e by DeSpelder/Strickland
Issue 1: Does Depression Make End-of-Life Decisions Untrustworthy?	**Chapter 6:** End-of-Life Issues and Decisions
Issue 2: Do Advance Directives Improve Care for Those Unable to Make Decisions?	**Chapter 6:** End-of-Life Issues and Decisions
Issue 3: Do Dying Persons Without Advocates Get a Different Quality of Care?	**Chapter 4:** Death Systems: Mortality and Society **Chapter 6:** End-of-Life Issues and Decisions
Issue 4: Compassion Fatigue: Does Burnout Occur in All Caregivers of Dying Patients?	**Chapter 5:** Health Care: Patients, Staff, and Institutions
Issue 5: Does a Dying Person with Severe Pain Have a Right to Effective Pain Management?	**Chapter 5:** Health Care: Patients, Staff, and Institutions
Issue 6: Should Pain Be Alleviated if It Hastens Death?	**Chapter 5:** Health Care: Patients, Staff, and Institutions **Chapter 6:** End-of-Life Issues and Decisions
Issue 7: Does Too Much Treatment Result in an Inhumane Dying?	**Chapter 3:** Perspectives on Death: Cultural and Historical
Issue 8: Are Feeding Tubes Obligatory?	**Chapter 5:** Health Care: Patients, Staff, and Institutions **Chapter 6:** End-of-Life Issues and Decisions
Issue 9: Does Withholding or Withdrawing Futile Treatment Kill People?	**Chapter 6:** End-of-Life Issues and Decisions
Issue 10: May a Dying Person Hasten Her Death?	**Chapter 6:** End-of-Life Issues and Decisions
Issue 11: Can Legal Suicide Really Safeguard Against Abuse?	**Chapter 12:** Suicide

(Continued)

Taking Sides: Clashing Views in Death and Dying	The Last Dance: Encountering Death and Dying, 9/e by DeSpelder/Strickland
Issue 12: Is Palliative Sedation Actually Euthanasia in Disguise?	**Chapter 6:** End-of-Life Issues and Decisions
Issue 13: Is Brain Death Dead Enough?	**Chapter 6:** End-of-Life Issues and Decisions **Chapter 13:** Risks, Perils, and Traumatic Death
Issue 14: Is It Better to Die in Hospice Than Hospitals?	**Chapter 6:** End-of-Life Issues and Decisions
Issue 15: Should Eldercare at the End of Life Be Subsidized?	**Chapter 4:** Death Systems: Mortality and Society
Issue 16: Is Dying Improved by Belonging to a Religious Community Rather Than Simply Being a Spiritual Person?	**Chapter 2:** Learning About Death: The Influence of Sociocultural Forces
Issue 17: Is Dying Made Better by Culturally Competent End-of-Life Care?	**Chapter 6:** End-of-Life Issues and Decisions
Issue 18: Do Funeral Rituals Help Grief?	**Chapter 8:** Last Rites: Funerals and Body Disposition

Topic Guide

This topic guide suggests how the selections in this book relate to the subjects covered in your course. You may want to use the topics listed on these pages to search the Web more easily. All issues and the articles that relate to each topic are listed below in the bold-faced term.

Advance Directives

2. Do Advance Directives Improve Care for Those Unable to Make Decisions?
7. Does Too Much Treatment Result in an Inhumane Dying?
8. Are Feeding Tubes Obligatory?
9. Does Withholding or Withdrawing Futile Treatment Kill People?
14. Is It Better to Die in Hospice Than Hospitals?

Assisted Suicide

5. Does a Dying Person with Severe Pain Have a Right to Effective Pain Management?
10. May a Dying Person Hasten Her Death?
11. Can Legal Suicide Really Safeguard Against Abuse?

Autonomy

1. Does Depression Make End-of-Life Decisions Untrustworthy?
12. Is Palliative Sedation Actually Euthanasia in Disguise?

Bereavement

16. Is Dying Improved by Belonging to a Religious Community Rather Than Simply Being a Spiritual Person?
18. Do Funeral Rituals Help Grief?

Brain Death

13. Is Brain Death Dead Enough?

Brain Injury

13. Is Brain Death Dead Enough?

Burial Practices

18. Do Funeral Rituals Help Grief?

Cancer

6. Should Pain Be Alleviated if It Hastens Death?
10. May a Dying Person Hasten Her Death?
14. Is It Better to Die in Hospice Than Hospitals?

Cardiac Death

13. Is Brain Death Dead Enough?

Communication

17. Is Dying Made Better by Culturally Competent End-of-Life Care?

Compassion Fatigue

4. Compassion Fatigue: Does Burnout Occur in All Caregivers of Dying Patients?

Coping

4. Compassion Fatigue: Does Burnout Occur in All Caregivers of Dying Patients?
16. Is Dying Improved by Belonging to a Religious Community Rather Than Simply Being a Spiritual Person?
18. Do Funeral Rituals Help Grief?

Cost of Care

7. Does Too Much Treatment Result in an Inhumane Dying?
15. Should Eldercare at the End of Life Be Subsidized?
18. Do Funeral Rituals Help Grief?

(Continued)

(Continued)

Introduction

"**C**hristina, please move Mrs. H into her room immediately, she is actively dying." I gestured at the frail older woman in a recliner chair, stationed near the desk, and urgently instructed the licensed practical nurse (LPN) behind the nursing station. The wide-eyed student shadowing me asked a question "How do you know she is dying?" It took moments to think through all of the years of professional experience with dying patients before I could really describe how I "knew" she was dying.

This book collaboratively gives many answers and raises many questions about dying. In my years as a geriatric nurse practitioner, I have often been asked to take students out to the nursing home with me so that they could observe the care that older adults receive in our long-term care system. The student with me that day had not practiced as a registered nurse yet, and had no "hands-on" nursing experience. She was observing my role as a nurse practitioner. Geriatric nurse practitioners provide primary care to older adults in these settings: conduct assessments, physical exams, and write orders for medical and nursing problems. I had seen the deaths of dozens of frail older adults over the years.

How did I know, with just a short observation, that this patient was actively dying? This book provides differing views on the questions about dying that are faced by millions. To know how she was *actively dying*—we had to learn more about decisions she made as she *actively lived among us.*

In the United States, there is a public argument emerging seeking changes to how we die. Mrs. H's dying is just a snapshot of larger realities. The way that we die has changed dramatically with the dawn of technological advances. This case demonstrates how much advanced directives can be a tool to improve dying. Best practices and better education of health professionals about dying demonstrate that good communication and collaboration also improve dying. Obstacles to good dying involve different, sometimes difficult practical decisions that conflict with diverse or divergent viewpoints of patients, family members, and health care professionals.

The collaborative coediting of this work with a bioethicist and comparative religious ethicist helps to fill out the philosophical and ethical views on dying. Mrs. H's case story reveals some of the needed changes in the public argument about how we die. For example, one recurrent question emerged: Who makes decisions about dying and on what do they base these decisions? Death often occurs as a rapidly unfolding clinical event. For Mrs. H, knowing her background issues and preferences provides meaning and direction for treatment decisions. To help the reader understand the procedural questions of decision making—who decides (patients or valid proxies) and on what basis treatments are elected or refused—we discuss these in Issues 1 and 2.

In the United States, the majority of dying happens in hospitals (45–55 percent), or nursing homes (20–25 percent). Although the most patients say they wish to die at home, the likelihood of this occurring is slim. About 2.4 million die in the USA each year. Of those that die in the hospital, eight of ten deaths result from decisions to withhold or withdraw treatment by patient-informed consent or designated surrogate(s) (Issue 2). Causes of death in the first world from chronic end stage diseases, such as cancer, heart disease, and dementia, are an "epidemiological transition" from earlier eras of infectious diseases and pandemic outbreaks. This shift compels hospitals in developed countries to rethink rationales for always providing aggressive care and transition to desisting inappropriate treatment.

Decisions about dying were not always a struggle of aggressive versus palliative treatment. Patients and caregivers in the early 1900s had completely different experiences of dying. Dying of infectious diseases, cancer, heart problems, or even "old age" generally occurred at home, with care being provided by family members. Because of this, the surrounding local community was much more aware of "how" people died, and perhaps more accepting of death as a natural end of the life cycle. Today 82 percent of Americans live in urban areas, with access to state-of-the-art medical care. The widespread mobility of family members complicates social networks of extended kinship for care of the dying. We discuss the controversy of whether it is better to die in hospitals or in hospice in Issue 14.

As we walked into Mrs. H's room, the student's question still tugged at me. My response to the student needed to include the theoretical knowledge, the years of learned clinical skills, and practical knowledge that other dying patients had taught me. Dying can in fact be made good (or less worse) through competent care and assistance. I began talking through my assessment with her. "See her respirations. Watch them. See now how she pauses, there . . . now check your watch, time it." The 20 second pause of apnea (from Greek, "without breath") seemed to last forever and then Mrs. H gasped and breathed again, rapidly at first, then slowing down, then stopping again. "We call this a Cheyne–Stokes pattern of breathing (1818, 1854). Look here at her arms and hands. What color are they?" I showed her how these pale arms had already turned a grayish blue color, the legs and feet were the same. "Aren't you going to do something?" she asked anxiously. "Yes," I said. "When Mrs. H was 92, she was much more alert and clear than she is today at 96. She gave advance directives that clearly indicate that she wants no more hospital stays. She wants comfort measures only, so that is what we are going to provide." "No," the student said, "I mean send her to the hospital. They could do something for her." The impulse for family members, health care providers, nurses, and students to suddenly "do something" often results in a prolonged hospital stay, tubes, equipment, and many tests at the end of life. It is difficult for newer nurses and health care providers to see that providing comfort *is* doing something. We discuss the controversy of whether too much treatment results in inhumane dying in Issue 7. Outcome-based knowledge about the experience of dying enables us to accurately interpret experience ("save the phenomena") for decisions to make it more comfortable.

Advance directives provide a *tool* for persons to clarify the types of care that they wish to receive when they have a terminal illness (Issue 2). In Mrs. H's case, these directives allowed her to focus on comfort rather than technology at the end of life. Often the problem with advance directives is that some are offered as a checklist of yes/no questions. If a patient checks "no" for all of them, they wonder if they will simply be abandoned at the end of life. It was important for this student to know that comfort care does not mean doing "nothing" at the end of life, but it does mean providing a lot of care that is comfortable. It also means that efforts are not made to simply extend survival with treatments judged by the patient as excessively burdensome that merely "prolonged dying" (Issue 9).

After a phone call to the patient's daughter and a request that the nurse contact the chaplain and the social worker in the home, we continued on our other rounds. *Best practices* show collaborative caregiving works. When we walked back into Mrs. H's room, the nurse asked, "Do you want her to get a little morphine?" Again, I turned to the student. "How does she look to you? Does she look comfortable?" The student paused. "She looks like she is sleeping peacefully, right now, but I get worried when she gasps for air like that and winces." I turned to the nurse again. "If you have the concentrated morphine, even 5 mg might be enough to make her a little more comfortable. Can we start some oxygen at 2 liters just to ease the breathing a bit?" The student turned to me. "Won't that morphine cause more respiratory problems? We were taught not to give morphine to people with respiration problems. It might kill her." We discussed the tiny dose that was being offered and how it met the goals of the patient for comfort. She was actively dying already. She would not die of this pain medication; she would die of her underlying disease. We discuss the controversy and fears of "hastening death" with the use of pain meds in Issues 5 and 6.

When we returned from seeing other patients, there were more changes in Mrs. H's room. Individual dying is part of social living—and art-filled caregiving at the end of life is essential and must embrace local and cultural customs. The social worker and chaplain had set up chairs in Mrs. H's room for family members as they arrived. Because this was a church-affiliated nursing home, the staff was very attentive to spiritual needs of family members and patients. A kitchen aide rolled in a cart with coffee and cups. The student looked at me again. "What are they doing?" I explained, "Dying can take a lot longer than you think. It may be a day or more before she finally passes. With the morphine and the oxygen, she may perk up a little bit. The staff bring in coffee to be supportive of the family during their vigil." Rituals at the end of life are important to family members. Mrs. H had a long Swedish heritage of drinking plenty of coffee. The staff knew that her daughter would appreciate this. After the daughter arrived, the chaplain announced a prayer service for interested staff in Mrs. H's room. We discuss whether dying is improved by being a part of a religious community in Issue 16.

The student looked at me and said, "In my country we would put a feeding tube in her like we do for all stroke patients. Why don't you place a feeding tube or an IV to bring her back?" I explained that Mrs. H's advance directives were guiding her care now. Also, the blue-gray signs of changes in her skin indicated that her whole body was starting to shut down. "That means that there is not much blood going to her stomach and intestines. She would have difficulty digesting the food put into her. When food and fluids are set aside at the end of life, the body's tissues are allowed to become slightly dehydrated. This allows for breathing to be more comfortable. Too much fluid makes breathing wet and rattling, and the patient struggles more." We discuss the controversies related to withholding or withdrawing feeding tubes in Issue 8.

Dying can be better when it more accurately reflects the patient and family views and values. Mrs. H had many advocates besides me. Better personal and social choices about dying are shaped by justice. Hence, the readings don't ask how death somehow is finally and completely "just." Rather, these readings probe how particular experiences of dying and death have empirically better outcomes based on *different understandings of justice, and respect for personal wishes*. These include interpretations of justice in dying as equality (informed consent, Issue 1), need (depression, Issue 1; pain management, Issue 5), merit (futility, Issue 9; brain death, Issue 13), productivity contribution (EOL costs, Issue 15), and justice as fairness (cultural competence, Issue 17).

Mrs. H died peacefully with her daughter at her side at noon the following day. Not all people have the luxury of a long life and a comfortable death. The debates and concerns about how we die are discussed in the challenging questions raised in this text. In cultures of demand-driven health care, some caregivers and persons at the end of life see themselves as consumers who should change laws to provide them with more control over end-of-life events and processes. "Death with Dignity" legislation in two states, Oregon and Washington, and more recently in Montana, came from concerns that dying was not handled well by professionals. People in these states have worked to exert control over their own dying processes and death events. Laws in these states apply only to persons who have a terminal illness; that is, they are expected to die within 6 months of their cancer or other serious illness. The requests cannot be made by family members of impaired patients (such as patients with dementia); the patient must be competent to make the request. Persons that meet these criteria must put forward three requests (verbal and written with a 2-week wait, followed by another request) to their physician for medications. The person must be able to self-administer these medications (they can't have a family member or health care provider to do this—although vague laws cause disputes about this). We provide challenging discussions of these controversies in Issues 10 and 11. In some European countries, legalization has decriminalized assisted death. In these American jurisdictions, one debate has shifted to prohibiting or effectively regulating legal, lethal self-administration for terminally ill.

Much of the writing on death and dying presumes a terminal disease (such as cancer or a degenerative neurological disease) that has a long drawn out course where patients and their family members slowly and gradually face dying. But dying doesn't happen this way to everyone. Some deaths are abrupt and unexpected. Mrs. H's daughter had never been through the dying experience with a parent before. "My father just dropped dead of a heart attack one day when I was away at college. I never even got to say goodbye. I just came home for the funeral." The rituals following dying are especially important for survivors. We discuss whether funerals help grief in Issue 18.

Decisions about care at the end of life can be most difficult when the dying person is an infant, a child, or a teenager. Family members are asked to make decisions about care when traumatic head injuries occur. In the midst of shock over a serious accident, parents are confronted with decisions that have unknown consequences: will their child survive this devastating injury or should they withdraw the tubes and machines? Physicians are not always certain about the eventual outcomes from brain injuries. Family members may hope for survival and not recognize the profound disability and years of nursing home costs that may follow. These critical decisions can haunt families for years.

End-of-life care and dying can be quiet and peaceful (like Mrs. H's case), or can be filled with pain that is completely out of control. Many different types of pain can be difficult to control, for example, cancer pain, pain from massive burns from an accident, etc. When patients are hospitalized for pain that is difficult or impossible to manage, physicians may start medications to sedate the patient while trying to control the pain. This practice of palliative sedation may mean that the patient will be sedated until they finally die. These practices are controversial because some clinicians view them as similar to euthanasia, that is, actively administering medications with the intent to cause death. We discuss this controversy in Issue 12.

Rather than having a single separate issue on children and dying, this book applies the same controversial questions through some of the additional readings, the introductory discussions, questions for critical thinking, and resource lists. Whether an adult or a child, the questions are the same: Who makes decisions? Is withholding or withdrawing treatment permitted in a terminally ill child? How is pain management handled? Does too much treatment create inhumane dying? Looking at these questions through the lens of a parent's eyes, who had hoped for a wonderful and long life for their child, brings special challenges to our discussions about dying. Does going too far with treatment reduce some of the quality time and experiences that the child might otherwise enjoy? Or does prolonged treatment provide a sense that "we did everything we could" for family members struggling with these difficult decisions?

Whether the dying person is young or old, when patients die at home the family caregivers take on the blessings and burdens of caregiving for a loved one who is dying. Family caregivers carry the internal emotional strain of the knowledge of what lies ahead (death) with an unknown time frame of "for how long." Some caregivers do this difficult caregiving job lovingly and willingly; others become overly burdened by the strain.

Professional caregivers (nurses, physicians, chaplains, social workers) are not immune to the emotional toll that working with dying patients can create.

However, some researchers indicate that professionals who experience compassion fatigue have been too inwardly focused on their own needs. Caregivers who are "other focused" in their approach to dying patients can be rejuvenated by caregiving. We approach whether all caregivers experience burnout from compassion fatigue in Issue 4.

Cultural backgrounds of family members and patients shape and influence all of the decisions about care at the end of life, approaches to and beliefs about dying, and funeral practices or rituals following death. Diverse cultural traditions, including religions, give different meanings to dying processes and death events. For most, death is not the enemy, nor all there is to dying. Most cultural traditions interpret transformations of dying and death as a spiritual rather than only a biomedical event for dying persons and caregivers. When there are differences in cultural views of patients and health care providers, communication can be challenging. Misunderstandings of what to expect from treatments and poor health literacy (understanding of health terminology) are more common in persons for whom English is a second language. Health care providers may not understand why families of one culture would want the terminal diagnosis kept secret from the patient. In the United States, physicians are required to provide full disclosure to patients about their disease and its prognosis (expected outcome). Culture clashes and differences in demands for treatment are discussed in Issue 17. Research about end-of-life decisions continues to explore and gauge how diverse populations view death and dying.

Finally, we explore bereavement with some of the new research that challenges the half century of bereavement inquiries pioneered by Kübler-Ross. Issue 18 invites readers to consider new cultural questions about how grief is experienced and performed in ways that promote resilience.

Obstacles to good dying are both *practical and theoretical. Clashing Views in Death and Dying* is a cross-disciplinary work for complex yet ultimately practical decisions. We practically weave diverse methods into the issues from the emerging multidisciplinary fields of nursing and medical practices, contemporary bioethics, and medical ethics. These include elements of decision science and economics (2 [brain injury], 9 [futile treatment], 15 [subsidized eldercare]), experimental methods (3 [dying without advocates]), quantitative surveys and qualitative research (1 [depression], 2 [advance directives], 4 [compassion fatigue], 14 [hospice vs. hospital]), ethnography (17 [cultural competencies]), law (5, 6 [right to pain management], 11 [can suicide by legally safeguarded]), casuistry (6, 7, 8, 10 [hastening death]), history (2 [advance directives]), professional codes (6, 10, 11, 12 [palliative sedation]), philosophy (6 [lethal pain relief], 8 [ANH obligatory]), religion and theology (16, [religious belonging vs. spiritual quest] 18 [rituals and grief]).

We have designed this book to address the reality of the challenges that patients and families address as they make a journey through the dying process. In discussing these challenging issues about dying, we present many sides of different complex issues. This journey is different for every person. Some experiences of death are swift and brief, and other journeys are fraught with pain, confusion, contradicting information, and difficult, emotionally charged decisions. Although the issues are arranged as yes/no questions, we recognize that there are more than two sides to most issues. Issues have been deliberately coedited to provide some balance in contested positions. Readers are encouraged to express opinions about diverse issues, both in agreement and in disagreement. We hope the readers will find this book raises awareness of the different perspectives and approaches to death, dying, and bereavement.

Internet References . . .

On Our Own Terms: Moyers on Dying: A 4-Part PBS series on end-of-life issues

www.pbs.org/wnet/onourownterms/

American Academy of Hospice and Palliative Medicine

Palliative care physician membership organization provides conferences and other tools to assist health care providers communicating with patients at the end of life.

www.aahpm.org

ANA End-of-Life Issues

List of online resources for end-of-life decision-making.

www.nursingworld.com/

Center for Palliative Care Education

This site is a well-organized compendium of educational resources with a particular focus on caring for patients with AIDS.

http://depts.washington.edu/pallcare

Help with Advance Care Directives by Concepts

This site provides a list of questions for persons to answer, which will help with developing advance directives.

www.tc.umn.edu/~parkx032/Q-L-WILL.html

Help with Advance Care Directives by State

These sites provide access to the various advance directive forms used by states. Laws in each state vary, so this is a useful guide for students exploring laws on advance directives.

www.noah-health.org/en/rights/endoflife/adforms.html
www.caringinfo.org/i4a/pages/index.cfm?pageid=3289

National Hospice and Palliative Care Organization

This site provides details for National Hospice and Palliative Care Organization, helps to locate hospice providers, and has discussions about end-of-life care.

www.nhpco.org/templates/1/homepage.cfm

End-of-Life Decision Making

*E*nd-of-life care is filled with decision making; whether done by the patient or family members, or by health care providers following professional guidance, decisions impact the experience of dying. In this unit we discuss decisional capacity of patients who make end-of-life decisions. Decisional capacity is the ability to fully grasp the implications of the decisions that are being made. Seriously ill patients may request aggressive care because they fear dying, or they may agree to futile treatments to please family members even though they would otherwise not want very aggressive care. Decision making at the end of life is influenced by age, culture, and religious background. We explore the issue of depression in dying patients, and whether the presence of depression could make decisions for or against care untrustworthy.

Advance directives are meant to describe what a person would want for care in the event that he or she was unable to make decisions at the end of life. Advance directives come in many different forms. State laws vary in their standards and requirements for health care directives. We discuss some of the problems with advance directives: vague language, patient's inability to anticipate all of the medical circumstances that might require decisions, and issues of health literacy, or patient's understanding of the decisions that are to be made. We examine whether patients who have established advance directives receive care that is congruent with their preferences.

- Does Depression Make End-of-Life Decisions Untrustworthy?

- Do Advance Directives Improve Care for Those Unable to Make Decisions?

ISSUE 1

Does Depression Make End-of-Life Decisions Untrustworthy?

YES: Benjamin Brody, from "Who Has Capacity?" *The New England Journal of Medicine* (July 16, 2009)

NO: National Ethics Committee of the Veterans Health Administration, from *Ten Myths About Decision-Making Capacity,* www.ethics.va.gov/docs/necrpts/NEC_Report_20020201_Ten_Myths_about_DMC.pdf (September 2002)

Learning Outcomes

After reading this issue, you should be able to:

- Gain an understanding of the meaning of term "decisional capacity" and how it is determined for patients making medical decisions.
- Describe the difference between "competence" (a legal term) and "decisional capacity."
- Understand the importance of diagnosing and treating depression for persons with terminal illnesses.
- Discuss the laws regarding the protection of persons with impaired decisional capacity.
- Identify and debate whether someone with depression can make an authentic or reasoned decision about the level of aggressiveness or type of care they prefer at the end of life.

ISSUE SUMMARY

YES: Benjamin Brody, a psychiatry resident physician, offers a discussion of cases he was called to evaluate for decisional capacity because of concerns about depression impairing decisional capacity. He demonstrates that each case must be uniquely approached and that in some cases depression can impair decisions related to end-of-life care.

NO: The National Ethics Committee of the Veterans Health Administration warns against using a single diagnosis as a criterion for the lack of decisional capacity. Instead they provide guidelines on what persons should be able to understand about their specific treatment in order to have decisional capacity.

Whether patients reach the end of life after a prolonged chronic illness or after an abrupt serious incident, they are often asked to make decisions about their care. Choices may be offered to continue treatment, or withdraw treatment, or may be related to specific treatment options that the patient would prefer. Some of these decisions are coached as yes/no questions: Do you want to try another round of chemotherapy? If you have difficulty with breathing, would you want to be kept alive on a ventilator? These are far from simple yes/no decisions. These decisions require patients to have a complex understanding of what the treatment entails, the length of time the treatment might be continued, the burden of the treatment, and the expected outcome of the treatment. Because end-of-life decisions greatly impact care approaches and treatment choices, health professionals are cautious about psychological problems that could impair decision making (Brody, 2009; Werth, 2004). In this issue, we explore two articles that discuss whether or not depression makes end-of-life decisions untrustworthy.

Some basic definitions are helpful in understanding this discussion. An untrustworthy decision would be one that doesn't appear authentic to the person's previously expressed or usual wishes or actions. "End of life" usually refers to the time frame prior to death. End of life does not always have a specific time frame for when death is expected. Many diseases are considered "terminal illnesses," that is, they eventually end in death. However in North America, the words "terminally ill" usually refer to patients who meet criteria for hospice, that is, they have less than 6 months to live. The 6-month criterion was established by insurance companies to aid physicians in determining when a patient is eligible for hospice benefits. In Europe, terminal illness generally means 1 year or less.

First, it is important to distinguish the difference between decision-making capacity and competence. Decision-making capacity is the ability to make a treatment decision based on the information and understanding of the treatment options. Competence is a legal presumption of reasonableness for making sound decisions (Grisso & Appelbaum, 1998; Ganzini et al. 2004, 264). In negative terms, "incompetent" refers to persons who are mentally constrained from making decisions (e.g., coma, developmentally challenged along a scale) (McArthur Treatment Competence Study, 2004; Friedman & Helm, 2010). In disputed cases, health care professionals and caregivers may be asked by courts to present evidence regarding a particular patient's competence (Friedman & Helm, 2010; Moberg & Rick, 2008). Unless a state court of law has determined incompetence, all adults are presumed competent (National Ethics Committee of the Veterans Health Administration, 2002). Health care professionals do not designate competence, but they do determine the current, functional, situation-specific decision-making capacity of a patient by assessing his or her understanding, evaluation, and communicative preferences about a given treatment.

There are several medical reasons that change or reduce the cognitive capacities of dying patients for treatment decisions. Hospitalized patients who are acutely ill may suffer from temporary decisional incapacity related to side effects of general anesthesia, pain medications, sedatives, or infections (this is called delirium or acute confusion). Decision-making capacity can be influenced by severe pain or overwhelming anxiety. Decision-making capacity for dying patients can be constrained by diseases (Alzheimer's disease, stroke, Parkinson's disease) that slowly impair cognitive ability (UCSD Task Force on Decisional Capacity, 2003). Even legally competent patients can lack decisional capacity if they are not able to grasp the burdens, benefits, and risks of a procedure. In health care professions, this capacity is called "health literacy" (Johnson, Kuchibhatla, & Tulsky, 2009).

Decision-making capacity is not all-encompassing; patients can have capacity for one type of medical decision, but lack capacity for others (Kapp, 2010). Decision-making capacity can be confounded by a patient's health literacy (the ability to comprehend medical terminology, description, and outcomes). For example, research has shown that African Americans seek much more aggressive care at the end of life compared with Caucasian patients (Johnson et al., 2009). But a recent study showed that the health literacy of patients, not race, was the independent predictor of aggressive end-of-life preferences. In that study, older patients who saw a video of a person with advanced dementia made different end-of-life decisions than those who were simply told about advanced dementia (Volandes et al., 2008).

Research has shown that depression can complicate and influence general decisions about health. When patients have depression in addition to other physical illnesses, they are less likely to follow treatment plans (adherence to treatment) and tend to be higher users of health services (Cimpean & Drake, 2011). Depression has been associated with increased disability, poor prognosis, and higher likelihood of death (mortality) for hospitalized patients (Cavanaugh, Furlanetto, Creech, & Powell, 2005; Ciro, Ottenbacher, Graham, Fisher, Berges, & Ostir, 2011). Severe depression can make life seem hopeless even for persons without terminal diseases. Clinically, severe depression can lead to suicide. Health care professionals are required to intervene when a patient is so incapacitated by depression that he or she is considered an immediate harm to himself or others (Schulberg et al., 2005).

Clinical depression is not a normal or inevitable part of the dying process (Rosenblatt & Block, 2001; Werth, 2004). In terminally ill patients, depressive symptoms can range from mild sadness to a complete inability to function. When a patient is already suffering from a disease like cancer, it is difficult to determine whether the symptoms of fatigue, pain, or sleep disturbances are related to the cancer or cancer treatment, or if they are signs of depression (Werth, 2004). When a patient is facing a serious terminal illness, it is common to experience anxiety, fear, sadness, loss, or distress. However, distress is not always a symptom of mental disorder (depression) that needs to be "medicalized" and treated. Normal sadness in the face of cancer may be related to a realistic feeling of loss and grieving for a future that has vanished. These psychological feelings may respond well to appropriate support, counseling, and guidance.

On the other hand, ignoring a real underlying diagnosis of a depressive disorder may reduce the patient's likelihood of receiving appropriate antidepressants and treatment. Physicians may have difficulties in distinguishing between true depression and the symptom of sadness at knowing the end of life was near (Lawrie, Lloyd-Williams, & Taylor, 2004). Health professionals generally agree that mild depression is very common in medically ill patients and cannot be assumed to lead to poor decision-making capacity.

The issue of depression that is serious enough to impair decisional capacity becomes a greater concern in states where terminal patients can elect physician-assisted death. Currently three states, Oregon, Washington, and Montana, have laws allowing patients with terminal conditions to request medications to end their lives. Patients requesting medications under these laws must have a confirmed terminal illness (6 months or less to live), with a consulting physician confirming patient's "competency" and "informed consent" with discretionary "counseling referral" for depression. Clinicians worry that the request for life-ending medications may be related to untreated depression, rather than an authentic and reasonable wish to ensure a quick and comfortable death in the face of a grave illness. Research indicates that about 15 to 25 percent of terminal patients requesting physician-assisted suicide could be classified as clinically depressed (Ganzini, Goy, & Dobscha, 2008). If health care professionals fail to recognize depression, they may be missing an opportunity to treat the psychological suffering of a patient at the end of life (Rosenblatt & Block, 2001).

Some depressed patients are capable of providing clear directives for the kind of treatment or care that they want. Wishes for the types of care or refusals of care at the end of life can be authentic and consistent with personal views despite the presence of depressive symptoms (Ganzini et al., 2008). Health professionals generally agree that mild depression is very common in medically ill patients and cannot be assumed to lead to poor decision-making capacity.

In the article for the YES position, Brody presents cases that he encountered as a psychiatric resident who was asked to determine if each of these patients had the capacity to understand their decision. In one of the cases he found the patient to be very clear about his choice and not depressed; in the other, he found the patient was refusing a treatment out of fear as a consequence of her depression.

In the article for the NO position, the National Ethics Committee provides a discussion of the 10 myths of decisional capacity. This guide for physicians discusses all of the issues that must be considered in evaluating the patient's capacity to make a health-related decision.

YES

Benjamin Brody

Who Has Capacity?

"**S**omeone else should get the liver," the patient told me, "somebody with kids or a family." Mr. D. was lying in his hospital bed with his hands folded atop his distended belly. Alcoholism had cost him his career as a software engineer, his marriage, and the goodwill of his siblings. Now it was threatening to cut his life short. He'd been sober for nearly 6 months and might qualify for placement on the transplant list. But no, Mr. D. told his medical team. Someone else should get the liver, somebody who deserved it more. That was when they called me for a psychiatry consult.

Now I was trying to sort through Mr. D.'s motives to be certain that he wasn't depressed or just making an angry, self-loathing decision that he would later reverse. A casual look at his lab work revealed electrolyte, renal, and liver-function abnormalities that could cause delirium and thus affect his judgment. I asked Mr. D. to recite the months of the year backward, to name simple objects, and to remember three random words for 5 minutes. He made mistakes with these tasks, so I was wary. Should he be permitted to refuse potentially lifesaving care? The question wasn't only about transplantation; before making it to surgery, he'd need dialysis. But Mr. D. was refusing that too. It wasn't a long-term solution, he explained. It would only help stabilize him for the transplant that he didn't want.

"If I got a new liver," he told me, "all I'd do is start drinking again. I'd just burn right through it. So you should give the liver to someone else."

He said this in a quiet, measured way that made me think he'd given the matter some thought—but that also made me uncomfortable. So I kept pressing him. No, he didn't feel depressed or guilty about his situation. He didn't actually want to be dead. When I asked about his mood, he shrugged and said, "Some days are better than others"—a statement that is, of course, true for us all.

As I sat by his bedside, I realized that what made me uncomfortable was my growing sense that, although he was probably delirious, he just might be making an informed decision based on a clear understanding of his options. In short, I suspected that we would have to allow him to refuse lifesaving care.

But that's not what I wrote in his chart. With Mr. D.'s life hanging in the balance, I didn't have confidence in my own judgment, so I recommended low-dose Haldol and punted. I would discuss the situation with my attending, and we'd follow the patient. Perhaps he'd change his mind.

As a psychiatry resident, I am routinely asked to make decisions about whether a patient's judgment is impaired. This past winter a young woman

From *The New England Journal of Medicine*, July 16, 2009, pp. 232–233. Copyright © 2009 by Massachusetts Medical Society. All rights reserved. Reprinted by permission.

with schizophrenia who was actively hallucinating was admitted to my service after she had violently pushed her mother into a wall. First thing the following morning, the patient asked to be discharged, but I didn't think she should go. Around the same time, a man who probably had bipolar disorder was brought in by his brother after acting bizarrely on vacation. By the time they arrived at the hospital, his behavior had returned to normal. Discharge the patient, I thought.

When I make these decisions, I have the supervision of an attending psychiatrist. But part of my job as a resident is to learn how to make them on my own. Residents in every field of medicine live with this tension: we need to be self-confident enough to apply what we know yet self-aware enough to ask for help when we've wandered too close to the edge of our competence.

That can be hard in some critical situations, when decisions have to be made on the spot. Around the same time as Mr. D. was refusing a liver transplant, I was called to the ER to see a middle-aged woman with AIDS who had arrived late the previous evening with severe pneumonia. To survive much longer Ms. P. would need to be mechanically ventilated. The ICU resident explained this to the patient, but despite the possibility that she wouldn't survive without intubation, she simply refused.

"Does she have capacity?" the resident asked me over the phone. "Please get down here as soon as you can. We don't have a lot of time."

Before leaving for the ER, I flipped through Ms. P.'s electronic record. In addition to AIDS she had a lifelong history of psychiatric problems. Several months earlier she had been hospitalized because of suicidal thoughts.

When I reached the ER a few minutes later, I found Ms. P. lying on a stretcher, laboring to breathe on her own. What, I asked, did she understand about her condition? She was able to give me the basics: she had not felt well over the past several days, and the doctors had told her that she had pneumonia. She also understood that the ICU team recommended intubation. So I asked, "Why won't you let us try to help you?"

"I'm scared," she said, looking embarrassed to admit it.

I let several moments pass. Her breathing was the only sound in the room. Then I asked her what, exactly, she was scared of. Ms. P. couldn't answer. I was worried about her recent suicidal thoughts. Had she been feeling depressed? She nodded and began to cry.

All the while, I had been watching her chest rise and fall. Feeling that I knew enough to make a firm decision, I excused myself. Talking to a psychiatry resident wasn't helping her breathe any easier.

I told the ICU team that the patient did not have the capacity to refuse intubation. A patient's fear isn't ground for withholding lifesaving care, despite her wishes. Ms. P.'s decision had been rash, made in the heat of a terrifying moment. Without the luxury of a longer interview, I couldn't fully assess her underlying depression and suicidal thoughts. I believed firmly that we needed to err on the side of treating her. And that's what I wrote in her chart.

Although my attending agreed entirely with this decision, she wasn't happy that I had made it by myself. "You should have called me right away when you got the consult," she said. In retrospect, that seemed painfully obvious.

Whenever possible, life-and-death decisions should be run up the flag-pole immediately. At this point in my training, the capacity consult was not something I was ready to complete on my own. But in the moment, pressed by the urgency of the patient's illness, I felt compelled to apply what I was sure I knew. We discussed the case a moment longer and then went to round on other patients, including Mr. D., whose liver failure was worsening.

After she saw Mr. D. herself, my attending agreed that he was delirious but that we could not yet say whether he had the capacity to refuse dialysis. Over the next several days he remained firm in his decision to forgo lifesaving treatment. Dialysis wouldn't cure his liver failure, he said. And no, he wouldn't reconsider being placed on the transplant list.

Given his delirium, we couldn't rule out underlying depression as an explanation for his decision. Theoretically, if we forced him to undergo dialysis and his delirium resolved and we then found him to be depressed, this could be treated. Would he then change his mind about the liver transplant? It seemed unlikely, but the stakes were high.

The medical team was pressing us for an answer. I found it unusually difficult to make a decision and told my attending so. "Tell the medical team to call Ethics," she suggested. The next morning an attending from the hospital ethics committee reviewed the case and agreed with everything we were doing, but she recommended that we try to find a friend of Mr. D. with whom he could discuss his situation.

That evening, my attending and I went back to see Mr. D. one last time. I realized that I must still have something fundamental to learn about capacity consults: as we entered Mr. D.'s room, I had no idea what my attending would say to him.

To my surprise, she just talked with him about his life. Was there a particular accomplishment he was proud of? Mr. D. paused for a moment and then described a piece of software he had written years earlier that elegantly solved a problem his company was facing. My attending pressed on. Mr. D. had talked to a lot of doctors about the decision he was making, but was there anyone else in his life he had discussed it with? There was an old friend in Texas he'd spoken to, he told us, who had agreed with his decision.

Significantly, Mr. D. laughed at times during our visit. His affect, as we would say, was reactive, which argued against a diagnosis of depression. As the conversation went on, I felt sad for Mr. D. but also relaxed, sure of the conclusion that I'd come to and that I knew my attending had also reached.

It was now dark outside on what would turn out to be one of the last nights of Mr. D.'s life. I would have to let him make a decision that I wasn't going to like, and I found it unusually difficult to say good-bye. As my attending and I finally excused ourselves and were leaving his room, I felt compelled to offer him one last safety net—just in case. "Please let me know," I said, "if there's anything else we can do."

**National Ethics Committee of the
Veterans Health Administration**

 **NO**

Ten Myths About
Decision-Making Capacity

Executive Summary

Assessment of decision-making capacity is critical, since it determines whether a patient's health care decisions will be sought and accepted. Because so much hinges on decision-making capacity, clinicians who care for patients have an ethical obligation to understand this concept.

This report by the National Ethics Committee of the Veterans Health Administration (VHA) provides clinicians with practical information about decision-making capacity and how it is assessed. As background for this report, we conducted an empirical study of clinicians and ethics committee chairs. Drawing from the results of this study, we identified ten common myths about decision-making capacity, which are explained in this report:

Myth 1. Decision-making capacity and legal competency are the same.

Myth 2. Lack of decision-making capacity can be presumed when patients go against medical advice.

Myth 3. There is no need to assess decision-making capacity unless patients go against medical advice.

Myth 4. Decision-making capacity is an "all or nothing" phenomenon.

Myth 5. Cognitive impairment equals lack of decision-making capacity.

Myth 6. Lack of decision-making capacity is a permanent condition.

Myth 7. Patients who have not been given relevant and consistent information about their treatment lack decision-making capacity.

Myth 8. Patients with certain psychiatric disorders lack decision-making capacity.

Myth 9. Patients who are involuntarily committed lack decision-making capacity.

Myth 10. Only mental health experts can assess decision-making capacity.

By describing and debunking these common misconceptions, the report aims to prevent potential errors in the clinical assessment of decision-making

From *NEC Report,* September 2002, pp. 1–11. Published by the National Ethics Committee (NEC) of the Veterans Administration.

capacity, thereby supporting patients' right to make autonomous choices about their own health care.

Introduction

Clinicians have both an ethical and a legal obligation to ensure that patients are informed about and allowed to participate in choices regarding their own health care. This obligation is rooted in the principle of respect for autonomy. Respect for autonomy requires, at a minimum, acknowledgment of an individual's right to have opinions, to make choices, and to take actions based on personal goals and values.[1]

Autonomous choices have three central characteristics: they are adequately informed, they are voluntary instead of coerced, and they are rational.[2] Patients who are unable to make autonomous choices are said to lack "decision-making capacity" (President's Commission, 1982).[3] The concept of decision-making capacity is pivotal, since assessments of decision-making capacity determine whether patients are empowered to make their own health care decisions, or whether someone else is empowered to make decisions for them. Without decision-making capacity, patients are considered unable to make autonomous choices.

For many patients, decision-making capacity is never in doubt. Some patients (e.g., those in a coma) are clearly incapable of making decisions about their care, while other patients are unquestionably capable. In routine clinical practice, decision-making capacity is often assessed informally or inconsistently.[4,5] But when decision-making capacity is questionable and important clinical decisions must be made, the process for assessing decision-making capacity should become more formal and explicit.

Responsibility for assessing decision-making capacity belongs with the clinician who is in charge of the patient's care. Because so much hinges on capacity assessments, all clinicians who care for patients have an ethical obligation to understand decision-making capacity and how it is assessed.

Misconceptions about decision-making capacity and its assessment are surprisingly common. As background for this report, we surveyed members of the Academy for Psychosomatic Medicine (most of whom are consultation liaison psychiatrists), geriatrician and psychologist members of the Gerontological Society of America, and chairs of ethics committees in VA Medical Centers. We asked respondents to rate, in their experience, the frequency and importance of 23 potential pitfalls in capacity assessment. Based on over 900 survey responses, we identified ten items that were rated as "common" by over 50% of survey respondents and "important" by over 70%. These ten "common myths" form the basis for this report. . . .

Myth 1. Decision-Making Capacity and Legal Competency Are the Same

Although decision-making capacity and competency both describe patients' ability to make decisions, they are *not* synonymous. Whereas competency is determined by a court of law, decision-making capacity is a clinical assessment.

Competency is a legal term—to say a person is incompetent indicates that a court has ruled the person unable to make valid decisions and has appointed a guardian to make decisions for the person.[6–8] Sometimes courts restrict the guardian's decision-making authority to particular domains in which the patient has a specific lack of capacity, such as financial decisions or health care decisions.[7] Though the legal process of determining incompetence varies from state to state, it is often lengthy, expensive, and emotionally draining.[6,7] For this reason, the legal process is typically reserved for people who are very impaired, not expected to recover, and making decisions that adversely affect their well-being.

In contrast to legal competency, decision-making capacity is assessed by clinicians as an everyday part of clinical care. Decision-making capacity is defined as the ability "to understand and appreciate the nature and consequences of health decisions and to formulate and communicate decisions concerning health care."[9] Although clinicians do not have the power to determine whether patients are incompetent as a matter of law, they do have the *de facto* power to determine that a patient is incapable of making health care decisions and to identify a surrogate decision maker to act on the patients' behalf. Moreover, legal challenges to clinician's capacity assessments are rare. . . .

Myth 2. Lack of Decision-Making Capacity Can Be Presumed when Patients Go Against Medical Advice

Clinicians should *not* conclude that patients lack decision-making capacity just because they make a decision that seems ill advised. Determining decision-making capacity involves assessing the process the patient uses to make a decision, not whether the final decision is correct or wise.[5,10] Sound decision-making requires the following four elements:[11]

1. Capacity to communicate choices;
2. Capacity to understand relevant information;
3. Capacity to appreciate the situation and its consequences;
4. Capacity to manipulate information rationally.

Clinicians should not automatically assume that a patient who makes an apparently unwise decision lacks decision-making capacity, nor should they accept without question a decision that markedly deviates from the patient's own previously stated values and goals. While the concept of patient autonomy requires that patients be permitted to make even idiosyncratic decisions, it is the responsibility of the clinician to assure that an idiosyncratic decision is not due either to a problem with decision-making capacity or to a misunderstanding that needs to be resolved.

Myth 3. There Is No Need to Assess Decision-Making Capacity Unless Patients Go Against Medical Advice

While clinicians should not presume incapacity in patients who make decisions that are contrary to medical advice, nor should they overlook incapacity in patients who go along with whatever clinicians recommend.[12] The fact that a patient is agreeable and cooperative should *not* be interpreted as evidence that the patient is capable of making an informed decision. A patient may assent to an intervention without understanding the risks and benefits or alternatives sufficiently to appreciate the consequences of that decision. Although it is unrealistic to expect clinicians to formally assess decision-making capacity with every patient decision, assessment is imperative for patients who, because of their medical conditions, are at risk of cognitive impairment. Assessment is also essential whenever the risks of a proposed medical intervention are relatively high in comparison to its expected benefits.

Myth 4. Decision-Making Capacity Is an "All or Nothing" Phenomenon

A patient who lacks the capacity to make one decision does *not* necessarily lack the ability to make all decisions. Instead, patients often have decision-making capacity with regard to some decisions but not others. In addition to assessing a patient's capacity to make health care decisions, a clinician may also be asked to assess a patients' ability to make choices about living independently, handling funds, or participating in research.[8,13] Each type of decision requires different skills and therefore requires a separate, independent assessment. Patients should be empowered to make their own decisions, except those for which they lack specific capacity.[5,9–10,12,14]

Even within the realm of health care decisions, capacity is not an "all or nothing" concept. Rather, because health care decisions vary in their risks, benefits and complexities, patients may be able to make some decisions but not others.[4,11,14–16] For example, a mildly demented patient may be able to decide that she wants antibiotic treatment for a urinary tract infection because the treatment allows her to pursue important goals, such as feeling well or staying out of the hospital, and its burdens and risks are low. On the other hand, the same patient may be unable to weigh the multiple risks and benefits of a complex neurosurgical procedure, with uncertain tradeoffs between quality and quantity of life. Therefore, when evaluating a patient's capacity to make health care decisions, clinicians must assess each decision separately.

Finally, capacity is not "all or nothing" in the sense that patients who lack decision-making capacity may still have wishes that should not be entirely ignored. Incapacitated patients, including those who are legally incompetent, should be allowed to participate in decision-making to the extent that they are able. For example, a patient may have a guardian appointed because of fluctuating capacity stemming from mental illness such as bipolar disorder or schizophrenia. In such a case, the clinician should, if possible, discuss proposed treatments with both the guardian and the patient. In the rare situation in which the patient is confronted by a treatment decision for which he or she has capacity and disagrees with the decision made by the guardian, the clinician should not disregard the patient's opinion, but attempt to resolve the disagreement, and if necessary, seek advice from an ethics committee and/or legal counsel.

Myth 5. Cognitive Impairment Equals Lack of Decision-Making Capacity

Decision-making capacity and cognitive ability are related, but they are *not* the same thing. Whereas decision-making capacity refers to the patient's ability to make a particular health care decision, cognitive ability encompasses a broad range of processes including attention, memory, and problem solving. Perhaps the simplest and most common cognitive test assesses "orientation to person, place, and time" by asking patients for their name, their location, and the date. Another widely used test called the Folstein Mini-Mental State Examination (MMSE), which takes about 5 minutes to administer, measures attention, concentration and memory.[17,18]

While cognitive ability and decision-making capacity are correlated, cognitive tests should not be used as a substitute for a specific capacity assessment.[19-21] Some patients who lack decision-making capacity may have high scores on the MMSE,[20,22] while patients who perform poorly on the MMSE may be capable of making some health care decisions.[4,13,23]

Unfortunately, there is no single gold standard test for determining decision-making capacity that is universally accepted. In fact, in complex cases, experts may disagree in their capacity assessments of the same patient.[8,24] In recent years, several instruments have been developed that increase the reliability of clinical assessments,[24-27] but none of these are in common use. . . .

Myth 6. Lack of Decision-Making Capacity Is a Permanent Condition

Lack of decision-making capacity is *not* always permanent; in fact, it is often only short-lived. Patients' capacity to make health care decisions may wax and wane over time, especially in patients with evolving medical or mental health disorders.[5] Patients may be temporarily incapacitated, for example, as a result of general anesthesia. Another common cause of temporary incapacity is delirium: a transient mental syndrome characterized by global impairments in cognition, especially inattention, that most often affects hospitalized patients. Delirium develops in the context of severe medical or surgical illness. In patients with delirium, capacity may fluctuate substantially over hours to days, or between one hospital admission and another.[28] In such patients, decision-making capacity needs to be regularly reassessed. In patients who are only intermittently incapacitated, important discussions should be timed to correspond to periods when the patient is capable of decision-making. Under such circumstances, conversations may need to be repeated to assure that any decisions made are an authentic reflection of the patient's values and goals.

Whenever loss of decision-making capacity is expected to be only temporary, important decisions should be delayed, if possible, while efforts are made to treat the underlying illness so that capacity may be restored. If delay is not possible, a surrogate should be selected to make decisions on the patient's behalf. Decisions made under these circumstances should not be considered immutable, however. As soon as patients recover capacity, authority for decision making should return to them.[16]

Myth 7. Patients Who Have Not Been Given Relevant and Consistent Information About Their Treatment Lack Decision-Making Capacity

A patient who has not received appropriate information, or who has received inconsistent information, cannot be expected to be able to make an informed decision. Therefore, lack of adequate information should *not* be mistaken for lack of decision-making capacity.

In many medical settings, especially teaching hospitals, patients receive information from many different sources including their inpatient treatment team, consultant specialists, primary care providers, and trainees at various levels. Not surprisingly, the information is not always uniform. . . .

The clinician must inform the patient of the expected benefits and known risks of the recommended intervention, as well as the risks and benefits of all reasonable alternatives, including no intervention. The legal standard for how much information a clinician is required to provide varies depending on the jurisdiction.

In addition to providing adequate information, clinicians should also assure that the information they provide is understood. Some patients may be capable of making health care decisions, but only if their clinicians make special efforts to help them. In some cases, all that is required is patience and repetition, or allowing extra time for patients to digest information or to consult with family and friends. Other strategies that may improve patient understanding include communicating both verbally and in writing, presenting information at the appropriate reading level, use of personnel specially trained to bridge language or cultural barriers, and enlistment of the patient's support system to convey information.[5,13,29,30]

Myth 8. Patients with Certain Psychiatric Disorders Lack Decision-Making Capacity

The fact that a patient has a particular psychiatric or neurologic diagnosis does *not* necessarily mean that the patient lacks the capacity to make health care decisions—in fact, patients with serious disorders such as Alzheimer's disease or schizophrenia often retain decision-making capacity.[5,13,31–34] Frequently, however, clinicians assume otherwise. In a survey of physicians in Massachusetts, for example, less than one third of respondents thought it possible that a person with dementia or with psychosis could be competent.[35]

Although a particular psychiatric diagnosis does not necessarily imply incapacity, the most common causes of incapacity include delirium and dementia. Therefore, the presence of such syndromes should alert clinicians to assess decision-making capacity with special care.[4–5,10]

Myth 9. Patients Who Are Involuntarily Committed Lack Decision-Making Capacity

In most states patients can be involuntarily committed for mental illness because they are a danger to themselves or others or unable to take care of themselves. Although involuntarily committed patients often lack the capacity to make health care decisions, this is *not* always the case. Even with involuntarily committed patients, incapacity should never be presumed, but must be assessed.

Like all other patients, those who are involuntarily committed should be allowed to make health care decisions, except decisions for which they lack specific capacity, and should be allowed to participate in all decisions to the extent that they are able. In addition, involuntarily committed patients may be entitled to extra protections under federal regulations and state law.[7] . . .

Myth 10. Only Mental Health Experts Can Assess Decision-Making Capacity

Although assessments of decision-making capacity are often conducted by mental health professionals, especially psychologists and psychiatrists, mental health experts are *not* the only clinicians who can assess decision-making capacity. Rather, all clinicians who are responsible for the care of patients should be able to perform routine capacity assessments. Psychiatrists and psychologists have specific expertise in the diagnosis and treatment of many of the disorders that cause incapacity; however, for many routine cases, decision-making capacity is best assessed by the clinician who is responsible for the patient's care.[36]

Assessment by the primary clinician may be advantageous for several reasons. First, while mental health professionals who are asked to evaluate decision-making capacity often must base their capacity assessments on only one or two encounters with the patient, the primary clinician has the advantage of multiple encounters over time. Second, a clinician who has a longitudinal relationship with the patient may be in a better position than a consultant to understand the patient as a person, and to assess whether the patient's decision is consistent with his or her goals and values.[5,10] Finally, the clinician who is responsible for the patient's care has the benefit of familiarity with the risks and benefits of the recommended intervention and its alternatives.

On the other hand, consultations from mental health professionals may be invaluable, especially in cases where capacity assessment is particularly challenging. For example, primary clinicians may need help from mental health consultants in assessing the capacity of patients with severe personality disorders, in whom distinguishing poor judgment from lack of decision-making capacity can be difficult.[37] . . .

Whether or not a mental health consultant renders an opinion about capacity, the final responsibility for capacity determination rests with the primary clinician.[10] In cases where professionals cannot reach agreement about a patient's decision-making capacity, an ethics committee should be consulted.

Conclusion

All clinicians have an ethical responsibility to support and respect patients' autonomous choices. To determine whether a patient is able to make an autonomous choice, clinicians must have an accurate understanding of decision-making capacity and how it is assessed. This report is intended to serve as a catalyst for education and discussion about the assessment of decision-making capacity, thereby promoting ethical health care practices essential to quality patient care.

References

1. Beauchamp TL, Childress JF. *Principles of Biomedical Ethics*. 5th ed. New York: Oxford University Press; 2001:63–64.

2. Beauchamp TL, Childress JF. *Principles of Biomedical Ethics*. 5th ed. New York: Oxford University Press; 2001:59.

3. President's Commission for the Study of Ethical Problems in Medicine and Biomedical and Behavioral Research. *Making Health Care Decisions*. Washington DC: U.S. Government Printing Office; 1982.

4. Karlawish JHT, Pearlman RA. Determination of decision making capacity. In: Cassel CK, Cohen HJ, Larson EB, Meier DE, Resnick NM, Rubenstein LZ, et al., eds. *Geriatric Medicine*. 4th ed. New York: Springer-Verlag. In press.

5. Grisso T, Appelbaum PS. *Assessing Competence to Consent to Treatment*. New York: Oxford University Press; 1998.

6. Kapp MB. Medical treatment and the physician's legal duties. In: Cassel CK, Cohen HJ, Larson EB, Meier DE, Resnick NM, Rubenstein, LZ, et al., eds. *Geriatric Medicine*. 3rd ed. New York: Springer-Verlag; 1997.

7. Gutheil TG, Appelbaum PS. *Clinical Handbook of Psychiatry and the Law*. 3rd ed. Philadelphia: Lippincott, Williams & Wilkins; 2000.

8. Moye J. Assessment of competency and decision making capacity. In: Lichtenberg PA, ed. *Handbook of Assessment in Clinical Gerontology*. New York: John Wiley & Sons, Inc.; 1999.

9. Veterans Health Administration. VHA Handbook 1004.1, August 1, 1996.

10. Lo B. *Resolving Ethical Dilemmas: A Guide for Clinicians*. Baltimore: Lippincott, Williams & Wilkins; 1995.

11. Applebaum PS, Grisso T. Assessing patient's capacities to consent to treatment. *N Engl J Med*. 1998;25:1635–1638.

12. Pomerantz AS, de Nesnera A. Informed consent, competency, and the illusion of rationality. *General Hospital Psychiatry*. 1991;13:138–142.

13. National Center for Cost Containment. *Assessment of Competency and Capacity of the Older Adult: A Practice Guideline for Psychologists*. Milwaukee: Department of Veterans Affairs; 1997.

14. Baker RR, Lichtenberg RA, Moye J. A practice guideline for assessment of competency and capacity of the older adult. *Prof Psychol: Res Pract.* 1998;29:149–154.

15. Gert B, Culver CM, Clouser KD. *Bioethics: A Return to Fundamentals.* New York: Oxford University Press; 1997.

16. Schwartz SI, Blank K. Shifting competency during hospitalization: a model for informed consent decisions. *Hosp Community Psychiatry.* 1986;37:1256–1260.

17. Tombaugh TN, McIntyre NJ. The Mini-Mental State Examination: a comprehensive review. *J Am Geriatr Soc.* 1992;40:922–935.

18. Folstein MF, Folstein SE, McHugh PR. "Mini-mental state": a practical method for grading the cognitive state of patients for the clinician. *J Psychiatr Res.* 1975;3:189–98.

19. Derse AR. Making decisions about life-sustaining medical treatment in patients with dementia: the problem of patient decision-making capacity. *Theor Med.* 1999;20:55–67.

20. Etchells E, Darzins P, Silberfeld M, Singer PA, McKenny J, Naglie G, et al. Assessment of patient capacity to consent to treatment. *J Gen Intern Med.* 1999;14:27–34.

21. Molloy DW, Silberfeld M, Darzins P, Guyatt GH, Singer PA, Rush B, et al. Measuring capacity to complete an advance directive. *J Am Geriatr Soc.* 1996;44:660–664.

22. Freedman M, Stuss DT, Gordon M. Assessment of competency: the role of neurobehavioral deficits. *Ann Intern Med.* 1991;115:203–208.

23. Fellows LK, Phil D. Competency and consent in dementia. *J Am Geriatr Soc.* 1998;46:922–926.

24. Marson DC, McInturff B, Hawkins L, Bartolucci A, Harrell LE. Consistency of physician judgments of capacity to consent in mild Alzheimer's disease. *J Am Geriatr Soc.* 1997;45:453–457.

25. Grisso T, Appelbaum PS, Hill-Fotouhi C. The MacCAT-T: a clinical tool to assess patients' capacities to make treatment decisions. *Psychiatr Serv.* 1997;48:1415–1419.

26. Bean G, Nishisato S, Rector NA, Glancy G. The psychometric properties of the Competency Interview Schedule. *Can J Psychiatry.* 1994;39:368–376.

27. Miller CK, O'Donnell DC, Searight R, Barbarash RA. The Deaconess Informed Consent Comprehension Test: an assessment tool for clinical research subjects. *Pharmacotherapy.* 1996;16:872–878.

28. Auerswald KB, Charpentier PA, Inouye SK. The informed consent process in older patients who developed delirium: a clinical epidemiologic study. *Am J Med.* 1997;103:410–418.

29. Sugarman J, McCrory DC, Hubal RC. Getting meaningful informed consent from older adults: a structured literary review of empirical research. *J Am Geriatr Soc.* 1998;46:517–524.

30. Roberts LW. Evidence-based ethics and informed consent in mental illness research. *Arch Gen Psychiatry.* 2000;57:540–542.

31. Carpenter WT, Gold JM, Lahti AC, Queern AC, Conley RR, Bartko JJ, et al. Decisional capacity for informed consent in schizophrenia research. *Arch Gen Psychiatry*. 2000;57:533–538.

32. Wirshing DA, Wirshing WC, Marder SR, Liberman RP, Mintz J. Informed consent: assessment of comprehension. *Am J Psychiatry*. 1998;155:1508–1511.

33. Grisso T, Appelbaum PS. Mentally ill and non-mentally-ill patients' abilities to understand informed consent disclosures for medication: preliminary data. *Law and Human Behavior*. 1991;15:377–388.

34. Grisso T, Appelbaum PS. The MacArthur treatment competence study. III: abilities of patients to consent to psychiatric and medical treatments. *Law and Human Behavior*. 1995;19:149–174.

35. Markson LJ, Kern DC, Annas GJ, Glantz LH. Physician assessment of patient competence. *J of Am Geriatr Soc*. 1994;42:1074–1080.

36. Gutheil TG, Duckworth K. The psychiatrist as informed consent technician: a problem for the professions. *Bull Menninger Clin*. 1992;56:87–94.

37. Katz M, Abbey S, Rydall A, Lowy F. Psychiatric consultation for competency to refuse medical treatment. *Psychosomatics*. 1995;36:33–41.

EXPLORING THE ISSUE

Does Depression Make End-of-Life Decisions Untrustworthy?

Critical Thinking and Reflection

1. If a patient is taking antidepressants, should he or she be excluded from making critical decisions about their care at the end of life? Can a patient have decisional capacity even if he is depressed?
2. Consider the situation of a 73-year-old patient with a history of mild depression who refuses dialysis for his kidney failure. The nephrologist indicates that the man could live comfortably for years with dialysis. The patient explains that he does not want to be "tethered to a machine." What questions would help the physician and family know that this patient has decisional capacity?
3. Why are health care providers concerned about the possibility of undiagnosed depression for persons who might be electing physician-assisted death in states that allow this? Aren't these patients dying anyway?
4. Can health care providers force treatments on depressed persons at the end of life? Why or why not?
5. Discuss the pros and cons: can an attempted suicide of a depressed patient be taken as reasonable grounds for proxies to withhold or withdraw medically futile treatment?

Is There Common Ground?

Depression is a common problem in persons with multiple medical issues. Most clinicians focus on a patient's decision-making capacity, rather than an underlying diagnosis (like depression). Reliable decision making requires that the patient has the capacity to understand and relate back the relevant treatment information, is able to identify each of the choices available, can appreciate the benefits and the burdens of each of the treatment choices, and is able to state the likely outcome of the treatment. Severe depression can compromise reasoning skills, such that a person may make decisions that don't reflect the approach they might take if their depression was relieved with treatment. However, many patients with depression symptoms can identify clearly their reasoning for treatment choices at the end of life.

Because public health concerns about end-of-life decisions are real, they deserve precise formulation of key issues: depression remains both widely un(der)treated and demonstrably capable of effective treatment; approximately 80 percent of persons with depressive disorders go untreated and 80–90 percent of those treated find relief (Public Broadcast Station, 2008). Older adults and dying patients experience depression in unique ways that impact end-of-life decisions (National Institute of Mental Health, 2011). Untreated or undertreated depression "is the most commonly identified reason that leads patients to seek hastened death," with prevalence of depression among terminal patients at 20–50 percent (Breitbart et al., 2010; Rosenblatt & Block, 2001). Yet depression is one of several mood disorders that occurs along the scale of situational diagnosis; it is not automatically equated with legal incompetence, nor decisional incapacity. Determining competence and capacity assesses the patient's ability to participate in decision making, but does not determine whether a final decision is correct or wise (Moberg & Rick, 2008).

References

Breitbart, W., Rosenfeld, B., Gibson, C., Kramer, M., Li, Y., Tomarken, A., et al. (2010). Impact of treatment for depression on desire for hastened death in patients with advanced AIDS. *Psychosomatics, 51*, 98–105.

Brody, B. (2009). Who has capacity? *New England Journal of Medicine, 36*(3), 232–233.

Cavanaugh, S., Furlanetto, L., Creech, S., & Powell, L. (2005). Medical illness, past depression, and present depression: A predictive triad for in-hospital mortality. *The American Journal of Psychiatry, 158*(1), 43–48.

Cimpean, D. & Drake, R. E. (2011). Treating co-morbid chronic medical conditions and anxiety/depression. *Epidemiology and Psychiatric Sciences, 20*(2), 141–150.

Ciro, C. A., Ottenbacher, K. J., Graham, J. E., Fisher, S., Berges, I., & Ostir, G. V. (2011). Patterns and correlates of depression in hospitalized older adults. *Archives of Gerontology and Geriatrics*, May 11. doi:10.1016/j.archger.2011.04.001

Friedman, S. & Helm, D. (2010). *End-of-life care for children and adults with intellectual and developmental disabilities.* Washington, D.C.: American Association on Intellectual and Developmental Disabilities.

Ganzini, L., Goy, E. R., & Dobscha, S. K. (2008). Prevalence of depression and anxiety in patients requesting physicians' aid in dying: Cross sectional survey. *British Medical Journal (International Edition), 337*(7676), 973–975.

Grisso, T. & Appelbaum, P. (1998). *Assessing competence to consent to treatment: A guide for physicians and other health professionals.* New York: Oxford University Press.

Johnson, K. S., Kuchibhatla, M., & Tulsky, J. A. (2009). Racial differences in self-reported exposure to information about hospice care. *Journal of Palliative Medicine, 12*(10), 921–927.

Kapp, M. B. (2010). Legal issues arising in the process of determining capacity in older adults. *Care Management Journal, 11*(2), 101–107. doi: 10.1891/1521-0987.11.2.101

Lawrie, I., Lloyd-Williams, M., & Taylor, F. (2004). How do palliative medicine physicians assess and manage depression. *Palliative Medicine, 18*, 234–238. doi:10.1191/0269216304pm865oa

Moberg, P. J. & Rick, J. H. (2008). Decision making capacity and competency in the elderly: A clinical and neuropsychological perspective. *NeuroRehabilitation, 23*, 403–413.

National Ethics Committee of the Veteran's Health Administration. (2002). *Ten myths about decision-making capacity*. Retrieved from www.ethics.va.gov/docs/necrpts/NEC_Report_20020201_Ten_Myths_about_DMC.pdf

National Institute of Mental Health. (2011). *Depression* (NIMH Publication No. 11-3561). Retrieved from www.nimh.nih.gov/health/publications/depression/complete-index.shtml

Public Broadcasting System. (2008). *Depression: Out of the shadows*. Retrieved from www.pbs.org/wgbh/takeonestep/depression/

Rosenblatt, L. & Block, S. D. (2001). Depression, decision making, and the cessation of life-sustaining treatment. *Western Journal of Medicine, 175*, 320–325.

Schulberg, H. C., Lee, P. W., Bruce, M. L., Raue, P. J., Lefever, J. J., Williams, J. W., et al. (2005). Suicidal ideation and risk levels among primary care patients with uncomplicated depression. *Annals of Family Medicine, 3*(6), 523–528.

UCSD Task Force on Decisional Capacity. (2003). *Procedures for determining decisional incapacity in persons participating in research protocols*. Retrieved from http://irb.ucsd.edu/decisional.shtml

Volandes, A., Paasche-Orlow, M., Gillick, M., Cook, E. F., Shaykevich, S., Abbo, E., et al. (2008). Health literacy not race predicts end-of-life care preferences. *Journal of Palliative Medicine, 11*(5), 754–762.

Werth, J. (2004). The relationships among clinical depression, suicide, and other actions that may hasten death. *Behavioral Sciences and the Law, 22*, 627–649. doi:10.1002/bsl.616

Additional Resources

Baumrucker, S. (2005). Ethics roundtable. *American Journal of Hospice and Palliative Medicine, 22*, 228–232. doi:10.1177/104990910502200313

Blumenthal, J. A., Babyak, M. A., Moore, K. A., Craighead, E., Herman, S., Khatri, P., et al. (1999). Effects of exercise training on older patients with major depression. *Archives of Internal Medicine, 159*(19), 2349.

Braun, M. & Moye, J. (2010). Decisional capacity assessment: Optimizing safety and autonomy for older adults. *Generations, 34*(2), 102–105.

Cullum, S., Metcalfe, C., & Brayne, C. (2008). Does depression predict adverse outcomes for older medical inpatients? A prospective cohort study of individuals screened for a trial. *Age Ageing, 37*(6), 690–695.

Donnelly, M. (2010). *Healthcare decision-making and the law: Autonomy, capacity and the limits of liberalism*. Cambridge: Cambridge University Press.

Dudley, M., Goldney, R., & Hadzi-Pavlovic, D. (2010). Are adolescents dying by suicide taking SSRI antidepressants? A review of observational studies. *Australasian Psychiatry, 18*(3), 242–245. doi:10.3109/10398561003681319

Frye, M. A. (2011). Bipolar disorder—A focus on depression. *New England Journal of Medicine, 364*(1), 51–59. doi:10.1056/NEJMcp1000402

Ganzini, L. & Dobscha, S. K. (2003). If it isn't depression. *Journal of Palliative Medicine, 6*(6), 927–930. doi:10.1089/109662103322654811

Ganzini, L., Leong, G. B., Fenn, D. S., Silva, J. A., & Weinstock, R. (2000). Evaluation of competence to consent to assisted suicide: Views of forensic psychiatrists. *American Journal of Psychiatry, 157*(4), 595–600.

Ganzini, L., Volicer, L., Nelson, W. A., Fox, E., & Derse, A. R. (2005). Ten myths about decision-making capacity. *Journal of the American Medical Directors Association, 6*(3), S100–S104. doi:10.1016/j.jamda.2005.03.021

Kross, E. K., Engelberg, R. A., Gries, C. J., Nielsen, E. L., Zatzick, D., & Curtis, J. (2011). ICU care associated with symptoms of depression and posttraumatic stress disorder among family members of patients who die in the ICU. *CHEST, 139*(4), 795–801. doi:10.1378/chest.10-0652

Kusz, H. & Dohrenwend, A. (2009). *Treatment refusal: Does depression affect decision-making capacity in end-of-life issues?* Retrieved from www.clinicalgeriatrics.com/articles/Treatment-Refusal-Does-Depression-Affect-Decision-Making-Capacity-End-Life-Issues

Lapid, M. I., Rummans, T. A., Poole, K. L., Pankratz, V. S., Maurer, M. S., Rasmussen, K. G., et al. (2003). Decisional capacity of severely depressed patients requiring electroconvulsive therapy. *Journal of ECT, 19*(2), 67–72.

Leven, I. & Parker, M. (2010). Prevalence of depression in granted and refused requests for euthanasia and assisted suicide: A systematic review. *Journal of Medical Ethics, 37*, 205–211. doi:10.1136/jme.2010.039057

Lightfoot, L. (2005). Incompetent decision makers and withdrawal of life-sustaining treatment: A case study. *Journal of Law, Medicine & Ethics,* Winter, 851–856.

Lorenz, K. A., Rosenfeld, K., & Wenger, N. (2007). Quality indicators for palliative and end-of-life care in vulnerable elders. *Journal of the American Geriatrics Society, 55*(S2), S318–S326. doi:10.1111/j.1532-5415.2007.01338.x

Moye, J., Karel, M. J., Edelstein, B., Hicken, B., Armesto, J. C., & Gurrera, R. J. (2007). Assessment of capacity to consent to treatment: Challenges, the "ACCT" approach, future directions. *Clinical Gerontologist, 31*(3), 37–66. doi:10.1080/07317110802072140

Mystakidou, K., Tsilika, E., Parpa, E., Smyrniotis, V., Galanos, A., & Vlahos, L. (2007). Beck depression inventory: Exploring its psychometric properties in a palliative care population of advanced cancer patients. *Journal of Cancer Care, 16*, 244–250.

Rayner, L., Price, A., Evans, A., Valsraj, K., Hotopf, M., & Higginson, I. (2011). Antidepressants for the treatment of depression in palliative care: Systematic review and meta-analysis. *Palliative Medicine, 25*(1), 36–51. doi:10.1177/0269216310380764

Reeve, J. L., Lloyd-Williams, M., & Dowrick, C. (2008). Revisiting depression in palliative care settings: The need to focus on clinical utility over validity. (Cover story). *Palliative Medicine, 22*(4), 383–391.

Robinson, J. & Crawford, G. (2005). Identifying palliative care patients with symptoms of depression: An algorithm. *Palliative Medicine, 19*(4), 278–287. doi:10.1191/0269216305pm1021oa

Roman, M. W. & Callen, B. L. (2008). Screening instruments for older adult depressive disorders: Updating the evidence-based toolbox. *Issues in Mental Health Nursing, 29*(9), 924–941. doi:10.1080/01612840802274578

Ruijs, C., Kerkhof, A., van der Wal, G., & Onwuteaka-Philipsen, B. (2011). Depression and explicit requests for euthanasia in end-of-life cancer patients in primary care in the Netherlands: A longitudinal, prospective study. *Family Practice, 28*(4), 393–399.

Sears, S. & Stanton, A. (2001). Physician-assisted dying: Review of issues and roles for health psychologists. *Health Psychology, 20*(4), 302–310.

Stacey, D., Menard, P., Gaboury, I., Jacobsen, M., Sharif, F., Ritchie, L., et al. (2008). Decision-making needs of patients with depression: A descriptive study. *Journal of Psychiatric & Mental Health Nursing, 15*(4), 287–295. doi:10.1111/j.1365-2850.2007.01224.x

Unutzer, J. (2007). Late-life depression. *New England Journal of Medicine, 357*(22), 2269–2276.

Werth Jr., J. L., Gordon, J. R., & Johnson Jr., R. R. (2002). Psychosocial issues near the end of life. *Aging & Mental Health, 6*(4), 402–412. doi:10.1080/1360786021000007027

Online Resources

Understanding and Managing Depression

www.pbs.org/wgbh/takeonestep/resources/didyouknow
.html#depression

On Our Own Terms: Moyers on Dying. A 4-part PBS Series on End-of-Life Issues

www.pbs.org/wnet/onourownterms/

National Institute of Mental Health

A detailed booklet that describes Depression symptoms, causes, and treatments, with information on getting help and coping.

"Depression,"

www.nimh.nih.gov/health/publications/depression/complete-index.shtml

"Older Adults and Suicide"

www.nimh.nih.gov/health/publications/older-adults-depression-and-suicide-facts-fact-sheet/index.shtml

U.S. National Library of Medicine and National Institutes of Health Offer a concise account of of Depression at

www.nlm.nih.gov/medlineplus/depression.html

National Alliance on Mental Illness (NAMI), weblinks to "Depression" include many resources at

www.nami.org/Content/NavigationMenu/Mental_Illnesses/Depression/
Mental_Illnesses_What_is_Depression.htm

ISSUE 2

Do Advance Directives Improve Care for Those Unable to Make Decisions?

YES: Maria J. Silveira, Scott Y. H. Kim, and Kenneth M. Langa, from "Advance Directives and Outcomes of Surrogate Decision Making Before Death," *The New England Journal of Medicine* (2010)

NO: Cees M. P. M. Hertogh, from "The Misleading Simplicity of Advance Directives," *International Psychogeriatrics* (2011)

Learning Outcomes

After reading this issue, you should be able to:

- Gain an understanding of how you can direct others to make health care decisions at the end of life if you could not speak for yourself. Who should decide the care you should receive and how should they base these decisions?
- Describe key ethical and legal evolutions of different advance care planning tools including living wills, advance directives, appointing a health care proxy, or durable power of attorney.
- Identify the impact of advance care planning on treatment decisions and preferences, by describing respective roles of patients, proxies, nurses, physicians, and others in advance planning processes.
- Understand differences between proxy directives, treatment directives, and values histories.
- Discuss differences between "substituted judgment" and "best interests" when a health care proxy provides informed consent for an incapacitated person.
- Identify and debate key obstacles to advanced care planning.

ISSUE SUMMARY

YES: University of Michigan physicians Silveira, Kim, and Langa found that if older adults had advance directives, the end-of-life care that they received was strongly associated with their previously stated preferences. In their study, about 25 percent of older adults were decisionally incapacitated at the end of life and required a surrogate decision-maker. The study found that those who had advance directives (AD) received care that was consistent with their previously expressed preferences.

NO: Professor of geriatric ethics in the Netherlands C. M. P. M. Hertogh argues that despite their history in enabling "prospective autonomy," many problems emerge for ADs. These include low frequency, low compliance, low adherence, changing preferences, unstable health, and a "disability paradox" that people change their minds as their health changes. To resolve potential conflicts between prior values of a competent person and best interests of one later incapacitated, he suggests patients shift instead to an ongoing dialogue between doctor and patient.

If you were seriously injured in a car accident tomorrow, who would make decisions about your health care? Since the early and mid-twentieth century, the American legal system has required that medical treatments be voluntary; that is, a person should give consent for treatments (*Schloendorff v. Society of New York Hospital*, 1914). Physicians are required to discuss a patient's condition, outcome, and risks of any procedures, and seek "informed consent" from the patient (Faden & Beauchamp, 1986, pp. 123–125; *Salgo v. Stanford*, 1957). In 1983, an important presidential commission document, "Decisions to Forego Life-Sustaining Treatment," clarified how informed consent included a patient's wishes to forego or refuse treatments. However, when patients lack decisional capacity (see Issue 1), valid proxies (family members and caregivers) are required to make these decisions for the patient. Advance directives (AD) are orders or guidelines that a person can write to direct their care if they are no longer able to speak for themselves. These directives spring from U.S. legislatures, courts, and documents that honor the "autonomy" of a patient. In this way, the wishes of an incapacitated person are understood as autonomous decisions that are directed "in advance" (Dworkin, 1993).

In the early years after they become part of legislation, the focus of living wills (1969) was to guide patient treatment decisions if they were terminally ill (expected to die within six months). If the patient had a written living will, health care providers had written evidence of prior wishes. For those lacking decision-making capacity, without written or oral directives, health care professionals usually seek to identify what families believe the patient would want (substituted judgment) first, and if family did not know, then health care professionals would seek a family (proxy) judgment about treatment based on patient well-being ("best interests"). In cases where there is no prior knowledge and no family, some health care professionals used a "reasonable treatment/provider/person" standard, that is, what would a usual medical provider do in cases that are similar (meeting a "standard of care").

Advanced directives evolved from a 1990 congressional "Patient Self-Determination Act" to include care decisions for persons who were incapacitated but not immediately terminally ill. These focused on real-time choices and "who decides." These take different forms in different states, but essentially can be set up in two ways; a patient can set out what treatments she wants under different possible medical conditions (treatment directives), and/or a patient can simply select a person (proxy designation) who can make explicit decisions when the patient no longer has capacity (Devettere, 2009). A patient must be initially competent to assign someone to act as one's "durable power of attorney for health care," essentially assigning them "proxy" status, for some future time when she or he is unable to make decisions. If this has not been designated and the patient loses decisional capacity, the court may assign a guardianship or conservatorship to that patient.

Since 1975, high-profile court cases have established precedents of valid "proxy rights" (that is, the right of the family to represent a patient's wishes) regarding refusal of life-sustaining therapies based on informed consent in Quinlan (1975–1985), Cruzan (1990–1993), Wanglie (1989–1991), Finn (1995–1998), and Schiavo (1990–2005). In each of these cases, patients did not have written advance directives, but family members represented patient wishes.

There have been challenges with advance directives. Very few younger patients have established a written directive. Even among elderly patients only about 30–40 percent have established directives. Some researchers have puzzled why so few patients have designated their directives. One of the reasons is that the types of documents required vary widely from state to state and laws can be difficult to read and understand. The 50 state jurisdictions may have different legal and clinical intepretations of key terms such as living will, advance directives, health care directive, and patient preferences (Meisel, Snyder, & Quill, 2000).

Most recently, a third generation of advanced planning combines personal values, goals of care, and treatment preferences. Health care professionals and ethicists have worked to clarify patient wishes with different terminologies; among these are a Values History (1988), Medical Directives (1989), Lifecare Advance Directives (1995), and "Five Wishes" from the Robert Wood Johnson Foundation (1996). However, consider that if a health care professional conducts a "values history" and writes the patient comments in his or her notes, it may be difficult to retrieve and translate that history at the time a decision must be made. Because of this, some states have worked to ensure patient wishes can be placed directly into physician orders to be upheld in the patient chart. These include Physician Orders for Life-Sustaining Treatment (POLST) and Medical Orders for Life-Sustaining Treatment (MOLST).

States that have adopted standardized "POLST" forms have ensured that these address a broad array of wishes that are physician orders on the record. These address four areas: whether the patient wants cardiopulmonary resuscitation (CPR), antibiotic use, artificial nutrition, and the degree of aggressive treatment or testing when a patient is at the end of life, even if they are not immediately terminally ill. For example, a patient with severe Parkinson's disease could indicate that she or he does not want CPR if his heart stopped, but may want antibiotic use for pneumonia. Some research shows that health care professionals misinterpret specific treatment orders such as "Do not resuscitate" (DNR), applying it so broadly that they think it means "do not treat" at all, which is inaccurate (Pearlman et al., 2000; Smith & O'Neill, 2008; Sulmasy et al., 2006). As indicated in the Parkinson's case above, these two requests are completely different for that patient.

Another difficulty with advance directives is that in many states, a health care directive is drafted by an attorney and written in legal language (Castillo et al., 2011). These directives do not have the status of a physician order even though they might be placed on the medical record. Health care professionals may not be certain when these legal documents must be implemented in patients who are not immediately terminally ill.

There is evidence that physicians ignore advance directives that have been made, because of uncertainty of the patient's potential response to treatments. One large study of patients in intensive care units at the end of life found that many advance directives were not followed (Castillo et al., 2011; SUPPORT, 1995). This may seem unusual to nonmedical persons. However, imagine the case of a healthy 65-year-old executive who is suddenly in a major car accident. Emergency services rush to save his life; they perform CPR (even though his advance directives say "no CPR") because he is not "terminally ill"—he was simply in an accident. Perhaps in the hospital he begins to show improvements, but then lands in the ICU again with a heart attack. He recently survived a major accident. When should the physicians follow the directives? The issue that advance directives cannot anticipate all medical circumstances is a great limitation (Sulmasy et al., 2006).

During the health care reform debate in 2010, physicians asked Medicare if they could be reimbursed for the lengthy conversations that are required when doing advance care planning with patients. The request came because physicians are reimbursed only for visits with a specific medical problem, not for lengthy discussions about patient wishes. Opponents of health care reform misinterpreted the request for these consultations, and launched an inflammatory campaign that referred to this as a request for "death panels." The view that this was a bureaucratic attempt to allow "killing grandma," did a great deal of damage to proponents who were simply seeking ways to have better discussions about reducing overtreatment at the end of life (Morone, 2010). Well-done advance care planning does not merely avoid litigation; it can prevent or resolve conflicts by enhancing open informal communication. Advance care planning assists decisions for incapacitated patients rather than merely complying with demands of families (Dobbins, 2005; Hopp, 2000).

The YES and NO selections address especially contested features of this debate.

In the YES selection, University of Michigan physicians Silveira, Kim, and Langa argue that for the 25 percent of older adults who require surrogate decision making because of decisional incapacity, care is improved because the outcomes of decision making reflect their treatment preferences. These are known with respect to life-sustaining treatment (such as living wills) or selection of surrogate decision makers (such as durable power of attorney for health care) or both (such as in advanced directives). These authors provide evidence that having advance directives makes a difference.

In the NO selection, Hertogh from the Netherlands argues that the history and North American culture of "prospective autonomy" has shown some of the limits of ADs. Their low usage and problems in interpretation signal better alternatives in that third stage of precommitments that are future-oriented and collaborative among care-givers and patients.

YES ←

Maria J. Silveira, Scott Y. H. Kim, and Kenneth M. Langa

Advance Directives and Outcomes of Surrogate Decision Making Before Death

Background

Recent discussions about health care reform have raised questions regarding the value of advance directives.

Methods

We used data from survey proxies in the Health and Retirement Study involving adults 60 years of age or older who had died between 2000 and 2006 to determine the prevalence of the need for decision making and lost decision-making capacity and to test the association between preferences documented in advance directives and outcomes of surrogate decision making.

Results

Of 3746 subjects, 42.5% required decision making, of whom 70.3% lacked decision-making capacity and 67.6% of those subjects, in turn, had advance directives. Subjects who had living wills were more likely to want limited care (92.7%) or comfort care (96.2%) than all care possible (1.9%); 83.2% of subjects who requested limited care and 97.1% of subjects who requested comfort care received care consistent with their preferences. Among the 10 subjects who requested all care possible, only 5 received it; however, subjects who requested all care possible were far more likely to receive aggressive care as compared with those who did not request it. Subjects with living wills were less likely to receive all care possible than were subjects without living wills. Subjects who had assigned a durable power of attorney for health care were less likely to die in a hospital or receive all care possible than were subjects who had not assigned a durable power of attorney for health care.

Conclusion

Between 2000 and 2006, many elderly Americans needed decision making near the end of life at a time when most lacked the capacity to make decisions. Patients who had prepared advance directives received care that was strongly

From *The New England Journal of Medicine*, April 1, 2010, pp. 1211–1218. Copyright © 2010 by Massachusetts Medical Society. All rights reserved. Reprinted by permission.

associated with their preferences. These findings support the continued use of advance directives.

Advance directives document patients' wishes with respect to life-sustaining treatment (in a living will), their choice of a surrogate decision maker (in a durable power of attorney for health care), or both. First sanctioned in 1976, advance directives were designed to protect patient autonomy[1] under the belief that patients who lose decision-making capacity are more likely to receive the care they want if they choose a surrogate decision maker, document their wishes in advance, or both. To promote the use of advance directives, Congress passed the Patient Self-Determination Act in 1990[2] mandating that all Medicare-certified institutions provide written information regarding patients' right to formulate advance directives. More recently, a proposal to reimburse providers for these activities through Medicare[3] stirred controversy and raised concern that advance directives would lead to denial of necessary care.

Currently, up to 70% of community-dwelling older adults have completed an advance directive.[4] The popularity of advance directives has grown tremendously, despite debate about their effectiveness.[5] Early evidence suggested that living wills have little effect on decisions to withhold or withdraw care[6-10] and do little to increase consistency between care received and patients' wishes.[11] More recently, studies have shown that patients with advance directives are less likely to receive life-sustaining treatment or to die in a hospital,[4,12] but it is unclear whether these outcomes were consistent with patients' wishes. Data on the effectiveness of a durable power of attorney for health care are limited.

In addition, it is unclear how often the circumstance in which advance directives would apply actually occurs—that is, how often patients face a treatable, life-threatening condition while lacking decision-making capacity. The prevalence of lost decision-making capacity and the frequency of surrogate decision making about life-sustaining therapies are unknown.

To better judge the need for and value of advance directives, we sought to determine the prevalence and predictors of lost decision-making capacity and decision making at the end of life. We also studied the association between advance directives and care received at the end of life, including the agreement between preferences stated in advance directives and the type of surrogate decision maker and decisions made at the end of life.

Methods

Data Sources and Study Population

We used data from the Health and Retirement Study,[12] a biennial longitudinal survey of a nationally representative cohort of U.S. adults 51 years of age or older.[13] We limited our study to persons 60 years of age or older who had died between 2000 and 2006 and for whom a proxy (a family member or knowledgeable informant) answered a study-directed exit interview after the participant's death. For most of these respondents, exit interviews occurred within 24 months after the subject's death. . . .

Outcomes

Our outcomes of interest were obtained from the responses of the proxies to the Health and Retirement Study exit surveys regarding the decedent's circumstances at death; specifically, whether the subject had completed a living will or durable power of attorney for health care, maintained decision-making capacity, and needed decision making at the end of life. . . . Questions used to determine outcomes of decision making mirrored those used to determine preferences. We examined predictors of and preferences for all care possible ("all care possible under any circumstances in order to prolong life"), limited care ("limit[ed] care in certain situations"), and comfort care ("comfortable and pain-free [while forgoing] extensive measures to prolong life").

Predictors

We investigated the influence of clinical and sociodemographic characteristics reported by subjects before death and by the proxy after the subject's death. Clinical factors included cognitive impairment ("fair" or "poor" memory 1 month before death), chronic conditions (cancer, lung disease, heart disease, cerebrovascular disease, or depression), the presence of pain ("often troubled with pain during the last year of life"), the duration of illness, and the year of death. Sociodemographic factors included age, sex, race or ethnic group (white, black, or other), marital status (married, living with a partner, or other), and educational level (less than high-school graduate, high-school graduate, or some college or more).

Statistical Analysis

For the entire sample, we tabulated the frequency of end-of-life decision making, completion of advance directives (stratified according to the type of advance directive), and preferences for treatment and a surrogate decision maker. In addition, for subjects who required decision making, we tabulated the prevalence of lost decision-making capacity. Among subjects who needed decision making and had lost decision-making capacity, we determined the prevalence of completion of advance directives. . . . We investigated the clinical and sociodemographic predictors of the requirement for decision making and the loss of decision-making capacity.

For subjects who required decision making and had lost decision-making capacity, we tested the association between the presence or absence of a living will or durable power of attorney for health care and the outcomes of decision making (hospitalization, all care possible, limited care, and comfort care).

For subjects with living wills, we tested the association between preferences and outcomes, . . . with adjustment for confounding by sociodemographic and clinical characteristics and stratification according to the type of preference. We also determined agreement between preferences and decisions made. . . .

For subjects who had appointed a durable power of attorney for health care, we . . . examine[d] the percent agreement between the appointed decision maker and the actual decision maker.

In all calculations and analyses, we accounted for the complex sampling design of the Health and Retirement Study[13,14] by using the appropriate sampling weight from the subject's last interview before death (while the subject was living in the community). . . .

Results

Study Population

A total of 4246 respondents to the Health and Retirement Study died between 2000 and 2006 according to their proxies, National Death Index data, or both. The Health and Retirement Study obtained exit data on 3963 of those decedents from proxies (93.3%); 3746 of the decedents (88.2%) were 60 years of age or older at the time of death. These data are representative of approximately 12 million deaths in the United States during the study period.

According to the study respondents, most deaths were "expected at about the time [they] occurred"[13] (58.6%); in 67.9% of the subjects, there was a week or more between the time of diagnosis and death. Before death, subjects commonly had heart disease (53.7%), depression (48.0%), cancer (35.0%), cerebrovascular disease (25.6%), lung disease (24.1%), or cognitive impairment (45.7%). The subjects were most likely to have died in hospitals (38.9%), in their homes (27.3%), or in nursing homes (24.5%).

Proxy Respondents

Proxy respondents were adult children (48.9%), spouses (32.5%), or other relatives (13.5%), who were most often interviewed by telephone (71.2%) or in person (28.3%) a mean (±SD) of 13±8.4 months after the subject's death. Three fourths of the interviews occurred between 1 and 19 months after the subject died. Proxies of decedents who required surrogate decision making were the decedent's actual decision maker 79.5% of the time.

Need for Decision Making at the End of Life

Of 3746 decedents, 42.5% required decision making about treatment in the final days of life (Figure 1). After adjustment for sociodemographic and clinical covariates, memory deficits, cerebrovascular disease, nursing home status, and loss of a spouse were associated with an increased likelihood of the need for decision making.

Prevalence of Lost Decision-Making Capacity

Of the 1536 decedents who required decision making, complete data were available for 1409, and of those subjects, 70.3% lacked decision-making capacity. . . . [S]ubjects who were less likely to retain decision-making capacity were those with cognitive impairment, those with cerebrovascular disease, and those residing in nursing homes. At least 76.6% of the overall population had at least one of these characteristics.

Figure 1

Schematic Representation of the Study Population.

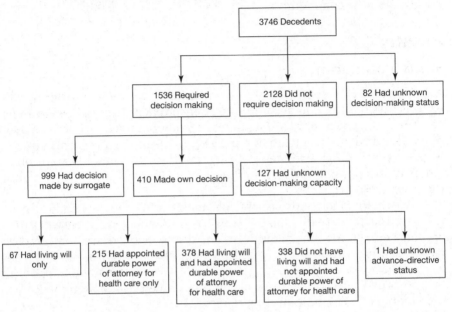

Actual numbers of subjects in the study are shown.

Advance Directives and Stated Preferences

Of 999 decedents who needed decision making and lacked decision-making capacity (29.8% of the subjects in the overall sample for whom complete data were available), 67.5% had an advance directive; 6.8% had appointed a living will only, 21.3% had appointed a durable power of attorney for health care only, and 39.4% had both prepared a living will and appointed a durable power of attorney for health care (Table 1). Among decedents who had living wills, 1.9% had requested all care possible, 92.7% had requested limited care, and 96.2% had requested comfort care. Among decedents who had appointed a durable power of attorney for health care, 64.6% had appointed a child or grandchild, 26.9% had appointed a spouse or partner, 6.6% had appointed another relative, and 1.9% had appointed a person who was not a relative. In a subgroup of women who had not been widowed, 67.0% had appointed spouses most often. The preferences of the subjects in the overall population were similar to those in the subgroup of subjects who required decision making and lacked decision-making capacity.

Living wills were completed a median of 20 months before death (mean, 43.5±57.5). A durable power of attorney for health care was completed a median of 19 months before death.

Table 1

Completion of and Preferences in Advance Directives.*

Variable	All Decedents (N = 3746)	Decedents Who Required Surrogate Decision Making (N = 999)
	percent	
Competed living will	44.9	46.4
Comfort care only	93.8	96.2
Limited care	91.3	92.7
All care possible	3.0	1.9
Assigned durable power of attorney for health care	54.3	61.0
Child or grandchild	60.3	64.6
Spouse or partner	29.6	26.9
Other relative	7.6	6.6
Nonrelative	2.7	1.9

*Percentages are weighted and were derived with the use of sampling weights from the Health and Retirement Study.

Living Wills and Care Received by Incapacitated Subjects

Incapacitated subjects who had prepared a living will (regardless of preferences) were less likely to receive all treatment possible and more likely to receive limited treatment than subjects without a living will (Table 2). Living wills were associated with increased odds of receiving comfort care and, although not significant, a trend toward decreased odds of dying in a hospital.

Among 435 incapacitated subjects who had prepared living wills and who had expressed a preference for or against all care possible, there was strong agreement between their stated preference and the care they received. However, outcomes appeared to vary according to the type of choice made. Of 425 subjects who did not indicate a preference for all care possible, 30 received it; among the 10 subjects who did indicate a preference for all care possible, 5 did not receive their choice. Of those subjects who did not receive their choice, four had appointed a durable power of attorney. Subjects who had requested all care possible were more likely to receive it than subjects who did not request it.

Of the 398 incapacitated subjects who had prepared a living will and had requested limited care, 331 (83.2%, unweighted percentage) received it; of the 36 subjects who had not requested limited care, 17 (47.2%, unweighted percentage) received it. . . . In adjusted analyses, subjects who had requested limited care were more likely to receive it than subjects who had not requested limited care (adjusted odds ratio, 8.11).

Table 2

Key Outcomes According to Advance-Directive Status among 999 Subjects.

Outcome	Living Will (N = 444)	No Living Will (N = 552)
	% of subjects	
Death in a hospital	38.8	50.4
All care possible	8.1	27.7
Limited care	80.6	66.0
Comfort care	96.8	91.3

Of 417 incapacitated subjects who had requested comfort care, 405 (97.1%) received it. Of the 29 subjects who did not request comfort care, 15 (51.7%) . . . received it. . . . However, in adjusted analyses, subjects who had requested comfort care were more likely to receive comfort care than subjects who had not requested it.

A total of 89.0% of the proxies reported that the living will was applicable to most decisions faced by surrogates. A total of 13.6% of proxies reported problems in following the subject's instructions (see the Supplementary Appendix for the exact wording of the question).

Durable Power of Attorney, Surrogate Decision Maker, and Treatment Received

Among subjects who required decision making, had lost decision-making capacity, and had appointed a durable power of attorney for health care, in 91.5% of subjects the actual decision maker matched the appointed surrogate. . . .

Subjects who had appointed a durable power of attorney for health care were less likely to die in a hospital or receive all care possible than those who had not appointed a durable power of attorney (Table 2). There were no significant differences between the two groups of subjects with respect to the receipt of limited or comfort care, after adjustment for potential confounding.

Discussion

We found that surrogate decision making is often required for elderly Americans at the end of life. Among our subjects, 42.5% needed decision making about medical treatment before death; in this group, 70.3% of subjects lacked the capacity to make those decisions themselves. In short, 29.8% required decision making at the end of life but lacked decision-making capacity. These findings suggest that more than a quarter of elderly adults may need surrogate decision making before death. Our data indicate that predicting which people will need surrogate decision making may be difficult. In our . . . analysis, cognitive impairment, cerebrovascular disease, and residence in a nursing home were associated with lost decision-making capacity before death; however, these characteristics were present in 76.6% of the entire study population.

Among subjects who needed surrogate decision making, 67.6% had an advance directive. This result confirms previous findings[3] and shows a great increase in the use of advance directives since the Study to Understand Prognoses and Preferences for Outcomes and Risks of Treatments[8] first reported that only 21% of seriously ill, hospitalized patients had an advance directive. The fact that so many elderly adults complete advance directives suggests that they find these documents familiar, available, and acceptable. Moreover, it suggests that elderly patients, their families, and perhaps their health care providers think that advance directives have value.

Subjects who had completed living wills and requested all care possible were much more likely to receive all care possible than were those who had not requested such care. Similarly, subjects who had requested limited or comfort care were more likely to receive such care than were subjects who had not indicated those preferences. In addition, most subjects who had appointed a durable power of attorney for health care had a surrogate decision maker who matched their choice. Although a causal relationship cannot be inferred, our findings suggest that advance directives do influence decisions made at the end of life.

Among the few subjects who wanted aggressive care, however, half did not receive it. Some persons might suggest that this finding indicates that advance directives are used to deny preferred health care. We believe that would be a misinterpretation of our findings, because our . . . analyses showed that documenting a preference for aggressive care significantly increased the likelihood of receiving such care as compared with not expressing such a preference. What might explain these findings? First, for many subjects, aggressive care may not have been an option regardless of their preferences. Second, among subjects who wanted all care possible, most had a durable power of attorney for health care to make real-time decisions on their behalf. Surrogates frequently override previously stated preferences, but usually because the circumstances require it, and data indicate that patients want it that way.[15] We suggest a more favorable interpretation of our data—namely, that living wills have an important effect on care received and that a durable power of attorney for health care is necessary to account for unforeseen factors. If we accept a durable power of attorney for health care as an extension of the patient, then we must also accept surrogate decisions as valid expressions of the patient's autonomy, even when those decisions conflict with the patient's written preferences before the onset of the terminal illness (as long as the durable power of attorney for health care acts with the patient's best interests in mind).

There were some important limitations of our study. The proxies who provided key data were subject to recall and social-desirability biases, especially with regard to subjective details such as patients' preferences. . . .

Another limitation of our study was the lack of data on preferences for subjects who did not have advance directives. . . .

Finally, our findings cannot be generalized to younger adults—a population that may not have the same need for surrogate decision making at the end of life.

In summary, we found that more than a quarter of elderly adults may require surrogate decision making at the end of life. Both a living will and a durable power of attorney for health care appear to have a significant effect on the outcomes of decision making. Thus, advance directives are important tools for providing care in keeping with patients' wishes. For more patients to avail themselves of these valuable instruments, the health care system should ensure that providers have the time, space, and reimbursement to conduct the time-consuming discussions necessary to plan appropriately for the end of life. Data suggest that most elderly patients would welcome these discussions.[17-19]

From the Veterans Affairs Center for Clinical Management Research (M.J.S., K.M.L.); and the Division of General Medicine (M.J.S., K.M.L.), Bioethics Program (M.J.S., S.Y.H.K.), Institute for Social Research (K.M.L.), Department of Psychiatry (S.Y.H.K.), and Center for Behavioral and Decision Sciences in Medicine (S.Y.H.K.), University of Michigan—both in Ann Arbor. Address reprint requests to Dr. Silveira at 300 N. Ingalls Bldg., Rm. 7C27, Box 5429, Ann Arbor, MI, 48901, or at mariajs@umich.edu.

References

1. Brown BA. The history of advance directives: a literature review. J Gerontol Nurs 2003;29:4–14.

2. Omnibus Budget Reconciliation Act of 1990, Pub. Law No. 101-508 (1990).

3. O'Brien M. Finance committee to drop end-of-life provision. The Hill. August 13, 2009. (Accessed March 5, 2010, at http://thehill.com/homenews/senate/54617-finance-committee-to-drop-end-of-life-provision.)

4. Teno JM, Gruneir A, Schwartz Z, Nanda A, Wetle T. Association between advance directives and quality of end-of-life care: a national study. J Am Geriatr Soc 2007;55:189–94.

5. Fagerlin A, Schneider CE. Enough: the failure of the living will. Hastings Cent Rep 2004;34:30–42.

6. Smedira NG, Evans BH, Grais LS, et al. Withholding and withdrawal of life support from the critically ill. N Engl J Med 1990;322:309–15.

7. Schneiderman LJ, Kronick R, Kaplan RM, Anderson JP, Langer RD. Effects of offering advance directives on medical treatments and costs. Ann Intern Med 1992;117:599–606.

8. Teno JM, Lynn J, Phillips RS, et al. Do formal advance directives affect resuscitation decisions and the use of resources for seriously ill patients? J Clin Ethics 1994;5:23–30.

9. Lo B, Saika G, Strull WM, Thomas E, Showstack J. 'Do not resuscitate' decisions: a prospective study at three teaching hospitals. Arch Intern Med 1985;145:1115–17.

10. Goodman MD, Tarnoff M, Slotman GJ. Effect of advance directives on the management of elderly critically ill patients. Crit Care Med 1998;26:701–4.

11. Danis M, Southerland LI, Garrett JM, et al. A prospective study of advance directives for life-sustaining care. N Engl J Med 1991;324:882–8.

12. Degenholtz HB, Rhee YJ, Arnold RM. The relationship between having a living will and dying in place. Ann Intern Med 2004;141:113–7.

13. Juster FT, Suzman R. An overview of the Health and Retirement Study. J Hum Resour 1995;30:Suppl:S7–S56.

14. Soldo BJ, Hurd MD, Rodgers WL, Wallace RB. Asset and health dynamics among the oldest old: an overview of the AHEAD Study. J Gerontol B Psychol Sci Soc Sci 1997;52:1–20.

15. Sehgal A, Galbraith A, Chesney M, Schoenfeld P, Charles G, Lo B. How strictly do dialysis patients want their advance directives followed? JAMA 1992;267:59–63.

16. Teno JM, Clarridge BR, Casey V, et al. Family perspectives on end-of-life care at the last place of care. JAMA 2004;291:88–93.

17. Smucker WD, Ditto PH, Moore KA, Druley JA, Danks JH, Townsend A. Elderly outpatients respond favorably to a physician-initiated advance directive discussion. J Am Board Fam Pract 1993;6:473–82.

18. Edinger W, Smucker DR. Outpatients' attitudes regarding advance directives. J Fam Pract 1992;35:650–53.

19. Steinhauser KE, Christakis NA, Clipp EC, et al. Preparing for the end of life: preferences of patients, families, physicians, and other care providers. J Pain Symptom Manage 2001;22:727–37.

Cees M. P. M. Hertogh  **NO**

The Misleading Simplicity of Advance Directives

The question of what constitutes a dignified old age has always been a topic of philosophical enquiry. Already in the writings of the stoic philosophers we can find relevant contributions to an ethic of "successful" aging. Seneca, for instance, reflects upon the pleasures of old age in several of his famous "Letters to Lucilius" (Seneca, 1967). However, he also writes about the bad years that may lie ahead and confides to his pupil: "Do not hear me with reluctance as if my statement applied directly to you, but weigh what I have to say. It is this. I shall not abandon old age, if old age preserves me intact for myself, and intact as regards to the better part of myself; but if old age begins to shatter my mind, and pull its various faculties to pieces, if it leaves me, not life, but only the breath of life, I shall rush out of a house that is crumbling and tottering. . . ."

Much has changed since Seneca wrote these words. Today, more and more people age successfully, enjoying increased physical and mental fitness and a high level of emotional and personal well-being. However, for those entering the fourth age, growing old still takes its toll, because of impending losses in learning potential and mental functioning and a strongly rising prevalence of dementia. In view of this grim perspective, Seneca's position appears to be far from anachronistic. For what dignity is there in being left with "only the breath of life"?

The instrument of the "advance directive"—or "living will" as this document was originally named when it was first introduced in 1969—can be seen as a contemporary, originally American alternative, to the more drastic solution to this challenging question proposed by Seneca in his day. In his book *Life's Dominion,* legal philosopher Ronald Dworkin—a strong advocate of advance directives—presents the case of Margo, a once intellectually vibrant and independent woman who, as a consequence of dementia, has become but a shadow of her former self and is now totally dependent on the care of strangers. Although there are no signs of suffering, Margo lives a life she would never have chosen if she still had a voice to speak. Yet, as Dworkin hypothesizes, if she had executed an advance directive, refusing any and all treatment, then pneumonia could offer her a dignified way out of her deteriorated state (Dworkin, 1993).

Over the years, the "Dworkinian" point of view has received much support. But do advance directives really offer a realistic solution to the complex

From *International Psychogeriatrics*, vol. 23, no. 4, 2011, pp. 511–515. Copyright © 2011 by International Psychogeriatric Association. Reprinted by permission of Cambridge University Press via Rightslink.

problem that called them into existence? What can we learn in this respect from more than 30 years of experience, at least in the USA, with advance directives? This is a relevant question in view of the fact that more and more countries are issuing legislation regarding advance directives. In addition, international organizations such as Alzheimer Europe (2005) promote the use of advance directives for decisions covering a wide range of health-related issues, including treatment and care.

Definition and Roles

A widely accepted definition describes advance directives as "written instructions executed by decisionally capable adults that pertain to future medical treatment preferences of the party executing the document. These directives take effect only if the patient is decisionally incapacitated at the time that specific decisions need to be made" (Kapp, 1995).

Advance directives can be classified into two categories: treatment directives and proxy directives. A treatment directive refers to a document specifying what kind of treatment the author desires under specific conditions in the event of incapacity, while a proxy directive empowers another person (e.g. health care proxy or durable power of attorney) to make decisions on behalf of the author. Both types of directives can also be combined (de Boer *et al.*, 2010). Morally, advance directives are rooted in the doctrine of informed consent. With expanding technology they became a key issue of the autonomy based bio-ethics movement of the 1970s. Central to this ethic is the judgment that autonomy is the core value to guide medical decision-making. Respecting autonomy allows individuals to shape their lives according to their personal values and preferences. In case of incompetence, when contemporaneous autonomy is no longer possible, so called "precedent" or "prospective autonomy" in the form of previous statements and expressed beliefs relevant to the treatment issues at stake should govern the outcome (Dworkin, 1986). This is especially true for advance statements that refuse treatment, since the informed consent doctrine holds that medical interventions are only allowed in the case of free and uncoerced consent—and consent can be withheld, even years ahead (Vezzoni, 2005).

Of course, advance directives were not designed with an exclusive focus on dementia and patients' fear of having to live through all its stages. In fact, their promotion was highly influenced by much-debated court cases on end-of-life decision-making in patients in a persistent vegetative state (PVS), such as the Karen Ann Quinlan case (Brown, 2003; Kirschner, 2005). Such cases enforced patients' feelings of powerlessness with regard to receiving care consistent with their preferences in case of incapacity. Hence, the anticipated role of advance directives was first and foremost to allow people to refuse "death-delaying" interventions in the event of incompetency and terminal illness or PVS.

Initially, the enthusiasm for advance directives was largely ideological, inspired as it was by the "new kid on the block" in medical ethics: the emphasis on patient autonomy (Faden and Beauchamp, 1986). Empirical knowledge on the subject was largely unavailable at the time and it was more or less taken for granted that advance directives would have a positive effect on medical culture and decision-making. However, these supposed positive effects were based on the assumption that the author of the advance directive is in a better position now than others will be in the future to decide how treatment decisions are to be made in the event of incompetency. Further, the author practices "auto-paternalism" by denying herself the right to a change of mind at a later moment and subordinates the interests of the future incompetent person to her prospective autonomy, just as Dworkin did in Margo's case. Moreover, Dworkin contended that prior choices should be implemented even if the patient with dementia explicitly expresses different wishes (Dworkin, 1986). Critical reflection on these premises and their consequences was scarce at the time and Rebecca Dresser (1992; 1995; 2003) was one of the few scholars who drew attention to the potential conflict between prior values of the still competent person and the welfare interests of the later incompetent person.

From Theory to Practice

With experience, however, came awareness of the problems, and empirical research gradually revealed that the reality was far from what proponents of advance directives had expected it to be. Since the disappointing findings of the first empirical study into the practice of advance directives, the SUPPORT study (SUPPORT, 1995), a plethora of research articles and critical reviews have been published and multiple interventions were designed to stimulate the uptake of advance directives, including several attempts to redesign them in order to increase their practicability and relevance to decision-making. Of the problems that all this research has revealed, some are more practical, while others are more fundamental in nature. First of all, with the exception of one recent study suggesting a prevalence of 67.6% in a cohort of Americans aged 60 years and older (Silveira *et al.*, 2010), the overall frequency of advance directives continues to be low, notwithstanding the existence of legal rules encouraging their completion, such as the Patient Self-Determination Act (PDSA) in the USA that came into force in 1990 and obliges hospitals and nursing homes to provide written information to all adults concerning their right to formulate an advance directive. Secondly, when they are completed, advance directives are often not complied with because they contain vague or ambiguous instructions, thus raising the question whether the author really understood what he conveyed to paper (Teno *et al.*, 1997). One way of dealing with this problem is to standardize advance statements on treatment preferences and/or stimulate consultation with health professionals when one considers drafting an advance directive (e.g. Emanuel and Emanuel, 1989). In practice however, physicians are seldom involved in this stage and the presentation of the directive is customarily the end of the inquiry instead of the beginning (Vezzoni, 2005). In addition, when advance directives do contain clear information, it may nevertheless be uncertain whether the author wants his directive to be followed. Research has revealed that authors regularly find that their families and physicians should have "leeway" to override their directives (Sehgal *et al.*,

1992). And to further complicate matters, it has been shown that proxies do a poor job in interpreting advance directives, as they are frequently biased by their own treatment preferences (Fagerlin *et al.*, 2001).

However, the most poignant problems of advance directives pertain to the stability of preferences and the effects of advance directives on the quality of care-giving in the final stage of life.

Stability of Preferences Over Time

Studies on the stability of treatment preferences have produced varying results and many of them are based on hypothetical not real-life decisions (Kirschner, 2005). We know, however, that our anticipatory beliefs often fail to recognize our ability to adapt and that it is notoriously difficult to imagine how one's current preferences will hold in a given situation (such as dementia) that one has never experienced before (Hertogh *et al.*, 2007). In general, preferences for life sustaining treatments are probably most stable in people with a stable health condition. Hence, advance directives are most applicable in case of acute (traumatic) disorders, such as severe brain injury resulting in PVS (Kirschner, 2005). Unstable health, on the other hand, will lead to changing preferences. This phenomenon is often so impressive that it has been termed "the disability paradox": a life that was once despised before the advent of chronic disease is accepted and even embraced with advancing illness (Albrecht and Devlieger, 1999). Dementia is no exception to this "rule," as is testified by a growing body of research on living with dementia from the patients' perspective (de Boer *et al.*, 2007). People do not become demented overnight; instead the gradual course of the disease allows for adaptation and a shift in response. As a rule of thumb, one may say that vulnerable persons often change their minds, particularly when their minds have changed (Kirschner, 2005). But what if they forget to change their advance directive, or are no longer able to do so? Here we touch upon a key obstacle for complying with advance directives.

Effect on Care-Giving in the Final Stage of Life

In several jurisdictions the condition of applicability of advance directives is restricted to terminal illness or imminent death situations; in others (e.g. the Netherlands) such restrictions do not exist and advance directives take effect from the outset of decisional incapacity. In dementia and associated neurodegenerative disorders, however, mental incapacity precedes the end of life and related medical decisions for an extended period. During this period patients may enjoy relatively good physical health, although they may suffer from intercurrent ailments (e.g. respiratory and urinary tract infections), exacerbation of comorbidity (e.g. heart failure), or trauma (hip fracture). Yet, advance directives offer no guidance with regard to routine medical care, and how they affect the many decisions that have to be taken during the final stage of life is largely unknown (Messinger-Rapport *et al.*, 2009; Gillick, 2010). Nonetheless, we do have some data. One qualitative study performed in the Netherlands showed that doctors and families of demented patients with an advance directive tend to base their decisions more often on a best interest standard, rather than on the advance directive: the directive is discussed repeatedly but seldom complied with (The et al., 2002). The findings of this study suggest that the conflict between precedent autonomy and current welfare interests, envisaged by Dresser, does not arise as such in actual practice and that the way past preferences are weighed is not influenced by the presence of an advance directive. However, research into the practice of advance directives for euthanasia in dementia has yielded some opposite results (Rurup et al., 2005). Although euthanasia was never performed, it can be gathered from this study that advance directives for euthanasia were occasionally respected by adopting a radical non-treatment policy, resulting in undertreatment of burdensome symptoms and insufficient palliative care. Thus, acting in accordance with prior instructions may very well conflict with the duty to protect incompetent persons from harm. In such a situation, strict adherence to an advance directive can result in the opposite of a dignified death and must be considered unethical.

Advance Care Planning Beyond the Living Will

In view of these dilemmas, what role can be accorded to advance directives in planning for future care? Looking back on more than three decades of prodigious efforts to implement and increase the uptake of advance directives, Muriel Gillick summarizes a growing consensus among experts when she writes that "the directives have been a resounding failure" (Gillick, 2010). They were a naive solution, proposed by an empirically uninformed bioethics for a human problem of overwhelming complexity. Yet, notwithstanding this failure, what the practice of advance directives does demonstrate is the relevance for health professionals to invest in helping people to plan ahead, specifically those who are facing a future of uncertainty with a high risk for incapacity, such as patients diagnosed with dementia and their families. The challenge now is to move on from static documents to a more dynamic practice of advance care planning, defined as a dialogical process of supporting patients and their proxies to think ahead and formulate goals of care as they confront the challenge of a progressive illness trajectory (Messinger-Rapport et al., 2009; Gillick, 2010, Hertogh, 2010). Such advance care planning should start early and must be firmly rooted in doctor-patient communication. It involves clarifying the patient's health status, determining his/her needs and values, and subsequently developing treatment plans that will be reassessed regularly and following any significant change in health. Furthermore, this process should be flexible and sensitive to the patient's views on autonomy. Indeed, the lesson that must be learned from the experience with advance directives is that clearly not everyone desires to manage and control their future (Winzelberg et al., 2005). Some people prefer to live life one day at a time and many wish to share the burden of decision-making with others, or even delegate this responsibility to their families and health professionals. Nonetheless, a timely start in exploring their ideas about how to deal with the challenges that lie ahead will allow others to better represent the interests of persons with dementia as the illness advances and capacity diminishes. It follows that this approach to advance care planning is time consuming and calls for high quality communicative skills, as well as for preparedness of doctors to take on a (pro)active role, using their knowledge of the disease trajectory in a way that is tailored to the patient's needs and preferences (Hertogh, 2010). Although they may feel a little uncomfortable with this responsibility after so many years of autonomy-centered decision-making, this approach is central to an ethic of care for people with dementia and will better serve their interests and those of their families than the mere signing of a form or the ticking of a checklist of interventions to be accepted or denied.

References

Albrecht, G. L. and Devlieger, P. J. (1999). The disability paradox: high quality of life against all odds. *Social Science and Medicine*, 48, 977–988.

Alzheimer Europe (2005). *Advance Directives: A Position Paper*, 6/2005. Available at: www.alzheimereurope.org/upload/SPTUNFUYGGOM/downloads/7939D9FD4CEE.pdf.

Brown, B. A. (2003). The history of advance directives. *Journal of Gerontological Nursing*, 29, 4–14.

de Boer, M. E., Hertogh, C. M., Dröes, R. M., Riphagen, I. I., Jonker, C. and Eefsting, J. A. (2007). Suffering from dementia: the patient's perspective. *International Psychogeriatics*, 19, 1021–1039.

de Boer, M. E., Hertogh, C. M., Dröes, R.M., Jonker, C. and Eefsting, J. A. (2010). Advance directives in dementia: issues of validity and effectiveness. *International Psychogeriatrics*, 22, 201–208.

Dresser, R. (1992). Autonomy revisited: the limits of anticipatory choices. In H. Binstock, S. G. Post and P. J. Whitehouse (eds.), *Dementia and Aging. Ethics, Values, and Policy Choices* (pp. 71–85). Baltimore/London: Johns Hopkins University Press.

Dresser, R. (1995). Dworkin on dementia: elegant theory, questionable policy. *Hastings Center Report*, 25, 6, 32–38.

Dresser, R. (2003). Precommitment: a misguided strategy for securing death with dignity. *Texas Law Review*, 81, 7, 1823–1847.

Dworkin, R. (1986). Autonomy and the demented self. *The Milbank Quarterly*, 64 (Suppl. 2), 4–16.

Dworkin, R. (1993). *Life's Dominion: An Argument about Abortion, Euthanasia, and Individual Freedom*. New York: Knopf.

Emanuel, L. L. and Emanuel, E. J. (1989). The medical directive: a new comprehensive advance care document. *JAMA*, 261, 3288–3293.

Faden, R. R. and Beauchamp, T. L. (1986). *A History and Theory of Informed Consent*. New York: Oxford University Press.

Fagerlin, A., Ditto, P. H., Danks, J. H., Houts, R. M. and Smucker, W. D. (2001). Projection in surrogate decisions about life-sustaining treatments. *Health Psychology*, 20, 166–175.

Gillick, M. R. (2010). Reversing the code status of advance directives? *New England Journal of Medicine*, 362, 1239–1240.

Hertogh, C. M. P. M. (2010). Advance care planning and palliative care in dementia: a view from the Netherlands. In J. C. Hughes, M. Lloyd-Williams, and G. A. Sachs (eds.), *Supportive Care for the Person with Dementia* (pp. 271–280). Oxford: Oxford University Press.

Hertogh, C. M. P. M., Boer, M. E. de, Dröes, R. M. and Eefsting, J. A. (2007). Beyond a Dworkinean view on autonomy and advance directives: response to open peer commentaries. *American Journal of Bioethics*, 7, W4–6.

Kapp, M. B. (1995). *Key Words in Ethics, Law and Aging.* New York: Springer Publishing Company.

Kirschner, K. L. (2005). When written advance directives are not enough. *Clinics in Geriatric Medicine*, 21, 193–209.

Messinger-Rapport, B., Baum, E. E. and Smith, M. L. (2009). Advance care planning: beyond the living will. *Cleveland Clinic Journal of Medicine*, 76, 276–285.

Rurup, M. L., Onwuteaka-Philipsen, B. D., van der Heide, A., van der Wal, G., and van der Maas, P. J. (2005). Physicians' experiences with demented patients with advance euthanasia directives in the Netherlands. *Journal of the American Geriatrics Society*, 53, 1138–1144.

Sehgal, A., Gailbraith, A., Chesney, M., Schoenfield, P., Charles, G. and Lo, B. (1992). How strictly do dialysis patients want their advance directives followed? *JAMA*, 267, 59–63.

Seneca (1967). *Ad Lucilium Epistulae Morales*, trans. R. M. Gummere. Cambridge, MA: Harvard University Press.

Silveira, M. J., Kim, S. Y. and Langa, K. M. (2010). Advance directives and outcomes of surrogate decision making before death. *New England Journal of Medicine*, 362, 1211–1218.

SUPPORT (1995). A controlled trial to improve care for seriously ill hospitalized patients in the Study to Understand Prognoses and Preferences for Outcomes and Risks of Treatment (SUPPORT). *JAMA*, 274, 1591–1598.

Teno, J. M. et al. (1997). Do advance directives provide instructions that direct care? *Journal of the American Geriatrics Society*, 45, 508–512.

The, B. A. M., Pasman, H. R. W., Onwuteaka-Philipsen, B. D., Ribbe, M. W. and van der Wal, G. (2002). Withholding the artificial administration of fluids and food from elderly patients with dementia: ethnographic study. *BMJ*, 325, 1–5.

Vezzoni, C. (2005). *The Legal Status and Social Practice of Treatment Directives in the Netherlands* (doctoral thesis). Groningen: Rijksuniversiteit Groningen. Available at http://irs.ub.rug.nl/ppn/28903504X.

Winzelberg, G. S., Hanson, L. C. and Tulsky, J. A. (2005). Beyond autonomy: diversifying end-of-life decision-making approaches to serve patients and families. *Journal of the American Geriatrics Society*, 53, 1046–1050.

EXPLORING THE ISSUE

Do Advance Directives Improve Care for Those Unable to Make Decisions?

Critical Thinking and Reflection

1. What are key general differences among living wills, durable power of attorney, advance directives, and understanding patient values? What are your state laws? See www.caringinfo.org/i4a/pages/index .cfm?pageid=3289; www.livingwillid.com/state.html.
2. How was each end-of-life decision-making tool both an improvement over its predecessor and a limit that needed to be surpassed (first-generation living wills, second-generation "directives," third-generation "goals")?
3. If you were to write your own advance directives, who might you select as a proxy for your care? What level of personhood would you want to preserve through medical care? Consider scenarios where you might be completely quadriplegic (unable to move arms and legs) but conscious, or cases like Alzheimer's disease, where you may be able to move about well, but are unable to remember, plan or safely care for yourself? Discuss the difficulties of having one simple document trying to capture all of the possible scenarios for future decisions. (See James Park, *Your Last Year: Creating Your Own Advance Directive for Medical Care,* Minneapolis, MN: Existential Books, www .existentialbooks.com, 2006, 81–94.)
4. In the above question, which personal or cultural values most/least influence your advanced planning (for example, personal values of being independent, self-directed, self-governing, or cultural/religious views that value vulnerable and dependent life in terms of possibilities that make caregiving generative, sticking together as a family)? Consider values of not wanting to be a financial or physical burden for your family; how do these weigh in your advance directives decision?
5. Consider the situation of an elderly mother who is 78 with mild Alzheimer's disease. She has designated her daughter to be her surrogate decision maker. When she was well, or last expressed decisional capacity, she said "no machines," with respect to end-of-life decision making. Her daughter and family members took that to mean "no CPR, comfort care only." When the patient is moved to a new state, her daughter seeks care for her there. This state requires an independent test of her decision-making capacity and a new clinician to ask about her preferences and to fill out an advanced directives. Discuss what challenges are faced when the patient is asked directly, "Do you want a CPR?" What if she says "yes"?

6. Debate and discuss: Do you think that time set aside for advanced directives should be reimbursed by insurance or federal subsidies? Do you think discussion of care approaches for an incapacitated person should be viewed as a "death panel"?

Is There Common Ground?

Advance directives are precommitments that have merits and limitations. These are practical and theoretical for different clinical and legal reasons. What some interpret as adaptable tools, others judge as having empirical problems that amount to three kinds of ethical and policy liabilities. Health care professionals characteristically refine different current decisional tools to help improve processes of care (Dobbins, 2005; Emanuel & Scandrett, 2010; Smith & O'Neill, 2008; Sulmasy & Snyder, 2010; Watson, 2010). Legal and policy critics are more skeptical about whether documented decisions accurately reflect the identity or needs of a vulnerable dying person. Patient underusage of advance planning (only 5–25 percent of persons have directives) and undercompliance with advance directions (most want "leeway"), are due in part to uncertainty or confusion about potential outcomes, or caregiver nonadherence to directives because of biases of proxies (1/3 make errors; see Emanuel & Scandrett, 2010; Shalowitz, Garrett-Mayer & Wendler, 2006; Sulmasy et al., 2006; Sulmasy & Snyder, 2010).

At least three kinds of objections emerge. First, some of the key terms or language which are used are ambiguous or inflexible to specific situations. New and simple technologies would have been "heroic measures" in years past. In setting an advance directive, one cannot anticipate the medical norms of the future. Secondly, the documentation of preferred choices at one point may confuse proxies who are faced with a very different situation. Some advance choices counterpose prior values of a previously competent person against the welfare/best interests of a currently incapacitated person. Treatment preferences may change as people adapt to disabilities—in the so-called "disability paradox"; patients change minds as minds change. More exploration is needed about the language of wish, preference, choice in relation to identity, incapacity, and treatment goals. Finally, some find the larger ambitions misguided of micromanaging death (Castillo et al., 2011; Dresser, 2003; Fagerlin & Schneider, 2004; Gillick, 2010; Hawkins, Ditto, Danks & Smuckers, 2005; Hertough, 2011).

Advanced planning makes people hopeful and fearful about who decides and how for the incapacitated. Part of the legislation that would have authorized reimbursement for physician counseling regarding advance directives once every 5 years was excluded in the 2010 Affordable Care Act because of public debates about alleged "death panels" (Pear, 2010, 2011). However, in the United States, when wishes are not known, physicians are more likely to "do everything," racking up health care costs for potentially futile approaches. If physicians are not reimbursed for the lengthy conversations required to sort out patient values, it may be less likely that these important discussions occur.

References

Castillo, L. S., Williams, B. A., Hooper, S. M., Sabatino, C. P., Weithorn, L. A., & Sudore, R. (2011). Lost in translation: The unintended consequences of advance directive law on clinical care. *Annals of Internal Medicine, 154,* 121–128.

Devettere, R. J. (2009). *Practical decision making in health care ethics: Cases and concepts* (3rd ed.). Washington, D.C.: Georgetown University Press.

Dobbins, E. H. (2005). Helping your patient to a "good death." *Nursing, 35*(2), 43–45.

Dresser, R. (2003). Precommitment: A misguided strategy for securing death with dignity. *Texas Law Review, 81*(7), 1823–1847.

Dworkin, R. (1993). *Life's dominion: An argument about abortion, euthanasia, and individual freedom.* New York: Knopf.

Emanuel, L. & Scandrett, K. (2010). Decisions at the end of life: Have we come of age? *BMC Medicine, 8,* 57–64.

Faden, R. R. & Beauchamp, T. L. (1986). *History and theory of informed consent.* Oxford: Oxford University Press.

Fagerlin, A. & Schneider, C. E. (2004). Enough. *Hastings Center Report, 34,* 30–42.

Gillick, M. R. (2010). Reversing the code status of advance directives? *New England Journal of Medicine, 362,* 1239–1240.

Hawkins, N., Ditto, P. H., Danks, J. H., & Smucker, W. D. (2005). Micromanaging death: Process preferences, values, and goals in end-of-life medical decision making. *Gerontologist, 45*(1), 107–117.

Hertough, C. P. (2011). The misleading simplicity of advance directives. *International Psychogeriatrics, 23*(4), 511–515.

Hopp, F. P. (2000). Preferences for surrogate decision makers, informal communication, and advance directives among community-dwelling elders: Results from a national study. *Gerontologist, 40*(4), 449–457.

Meisel, A., Snyder, L., & Quill, T. (2000). Seven legal barriers to end-of-life care: Myths, realities, and grains of truth. *Journal of the American Medical Association, 284*(19), 2495–2501.

Morone, J. A. (2010). Presidents and health reform: From Franklin D. Roosevelt to Barack Obama. *Health Affairs, 29*(6), 1096–1100. doi:10.1377/hlthaff.2010.0420

Pear, R. (2010, December 25). Obama returns to end of life plan that caused stir. *The New York Times.* Retrieved from www.nytimes.com/2010/12/26/us/politics/26death.html?pagewanted=all

Pear, R. (2011, January 04). U.S. alters rule on paying for end of life planning. *The New York Times.* Retrieved from www.nytimes.com/2011/01/05/health/policy/05health.html?_r=1

Pearlman, R. A., Cain, K. C., Starks, H., Cole, W. G., Uhlmann, R. F., & Patrick, D. L. (2000). Preferences for life-sustaining treatments in advance care planning and surrogate decision making. *Journal of Palliative Medicine, 3*(1), 37–48.

Salgo v. Leland Stanford Jr. University Board of Trustees. Civ. No. 17045. California App. Div. 2d 560, 1957.

Schloendorff v. The Society of the New York Hospital. (105 NE 92). Court of Appeals of New York. 149 App. Div. 915, 1914.

Shalowitz, D. I., Garrett-Mayer, E., & Wendler, D. (2006). The accuracy of surrogate decision makers: A systematic review. *Archives of Internal Medicine, 166*(5), 493–497.

Silveira, M. J., Kim, S. H., & Langa, K. M. (2010). Advance directives and outcomes of surrogate decision making before death. *The New England Journal of Medicine, 362*(13), 1211–1218.

Smith, C. B. & O'Neill, L. B. (2008). Do not resuscitate does not mean do not treat: How palliative care and other modalities can help facilitate communication about goals of care in advanced illness. *Mount Sinai Journal of Medicine, 75*, 460–465.

Sulmasy, D. P. & Snyder, L. (2010). Substituted interests and best judgments: An integrated model of surrogate decision making. *Journal of the American Medical Association, 304*(17), 1946–1947.

Sulmasy, D. P., Sood, J. R., Texiera, K., McAuley, R. L., McGugins, J., & Ury, W. A. (2006). A prospective trial of a new policy eliminating signed consent for do not resuscitate orders. *Journal of General Internal Medicine, 21*(12), 1261–1268.

SUPPORT. (1995). A controlled trial to improve care for seriously ill hospitalized patients in the study to understand prognoses and preferences for outcomes and risks of treatment (SUPPORT). *Journal of the American Medical Association, 274*, 1591–1598.

Watson, E. (2010). Advance directives: Self-determination, legislation and litigation issues. *Journal of Legal Nurse Consulting, 21*(1), 9–14.

Additional Resources

Brewer, B. (2008). Do not abandon, do not resuscitate: A patient advocacy position. *Journal of Nursing Law, 12*(2), 78–84.

Caprio, A. J., Hanson, L. C., Munn, J. C., Williams, C. S., Dobbs, D., Sloane, P. D., & Zimmerman, S. (2008). Pain, dyspnea, and the quality of dying in long-term care. *Journal of the American Geriatrics Society, 56(4)*, 683–688. doi:10.1111/j.1532-5415.2007.01613.x

Cochrane, T. I. (2009). Unnecessary time pressure in refusal of life-sustaining therapies: Fear of missing the opportunity to die. *American Journal of Bioethics, 9*(4), 47–54.

Feeg, V. & Elebiary, H. (2005). Exploratory study on end-of-life issues: Barriers to palliative care and advance directives. *American Journal of Hospice and Palliative Medicine, 22*(2), 119–124.

Fields, L. (2007). DNR does not mean no care. *Journal of Neuroscience Nursing, 39*(5), 294–296.

Fry, S., Veatch, R., & Taylor, C. (2010). *Case studies in nursing ethics* (4th ed.). Sudbury, MA: Jones and Bartlett.

Gallo, J. J., Straton, J. B., Klag, M. J., Meoni, L. A., Sulmasy, D. P., Wang, N., & Ford, D. E. (2003). Life-sustaining treatments: What do physicians want and do they express their wishes to others? *Journal of the American Geriatrics Society, 51*(7), 961–969.

Golbert, C. (2010). Health care surrogate decision making and bioethics: Case studies from the files of the office of the cook country public guardian. *NAELA Journal, 6*(2), 155–179.

Goodie, J. & McGlory, G. (2010). Compassionate care: A focus on dying well. *Nursing, 40*(5), 12–14.

Helping caregivers cope with a patient's dementia. (2005). *Nursing, 35*(9), 22.

Parkman, C. & Calfe, B. (1997). Advance direct: Honoring your patient's end of life wishes. *Nursing, 97*, 48–53.

Perkins, H. S. (2007). Controlling death: The false promise of advance directives. *Annals of Internal Medicine, 147*(1), 51–57.

Puopolo, A. (1999). Gaining confidence to talk about end-of-life care. *Nursing, 29*(7), 49–51.

Silveira, M. J., DiPierro, A., Gerrity, M. S., & Feudtner, C. (2000). Patients' knowledge of options at the end of life: Ignorance in the face of death. *Journal of the American Medical Association, 284*(19), 2438–2488.

Stefanou, N. & Faircloth, S. (2010). Exploring the concept of quality care for the person who is dying. *British Journal of Community Nursing, 15*(12), 588–593.

Sulmasy, D. P. (2010). The last word: The Catholic case for advance directives. *America, 203*(16), 13–16.

Sulmasy, D. P., Sood, J. R., & Ury, W. A. (2004). The quality of care plans for patients with do-not-resuscitate orders. *Archives of Internal Medicine, 164*(14), 1573–1578.

Surrogate model focuses on substituted interests. (2010). *Medical Ethics Advisor, 26*(12), 133–135.

Taylor, C. (2008). Advance directives. In K. K. Kuebler & P. Esper, *Palliative practices from A-Z for the bedside clinician* (pp. 1–4). Pittsburg, PA: Oncology Nursing Society Press.

Teno, J. M., Gruneir, A., Schwartz, Z., Nanda, A., & Wetle, T. (2007). Association between advance directives and quality of end-of-life care: A national study. *Journal of the American Geriatrics Society, 55*(2), 189–194.

Tulsky, J. A. (2005). Beyond advance directives importance of communication skills at the end of life. *Journal of the American Medical Association, 294*(3), 359–365.

Online Resources

American Academy of Hospice and Palliative Medicine

Palliative care physician membership organization provides conferences and other tools to assist health care providers communicating with patients at the end of life.

www.aahpm.org

American Bar Association

The American Bar Association provides a consumer guide to advance directives.

www.abanet.org/aging/toolkit

www.americanbar.org/groups/law_aging/resources/consumer_s_toolkit_for_
health_care_advance_planning.html

ANA End of Life Issues

List of online resources for end-of-life decision making.

www.nursingworld.org/MainMenuCategories/EthicsStandards/Resources/Endof-
Life.aspx

Center for Palliative Care

Research and education devoted to physician–patient communication and end-of-life care provides research and teaching resources.

www.durham.hsrd.research.va.gov/palliative.asp

Center for Palliative Care Education

Well-organized compendium of educational resources with a particular focus on caring for patients with AIDS.

http://depts.washington.edu/pallcare

End of Life/Palliative Education Resource Center (EPERC)

Online site with peer-reviewed educational resources, including materials on communication and end-of-life decision making.

www.eperc.mcw.edu

Growth House Inc.

Online information clearinghouse for all information related to end-of-life care.

www.growthhouse.org

Help with Advance Care Directives by Concepts

www.tc.umn.edu/~parkx032/Q-L-WILL.html

Help with Advance Care Directives by State

www.noah-health.org/en/rights/endoflife/adforms.html

www.caringinfo.org/i4a/pages/index.cfm?pageid=3289

The National Academy of Elder Law Attorneys

www.naela.org

National Hospice and Palliative Care Organization

Details for National Hospice and Palliative Care Organization.

www.nhpco.org/templates/1/homepage.cfm

OncoTalk

National Cancer Institute–supported biannual retreat for oncology fellows to improve communication skills at the end of life.

www.oncotalk.info

Internet References . . .

National Institutes of Health: National Institute of Neurological Disorders and Stroke

These sites offers news, funding, training and research from the National Institute of Neurological Disorders and Stroke to reduce the burden of neurological disease.

http://stroke.nih.gov/

http://health.nih.gov/topic/Stroke

Compassion Fatigue Articles

This Web site offers a virtual library of articles on compassion fatigue.

www.vaonline.org/doc_compassion.html

Compassion Fatigue Links

This site offers links to other sites that includes crisis, grief and healing, and suicide prevention.

www.vaonline.org/care.html

Compassion Fatigue Self-Test

This site aids people in detecting their fatigue threshold.

www.compassionfatigue.org/pages/CompassionFatigueSelfTest.html

How Compassion Fatigue Can Overwhelm Charity Workers

This presents an article on compassion fatigue in volunteers and charity workers.

http://philanthropy.com/jobs/2002/03/21/20020321-974239.htm

Overcoming Compassion Fatigue

Compassion fatigue is addressed and discussed in this excellent site.

http://pspinformation.com/caregiving/thecaregiver/compassion.shtml

American Foundation for Suicide Prevention (AFSP)

This site provides basic information on suicide as well as information on suicide-prevention programs and surviving suicide loss.

www.afsp.org/

Suicide Awareness

This site provides a variety of articles and information on suicide including rape and suicide, domestic violence and suicide, and links for help.

www.suicide.org

Caregiver End-of-Life Decision Making

*W*hen patients are unable to make decisions and have no advance directives, health care professionals rely on family members or caregivers to assist with end-of-life decision making. Family members who make these decisions are supposed to base them on what the patient would want. But under some circumstances, families are ill-prepared for decisions about end of life. Teenagers in car accidents can sustain severe brain injuries. Parents must be ready to face the death of a child when making care decisions for stopping treatment. Physicians may realize that the brain injury is so severe that survival would mean a lifetime of nursing home care for that teen. In this unit, we discuss the unique issues faced by family members of brain-injured patients and whether care should be withdrawn. Some patients who are dying have no family members or advocates to speak for them. In these cases, health professionals have to use a "standard of care" rule for patients of this kind. We explore whether patients without advocates receive different care than patients with advocates.

Most caregivers for dying patients are women, although there are many men who provide care to dying spouses. Caregiving for a loved one at the end of life can be an exhausting. We examine the issue of caregiver fatigue in persons who care for dying patients. What happens when care becomes overwhelming for family caregivers? Finally, we address the issue of homicide and suicide in intimate relationships. These tragic deaths often leave family members stunned and distraught as they try to sort through feelings of loss.

- Do Dying Persons Without Advocates Get a Different Quality of Care?

- Compassion Fatigue: Does Burnout Occur in All Caregivers of Dying Patients?

ISSUE 3

Do Dying Persons Without Advocates Get a Different Quality of Care?

YES: Elizabeth Barnett Pathak, Michele L. Casper, Jean Paul Tanner, Steven Reader, and Beverly Ward, from "A Multilevel Analysis of Absence of Transport to a Hospital Before Premature Cardiac Death," *Preventing Chronic Disease* (vol. 7, no. 3, 2010)

NO: Linda S. Wasserman, from "Respectful Death: A Model for End-of-Life Care," *Clinical Journal of Oncology Nursing* (vol. 12, no. 4, 2008)

Learning Outcomes

After reading this issue, you should be able to:

- Gain an understanding of the challenges of dying patients without advocates.
- Describe the findings of studies on end-of-life care in homeless persons without identified family or surrogates.
- Discuss the laws regarding providing care when there is no one to represent patient wishes.
- Identify and debate the issues related to aggressiveness of treatments in persons without advocates.
- Describe the challenges in providing end-of-life care to homeless persons with chemical dependency issues.

ISSUE SUMMARY

YES: Elizabeth Barnett Pathak, Jean Paul Tanner, Steven Reader, and Beverly Ward, of the University of South Florida, and Michele L. Casper, from the Centers for Disease Control and Prevention, found that people who are unmarried and live alone are vulnerable to dying from cardiac events without medical aid or a witness.

NO: Linda Wasserman, an advance practice nurse proposes a "respectful death" model of care that would be used as an approach to all patients, regardless of whether they have an advocate. The model includes identifying a caregiver for dying patients, with or without advocates.

$\mathbf{M}$uch of the literature related to dying assumes that the dying individual will be surrounded by loved ones in a health care system or in their own home with the physical and emotional support that they need at the end of life. Researchers have demonstrated that family advocates who visit frequently can make a difference in the quality of end-of-life care for patients in nursing home settings (Shield, Wetle, Teno, Miller, & Welch, 2010). However, several researchers have identified a fundamental deficiency in the assumption that patients are always surrounded by loved ones in their dying days. Our society does not address the needs of dying homeless individuals who are alienated from family or individuals who other patients who have no advocate or other supportive resources (Kushal & Miaskowski, 2006; Markowitz & McPhee, 2007; Song et al., 2007). In this issue, we discuss the concerns of individuals who have no advocates at the end of life and the challenges faced by the medical community in addressing these issues.

There are few research studies that have examined end-of-life care for persons without advocates or who are homeless. Data from the 2010 Annual Homeless Assessment Report (AHAR) indicates that on any given night there are approximately 649,000 homeless persons in the United States. Over the course of a year, homelessness affects an estimated 1.5 million individuals who transition in and out of living on the streets to living in temporary shelters or housing in the United States. Rates of substance abuse and mental illness and medical problems are high among those who are homeless. One study of deaths of 77 homeless persons in King County, Washington, showed that the manner of death was accidental (35 percent), followed by natural causes (29 percent). Examples of accidental deaths included intoxication with alcohol, street drugs, prescription drugs, or a combination of these; traffic accidents (pedestrian); and drowning, choking, or homicide. Sadly, 55 percent of these persons died outdoors (Public Health–Seattle & King County, 2004). The natural causes in the King County study of homeless persons included cardiovascular disease, cirrhosis, infection, diabetes, cancer, chronic obstructive lung disease, pneumonia, and AIDS. For homeless patients who continue to use illicit substances while receiving end-of-life care, there are challenges in writing prescriptions for end-of-life pain management for diseases like cancer (Kushel & Miaskowski, 2006).

Most homeless people lack social support and have no medical insurance. This becomes particularly problematic as medical problems increase. Homeless people are less likely to have a surrogate decision maker. One study reported that homeless patients were usually estranged from family members and the majority of them did not want family members contacted when they were dying. In addition, that research reports that the homeless feel that they are not treated with respect and that there is a palpable bias among health professionals that the homeless are not deserving of basic health care (Song et al., 2007).

When homeless persons face terminal illnesses, they face other challenges. They may have difficulty in understanding the process of end-of-life planning, may be unable to adhere to medication regimens, and may be unable to find a place to provide them with the terminal care that they require (Kushel & Miaskowski, 2006). For example, hospice services in the community require the patient to have a designated caregiver, an identified location of care, and resources (insurance or Medicaid) to cover the hospice costs. Homeless persons with mental illness may be suspicious or unable to designate a caregiver. If the patient is accustomed to shifting from place to place, they cannot be managed by hospice if they are too difficult to track.

Clinicians face specific challenges in approaching end-of-life care for persons without advocates. If there is no advance directive (see Issue 2), or surrogate designated, how can they best serve the interests of the patient? Kushel and Miaskowski (2006) recommend that clinicians document conversations with these patients about end-of-life wishes so that the record can show a pattern of the patient values, regardless of any formal signed advance directives.

One way to address the needs of homeless persons at the end of life is to ensure that hospitals have services that respond to their unique issues. Hospitals that serve greater numbers of homeless people should develop inpatient palliative care services to improve the end-of-life care these patients receive (Kushel & Miaskowski, 2006; Markowitz & McPhee, 2007), followed up with a physician serving the homeless patient in the Kushel case report. The patient did develop a good relationship with a health care provider as he faced renal cancer. However, because he was unwilling to stay in one place very long for care, hospice could not continue providing services. The challenge of the palliative care team model is that one cannot assume that all persons without surrogates would be in the hospital at the end of life where they have access to a team.

In addition, not all patients without advocates are homeless. Single persons, living alone, or elderly persons who have no living family members may also be at risk for not having an advocate at the end of life. Approximately 5 percent of patients who die in the intensive care units at hospitals lack a surrogate decision maker and an advance directive (White et al., 2007). A study of timing of transport to the hospital after a cardiac event showed that persons who lived alone or had no surrogate were more likely to die of the cardiac event because of the delay of transport (Pathak, Casper, Tanner, Reader, & Ward, 2010). If a patient arrives in an emergency room or the hospital without expressed wishes and without an advocate, physicians are legally required to provide the standard of care that they would offer to other patients in similar circumstances. However, laws about who can make decisions about care withdrawal from these types of patients vary from state to state. Some states allow physicians to issue a do not resuscitate order if the medical care is seen as futile and the physician receives written agreement from another physician (NY state law) (White et al., 2007). However, other states require a guardian to be appointed to represent the patient (Washington case law), and still other states have no explicit law regarding how end-of-life care should be handled for patients without surrogates or advance directives.

In the YES article, Elizabeth Barnett Pathak, Jean Paul Tanner, Steven Reader, and Beverly Ward, of the University of South Florida, and Michele L. Casper, from the Centers for Disease Control and Prevention, found that people who are unmarried and live alone are vulnerable to dying from cardiac events without medical aid or a witness. The quality of medical outcomes for these patients at the end of life is definitely impacted by the lack of an advocate or surrogate decision maker.

In the NO article, Linda Wasserman, an advance practice nurse, proposes an approach to ensure quality of care to all dying patients, regardless of whether they have an advocate. In her essay, Wasserman identifies a holistic and practical model for end-of-life care to improve the quality of care offered to patients. She discusses the need to develop relationships with dying patients and have clear conversations about values and wishes for end-of-life care.

A Multilevel Analysis of Absence of Transport to a Hospital Before Premature Cardiac Death

Abstract

Introduction

Prompt transportation to a hospital and aggressive medical treatment can often prevent acute cardiac events from becoming fatal. Consequently, lack of transport before death may represent lost opportunities for life-saving interventions. We investigated the effect of individual characteristics (age, sex, race/ethnicity, education, and marital status) and small-area factors (population density and social cohesion) on the probability of premature cardiac decedents dying without transport to a hospital.

Methods

We analyzed death data for adults aged 25 to 69 years who resided in the Tampa, Florida, metropolitan statistical area and died from an acute cardiac event from 1998 through 2002 (N = 2,570). Geocoding of decedent addresses allowed the use of multilevel (hierarchical) logistic regression models for analysis.

Results

The strongest predictor of dying without transport was being unmarried (odds ratio, 2.13; 95% confidence interval, 1.79–2.52, $P < .001$). There was no effect of education; however, white race was modestly predictive of dying without transport. Younger decedent age was a strong predictor. Multilevel statistical modeling revealed that less than 1% of the variance in our data was found at the small-area level.

Conclusions

Results contradicted our hypothesis that small-area characteristics would increase the probability of cardiac patients receiving transport before death. Instead we found that being unmarried, a proxy of living alone and perhaps

From *Preventing Chronic Disease*, May 2010, pp. 1–11. Published by Centers for Disease Control and Prevention.

low social support, was the most important predictor of people who died from a cardiac event dying without transport to a hospital.

Introduction

Premature deaths from heart disease usually result from a severe, acute event such as an acute myocardial infarction (AMI) ("heart attack") or, less commonly, a sudden cardiac arrest (SCA). In most cases, the onset of these life-threatening events begins at home.[1] Prompt transportation to a hospital and aggressive medical care can often prevent death in these severe cases; however, many victims die at home without initiating an attempt at transport to a hospital.[1] Transportation to a hospital in the United States occurs both by professional emergency medical services (EMS) and by self-transport (usually by private motor vehicle). It is not uncommon for people with AMI to attempt to drive themselves to the nearest hospital.

In the United States, as in many industrialized nations, most decedents die in a hospital.[2] This situation reflects both the extensiveness of medical services and intensiveness of medical interventions for chronic diseases at the end of life. Consequently, we can view deaths from cardiac events that occur before transport as a result of 3 general scenarios: 1) onset of cardiac symptoms is severe and death follows rapidly, with no time to solicit or initiate transportation (eg, sudden cardiac death); 2) the patient delays or avoids seeking medical treatment and death follows at some point hours later; 3) the patient desires transport to a hospital but is unable to access transportation before death. Under the last scenario, the patient's inability to access transportation could result from several factors, including lack of family member, neighbor, or bystander support for communication and transportation; lack of telephone; lack of vehicle for personal transportation; lack of local availability of EMS; being a long distance from the nearest hospital; and lack of insurance or financial means to obtain transportation.

Many, if not most, people experiencing cardiac symptoms delay seeking medical treatment.[1] Early professional approaches to this problem assumed that lack of knowledge of heart attack symptoms was the source of patient delays. However, more recent research has demonstrated that lack of knowledge is rarely the most important reason for patient delays in seeking treatment.[1] Rather, reasons for delays in treatment seeking are complex and relate to patients' age, sex, cultural and racial/ethnic background, socioeconomic status, insurance coverage, geographic location, medical history, availability of social support, and cognitive and emotional factors.[1]

We have previously described how "no transport" deaths from cardiac events may represent lost opportunities for life-saving medical intervention.[3] Although SCAs are rapid-onset events that require immediate medical intervention to ensure resuscitation and reperfusion of the heart,[4] the typical clinical development of an AMI opens a wider time frame for medical intervention.[5] Both individual (patient) factors[1,2,3] and local social environmental (small-area) factors[3,7,8] may influence the use of medical care resources during an acute cardiac event. Availability of an acute-care hospital and local EMS are essential requirements, but even in areas with reasonable availability of services, many deaths from cardiac events occur without transport.[8]

On the basis of findings from previous research, we hypothesized that both sociodemographic characteristics of decedents (unmarried, male, younger age, white race, and lower educational attainment) and social environmental characteristics of small areas (low population density and low social cohesion) would increase the probability that people would die from a cardiac event without transport to a hospital. Social cohesion is an ecologic construct that attempts to capture the overall extent of social ties and connectedness in a defined community. Low community social cohesion has been independently associated with heart disease risk.[9,10] We focused on premature deaths because complex factors influence the desirability of hospitalization and aggressive medical intervention among elderly patients, particularly the very elderly.[2] In contrast, for nonelderly persons who experience cardiac events, there exists a social and cultural presumption about the importance and necessity of medical intervention in industrialized countries such as the United States.[2]

Methods

Study Population and Definitions

Our study population consisted of adults aged 25–69 years who died from an acute cardiac event during 1998 through 2002 in Tampa, Florida. We ascertained cardiac decedent status from death certificates. An acute cardiac death was defined as any death for which the coded underlying cause was AMI, cardiac arrest/cardiac dysrthymias, cardiovascular disease unspecified or ill-defined and unknown causes. We included cardiovascular disease unspecified because under ICD-9, this code was used for cases of myocardial infarction and ischemic heart disease with insufficient diagnostic information.[11] Because the likelihood of misclassification of cause-of-death coding for heart disease is not independent of place of death (the basis of our main study outcome), we used a definition of acute cardiac deaths that included definite, probable, and possible AMIs and sudden cardiac deaths.

The cause-of-death category ill-defined and unknown causes (ID) is used when postmortem evidence is insufficient to support assigning a specific disease as cause of death.[12] Earlier research on SCA fatalities indicated that these were often coded as ID on the death certificate.[13] A study from Belgium found that approximately 5% of definite or possible cases of AMI had been coded as ID on the death certificate.[11]

Our outcome in this study was no transport before cardiac death. We obtained transport status information for each decedent from the place of death variable on the death certificate. We categorized a cardiac death as occurring with no transport if the place of death was reported as either at home or in another location in the community. Deaths that occurred during or after transport had place of death reported as 1 of the following: 1) dead on arrival (at hospital), 2) emergency room/outpatient, 3) hospital inpatient, or 4) hospital, unknown inpatient or outpatient status. Variables we examined were age by group (25–49, 50–59, 60–64, and 65–69 years), sex, race/ethnicity (non-Hispanic whites vs Hispanics and non-Hispanic blacks), educational attainment (no college degree vs college degree) and marital status (unmarried vs married).

Small-Area Variables

Our study area was the Tampa-St. Petersburg-Clearwater metropolitan statistical area (Tampa MSA). This ethnically and geographically diverse area of more than 2 million people encompasses 2,600 square miles of central cities, suburbs, small towns, and rural farms spread across 4 counties. Our geographic unit of analysis was the public use microdata area (PUMA).[14] Population and housing data for the 20 PUMAs in our study area were obtained from the public use microdata 5% sample from the 2000 census.[14] . . .

We examined 2 dimensions of the social environment that we hypothesized would influence access to and use of transportation (whether private or EMS). The first was low population density. . . . The second dimension was low social cohesion. We looked at 3 indicators for the population aged 25 to 69 years: percentage who lived alone, percentage who had resided at the same address for less than 5 years, and percentage who had resided at the same address for more than 10 years. . . .

Discussion

. . . [W]e found that being unmarried, a proxy of living alone and perhaps of a lack of social support, was the strongest predictor of dying without transport for cardiac decedents. Previous research findings have consistently shown heart disease death rates are higher for unmarried people than for married people,[18-22] which could be due to higher incidence of heart disease,[23,24] higher case fatality,[21] or both. Our study suggests that at least some portion of this excess is due to higher case fatality: unmarried people who live alone may have impaired access to life-saving EMS. Future studies could directly test this hypothesis through linked EMS and patient outcome data.

Our results showing a higher probability of whites dying with no transport compared with blacks and Hispanics are consistent with earlier national findings.[3] This result is surprising from the perspective of patient delays in seeking treatment, because several studies have shown that blacks in particular delay seeking treatment longer than whites. However, our findings could result from unmeasured differences in household composition between whites and other racial/ethnic populations. National census data reveal that racial/ethnic minorities are less likely to live alone than whites and are more likely to live in extended family households.[25,26]

The REACT trial found that people who lived alone were more likely than others to use EMS for transportation to a hospital, perhaps reflecting a lack of other transportation options.[27] However, the study's respondents were much more likely to call EMS when they were bystanders to the cardiac event of a stranger than when they were personally experiencing cardiac symptoms.[27]

Although the symptoms experienced in cardiac events often differ from typical and expected symptoms,[28] the incongruity in symptoms does not explain delays in seeking treatment.[29] In a study of rural residents, the most important predictors of decision time to seeking treatment were lack of ability to carry out normal activities and extent of anxiety.[29]

Notable strengths of our study include accurate geocoding, specificity of cardiac causes of death, and the use of multilevel modeling. In addition, the validity of death certificate data on Hispanic ethnicity, black race, white race, and educational attainment has been high.[30-32] We included both suspected and definite acute cardiac deaths to avoid selection bias, because many out-of-hospital deaths (eg, nontransported) lack accurate cause-of-death coding. However, it is likely that we also introduced some degree of misclassification, as some of the ID deaths may not have been cardiac in origin. Furthermore, our use of death certificate data entails other limitations. Primarily, we did not have access to data for a true denominator of all acute cardiac events that occurred in our study area during the study period (ie, a study population that included both decedents and survivors). Unlike the case for cancer, no surveillance system of incident coronary heart disease exists in the United States. In addition, data about decedent medical history and socioeconomic status were not available.

Our study was conducted in a large ethnically and geographically diverse area, which improves the generalizability of our findings. However, none of the rural areas in the Tampa MSA could be considered isolated or remote. Future studies in remote rural areas may well find a stronger effect of geographic and social environmental factors. Furthermore, our study area has well-funded and extensive local EMS provider agencies, which may minimize the barriers of location and distance on transport status once medical aid is requested.

Our study showed that low population density and low population social cohesion were not impediments to transport before cardiac death. It appears that a smaller geographic scale (ie, the household) is the critical level for interventions to reduce delay times for seeking treatment for acute cardiac events. Previous research has shown that the public is more willing to intervene and help a stranger or family member than to seek aid and treatment for self-suffering.[27] Interventions are needed to overcome the reluctance of many patients to take action to help themselves. People who are unmarried and live alone are particularly vulnerable to dying from cardiac events without medical aid or witness.

References

1. Moser DK, Kimble LP, Alberts MJ, Alonzo A, Croft JB, Dracup K, et al. Reducing delay in seeking treatment by patients with acute coronary syndrome and stroke: a scientific statement from the American Heart Association Council on Cardiovascular Nursing and Stroke Council. Circulation 2006;114(2):168–82.

2. Seale C. Changing patterns of death and dying. Soc Sci Med 2000;51(6):917–30.

3. Barnett E, Reader S, Ward BG, Casper ML. Social and demographic predictors of no transport prior to premature cardiac death, United States, 1999–2000. BMC Cardiovasc Disord 2006;6:45.

4. Wu LA, Kottke TE, Brekke LN, Brekke MJ, Grill DE, Goraya TY, et al. Opportunities to prevent sudden out-of-hospital death due to coronary heart disease in a community. Resuscitation 2003;56(1):55–8.

5. Faxon D, Lenfant C. Timing is everything: motivating patients to call 9-1-1 at onset of acute myocardial infarction. Circulation 2001;104(11):1210–1.

6. Schoenberg NE, Peters JC, Drew EM. Unraveling the mysteries of timing: women's perceptions about time to treatment for cardiac symptoms. Soc Sci Med 2003;56(2):271–84.

7. Pearson TA, Bazzarre TL, Daniels SR, Fair JM, Fortmann SP, Franklin BA, et al. American Heart Association guide for improving cardiovascular health at the community level: a statement for public health practitioners, health-care providers, and health policy makers from the American Heart Association Expert Panel on Population and Prevention Science. Circulation 2003;107(4):645–51.

8. Tydén P, Engström G, Hansen O, Hedblad B, Janzon L. Geographical pattern of female deaths from myocardial infarction in an urban population: fatal outcome out-of-hospital related to socio-economic deprivation. J Intern Med 2001;250(3):201–7.

9. Chaix B. Geographic life environments and coronary heart disease: a literature review, theoretical contributions, methodological updates, and a research agenda. Ann Rev Public Health 2009;30:81–105.

10. Stjärne MK, Ponce de Leon A, Hallqvist J. Contextual effects of social fragmentation and material deprivation on risk of myocardial infarction—results from the Stockholm Heart Epidemiology Program (SHEEP). Int J Epidemiol 2004;33(4):732–41.

11. De Henauw S, de Smet P, Aelvoet W, Kornitzer M, De Backer G. Misclassification of coronary heart disease in mortality statistics. Evidence from the WHO-MONICA Ghent-Charleroi Study in Belgium. J Epidemiol Community Health 1998;52(8):513–9.

12. Armstrong DL, Wing SB, Tyroler HA. United States mortality from ill-defined causes, 1968–1988: potential effects on heart disease mortality trends. Int J Epidemiol 1995; 24(3):522–7.

13. Armstrong D, Wing S, Tyroler HA. Race differences in estimates of sudden coronary heart disease mortality, 1980–1988: the impact of ill-defined death. J Clin Epidemiol 1996;49(11):1247–51.

14. Census 2000, Public-use microdata sample (PUMS), United States, technical documentation. Washington (DC): US Census Bureau; 2003.

15. Schabenberger O. Growing up fast: SAS 9.2 enhancements to the GLIMMIX procedure. Paper presented at: SAS Global Forum 2007; April 16–19, 2007; Orlando, Florida.

16. Martikainen P, Kauppinen TM, Valkonen T. Effects of the characteristics of neighbourhoods and the characteristics of people on cause specific mortality: a register based follow up study of 252,000 men. J Epidemiol Community Health 2003;57(3):210–7.

17. Guo G, Zhao H. Multilevel modeling for binary data. Ann Rev Sociol 2000;26:441–62.

18. Johnson NJ, Backlund E, Sorlie PD, Loveless CA. Marital status and mortality: the National Longitudinal Mortality Study. Ann Epidemiol 2000;10(4):224–38.

19. Ebrahim S, Wannamethee G, McCallum A, Walker M, Shaper AG. Marital status, change in marital status, and mortality in middle-aged British men. Am J Epidemiol 1995;142(8):834–42.

20. Malyutina S, Bobak M, Simonova G, Gafarov V, Nikitin Y, Marmot M. Education, marital status, and total and cardiovascular mortality in Novosibirsk, Russia: a prospective cohort study. Ann Epidemiol 2004;14(4):244–9.

21. Mendes de Leon CF, Appels AW, Otten FW, Schouten EG. Risk of mortality and coronary heart disease by marital status in middle-aged men in The Netherlands. Int J Epidemiol 1992;21(3):460–6.

22. Ben-Shlomo Y, Smith GD, Shipley M, Marmot MG. Magnitude and causes of mortality differences between married and unmarried men. J Epidemiol Community Health 1993;47(3):200–5.

23. Engström G, Tydén P, Berglund G, Hansen O, Hedblad B, Janzon L. Incidence of myocardial infarction in women. A cohort study of risk factors and modifiers of effect. J Epidemiol Community Health 2000;54(2):104–7.

24. Engström G, Hedblad B, Rosvall M, Janzon L, Lindgärde F. Occupation, marital status, and low-grade inflammation: mutual confounding or independent cardiovascular risk factors? Arterioscler Thromb Vasc Biol 2006;26(3):643–8.

25. Ramirez RR. We the people: Hispanics in the United States: Census 2000 special reports. Washington (DC): US Census Bureau, 2004. p. 1–18. Publication CENSR-18.

26. McKinnon JD, Bennett CE. We the people: blacks in the United States: Census 2000 special reports. Washington (DC): US Census Bureau, 2005. p. 1–17. Publication CENSR-25.

27. Brown AL, Mann NC, Daya M, Goldberg R, Meischke H, Taylor J, et al. Demographic, belief, and situational factors influencing the decision to utilize emergency medical services among chest pain patients. Rapid Early Action for Coronary Treatment (REACT) study. Circulation 2000;102(2):173–8.

28. Albarran JW, Clarke BA, Crawford J. 'It was not chest pain really, I can't explain it!' An exploratory study on the nature of symptoms experienced by women during their myocardial infarction. J Clin Nurs 2007;16(7):1292–301.

29. Morgan DM. Effect of incongruence of acute myocardial infarction symptoms on the decision to seek treatment in a rural population. J Cardiovasc Nurs 2005;20(5):365–71.

30. Arias E, Schauman WS, Eschbach K, Sorlie PD, Backlund E. The validity of race and Hispanic origin reporting on death certificates in the United States. Vital Health Stat 2 2008 Oct;(148):1–23.

31. Sorlie PD, Johnson NJ. Validity of education information on the death certificate. Epidemiology 1996;7(4):437–9.

32. Rosamund WD, Tyroler HA, Chambless LE, Folsom AR, Cooper L, Conwill D. Educational achievement recorded on certificates of death compared with self-report. Epidemiology 1997;8(2):202–4.

Linda S. Wasserman

 **NO**

Respectful Death: A Model for End-of-Life Care

The Respectful Death Model (RDM) is a research-based, holistic, and practical model developed to improve end-of-life care. A respectful death is one which supports dying patients, their families, and professionals in the completion of life cycles and can be used by all members of the healthcare team. The model is a process method commencing with the establishment of a therapeutic relationship with the dying patient and his or her family and, as a result, their stories are heard and incorporated into the care plan. This article demonstrates that hospice and palliative care nurses have been practicing this model since the origination of care of the dying. Other topics addressed are the current culture toward death in the United States, the roles of nurses in the RDM, and the barriers and benefits of the RDM. Recommendations for future research in end-of-life care also are addressed.

About 2 million Americans died in 2007 (U.S. Department of Health and Human Services, 2008), but the demographics of those who have died has changed dramatically since the early 1900s. Death in childhood was more common at that time (Teno, McNiff, & Lynn, 2000) but, with the introduction of antibiotics, immunizations, and sanitation practices, morbidity and mortality rates began to drop and a longer life expectancy was realized (Teno et al.). Today, older adults typically die from chronic illnesses with a gradual period of deterioration and disability (Teno et al.).

Unfortunately, many Americans still die in physical, emotional, social, psychological, and spiritual pain (Steinhauser et al., 2000; Vig, Davenport, & Pearlman, 2002) despite research such as the Study to Understand Prognoses and Preferences for Outcomes and Risks of Treatment (Covinsky et al., 1994); the formation of groups such as Compassion and Choices (formerly known as the Hemlock Society), Americans for Better Care of the Dying, and Dying Well; enactment of laws to protect older Americans; and professional educational changes (Bookbinder & Kiss, 2001).

Current Culture Surrounding Death in the United States

The current culture surrounding death in the United States is highlighted from various perspectives: attitudes and perceptions, the realities of death, and the dying process and discourses.

From *Clinical Journal of Oncology Nursing*, August 2008, pp. 621–626. Copyright © 2008 by Oncology Nursing Society. Reprinted by permission.

AT A GLANCE

- The Respectful Death Model (RDM) is a practical, research-based holistic tool meant to foster the education of varied disciplines in end-of-life care.
- The RDM details the establishment of therapeutic relationships with patients and their families and, as a result, their stories are heard and incorporated into the care plan.
- Nurses establish therapeutic relationships with their patients and families, ensuring frank dialogues about death and resultant respectful deaths.

Attitudes and Perceptions

Byock (2002) and Kastenbaum (2004) described the historic and current U.S. culture as one that denies and fears death. Examples include expressions such as "he or she passed on" or "he or she is at rest," rather than saying "he or she died." Death is still a taboo topic. Becker (1973) stated that the fear of death is universal, and Kastenbaum (1978) noted that the study of death may improve the quality of all civilization by eliminating painful deaths.

In any discussion about death, suffering often is used simultaneously. The Respectful Death Model (RDM) requires healthcare professionals to listen to the dying to help relieve their suffering (Farber & Farber, 2006). Cassell (2004) defined suffering as the stress that occurs as a result of losses, including loss of family, friends, possessions, roles, relationships, a future, and physical losses related to bodily functions. Suffering occurs within relationships; the nature of these relationships, according to Cassell, influences the degree of suffering that is experienced. However, this thought is contrary to some current theories about death and suffering because of the tendency to use medication to relieve suffering (Byock, 1996).

Pioneers in Changing Attitudes

Although some 30–40 years have passed since champions such as Saunders, Feifel, Quint Benoliel, Folta, Glaser and Strauss, and Kubler-Ross pioneered work with the dying, U.S. culture has not significantly changed its attitude toward death.

Saunders, a nurse, social worker, and doctor, began her work in the East End of London in the late 1950s and founded St. Christopher, the first hospice (Clark, 1999). She defined and described a theory of total pain: that the dying suffered not only physical pain but "emotional, spiritual, psychological, and social pain" (Clark, p. 729). Feifel edited the first comprehensive book in 1959, *The Meaning of Death*, in which topics such as modern art and death, the treatment of the dying, and attitudes toward death by healthy and mentally ill populations were addressed.

Quint Benoliel, a nurse researcher, published a book and several articles on caring for the dying and was one of the first to do research on the dying in teaching hospitals (Quint Benoliel, 1977). She described the care/cure dilemma and that the existential or human aspect was missing from this care.

Folta, also a nurse researcher, described death as "multicomplex." She studied the attitudes and perception of death of various nurses at several sites (Folta, 1965). Her research revealed that, despite the fact that death was perceived as peaceful, nurses described their attitudes as fearful and anxious. Folta concluded that this fear might be a universal human reaction or that it may be because her particular groups of nurses feared death and, therefore, chose nursing as a career to help prevent it.

Glaser and Strauss (1965) also studied the dying in hospitals and developed a theory about the awareness context surrounding death, referring to the knowledge that the dying patient, caregivers, and family hold regarding the fate of the patient (Glaser & Strauss).

Kubler-Ross, a psychiatrist, talked with dying patients in hospitals in the 1960s and was one of the first to address the public about dying (Kubler-Ross, 1969). She developed a stage theory describing various emotions and considerations that people experienced when confronted with death (Clark, 1999).

Realities of Death

We are mortal and aware that we will die. We mourn and bury our dead with some cultures believing that death is a personal, unique, and private journey of an individual whereas others see it as a public event (Byock, 2002; Vig et al., 2002). The responsibility of caring for the dying rests with individuals and communities because of shared mortality and the effects each death has on individuals and communities (Braun, Zir, Crocker, & Seely, 2005; Byock, 2003).

Another thought on death is that it is a natural part of life, a stage in which the dying attempt to find meaning in their lives and of life in general (Byock, 2002). The old die to make way for the new; death makes way for the birth of children (McCue, 1995). Many authors today, just as the early pioneers did, advocate for a holistic approach to end-of-life (EOL) care, bringing attention to the physical, spiritual, emotional, and social needs of the patient (Dobratz, 2005; Mariano, 2001).

The Dying Process

Western medical and bioethical decisions reflect the importance of individual autonomy and personal choice in health-care decisions (Volker, Kahn, & Penticuff, 2004). The Patient Self-Determination Act of 1991 gave hospitalized patients the right to make treatment decisions, which led to the formation of advance directives and gave patients the right to refuse life-sustaining treatments (Bookbinder & Kiss, 2001).

A study of more than 4,400 seriously ill and older adult patients by Lynn et al. (1997) revealed that most died in acute care hospitals and often suffered from pain and other symptoms. The study also revealed that family members interviewed after the death of a loved one confirmed that life-sustaining treatments were performed despite their wishes for comfort only. The U.S. Department of Health and Human Services (2006) revealed that, in 2004, 2,401,400 U.S. residents died. Of those, 903,953 (37%) died in inpatient hospitals or medical centers, the highest percentage for any one location. Other locations included at home, in nursing care facilities, and in emergency rooms.

Walter (1996) suggested that the original discourse on death emanated from the church, which supported the dying and their families. However, the 20th century saw a shift from the church to modern medicine and the hospital setting (Walter). Sullivan (2002) described hospitals as institutions that value saving lives and favor acute care rather than care of the dying. The discourse changed in the late 20th century to "living with dying" because of the extended life expectancy of patients living with life-threatening diseases (Walter).

The culture of dying in the United States, however, has been rocked by media coverage of the Terri Schiavo case; the death of Pope John Paul II (Lazar, 2005); the deaths from the September 11, 2001, terrorist attacks; and the deaths of soldiers and civilians in Iraq and Afghanistan in the war on terror (Gallo-Silver & Damaskos, 2004). How those events will affect cultural views on dying is unknown.

The Respectful Death Model

The RDM is a research-based and holistic model developed out of a qualitative study of patients with cancer funded by a grant from the Project on Death in America (Open Society Institute, 2008). The original purpose of the research was to establish an EOL curriculum for family practice residents in the School of Medicine at the University of Washington (Farber, Egnew, & Farber, 2004). Working collaboratively with patients with cancer, their families, and their healthcare providers, researchers were able to conduct focus group studies about EOL concerns. RDM evolved from the focus groups and a workbook was created to assist patients and their families with EOL concerns (Farber et al.).

Respectful death and the RDM of EOL care can be used by all members of care teams. The process method and the roles of nursing in the RDM will be described and the benefits and barriers will be discussed and support for the model provided (see Figure 1).

Respectful Death and the Model of Care

A respectful death is one which supports dying patients, their families, and healthcare professionals in the completion of the life cycle (Farber et al., 2004). This necessitates an intimate and personal relationship with patients and families; therefore, it is a model "that acknowledges the power of relationships and invites [professionals] to be mindful, curious, and open to surprises" (Farber & Farber, 2006, p. 223). An intimate and personal relationship is natural for many hospice, palliative care, and other nurses, but some members of the healthcare team may need mentoring by experienced nurses to practice these roles. Nurses have always formed therapeutic relationships with their

Figure 1

Study Schema

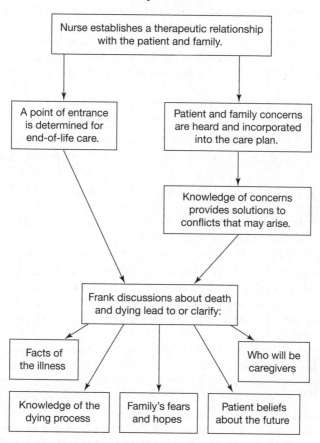

Nurse establishes a therapeutic relationship with the patient and family.

A point of entrance is determined for end-of-life care.

Patient and family concerns are heard and incorporated into the care plan.

Knowledge of concerns provides solutions to conflicts that may arise.

Frank discussions about death and dying lead to or clarify:

Facts of the illness

Who will be caregivers

Knowledge of the dying process

Family's fears and hopes

Patient beliefs about the future

Note: Based on information from Farber et al., 2004.

patients and have been in the forefront in caring for the dying, as evidenced by the hospice movement in the United States. . . .

One result of the formation of these intimate and therapeutic relationships is that patients' and families' stories are heard, and, as a result, are incorporated into the care plan (Farber & Farber, 2006). Each individual has different tasks he or she would like to complete at EOL, including reconnecting with lost family, saying goodbyes, and forgiving others. One role of healthcare professionals in the RDM is to help the dying and their families complete these tasks (Farber & Farber).

Farber et al. (2004) clarified that the point of entrance for EOL care should occur when the professional determines that a patient could die within a year. The model describes how to begin communication about death and how to explore patients' and families' knowledge of death (Farber & Farber, 2006).

Nurses in all settings must begin this communication about death with their dying patients and families.

Farber and Farber (2006) discussed the issue of cultural diversity and claimed that every relationship is cross-cultural. A patient's experiences, beliefs, race, gender, and socioeconomic class help define who the patient is and his or her meaning of life (Farber & Farber). The responsibility of healthcare professionals is to discover and understand the individual cultural experience and use that information in the care of patients and their families.

Establishing a Therapeutic Relationship

The story of the patient and his or her family is obtained by establishing a therapeutic relationship and "mindful listening" (Farber & Farber, 2006, p. 223). Professionals must first examine their own values and beliefs surrounding death prior to working with the dying (Farber et al., 2004). Establishing relationships and mindful listening is accomplished through "commitment, connection, and consciousness" (Farber & Farber, p. 223). Commitment refers to the fact that professionals will not abandon the patient when they are dying and will remain by their side until the end (Farber & Farber). Establishing connections means that the patient and family can discuss all topics of importance, such as the existential questions of life, and receive responses from the healthcare professional caring for them (Farber & Farber). Consciousness refers to experiences and life meanings shared by the patient and his or her family (Farber & Farber).

Farber and Farber (2006) also informed healthcare professionals on how to begin dialogues about death. One of the first pieces of knowledge to ascertain from the patient is what understanding he or she has of the illness (Farber & Farber). Another important question is "who would you like involved in your healthcare decisions?" (Farber & Farber, p. 233). A patient's beliefs about the future also should be determined (Farber & Farber) and an understanding of the dying process should be clarified if misunderstood (Farber & Farber). A patient's fears and hopes also are critical pieces of information, as is determining the patient's past experiences with crises (Farber & Farber).

Benefits of the Model

The formation of the therapeutic relationship, the exploration of the patient's and family's knowledge of death, and listening to their stories aids in the clarification of EOL issues and helps provides solutions that reduce conflict and suffering (Farber & Farber, 2006). Life stories often are remembered and retold, or are written down, to benefit future generations in their understanding of life and death (Farber & Farber). Another benefit of the model is the potential for growth and learning experiences for the patient, family, healthcare professionals, and community (Farber & Farber) and the ability of the patient to achieve respectful death and complete his or her life cycle.

Caring for patients in EOL can be a privilege. Healthcare professionals experience the personal satisfaction of helping to heal during this time, are reminded of the beauty of life and nature, and may experience a deeper under-standing of life and death. Healthcare professionals have the satisfaction of providing a service to the community, such as being a witness to suffering or educating others about EOL issues (Farber & Farber, 2006). Farber and Farber defined for healthcare professionals when patients should be informed that they are dying, which has been lacking in other models of care, and instructed healthcare professionals on how to communicate the important issues of EOL to patients and families. The RDM is, therefore, a practical model that can help educate professionals in the holistic care of the dying. Decisions regarding the myriad of choices that are required will be less of a burden to families and communities because of these dialogues.

The RDM dissolves the value judgments of healthcare professionals and returns the process to the patient and family. The lived experiences of the patient and their family are important in this model (Farber & Farber, 2006). The focus on patients and families and their preferences and meanings, along with needed healthcare system and policy changes, can pave the way for respectful deaths.

Support for the Concept of Respectful Death

Many authors have written about the importance of patient-provider commu-nication and obtaining stories from patients and their families. Saunders used patient narratives as an important methodologic tool in her research (Clark, 1999). Suchman and Matthews (1988) described healing as a connection between the patient and provider in which the patient feels that his or her con-cerns are listened to and heard. Amato (1990) acknowledged that people have to tell their stories and that the stories provide truths and legacies for those who survive. Nuland (1994) stressed listening to the patient and stated that "I would listen more to the patient and ask [him or her] less to listen to me" (p. 253).

Chokyi and Shlim (2004) stated that the healthcare professional is the main focus of hope for ill and dying patients. Kubler-Ross (1969) also said that EOL care should be based on the experiences, needs, and responses of the patient. The words of a patient in *Crossing Over: Narratives of Palliative Care* (Barnard, Towers, Boston, & Lambrinidou, 2000) illustrate the importance and benefits of the therapeutic relationship and mindful listening.

> Well, you know, you got to find out about the identity of a person to get to know them. Because if you don't know a person, you got to find out about his identity, go where he lives, where he goes, where he was born, who's in his family. He's got to open up, and tell you these things. Because the more you know about this person, his family, then that'll make you know more about you. (Barnard et al., 2000, p. 2993).

Frank's (1995) *The Wounded Storyteller: Body, Illness, and Ethics* describes the telling of stories during illness and dying. According to Frank, the stories are told because of the changes that illness brings to the body. Frank believed that the stories served two functions: a personal one in which the stories help the individual make sense of the illness and the changes to his or her concept of self, and a social one, in which stories require a listener to hear them. Frank also described storytelling as the turning of suffering into testimony and that the listeners, in turn, become witnesses and bear responsibilities of communicating the knowledge to others.

Barriers to the Respectful Death Model

Linda Emmanuel, vice president of ethics at the American Medical Association and an author in EOL care, said, "We have an entire healthcare system not friendly to EOL care, a workforce not educated to EOL care, and an entire population just climbing out of the era when it was taboo to talk about it" (Grady, 2000, p. A1). That sentence succinctly describes the barriers to all EOL models of care.

The first barrier with the RDM that Farber and Farber (2006) identified was that the medical culture in the United States does not usually allow time for, or ignores, patient and family input. Physicians often are not compensated for "just" talking with patients and nurses often are focused on the physical tasks of intensive care and oncology units with little time left to listen to patients and families.

A second barrier is that healthcare professionals must let go of their views as experts and become "guides, collaborators and consultants" (Farber et al., 2004, p. 115), a difficult task because of the loss of control they feel and their adherence to a biomedical model of care (Farber & Farber, 2006). The model of care refers to the fact that death is viewed as "a lingering biological accident rather than a biological inevitability" (Callahan, 2005, p. 11).

Another barrier that Farber et al. (2004) addressed is the comfort level in practicing something new. The therapeutic relationship of the nurse and the dying patient has been well documented (Perrin, 2001; Quint Benoliel, 1977; Rando, 1984). Nurses are the ideal providers to elicit stories or narratives, as they spend the most time with patients and interact with their families and other caregivers (Krammer, Ring, Martinez, Jacobs, & Williams, 2001; Witt Sherman & LaPorte Matzo, 2001).

Conclusion and Discussion

This article has highlighted the current culture of death in the United States, which is still one of denial and fear. However, the culture and discourse may be changing because of media coverage of high-profile deaths, tragedies such as the September 11, 2001, terrorist attacks, and deaths of soldiers and civilians in the war on terror (Gallo-Silver & Damaskos, 2004; Lazar, 2005). However, many Americans still die in physical, emotional, social, psychological, and spiritual pain (Steinhauser et al., 2000; Vig et al., 2002).

The RDM is a holistic and research-based model describing the establishment of a therapeutic relationship with the dying patient and his or her family and listening to and incorporating their stories into the care plan (Farber & Farber, 2006). This exploration and resulting knowledge aid in the clarification of and offer solutions to issues that occur in the EOL setting, thereby reducing conflict and suffering (Farber & Farber). Many hospice, palliative care, and other nurses have been practicing this model for many years, but others should incorporate it into their care by mentoring with experienced nurses and practicing the RDM.

The U.S. culture is trending toward a change in EOL care. Patients will benefit from dialogues about death with healthcare professionals, their families, and their neighbors. The RDM encourages dialogue to take place. The collective voice of professionals in the field of EOL care and health care in general has a responsibility to the community to foster dialogue for the good of the entire patient population (Byock, 2003). In addition, dialogue should take place prior to patients becoming too ill or unable to speak, so that their beliefs, values, and stories can be told and incorporated into care plans. . . .

References

Amato, J.A. (1990). *A history and a theory of suffering.* New York: Greenwood Press.

Barnard, D., Towers, A., Boston, A., & Lambrinidou, Y. (2000). *Crossing over: Narratives of palliative care.* New York: Oxford University Press.

Becker, E. (1973). *The denial of death.* New York: Free Press.

Bookbinder, M., & Kiss, M. (2001). Death and society. In M. LaPorte Matzo & D. Witt Sherman (Eds.), *Palliative care nursing* (pp. 89–117). New York: Springer Publishing.

Braun, K.L., Zir, A., Crocker, J., & Seely, M.R. (2005). Kokua mau: A statewide effort to improve end-of-life care. *Journal of Palliative Medicine, 8*(2), 313–323.

Byock, I.R. (1996). The nature of suffering and the nature of opportunity at the end of life. *Clinics in Geriatric Medicine, 12*(2), 237–252.

Byock, I.R. (2002). The meaning and value of death. *Journal of Palliative Medicine, 5*(2), 279–288.

Byock, I.R. (2003). Rediscovering community at the core of the human condition and social covenant. Retrieved January 30, 2006, from www.dyingwell.org/hastings07.10.03.htm

Callahan, D. (2005, Fall). Conservatives, liberals, and medical progress. *New Atlantis, 10,* 3–16.

Callanan, M., & Kelly, P. (1997). *Final gifts.* New York: Bantam.

Cassell, E.J. (2004). *The nature of suffering and the goals of medicine.* Oxford, UK: Oxford University Press.

Chokyi, N.R., & Shlim, D.R. (2004). *Medicine and compassion: A Tibetan lama's guidance for caregivers.* Boston: Wisdom.

Clark, D. (1999). 'Total pain,' disciplinary power and the body in the work of Cicely Saunders, 1958–1967. *Social Science and Medicine, 49*(6), 727–736.

Covinsky, K.E., Goldman, L., Cook, E.F., Oye, R., Desbiens, N., Reding, D., et al. (1994). The impact of serious illness on patients' families. SUPPORT investigators. Study to understand prognoses and preferences for outcomes and risks of treatment. *JAMA, 272*(23), 1839–1845.

Dobratz, M.C. (2005). Gently into the light: A call for the critical analysis of end-of-life outcomes. *Advances in Nursing Science, 28*(2), 116–127.

Farber, A., & Farber, S. (2006). The respectful death model: Difficult conversations at the end of life. In R.S. Katz & T.A. Johnson (Eds.), *When professionals weep* (pp. 221–236). New York: Routledge.

Farber, S., Egnew, T., & Farber, A. (2004). What is a respectful death? In J. Berzoff & P.R. Silverman (Eds.), *Living with dying* (pp. 102–127). New York: Columbia University Press.

Feifel, H. (1959). Introduction. In H. Feifel (Ed.), *The meaning of death* (pp. xi–xvii). New York: McGraw-Hill.

Folta, J.R. (1965). The perception of death. *Nursing Research, 14*(3), 232–235.

Frank, A.W. (1997). *The wounded storyteller: Body, illness, and ethics.* Chicago: University of Chicago Press.

Gallo-Silver, L., & Damaskos, P. (2004). September 11: Reflections on living with dying. In J. Berzoff & P.R. Silverman (Eds.), *Living with dying* (pp. 72–93). New York: Columbia University Press.

Glaser, B.G., & Strauss, A.L. (1965). *Awareness of dying.* Chicago: Aldine.

Grady, D. (2000, May 29). At life's end, many patients are denied peaceful passing: Planning for death. *New York Times*, p. A1.

Kastenbaum, R.J. (1978). *Death, society, and human experience.* Boston: Allyn and Bacon.

Kastenbaum, R.J. (2004). *On our way: The final passage through life and death.* Berkeley, CA: University of California Press.

Krammer, M.L., Ring, A.A., Martinez, J., Jacobs, M.J., & Williams, M.B. (2001). The nurse's role in interdisciplinary and palliative care. In M. LaPorte Matzo & D. Witt Sherman (Eds.), *Palliative care nursing* (pp. 118–139). New York: Springer Publishing.

Kubler-Ross, E. (1969). *On death and dying.* New York: Macmillan.

Lazar, K. (2005, April 3). Living with death: More seek a voice after Schiavo case. *Boston Globe*, p. 1.

Lynn, J.L. (2005). Living long in fragile health. *Hastings Center Report, 35*(6, Suppl.), SI14–S118.

Lynn, J.L., Teno, J.M., Phillips, R.S., Wu, A.W., Desbiens, N., & Harrold, J. (1997). Perceptions by family members of the dying experience of older and seriously ill patients. *Annals of Internal Medicine, 126*(2), 97–106.

Mariano, C. (2001). Holistic integrative therapies in palliative care. In M. LaPorte Matzo & D. Witt Sherman (Eds.), *Palliative care nursing* (pp. 48–86). New York: Springer Publishing.

McCue, J. (1995). The naturalness of dying. *JAMA, 273*(13), 1039–1043.

Nuland, S.B. (1994). *How we die.* New York: Alfred A. Knoff.

Oldenburg, B., & Parcel, G.S. (2002). Diffusion of innovations. In K. Glanz, B.K. Rimer, & F.M. Lewis (Eds.), *Health behavior and health education: Theory, research, and practice* (pp. 312–334). San Francisco: Jossey-Bass.

Open Society Institute. (2008). Project on death in America. Retrieved June 10, 2008, from www.soros.org/initiatives/pdia

Perrin, K.O. (2001). Communicating with seriously ill and dying patients, their families, and their health care providers. In M. LaPorte Matzo & D. Witt Sherman (Eds.), *Palliative care nursing* (pp. 219–244). New York: Springer Publishing.

Quint Benoliel, J. (1977). *A care-cure problem: Dying in teaching hospitals: Final report* [Grant No. NU 00463]. Seattle, WA: School of Nursing, Community Health Care Systems Department.

Rando, T.A. (1984). *Grief, dying, and death: Clinical interventions for caregivers.* Champaign, IL: Research Press.

Steinhauser, K.E., Christakis, N.A., Clipp, E.C., McNeilly, M., McIntyre, L., & Tulsky, J.A. (2000). Factors considered important at the end-of-life by patients, family, physicians, and other care providers. *JAMA, 284*(19), 2476–2483.

Suchman, A.L., & Matthews, D.A. (1988). What makes the patient-doctor relationship therapeutic? Exploring the connexional dimension of medical care. *Annals of Internal Medicine, 108*(1), 125–130.

Sullivan, M.D. (2002). The illusion of patient choice in end-of-life decisions. *American Journal of Geriatric Psychiatry, 10*(4), 365–372.

Teno, J.M., McNiff, K., & Lynn, J. (2000). Measuring quality of medical care for dying persons and their families: Preliminary suggestions for accountability. *Annual Review of Gerontology and Geriatrics, 20*(1), 97–119.

U.S. Department of Health and Human Services. (2006). Births, marriages, divorces, and death. *National Vital Statistics Report, 54*(20), 1–4.

U.S. Department of Health and Human Services. (2008). Births, marriages, divorces, and death. *National Vital Statistics Report, 56*(18), 1–14.

Vig, E.K., Davenport, N.A., & Pearlman, R.A. (2002). Good deaths, bad deaths, and the preferences for the end of life: A qualitative study of geriatric outpatients. *Journal of American Geriatrics Society, 50*(9), 1541–1548.

Volker, D.L., Kahn, D., & Penticuff, J.H. (2004). Patient control and end-of-life care part 1. The advanced practice nurse perspective. *Oncology Nursing Forum, 31*(5), 954–960.

Walter, T. (1996). Developments in spiritual care of the dying. *Religion, 26*(4), 353–363.

Witt Sherman, D., & LaPorte Matzo, M. (2001). Palliative care nursing: Changing the experience of dying in America. In M. LaPorte Matzo & D. Witt Sherman (Eds.), *Palliative care nursing* (pp. xvii–xxiv). New York: Springer Publishing.

Witt Sherman, D., LaPorte Matzo, M., Rogers, S., McLaughlin, M., & Wyden, R. (2000). Steps to improve the quality of life for people who are dying. *Psychology, Public Policy, and Law, 6*(2), 575–581.

EXPLORING THE ISSUE

Do Dying Persons Without Advocates Get a Different Quality of Care?

Critical Thinking and Reflection

1. What are three challenges for health care providers facing end-of-life care decisions for patients without a surrogate or a written advance directive?
2. Consider the situation of a homeless person admitted to the intensive care unit on a respirator with pneumonia. Because of years of drinking, he has severe cirrhosis of liver and has no gag reflex. What would physicians and nurses want to know about this patient's ideas, values, and life style as they made decisions about his end-of-life care?
3. How do the issues of homelessness complicate end of life care? Does the type of terminal illness or the level of care need make a difference in where this person might receive care?
4. What are the laws in your state regarding who makes decisions for seriously ill patients without advocates? Should health care professionals make attempts to contact distant family members who have not been involved with these patients? Why or why not?
5. Who would you want as a decision maker for your care if you had no relatives? How would you designate this or let your wishes be known?

Is There Common Ground?

All health professionals are taught to provide care for all patients based on recommended medical guidelines and not on the patient's income status, educational level, or psychiatric status. However, the research of Song et al. (2007) indicates that homeless patients are acutely aware of the "problem" they pose to the health care system. When patients have acute mental illness problems or substance abuse problems, professionals may struggle to try to provide an objective approach to managing the dying process. Patients without advocates or surrogate decision makers may receive medical care that is not based on their wishes, but rather based on what professionals perceive may be best for that patient. Physicians who recognize that a patient may abuse or sell the pain medications ordered for end-of-life care may be reluctant to provide the same level of comfort for a patient with chronic substance abuse problems. However, if a model of care is followed to develop relationships with patients despite differences in background, socioeconomic status, psychiatric status or housing, patients should receive the same quality of care at the end of life regardless of their status.

References

Kushel, M. B. & Miaskowski, C. (2006). End of life care for homeless patients: "She says she'll be there to help me in any situation." *Journal of the American Medical Association, 296*(24), 2959–2966.

Markowitz, A. J. & McPhee, S. J. (2007). End of life care for homeless patients: "She says she is to help me in any situation." *Journal of the American Medical Association, 297*(3), 305.

Pathak, E. B., Casper, M. L., Tanner, J. P., Reader, S., & Ward, B. (2010). A multi-level analysis of absence of transport to a hospital before premature cardiac death. *Preventing Chronic Disease, 7*(3), 1–11.

Public Health–Seattle and King County. (2004). King County 2003 Homeless Death Review. Retrieved from www.kingcounty.gov/healthservices/health/personal/HCHN/providers.aspx

Shield, R. R., Wetle, T., Teno, J., Miller, S. C., & Welch, L.C. (2010). Vigilant at the end of life: Family advocacy in the nursing home. *Journal of Palliative Medicine, 13*(5), 573–579. doi:10.1089/jpm.2009.0398

Song, J., Bartels, D. M., Ratner, E. R., Alderton, L., Hudson, B., & Ahluwalia, J. S. (2007). Dying on the streets: Homeless persons' concerns and desires about end of life care. *Journal of General Internal Medicine, 22*(4), 435–441. doi:10.1007/s11606-006-0046-7

U.S. Department of Housing and Urban Development. (2010). *Annual Homeless Assessment Report (AHAR).* Retrieved from www.hudhre.info/documents/2010HomelessAssessmentReport.pdf

Wasserman, L. S. (2008). Respectful death: A model for end of life care. *Clinical Journal of Oncology Nursing, 12*(4), 621–626. doi:10.1188/08.CJON.621-626

White, D. B., Curtis, J., Wolf, L. E., Prendergast, T. J., Taichman, D. B., Kuniyoshi, G., et al. (2007). Life support for patients without a surrogate decision maker: Who decides? *Annals of Internal Medicine, 147*(1), 34–40.

Additional Resources

Ball, S. (2006). Nurse-patient advocacy and the right to die. *Journal of Psychosocial Nursing, 44*(12), 36–42.

Beckstrand, R. L., Smith, M. D., Heaston, S., & Bond, E. (2008). Emergency nurses' perceptions of size, frequency, and magnitude of obstacles and supportive behaviors in end-of-life care. *Journal of Emergency Nursing, 34*(4), 290–300. doi:10.1016/j.jen.2007.09.004

Camhi, S. L., Mercado, A. F., Morrison, R., Du, Q., Platt, D. M., August, G. I., et al. (2009). Deciding in the dark: Advance directives and continuation of treatment in chronic critical illness. *Critical Care Medicine, 37*(3), 919–925. doi:10.1097/CCM.0b013e31819613ce

Fields, L. (2007). DNR does not mean no care. *Journal of Neuroscience Nursing, 39*(5), 294–296.

Grunier, A., Mor, V., Weitzen, S., Truchil, R., Teno, J., & Roy, J. (2007). Where people die: A multilevel approach to understanding influences on site of death in America. *Medical Care Research and Review, 64*(4), 351–378.

Kyusuk, C., Essex, E., & Samson, L. F. (2008). Ethnic variation in timing of hospice referral: Does having no informal caregiver matter? *Journal of Palliative Medicine, 11*(3), 484–491. doi:10.1089/jpm.2007.0149

Moinpour, C. M., Lyons, B. B., Schmidt, S. P., Chansky, K. K., & Patchell, R. A. (2000). Substituting proxy ratings for patient ratings in cancer clinical trials: An analysis based on a southwest oncology group trial in patients with brain metastases. *Quality of Life Research, 9*(2), 219–231.

Seale, C. (2004). Media constructions of dying alone: A form of "bad death." *Social Science & Medicine, 58*(5), 967–974. doi:10.1016/j.socscimed.2003.10.038

Song, J., Wall, M. M., Ratner, E., Bartels, D., Ulvestad, N., & Gelberg, L. (2008). Engaging homeless persons in end of life preparations. *Journal of General Internal Medicine, 23*(12), 2031–2045. doi:10.1007/s11606-008-0771-1

Sulmasy, D. P., He, M. K., McAuley, R., & Ury, W. (2008). Beliefs and attitudes of nurses and physicians about do not resuscitate orders and who should speak to patients and families about them. *Critical Care Medicine, 36*(6), 1817–1822.

United States Interagency Council on Homelessness. (2010). *Opening doors: Federal strategic plan to prevent and end homelessness.* Retrieved from www .usich.gov/PDF/OpeningDoors_2010_FSPPreventEndHomeless.pdf

White, D. B., Curtis, J. R., Lo, B., & Luce, J. (2006). Decisions to limit life-sustaining treatment for critically ill patients who lack both decision-making capacity and surrogate decision-makers. *Critical Care Medicine, 34*(8), 2053–2059.

ISSUE 4

Compassion Fatigue: Does Burnout Occur in All Caregivers of Dying Patients?

YES: **Nancy Jo Bush,** from "Compassion Fatigue: Are You at Risk?" *Oncology Nursing Forum* (vol. 36, no. 1, 2009)

NO: **Dorothy J. Dunn,** from "The Intentionality of Compassion Energy," *Holistic Nursing Practice* (vol. 23, no. 4, 2009)

Learning Outcomes

After reading this issue, you should be able to:

- Gain an understanding compassion fatigue and burnout in caregivers for dying patients.
- Discuss the differences of Eastern and Western philosophical views of compassion.
- Identify the behaviors, symptoms, and attitudes of professional and family caregivers of dying patients who are showing signs of compassion fatigue.
- Understand the potential interventions to reduce compassion fatigue and address the needs of "wounded healers."

ISSUE SUMMARY

YES: Nancy Jo Bush, an assistant professor at the University of California, identifies the phenomenon of compassion fatigue in nurses. She discusses caregivers at risk for emotional exhaustion related to their work.

NO: Dorothy Dunn of Florida Atlantic University describes compassion energy as the converse of compassion fatigue. She believes that nurses and other caregivers can grow and thrive if they understand how to prevent burnout by self-generating vigor as compassion energy.

"The dew of compassion is a tear." (Lord Byron)

"A tear is an intellectual thing." (William Blake)

Professional caregivers of dying persons often experience stress and fatigue while trying to provide compassionate care to patients. One common thread of professional programs for health care workers, chaplains, and social workers is that they must be empathetic to their clients' needs and provide them with compassionate care. Compassion fatigue is a term that was initially coined to describe emergency room nurses who appeared to have lost their ability to nurture (Joinson, 1992). Other nurse researchers have examined this phenomenon to help identify those caregivers who are at risk for compassion fatigue (Bush, 2009; Coetzee & Klopper, 2010; Figley, 1995). In this issue, we define compassion and examine compassion fatigue. We discuss the different viewpoints on the challenges and emotional tolls of providing compassionate care to dying patients.

Philosophical and religious thought in the west historically interpreted the term "compassion" as the tragic compassion (in Aristotle) of identification with seriously undeserved suffering taken on by an outsider (Nussbaum, 2001; Roberts, 2011). Teresa of Calcutta identifies compassion as Christ-like suffering: ". . . there is nothing heavier than compassion; not even one's own pain weighs so heavy as the pain one feels with someone, for someone, pain intensified by the imagination, and prolonged by a hundred echoes" (Kundera, 2009, p. 31). In Buddhist traditions, loving kindness (*metta*) and compassion (*karuna*) are not about tragic identification between a self and another. Rather, these are viewed as a mechanism for practical personal transformation. In these traditions, compassion relinquishes self-constraining empathies and ego-imprisoning sympathies to transform oneself in order to help all (Harvey, 2000; Suh, 2004). "Whoever, O monks, would nurse me, he should nurse the sick" (Buddha, Mahavagga 8.26.3, Buddhist Pali Canon). Compassion does not aim for deep empathy with another, or idealized sympathy for another, or future transformation into some other. Compassion requires daily engagement with the other also struggling with emotions (*com-passio*). Eastern philosophy influence has helped Western philosophers to rediscover the centrality of compassion: "The whole idea of compassion is based on a keen awareness of the interdependence of all these living beings, which are all part of one another, and all involved in one another" (Merton, 1975, pp. 341–342).

Lewin (1996) defined the complex emotion of compassion in the nursing profession as a balancing act: nurses hold their patients' despair in one hand and their own hopefulness in the other. Not all health professionals experience compassion fatigue. Marr (2009) argues that compassion is not a static state; we are not simply compassionate or not compassionate. Her work embraces the Eastern philosophers' approach. She believes that health care professionals who are truly engaged in the moment of interaction with patients (and not preoccupied with themselves) will find compassion can arise anew in each situation. Similar to Eastern philosophers, she believes that by forgetting ourselves, listening intently, and "dancing in the moment with the other," our energy is saved. "If we are worried about ourselves, our status, our role, who we are ('Look at me! I'm so compassionate!'), or believe that being compassionate means flailing yourself against the rocks over and over again so you are physically or mentally exhausted (martyrdom), then burnout is likely" (Marr, 2009, p. 739).

Marr's Buddhist approach to professional interactions may be the ideal. However, the reality of caring for 6–8 seriously ill patients with competing needs and demands at the end of a 12-hour shift can strain the philosophical ideals of any altruistic sole. Hospice chaplains who become spiritually exhausted providing care to families of dying patients may refer to themselves as "wounded healers" (Nouwen, 1979). Observations of emotionally exhausted nurses have led nurse researchers to seek a better understanding of the construct of compassion fatigue.

Coetzee and Klopper (2010) define compassion fatigue as the end outcome of progressive and cumulative processes that are described in three distinct stages. These stages begin after prolonged continuous, intense work with patients. In the early stage, the caregiver experiences "compassion discomfort," a stage of physical weariness, and lessened emotional enthusiasm, desensitization, and weakening attention. When symptoms are detected at this stage, they can be relieved by rest and renewal. However, prolonged exposure to stressful caregiving leads to a second stage called compassion stress and is characterized by physical symptoms, emotional symptoms, and social/spiritual symptoms. The third and final stage of extended stressful caregiving is compassion fatigue, where energy expenditure outstrips the restorative process (Coetzee & Klopper, 2010). In this final stage, they sum up the symptoms that lead to a positive diagnosis of compassion fatigue. "The physical effects include weariness, loss of strength, reduced output, diminished performance, loss of endurance, and increased physical complaints. The emotional effects include lessened enthusiasm, desensitization, diminished ability, irritability, and being emotionally overwhelmed. The social effects include an inability to aid and share in the suffering of patients. The spiritual effects include a decrease in discernment and a lack of spiritual awareness. The intellectual effects include weakening attention, boredom, and an impaired ability to concentrate" (Coetzee & Klopper, 2010, p. 241). This description is similar to the emotional exhaustion of burnout and the symptoms similar to posttraumatic stress disorder (Bush, 2009).

Although not all caregivers experience these changes, health professionals and spiritual guides (physicians, nurses, therapists, ministers, counselors, social workers) who work with dying patients are at risk for compassion fatigue. Informal caregivers, family members of dying patients, are also at risk for compassion fatigue for reasons similar to caregiving professionals. Any situation of caring for another with prolonged periods of being overwhelmed or demoralized by the work of compassionate giving can manifest as emotional burnout (Joinson, 1992).

Family members caring for hospice patients may be able to do the physical care, but may be privately overwhelmed by the prolonged stress of not knowing when the person will die. They may have additional stressors of second guessing decisions that were made prior to finally ending treatments and enrolling in hospice. The emotional angst of not knowing whether one has "done enough" can add to the stressors of caregiving. This exposure to trauma can change a caregiver's cognitive schema and can even lead to an acute disorder with symptoms of intense fear and hopelessness secondary to posttraumatic stress disorder (Figley, 1999, 2002).

Researchers are beginning to develop scales for assessing compassion fatigue as a way of detecting those caregivers who need respite, counseling, or relief. However, there are few validation studies and little information on the psychometric properties for these assessment tools (Najjar, Davis, Beck-Coon, & Doebbeling, 2009). Coetzee and Klopper (2010) encourage health care organizations to provide education to nurses on compassion fatigue and the gradual stages that preclude complete burnout. They recommend that persons working with dying patients or in traumatic caregiving situations should become skilled in recognizing the risk factors and causes of compassion fatigue. These caregivers should be taught about the cumulative and progressive process from early manifestations of compassion discomfort, to the secondary stages of compassion stress, and compassion fatigue. Nurses and caregivers with better awareness may be able to institute measures to prevent the development and progression of compassion fatigue. These could include encouraging caregiver respite, leave of absence, reduction of shift time, or support groups to discuss stressors.

Knowledge about the existence and symptoms of compassion fatigue may help nurses identify these in patient caregivers/family members of dying patients. The establishment of support groups for family caregivers and professional caregivers could allow them an opportunity to seek assistance before experiencing burnout. Organizations that are concerned about retaining skilled workers in the health care workforce should consider screening programs and assistance programs for caregivers. Employee assistance programs that provide counseling and life skills education should be sensitive to the reluctance that many professionals experience in seeking help for their own needs. Easing the emotional burden of caregiving work may prevent the development and progression of compassion fatigue (Bush, 2009; Coetzee & Klopper, 2010; Newsom, 2010).

In the YES article, Nancy Jo Bush, an assistant professor at the University of California, identifies the phenomenon of compassion fatigue in nurses. She discusses caregivers at risk for emotional exhaustion related to their work. Bush identifies the risk factors of empathetic engagement and discusses the similarities and differences between compassion fatigue, burnout, secondary trauma stress, and vicarious trauma. Bush recommends problem-solving coping mechanisms, the need to establish empathetic boundaries, and to have self-awareness and self-forgiveness.

In the NO article, Dorothy Dunn of Florida Atlantic University describes compassion energy as the converse of compassion fatigue. She believes that nurses and other caregivers can grow and thrive if they understand how to prevent burnout by self-generating vigor as compassion energy. Her view fits with more of the Eastern philosophy of compassion, as compassion energy. "Nurses initiate the experience of compassion energy when they answer the call from a patient. The 3 attributes of compassion energy are compassionate presence, patterned nurturance, and intentionally knowing the nursed and self as whole."

YES

Nancy Jo Bush

Compassion Fatigue: Are You at Risk?

E.P., a 34-year-old oncology staff nurse, felt like she was losing control of her life. She felt a sense of dread and fatigue each morning when her alarm went off. How could she make it through one more day trying to balance her family life, her job, and caring for her mother, whose senile dementia was gradually worsening every day? E.P. could not really remember the last time she felt energetic and positive, nor could she pinpoint when she began to feel so overwhelmed.

E.P. had been married for 13 years to her college sweetheart. He was in sales and worked out of the home, which, she felt, often added to the chaos of their lives. Their children came soon after marriage and were now embarking on adolescence—a daughter, 12, and a son, 10. The children seemed to fight continuously for inconsequential reasons, and her daughter was beginning to challenge E.P. in every arena: clothes, music, friends, homework, and curfew. E.P.'s husband played a passive role in their childrearing, and E.P. often did not feel supported when she attempted to set guidelines or expectations for the children. Caring for her mother was adding additional stress and her only sibling lived out of state and was not available to assist her in handling the physical, emotional, or financial aspects of their mother's care.

E.P. had studied nursing in college and began working immediately after graduation. She worked in general medical-surgical units initially; looking back, she remembered being enthusiastic and eager to go to work every day. Nursing was not just a job for her. E.P. felt that nursing was a profession and, at one time, she had hoped to further her education and become a nurse practitioner. She did not plan to become an oncology nurse but worked the float pool for several months and soon found that her work with patients with cancer and their families was rewarding. E.P. enjoyed the challenges of working in a specialty area, learning new skills, and felt that the environment reinforced the ideals that made her enter the profession in the first place: empathy, compassion, caring, and making a difference in the lives of her patients and their families.

The years passed quickly—her children kept her outside life very busy, her colleagues at work became her dearest friends, and she had started to take classes to get a master's degree in oncology nursing. She worked 12-hour day shifts that initially made her feel like she could juggle family, work, school,

From *Oncology Nursing Forum,* January 2009, pp. 24–28. Copyright © 2009 by Oncology Nursing Society. Reprinted by permission.

her mother's care, and, if possible, some time for herself to continue jogging, her favorite form of exercise. Her first semester was a difficult transition and, at times, she felt overwhelmed by the amount of reading and studying required. Her husband and her children did not seem to understand the demands of her studies, and their expectations of her remained the same. Her husband did not understand her desire to further her education; he would express his feelings that "a nurse is a nurse; just a nurse." Unexpectedly, rearing her daughter began to feel more, not less, demanding. At times, E.P. felt that her daughter would challenge her on every occasion and keep their relationship at arm's length. She missed feeling close to her daughter but tried to understand her need for independence. Her son seemed unaffected by any family crisis that would occur but he would fight with his sister, refuse to do homework, and had to be constantly reminded to do his chores around the house.

The hospital environment and work demands also were making E.P. feel "down." The nursing shortage had increased the nurse-patient ratio, so, most days, she came home feeling physically and emotionally drained. It was hard for her to rationalize going to school when she could no longer practice nursing at the bedside with the time to care for her patients and their families as she once had. The inpatient oncology population also was becoming more acutely ill, and the nursing staff was experiencing more deaths, family grief, and loss, without a balance of caring for patients who were being treated in outpatient settings or who were survivors. As hospital finances became worse, other resources, such as social services and advanced practice nurses, became scarce. Gone were the days of support groups on the unit for the staff or educational programs at work to help the nurses feel competent with technological changes and the demand for new skills. Over time, E.P. began to feel that nursing was a job, not a profession, and not supported or recognized for the hard work, both emotional and physical, that oncology nursing demanded.

E.P. began to feel a sense of hopelessness and helplessness when it came to making any changes in her home or work environment. She would stay up late to study and, even with eight hours of sleep on a weekend night, was constantly fatigued. Her husband and children said that she was "irritable" and always distant. When she would visit her mother, she would leave feeling depressed; as if her mother was dying slowly in front of her. At work, E.P. continued to feel emotionally close to her patients and their families but, unknowingly, she was unable to leave their grief and issues at work. She began to wake up at night dreaming about a patient or fearing that a patient she cared for would die before she got back to work in the morning. Several nightmares included fears of injury to her children resulting in their own death. Months had passed since she had gone jogging, and she was unable to concentrate on her studies, often finding herself sitting for hours preoccupied with feelings of fear or anxiety. She began to feel incompetent at work, at home, and with her studies. E.P. felt angry at her husband for his lack of understanding and support in all areas of her life and she would shutter if he attempted to show any signs of affection or intimacy. She felt her life was like a roller coaster out of control and that no one, not even her own friends and colleagues, could keep her on the track. As her isolation increased, so did her loneliness. Feelings of despair would erupt when a patient or family member was in despair, and she began to feel their loss as her loss, too.

What Is Compassion Fatigue?

Lewin (1996) described compassion as a complex emotion that allows caregivers to hold and sustain themselves in emotional balance while holding patients' despair in one hand and their hopefulness in the other. Compassion requires an inner conviction and resiliency—a passion of personal ethics, personal beliefs, and a personal way of being. Lewin explained that compassion requires us to ask who we are, what we wish to be, what are our joys and commitments, and what values do we hold dear and defend? He described compassion as the core value of the caregiver's work, and that the essence of compassion is what gives nursing its soulfulness, staying power, and healing resources. Poignantly, Lewin encapsulated what all nurse caregivers come to know, "Our patients instruct us in so much that is painful, but our patients lead us to love, appreciate, and enjoy so much that we would not otherwise have known to cherish. We come to care about what they care about because they care about it and we care for them" (p. 25).

Compassion fatigue is a term first coined by Joinson (1992) to describe the unique stressors that affect people in caregiving professions (e.g., nurses, psychotherapists, ministers). Joinson envisioned compassion fatigue as a unique and expanded form of burnout, not only environmental stressors of the workplace negatively affecting nurse caregivers but the patient's physical needs (e.g., pain, discomfort) and emotional needs (e.g., fear, anxiety) contributing to nurses becoming tired, depressed, angry, ineffective, and, at the end of the continuum, apathetic and detached. Compassion fatigue and burnout in the nursing profession often have been addressed in the specialty of palliative care when nurse caregivers must come to terms with their own grief and loss related to caring for dying patients (Mulder, 2000). Joinson addressed the cost of compassion fatigue (evidenced in the case study). Nurse caregivers may feel as if they are working two jobs, giving of themselves all day at work and returning home to nurture and care for family, constant stress eating away at the commitment and the foundation on which the career was built. As a result of compassion fatigue, somatic complaints range on a continuum from headaches to depression, and emotional symptoms range from irritability to anger. If unaddressed, isolation, withdrawal, and detachment occur. Compassion fatigue is a complex phenomenon that escalates gradually as a product of cumulative stress over time, often when caregivers ignore the symptoms of stress and do not attend to their own emotional needs.

How Is Compassion Fatigue Differentiated from Similar Theories Such as Burnout?

Burnout is a well-known construct and is experienced by oncology nurses beginning with the continual changes and increased demands of the health-care and work environment, such as cutbacks, cost-containment, and demands to do more with less. The phenomenon of burnout has been well researched over the past 30 years and appeared in the literature prior to the concept of compassion fatigue. Burnout has been described as having feelings of failure, being worn out, or becoming exhausted by excessive demands on energy, strength, or resources (Freudenberger, 1974). Burnout manifests as physical, psychological, and behavioral reactions: emotional exhaustion, diminished caring, and a profound sense of demoralization (Maslach, 1993). The literature on burnout shows that committed professionals such as E.P. begin their careers with energy, involvement, and efficacy, and emotional exhaustion is viewed as the main component of burnout, with involvement becoming cynicism and efficacy becoming ineffectiveness (Lederberg, 1998; Maslach, Schaufeli, & Leiter, 2001).

Vicarious traumatization is a term closely related and often used interchangeably with compassion fatigue. The stresses experienced by oncology caregivers are twofold and intertwined. Inherently, the heart of oncology care is the relationships that develop between caregivers and patients and their families. To be truly effective in oncology care, in the process of helping others heal through the trauma of a cancer diagnosis and treatment, the nurse must give of himself or herself from a deeply personal and spiritual level. The empathic engagement that takes place between nurse and patient must maintain a fine balance with appropriate emotional boundaries to safeguard the mental health of both. A risk for oncology nurses, and other nurse caregivers in trauma centers, intensive care units, and burn units, is that after prolonged exposure to trauma and loss, the caregivers begin to integrate the emotions, fears, and grief of their patients, ultimately increasing their own stress and emotional pain (see Figure 1). The construct of vicarious trauma posits that the psychological distress that incurs over prolonged exposure to trauma actually changes the cognitive schema or perspective of the caregiver related to such life issues as intimacy, trust, safety, self-esteem, and control (Saakvitne & Pearlman, 1996). Nurses experiencing vicarious traumatization no longer feel grounded in the world around them; they begin to question the meaning of life, risk losing a sense of purpose, and pervasive hopelessness may set in (Figley, 2002; Larson & Bush, 2006). As the case study demonstrates, E.P. began to feel a sense of hopelessness and ineffectiveness in her ability to change the circumstances of her life. Figley (1999) described this phenomenon as the cost of caring.

Secondary traumatic stress incorporates the concepts of compassion fatigue and vicarious trauma caused by empathic engagement, but the subsequent emotions and behaviors may result in an acute stress disorder or symptoms similar to post-traumatic stress disorder (PTSD). According to the American Psychiatric Association (2000), "any person who has experienced, witnessed, or been confronted with an event or events that involve actual or threatened death or serious injury, or a threat to the physical integrity of oneself or others" (p. 426) is a criterion for the diagnosis of PTSD. Another criterion is that the person's response can involve intense fear and hopelessness. E.P. began to fear for the safety of her own family during nightmares that concerned death and dying. Many experiences reported by emotionally exhausted

Figure 1

The Risks of Empathic Engagement

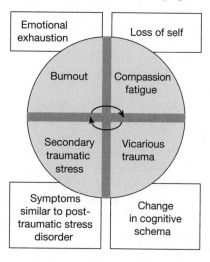

caregivers are similar to the experiences of people with acute stress response or PTSD: recurrent recollections, distressing dreams, psychological distress (e.g., anxiety), reminders of the event or death of the person being cared for, in addition to physical symptoms including irritability, difficulty concentrating, and insomnia (Figley, 1999). The individual's experience in relation to the traumatic event, combined with a lack of personal and supportive resources to cope, exacerbate the feelings of fear and loss, challenging the person's belief system, faith, and trust in others and themselves (Figley).

Who Is at Risk?

All caregivers are at risk for emotional exhaustion from their work and in any level or all degrees described by the constructs proposed in the literature (Badger, 2000). Figley (1999) stated that "The capacity for compassion and empathy seems to be at the core of our ability to do the work and at the core of our ability to be wounded by the work" (p. xv). Stamm (1999) warned that we may begin our careers with the illusion that we will be protected from the pain and loss of those we care for by our educational preparation and our "white coats," believing that our educational training, our clinical work, our research, or our teaching will help us keep our balance and objectivity. Figley (1999) stressed that compassion fatigue, vicarious trauma, and secondary traumatic stress are natural, predictable, treatable, and unpreventable consequences of working with suffering and traumatized patients.

Stress and coping theories commonly assert that it is not the stressors themselves but how the individual responds to them that influences stress and coping responses (Lazarus & Folkman, 1984). Adaptive coping responses are viewed as action-oriented, problem-solving approaches. Ultimately, can the nurse identify and feel effective to modify, adapt, and change within the work environment to meet the challenges? If not, the chronic stress, disillusionment, and frustration may lead to ineffective coping responses and use of defensive mechanisms such as avoidance approaches (e.g., withdrawal, apathy, food or substance abuse). E.P. began to withdraw from her husband in addition to feeling disappointment about her children's lack of support. Personal stressors, a lack of adequate support systems, and personal trauma will all place the nurse caregiver at a higher risk for compassion fatigue.

Understanding the countertransference between the caregiver and the patient is important when speaking about vicarious trauma or secondary traumatic stress. In psychodynamic therapy, countertransference is the emotional reaction to the patient by the therapist because of a process by which the therapist sees oneself or one's past experiences played out by the patient. The issue is the risk of overidentifying with the patient or attempting to meet one's personal needs through the patient (Figley, 1999, 2002). In the case study, E.P. is experiencing anticipatory grief related to her mother's illness, cognitive deterioration, and imminent death.

Research has identified that organizational stressors, such as the workplace, role ambiguity, and workload, contribute to nursing burnout. Prolonged exposures to stressful environments that consist of low staffing and a lack of administrative and colleague support keep nurses in a constant state of alertness and isolation that eventually create physical and mental exhaustion (Cohen, 1995; Duquette, Kerouac, Sandu, & Beaudet, 1994; Medland, Howard-Rubin, & Whitaker, 2004). Studies on sociodemographic factors have not demonstrated that gender, employment status, specialty units, or educational preparation contribute to burnout. Interestingly, age has been found to be positively correlated with burnout, with younger nurses being most vulnerable, possibly because they are unprepared for role ambiguity, heavy workloads, and changing environments (Duquette et al.). In a review of research to identify workplace stress associated with oncology caregivers, identified stressors included physician-and coworker-related stress, organizational and environmental factors, inadequate resources, and emotional stress (e.g., observing suffering), ethical issues, low self-esteem, and death and dying (Medland et al.).

Nurses who are idealistic, highly motivated, and committed also are at high risk to experience burnout and compassion fatigue, possibly the result of the cumulative losses they experience that cause disappointment and despair or if they perceive that they are not moving toward their care goals and do not feel effective in changing the environment to do so. For these reasons, idealistic, highly motivated, and highly empathic helpers often are the first to burn out, as does a bright flame by virtue of its intensity (Larson, 1993). Oncology nurses who work in palliative care are at an increased risk for compassion fatigue and secondary trauma because they experience multiple deaths within a short period of time. The associated grief and loss can lead to depression and chronic grief reactions (Vachon, 2001). Vachon has described oncology caregivers as "wounded healers." In a personal journal of her experiences in palliative care medicine, Mulder (2000) described the healing and wisdom gained amidst the suffering of palliative care and reflected on the adage, "healer, heal thyself."

Compassionate Care for the Self

Stebnicki (2008) stated, "In traditional Native American teaching, it is said that each time you heal someone you give away a piece of yourself until, at some point, you will require healing" (p. 3). Empathic engagement is essential to the healing process in disciplines such as nursing, medicine, and psychotherapy. Stebnicki stressed that caregiving professionals must prepare their minds, bodies, souls, and spirits to become resilient in working with patients at intense levels of interpersonal functioning. Stebnicki expanded upon the fatigue syndromes and has coined the term "empathy fatigue." He investigated the interaction of variables that influence empathy fatigue, including caregiver personality traits (e.g., resiliency), coping resources, age, developmental experience, and, ultimately, the inter-relationship between the caregiver's mind, body, and spiritual development. Stebnicki emphasized that empathy is a way of being and a form of communication; that caregivers develop the skills of empathic engagement is essential: positive beliefs about themselves as well as their patients, a healthy self-concept, embracing values that respect other people and cultures, and the capability to listen to and understand the needs of others.

To avoid end points of the continuum between emotional overinvolvement with patients to the other extreme of emotional distance or burnout, the key may be compassionate care for the self and "balanced" empathy (Larson & Bush, 2006). What may contribute to the long-term coping resources of many oncology nurses is what they learn from the patients themselves. Oncology nurses learn about courage and resiliency from many of their patients who transform their adversity into challenge and who find hope in often hopeless situations (Larson & Bush). Nurses must be as compassionate, understanding, and forgiving of themselves as they are for their patients and loved ones; balancing their giving to others with giving to themselves. Welsh (1999) called this "practicing responsible selfishness." As highly motivated and committed caregivers, nurses must engage in activities that comfort, restore, and rejuvenate empathic caring. Hill (1991) proposed that, for caregivers to be most helpful to their patients, they must use reflection and inner awareness to attend to the emotional needs of their inner lives. A shared "duality" of time and life exist with patients—the existential concerns and the blessing and burden of searching for life's meaning. Both are central themes in the lives of patients experiencing cancer and nurses experience the illness through empathic engagement. The patient with cancer often asks, "Why me?" and the oncology caregiver often asks "Why not me?" (Hill).

Empathy can be viewed as a double-edged sword, an honorable personality trait and a point of vulnerability at the same time (Larson & Bush, 2006). The compassionate qualities that attract oncology nurses to their profession are the same ones that make them vulnerable to burnout, vicarious trauma, or secondary traumatic stress over the long haul. Preventive self-care strategies are essential ingredients for professional survival and also are necessary for personal growth. Only when nurses take time to heal themselves can they be

Figure 2

Healing the Spirit

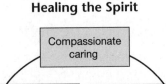

truly available to aid in the healing of others. The major preventive self-care tasks are well understood by the majority of nurse caregivers: exercising, relaxation, maintaining adequate sleep and nutrition, and reaching out for support from others. Why are these strategies so difficult to maintain on an ongoing basis? It may be because the strategies are straightforward and simplistic and do not touch upon the deeply spiritual needs that are essential for self-care. Prevention and treatment of compassion fatigue must begin with care for, protection of, and healing of the spirit (see Figure 2). Nurses should continue to work with compassion, vulnerability, and tenderness but learn how to manage sadness in growth-enhancing rather than destructive ways. Nurses should be alert to countertransference reactions and symptoms of vicarious trauma, such as overinvolvement or withdrawal. Learn to set boundaries and limits; learn to reach out for support from coworkers, peers, family, and friends. Apply action-oriented, problem-solving behaviors to find solutions to the stressful health-care environment and how to deliver the best quality care with the resources available. Do your best—what Larson and Bush (2006) called practicing the art of the possible. Lastly, learning forgiveness and self-love is inherent in healing and preventing compassion fatigue. Being gentle, kind, and patient with themselves is one way nurses can effectively cope. Nurses should treat themselves with the empathy and compassion that they give others.

References

American Psychiatric Association. (2000). *Diagnostic and statistical manual of mental disorders* (4th ed.). Washington, DC: Author.

Badger, J.M. (2000). Understanding secondary traumatic stress. *American Journal of Nursing, 101*(7), 26–32.

Cohen, M.Z. (1995). The meaning of cancer and oncology nursing: Link to effective care. *Seminars in Oncology Nursing, 11*(1), 59–67.

Duquette, A., Kerouac, S., Sandu, B.K., & Beaudet, L. (1994). Factors related to nursing burnout: A review of empirical knowledge. *Issues in Mental Health Nursing, 15*(4), 337–358.

Figley, C.R. (1999). Compassion fatigue: Toward a new understanding of the costs of caring. In B.H. Stamm (Ed.), *Secondary traumatic stress: Self-care issues for clinicians, researchers and educators* (2nd ed., pp. 3–29). Lutherville, MD: Sidran Press.

Figley, C.R. (2002). *Treating compassion fatigue.* New York: Brunner-Routledge.

Freudenberger, H.J. (1974). Staff burnout. *Journal of Social Issues, 30*(1), 159–165.

Hill, H.R. (1991). Point and counterpoint: Relationships in oncology care. *Journal of Psychosocial Oncology, 9*(2), 97–112.

Joinson, C. (1992). Coping with compassion fatigue. *Nursing, 22*(4), 116–121.

Larson, D.G. (1993). *The helper's journey: Working with people facing grief, loss, and life-threatening illness.* Champaign, IL: Research Press.

Larson, D.G., & Bush, N.J. (2006). Stress management for oncology nurses: Finding a healing balance. In R. Carroll-Johnson, L. Gorman, & N.J. Bush (Eds.), *Psychosocial nursing along the cancer continuum* (pp. 587–601). Pittsburgh, PA: Oncology Nursing Society.

Lazarus, R.A., & Folkman, S. (1984). *Stress, appraisal, and coping.* New York: Springer.

Lederberg, M.S. (1998). Oncology staff stress and related interventions. In J.C. Holland (Ed.), *Psycho-oncology* (pp. 1035–1048). New York: Oxford University Press.

Lewin, R.A. (1996). *Compassion: The core value that animates psychotherapy.* Northvale, NJ: Jason Aronson.

Maslach, C. (1993). Burnout: A multidimensional perspective. In W.B. Schaufeli, C. Maslach, & T. Marek (Eds.), *Professional burnout: Recent developments in theory and research* (pp. 19–32). Washington, DC: Taylor and Francis.

Maslach, C., Schaufeli, W.B., & Leiter, M.P. (2001). Job burnout. *Annual Review of Psychology, 52,* 397–422.

Medland, J., Howard-Rubin, J., & Whitaker, E. (2004). Fostering psychosocial wellness in oncology nurses: Addressing burnout and social support in the workplace. *Oncology Nursing Forum, 31*(1), 47–54.

Mulder, J. (2000). Transforming experience into wisdom: Healing amidst suffering. *Journal of Palliative Care, 16*(2), 25–29.

Saakvitne, K.W., & Pearlman, L.A. (1996). *Transforming the pain: A workbook on vicarious traumatization for helping professionals who work with traumatized clients.* New York: W.W. Norton.

Stamm, B.H. (1999). *Secondary traumatic stress: Self-care issues for clinicians, researchers, and educators* (2nd ed.). Lutherville, MD: Sidran Press.

Stebnicki, M.A. (2008). *Empathic fatigue: Healing the mind, body, and spirit of professional counselors.* New York: Springer.

Vachon, M.L. (2001). The nurse's role: The world of palliative care nursing. In B.R. Ferrell & N. Coyle (Eds.), *Textbook of palliative nursing* (pp. 647–662). New York: Oxford University Press.

Welsh, D.J. (1999). Care for the caregiver: Strategies for avoiding "compassion fatigue." *Clinical Journal of Oncology Nursing, 3*(4), 183–184.

CLINICAL HIGHLIGHTS: COMPASSION FATIGUE

Definition

Compassion fatigue refers to an emotional state with negative psychological and physical consequences that emanate from acute or prolonged caregiving of people stricken by intense trauma, suffering, or misfortune. Compassion fatigue occurs when emotional boundaries become blurred and the caregiver unconsciously absorbs the distress, anxiety, fears, and trauma of the patient (also termed countertransference). The cumulative effects of untreated compassion fatigue can have a negative effect on personal and professional psychological, physical, social, and work-related health. Depending upon empirical research and the discipline, compassion fatigue also has been interchangeably described as burnout, vicarious traumatization, secondary traumatic stress, and empathy fatigue.

Pathophysiology

Stress and coping theories commonly assert that the appraisal of a situation as stressful or threatening and individuals' perceptions of their ability to cope with the situation ultimately determine their response. If caregivers appraise their personal-life or work-environment demands and exceed their abilities to cope effectively, ultimately, they may be functioning in a constant state of alertness such as "fight or flight" stimulation. If chronic stress continues, individuals may use ineffective coping strategies to self-medicate their emotional and physical pain with defensive or avoidant strategies (e.g., alcohol or substance abuse, risky behaviors, isolation or withdrawal) or become apathetic, cynical, angry, or depressed.

Risk Factors

Caregivers who inherently demonstrate the ability to show compassion and express empathy are at the greatest risk for compassion fatigue when exposed to cumulative grief and loss in their work (Figley, 1995). Oncology nurses enter the field to be healers but are faced with multiple losses, trauma, and grief despite their best efforts. The oncology nursing specialty forces nurses to face the same existential issues confronting patients and serve as a constant reminder of their own mortality and the fragile hold on life (Hill, 1991). Sociodemographic variables, such as stressful work environments, lack of social support systems, and personal life stressors and experiences, also may leave a caregiver more vulnerable.

Clinical Presentation

Symptoms of compassion fatigue can occur on a continuum from acute to chronic and affect seven domains: cognitive, emotional, behavioral, personal relations, somatic, work performance, and spiritual (Figley, 2002). Cognitive symptoms may include decreased concentration, low self-esteem, and apathy. Emotional symptoms may range from feelings of anxiety, guilt, and anger to feelings of powerlessness and helplessness. Often the most noticeable behavioral symptoms include irritability, moodiness, appetite changes, and sleep disturbances. Relationships suffer when an individual experiences compassion fatigue. Symptoms of withdrawal, mistrust, and isolation serve to exacerbate the loneliness the nurse is experiencing. Somatic complaints may range from generalized aches and pains to impaired immunity. All of the symptoms can have a negative effect on work performance, including exhaustion, low motivation, absenteeism, and detachment or apathy. The nurse may start to question the meaning of life, his or her own purpose in life, and question the very belief systems, values, and commitment that provide feelings of emotional safety and trust.

Treatment

Hill (1991) proposed that, for caregivers to provide healing to their patients, they must use reflection and inner awareness to attend to their spiritual lives. Each individual nurse must learn to recognize his or her own coping mechanisms and to find a balance of mental and physical health. Buffering factors to prevent compassion fatigue include the use of problem-solving coping strategies, hardiness, and social support. Effective coping includes positive reappraisal, self-control, and seeking support from others. Certain individuals demonstrate personality traits such as openness to change or challenge, a capacity to commit to personal goals, and feeling control over themselves and their situations (Duquette, Kerouac, Sandu, & Beaudet, 1994). Social support in the workplace that protects against compassion fatigue includes the support of colleagues and superiors. Nurses often feel that identifying their own emotional needs are signs of weakness or failure. By expressing and sharing emotional angst with colleagues, friends, and family, the nurse has the opportunity to problem-solve and reflect. Reaching out to others also helps the nurse normalize feelings and let go of self-blame and guilt. In cases of cumulative grief and what Levine (2005) terms "unattended sorrow," psychotherapy is a very effective treatment for healing.

Implications for Nursing

Nurses heal with compassion and empathic engagement with their patients and, ". . . we must bear loss as deeply as we cared" (Levine, 2005, p. 15). Oncology healthcare professionals at all levels must support each other, respect the contributions of all involved in oncology care, and reach out to others, particularly nurses in need of nurturing and renewal. Nursing research is required to identify the most pressing variables affecting the occurrence of compassion fatigue and delineate the association between personal stressors, professional stressors, and workplace stressors that contribute to specific negative behaviors and somatic complaints. The information could be used in educational programs to prepare new oncology nurses for the exposure to suffering and to provide treatment programs and supportive measures to prevent what Levine calls "the wounding of hope" (p. 27).

References

Duquette, A., Kerouac, S., Sandu, B.K., & Beaudet, L. (1994). Factors related to nursing burnout: A review of empirical knowledge. *Issues in Mental Health Nursing, 15*(4), 337–358.

Figley, C.R. (1995). Compassion fatigue as secondary traumatic stress disorder: An overview. In C.R. Figley (Ed.), *Compassion fatigue: Coping with secondary traumatic stress disorder in those who treat the traumatized* (pp. 1–20). New York: Brunner/Mazel.

Figley, C.R. (2002). *Treating compassion fatigue.* New York: Brunner-Routledge.

Hill, H.R. (1991). Point and counterpoint: Relationships in oncology care. *Journal of Psychosocial Oncology, 9*(2), 97–112.

Levine, S. (2005). *Unattended sorrow: Recovering from loss and reviving the heart.* New York: Holtzbrinck.

Dorothy J. Dunn  **NO**

The Intentionality of Compassion Energy

Compassion energy is the converse of compassion fatigue. Nurses will grow and thrive if they understand how to self-generate vigor as compassion energy, preventing compassion fatigue or burnout. The compassion energy experience can elicit implications for nursing practice to add to the caring process.

[The devastation of suffering encountered in the lives of the nursed often causes nurses to protect themselves from the nursed. Relating from a distance, the nurse shields herself or himself from the perceived vulnerability of suffering, even though this is incongruent with nurses' commitment to remain engaged and to care compassionately. Nurses need to strengthen the capacity of compassion to remain fully present to individuals and their families during times of suffering.]

Compassion energy is new to the literature. Nurses who self-generate vigor as compassion energy find meaning in caring for others. When nurses self-generate vigor, they regenerate the capacity to foster interconnectedness with the nursed. I will argue that nurses transform nursing care by using my newly developed concept of compassion energy in practice to restore positive meaning in the lifeworld of both the nurse and the nursed.

This article defines *compassion energy* as the regeneration of nurses' capacity to foster interconnectedness when the nurse activates the intent to nurse. This article explores compassion energy through the lens of caring theory. The purpose of this article is to explain the attributes of compassion energy within the context of valuing the uniqueness of answering the nursing call with compassionate presence, patterned nurturance, and intentionally knowing the nursed.

Background

Almost from the onset of modern nursing in America, the term *compassion* has been used to depict a recommended quality associated with nursing activities.[1] In the mid-20th century, Rogers and others investigated "energy" and energy fields as of particular interest to nursing practice.[2,3] In the later 20th and early

From *Holistic Nursing Practice*, July/August 2009, pp. 222–229. Copyright © 2009 by Lippincott Williams. Reprinted by permission of Wolters Kluwer Health via Rightslink.

21st centuries, caring theory has emerged as a compelling conceptual basis for nursing practice.[4–10]

For the purpose of this article, compassion will be regarded as an active, positive emotion with volitional qualities.[11] This article argues that the nursing situation lends itself to nurturing energetic compassion,[10] compassion for the nursed leads the nurse to discover a source of energy,[2,4,12] and finally authentic compassionate presence is the "quality of presence that allows one to share with and make room for the other."[13(p89)]

Data Sources

Compassion

Fox[14] asserts that the interdependence of human beings means that all are a part of one another and all are involved in one another. According to Fox, "compassion operates at the same level as celebration. The awareness of togetherness urges us to rejoice at another's joy (celebration) and to grieve at another's sorrow."[14(p4)] Celebration is considered a letting go of ego and overcoming the difficulty of entering into others' suffering to relieve others' suffering.[4,5]

Lundberg and Boonprasabhai's[15] ethnographic study defined *compassion* as giving care from the heart, valuing people, respect, trust, and loving concern. Experiencing compassion, the nurse seeks to know and understand interconnectedness to others to alleviate suffering and celebrate joy with the nursed.[13,14] Roach[13] defines *compassion* as

> a way of living born out of an awareness of one's relationship to all living creatures. It engenders a response of participation in the experience of another's sensitivity to the pain and brokenness of the other and a quality of presence that allows one to share with and make room for the other. [13(p50)]

Compassion involves a simple, unpretentious presence with the other.[13] A nurse's lack of presence may indicate avoidance behavior. Suffering seems to call forth a natural human tendency to distance one's self from exposure to vulnerability.[16]

A nurse may perform actions for the nursed with a sense of duty or moral obligation. The nurse, in this case, acts out of duty, not out of compassion. The value of human care and caring involves a higher sense of spirit of self.[4] Compassion is a gift and cannot be acquired by advanced skills and techniques.[13(p51)]

Nurturance

Common usage defines *nurturance* as affectionate care and attention.[17] Nurturing acts are behaviors directed toward another with the intention of providing physical or psychological nourishment.[18] This definition illuminates how nurses will care in a manner that respects the uniqueness and value of the nursed. An important dimension of a successful nurturing act requires the nurse to assess and respond to the emotions and needs of the nursed.[18]

Nurturance is an attribute within compassionate presence.[4,13,14,16] Quality presence transforms compassion for the nurse and the nursed to promote and nurture health and well-being with each other.[2,13] The nurse answers the call to nurse with the intent to know the nursed by alleviating suffering and seeking interconnectedness with the nursed.[10,13,14,19]

Caring Theory

Caring theory explores compassion as an attribute of the nurse that enhances well-being by transforming experiences for both the nurse and the nursed.[2,11,13] Nurses enhance personhood by participating in nurturing relationships with caring others in the moment.[10] When the nurse answers the call of the nursed with compassionate intent to alleviate suffering or to celebrate joy, a processing of energy occurs.[2,11,3,13,14,19] This energy transforms the nurse and the nursed to a higher level of consciousness.[1,2]

Compassion is one of the essences of care. The nurse compassionately nurtures the nursed. The call from the nursed is heard by the nurse. The nurse response is compassionate intention in the context of the nursing situation.[10,19]

Locsin's Theory . . . describes the necessity of establishing rapport, trust, confidence, commitment, and compassion to know the other fully as person. This is integral in the process of values experienced in the nursing situation.[8,10] The nurse comes to know the nursed with quality presence. An energized process occurs between the nurse and the nursed, as the nurse is being-with and doing-with the nursed.[9] In consequence, both will experience the encounter with intention.[19]

Nurse's work may impact the ability of the nurse to be present with the nursed. When the call for the nurse is fear, pain, suffering, sadness, loss, anxiety, or frustration, it can be perceived as threatening to the nurse. As a defense, the nurse may relate from a distance or hide behind the technical equipment and be present with the monitor rather than with the nursed.

Intentionality

The intention of nurses is to nurture a person.[10] Henderson defines *nursing* as

> . . . to assist the individual, sick or well, in the performance of those activities contributing to health or its recovery (or a peaceful death) that he would perform unaided if he had the necessary strength, will, or knowledge. And to do this in such a way as to help him gain independence as rapidly as possible.[20(p42)]

Common usage defines *intentionality* as the property of being about or directed toward a subject, as inherent in conscious states, beliefs, or creations of the mind.[21] Intentionality and authentic presence allow the nurse to hear the call.[10,19] The nurse enters into the nursing situation with the intentional commitment of knowing the nursed as a caring person. . . .

Using intention, the nursing response is a caring expression of nurturing to sustain, enhance, and energize the nurse and the nursed in the nursing situation. . . .[10,11]

In the caring between the nurse and the nursed, energy processing is initiated and personhood is enhanced.[10,11,19] As the nurse intentionally comes to know self as caring, she or he lets go of ego to experience the interconnectedness that enables the nurse to know self and other as living caring.[4,5]

Intentionality promotes a healing caring consciousness as energy within the human environment field of a caring moment.[5] Watson states that

> cultivation of sensitivity to one's self and to others becomes a cultivation of one's own spiritual practices and transpersonal self, going beyond ego self, opening to others with sensitivity and compassion.[6(p298)]

In a caring consciousness, the nurse and the nursed experience a subtle energy environment whereby compassionate love and caring come together intentionally to form a deep transpersonal caring occasion. . . .[4]

Thus, the nurse is viewed as a coparticipant in the human care process with high value placed on the relationship between the nurse and the nursed.[5(p35)]

Compassion is experienced as deep transpersonal caring. Compassion energy depends on the intention of nurses' authentic quality presence with the nursed.[3,4,10,19,22]

Compassion Energy

Nurses initiate the experience of compassion energy when they answer the call from a patient. The 3 attributes of compassion energy are compassionate presence, patterned nurturance, and intentionally knowing the nursed and self as whole.[23]

When the nurse answers the call of the nursed with the intent to alleviate suffering, the nursed reveals her or his hopes, dreams, and aspirations. The nurse and nursed's individual expressions of affirmation, support, and celebration are exchanged as energy via compassionate presence.[8] Compassion becomes the energy of caring.[24]

In the nursing situation, the nurse answers the call with patterned nurturance that yields energy to be compassionately present. The dynamic unfolding of the energy exchange is experienced as patterned nurturance through listening, knowing, and being with the nursed in authentic compassionate presence.[5,9]

In intentional caring consciousness, the nurse intentionally knows the nursed as whole. The patient has the choice of letting the nurse know her or him as a person.[8,10] Compassion energy is the intersubjective gift of compassion that gives nurses the opportunity to be with the nursed. Alleviating suffering or celebrating joy, the nurse and the nursed express a warm approval while sharing joyful satisfaction in the nursing situation by enhancing compassionate presence, patterned nurturance, and intentionally knowing the nursed and self as whole.[23]

Discussion

. . . Johns describes 6 factors that pattern within a nursing situation to determine "the extent the nurse is available to the nursed: compassion and love, vision and intentionality, knowing the person, the aesthetic response, knowing and managing self in a relationship, and creating and sustaining a practice environment."[24(p39)] Compassion is the energy of caring and it is experienced in the nursing situation.[10,24]

Compassion energy occurs when the nurse values the uniqueness of answering the call with compassionate presence, patterned nurturance, and intentionally knowing the nursed and self as whole.[23] The following mini-saga depicts a compassion energy nursing situation:

> I was overdue for lunch and hungry when LC arrived pale, diaphoretic, holding his chest with one hand and grabbing my arm with his other. The nursing call was loud and clear, "call my wife and don't let me die." Lunch and hunger were no more. Compassion became the feast.[23]

In the above story, the nurse discovered compassion energy in the call of the nursed and her or his personhood was enhanced.[10] Compassion for the nursed leads the nurse to discover a source of energy. Through intention, the nurse regenerates compassion within her or his capacity to foster interconnectedness.

Nurses enter into a partnership with the nursed and engage in meaningful dialogue as the dynamic pattern unfolds.[2,11] What matters most to the nursed becomes transparent as the nursed guides the discussion. . . .

Implication for Nursing Research, Practice, and Education

Human beings live in the world with meaningful compassionate relationships. I have argued in this article that the culture of nursing should be considered and nurtured as compassion in present-day practice. Nurses will grow and thrive if they understand how to self-generate vigor as compassion energy to find meaning in caring others. Nurses confronted with high physical job demands and have low physical job resources are at risk for physical complaints and burnout.[25(p82)] If the nurse intends to be caring, she or he initiates an energy exchange that promotes compassion energy and prevents experiencing compassion fatigue or burnout. Exploring compassion energy through research will contribute to the body of nursing knowledge and practice.

Research

Quantitative and qualitative research methods to study compassion energy will add to the body of nursing knowledge. Quantitative research methods will describe how prevalent, how often, and what are the characteristics of compassion energy. . . .

Qualitative research methods begin with identification of what is compassion energy to the nurse, what is important about it, and how does it work for the nurse and the nursed. . . .

Benner describes clinical knowledge as an interpretative approach. The intentions and understanding of the participants are taken into consideration and seen as dependent on a shared world of meaning.[26(p40)] The novice nurse interpretation of compassion compared with the expert nurse interpretation of compassion could be examined with ethnographical fieldwork methods. Researchers can learn from members of the nursing culture regarding differences and similarities when providing compassionate care. The assumption is that all nurses desire to care with compassion.

Nursing situations present the novice nurse with a set of tasks that must be accomplished.[27] Overwhelmed by the patient's biomedical needs, novice nurses may feel unable to attend to their psychosocial needs. . . . The novice nurse will learn to increase her or his vigor and energy that nurtures her or his creativity and self-care. . . . Caring-for-self strategies that enhance emotional growth include techniques such as balanced humor, relaxation, and stress reduction while caring for the nursed will be encouraged to maximize the novice nurse's potential. Once an awareness and willingness to utilize caring-for-self strategies is unfolding, the novice nurse can practice compassion for self. Then, the novice nurse can be open to intentionally ask the nursed compassionately what matters most. . . .

Research in Practice

First-hand perspective on the compassion energy experience can elicit implications for nursing practice to revise or add to the caring process. Compassionate caring can be provided for the nursed in an efficient and timely manner, to benefit the nurse and the nursed. . . .

The nursing situation is an interactive qualitative place to dwell and study the dynamic and evolving energetic process of compassion. . . .

The notion that compassion is a necessary condition to the "being" of a nurse is not new.[1] Hamilton's historical study of Lillian Wald, Lavina Dock, and Annie Goodrich discusses compassion as an expected attitude that Wald and Dock created in the context of the Henry Street Settlement House.[1(p248)]

Systematically collecting, critically evaluating, and interpreting historical evidence from compassionate nurses from the 19th to 21st century will provide the needed historical evidence for compassion energy by investigating nurses' compassion over time to build nursing knowledge.[28] Hamilton declares "the idea of compassion and caring as a central virtue in nursing appeals to the core of nursing."[1(p256)]

Qualitative research methods enable exploration of everyday experiences of compassion and suffering to give meaning to suffering and experiencing vulnerability of the nurse and the nursed. . . .

Education

Overcoming the tendency to care at a distance requires a new discourse. Heidegger's idea of empty busywork in which the nurse may use technology as a barrier against developing a relationship with the nursed should be investigated.[8,29] Nurses can assist the nursed in the work of suffering by understanding how to be compassionately present.

Being present with another who is suffering is an important part of the healing process for those who are seeking meaning in their life. Teaching nursing students to focus their intent on compassionate caring to trigger the energy exchange, rather than focusing on task-oriented "doing the job" or "getting tasks done," should be implemented into academic curricula and orientation programs in the workplace. . . .

Presently, education is focused on care, cure, and restorative function and does not address "relief of suffering" adequately.[30] Narrative education is considered the phenomenology of human suffering by assisting students in learning to dwell patiently, humbly, and attentively with the suffering nursed.[30] Integrating substantive philosophical content in nursing education curricula will enable students to come to know what it means to be human and to suffer. Students will thereby have an opportunity for deep reflection, intense dialogue, and meaningful research.

Critical reflection using narrative story is a way of gaining self-awareness and personal growth, as well as the notion that caring can be learned through reflection. There is a philosophical link between self-care, caring, and holistic nursing practice.[31] The process of self-reflection is a way to gain self-awareness and learn to care for self. Sherwood[32] acknowledged the importance of a caring connection centered on caring for self. . . .

Conclusion

In conclusion, this article has argued that it is necessary to understand and nurture the ability of the nurse to self-generate vigor as compassion energy. With compassion energy, the nurse will find meaning in caring for self and the nursed with the intent to alleviate suffering or celebrate joy. The compassion energy exchanged is transformative and can restore positive meaning in the lifeworld of both the nurse and the nursed.

References

1. Hamilton D. Constructing the mind of nursing. *Nurs Hist Rev*. 1994;2:3–28.

2. Newman MA. *Health as Expanding Consciousness*. 2nd ed. New York, NY: NLN; 1994.

3. Rogers ME. *An Introduction to the Theoretical Basis of Nursing*. Philadelphia, PA: FA Davis; 1970.

4. Watson J. *Nursing: Human Science and Human Care*. Norwalk, CT: Appleton-Century-Crofts; 1985.

5. Watson J. Jean Watson's theory of human caring. In: Parker ME, ed. *Nursing Theories and Nursing Practice.* 2nd ed. Philadelphia, PA: FA Davis; 2006:295–301.

6. Leininger MM. Leininger's theory of nursing: culture care diversity and universality. *Nurs Sci Q.* 1988;1:152–160.

7. Ray M. The theory of bureaucratic caring for nursing practice in the organizational structure. *Nurs Adm Q.* 1989;13:31–42.

8. Locsin R. Technologic competence as expression of caring in critical care settings. *Holis Nurs Pract.* 1998;12:50–56.

9. Swanson KM. Empirical development of middle range theory of caring. *Nurs Res.* 1991;40:161–166.

10. Boykin A, Schoenhofer S. *Nursing as Caring: A Model for Transforming Practice.* Sudbury, MA: NLN; 2001.

11. Newman MA. *Transforming Presence: The Difference That Nursing Makes.* Philadelphia, PA: FA Davis; 2008.

12. Todaro-Franceschi V. The idea of energy as phenomenon and Rogerian science: are they congruent? *Visions.* 1999;7:30–41.

13. Roach MS. *Caring, the Human Mode of Being: A Blueprint for the Health Professions.* Ottawa, ON, Canada: CHA Press; 2002.

14. Fox M. *A Spirituality Named Compassion.* New York, NY: HarperCollins; 1979.

15. Lundberg PC, Boonprasabhai K. Meanings of good nursing care among Thai female last-year undergraduate nursing students. *J Adv Nurs.* 2001;34:35–42.

16. Johnston NE. Finding meaning in adversity. In: Johnston NE, ed. *Meaning in Suffering: Caring Practice in the Health Professions.* Madison: University of Wisconsin Press; 2007:98–141.

17. *Merriam-Webster Online Dictionary.* Springfield, MA: Merriam-Webster, Inc; 2008. www.merriamwebster.com/dictionary/nurturance. Accessed June 4, 2008.

18. Sappington J. Nurturance: the spirit of holistic nursing. *J Holist Nurs.* 2003;21:8–19.

19. Paterson JG, Zderad LT. *Humanistic Nursing.* New York, NY: NLN; 1988.

20. Henderson V. *Basic Principles of Nursing Care.* London, England: International Council of Nurses; 1961.

21. *American Heritage Dictionary of the English Language.* Boston, MA: Houghton Mifflin; 2008. www.bartleby.com/61/5/10180587/intentionality.html. Accessed June 9, 2008.

22. Watson J. *Caring Science as Sacred Science.* Philadelphia, PA: FA Davis; 2005.

23. Dunn DJ. A way of knowing, being, valuing and living with compassion energy: a unitary science perspective. Paper presented at: The Conference of the Rogerian Scholars; October 12–14, 2007; Cleveland, OH.

24. Johns C. With just a little bit of love: reflection on dwelling with Kristen. *Int J Hum Caring.* 2005;9:36–42.

25. Van den Tooren M, de Jonge J. Managing job stress in nursing: what kind of resources do we need? *J Adv Nurs.* 2008;63:75–84.

26. Benner P. *From Novice to Expert: Excellence and Power in Clinical Nursing Practice.* Menlo Park, CA: Addison-Wesley; 1984.

27. Benner P, Tanner CA, Chesla CA. *Expertise in Nursing Practice: Caring, Clinical Judgment and Ethics.* New York, NY: Springer; 1996.

28. Polit DF, Beck CT. *Nursing Research: Principles and Methods.* 7th ed. Philadelphia, PA: Lippincott Williams & Wilkins; 2004.

29. Heidegger M. *The Question Concerning Technology and Other Essays.* New York, NY: Harper & Row; 1977.

30. Swenson MM, Sims SL. Listening to learn: narrative strategies and interpretive practices in clinical education. In: Dickelmann NL, ed. *Teaching the Practitioners of Care: New Pedagogies for the Health Profession.* Madison: University of Wisconsin Press; 2003:154–193.

31. Wilson CB, Grams K. Reflective journaling and self-care: the experience of MSN students in a course on caring. *Int J Hum Caring.* 2007;11:16–21.

32. Sherwood G. Patterns of caring: the healing connection of interpersonal harmony. *Int J Hum Caring.* 1997;1:30–38.

EXPLORING THE ISSUE

Compassion Fatigue: Does Burnout Occur in All Caregivers of Dying Patients?

Critical Thinking and Reflection

1. Is compassion fatigue simply exhaustion from too much work? Would caregivers who work with dying patients suffer less compassion fatigue if they were allotted shorter work weeks or adequate breaks?
2. Why should caregivers recognize effects of stress and develop coping strategies that balance self-regard (nurturing) and other-regard (generativity)? Do all caregivers need to do this?
3. A daughter cares for her dying father who has chronic obstructive pulmonary disorder and has lost the ability to recognize her or all the care she is providing. His irritability and lack of gratitude, along with his slow decline, affect her emotionally. What can strategies might she use to balance healthy self-care and care giving?
4. What special risks are faced by caregivers who are sole caregivers of those with special needs in prolonged end stage illnesses such as ALS or AIDS? What help should be offered to individuals with minimal or no family support who are most at risk?
5. Discuss the pros and cons: you know someone exhausted by compassion fatigue but who refuses to admit it (she claims it is her "cross"). What can you say?

Is There Common Ground?

Some caregivers boast of being "wounded healers"—a translation of Carl Jung's interpretation of counter-transference based on Greek mythology, "Only wounded physicians heal" (Conti-O'Hara, 2001; Jung, 1989; Nouwen, 1979; Sulmasy 1997, p. 109; 2006: p. 24). However, the risk of being that wounded healer with compassion fatigue is that one loses empathy. Research in psychology and the neurosciences has demonstrated that a person must have empathy to be able to recognize emotional states in facial expressions of others. This ability is the basis of being able to identify with another's situation by means of congruent emotions (Stueber, 2006).

In examining relationships of caregivers to dying patients, we cannot provide specific measurement of compassion. Although patients may identify that "she didn't care enough," it is difficult to identify a threshold of compassion. Our concern for others must balance self-regard (care for the self) with generativity (other-regard called altruism) (Browning & Cooper, 2004). Caring for a dying patient is not confined to physical health, but the whole of the person (Kauffman, 1999; Marty, 2005; Orsi, 2005). Persons and communities who provide care to the suffering are also those who may be suffering and grieving. What comforts afflicted can afflict the comfortable.

References

Browning, D. & Cooper, T. (2004). *Religious thought and the modern psychologies.* Minneapolis, MN: Fortress Press.

Bush, N. (2009). Compassion fatigue: Are you at risk? *Oncology Nursing Forum, 36*(1), 24–28. doi:10.1188/09.ONF.24-28

Coetzee, S. & Klopper, H. C. (2010). Compassion fatigue within nursing practice: A concept analysis. *Nursing & Health Sciences, 12*(2), 235–243. doi:10.1111/j.1442-2018.2010.00526.x

Conti-O'Hara, M. (2001). *The nurse as wounded healer: From trauma to transcendence.* Sudbury, MA: Jones and Bartlett Publishers.

Dunn, D. J. (2009). The intentionality of compassion energy. *Holistic Nursing Practice, 23*(4), 222–229.

Figley, C. R. (1995). The transmission of trauma. In C. R. Figley (Ed.), *Compassion fatigue: Coping with secondary traumatic stress disorder in those who treat the traumatized* (pp. 248–254). London: Brunner-Routledge.

Figley, C. R. (1999). Compassion fatigue: Toward a new understanding of the costs of caring. In B. H. Stamm (Ed.), *Secondary traumatic stress: Self-care issues for clinicians, researchers and educators* (2nd ed., pp. 3–29). Lutherville, MD: Sidran Press.

Figley, C. R. (2002). *Treating compassion fatigue.* New York: Brunner-Routledge.

Harvey, B. (2000). *An introduction to Buddhist ethics: Foundations, values, and issues.* Cambridge: Cambridge University Press.

Joinson, C. (1992). Coping with compassion fatigue. *Nursing, 22*(4), 116–121.

Jung, C. G. (1989). *Memories, dreams, reflections.* New York: Vintage Books Edition.

Kauffman, C. (1999). Catholic health care in the United States: American pluralism and religious meanings. *Christian Bioethics, 5*(1), 44–65. doi:10.1093/chbi.5.1.44.3797

Kundera, M. (2009). *The unbearable lightness of being: A novel.* New York: Harper Perennial Modern Classics.

Lewin, R. A. (1996). *Compassion: The core value that animates psychotherapy.* Northvale, NJ: Jason Aronson.

Marr, L. (2009). Can compassion fatigue? *Journal of Palliative Medicine, 12*(8), 739–740. doi:10.1089/jpm.2009.9577

Marty, M. (2005). Religion and healing: The four expectations. In L. L. Barnes & S. S. Sered (Eds.), *Religion and healing in America* (pp. 487–504). New York: Oxford University Press.

Merton, T. (1975). *The Asian journal of Thomas Merton.* New York: New Directions.

Najjar, N., Davis, L. W., Beck-Coon, K., & Doebbeling, C. (2009). Compassion fatigue: A review of the research to date and relevance to cancer-care providers. *Journal of Health Psychology, 14*(2), 267–277. doi:10.1177/1359105308100211

Newsom, R. (2010). Compassion fatigue: Nothing left to give. *Nursing Management, 41*(4), 42–45.

Nouwen, H. (1979). *The wounded healer: Ministry in contemporary society.* New York: Doubleday.

Nussbaum, M. (2001). *Upheavals of thought: The intelligence of emotion.* Cambridge: Cambridge University Press.

Orsi, R. (2005). The cult of the saints and the reimagination of the space and the time of sickness in twentieth century American Catholicism. In L. L. Barnes & S. S. Sered (Eds.), *Religion and healing in America* (pp. 29–47). New York: Oxford University Press.

Roberts, R. (2011). Emotions in the Christian tradition. In E. Zalta, *The Stanford Encyclopedia of Philosophy* (Summer 2011 ed.). Retrieved from http://plato.stanford.edu/archives/sum2011/entries/emotion-Christian-tradition

Stueber, K. (2006). *Rediscovering empathy: Agency, folk psychology, and the human sciences.* Cambridge, MA: MIT Press.

Suh, S. (2004). *Being Buddhist in a Christian world: Gender and community in a Korean American temple.* Seattle, WA: University of Washington Press.

Sulmasy, D. P. (1997). *The healer's calling: A spirituality for physicians and other health care professionals.* Mahwah, NJ: Paulist Press.

Sulmasy, D. P. (2006). *The rebirth of the clinic: An introduction to spirituality in healthcare.* Georgetown: Georgetown University Press.

Additional Resources

Adams, R. E., Figley, C. R., & Boscarino, J. A. (2008). The compassion fatigue scale: Its use with social workers following urban disaster. *Research on Social Work Practice, 18*(3), 238–250. doi:10.1177/1049731507310190

Aristotle. 1385b Compassion. In *The art of rhetoric.*

Boyle, D. A. (2011). Countering compassion fatigue: A requisite nursing agenda. *Online Journal of Issues in Nursing, 16*(1), Manuscript 2. doi:10.3912/OJIN.Vol16No01Man02

Chase, D. M., Monk, B. J., Wenzel, L. B., & Tewari, K. S. (2008). Supportive care for women with gynecologic cancers. *Expert Review of Anticancer Therapy, 8*(2), 227–241.

Dikkers, J. E., Geurts, S. E., Kinnunen, U., Kompier, M. J., & Taris, T. W. (2007). Crossover between work and home in dyadic partner relationships. *Scandinavian Journal of Psychology, 48*(6), 529–538. doi:10.1111/j.1467-9450.2007.00580.x

Doorenbos, A., Wyatt, G., Gift, A., Rahbar, M., Given, S. J., & Given, C. (2004). The impact of end-of-life care on caregivers of family members over 65 with cancer. *The Gerontologist, 44*(1), 644.

Emslie, C., Whyte, F., Campbell, A., Mutrie, N., Lee, L., Ritchie, D. et al. (2007). "I wouldn't have been interested in just sitting round a table talking about cancer": Exploring the experiences of women with breast cancer in a group exercise trial. *Health Education Research, 22*(6), 827–838.

Fleming, D. A., Sheppard, V. B., Mangan, P. A., Taylor, K. L., Tallarico, M., Adams, I., et al. (2006). Caregiving at the end of life: Perceptions of health care quality and quality of life among patients and caregivers. *Journal of Pain & Symptom Management, 31*(5), 407–420. doi:10.1016/j.jpainsymman.2005.09.002

Fry, S. (2003). Nursing ethics. In S. Post (Ed.), *Encyclopedia of bioethics* (3rd ed., pp. IV: 1898–1903). New York: Macmillan Reference USA.

Fry, S. & Johnstone, M. J. (2002). *Ethics in nursing practice: A guide to ethical decision making* (2nd ed.). Oxford: Blackwell Publishing.

Gilligan, C. (1993). *In a different voice: Psychological theory and women's development*. Cambridge, MA: Harvard University Press.

Gray, R. W. (2008). Avoid compassion fatigue. *Tennessee Medicine: Tennessee Medical Foundation, March,* 27.

Hayes, C. (2004). Ethics in end-of-life care. *Journal of Hospice and Palliative Nursing, 6*(1), 36–43.

Henry, J. & Henry, L. (2004). *The soul of the caring nurse: Stories and strategies for revitalizing professional passion*. Washington, D.C.: American Nurses Association.

Holstein, M. & Mitzen, P. (2001). *Ethics in community-based elder care*. New York: Springer Publishing Company.

Jecker, N. & Reick, W. (2003). Contemporary ethics of care. In S. Post (Ed.), *Encyclopedia of bioethics* (3rd ed., pp. I: 367–374). New York: Macmillan Reference USA.

Lai, W. (1981). The Buddhist "prodigal son": A story of misperceptions. *Journal of the International Association of Buddhist Studies, 4*(2), 91–98.

Lester, N. (2010). Compassion fatigue. *Mental Health Practice, 14*(2), 11.

Levine, C. (2004). *Always on call: When illness turns families into caregivers*. Nashville, TN: Vanderbilt University Press.

Malterud, K. (2000). Symptoms as a source of medical knowledge: Understanding medically unexplained disorders in women. *Family Medicine Journal, 32*(9), 603–611.

McGibbon, E., Peter, E., & Gallop, R. (2010). An institutional ethnography of nurses' stress. *Qualitative Health Research, 20*(10), 1353–1378. doi:10.1177/1049732310375435

McHolm, F. (2006). Rx for compassion fatigue. *Journal of Christian Nursing, 23*(4), 12–19.

Mulder, J. & Gregory, D. (2000). Transforming experience into wisdom: Healing amidst suffering. *Journal of Palliative Care, 16*(2), 25–29.

Perry, B., Dalton, J. E., & Edwards, M. (2010). Family caregivers' compassion fatigue in long-term facilities. *Nursing Older People, 22*(4), 26–31.

Pfifferling, J. & Gilley, K. (2000). Overcoming compassion fatigue. *Family Practice Management, 7*(4), 39–44.

President's Council on Bioethics. (2005). *Taking care: Ethical caregiving in our aging society*. Retrieved from http://bioethics.georgetown.edu/pcbe/reports/taking_care/taking_care.pdf

Reich, W. (1995). History of the notion of care. In *Encyclopedia of bioethics* (2nd ed., pp. I: 319–331). New York: Simon & Schuster Macmillan.

Risse, G. (1999). A history of hospitals: The future of hospitals as healing spaces. In *Mending bodies, saving souls: A history of hospitals* (pp. 675–687). New York: Oxford University Press.

Running, A., Tolle, L., & Girard, D. (2008). Ritual: The final expression of care. *International Journal of Nursing Practice, 14*(4), 303–307. doi:10.1111/j.1440-172X.2008.00703.x

Sawyer, L. M. (1989). Nursing code of ethics: An international comparison. *International Nursing Review, 36*(5), 145–148.

Sevilla, A. L. (2010). Founding human rights within Buddhism: Exploring Buddha-nature as an ethical foundation. *Journal of Buddhist Ethics, 17*, 212–252.

Sinclair, H. & Hamill, C. (2007). Does vicarious traumatisation affect oncology nurses? *European Journal of Oncology Nurses, 11*(4), 348–356.

Varner, J. M. (2004). ASNA independent study activity—compassion fatigue. *Alabama Nurses, 31*(1), 30.

Online Resources

Compassion Fatigue Articles

www.vaonline.org/doc_compassion.html

Compassion Fatigue Links

www.vaonline.org/care.html

Compassion Fatigue Self-Test

www.compassionfatigue.org/pages/CompassionFatigueSelfTest.html

How Compassion Fatigue Can Overwhelm Charity Workers

http://philanthropy.com/jobs/2002/03/21/20020321-974239.htm

Overcoming Compassion Fatigue

http://pspinformation.com/caregiving/thecaregiver/compassion.shtml

Internet References . . .

Alliance of State Pain Initiatives
>http://trc.wisc.edu/

American Pain Foundation
>www.painfoundation.org/

American Pain Society
>www.ampainsoc.org/

Center to Advance Palliative Care
>www.getpalliativecare.org/

Emerging Solutions in Pain
>www.emergingsolutionsinpain.com/

Federation of State Medical Boards
>www.fsmb.org/

Federation of State Medical Boards: Responsible Opioid Prescribing
>www.fsmb.org/pain-overview.html

International Association for the Study of Pain
>www.iasp-pain.org//AM/Template.cfm?Section=Home

National Foundation for the Treatment of Pain
>www.paincare.org/pain_management/advocacy/ca_bill.php

Pain & the Law
>www.painandthelaw.org/statutes/state_pain_acts.php

Pain & Policy Studies Group
>www.painpolicy.wisc.edu/

Pain Control: Support for People with Cancer
>www.cancer.gov/cancertopics/coping/paincontrol

American Hospital Association Statistics
>www.aha.org/research/rc/stat-studies/fast-facts.shtml

Treatment Requests and Decisions: Pain and Futility

*M*ost dying patients have one request, to be kept comfortable through the dying process. There are many barriers to good pain management at the end of life: underprescribed medication, too little medication, worries about overdosing medication, patient or family concerns about oversedation or addiction. This unit explores several issues related to pain management at the end of life. Providing comfort is an ethical obligation of health care professionals and we discuss whether patients have a right to effective pain management at the end of life. We explore the concerns that health care professionals and family members raise when treatment of pain means hastening death.

Patients and families sometimes have difficulties understanding that treatments at the end of life are futile. Demanding treatments that offer no benefit can create additional pain and suffering at the end of life. In this unit, we describe overtreatment and the issues of futility at the end of life. Essays are included that specifically address the unique burdens of tube feedings in dying patients and the challenges that withholding and withdrawing tube feedings present to family members. Family members particularly struggle with the decision to withhold or withdraw futile treatment in dying patients, because they fear that this withdrawal "kills" the patient. Understanding that the patient is dying of the underlying disease process is an important step in working through these concerns.

- Does a Dying Person with Severe Pain Have a Right to Effective Pain Management?
- Should Pain Be Alleviated if It Hastens Death?
- Does Too Much Treatment Result in an Inhumane Dying?
- Are Feeding Tubes Obligatory?
- Does Withholding or Withdrawing Futile Treatment Kill People?

ISSUE 5

Does a Dying Person with Severe Pain Have a Right to Effective Pain Management?

YES: Kathryn L. Tucker, from "Medico-Legal Case Report and Commentary: Inadequate Pain Management in the Context of Terminal Cancer. The Case of Lester Tomlinson," *Pain Medicine* (vol. 5, no. 2, 2004)

NO: Rodney Syme, from "Necessity to Palliate Pain and Suffering as a Defence to Medical Homicide," *Journal of Law & Medicine* (vol. 17, no. 3, 2009)

Learning Outcomes

After reading this issue, you should be able to:

- Describe differences between pain relief as a human right, a civil liberty, a civil right, and a risk of criminal homicide or civil duty according to a standard of care.
- Learn about how pain relief can be ethically justified in terms of utilitarianism, duty, or rights.
- Identify and debate structural barriers to undertreatment for dying persons with severe pain among patients, caregivers, providers, and policymakers.
- Discuss and distinguish different kinds of accountability that physicians must address in pain management of dying patients.

ISSUE SUMMARY

YES: Kathryn L. Tucker, the Director of Legal Affairs for the Compassion and Choices in Seattle, discusses the case of Lester Tomlinson, an 85-year-old patient dying of cancer whose family was successful in reaching an agreement after a lawsuit against the hospital and health providers for inadequate pain treatment. Brushwood (2004) and Johnson (2004) qualify Tucker's claims.

NO: Rodney Syme argues that it is surprising that under current laws more physicians are not prosecuted for homicide when delivering high doses of pain medications at the end of life. He identifies a need for a defense for medical homicide based on the necessity to relieve pain.

We must all die. But that I can save him from days of torture, that is what I feel as my great and ever new privilege. Pain is a more terrible lord of mankind than even death itself.

Albert Schweitzer (1931)

One of the major concerns for dying patients and their family members is that the patient should not suffer or die in pain. This issue discusses the issue of having a "right" to effective pain management. The use of the word "rights" suggests that laws or standards should be in place to guide and regulate health care professionals who have a role in controlling pain. Providers, patients, regulators, and laws should agree on three key areas. First, the pain in a dying patient must be accurately diagnosed, effectively managed, and is treated as best possible even if complete relief cannot be attained. Second, the clinicians, regulators, and laws must accept an underlying ethical consideration that pain "ought to be relieved" and is respected as an obligation or duty based on different kinds of rights. Finally, adequate pain relief is supported by legal, professional, and regulatory agencies.

To address the first issue, one must understand the current problems with pain management practices. Because of the unpredictable nature of dying, nearly 8 out of every 10 hospital deaths occur without a palliative care consultation and formal pain management plan (Pan et al., 2001; Smits, Furletti, & Vladeck, 2002). Research shows that between 26 percent and 50 percent of patients are reported to have pain that was undertreated at the end of life (Fineberg, Wenger, & Brown-Saltzman, 2006; Smith et al., 2010; SUPPORT, 1995). Health care professionals believe that only 10 percent of pain is not able to be relieved by appropriate measures (American Pain Society, 1997; Ingham, Mohamudally, & Portenoy, 2009).

Barriers to undertreatment come from many sources: patients who are worried about being too sedated or becoming addicted; caregivers who are reluctant to give pain doses because they are afraid they will "kill" the patient (see Issue 8); providers may not adequately assess the patient's real level of pain or prescribe doses lower than needed; and regulators may review prescribing practices and sanction physicians for high narcotic prescribing. Physicians who are focusing on fighting the disease may lose sight of the pain and suffering of the patient or delay referral to hospice for comfort (Howell & Lutz, 2008). Palliative care or pain management teams can expertly diagnose types of pain and effectively work to relieve this pain.

Researchers have recognized the need for health care provider education on appropriate pain treatment, and professional guidelines for the treatment of pain have been developed. However, laws that were established to prevent diversion can also produce a "culture of underprescription" because physicians deal with regulatory standards of triplicate prescriptions and documentation (Imhof & Kaskie, 2008; Ingham et al., 2009). The Model Pain Relief Acts have created a "safe harbor" (legal protection) for health care professionals "who prescribe pain medication as long as the physician substantially complied with accepted practice and care guidelines for pain management" including risk disclosure, documentation, and consultation (Project on Legal Constraints, 1996; Tucker, 2001, p. 935).

Another key aspect of the right to adequate pain relief is that it is ethically justified in three ways. Utilitarians would argue that undertreatment has huge social impacts and personal costs of needless suffering (Institute of Medicine, 2011). Others suggest a duty-based approach to pain. Providers must treat pain because they are required to do no harm (nonmaleficence) and must provide comfort based on a positive duty of beneficence (Bernat, 2008)—others propose rights.

In reviewing clinical guidelines and legal cases over the past few decades, pain relief can be seen as one of five different kinds of rights: a basic human right (Human Rights Watch, 2009; International Association for the Study of Pain (IASP), 2004), a civil liberty (California Pain Patient's Bill of Rights, 1997), a civil right (Pettus, 2011), a risk of criminal homicide (Syme, 2009), and a civil duty (Tucker, 2004). The emerging clinical practice guidelines from almost every subspecialty reinforce pain relief as a public health goal. These guidelines clarify how an ethical ideal as the right to adequate pain treatment is transformed into public policy. Acknowledging pain management as a right influences both private and civic practices, including practices that legislate or regulate physician care or hospital review and judicial oversight of such practices.

Adequate pain relief for the dying as a human right, a civil liberty, or a civil right carries a risk of civil duty or sanctions (including criminal sanctions) if a standard of care is not met. Pain relief for dying is guided not only by clinical practice guidelines but also by legislative rulings. In 1971, the Controlled Substances Act placed medicines under the jurisdiction of the DEA and FDA and provides oversight of prescribers. In 1976, the International Association of the Study of Pain defined pain as both physical and psychological (Stahl, 2008, p. 777) and provided recommendations for treatment. In 1986, the World Health Organization proposed a three-step pain relief standard for cancer that has been adopted, applied, and modified over the years (Vargas-Schaffer, 2010).

Some expand adequate end-of-life pain relief to being a general *human right*, with implications for how resources are organized for care of dying patients. This view could provide support for health care professionals who seek to reduce severe and intractable pain at the end of life but worry about legal sanctions (Brennan, Carr, & Cousins, 2007; Human Rights Watch, 2009; IASP, 2004; Nussbaum, 1999, 2001).

American constitutional law and corresponding political theory of common law narrow excessive treatment of pain to *homicide*. State jurisdictions must decide if the extremely high doses of pain medications used in dying patients are given with intent to cause death and thus considered a *criminal act*

(Syme, 2009). Another approach is to look at state regulations for whether and how comfort care is a *civil duty*. This means that persons who fail to provide adequate pain relief have failed their civil duty to meet the standard of care and could be sued for such failure (Tucker, 2004). Some explore whether adequate pain relief is a *civil liberty* with the possibility of examining government-related care that fails to meet this as not meeting a standard to avoid "cruel and unusual punishment." Still others identify adequate pain relief as a *civil right*—or an obligation imposed on the government to take positive action to protect citizens from any illegal action of government agencies as well as of other private citizens (e.g., debating DEA/FDA classifications of painkillers; Ginsberg, Lowi, & Weir, 2005, pp. 119, 164). A "right to palliative care" protects the "vulnerable autonomy" of end-stage dying persons based on citizenship (Pettus, 2011).

Who is responsible for un(der)treated pain? Accountability for adequate pain management comes through civil courts as a *civil duty*. Professionals are monitored and disciplined by State Medical Boards and regulatory agencies (DEA). A "right to aggressive pain management" has been litigated in cases involving end-stage cancers that were undertreated. These are made as claims of medical negligence. Plaintiffs may seek compensation for "pain and suffering" in any lawsuit that involves severe injury and/or death. States vary as to whether pain and suffering damages survive a patient's death under medical negligence laws (e.g., no in California, yes in Louisiana). Other cases pursue poor pain control under statutes that govern elder abuse; litigation has been successful in meeting this additional proof of recklessness (Tucker, 2004). Civil litigation (i.e., "medical malpractice") seeks monetary redress for negligence. To prevail in such a lawsuit, a plaintiff must prove four elements: (1) existence of a duty to care (between a specific doctor and a specific patient), (2) negligence (i.e., a breach of the duty to provide reasonable care), (3) blameworthy harm (injury and/or death), and (4) a consequence of that negligence (not too remote) (Baker, 2007). Brushwood (2004) argues that holding physicians accountable through elder abuse or medical negligence won't improve pain management, because pain management is related to the structural flaws (provider training, patient fears).

In the article for the YES position, Kathryn L. Tucker, the Director of Legal Affairs for the Compassion and Choices in Seattle, discusses the case of Lester Tomlinson, an 85-year-old patient dying of cancer whose family was successful in reaching an agreement after a lawsuit against the hospital and health providers for inadequate pain treatment. Tucker explains how the settlement of her court litigation among different jurisdictions (State Medical Board, State Health Services, Center for Medicare/Medicaid) reveals there were violations of standards of care among hospital, providers, and nursing home. Johnson (2004) argues that this case fell within "safe harbor guidelines" of permissible aggressive care, but variable state policies may limit compensation for substandard care.

In the article for the NO position, Rodney Syme argues that it is surprising that under current laws more physicians are not prosecuted for homicide when delivering high doses of pain medications at the end of life. He suggests that a better law should focus on palliation and consent, rather than criminal law of causation focused on intention and cause of death.

YES

Kathryn L. Tucker

Medico-Legal Case Report and Commentary: Inadequate Pain Management in the Context of Terminal Cancer. The Case of Lester Tomlinson

Abstract

Presented is a review of the pain management provided to an elderly male patient dying of mesothelioma in an acute care hospital and, subsequently, in a nursing home. Discussed are the medico-legal aspects of the case, including the patient's survivors' efforts to hold the treating physicians, hospital, and nursing home accountable for inadequate pain management through complaints submitted to the state medical boards, the state department of health services, and the Center for Medicaid/Medicare Services, and in state court.

Introduction

Lester Tomlinson, 85 years old, was dying from mesothelioma, an invasive, progressive, and painful terminal cancer of the lining of the lung. Lester suffered significant pain caused by his cancer. He had made his wishes for aggressive pain management known in various ways, including by executing a written advance directive, which specifically addressed this aspect of his care. Ginger and Rosa Tomlinson, Lester's daughter and wife, were present daily during Lester's last weeks of life. This article provides an overview of the end-of-life care provided to Lester, discusses the pursuit of accountability by the patient's survivors of the involved facilities and physicians, and offers commentary.

Factual Overview of Care Provided in Acute Care Hospital and Nursing Home

Acute Care Hospital

Lester was a patient of M. D. Medical Center (MD), an acute care hospital in northern California, between January 18, 2001 and January 23, 2001. Dr V. was Lester's attending physician at MD. Dr. V. prescribed pain medication

From *Pain Medicine*, June 2004, pp. 214–217, 218–221. Copyright © 2004 by American Academy of Pain Medicine. Reprinted by permission of Wiley-Blackwell via Rightslink.

that could only be given "as needed," that is, when it came to the provider's attention that Lester was already in pain. The nursing staff at MD did not monitor, assess, or respond to Lester's pain. On January 23, 2001, Lester was discharged from MD to a nursing home, BCC. Dr. V. prescribed no pain medication on discharge for Lester. Lester suffered severe pain during and following his transfer to BCC.

Nursing Home

Lester was a resident at BCC from January 23, 2001 until his death on February 12, 2001. When Lester was transferred to BCC from MD, his care was transferred to BCC's attending physician, Dr. W. Although Lester had been receiving pain medication while in the hospital, pain medication was not ordered for him on admission to BCC, or for the next 3 days. Dr. W. did not visit or examine Lester for 17 days. Lester's family members were by his bedside daily and frequently informed the staff that Lester was in unrelieved pain. At times, Lester cried out and asked his daughter to help him die because the pain was so terrible.

In response to the family's requests for pain relief, Dr. W. eventually ordered acetaminophen/hydrocodone to be provided every 4 hours as needed. Lester continued to suffer. When Ginger, the patient's daughter, called Dr. W. regarding the need for stronger pain medicine he refused to talk with her. Dr. W. eventually ordered a fentanyl patch; however, during the time the transdermal medication was reaching an effective level, Lester continued to suffer. The nursing staff did not advocate for more pain medication for Lester, nor did nurses insist that Dr. W. visit him. Several days later, the same daughter urged Dr. W. to order morphine. He ordered morphine in liquid form to be given every 6 hours. He also ordered that controlled-release morphine be given every 4 hours as needed. At no time did Dr. W. call for a consult with a pain or palliative care specialist.

Lester frequently cried out in pain, moaned, and grimaced. Every order for pain medication was done in response to family demands. The patients daughter, Ginger, finally called Dr. Messer, Mr. Tomlinson's oncologist, who intervened and ordered stronger pain medication. Lester died 4 days after Dr. W's first visit.

Pursuit of Accountability: Complaints Filed with Medical Board of California, the Center for Medicaid/Medicare Services, the California Department of Health Services, and Tort Suit

Ginger Tomlinson had heard of the case *Bergman v. Eden Medical Center*, a case involving an elderly cancer patient who did not receive adequate pain management, that had recently been tried to a jury in Alameda County, California. The jury in that case found that the physician had been reckless, entered a finding of elder abuse, and returned a verdict of $1.5 million for the patient's pain and suffering. After her father's death, Ginger contacted the patient advocacy group that had assisted the Bergman family, the Compassion in Dying Federation (CIDF), to explore what could be done to ensure that no other patient or family suffered needlessly.

The CIDF's Director of Clinical Case Management, an experienced hospice nurse, interviewed Ginger and reviewed Lester's medical records from MD and BCC. The Case Manager concluded that there had been serious failings in the pain management provided to Lester. The CIDF's Director of Legal Affairs recommended that complaints be filed with the Medical Board of California (MBC) regarding Dr. W. and with the Center for Medicaid/Medicare Services (CMS, formerly HCFA) as well as the state counterpart agency, the California Department of Health Services (DHS), regarding BCC. The complaints to these agencies were submitted accompanied by a written expert opinion obtained by CIDF from an experienced palliative care physician.

In addition, the CIDF's Director of Legal Affairs recommended that a tort suit be filed against Dr. V., MD, Dr. W., and BCC in California state court, alleging that the failure to treat Lester's terminal cancer pain adequately constituted elder abuse. A complaint was filed in Contra Costa County on January 15, 2002. It is important to note that, in California, pain and suffering damages do not survive the death of the patient under the state's medical negligence laws, thus there would be no damages recoverable for Mr. Tomlinson's pain and suffering under a medical negligence claim in California. The plaintiffs' counsel thus opted to litigate the claim under the elder abuse statute, which permits survival of an elder's pain and suffering claim. This strategy, however, presented the additional significant burden of needing to establish that the defendants' conduct in failing to treat the patient's pain constituted recklessness, rather than simply negligence. A greater degree of departure from standard of care must be shown to prevail in a claim that a defendant physician was reckless than would be required to prevail in a claim of negligence. Plaintiffs establish that defendants have been reckless, rather than simply negligent, by showing that they were practicing in an environment rich with information about the defendants' duties and responsibilities to treat pain aggressively and attentively. In states where a patient's pain and suffering prior to death due to medical negligence survives and accrues to the estate, a claim for failure to treat pain adequately could be more easily litigated as a medical negligence claim.

Resolution of the MBC Complaint

In response to the complaint submitted to the MBC regarding Dr. W., . . . a decision adopting a Stipulation for Public Reprimand was entered in this matter, specifying that Dr. W. was to receive a Public Reprimand, must undergo an assessment of knowledge and skills, must complete a minimum of 40 hours of CME in the area of deficiency, and must complete a physician/patient communication course.

Resolution of the CMS/DHS Complaint

The California DHS issued a Class A Notice of Deficiency to BCC, finding numerous violations of code provisions pertaining to pain and symptom management and ordered extensive corrective action.

Resolution of the Tort Suit

After extensive discovery and multiple motions, the tort case . . . [s]ettlement was reached with all four defendants prior to the start of the trial. Settlement with the hospital physician, Dr. V., was reached in December, 2002. The terms of that settlement are confidential.

Soon after the settlement with the hospital physician was reached, settlement was reached with MD, which acknowledged that it had implemented pain and palliative care training as a result of the suit. The financial aspect of the settlement is confidential. Dr. W., the nursing home physician, settled by agreeing to take 16 hours of CME in pain/palliative care in 2003. . . . Media coverage of the Tomlinson case was strongly sympathetic to the plaintiffs.

Commentary

Acute Care Hospital Care and Discharge

Neither Dr. V. nor the nurses at MD performed consistent, appropriate, and necessary assessments of Lester's pain. Nor did they initiate a pain management program that would relieve his pain. Dr. V.'s order for pain medication was written "as needed," meaning that Lester Tomlinson had to descend into pain and then ask for relief every time he needed pain medication. This *virtually guaranteed* that Lester would suffer significant pain while hospitalized. There is consensus throughout the medical community that pain medication for terminal cancer patients should be provided around the clock, with additional medication available to manage breakthrough pain. With regard to Lester's discharge, Dr. V. knew of the plan to discharge Lester and had a duty to prescribe appropriate discharge medication, including pain medication. He failed to fulfill this duty. This caused a period of unnecessary suffering, a problem compounded following admission to BCC, when the physician and staff that assumed his care at that facility failed to promptly provide pain medication.

Care at BCC

The failure to provide any pain medication for 3 days following admission is inexcusable in this case. An immediate pain assessment should have been done upon admission. A pain management plan should have been immediately put into place to get the patient's pain controlled. An appropriate pain management plan for a terminally ill cancer patient should include around-the-clock administration of opioid analgesics in doses sufficient to achieve good pain relief. Determination of an adequate dose should be made based upon careful assessments, with the dosage titrated upward until relief is attained. Additional medication should have been made available for breakthrough pain. Regular assessments of pain should have been initiated to ensure that the patient's pain was kept under control. Management of the pain of a terminal cancer patient is addressed in many authoritative clinical practice guidelines; reference to any one of these would have informed the providers regarding appropriate care for this patient.

Dr. W.'s pain medication orders reflect that he did not know which medications would be appropriate to treat Lester. This is revealed both by his order for liquid morphine to be given every 6 hours (instead of every hour as would be usual) and his order for controlled-release morphine to be given every 4 hours as needed (a long-acting medication typically given every 12 hours). Dr. W. should have called a pain consult with a pain or palliative care specialist.

There can be little doubt that with proper pain care Lester Tomlinson would not have suffered so horribly and that his final days could have been spent in comfort, surrounded by his family, saying goodbye in peace and dignity. He was robbed of this opportunity because he was left in such terrible pain that he could think of nothing else. What happened to Lester Tomlinson should not have happened. The health care providers involved in caring for him as he approached death were either ignorant of appropriate, modern pain medications and principles of pain treatment or callously indifferent to Lester's terrible suffering.

At the time that Lester Tomlinson was dying, all California physicians and medical facilities had ample notice of their obligations, duties, and responsibilities to treat pain attentively and aggressively, and should have been fully aware that terminally ill patients experiencing pain have the right to receive pain medication to relieve that pain. Lester's caregivers were either ignorant of all this information regarding the patient's right and the provider's corresponding duties or were aware of the patient's right and their corresponding duties but chose to ignore them.

Resolution of the MBC Action

The filing of charges against Dr. W. by the MBC and the ultimate entry of a Stipulation for Public Reprimand, which compels the physician to devote significant time to education in pain management, palliative care, and communication, reflect a significant change in how the MBC perceives and handles complaints involving the failure to adequately treat pain. The MBC is now accepting its responsibility to correct physicians who fail to employ modern practices and principles of pain management. This MBC's willingness to take action in an undertreated pain case will hopefully serve as an example to other medical boards considering such complaints.

Issuance of the California DHS Citation

The issuance of a Notice of Deficiency by the California DHS reflects a willingness by that agency, and the federal counterpart agency, CMS, to sanction facilities that fail to provide adequate pain management. This is a powerful corrective tool.

Tort Settlements

The settlement by all four defendants of the tort suit prior to the start of a trial reflects awareness in the defense bar, and among health care providers, that a case involving failure to adequately treat the pain of a dying patient carries great risk and exposure for defendants. This is so even when the state where the suit is filed requires that a plaintiff show reckless, as opposed to merely negligent, conduct. This case, like the *Bergman v. Eden Medical Center* case before it, vividly illustrates that cases of inadequate pain treatment can result in significant exposure to tort claims, with significant financial implications. This is appropriate because knowledge of how to treat pain is available. The problem is that, without outside motivation, physicians fail to acquire and apply the available knowledge. Physicians must be motivated to acquire and apply this available knowledge.

Commentary: David B. Brushwood, RPh, JD

The system "sets up" doctors to fail in their provision of adequate pain relief to their patients. Holding doctors liable for their failures, based on elder abuse or medical negligence, is unfair and ineffective. Threatening doctors with legal liability will not improve the quality of pain management in America.

The system works this way:

- Doctors are taught virtually nothing about pain management in medical school. This was absolutely true in the past and is a qualified truth for the present. Despite considerable brave talk and several noteworthy exceptions, the future of comprehensive pain management education appears grim unless a significant commitment to change is made.
- Residency training adds little knowledge or skill to a doctor's pain management resumé. The standard advice is to "start low" (so low there is little or no analgesia) and "go slow" (so slow there never will be analgesia).
- Most pain management CME is unproductive. It is mostly about "telling," a bit about "showing," but rarely is there any "doing." Anyone who can sit still for a few hours and fog a mirror at the end receives credit for successful completion.
- New rules from various agencies arrogantly mandate greater attention to pain management, but the agencies do no advocacy with insurance companies that refuse payment for adequate pain management, and they do not address staffing shortages that often make it impossible to do pain management well.
- Many patients (and their families) fear "narcotics," because they have been told that only weak-willed people use them and that there is an inevitable free-fall down the slippery slope from the issuance of one hydrocodone/acetaminophen prescription to hopeless drug abuse and addiction.
- Regulators adopt guidelines that they hope will be a "safe harbor" for legitimate pain medicine, shielded from irrational regulatory oversight, but these guidelines have the opposite effect. They are useless in

clinical practice, but priceless as a list of "gotchas" when regulators target heavy opioid prescribers.

- Law enforcement personnel who detect diversion problems in a doctor's practice rarely consult early on. Instead they conduct discreet surveillance, waiting for a small problem to become a large one. Then they swoop in with swat teams and attendant media coverage. They overcharge doctors with crimes that were not committed, and they dismiss the charges years later with no apology.
- So-called "expert witnesses" gladly accept hundreds of dollars per hour to second-guess their colleagues' clinical judgments, helping the police build an irrelevant records case against other doctors, by finding fault with the drugs their colleagues prescribed, the doses they used, and the frequency of their prescribing.

Within such a system, it is no wonder that some doctors adopt covert or overt policies against the use of opioids for pain. It is tragic and shameful for this to happen, but it is understandable. The doctors have been set up to fail by the flawed system.

Threatening doctors with legal liability for underprescribing pain medications will not fix the underlying systematic problems. But the simplicity of threatening legal liability has tremendous appeal—just like threatening to spank a child who brings home an unsatisfactory report card. . . .

The threat of liability for undertreating pain will not produce a rational, consistent, caring response from doctors. There are too many other variables affecting the quality of pain management. In fact, the inconsistency of tort liability will make things worse. Because tort standards are developed on a case-by-case basis through polarized advocacy, rather than negotiated deliberation, doctors will be forced to guess what the tort standard might become and then adopt practices that they hope will hit this moving target. The purpose of tort liability is to compensate victims, not establish comprehensive public health policy.

No good will come to the pain management movement from expansions in liability for undertreating pain. The plaintiffs' lawyers can't solve this problem. . . . We must all work harder to solve this terrible problem.

What must we do?

- Develop interdisciplinary, comprehensive pain management education. Students in medicine, nursing, pharmacy, and dentistry must learn together their mutual responsibilities for pain management and steps to take in diversion prevention. Every case study used in basic education should incorporate a relevant pain management component.
- Implement mini-residencies for law enforcement personnel to teach them that pain management is not about drugs, it is about people who suffer and who seek caring, respectful medical treatment so they can simply go about their activities of daily living.
- Require skills demonstration as a condition of CME participation. All doctors should be able to assess pain, select an appropriate treatment—pharmaceutical or nonpharmaceutical—titrate to effect without adverse

effects, convert from one drug to another, manage adverse effects, and prevent drug diversion.

- Help the media understand that there is an epidemic of untreated and undertreated pain. Show them how to teach the public that pain can be managed without a significant risk of addiction. The "hillbilly heroin" story is old news.
- Cooperate with law enforcement in an "early consult" when a doctor is suspected of being duped into inappropriate prescribing. This should be a fair but firm colleague-to-colleague explanation of the dangers of drug diversion, the methods to prevent it while continuing to meet the needs of patients, and the consequences of failing to be vigilant.
- Make a clear distinction between criminal misconduct outside the practice of medicine and malpractice within medicine. Stop testifying that colleagues have occasionally failed to use the best professional judgment and therefore should be found guilty of a crime. Nobody is consistently at their best and it is not a crime to be adequate but less than the best.

Everyone who practices any health care profession is responsible for meeting the standard of care. When there is a bad outcome from care, health care professionals should be held accountable. If the accounting is inadequate, then they should be held liable. Corrective justice requires that one who is at fault for harm caused to another provides compensation to the harmed party. Those who provide medical services and products to patients in pain should be held to the relevant standard. But a finding of individual liability does nothing to promote comprehensive improvements in the quality of care. It is not even a step in the right direction. This is a difficult problem that defies simple solutions. The small number of settlements and judgments of liability for undertreating pain over the past several years are outliers. They do not constitute even the hint of a legal trend, and they should not be used to coerce desired behaviour from those responsible for providing services and products to patients.

For decades, doctors, nurses, and pharmacists have been frightened into doing the wrong thing. They cannot not be frightened into doing the right thing. If you put a frightened doctor, nurse, or pharmacist into a dysfunctional system, the system will win every time. What is needed is systemic change, not frightening threats of legal liability.

David B. Brushwood, RPh, JD
Professor of Pharmacy Health Care Administration
The University of Florida College of Pharmacy

Commentary: Sandra H. Johnson JD, LLM

Prior to the Bergman and Tomlinson cases described in this note, research on legal risk in pain management consistently and uniformly concluded that legal risk for neglect of pain was nearly nonexistent. Medical disciplinary actions were brought against physicians who treated patients for pain with controlled substances, but none had been brought against physicians who allowed patients to suffer through neglect or ignorance. Physicians had been sued by patients for malpractice for their use of controlled substances in treating pain, with patients claiming that they had become addicted or had injured someone while under the influence of drugs, but only one known case had been successfully brought against a health care provider for negligence in failing to treat pain. Federal activity, primarily through the U.S. Drug Enforcement Administration (DEA), because of the scope of their jurisdiction and the authorizing statute, has focused on physicians prescribing controlled substances, but not on physicians who fail to do so.

Advocates have made significant efforts to assure that medical disciplinary actions against physicians for their prescribing practices now use appropriate standards to evaluate those practices. There has been some success in changing medical board policies and practices through the development and adoption of guidelines for the boards. A few medical boards, including California's, have taken action to discipline doctors who have breached medical standards in caring for their patients in pain, although such actions are still rare for several reasons. Legislatures, with California in the lead, have enacted statutes to protect physicians from inappropriate disciplinary action; to encourage effective treatment of patients in pain; and to ensure that physicians receive appropriate training. The DEA and the leading associations involved in the treatment of patients in pain joined forces to issue a statement recognizing that effective pain management was a critical public issue.

These approaches have all focused on righting the course of regulatory efforts focused on drug control to make sure that they recognize the adverse impact such efforts can have on the quality of medicine. They have been successful on many fronts, but not entirely so. Cases of inappropriate arrests, prosecutions, and disciplinary sanctions still seem to occur, although there is evidence of improvement.

Another approach to addressing the imbalance of legal sanctions that may encourage physicians to neglect patients in pain is to enforce medical standards for pain treatment through private litigation against individual doctors by patients who have been injured by substandard care. The Bergman and Tomlinson cases represent this strategy. Such litigation does something that no other legal remedy can do: it provides compensation to victims. It also clearly establishes a legally enforceable duty to the individual patient to treat pain in accordance with professional medical standards. As the author of the case commentary notes, litigation can also attract media attention to the problem of neglect in a way that policy statements can never do.

Advocates for patients in pain can use such litigation to right the wrong done to the individual and to send a message that pain treatment is legally required. One response to the threat of litigation, however, is that it doesn't simply level the playing field by equalizing risks so that doctors can practice good medicine. Rather, it creates an environment in which the doctor believes that "you're damned if you do and damned if you don't." Unfortunately, malpractice and negligence can be unpredictable, with many, many injured patients failing to file suits against seriously negligent physicians and some suits filed without a firm foundation in medical standards.

Neither Bergman nor Tomlinson are cases of "damned if you do, and damned if you don't." These cases fell squarely within the most well-established legal and policy "safe harbors" for the most aggressive pain treatment. Aggressive treatment of patients in severe pain from cancer is not controversial legally or as a matter of policy. The use of controlled substances for the relief of cancer pain has long been established, although many of us still have memories of older family members who screamed in pain from cancer and who had to wait for the next dose out of fear that these patients would become addicted. Medical boards have recognized for years now that aggressive treatment for cancer pain does not raise issues for disciplinary action. Most especially for cancer patients in the final stages of a terminal form of the disease, there is absolutely no concern over addiction or diversion, for example. In addition, improving palliative care for the dying, including relief of pain, has been a national policy priority for nearly a decade. There is broad and deep agreement that pain management is a core medical and ethical duty for the dying patient.

On the legal side of the ledger, these two lawsuits faced significant obstacles as well. The legal basis for these cases and for others like them lies in state law, and, by definition, state law is particular to each state with wide variations between one state and another. Nevertheless, some general observations are possible. Damages for "pain and suffering," which the legal system terms "noneconomic damages," are not favored in law. The commentary on the Tomlinson case notes specifically that claims for pain and suffering are extinguished upon the death of the patient in California, as is true in other states as well. Furthermore, many states cap or limit the amounts that can be awarded for noneconomic damages in the range of $250,000 or so. The effect of this limitation in itself is to make litigation in which noneconomic damages are key, such as these cases, unattractive, if not impossible, to bring because the recovery is not likely to cover the costs of the lawsuits. . . .

Beyond the question of damages, cases outside the paradigmatic Bergman and Tomlinson cases would be much more difficult to prove. Neither Mr. Bergman nor Mr. Tomlinson appeared to have required a highly sophisticated level of pain management, and so the suits did not face the problems of establishing medical standards and the cause of the patient's pain. . . . The location of the treatment is also relevant. In each of these cases, the patient was resident in a health care facility, which placed him under the full control of the institution. There can be no argument about patient noncompliance. Nor did the patient or family have full freedom to involve other physicians. From the description provided in the commentary, it would appear that deficient administration or management by the facility could be argued, making the case much easier to prove than one that relied solely on deficiencies in medical judgment.

The physicians and health care facilities in the Bergman and Tomlinson cases had no realistic fear that they would be damned if they treated these patients, even very aggressively, for pain. Nor should these cases be taken as heralds of an avalanche of cases to come. They were extreme situations and engendered an extreme response from the jury in the Bergman case and from the media in the Tomlinson case. That is not to say that physicians and health care facilities should ignore their duties to make every effort to treat pain effectively, nor should they feel immune from accountability through private litigation or public regulation for neglect.

Rodney Syme

 **NO**

Necessity to Palliate Pain and Suffering as a Defence to Medical Homicide

The courts, in applying the criminal law in relation to homicide, rely heavily on determining the cause of death, and the existence of intention to cause death. The inadequacy of such processes in relation to prosecutions for medical actions at the end of life is discussed. The principle that there is no "special defence" for doctors is refuted. The legal and ethical obligation of doctors to respect their patients' autonomy, and maximally relieve their pain and suffering, creates a special and exposed position for doctors treating patients near life's end. The result is a quasi-legal practice in which doctors achieve such relief, even though it may commonly hasten death. This medical and legal position has its basis in hypocrisy and obfuscation. The astonishing rarity of prosecution of doctors indicates a "benign conspiracy" on the part of prosecutorial authorities in this regard. It is argued that a transparent and objectively sustainable defence to medical homicide would be a defence based on the necessity to palliate pain and suffering, combined with documented consent by the sufferer to the provision of such palliation.

Introduction

The principles of the criminal law relating to homicide have evolved over time, and are today well established. The pillars are the actus reus (that the defendant caused the death) and the mens rea (that the defendant intended to cause death). Associated principles are that motive is of no consequence, that the time of the intended death in relation to the expected time of natural death is irrelevant, that consent of the deceased is of no consequence, and that the law is to be applied without partiality.

Medical practice has for centuries involved assistance for the dying, of relieving suffering at the end of life. Modern medical practice, after the Second World War, has evolved to include the withholding and withdrawal of life-preserving treatment. It has also resulted in organised palliative care of the dying person. In addition, there have been significant changes in medical

From *Journal of Law and Medicine*, December 2009, pp. 439–451. Copyright © 2009 by Thomson Reuters Professional Ltd, Australia. Reprinted by permission.

ethics and in community expectations. The actions of doctors are now very closely associated with the causation and timing of death. . . .

If . . . the doctor hastens death, with or without consent, to relieve a patient's agony, the doctor may face the full rigour of the law.

Courts have repeatedly stated that there is no special defence for doctors threatened with prosecution for hastening the death, or assisting in the suicide, of a suffering patient. Nevertheless, there has evolved an ambiguous and inconsistent set of arguments, based on intention and causation, that in practice does provide a poorly articulated and unacknowledged defence for doctors.

There is, however, a single argument which covers end-of-life situations with transparency and consistency, and acknowledges medical ethics and community expectations. It is a defence based on the necessity to palliate pain and suffering.

Relevant Principles of the Criminal Law

The law relating to murder will apply if a person intends to cause death or serious bodily harm, and death occurs as a result of that person's act, provided there is no legal defence (such as self-defence). This law is very likely to apply if there is foresight of the probability that death or serious bodily harm will occur as a result of an act. The criminal law does not distinguish between the intended result of a defendant's action (the primary effect) and the unintended but inevitable consequence of that action (the secondary effect).

With regard to causation in a medical context, it matters not whether a person is dying. Any action which interrupts life to cause or hasten death is regarded as the actus reus for legal purposes. . . .

It is the proximate action that is the responsible one, not any precedent causes.

Equally, it is of no consequence how little the time between the expected natural death and the contrived death. If a daughter smothers her mother who is imminently dying of cancer, the daughter will be liable to prosecution for murder. As Ognall J said in the trial of Dr Nigel Cox for attempted murder, "it matters not by how much or by how little her death was hastened or intended to be hastened," or as Devlin LJ observed in *R v Adams (Bodkin)* [1957] Crim LR 365 at 365, "It does not matter for this purpose that her death was inevitable and her days were numbered." Thus no doctor can lawfully, in theory, take any steps deliberately to hasten a patient's death by however short a period of time.

The law repeatedly states that it recognises no special defence for doctors. In *R v Adams* Devlin LJ stated (at 375):

> We have heard a good deal of discussion . . . about the circumstances in which doctors might be justified in administering drugs which would shorten life. Cases of severe pain have been suggested and generally approved by the witnesses . . . and also there have been suggested cases of helpless misery. It is my duty to tell you that the law knows no special defence of this character.

It is considered proper that all persons should be treated equally under the law.

Thus, the principles of criminal law, strictly applied, do not provide any special defence for doctors, do not allow them to hasten death by intention or foresight, by any margin of time. Yet most educated people know that things do not work that way. In *Compassion in Dying v Washington* 79 F 3d 790 (1996) Reinhardt J stated (at 823):

> As part of the tradition of administering comfort care, doctors have been supplying the causal agent of patients' deaths for decades. Physicians routinely and openly provide medication to terminally ill patients with the knowledge that it will have a double effect—reduce the patient's pain and hasten his death.

. . . Humanity and individuality, sidelined in law, are key considerations in ethics. The law often represents the lowest level of acceptable behaviour, and clinicians should strive for higher standards than the bare minimum. . . .

The Reality of Medical Practice and Its Conflict with the Law

Dr John Gregory, in his 18th century lectures on the duties of a physician, stated: "It is as much the business of a physician to alleviate pain, and to smooth the avenues to death when unavoidable, as to cure diseases." . . .

The reality of modern medical practice for the dying can be summed up in six "givens" or unarguable facts:

- dying may be associated with intolerable suffering, and there may be a crescendo of suffering as death approaches;
- the doctor's duty is to relieve suffering;
- some suffering will only be relieved by death;
- the doctor's duty is to respect patient autonomy;
- some patients rationally and persistently request assistance to die; and
- palliative care cannot relieve all the pain and suffering of dying patients.

It is an inescapable fact that a majority of deaths in modem medicine are affected to a greater or lesser degree by the actions or inactions of the doctor. This may lead to either the hastening of death or prolonging of dying.

There are two particular situations where these "givens" come into play. First, these situations occur in cases of "interrupted dying," when death has been prevented by invasive medical procedures such as artificial ventilation and artificial nutrition and hydration; and secondly, in cases where there is intolerable and unrelievable suffering of terminally and hopelessly ill patients.

The first situation occurs, e.g., when a patient who is fully competent to make rational decisions requests that life-prolonging treatment be withheld or cease. In that situation, the doctor is obliged to respect the patient's autonomy. Such a withdrawal of life-sustaining treatment may foreseeably result in death, and in fact such action can become the immediate cause of death. Indeed, a competent person may refuse treatment with that clear intention. Not only that, but the doctor may also be obliged to provide medication such as opiates and sedatives in order to palliate the suffering associated with a difficulty in breathing, or dehydration associated with withdrawal of food and fluids. These palliating drugs may even further hasten death.

For an incompetent person, a legally appointed agent or surrogate decision-maker may make the same decision. Alternatively, an argument of medical futility may be used by the doctor to justify withdrawal of treatment which has not met its intended aim (to restore that person to health). . . .

The necessity for the doctor to comply with refusal or withholding of treatment must be recognised, and the doctor protected in such action, since the alternative could have dire consequences. Lack of protection could result in doctors refraining from commencing potential but unpredictable life-sustaining treatments in the first place, or refraining from withdrawing futile treatments, or not providing adequate palliation to dying patients.

Because of the medical profession's adherence to the "givens," those dire outcomes have not commonly occurred, despite the obvious conflict between the doctor's actions and the law. Nevertheless, there have been occasions where the lack of clarity in the law has resulted in continuation of arguably futile treatment for long periods, and of minimal and inadequate palliation.

In the second situation, the sixth "given" (that palliative care cannot relieve all pain and suffering) becomes critically important. Support of institutional palliative care has become the formal response of government regarding end-of-life suffering, but Palliative Care Australia acknowledges that it cannot relieve all the pain and suffering of dying persons. Yet the second "given" indicates that the doctor has an obligation to do so, and the third "given" indicates that such relief may only occur through death. This is the doctor's perennial dilemma . . . of risking or actually hastening death in order to relieve suffering, in clear conflict with the criminal law. Often hastening death has been achieved rather crudely by increasing doses of opioids. Over the last 20 years this has increasingly occurred by the more sophisticated continuous deep sedation. In some jurisdictions, recognition of the fourth "given" (the doctor's duty to respect autonomy) and fifth "given" (some patients rationally and persistently request assistance to die) has led to legislation for physician-assisted dying by the most appropriate agreed medical means, either by way of a lethal injection (The Netherlands), or the prescription of lethal oral medication (Oregon). It is also clear that some doctors have prescribed oral medications rather than injectables in order to give control over death to their patients.

Thus, it is not sufficient to consider this problem from the sole point of view of injectable opioids. Oral medication is increasingly involved, and coma-inducing sedatives are playing an equally significant and increasing role, with or without opioids, in end-of-life palliation.

Deep Continuous Sedation

Deep continuous sedation was developed as a response to the moral imperative to provide maximum palliation. Initially described as "pharmacological oblivion," subsequently as "terminal sedation" or "palliative sedation," this practice was first revealed in palliative care literature in the late 1980s. Terminal sedation involved using sedatives, often with opioids, to maintain a patient with intolerable suffering in a continuing coma whereby their suffering was not apparent. As Hunt said, "permanent unconsciousness is, in the patient's view similar to being dead." As pharmacological oblivion was usually accompanied by the withdrawal of food and fluids, patients never survived the coma.

The cause of such an inevitable death could be contentious, a competition between the terminal illness and the lethal effects of cardio-respiratory depression, dehydration and secondary pulmonary complications due to the treatment. Forensic examination could rarely distinguish the exact cause of death.

Terminal sedation treatment became readily and widely accepted in palliative care, because, as Burke et al. said, "it provided a readily available means of controlling symptoms and overcoming patient distress where no feasible alternative existed previously." It was initially used for terminal anguish, confusion and delirium, but this steadily evolved to encompass unrelievable pain, breathlessness, severe nausea and vomiting, cachexia and exhaustion, and psychological and existential distress—in other words, intolerable or refractory suffering, all possible indications for a request for medically assisted dying.

Some doctors have tried to argue that terminal sedation, properly used, does not hasten death. The use of coma-inducing sedatives and opioids is normally strongly contraindicated in severe breathlessness, as it is certain to depress respiration and seriously threaten life. Many palliative care specialists attest to the risk, and the actuality, of hastening or causing death by this means, in breathlessness and other circumstances. The justification of such action in moral terms is the doctrine of double effect. Clearly, there would be no need to refer to this doctrine if terminal sedation did not hasten death.

While some doctors using deep continuous sedation might have been comfortable that they had no intention to hasten death, the ambiguity of this situation did not escape others. Palliative care specialists, Billings and Block, likened it to "slow euthanasia," defined as "the clinical practice of treating a terminally ill patient in a fashion that will assuredly lead to a comfortable death, but not too quickly." One could argue that the singular distinction between deep continuous sedation and euthanasia was the time taken to die. Emanuel was well aware of the death-hastening effect of terminal sedation, and therefore advocated "anaesthetic coma"—continuous sedation with full hydration and monitoring to prevent either anaesthetic-induced death or unwanted return to consciousness. She confirmed, apparently without concern, that patients "may continue for days in this state before dying," as if the time taken for them to die was of no consequence. Whatever the reality regarding intention, there is no doubt that the possibility or probability of hastening death can be foreseen on many occasions when it is used, creating potential conflict with the criminal law. This clear potential conflict has a significant influence in diminishing the appropriate deployment of deep continuous sedation.

Loewy wrote of terminal sedation:

[C]learly the intent here is more than just the clear goal of relieving pain and suffering. Because the goal of relieving pain and suffering adequately can be attained only by obtunding the patient until death ensues, the patient's death becomes the end point and, therefore, one of the intended goals. These goals do not differ from those of physician assisted suicide, or, for that matter, voluntary euthanasia. . . . Terminal sedation, we would claim, differs from some form of voluntary euthanasia mainly in that it has not been and is unlikely to be legally challenged.

Of course, the reason doctors have not been challenged over terminal sedation is that they can argue their intention to relieve suffering with confidence, particularly if the sedation is induced slowly. Indeed, the patient may become the unwitting agent of the doctor's defence in the sense that the slower the death is hastened the more protection there is for the doctor.

Billings and Block were not critical of the practice itself, but only of the hypocrisy which accompanied it, as was Loewy:

Although such a practice may shorten life, I do not in any way oppose maximal sedation and analgesia for patients at this stage of life. Indeed I can see no rational or humane argument against such a practice. But I do oppose the idea that we should engage in this practice for our own or the court's sake. Ethics, if it must be anything, must be honest.

Loewy seriously challenges the intention behind terminal sedation. Jessica Corner, Director of the Centre for Cancer and Palliative Care Studies at Royal Marsden Hospital in the United Kingdom, also does so, stating:

[T]he easing of death, as an intentional double effect, is commonplace in palliative care and in general practice. . . . Palliative care needs to take the lead by making clear the strategies it employs for managing difficult situations at the end of life, and, when double effect is used with a view that death is a likely and welcome secondary consequence, to be open about this.

This acknowledgment that death can be a "welcome secondary consequence" places the doctrine of double effect in perspective because it is premised on the notion that hastening death is morally bad. Hunt also criticises this "morally bad" notion, and Randall and Downie see no place for the "double effect" argument in palliative care. Asch wrote: "In practice, however, terminal sedation is often used not only with the intent of providing comfort, but also with the unstated—and 'winked at'—intent to hasten death." At an official rather than personal level, the statement of the Council of Judicial and Ethical Affairs of the American Medical Association is worth noting:

The ethical distinction between providing palliative care that may have fatal side effects and providing euthanasia is subtle because in both cases the action that caused death is performed with the purpose of relieving suffering.

Why has continuous deep sedation become increasingly common over time? Dutch research indicates that it occurred in 10% of deaths in The Netherlands in 2001, and has been used by half of all Dutch physicians. One obvious conclusion is that doctors find its use necessary in order to adequately relieve the pain and suffering of dying patients. To state that another way, much of the pain and suffering of dying patients will only be relieved by their death, or by induced medical coma until their death (the third "given"). In some circumstances, there is a legitimate palliative need to induce coma which leads to a hastened death. It is worth noting that once a terminally ill patient with intolerable suffering is sedated to unconsciousness, the dosage of sedating drugs is maintained until death, even though, as clinical deterioration occurs and urine output falls, the blood levels of toxic and lethal drugs will rapidly rise. If there were a genuine intention not to hasten death, the level of sedative and other drugs would be titrated down to minimal levels. This is not done because to do so would simply run the risk of prolonging a bizarre medical state, deliberately induced lethal coma. When such a process is prolonged, it causes significant distress to most doctors, nurses and families. It can also be stated that if there was a genuine intention not to hasten death, hydration would be provided. Quite properly it is not, because to do so would prolong the dying in a drug-induced coma. Prolonged sedation is a grinding, thoroughly distasteful and demoralising process. The time taken for patients to die in a deliberate medically induced coma is important to all who are involved. It is hard to imagine that many doctors who employ terminal sedation don't wish to see it come to an end, even if this means deliberately hastening death. The law has little comprehension of medicine and of decent human nature if it does not comprehend this fact.

The Application of the Law in Practice

How, then, does the legal process deal with this fundamental conflict between law and medicine? Since the law says there is no special defence for doctors, one would expect many prosecutions. However, in Australia in the last 50 years there have been only two. . . . Over the same period, there have been many prosecutions of laypersons for murder, attempted murder and assisted suicide in circumstances commonly described as "mercy killings."

What, then, is going on? Are doctors being deliberately protected and not prosecuted in circumstances where, if they were laypersons, they would be? Does there exist a covert "doctor's defence," or is there a "benign conspiracy" not to investigate or prosecute doctors who act compassionately? Certain United Kingdom judicial decisions throw some light on these questions.

The Problem with Causation

Perhaps Devlin LJ had this problem in mind when he directed the jury in the celebrated case of *R v Adams (Bodkin)* [1957] Crim LR 365. It is hard to imagine that the form of words that he used, or the implications flowing from them, were not carefully thought through. Dr Bodkin Adams had delivered large and potentially lethal doses of opioids to his 81-year-old patient who had suffered a severe stroke, not a notoriously painful condition. In addressing the jury, Devlin LJ made some very significant remarks. He indicated that the jury should take a "commonsense" approach to the question of causation, stating that "because a doctor had done something, death occurs at eleven o'clock instead of twelve o'clock, or even Monday instead of Tuesday, no people of common sense would say 'Oh, the doctor caused her death'." He understood that timing in relation to death is something well within the doctor's ambit to control. Yet he went on to say that the cause of death was the illness or injury that necessitated the doctor's act. While this assessment of causation is comforting to doctors, patients and their families, and, perhaps, to the judges themselves, it is illogical. If a layperson delivered the same injection and hastened death by hours or a day, they would certainly be seen to have caused the death. The use of causation cannot be selective if legal principles are to be applied impartially.

The soft nature of causation as a significant factor in end-of-life criminality was summed up by Reinhardt J in *Compassion in Dying v Washington* 79 F 3d 790 at 823 (1996):

> Contrary to the State's assertion, given current medical practices and current medical ethics, it is not possible to distinguish prohibited from permissible medical conduct on the basis of whether the medication provided by the doctor will cause the patient's death.

The same selective argument regarding causation has been used in relation to the withdrawal of treatment such as respirators, or artificial nutrition and hydration, as in the celebrated case of *Bland*. Of this argument Grubb says, "[A]s a matter of factual causation, of course the doctor's act caused the patient's death." Lord Mustill, also commenting on this argument, said it "seems to . . . require not manipulation of the law so much as its application in an entirely new and illogical way." Of course, from a moral and ethical point of view, the doctor is acting appropriately, and the act which causes death ("kills" is not an appropriate word) should be seen as justified by necessity, rather than confusing the issue by obfuscation and illogic. . . . On the other hand, it is certain that a layperson, or a nurse, who disconnected a ventilator without medical direction, or who ceased feeding a patient in their care via a stomach tube, would be prosecuted.

The Problem with Intention

In *R v Adams* (*Bodkin*) [1957] Crim LR 365 Devlin LJ went on to say (at 375):

> If the first purpose of medicine, the restoration of health, can no longer be achieved, there is still much for the doctor to do, and he is entitled to do all that is proper and necessary to relieve pain and suffering even if measures he takes may incidentally shorten life.

The principal critical focus of this direction has been on the implications regarding intention. However, in passing, two other aspects deserve notice:

first, that the person Devlin LJ describes need not be terminally ill; and secondly, that it was not pain alone that required relief but also suffering.

Devlin LJ's direction on intention further improved the doctor's position, removing "foresight" as a criterion for homicide in a medical sense, the only circumstance in law where this applies. Despite acknowledging that doctors had no special protection, he created not one but two protections—on intention as well as causation. Devlin LJ's statement that a doctor could hasten death with foresight provided his intention was to relieve suffering and not to hasten death, has been regarded by many legal, medical and ethical experts as an expression of the "doctrine of double effect." However, this doctrine is a moral doctrine and only two of its four principles are covered by Devlin LJ's statement. Be that as it may, there is again no doubt that it has been gratefully received by the medical and legal professions as a way out of a difficult situation. Effectively, Devlin LJ had created a legal justification for hastening death, namely the relief of pain and suffering. . . . Even though he indicated that doctors should "provide proper and necessary" pain relief, that direction was not given on the basis that the relief of pain justified an act that would otherwise be murder in law.

However, Skene contends that the conceptual basis of the doctrine is not entirely clear. She indicated it has been argued that the doctor commits no offence because there is no criminal intent. However, as Grubb points out, "The English criminal law . . . does not distinguish between the desired result of a defendants' action (the primary effect) and the undesired but inevitable consequence of his action (the secondary effect)." Devlin LJ had turned this principle on its head, making an exception on "foreseeing" solely for the medical profession. So there has developed a range of words that are applied to this situation such as primary or secondary effect, consequence or intention. The medical profession, not surprisingly, has grasped onto these distinctions. The Australian Medical Association has stated that "the AMA supports doctors whose primary intent is to relieve the suffering and distress of terminally ill patients, in accordance with the patients' wishes and interests, even though a foreseen secondary consequence is the hastening of death."

The Abuse of Intention: *R v Cox*

Another celebrated English case of medically accelerated death is *R v Cox* (1992). Dr Nigel Cox was a rheumatologist of "exemplary character" (Ognall J's words) who had treated Mrs Lillian Boyes for progressive, severe rheumatoid arthritis for over 13 years. She trusted him implicitly, and, suffering grievously with pain in the terminal stages of her illness, she refused all treatment, asking only that her pain and suffering be relieved. Massive doses of heroin did not relieve her distress. This was clearly a situation in which suffering would only be relieved by death (the third "given"). Cox indicated that it was his intention to relieve Mrs Boyes' suffering; but if her suffering could only be relieved by her death, was a parallel intention to cause death not also valid? No matter how much the court might like to think differently, relieving suffering and hastening death are sometimes inextricably linked. . . .

So a dedicated, compassionate doctor, doing his utmost to fulfil the trust of his patient and relieve her extreme pain and suffering, was convicted of a major offence, on the simple premise that he used the wrong drug, in order to preserve the holy grail of intention. . . . Cox should have been admonished for using the wrong drug, instructed in terminal sedation, but not charged with attempted murder.

But there were other twists. Cox was charged with attempted murder rather than murder because Mrs Boyes was cremated before an autopsy could be performed, denying certainty . . . that the potassium caused her death, since she was already very close to death. [A] large dose of potassium causes death extremely rapidly; to a doctor, this argument about causation is implausible, a comfortable legal fiction, which may have saved Cox being charged with murder, but ironically may have resulted in his conviction. If he had been charged with murder, there is a strong probability that the jury would not have agreed with such a verdict, since it carried a mandatory life sentence. As it happened, the judge imposed a sentence of one year's imprisonment, which was suspended. The General Medical Council merely reprimanded Cox (for an act that would normally result in being "struck off") and allowed him to continue to practise!

The presiding judge said, "deliberate conduct by a doctor aimed at bringing about the death of a patient required, *as a matter of principle*, to be marked by a term of imprisonment." On this principle, of supposed intent, a humane doctor was to be imprisoned. The judge meant to send a signal about medical behaviour. All it did was ensure that doctors did not use potassium chloride. . . .

The Lack of Successful Prosecutions: Why?

The 50 years since *Adams* have been notable for the remarkable lack of prosecutions of doctors for deliberate hastening of death. There have been none in Victoria, only two in Australia (Stephens, Hollo), and a handful in the United Kingdom (Adams, Cox, Arthurs, Moor). None have been successful except Cox, and in his case, simply because he used the wrong drug. Cox's prosecution occurred simply because a nurse with a contrary moral view made a complaint after the event, and the process could not be stopped.

It is remarkable because, during this time, there have been numerous published, refereed articles which indicate that many doctors not infrequently deliberately hasten the death of their patients. At the same time, many laypersons have been charged and convicted of murder, attempted murder, manslaughter and aiding or abetting suicide, although very few have been punished. This suggests two conclusions: first, that there is a special protection (defence) for doctors; and secondly, that the judiciary sees lay mercy killing as a regrettable but "benign crime," something to be prevented but forgiven.

Why does this situation prevail? Perhaps it is because the public expect their doctor to be free to assist them with a humane and dignified death, and do not complain when this happens. Respected public opinion polls around the Western world consistently find that 80% of citizens support law reform to allow this to happen. The prosecution of a doctor for such action inevitably would send a profoundly negative signal to doctors who actively palliate their patients—even more so would a successful prosecution. Abraham Lincoln famously stated that "no law is stronger than the public sentiment where it is to be enforced." Thus, the criminal law in relation to two of the most serious crimes—murder or aiding or abetting suicide—is not actively applied in relation to medical end-of-life practice, although the façade is maintained, with harmful consequences, that this is not so. These harmful consequences, of course, are that medical end-of-life practices are entirely arbitrary, and covert, not behaviour of which the rule of law would approve. One can argue that there is a benign, unstated "conspiracy" to allow the status quo to continue. The decidedly uncomfortable "conspirators" are the police, coroners, prosecutorial authorities and the "law," who are placed in this position by government which refuses to provide clarity and guidance for them. The "conspiracy" is "benign" only because it operates to protect doctors who need this protection in order to treat their patients with compassion, according to their needs and best interests, at the end of life.

The Inadequacy of Intention

The use of intention as a basis for criminality in medical matters is exceedingly contentious. The determination of intention at the end of life is complex. Miller states:

> [T]he intentions of clinicians, however, may be multiple and ambiguous, and the causal contributions of escalating dosages of morphine to the timing of terminally ill patients' deaths may be difficult to discern. Therefore there exists a grey zone between standard palliative care and active euthanasia. . . .

Further, Quill writes that "Multi-layered intentions are present in most, if not all, end-of-life decisions," and that "the subjective realm of intention . . . cannot be reliably measured, evaluated or verified." Dr Marcia Angell, editor of the *New England Journal of Medicine,* concurred, saying, "when the suffering of a dying patient is prolonged and intractable, a doctor who administers large doses of a controlled substance [opioids or barbiturates] may well have mixed intentions." Is a doctor's intention what he says it is, or is it what someone else thinks it is—it is clearly merely someone's opinion as to how another person is thinking. The clear distinction that the court might prefer is lacking. The use of double effect to justify a doctor's intention has been strongly criticised. . . .

It should be clear that the doctor's intention is a flawed measure for determining legal culpability. . . .

The Necessity to Palliate Suffering as a Transparent Defence

A few commentators on Devlin LJ's decision have correctly pointed out the more effective justification for his direction, and it is in his own words. He used the phrase "necessary to relieve pain and suffering"; if it is necessary to do something, then there is a necessity to do so. Williams regarded the defence of necessity as being a more straightforward argument for Devlin LJ's direction. The necessity to relieve pain and suffering encompasses the philosophy of palliation as a moral principle at the end of life (the second "given").

As Cherny et al. said, "there is an ethical imperative to offer care and to provide adequate relief of suffering" and there is "an overwhelming obligation to optimize comfort until death ensues." . . .

There is a need for a principle more concrete and transparent than intention, and it is the observable and assessable necessity for palliation, supported by the recorded request for that palliation. The fact that a person has a terminal or advanced incurable disease is provable, and the fact that they have intolerable and unrelievable suffering can be determined by detailed discussion. While the existence of unrelievable suffering can be verified medically, the presence of intolerable suffering is admittedly subjective. . . .

Other legal authorities have alluded to necessity as a defence to hastening or causing death. This article is not an argument for "necessity" as a defence to homicide in a general sense, but only in the limited medical sense. In that sense, it is linked to a necessity to achieve an appropriate medical end. . . .

A request for maximum palliation that might or would have the effect of hastening death can be recorded as consent to maximum palliation. For necessity to be a valid defence, it must not only be the doctor's, but also the patient's, view that it is necessary. Consent is an essential element to ensure that necessity is not merely the non-consensual view of the doctor. While consent is never a defence to murder, consent to palliation is a different matter. Informed consent is a central element in medical practice—it allows for the legal refusal of treatment, and it changes assault into legitimate surgery. . . . It is an important adjunct to the question of necessity to palliate suffering.

These medical states can be confirmed by a second opinion. If these two circumstances exist concurrently, there are clear grounds for palliation of the suffering. As argued, sometimes such palliation may necessitate hastening of death. If the request for such palliation is rational and persistent or enduring (again verifiable phenomena), then the doctor should be protected in providing that palliation. Rational patients must be trusted to act in their own best interests, and to have no intention to end their own life except in exceptional circumstances. Equally, the doctor must be trusted to provide such palliation in a secure and dignified way that is acceptable to the patient, and only to do so in extreme circumstances.

Conclusion

Intention and causation are the pillars upon which criminal charges relating to murder stand. It has been shown that these pillars are inadequate when applied to medical acts at the end of life. Legal authority states that there is no special defence for doctors, yet by manipulation of the law, and by illogical application of causation, an unacknowledged defence for doctors has been created. Prosecutions of doctors for hastening death in a foreseen manner rarely occur, despite the fact that such hastening commonly occurs. This "benign conspiracy" is well known, and damaging to the rule of law. . . .

The "benign conspiracy" exists because it is recognised that the medical profession operates in a dangerous and exposed position which does not apply to any other group in society. Society generally, and patients specifically, expect their doctors to be protected so that they can provide maximum relief of pain and suffering without fear of prosecution. Public policy covertly acknowledges this, but the conspiracy involved is harmful to many patients, and to the rule of law. . . .

Because of the special position of doctors in relation to their dying patients, there should be an open and acknowledged special defence for doctors in relation to hastening death. This special defence should be based on necessity—not necessity per se, but the necessity to palliate pain and suffering (or to borrow the words of the *Medical Treatment Act 1988* (Vic)—"dying patients should receive maximum relief of pain and suffering"). The presence of unrelievable pain and suffering is verifiable and recordable, and is a transparent guide. Further, the defence of necessity to palliate must be supported by consent to be given maximum relief.

"Surely openness and clarity are legal virtues that deserve realization." Currently, there is a pointless argument about words, such as intention, causation, double effect and foresight, about their meaning and use, which loses sight of the suffering patient. In the end, necessity to relieve suffering, combined with consent to such action, is a clear, verifiable basis for both legal and medical practice.

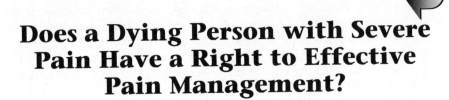

Does a Dying Person with Severe Pain Have a Right to Effective Pain Management?

Critical Thinking and Reflection

1. Do you think patients can demand pain medications at the end of life, even though a health care professional assessment indicates that they don't appear to be in pain?
2. What new standard for pain relief is emerging from clinical practice guidelines?
3. What would a "right to pain relief" mean? Is adequate pain relief the obligation of a just society? How would reducing obstacles such as widespread lack of understanding of pain relief and risks of pain-relieving meds, high regulatory scrutiny, or potential penalties improve the treatment of pain?
4. With respect to improving pain relief, are health care professionals or lawyers part of the problem or solution to good pain relief? Standard of care discussions about pain are part of larger civil litigation called tort reform debates. A wide public debate continues among many who see medical malpractice as either key to health care problems or tort (liability) reform as essential to effective health care reform (Studdert et al., 2006). What do you think?
5. Given that pain medications are prescribed by physicians but usually administered by nurses, should laws be in place that sanction nurses equally to physicians if pain relief is inadequate?
6. Debate whether undertreated pain promotes requests for death. North American jurisdictions link "pain and suffering" for damages in civil law but distance themselves from some central European jurisdictions, where practices and laws permitted self-killing and assisted suicide not only for terminal conditions but also for "the unbearable and hopeless suffering of the patient" (Buiting et al., 2009; Netherlands Law, 2002).

Is There Common Ground?

"There is no pain [...] without pain behaviour." (Wittgenstein, 1953, p. 97, §281) Why focus on pain? Nurses and health care professionals have remained advocates for patient-centered determinations and applications against counter-pressures that are regulatory, practical, and legal.

Since 1971 the manufacture, importation, possession, use, and distribution of certain substances for pain have been regulated by the Congressional

Controlled Substances Act that classifies (schedules) medicines under the jurisdiction of two federal agencies (DEA and FDA). Medical organizations have established standards or guidelines for pain treatment; these include the "World Health Organization (1986), the American Pain Society (1993), the American Medical Association, Agency for Health Care Policy and Research (AHCPR) (1992), the Federation of State Medical Boards (1998), and the Joint Commission on Accreditation of Healthcare Organizations (JCAHO) (2000)" (Tucker, 2001, p. 936). Medical and nursing organizations in the last decade "have given detailed clinical practice guidelines for providing pain management as part of routine EOL care" (American Academy of Pain Medicine (AAPM) and American Pain Society (APS), 1996; Oncology Nursing Society, 2002; American Nurses Association, 2003; Imhof & Kaskie, 2008, p. 908). Even though these guidelines exist, health care professionals find themselves at complex interdisciplinary crossroads of clinical care. They face jurisdictional disputes among professions, regulatory agencies, and insurance coverage about what kind and how much pain treatment will be allowed.

Patterns of positive pain policy adoptions are telling: from 1988–2003 some 19 states adopted four medical board pain-management policies that help determine a "good death": "(a) pain management is part of general medical practice, (b) opioids are a legitimate form of professional practice, (c) dosage amount alone does not determine prescription legitimacy, and (d) reduce physicians' fears of regulatory scrutiny" (Imhof & Kaskie, 2008, p. 922). Legal counsel on medical boards has helped positive pain policies to ensure that patients have a right to good pain management (Imhof & Kaskie, 2008).

References

American Pain Society Task Force on Pain. (1997). Treatment of pain at the end of life: A position statement from the American Pain Society. *APS Bulletin, 7*(1). Retrieved from www.ampainsoc.org/library/bulletin/jan97/treatment.htm

Baker, T. (2007). *The medical malpractice myth.* Chicago, IL: University of Chicago Press.

Bernat, J. (2008). *Ethical issues in neurology* (3rd ed.). New York: Lippincott Williams & Wilkins.

Brennan, F., Carr, D. B., & Cousins, M. (2007). Pain management: A fundamental human right. *Anesthesia & Analgesia, 105*(1), 205–221.

Buiting, H., van Delden, J., Onwuteaka-Philpsen, B., Rietjens, J., van Tol, D., Gevers, J., et al. (2009). Reporting of euthanasia and physician-assisted suicide in the Netherlands: Descriptive study. *BMC Medical Ethics, 10*, 18. doi: 10.1186/1472-6939-10-18

Bushwood, D. (2004). Comment: The debate on elder abuse for under treated pain. *Pain Medicine, 5*(2), 218.

California Pain Patient's Bill of Rights. (1997). *California Health & Safety Code 124961.* Retrieved from www.medsch.wisc.edu/painpolicy/domestic/states/CA/calaw2.htm

Fineberg, I., Wenger, N. S., & Brown-Saltzman, K. (2006). Unrestricted opiate administration for pain and suffering at the end of life: Knowledge and attitudes as barriers to care. *Journal of Palliative Medicine, 9*(4), 873–883. doi:10.1089/jpm.2006.9.873

Ginsberg, B., Lowi, T. J., & Weir, M. (2005). *We the people: An introduction to American politics* (5th ed.). New York: W. W. Norton.

Howell, D. D. & Lutz, S. (2008). Hospice referral: An important responsibility for the oncologist. *Journal of Oncology Practice, 4*(6), 303–304.

Human Rights Watch. (2009). *"Please, do not make us suffer any more . . .": Access to pain treatment as a human right.* Retrieved from www.hrw.org/reports/2009/03/02/please-do-not-make-us-suffer-any-more

Imhof, S. L. & Kaskie, B. (2008). Promoting a "good death": Determinants of pain-management policies in the United States. *Journal of Health Politics, Policy and Law, 33*(5), 907–941. doi: 10.1215/03616878-2008-024

Ingham, J., Mohamudally, A., & Portenoy, R. (2009). Measurement of pain and other symptoms. In G. Hanks, N. I. Cherny, N. A. Christakis, M. Fallon, S. Kaasa, & R. Portenoy, *Oxford textbook of palliative medicine* (4th ed., pp. 203–222). New York: Oxford University Press.

Institute of Medicine. (2011). *Relieving pain in America: A blueprint for transforming prevention, care, education, and research.* Retrieved from www.iom.edu/Reports/2011/Relieving-Pain-in-America-A-Blueprint-for-Transforming-Prevention-Care-Education-Research.aspx

International Association for the Study of Pain. (2004). Pain relief as a human right. *Clinical Update 12*(5), 1–4.

Johnson, S. (2004). Comment: The debate on elder abuse for under treated pain. *Pain Medicine, 5*(2), 219.

Netherlands Law. (2002). *Wet toetsing levensbeëindiging op verzoek en hulp bij zelfdoding* (Termination of Life on Request and Assisted Suicide Law) See "uitzichtloos en ondraaglijk lijden van de patiënt" ("the unbearable and hopeless suffering of the patient"). Retrieved from www.nvve.nl/nvve2/pagina.asp?pagkey=71892#staatsblad

Nussbaum, M. (1999). *Sex and social justice.* New York: Oxford University Press.

Nussbaum, M. (2001). *Women and human development: The capabilities approach.* Cambridge: Cambridge University Press.

Pan, C. X., Morrison, R. S., Meier, D. E., Natale, D. K., Goldhirsch, S. L., Kralovec, P., et al. (2001). How prevalent are hospital-based palliative care programs? Status report and future directions. *Journal of Palliative Medicine, 4*(3), 315–324.

Pettus, K. (2011). Palliative care as a late modern citizenship right. In *APSA Annual Meeting Paper.* Retrieved from http://papers.ssrn.com/sol3/papers.cfm?abstract_id=1902073##

Project on Legal Constraints on Access to Effective Pain Relief. (1996). The pain relief act. *Journal of Law, Medicine & Ethics, 24*(4), 317–318. Retrieved from www.painandthelaw.org/statutes/model_act.php

Schweitzer, A. (1931). *The primeval forest.* New York: MacMillan Company.

Smith, A. K., Cenzer, I., Knight, S. J., Puntillo, K. A., Widera, E., Williams, B. A., et al. (2010). The epidemiology of pain during the last 2 years of life. *Annals of Internal Medicine, 153*(9), 563–569.

Smits, H. L., Furletti, M., & and Vladeck, B. C. (2002). *Palliative care: An opportunity for medicare.* New York: Mount Sinai School of Medicine.

Stahl, S. (2008). *Stahl's essential psychopharmacology: Neuroscientific basis and practical applications* (3rd ed.). Cambridge: Cambridge University Press.

Studdert, D. M., Mello, M., Gawande, A., Gandhi, T. K., Kachalia, A., Yoon, C., et al. (2006). Claims, errors, and compensation payments in medical malpractice litigation. *New England Journal of Medicine, 354*(19), 2024–2033. doi:10.1056/NEJMsa054479

SUPPORT. (1995). A controlled trial to improve care for seriously ill hospitalized patients in the study to understand prognoses and preferences for outcomes and risks of treatment (SUPPORT). *Journal of the American Medical Association, 274,* 1591–1598.

Syme, R. (2009). Necessity to palliate pain and suffering as a defence to medical homicide. *Journal of Law & Medicine, 17*(3), 439–451.

Tucker, K. (2001). Provider accountability for inadequate pain management. In R. S. Weiner (Ed.), *Pain management: A practical guide for clinicians* (6th ed., pp. 935–938). New York: CRC Press.

Tucker, K. (2004). Medico-legal case report and commentary: Inadequate pain management in the context of terminal cancer. The case of Lester Tomlinson. *Pain Medicine, 5*(2), 214–217.

Vargas-Schaffer, G. (2010). Is the WHO analgesic ladder still valid? Twenty-four years of experience. *Canadian Family Physician, 56*(6), 514–517.

Wittgenstein, L. (1953/1989). *Philosophical investigations.* Oxford: Basil Blackwell.

Additional Resources

Baszanger, I. (1998). *Inventing pain medicine: From the laboratory to the clinic.* New Brunswick, NJ: Rutgers University Press.

Baumann, A., Audibert, G., Claudot, F., & Puybasset, L. (2009). Ethics review: End of life legislation—the French model. *Critical Care, 13*(1), 204. doi:10.1186/cc7148

Burt, R. A. & Gottlieb, M. K. (2007). Palliative care: Ethics and the law. In A. M. Berger, J. L. Shuster, & J. H. Von Roenn (Eds.), *Principles and practice of palliative care and supportive oncology* (3rd ed., pp. 723–724). Philadelphia, PA: Lippincott Williams & Wilkins.

California Intractable Pain Treatment Act. (1990). *California Business & Professional Code § 2241.5.* Retrieved from www.medsch.wisc.edu/painpolicy/domestic/states/CA/calaw.htm

Cassell, E. J. (1982). The nature of suffering and the goals of medicine. *New England Journal of Medicine, 306*(11), 639–645.

Cassell, E. J. (1991). *The nature of suffering and the goals of medicine.* New York: Oxford University Press.

Cassell, E. J. (1999). Diagnosing suffering: A perspective. *Annals of Internal Medicine, 131*(7), 531–534.

Cellarius, V. (2011). "Early terminal sedation" is a distinct entity. *Bioethics, 25*(1), 46–54. doi:10.1111/j.1467-8519.2009.01747.x

Charleton, J. E. (2005). *Core curriculum for professional education in pain* (3rd ed.) Seattle, WA: International Association of the Study of Pain Press.

Controlled Substances Act. (1971). *Title 21 United States Code*. Retrieved from www.deadiversion.usdoj.gov/21cfr/21usc/index.html

Field, M. J. & Casell, C. K. (1997). *Approaching death: Improving care at the end of life*. Washington, D.C.: National Academy Press.

Fitzpatrick, M. (2000). *The tyranny of health: Doctors and the regulation of lifestyle*. London: Routledge.

Graham, S. S. & Herndl, C. G. (2011). Talking off-label: The role of stasis in transforming the discursive formation of pain science. *Rhetoric Society Quarterly 41*(2), 145–167.

Green, C. R., Hart-Johnson, T., & Loeffler, D. R. (2011). Cancer-related chronic pain: Examining quality of life in diverse cancer survivors. *Cancer, 117*(9), 1994–2003.

Medicare Payment Advisory Commission. (2006). *Report to the congress: Increasing the value of medicare*. Retrieved from www.medpac.gov/documents/Jun06_EntireReport.pdf

Melzack, R. (1988). The tragedy of needless pain: A call for social action. In R. Dubner, G. F. Gebbart, & M. R. Bond (Eds.), *Proceedings of the 5th world congress on pain* (pp. 1–11). New York: Elsevier.

Melzack, R. & Wall, P. D. (1996). *The challenge of pain*. New York: Penguin Global.

President's Council on Bioethics. (2008). A summary of the council's debate on the neurological standard for determining death. In Pellegrino, E., Bloom, F., Carson B., et al. (Eds.), *Controversies in the determination of death: A white paper* (pp. 89–94). Retrieved from www.thenewatlantis.com/docLib/20091130_determination_of_death.pdf

Rich, B. (2000). A prescription for the pain: The emerging standard of care for pain management. *William Mitchell Law Review, 26*(1) 1–37.

Saunders, C. (1963). The treatment of intractable pain in terminal cancer. *Journal of the Royal Society of Medicine, 56*, 195–197.

Scarry, E. (1985). *The body in pain: The making and unmaking of the world*. New York: Oxford University Press.

Sontag, S. (2003). *Regarding the pain of others*. New York: Picador, Farrar, Straus & Giroux.

Stahl, S. (2011). *The prescriber's guide: Stahl's essential psychopharmacology*. Cambridge, MA: Cambridge University Press.

Sullum, J. (2010, June 25). *Pain doctor faces twenty years to life for trusting patients*. Retrieved from http://reason.com/blog/2010/06/25/kansas-pain-doctor-faces-20-ye

Sussex, R. (2009). The language of pain in applied linguistics: Review article of Chryssoula Lascaratou's The language of pain. *Australian Review of Applied Linguistics, 32*(1), 6.1–6.14. doi: 10.2104/aral0906

Teno, J. M., Kabumoto, G., Wetle, T., Roy, J., & Mor, V. (2004). Daily pain that was excruciating at some time in the previous week: Prevalence, characteristics, and outcomes in nursing home residents. *Journal of the American Geriatrics Society, 52*(5), 762–767. doi:10.1111/j.1532-5415.2004.52215.x

Teno, J. M., Shu, J. E., Casarett, D., Spence, C., Rhodes, R., & Connor, S. (2007). Timing of referral to hospice and quality of care: Length of stay and bereaved family members' perceptions of the timing of hospice referral. *Journal of Pain & Symptom Management, 34*(2), 120–125. doi:10.1016/j.jpainsymman.2007.04.014

Tucker, K. (2001). Medical board corrective action with physicians who fail to provide adequate pain care. *Journal of Medical Licensure and Discipline, 87*(4), 130–131.

Tucker, K. (2002). Pain management: Advising and advocating for good care; seeking redress and accountability for inadequate care. *NAELA Quarterly, 15*(4), 17–21.

Tucker, K. (2003). End of life care: A human rights issue. *Human Rights: Section of Individual Rights and Responsibilities, American Bar Association, 30*(2), 11–23.

Tucker, K. (2004). The chicken and the egg: The pursuit of choice for a human hastened-death as a catalyst for improved end-of-life care; improved end-of-life care as a precondition for legalization of assisted dying. *NYU Annual Survey of American Law, 60*, 355–378.

Tucker, K. (2007). Privacy and dignity at the end of life: Protecting the right of Montanans to choose aid in dying. *Montana Law Review, 68*(2), 317–333.

Waldman, S. D. (2006). *Pain management*. Philadelphia, PA: Saunders.

Wall, P. (2002). *Pain: The science of suffering*. New York: Columbia Univesity Press.

World Health Organization. (n.d.). *WHO's pain ladder*. Retrieved from www.who.int/cancer/palliative/painladder/en/

Online Resources

Alliance of State Pain Initiatives

http://trc.wisc.edu/

American Academy of Pain Medicine

www.painmed.org/

American Pain Foundation

www.painfoundation.org/

American Pain Society

www.ampainsoc.org/

Center to Advance Palliative Care

www.getpalliativecare.org/

Emerging Solutions in Pain

www.emergingsolutionsinpain.com/

Federation of State Medical Boards

www.fsmb.org/

Federation of State Medical Boards: Responsible Opioid Prescribing

www.fsmb.org/pain-overview.html

International Association for the Study of Pain

www.iasp-pain.org//AM/Template.cfm?Section=Home

International Association for the Study of Pain: Guide to Pain Management in Low Resource Settings

www.iasp-pain.org/AM/Template.cfm?Section=Home&Template=/CM/ContentDisplay.cfm&ContentID=12172

National Foundation for the Treatment of Pain

www.paincare.org/pain_management/advocacy/ca_bill.php

Pain & the Law

www.painandthelaw.org/statutes/state_pain_acts.php

Pain & Policy Studies Group

www.painpolicy.wisc.edu/

Pain Control: Support for People with Cancer

www.cancer.gov/cancertopics/coping/paincontrol

Glossary for Essays

International Association for the Study of Pain: Pain Terms Defined

www.iaspiasppain.org/AM/Template.cfm?Section=Pain_Defi...isplay.cfm&ContentID=1728

Glossary

Pain

Acetaminophen: nonopioid pain reliever

Analgesic: also known as a painkiller, this refers to any group of drugs used to relieve pain

Anesthetics: reversibly eliminate sensation

Break-through pain: pain that (1) comes through for a short periods of time and (2) is not alleviated by pain management (3) characteristic of cancer (4) that varies from person to person (American Chronic Pain Association, American Pain Society, American Academy of Pain, Breakthrough Cancer Pain)

CME: Continuing Medical Education: Continuing education (CE) for those in a medical field to maintain competence and learning new developments in their fields of knowledge and skills

Elder abuse: blameworthy harm of elderly, in reference to lack of appropriate attention in expectations of trust

Fentanyl patch: medicated adhesive patch with opioid to treat breakthrough pain with rapid onset and short duration

Hillbilly heroin

Hydrocodone: opioid pain reliever

Morphine: opioid painkiller (analgesic)

Negligence: failure to exercise care that a prudent person would exercise in like circumstances

Opioid: chemicals that bind to receptors in the brain, spinal cord, and digestive tract

Standard of care

Tort suit: a wrong that involves breach of a civil duty that is owed to someone (a medical "standard of care")

ISSUE 6

Should Pain Be Alleviated if It Hastens Death?

YES: Richard A. Mularski, Kathleen Puntillo, Basil Varkey, Brian L. Erstad, Mary Jo Grap, Hugh C. Gilbert et al., from "Pain Management Within the Palliative and End-of-Life Care Experience in the ICU," *CHEST* (vol. 135, no. 5, 2009), doi:10.1378/chest.08-2328

NO: Charles L. Sprung, Didier Ledoux, Hans-Henrik Bulow, Anne Lippert, Elisabet Wennberg, Mario Baras et al., from "Relieving Suffering or Intentionally Hastening Death: Where Do You Draw the Line?" *Critical Care Medicine* (vol. 36, no. 1, 2008)

Learning Outcomes

After reading this issue, you should be able to:

- Gain an understanding of the types of pain experienced at the end of life.
- Describe the challenge of pain management for dying patients.
- Understand the importance of intent in the treatment of pain at the end of life.
- Discuss and distinguish the difference between terminal sedation and euthanasia.
- Identify and debate whether there should be more clinical oversight of pain management practices at the end of life.

ISSUE SUMMARY

YES: Richard A. Mularski, a physician from the Center for Health Research at Kaiser Permanente Northwest, and colleagues from around the country discuss palliative care and end-of-life care in the intensive care unit. They identify that the intent of pain medications in this setting is the relief of pain and suffering, even if the possibility exists that these treatments will hasten death.

NO: Charles L. Sprung, MD, JD, a physician, lawyer, and professor at Haddasah University Hospital, in Jerusalem, writes with colleagues from around the world about their concerns with treatments and medications in the ICU that actively shorten the dying process. They raise concerns about the lack of distinction between alleviating suffering and active euthanasia and that inappropriately large doses of pain medications may be given to hasten death "in the guise" of relieving pain and suffering.

The dying experience is unique to each individual depending on the underlying disease or injury. In many cases, dying can bring a peaceful end to a long disease process. However, this experience is not always peaceful and pain free. Although the cornerstone of hospice care is high-quality management of the symptoms of dying (pain, restlessness, difficulty breathing, loss of appetite, etc.), these symptoms cannot be managed in all patients (Fineberg, Wenger, & Brown-Saltzman, 2006). Pain that remains severe or intolerable even with the best medication and other treatments is called "intractable pain." Physicians and nurses have developed pain management clinical practice guidelines to improve the possibility of good pain management for most dying patients. But research shows that between 26 percent and 50 percent of patients are reported to have pain that was undertreated at the end of life (Fineberg, Wenger, & Brown-Saltzman, 2006; Smith et al., 2010; SUPPORT, 1995). This issue debates the challenge of whether high doses of pain medications at the end of life are justified even if they may cause the death of the patient.

There are many different sources of pain in dying patients. Extensive burns can cause horrible pain, because of the sensitive pain nerve endings in the skin that has been burned. Traumatic accidents may fracture bones and damage internal organs. Patients dying from cancer have many sources of pain: tissue compression or displacement by the cancerous tissue, bone pain related to metastases to the bone, and bowel pain related to obstruction caused by invasive cancer tissue. Long-term smokers or diabetic patients often have extensively damaged blood vessels at the end of life. They may experience vascular pain, ischemic (dead) tissue pain, or neuropathic pain (damage to nerve endings) because of their inability to transport oxygen into the cells. Pain at the end of life can also be caused by treatments, interventions, or diagnostic procedures that patients are receiving for their cancer (Bass, 2010; Beckstrand, Smith, Heaston, & Bond, 2008).

Aggressive pain treatment practices for dying patients can provide relief and comfort. The first line medications for severe pain are opioids (these include medications such as morphine, dilaudid, codeine, and oxycodone). These medications can be taken orally or given intravenously to try to reduce pain (Bass, 2010). One recent study showed that the use of high dose opioids for cancer patients had no effect on mortality, indicating that those patients receiving higher doses of pain medications did not die sooner than those without high doses of pain meds (Azoulay, Jacobs, Cialic, Mor, & Stessman, 2011).

Not all pain at the end of life responds well to opioid medications. When patients are experiencing intractable pain, physicians may resort to a practice called "palliative sedation" or "terminal sedation." The practice of treating patients with high doses of sedatives along with pain medications to reduce the patient's awareness of symptoms of suffering has become a standard procedure when trying to control intractable pain of dying patients (Billings, 2011; Boyle, 2004; Olsen, Swetz, & Mueller, 2010). Some physicians refer to this practice as "terminal sedation" although many clinicians argue that this very term implies a different intent of the medications (Lo & Rubenfeld, 2005). These high doses of sedatives and pain medications may also have the effect of shortening the patient's life.

Bioethicists use the term "double effect" to describe actions that are intended to do good (relieve pain), but also have a bad outcome (a hastened death). By invoking the rule of double effect in the cases of terminal sedation, physicians focus on their intent of relieving or controlling suffering and not the secondary outcome of shortening a dying patient's life (Billings, 2011; Boyle, 2004; Olsen et al., 2010). The role of the physician and nurse is to provide relief from pain and suffering. However, when very aggressive interventions are used for pain management, colleagues may question the intent of the physician prescribing the treatment or the nurse administering the treatment. Clinicians and ethicists have debated whether this aggressive treatment of pain is any different than voluntary active euthanasia (intentionally causing a patient's death), which is illegal and morally objectionable to many health care professionals (Billings, 2011; Boyle, 2004; Lo & Rubenfeld, 2005).

In the essay in favor of pain treatments that relieve suffering (the YES article), even if they cause the death of the patient, Mularski discusses pain management for end of life care in the intensive care unit. She argues that pain management should be the primary focus of end of life care and that suffering should be addressed by the interdisciplinary team. She reinforces the need for good communication with family members of patients to assist them in understanding that the goal of pain medications and other management strategies are to relieve suffering at the end of life (Mularski et al., 2009).

Clinicians from the opposing point of view raise questions about the real intent of many of the physicians who initiate palliative sedation. The ETHICUS study group examined the use of medication for sedation and pain treatment for seriously ill patients who died in intensive care units (Sprung et al., 2008). This collection of intensive care physicians from several European countries identify that deliberately terminating the life of another person is illegal. However, it can be exceedingly difficult to distinguish between measures taken to provide relief from pain and suffering and those done with the intention of shortening the dying process (Sprung et al., 2008).

YES

Richard A. Mularski et al.

Pain Management Within the Palliative and End-of-Life Care Experience in the ICU

In the ICU where critically ill patients receive aggressive life-sustaining interventions, suffering is common and death can be expected in up to 20% of patients. High-quality pain management is a part of optimal therapy and requires knowledge and skill in pharmacologic, behavioral, social, and communication strategies grounded in the holistic palliative care approach. This contemporary review article focuses on pain management within comprehensive palliative and end-of-life care. These key points emerge from the transdisciplinary review: (1) all ICU patients experience opportunities for discomfort and suffering regardless of prognosis or goals, thus palliative therapy is a requisite approach for every patient, of which pain management is a principal component; (2) for those dying in the ICU, an explicit shift in management to comfort-oriented care is often warranted and may be the most beneficial treatment the health-care team can offer; (3) communication and cultural sensitivity with the patient-family unit is a principal approach for optimizing palliative and pain management as part of comprehensive ICU care; (4) ethical and legal misconceptions about the escalation of opiates and other palliative therapies should not be barriers to appropriate care, provided the intention of treatment is alleviation of pain and suffering; (5) standardized instruments, performance measurement, and care delivery aids are effective strategies for decreasing variability and improving palliative care in the complex ICU setting; and (6) comprehensive palliative care should addresses family and caregiver stress associated with caring for critically ill patients and anticipated suffering and loss.

Pain management is an essential component of medical care for the critically ill patient. The ICU is a unique care setting where critically ill patients receive expeditious and aggressive life-sustaining interventions and where suffering is common. Thus high-quality pain management and optimal palliative therapy are part of the therapeutic targets for every patient. Pain assessment and management fall within the comprehensive scope of palliative care that should be provided concurrently with curative interventions and supportive care in the ICU.[1-12] Appropriate pain management begins with recognizing, evaluating, and monitoring pain. Achieving excellent pain management

From *Chest*, May 2009, pp. 1360–1369. Copyright © 2009 by American College of Chest Physicians. Reprinted by permission of American College of Chest Physicians via Rightslink.

requires knowledge and skill in pharmacologic, behavioral, social, and communication strategies that are grounded in the holistic palliative care approach.

Dying patients in the ICU are common and warrant a focused palliative approach. Polling reveals that most people wish to die at home;[13–15] however, > 50% of death continues to occur in the hospital setting, most with ICU care.[13,16,17] Approximately 15% of patients admitted to the ICU, or > 500,000 per year in the United States, experience death in the ICU.[17–22] Pain management should be a primary therapeutic focus, especially at the end of life, and delivered within the spectrum of comprehensive palliative care.

Palliative care consists of treatment and support designed to improve the quality of life for patients and their families and reduce suffering from problems associated with life-threatening illness or injury.[6,23] Eric Cassel[24,25] has characterized suffering as both the human experience of physical distress and the emotive aspect of anything that threatens the intactness of the person. The therapies and the rapid pace common to the ICU setting create frequent opportunity for both of these experiences. In fact, most ICU patients experience moderate to severe pain and other sources of suffering.[16,26–28]

Dying patients experience a range of symptoms that are best managed within a comprehensive care model that includes the family and close friends of the patient.[29–34] For those dying in the ICU, an explicit shift in management from curative therapy to comfort-oriented care is warranted.[35–38] Palliative care may be among the main benefits offered by the health-care team in the ICU for those actively dying.

Health-care providers play an active role in managing end-of-life care for ICU patients.[35,36] In 1997, the Institute of Medicine formulated the following three aspects of good dying: (1) avoidance of distress and suffering; (2) in general accord with patient's preferences and wishes; and (3) consistent with clinical and cultural standards.[13] Since that time, the palliative care field has identified core strategies that relate to quality end-of-life care.[1,5,6,39–42] This article focuses on pain therapy as part of optimal palliative and end-of-life care in the ICU. . . .

When changes in status or symptoms such as pain vary frequently, shorter time intervals and reassessments are necessary, including keeping in touch with the family unit. . . .

Suffering and Comprehensive Palliative Care

The management of pain is just one aspect of palliative and end-of-life care in the ICU that addresses the broad goal of relief of suffering. Cassel[24] defines suffering as a state of severe distress that threatens the intactness of the person, and Saunders[43] recognized that "pain" may be more than a physical symptom for a patient and could be "total pain" with multiple dimensions. Suffering is multidimensional and is caused and modulated by physical (pain and other symptoms), psychological (anxiety, depression, body image, and loss of control), social (changed roles, family issues, isolation, finances, and unfinished business), and spiritual/existential aspects (meaning of symptoms and disease, religious beliefs, and fears of death). Spiritual well-being is important to many patients as they near end of life and positively correlates with quality of life.[44] To find meaning for suffering is innate to the human experience. Some view suffering as caused by undue attachment to worldly possessions; others attribute a redemptive value to suffering. In addition to religious influences, past experiences and traditions influence behaviors such as acceptability of outward expressions of suffering.

Cassel[24,45] has further clarified the importance of balancing medical care objectives, recognizing that both the relief of suffering and the cure of disease are equal and appropriate goals in a profession dedicated to the care of the sick. Palliative care in the ICU is a complementary approach to appropriate life-prolonging treatments and, by its very nature, is directed at the patient-family unit. A systematic approach that balances the values of patients and families with available knowledge and responses to therapy can assist in promoting comprehensive palliative care simultaneously with the administration of curative interventions.[6,41] Care delivery is best accomplished by an interdisciplinary palliative care team where individual members can use their aptitude and expertise in exploring different dimensions of suffering and means to lessen or relieve suffering.

Optimizing Pain Management at the End of Life

When curative approaches are not expected to be successful, a transition to primary comfort-focused care and the withdrawal of ineffective or burdensome therapies is often necessary. Although guidelines and detailed strategies have been developed for analgesic therapy during the removal of life-sustaining interventions, communication about what to expect and how things may proceed remain paramount to negotiating this care transition.[46-50] As part of ICU end-of-life care during withdrawal of life-sustaining therapies, patients and their families expect pain management to be responsive and effective.[6,7,28,29,37,51-54] Some patients and families may be able to have meaningful interactions at the end of life, and thus brief interruption of sedatives and analgesics may be reasonable.

Optimal pain management at an ICU patient's end of life is predicated on an assessment of what the patient is experiencing. Rarely are dying ICU patients able to self-report information about their pain. Thus it is incumbent on the critical care health professionals, perhaps with the assistance of the patient's family members, to do as complete a pain assessment as possible without self-report input from the patient. In an accompanying article in this series (Puntillo, Pasero, Li, et al, on evaluation of the ICU patient with pain), we presented information about some pain assessment instruments that have had the most validity testing, the Behavioral Pain Scale[55] and the Critical-Care Pain Observation Tool.[56] Both tools contain descriptors of specific observations that the patient's ICU care providers can make that, when present, could indicate the patient is experiencing pain. Providers could also choose to develop a brief pain behaviors checklist that would include specific behaviors noted in research to correlate with patients' self-reports of pain: grimacing, rigidity, wincing, shutting of eyes, clenching of fists, verbalization, and moaning.[57]

A close family member's assessment of pain should not be overlooked. Although the evidence regarding the validity of surrogates' reports is equivocal, some findings are promising enough that they should be considered in situations such as this, when an ICU patient is close to death. Indeed, in the cohort of 2,645 Study to Understand Prognosis and Preference for Outcomes and Risks of Treatment (or SUPPORT) patients and their surrogates,[58] surrogates had a 73.5% accuracy rate in estimating presence or absence of patient's pain, with a tendency for the surrogates to overestimate patient pain. Accuracy in estimating the exact level of patients' pain was poorer (53%). However, certain factors increased surrogates' levels of accuracy, as follows: (1) when patients' levels of pain were at the lowest and highest extremes (9.1 and 3.2 times greater odds for accuracy, respectively; 89% accuracy when patients reported severe pain); (2) estimating within one level of the patients' pain (increase from 73.5 to 82% accuracy); and (3) providers completing their pain assessment on the same day as the patient pain reports.[59] It appears that the visibility of the functional problem could influence patient-proxy agreement. For example, agreement between raters has been closer for pain than for anxiety,[60] fatigue, insomnia,[59] or overall health.[61] Research has also demonstrated that agreement about symptoms did not depend on the type of proxy rater (ie, family member, nurse, or physician), indicating that one type of rater is not preferable over another.[62] Erring on the side of treatment and symptom control may help reduce patient and family suffering.[59] Indeed, an integrated approach that incorporates multiple proxy raters of patients' symptoms may be the most valuable in accurately assessing patients' symptoms,[62] in this case pain.

Overcoming Pain Management

One barrier to good pain management at the end of life occurs when there are ethical misconceptions or legal concerns about the escalation of opiates or other palliative therapies. Although ethical and legal consensus upholds the appropriateness of withdrawing unwanted or unhelpful therapies to avoid the prolongation of the dying process and the administration of medications with the intent of relieving suffering, concern may mitigate optimal administration of therapies.[63-67] When providers administer pain medications and other palliative therapies for the dying patient in the ICU, the intent should explicitly be on relief of symptoms, and communication with the family must stress this goal, even if the possibility exists that such treatments could hasten death.

The doctrine of double effect supports the aggressive palliation of pain as different from the active hastening of death and is ethically justifiable as long as the caregiver's primary intent is alleviating suffering.[65-67] ICU health-care providers should communicate this strategy with patient and families, document the reason for and titration of agents used for the alleviation of pain, and consider engaging the family members in discussions of the process to avoid under- or overtreatment of pain. Research findings suggest that aggressive pain management at the end of life does not necessarily shorten life, but rather pain management may be life-prolonging by decreasing the systemic effects of uncontrolled pain that can compromise vital organ function.[68-74] Indeed, Chan and colleagues[74] found no statistically significant relationship between opiate doses and time to death (from 1 h before ventilator withdrawal to time of death) in a cohort of critically ill patients.

Pain Management During Withdrawal of Therapies

Currently there is no one best way to medicate patients for pain and other discomfort during withdrawal of life-sustaining therapies in the ICU. In a systemic review of relevant literature, Campbell[75] noted a great variation in the types and amounts of medications used during ventilator withdrawal. Morphine doses in the final 12 h of life have ranged from 1 mg to 698 mg in a group of 174 patients[76] and have ranged from 2 to 450 mg in the 4 h before death in another group of 155 ICU patients.[77] . . .

Palliative Sedation

Palliative sedation, also known as total sedation, terminal sedation, or controlled sedation, can be defined as sedation for intractable distress or suffering in the dying.[78,79] Palliative sedation is differentiated from usual ICU sedation in that the goal of the former is to reduce a patient's awareness of distressing symptoms that cannot be adequately controlled by symptom-specific interventions, as opposed to the treatment of anxiety or agitation as in the ordinary use in the ICU targeting safety and comfort in patient care. The distinction between a difficult vs a refractory symptom is important as only in the latter case should palliative sedation be considered. Cherney and Portenoy[80] note three characteristics of a refractory symptom: (1) aggressive efforts fail to provide relief, (2) additional invasive/noninvasive treatments are incapable of providing relief, and (3) additional therapies are associated with excessive or unacceptable morbidity unlikely to provide relief in a reasonable time frame.

The literature provides insight into how often and for what purpose palliative sedation is used in terminally ill patients in a hospice or palliative care unit setting. In an international study from four centers (three hospices and one palliative care unit) in Israel, Spain, and South Africa, palliative sedation was deemed appropriate for terminally ill patients with delirium (9 to 23%), dyspnea (2 to 13%), and existential distress (1 to 5%).[81] In another study from Germany, the main indications for palliative sedation were anxiety/psychological distress (40%), dyspnea (35%), and delirium/agitation (14%).[82] In both of these series, pain was rarely (< 3%) the cited indication for palliative sedation.

Practitioners in the ICU setting are unlikely to encounter patients with sufficient refractory pain to consider the use of palliative sedation. Yet it is important that they understand the ethical and legal basis, guidelines and requirements, and appropriate use of drugs for palliative sedation.[78] From an ethical and legal standpoint, the difference in intent separates palliative sedation from provider-assisted death or euthanasia. The intent in palliative sedation is to relieve refractory suffering, not to hasten death. Guidelines must be in place in all settings, including ICUs, where care is provided to the terminally ill.[83] Criteria for palliative sedation should include the following: (1) confirmation of a terminal illness whose symptom(s) are refractory to all available treatments, (2) psychological and spiritual assessments have been completed by a skilled clinician, clergy, or skilled palliative care team member, (3) a do not resuscitate order is in effect and informed consent has been obtained and documented, and (4) nutrition and hydration issues have been addressed and documented. Palliative sedation should be considered as a rare and very selectively used modality at the end of the continuum of palliative care.[84]

Caring for Caregivers

Although the relief of suffering for patients in the critical care setting is of prime importance, suffering experienced by their family members and those engaged in caregiving also deserve attention. Of 906 critical care nurses surveyed about their experiences with ICU patients at end of life, 78% thought that dying ICU patients frequently (31%) or sometimes (47%) received inadequate pain medicine.[85] Nurses who understood the principle of double effect (98% of 906 surveyed) agreed that administering analgesics to decrease patient pain, even though there might be an unintended consequence of hastening death, is an ethical way to treat a dying patient.[85] Yet other nurses have identified lack of adequate pain relief for their patients as one obstacle to providing good end-of-life care,[86] and they believe that effective symptom control is a prerequisite for a dignified death.[87] When nurses provide care that does not relieve their patient's suffering or when they follow orders for pain medication even when the medications prescribed do not control the patient's pain, they are at high risk for suffering moral distress.[88] ICU nurses can be prepared with the knowledge and skills to make decisions about patients' analgesic needs and be provided guidelines or protocols that will assist them in making analgesic treatment decisions.[89] If they are provided the time necessary to titrate analgesics according to the patient's response by being relieved of some of their other responsibilities during this period,[90] their contributions to patient comfort may increase while their vicarious suffering decreases. . . .

Achieving Quality Palliative and End-of-Life Care in the ICU

Despite well agreed-on goals for quality palliative and end-of-life care in the ICU,[8–10] many patients experience discomfort and other undesirable states during end-of-life time in the ICU. Because of this disconnect, the health-care enterprise is beginning to emphasize research, evaluation, and quality improvement for palliative care in the ICU.[1,5,6,16,41,91,92] A structured and deliberate approach is required to achieve high-quality pain management. Health-care providers play an active role in managing the deaths of critically ill patients, suggesting a level of accountability for optimizing palliative and end-of-life comfort care for those in the ICU.[93–95]

Across health-care settings and situations, quality can be defined as the "degree to which health services for individuals and populations increase the likelihood of desired health outcomes and are consistent with current professional knowledge."[96] This definition emphasizes that care should be in alignment with patient-family preferences and should be guided by our emerging evidence base. It further suggests that before care can be improved, its performance needs reliable measurement. Quality measurement of palliative care in the ICU requires that measures have a strong relationship between processes of care (that is, the things we as health-care practitioners do in caring for patients in pain) and management outcomes (those that ICU patients and families highly value). A number of general quality of care measure sets have begun to incorporate palliative and end-of-life care measures[2,5,6,97,98] that share an emphasis on pain management.

Conclusion

In summary, ICU care should strive to provide optimal pain management and palliative care in the ICU environment. Such care should attend to multiple sources of patient pain and suffering and target communication among patients, families, and ICU professionals that promote patient comfort. Indeed, such a focused approach to pain management is perhaps one of the most crucial aspects of optimizing delivery of care in the complex critical care setting. Care delivery using the interdisciplinary model will facilitate comprehensive care that includes pain management and alleviation of human suffering by utilizing multiple members of a team who interact in a coordinated fashion. To achieve high-quality pain management and palliative care in the ICU, processes and outcomes of such care need to be evaluated and revised accordingly. With careful attention to palliative care and pain management, patients and their families can avoid suffering while pursuing healing or comfortable dying in the ICU.

References

1. Nelson JE, Mulkerin CM, Adams LL, et al. Improving comfort and communication in the ICU: a practical new tool for palliative care performance measurement and feedback. *Qual Saf Health Care* 2006; 15:264–271.

2. Mularski RA, Curtis JR, Billings JA, et al. Proposed quality measures for palliative care in the critically ill: a consensus from the Robert Wood Johnson Foundation Critical Care Workgroup. *Crit Care Med* 2006; 34(suppl):S404–S411.

3. Ferrell BR. Overview of the domains of variables relevant to end-of-life care. *J Palliat Med* 2005; 8(suppl):S22–S29.

4. Lorenz K, Lynn J, Morton SC, et al. End-of-life care and outcomes. *Evid Rep Technol Assess (Summ)* 2004; 110:1–6.

5. Mularski RA. Defining and measuring quality palliative and end-of-life care in the intensive care unit. *Crit Care Med* 2006; 34(suppl):S309–S316.

6. National Consensus Project. Clinical practice guidelines for palliative care; 2004. at: www.nationalconsensusproject.org. Accessed November 18, 2008.

7. Steinhauser KE, Christakis NA, Clipp EC, et al. Factors considered important at the end of life by patients, family, physicians, and other care providers. *JAMA* 2000; 284:2476–2482.

8. Selecky PA, Eliasson CA, Hall RI, et al. Palliative and end-of-life care for patients with cardiopulmonary diseases: American College of Chest Physicians position statement. *Chest* 2005; 128:3599–3610.

9. Lanken PN, Terry PB, Delisser HM, et al. An official American Thoracic Society clinical policy statement: palliative care for patients with respiratory diseases and critical illnesses. *Am J Respir Crit Care Med* 2008; 177:912–927.

10. Truog RD, Campbell ML, Curtis JR, et al. Recommendations for end-of-life care in the intensive care unit: a consensus statement by the American College of Critical Care Medicine. *Crit Care Med* 2008; 36:953–963.

11. Mularski RA, Rosenfeld KE, Sloan JA, et al. International conference on malignant bowel obstruction: a model for randomized prospective trials in palliative care: measuring outcomes in randomized prospective trials in palliative care. *J Pain Symptom Manage* 2007; 34(suppl):S7–S19.

12. Patrick DL, Curtis JR, Engelberg RA, et al. Measuring and improving the quality of dying and death. *Ann Intern Med* 2003; 139:410–415.

13. Field MJ, Cassel CK. Approaching death: improving care at the end of life Washington, DC: National Academy Press, 1997.

14. Pritchard RS, Fisher ES, Teno JM, et al. Influence of patient preferences and local health system characteristics on the place of death: SUPPORT Investigators; Study to Understand Prognoses and Preferences for Risks and Outcomes of Treatment. *J Am Geriatr Soc* 1998; 46:1242–1250.

15. Weitzen S, Teno JM, Fennell M, et al. Factors associated with site of death: a national study of where people die. *Med Care* 2003; 41:323–335.

16. SUPPORT Principal Investigators. A controlled trial to improve care for seriously ill hospitalized patients: the Study to Understand Prognoses and Preferences for Outcomes and Risks of Treatments (SUPPORT). *JAMA* 1995; 274:1591–1598.

17. Center for the Evaluative Clinical Sciences at Dartmouth Medical School. The Dartmouth Atlas of Health Care, 2002; Available at: www.dartmouthatlas.org. Accessed November 18, 2008.

18. Angus DC, Barnato AE, Linde-Zwirble WT, et al. Use of intensive care at the end of life in the United States: an epidemiologic study. *Crit Care Med* 2004; 32:638–643.

19. Lynn J, Harrell F Jr, Cohn F, et al. Prognoses of seriously ill hospitalized patients on the days before death: implications for patient care and public policy. *New Horiz* 1997; 5:56–61.

20. Lunney JR, Lynn J, Foley DJ, et al. Patterns of functional decline at the end of life. *JAMA* 2003; 289:2387–2392.

21. Mularski RA. Pain management in the intensive care unit. *Crit Care Clin* 2004; 20:381–401.

22. Mularski RA. Defining and measuring quality palliative and end-of-life care in the intensive care unit. *Crit Care Med* 2006; 34(suppl):S309–S316.

23. World Health Organization. WHO definition of palliative care, 2005. Available at: www.who.int/cancer/palliative/definition/en/. Accessed November 18, 2008.

24. Cassel EJ. The nature of suffering and the goals of medicine. *N Engl J Med* 1982; 306:639–645.

25. Cassel EJ. Diagnosing suffering: a perspective. *Ann Intern Med* 1999; 131:531–534.

26. Desbiens NA, Wu AW, Broste SK, et al. Pain and satisfaction with pain control in seriously ill hospitalized adults: findings from the SUPPORT research investigations; for the SUPPORT investigators—Study to Understand Prognoses and Preferences for Outcomes and Risks of Treatment. *Crit Care Med* 1996; 24:1953–1961.

27. Desbiens NA, Wu AW. Pain and suffering in seriously ill hospitalized patients. *J Am Geriatr Soc* 2000; 48(suppl):S183–S186.

28. Nelson JE, Meier DE, Oei EJ, et al. Self-reported symptom experience of critically ill cancer patients receiving intensive care. *Crit Care Med* 2001; 29:277–282.

29. Oxford textbook of palliative medicine. 2nd ed. Oxford, UK: Oxford University Press, 1998.

30. Lanken P: Optimal care for patients dying in the ICU, International consensus conference in intensive care medicine, Brussels, 2003. Available at: www.esicm.org. Accessed November 18, 2008.

31. Curtiss CP, Haylock PJ. Managing cancer and noncancer chronic pain in critical care settings: knowledge and skills every nurse needs to know. *Crit Care Nurs Clin North Am* 2001; 13:271–280.

32. Cullen L, Greiner J, Titler MG. Pain management in the culture of critical care. *Crit Care Nurs Clin North Am* 2001; 13:151–166.

33. Foley KM. Management of cancer pain. In: DeVita VT, Hellman S, Rosenberg SA, eds. Principles and practices of oncology. Philadelphia, PA: Lippincott, 1994; 2417–2448.

34. World Health Organization. Cancer pain relief and palliative care. Geneva, Switzerland: WHO, 1996.

35. Prendergast TJ, Claessens MT, Luce JM. A national survey of end-of-life care for critically ill patients. *Am J Respir Crit Care Med* 1998; 158:1163–1167.

36. Luce JM, Prendergast TJ. The changing nature of death in the ICU. In: Curtis JR, Rubenfield GD, eds. Managing death in the intensive care unit: the transition from cure to comfort. New York, NY: Oxford University Press, 2001; 19–29.

37. Curtis JR, Rubenfeld GD. Managing death in the intensive care unit: the transition from cure to comfort. New York, NY: Oxford University Press, 2001.

38. Curtis JR, Rubenfeld GD. Improving palliative care for patients in the intensive care unit. *J Palliat Med* 2005; 8:840–854.

39. Clarke EB, Curtis JR, Luce JM, et al. Quality indicators for end-of-life care in the intensive care unit. *Crit Care Med* 2003; 31:2255–2262.

40. Promoting Excellence in End-of-Life Care. Innovative models and approaches for palliative and end-of-life care: promoting palliative care excellence in intensive care. Available at: www.promotingexcellence.org. Accessed November 18, 2008.

41. Curtis JR, Rubenfeld GD. Managing death in the intensive care unit: the transition from cure to comfort. New York, NY: Oxford University Press, 2001.

42 Lorenz K, Lynn J, Dy S, et al. Cancer care quality measures: symptoms and end-of-life care; summary, evidence report/technology assessment—Number 137. Available at www.ahrq.gov/clinic/tp/eolcanqmtp.htm#Report. Accessed February 27, 2009.

43. Saunders C. Foreword. In: Oxford textbook of palliative medicine. 3rd ed. Oxford, UK; New York, NY: Oxford University Press, 2004.

44. Prince-Paul MJ. Relationships among communicative acts, social well-being, and spiritual well-being on the quality of life at the end of life in patients with cancer enrolled in hospice. *J Palliat Med* 2008; 11:20–25.

45. Cassel EJ. Diagnosing suffering: a perspective. *Ann Intern Med* 1999; 131: 531–534.

46. Hawryluck LA, Harvey WR, Lemieux-Charles L, et al. Consensus guidelines on analgesia and sedation in dying intensive care unit patients. *BMC Med Ethics* 2002; 3:E3.

47. Wilson WC, Smedira NG, Fink C, et al. Ordering and administration of sedatives and analgesics during the withholding and withdrawal of life support from critically ill patients. *JAMA* 1992; 267:949–953.

48. Cullen L, Greiner J, Titler MG. Pain management in the culture of critical care. *Crit Care Nurs Clin North Am* 2001; 13:151–166.

49. Task Force on Ethics of the Society of Critical Care Medicine. Consensus report on the ethics of foregoing life-sustaining treatments in the critically ill. *Crit Care Med* 1990; 18:1435–1439.

50. Rubenfeld GD. Principles and practice of withdrawing life-sustaining treatments. *Crit Care Clin* 2004; 20:435–451.

51. American Medical Association. Pain management: the online series. 2004.

52. American Medical Association. Pain management: the online series. Available at: www.ama-cmeonline.com/pain_mgmt. Accessed February 27, 2009.

53. American Medical Association Education for physicians on end-of-life care. Available at: www.epec.net/EPEC/webpages/index.cfm. Accessed February 27, 2009.

54. Mularski RA, Heine CE, Osborne ML, et al. Quality of dying in the ICU: ratings by family members. *Chest* 2005; 128:280–287.

55. Payen JF, Bru O, Bosson JL, et al. Assessing pain in critically ill sedated patients by using a behavioral pain scale. *Crit Care Med* 2001; 29:2258–2263.

56. Gelinas C, Fillion L, Puntillo KA, et al. Validation of the Critical-Care Pain Observation Tool in adult patients. *Am J Crit Care* 2006; 15:420–427.

57. Puntillo KA, Morris AB, Thompson CL, et al. Pain behaviors observed during six common procedures: results from Thunder Project II. *Crit Care Med* 2004; 32:421–427.

58. Desbiens NA, Mueller-Rizner N. How well do surrogates assess the pain of seriously ill patients? *Crit Care Med* 2000; 28:1347–1352.

59. Lobchuk MM, Kristjanson L, Degner L, et al. Perceptions of symptom distress in lung cancer patients: I. Congruence between patients and primary family caregivers. *J Pain Symptom Manage* 1997; 14:136–146.

60. Nekolaichuk CL, Bruera E, Spachynski K, et al. A comparison of patient and proxy symptom assessments in advanced cancer patients. *Palliat Med* 1999; 13:311–323.

61. Sneeuw KC, Aaronson NK, Sprangers MA, et al. Evaluating the quality of life of cancer patients: assessments by patients, significant others, physicians and nurses. *Br J Cancer* 1999; 81:87–94.

62. Nekolaichuk CL, Maguire TO, Suarez-Almazor M, et al. Assessing the reliability of patient, nurse, and family caregiver symptom ratings in hospitalized advanced cancer patients. *J Clin Oncol* 1999; 17:3621–3630.

63. American Thoracic Society Bioethics Task Force. Withholding and withdrawing life-sustaining therapy. *Ann Intern Med* 1991; 115:478–485.

64. Behavioral research. Making health care decisions: a report on the ethical and legal implications of informed consent in the patient-practitioner relationship. Washington, DC: US Government Printing Office, 1982.

65. Beauchamp TL, Childress JF. Principles of biomedical ethics. 5th ed. Oxford, UK: Oxford University Press, 2001.

66. Paris JJ, Muir JC, Reardon FE. Ethical and legal issues in intensive care. *J Intensive Care Med* 1997; 12:298–309.

67. Jonsen AR, Siegler M, Winslade WJ. Clinical ethics. 4th ed. New York, NY: McGraw-Hill, 1998.

68. Bercovitch M, Waller A, Adunsky A. High dose morphine use in the hospice setting: a database survey of patient characteristics and effect on life expectancy. *Cancer* 1999; 86:871–877.

69. Vella-Brincat J, Macleod AD. Adverse effects of opioids on the central nervous systems of palliative care patients. *J Pain Palliat Care Pharmacother* 2007; 21:15–25.

70. Estfan B, Mahmoud F, Shaheen P, et al. Respiratory function during parenteral opioid titration for cancer pain. *Palliat Med* 2007; 21:81–86.

71. Citron ML, Johnston-Early A, Fossieck BE Jr, et al. Safety and efficacy of continuous intravenous morphine for severe cancer pain. *Am J Med* 1984; 77:199–204.

72. Edwards MJ. Opioids and benzodiazepines appear paradoxically to delay inevitable death after ventilator withdrawal. *J Palliat Care* 2005; 21:299–302.

73. Mularski RA. Pain management in the intensive care unit. *Crit Care Clin* 2004; 20:381–401.

74. Chan JD, Treece PD, Engelberg RA, et al. Narcotic and benzodiazepine use after withdrawal of life support: association with time to death? *Chest* 2004; 126:286–293.

75. Campbell ML. How to withdraw mechanical ventilation: a systematic review of the literature. *AACN Adv Crit Care* 2007; 18:397–403.

76. Hall RI, Rocker GM. End-of-life care in the ICU: treatments provided when life support was or was not withdrawn. *Chest* 2000; 118:1424–1430.

77. Rocker GM, Heyland DK, Cook DJ, et al. Most critically ill patients are perceived to die in comfort during withdrawal of life support: a Canadian multicentre study. *Can J Anaesth* 2004; 51:623–630.

78. Salacz M, Weissman D. Fast fact and concept #106 and #107: controlled sedation for refractory suffering; part I and II. Available at: www.eperc.mcw .edu/ff_index.htm. Accessed February 27, 2009.

79. National Ethics Committee, Veterans Health Administration. The ethics of palliative sedation as a therapy of last resort. *Am J Hosp Palliat Med* 2007; 23:483–491.

80. Cherny NI, Portenoy RK. Sedation in the management of refractory symptoms: guidelines for evaluation and treatment. *J Palliat Care* 1994; 10:31–38.

81. Fainsinger RL, Waller A, Bercovici M, et al. A multicentre international study of sedation for uncontrolled symptoms in terminally ill patients. *Palliat Med* 2000; 14:257–265.

82. Muller-Busch HC, Andres I, Jehser T. Sedation in palliative care: a critical analysis of 7 years experience. *BMC Palliat Care* 2003; 2:2.

83. Rousseau P. Existential suffering and palliative sedation: a brief commentary with a proposal for clinical guidelines. *Am J Hosp Palliat Care* 2001; 18:151–153.

84. Carr MF, Mohr GJ. Palliative sedation as part of a continuum of palliative care. *J Palliat Med* 2008; 11:76–81.

85. Puntillo KA, Benner P, Drought T, et al. End-of-life issues in intensive care units: a national random survey of nurses' knowledge and beliefs. *Am J Crit Care* 2001; 10:216–229.

86. Kirchhoff KT, Beckstrand RL. Critical care nurses' perceptions of obstacles and helpful behaviors in providing end-of-life care to dying patients. *Am J Crit Care* 2000; 9:96–105.

87. Nordgren L, Olsson H. Palliative care in a coronary care unit: a qualitative study of physicians' and nurses' perceptions. *J Clin Nurs* 2004; 13:185–193.

88. Elpern EH, Covert B, Kleinpell R. Moral distress of staff nurses in a medical intensive care unit. *Am J Crit Care* 2005; 14:523–530.

89. American Association of Critical Care Nurses. AACN protocols for practice: palliative care and end-of-life issues in critical care. Boston, MA: Jones & Bartlett, 2006.

90. Chapple HS. Changing the game in the intensive care unit: letting nature take its course. *Crit Care Nurse* 1999; 19:25–34.

91. Desbiens NA, Mueller-Rizner N, et al. The symptom burden of seriously ill hospitalized patients: SUPPORT Investigators; Study to Understand Prognoses and Preferences for Outcome and Risks of Treatment. *J Pain Symptom Manage* 1999; 17:248–255.

92. Nelson JE, Meier DE, Oei EJ, et al. Self-reported symptom experience of critically ill cancer patients receiving intensive care. *Crit Care Med* 2001; 29:277–282.

93. Prendergast TJ, Claessens MT, Luce JM. A national survey of end-of-life care for critically ill patients. *Am J Respir Crit Care Med* 1998; 158:1163–1167.

94. Faber-Langendoen K. A multi-institutional study of care given to patients dying in hospitals: ethical and practice implications. *Arch Intern Med* 1996; 156:2130–2136.

95. Smedira NG, Evans BH, Grais LS, et al. Withholding and withdrawal of life support from the critically ill. *N Engl J Med* 1990; 322:309–315.

96. Blumenthal D. Part 1: quality of care; what is it? *N Engl J Med* 1996; 335:892.

97. Lorenz K, Lynn J, Dy S, et al. Cancer care quality measures: symptoms and end-of-life care. 137th ed. Rockville, MD: Agency for Healthcare Research and Quality, 2006.

98. Lorenz KA, Lynn J, Dy S, et al. Quality measures for symptoms and advance care planning in cancer: a systematic review. *J Clin Oncol* 2006; 24:4933–4938.

Charles L. Sprung et al.    **NO**

Relieving Suffering or Intentionally Hastening Death: Where Do You Draw the Line?

End-of-life actions are common in intensive care units (ICUs) around the world.[1–4] Despite a widespread perception of excessive and inappropriate use of life-sustaining technology, withholding or withdrawing of treatment occurs in more than two thirds of patients dying in ICUs[1,4] and has actually increased.[5] The use of aggressive therapy has decreased.[5–7] While in the past most patients died in ICUs after cardiopulmonary resuscitation (CPR),[8] presently only approximately 20% of ICU patients who die undergo CPR.[1,4]

Discussions of end-of-life practices in ICUs generally imply that the lines between these practices are clear and well defined. Actions undertaken in the care of dying patients are grouped into distinct categories, including CPR, withholding or withdrawing treatment, and active euthanasia or active shortening of the dying process (SDP).[1–5] Active euthanasia or SDP is assumed to be distinct from legal and ethically acceptable practices, such as withholding and withdrawing treatment.

Even though limitation of therapy is common, active euthanasia is controversial and only legal in The Netherlands and Belgium (on the patient's direct request),[9,10] and physician-assisted suicide is only allowed in Switzerland and Oregon in the United States.[11] In these countries, where the law defines euthanasia as the act of deliberately terminating the life of another person at his or her request, active euthanasia practiced in the ICU for incompetent patients would be viewed as illegal. Palliative care, on the other hand, is widely practiced and encouraged.[12] It is well known that the same medications given to ease pain and suffering can potentially cause or hasten death. It is exceedingly difficult to determine whether and when relief measures are undertaken with the implicit or explicit intention to shorten the dying process as opposed to just relieve pain and suffering.

Only three studies have examined the use of life-shortening practices in adult ICUs. In an attitudinal survey conducted in 16 European countries, 40% of physicians admitted to sometimes deliberately administering drugs to patients with no hope of survival until death ensues.[13] The ETHICUS study documented SDP in seven of 17 European countries.[4] Asch[14] noted that 17% of critical care nurses were asked by patients or relatives to perform euthanasia or assist in suicide, and 16% reported that they had engaged in such practices.

From *Critical Care Medicine,* January, 2008, pp. 8–13. Copyright © 2008 by Society of Critical Care Medicine. Reprinted by permission of Lippincott Williams/Wolters Kluwer Health via Rightslink.

The purpose of this article is to make the argument and show evidence that there is no clear-cut distinction between treatments administered to relieve pain and suffering when withdrawing life-sustaining treatment and those intended to shorten the dying process. An in-depth examination of this gray area in end-of-life care has important moral and ethical implications for the practice of intensive care medicine. It also has implications for other acute care areas, long-term care, and community care, where there are similar concerns about pain management vs. actively assisting in the dying process. The article elaborates on the previous report,[4] which only briefly touched on the findings on SDP. It analyzes the overlap between SDP and other end-of-life practices relying on three variables: doses of potentially life-shortening intravenous drugs, the time for patients to die after limitation of therapy, and the intent of the doctors who prescribed the medications.

Methods

Study Population. This report is a secondary analysis of a previous prospective study.[4] All consecutive adult patients who died or had any limitation of life-saving interventions in the ICU from January 1, 1999, to June 30, 2000, were studied prospectively.[4] Patients were followed until discharge from ICU, death, or 2 months from the decision to limit therapy.[4]

Definitions of End-of-Life Categories. End-of-life categories were defined prospectively as CPR, brain death, withholding life-sustaining treatment, withdrawing life-sustaining treatment, and SDP as previously reported.[4] SDP was defined in the questionnaire as a circumstance in which someone performed an act with the specific intent of shortening the dying process. These acts did not include withholding or withdrawing treatment, and examples included intentional overdose of narcotics, anesthetics, or potassium chloride.[4] . . . Patients were classified as "withhold" only if that was the sole limitation made; "withdraw" included patients for whom treatment was both withheld and withdrawn; and "SDP" included cases involving withholding or withdrawing and SDP decisions.

Ethical and Legal Considerations. No interventions or treatments were given, withheld, or withdrawn from patients as part of the initial observational study.[4] . . .

Study Centers and Data Collection. . . . The prospectively collected data used specifically for this secondary analysis included type of end-of-life category (SDP and other categories were self-identified by the responsible physician) and dates and times of 1) ICU admission; 2) death or discharge; and 3) decisions to limit therapy, medication, and doses used for SDP and the intent of the doctors prescribing the medication or extubation. Physicians retrospectively classified the acts used for SDP as definitely, probably, or probably not the cause of the patient's death. . . .

Results

During the initial study, 31,417 patients were admitted to ICUs in 37 centers located in 17 countries.[4] Of the 31,417 patients, 4,248 who died or had limitations of life-sustaining treatments comprised the study population. Limitation of life-sustaining therapy occurred in 3,086 (72.6%) of 4,248 patients, 9.8% of all ICU admissions, and 76.0% of dying patients. The frequencies of the different end-of-life categories were as follows: 832 (19.6%) of the patients received CPR, 330 (7.8%) were diagnosed with brain death, 1,594 (37.5%) had therapies withheld, 1,398 (32.9%) had therapies withdrawn, and 94 (2.2%) underwent SDP.

All SDP patients already had previous therapies withheld or withdrawn. SDP was performed in nine of the 37 centers in seven of the 17 countries, which was a minority of centers. Of the SDP patients, types of medications were available for all patients, and doses used for SDP were available for 66 (70%) patients. . . . Treatment modalities used for the patients who underwent SDP included administration of opiates or benzodiazepines alone or in combination; four patients also received muscle relaxants and seven received barbiturates. Potassium chloride was not used in any of the SDP cases. The most commonly used opiate was morphine (administered to 71 patients alone or in combination). The most commonly used benzodiazepine was diazepam (administered to 54 patients alone or in combination). . . . Although mean doses of opiates and benzodiazepines used for SDP were higher than mean doses used with withdrawing in previous studies,[2,3] they were no higher in 20 of 66 patients and were within the ranges of doses used in all but one patient. In retrospect, doctors considered that the doses of medications they gave for SDP definitely led to the patient's death in 72 patients (77%), probably led to the patient's death in 11 (12%), and were unlikely to have led to the patients death in 11 (12%).

The median (IQR) time from the first decision to limit treatment until death was 14.7 hrs (51.0 hrs). The median (IQR) time from the decision for the most active form of limitation of therapy until death was 6.6 hrs (30.2 hrs) for all patients, 14.3 hrs (64.6 hrs) for withholding, 4.0 hrs (16.2 hrs) for withdrawing, and 3.5 hrs (7.0 hrs) for SDP ($p < .001$). Increasing doses of opiates and benzodiazepines were associated with a shorter time to death. . . .

Discussion

Although end-of-life medical actions are commonly grouped into distinct categories, in actual practice they form a continuum—from aggressive resuscitation to active euthanasia—and the dividing lines between different actions are not always easy to define. A thorough and frank discussion of the differences, similarities, and overlaps between different end-of-life practices is vital to ensure optimal and responsible critical care.

An example of the complexity in defining different categories of ICU care is the relationship between withholding and withdrawing life-sustaining therapies. The conventional ethical view is that there is no moral distinction between the two,[13] but this belief is not universal,[15] and studies show that some healthcare professionals are more reluctant to withdraw than withhold therapies.[13,16] In fact, different studies have defined not restarting an intravenous vasopressor infusion as either withholding[17] or withdrawing.[4]

The blurred line between different categories is also exemplified by the confusion among physicians, which causes them to misclassify or misrepresent their own actions: A U.S. survey suggested that the actual practice of euthanasia or physician-assisted suicide in the United States and other countries may be overstated by >20%.[18] In the survey, many oncologists who initially reported that they had intentionally ended a patient's life revealed through in-depth interviews that in fact they had performed withholding of life-sustaining treatment or provided potentially life-shortening narcotics for pain relief, which are neither euthanasia nor assisted suicide.[18]

Only one previous study in neonatal ICUs specifically evaluated the controversial overlap between the use of potentially life-shortening drugs and mercy killing.[19] Van der Heide et al.[19] found "a rather large overlap between decisions to administer drugs with and without the intention of hastening death, with respect to the type and dose of the drugs given, aspects of decision making, [and] prognostic factors." They reported that potentially life-shortening drugs were given in 37% of 299 deaths; of these, the possibility that death would be hastened was taken into account in 52% of patients, hastening of death was partly intended in 22%, and hastening of death was explicitly intended in 26%.[19] All respondents who explicitly intended to hasten death stated that they also acted to alleviate pain or other symptoms.[18] Median doses of drugs and length of time by which life was shortened were higher when hastening death was explicitly intended.[19] The authors stated that whether drugs were administered with or without the intention of hastening death was not always clear.[19] Wilson et al.[3] showed that physicians ordered drugs to hasten death in 39% of cases but always with other reasons, such as relieving pain. A Dutch governmental multidisciplinary task force on end-of-life decisions also underlined that hastening death in patients may be difficult to distinguish from the palliative effects of drugs.[20] The issue is further complicated by the fact that medications given concomitantly with withdrawal of therapy may instead of shortening the time to death actually sometimes delay an inevitable death.[21,22]

The purpose of this article is to shed light on one of the most controversial areas in end-of-life practices: the lack of clear or easily determined distinctions between SDP or euthanasia and therapies intended to relieve pain and suffering administered when withdrawing life-sustaining therapies. Differentiation between the two is complicated and may be impossible because the physicians' true intentions are often difficult to ascertain. In an emotionally charged, life-and-death setting, such as the ICU, these intentions are likely to be multilayered, complex, and ambiguous.[12,23,24]

Figure 1 demonstrates the spectrum of actions between palliative care and euthanasia. Palliative care is given to relieve pain and suffering with doses of drugs that are usually inadequate to shorten a patient's life but may at times hasten death without the intent to do so. Euthanasia or SDP occurs when a doctor administers drugs in doses adequate to shorten a patient's life with the explicit intent to hasten death. Differentiation may be difficult as intentions are subjective and private and only self-reporting or an analysis of extreme actions will be determinant.[12] This study is one of the few that prospectively recorded the intensivists' intentions along with their practices. The most striking finding of the study was that although doses of opioids and benzodiazepines reportedly used to shorten the dying process with the intention to cause death were higher than those used for symptom relief in earlier studies,[2,3] mean doses

Figure 1

The Spectrum of Actions Between Palliative Care and Euthanasia

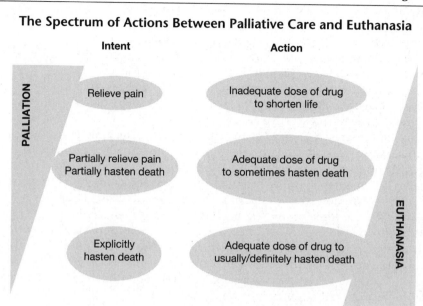

Intent

Action

PALLIATION

EUTHANASIA

Relieve pain

Inadequate dose of drug
to shorten life

Partially relieve pain
Partially hasten death

Adequate dose of drug
to sometimes hasten death

Explicitly
hasten death

Adequate dose of drug to
usually/definitely hasten death

in close to one third of patients were similar and ranges for all patients were analogous to those in earlier studies. Surprisingly, the time to death for SDP patients was not different than that for patients in whom withdrawal was performed. This is probably related to the fact that doses of drugs used for SDP were not sufficient to cause an immediate death. Some physicians who performed SDP may have thought of their actions as "the double effect" and not as euthanasia despite the definition. An important finding of this study was that larger doses used for SDP did, however, correlate with a quicker death. Previous smaller studies have not shown a correlation between higher doses of narcotics and/or benzodiazepines and shorter patient survival.[21,25] Although the practices of palliative care and SDP are very different, distinguishing the two may be extremely difficult.

The confusion in end-of-life decisions is also seen within the SDP patients. All doctors explicitly intended to hasten death in SDP patients. In a retrospective evaluation of these actions based on doses of medications given and the length of time until death, the actions were not so clear. Physicians believed that the doses they gave were definitely the cause of death in 77% of patients, probably the cause in 12%, and probably not the cause in 11%. It is recognized that absolute doses may not be indicative of euthanasia or SDP, because prior exposure, tolerance, and duration of medications are important. Inadequate doses of drugs might be related to a doctor's feelings of guilt or fear of prosecution and may explain the surprising finding that even when SDP was intended, patients took several hours to die, almost as long as cases of in therapy withdrawal. Another unexpected discovery was that extubated patients lived longer than nonextubated patients. These findings suggest that the gray area between relief measures and SDP extends in both directions: While in some cases physicians may be hastening the patient's death by providing what is classified as relief measures, in other cases physicians supposedly intending to cause death may in fact be providing drugs that are only capable of relieving pain and suffering. Therefore, the distinction between therapies intended to relieve pain and suffering and those intended to cause death may not be as clear as previously thought.

A major strength of the present study is that it provides empirical data for an ethical debate that often remains theoretical due to scarcity of facts. Other strong features include the prospective design, enrollment of a large number of consecutive patients from 37 ICUs in 17 countries, evaluation of all limitations and deaths in all admitted patients, and analysis of the intent and self-reporting of actions rather than theoretical responses to a questionnaire. Anonymity and contemporaneous documentation probably resulted in honest and more accurate reporting.

There are, however, limitations to the present study. Drug doses were not available for some of the SDP patients and for patients who had therapies withheld or withdrawn. There may have been a selection bias in the doses that were reported. In addition, participants by their special interest in ethical issues may not necessarily share the attitudes of unselected ICU physicians. Severity scores of the patients were not analyzed, and underreporting of practices for fear of legal ramifications cannot be excluded.

The present report provides evidence that some physicians may be giving much larger doses of medications than needed for relief of pain or suffering so that the patient can die with dignity, but these physicians do not call this practice euthanasia. Yet in fact, physicians administering these perfectly legal relief treatments may in fact consciously or unconsciously be practicing a disguised form of mercy killing. It is unclear how many physicians or nurses around the world, in providing relief measures to terminal patients, also intend to shorten the dying process.

This complex empirical picture of actual ICU practice, rather than an idealized list of distinct, neatly separated actions, should form the basis for an open discussion of end-of-life practices. We need to arrive at a level of transparency at which proper safeguards for end-of-life medical care[17,21] can be developed and maintained. Palliation with potentially life-shortening drugs may be given with no intent, partial intent, or explicit intent to hasten death. Markedly increasing doses of these drugs may be considered homicide by some and an appropriate form of terminal care by others. Physicians should administer drugs in sufficient amounts to relieve pain and suffering because the importance of palliative care cannot be overemphasized, but the drugs should not be intended to directly cause death.[12] Physicians must recognize that appropriate palliative care may lead to a patient's death although unintended. One important safeguard should be proper documentation of the use of potentially life-shortening measures, including keeping records on the timing and doses of the drug and the physician's intention at each step.

Such documentation can help protect the physician wrongly accused of deliberately ending a patient's life. No less important, it may reduce the use of inappropriately large doses of medications to shorten the dying process given in the guise of relieving pain and suffering.

References

1. Prendergast TJ, Claessens MT, Luce JM: A national survey of end-of-life care for critically ill patients. *Am J Respir Crit Care Med* 1998; 158:1163–1167.

2. Keenan SP, Busche KD, Chen LM, et al: A retrospective review of a large cohort of patients undergoing the process of withholding or withdrawal of life support. *Crit Care Med* 1997; 25:1324–1331.

3. Wilson WC, Smedira NG, Fink C, et al: Ordering and administration of sedatives and analgesics during the withholding and withdrawal of life support from critically ill patients. *JAMA* 1992; 267:949–953.

4. Sprung CL, Cohen SL, Sjokvist P, et al: End-of-life practices in European intensive care units. The Ethicus Study. *JAMA* 2003; 290: 790–797.

5. Prendergast TJ, Luce JM: Increasing incidence of withholding and withdrawal of life support from the critically ill. *Am J Respir Crit Care Med* 1997; 155:15–20.

6. Wilson D: A report of an investigation of end-of-life care practices in health care facilities and the influences on those practices. *J Palliat Care* 1997; 13:34–40.

7. Wilson D: Addressing myths about end-of-life care: Research into the use of acute care hospitals over the last five years of life. *J Palliat Care* 2002; 18:29–38.

8. Sprung CL, Eidelman LA, Pizov R: Changes in forgoing life-sustaining treatments in the United States: Concern for the future. *Mayo Clin Proc* 1996; 71:512–516.

9. Van der Maas BJ, Van der Wal, Haver Kate I, et al: Euthanasia, physician-assisted suicide and other medical practices involving end of life in the Netherlands, 1990–1995. *N Engl J Med* 1996; 335:1699–1705.

10. Delliens L, Mortier F, Bilsen J, et al: End-of-life decisions in medical practice in Flanders, Belgium: A nationwide survey. *Lancet* 2000; 356:1806–1811.

11. Burkhardt S, La Harpe R, Harding TW, et al: Euthanasia and assisted suicide: Comparison of legal aspects in Switzerland and other countries. *Med Sci Law* 2006; 46:287–294.

12. Truog RD, Cist AFM, Brackett SE, et al: Recommendations for end of life care in the intensive care unit: The Ethics Committee of the Society of Critical Care Medicine. *Crit Care Med* 2001; 29:2332–2348.

13. Vincent JL: Forgoing life support in western European intensive care units: The results of an ethical questionnaire. *Crit Care Med* 1999; 27:1626–1633.

14. Asch DA: The role of critical care nurses in euthanasia and assisted suicide. *N Engl J Med* 1996; 334:1374–1379.

15. Steinberg A, Sprung CL: The dying patient: New Israeli legislation. *Intensive Care Med* 2006; 32:1234–1237.

16. The Society of Critical Care Medicine Ethics Committee. Attitudes of critical care medicine professionals concerning forgoing life-sustaining treatments. *Crit Care Med* 1992; 20:320–326.

17. Eidelman LA, Jakobson DJ, Pizov R, et al: Forgoing life-sustaining treatment in an Israeli ICU. *Intensive Care Med* 1998; 24: 162–166.

18. Emanuel EJ, Daniels ER, Fairclough D, et al: The practice of euthanasia and physician-assisted suicide in the United States. Adherence to proposed safeguards and effects on physicians. *JAMA* 1998; 280:507–513.

19. Van der Heide A, van der Maas P, van der Wal G, et al: Using potentially life-shortening drugs in neonates and infants. *Crit Care Med* 2000; 28:2595–2599.

20. Overleggoep Toetsing Zorgvuldig Medische Handelen Rond het Levenseinde bij Pasgeborenen: Toetsing als Spiegel van de Medische Praktijk. Ministerie van Volksgezondheid, Welzijn en Sport, 1997.

21. Chan JD, Treece PD, Engleberg RA, et al: Narcotic and benzodiazepine use after withdrawal of life support. *Chest* 2004; 126: 286–293.

22. Edwards MJ: Opioids and benzodiazepines appear paradoxically to delay inevitable death after ventilator withdrawal. *J Palliat Care* 2005; 21:299–302.

23. Quill TE: The ambiguity of clinical intentions. *N Engl J Med* 1993; 329:1039–1040.

24. Quill TE, Lo B, Brock DW: Palliative options of last resort. *JAMA* 1997; 278:2090–2104.

25. Campbell ML, Bizek KS, Thill M: Patient responses during rapid terminal weaning from mechanical ventilation: A prospective study. *Crit Care Med* 1999; 27:73–77.

EXPLORING THE ISSUE

Should Pain Be Alleviated if It Hastens Death?

Critical Thinking and Reflection

1. Consider the issue of palliative sedation for a child who is having unbearable pain from cancer. In what way would the arguments for or against palliative sedation be different if the dying patient is a child?
2. Consider the case of Miss A. F., a 36-year-old dying of cardiomyopathy (a weakened heart) from years of cocaine and drug use. Her condition causes her to have terrible pains in her feet and legs, and she is very short of breath, restless, and delirious. Should doctors and nurses treat pain differently at the end of life when the patient is a drug addict? Discuss your concerns about the use of pain meds in this case.
3. Physicians are often reluctant to order pain medications in high doses, even though patients report pain has not been relieved. Is the treatment of pain at the end of life any different than treating pain at any other time of life? Why or why not?
4. A family is providing care for their dying mother in hospice. Even though the patient is crying out with pain, the daughter says that she is afraid to give more pain medicine because she does not want to be the one who "kills" her mother. Is this an accurate statement? Why or why not?
5. If you were in a fire and sustained such severe burns that the doctors did not think you would survive, would you prefer palliative sedation? Discuss the challenge that this presents to your family, friends, or classmates.

Is There Common Ground?

Patients who are suffering at the end of life may require palliative sedation to control the intense discomfort of dying. The use of palliative sedation may vary based on patient symptoms, but it has become a standard of care for patients in intractable pain. The ethical concerns are raised when a patient requires sedation along with pain medication in high doses to control suffering. In these cases, the treatment of suffering may hasten the patient's death. If palliative sedation can be misused, or offered with the wrong intent, then it would be indistinguishable from euthanasia, which is illegal. Health professionals are wise to consider oversight and standards for these practices to monitor clinicians who violate the ethical standard.

Health professionals are challenged by the suffering of the dying patients under their care. It is difficult to see a patient suffering despite attempts for relief of pain. The rule of double effect addresses this ethical concern. When the physician prescriber or the nurse who administers the life-shortening analgesics understands the goal of that treatment is to relieve the patient's suffering, not to shorten the patient's life.

References

Azoulay, D., Jacobs, J., Cialic, R., Mor, E., & Stessman, J. (2011). Opioids, survival, and advanced cancer in the hospice setting. *Journal of the American Medical Directors Association, 12*(2), 129–134. doi:10.1016/j.jamda.2010.07.012

Bass, M. (2010). Anatomy and physiology of pain and the management of breakthrough pain in palliative care. *International Journal of Palliative Nursing, 16*(10), 486–492.

Beckstrand, R. L., Smith, M. D., Heaston, S., & Bond, A. E. (2008). Emergency nurses' perceptions of size, frequency and magnitude of obstacles and supportive behaviors in end-of-life care. *Journal of Emergency Nursing, 34*(4), 290–300.

Billings, J. (2011). Double effect: A useful rule that alone cannot justify hastening death. *Journal of Medical Ethics, 37*(7), 437–440. doi:10.1136/jme.2010.041160

Boyle, J. (2004) Medical ethics and the double effect: The case of terminal sedation. *Theoretical Medicine, 25*, 51–60.

Fineberg, I. C., Wenger, N. S., & Brown-Saltzman, K. (2006). Unrestricted opiate administration for pain and suffering at the end of life: Knowledge and attitudes as barriers to care. *Journal of Palliative Medicine, 9*(4), 873–879. doi:10.1089/jpm.2006.9.873

Lo, B. & Rubenfeld, G. (2005). Palliative sedation in dying patients: "We turn to it when everything else hasn't worked." *Journal of the American Medical Association, 294*(14), 1810–1816.

Mularski, R. A., Puntillo, K., Varkey, B., Erstad, B. L., Grap, M., Gilbert, H. C., et al. (2009). Pain management within the palliative and end-of-life care experience in the ICU. *CHEST, 135*(5), 1360–1369. doi:10.1378/chest.08-2328

Olsen, M. L., Swetz, K. M., & Mueller, P. S. (2010). Ethical decision making with end-of-life care: Palliative sedation and withholding or withdrawing life-sustaining treatments. *Mayo Clinic Proceedings, 85*(10), 949–954.

Smith, A. K., Cenzer, I., Knight, S. J., Puntillo, K. A., Widera, E., Williams, B. A., et al. (2010). The epidemiology of pain during the last 2 years of life. *Annals of Internal Medicine, 153*(9), 563–569.

Sprung, C. L., Ledoux, D., Bulow, H., Lippert, A. Wennberg, E., Baras, M., et al. (2008). Relieving suffering or intentionally hastening death: Where do you draw the line? *Critical Care Medicine, 36*(1), 8–13.

SUPPORT Principal Investigators. (1995). A controlled trial to improve care for seriously ill hospitalized patients. The Study to Understand Prognoses and Preferences for Outcomes and Risks of Treatments (SUPPORT). *Journal of the American Medical Association, 274*(20), 1591–1598.

Additional Resources

Baron, M. G., Raposo, C. G., & Marin, A. P. (2005). Sedation in clinical oncology. *Clinical Translational Oncology, 7*(7), 295–301.

Caprio, A. J., Hanson, L. C., Munn, J. C., Williams, C. S., Dobbs, D., Sloane, P. D., et al. (2008). Pain, dyspnea, and the quality of dying in long-term care. *Journal of the American Geriatrics Society, 56*(4), 683–688. doi:10.1111/j.1532-5415.2007.01613.x

Cellarius, V. (2011). "Early terminal sedation" is a distinct entity. *Bioethics, 25*(1), 46–54. doi:10.1111/j.1467-8519.2009.01747.x

Federico, A. (2009). Assessing pain in patients with dementia. *Nursing, 39*(12), 64.

Hanson, L. C., Eckert, J., Dobbs, D., Williams, C. S., Caprio, A. J., Sloane, P. D., et al. (2008). Symptom experience of dying long-term care residents. *Journal of the American Geriatrics Society, 56*(1), 91–98. doi:10.1111/j.1532-5415.2007.01388.x

LeGrand, S. & Walsh, D. (2010). Comfort measures: Practical care of the dying cancer patient. *American Journal of Hospice & Palliative Medicine, 27*(7), 488–493. doi:10.1177/1049909110380200

Levy, M. H. & Cohen, S. D. (2005). Sedation for the relief of refractory symptoms in the imminently dying: A fine intentional line. *Seminars in Oncology, 32*(2), 237–246.

Manninen, B. A. (2006). A case for justified non-voluntary active euthanasia: Exploring the ethics of the Groningen Protocol. *Journal of Medical Ethics, 32*(11), 643–651. doi:10.1136/jme.2005.014845

Munn, J. C., Hanson, L. C., Zimmerman, S., Sloane, P., & Mitchell, M. (2006). Is hospice associated with improved end-of-life care in nursing homes and assisted living facilities? *Journal of the American Geriatrics Society, 54*(3), 490–495.

Rifkinson-Mann, S. (2003). Legal consequences and ethical dilemmas of pain perception in persistent vegetative states. *Journal of Health Law, 36*(4), 523–548.

Tu, M. S. & Chiou, C. P. (2007). Perceptual consistency of pain and quality of life between hospice cancer patients and family caregivers: A pilot study. *International Journal of Clinical Practice, 61*(10), 1686–1691. doi:10.1111/j.1742-1241.2007.01347.x

Wentz, J. (2003). Assessing pain at the end of life. *Nursing, 33*(8), 22.

Yabroff, K., Mandelblatt, J., & Ingham, J. (2004). The quality of medical care at the end-of-life in the USA: Existing barriers and examples of process and outcome measures. *Palliative Medicine, 18*(3), 202–216. doi:10.1191/0269216304pm880oa

Younger, J., McCue, R., & Mackey, S. (2009). Pain outcomes: A brief review of instruments and techniques. *Current Pain and Headaches Report, 13*(1), 39–43.

ISSUE 7

Does Too Much Treatment Result in an Inhumane Dying?

YES: **Shannon Brownlee**, from "Afterward," In *Overtreated: Way Too Much Medicine Is Making Us Sicker and Poorer* (New York, NY: Bloomsbury, pp. 305–312, 2008)

NO: **Amanda Bennett and Charles Babcock**, from "Lessons of a $618,616 Death," *BusinessWeek* (no. 4170, 2010)

Learning Outcomes

After reading this issue, you should be able to:

- Gain an understanding of the meaning of unnecessary therapies or overtreatment.
- Discuss how overtreatment can dehumanize, depersonalize, individualize, and consumerize dying and death.
- Distinguish overtreatment caused by increased access to technological advances from inappropriate treatments that misapply specific therapies.
- Understand how both health professionals and families of dying patients contribute to the problem overtreatment at the end of life.

ISSUE SUMMARY

YES: In the Afterword of her book, medical journalist Shannon Brownlee offers a poignant story of an elderly man with an implanted small battery-powered electrical impulse generator to correct an irregular heartbeat (called an implanted cardiac defibrillator or ICD). She raises serious concerns about whether we can sustain a "do everything" approach in health care, and what this means for end of life care.

NO: Amanda Bennett, an executive editor with Bloomberg News, and Charles Babcock, editor-at-large for *InformationWeek*, write about Mrs. Bennett's experience of the last years of her husband's life. She balances the discussion of the costs of his care with the value of his last years of life, the important family events and experiences that made it worth it to go through expensive treatments.

[The task of medicine] is to do away with sufferings of the sick, to lessen the sufferings of their disease, and to refuse to treat those who are overmastered by their diseases, realizing that in such cases medicine is powerless. (Hippocrates, 1995)

Death is inevitable; dying badly is not. (Jennings, Kaebnick, & Murray, 2005, p. S57)

One of the challenges of dying in the United States is knowing when to stop treatment and allow nature to take its course. Although most patients say that they would like to have a peaceful death at home, dying most often occurs in hospitals. Technological innovations for acute interventions have unquestioned life-saving benefits. There has been a gradual introduction of increasingly more technical treatments over the past century. Given media reports of incredible life-saving stories, the availability of microsurgeries and implantable technologies, it is not surprising that 40 percent of Americans believe that medical technology can *always* save their lives (Callahan, 2008). In this issue, we will explore overtreatment and its impact on end of life care.

Dying persons may receive too much treatment when health care professionals continue (or family members demand) aggressive therapies even though these therapies are unlikely to change the final outcome. Overtreatment can tie up scarce medical resources such as ICU beds (Crippen et al., 2010). In one study, emergency room nurses identified that unrelieved pain was a significant problem for end of life care because families had unrealistic expectations of life saving and continued painful treatments instead of allowing adequate analgesia and comfort treatments for patients (Beckstrand, Smith, Heaston, & Bond, 2008). On a broader scale, overtreatment drives up health care costs by using funds from insurance that might be otherwise used for health care in prevention and screening areas (Brownlee, 2008; Callahan, 2008).

The initiation or demand for inappropriate treatment can come from health care providers or from family members. Providers and hospitals receive more financial reimbursement from expensive tests and procedures, and thus have a financial interest in trying more treatments (Barnato et al., 2007; Wilkinson & Savulescu, 2011). Fragmented health care means that specialist physicians who only address one area of physiology (kidney function or respiratory function) may ignore the need for end-of-life discussions or a more team based approach to directly address the issue of dying. Families may not understand the information they are being given (have low health literacy) or may be in conflict about goals of care for their loved one. Some families believe that by waiting longer, a miracle will occur, and are completely unrealistic about the likelihood of survival (Bradley & Brasel, 2009; DeLisser, 2009).

One in five of all Americans who die use intensive care services (Curtis & Vincent, 2010). Although elders make up only 14 percent of our population, most ICU patients are over age 65. Almost half of the patients who die in hospitals have received intensive care at some time during their hospital stay. The aggressive treatment of very old patients with many more chronic diseases is the greatest contributor to ICU mortality in the United States (Niederman & Berger, 2010). Patients who die in intensive care, usually die as a direct result of decisions to cut back on aggressive approaches or stop life-sustaining treatment (Bernat, 2005).

If physicians and hospitals can provide the world's most advanced treatment, why is the experience of dying so poorly addressed (Barnato et al., 2007; Teno et al., 2005)? Part of the reason is that physicians are uncomfortable with prognoses (predicting the outcome of the disease). They offer treatments to families without a clear, honest direct communication that the treatment being offered is not a cure, but rather simply an approach to sustain life as it is. For some patients, overtreatment is a result of poorly understood language as physicians discuss treatments that are not curative (designed to cure a disease), but rather are palliative (designed to treat symptoms and provide comfort). Cancer patients who overestimate their ability to survive or "beat" the cancer are more likely to die a death in an intensive care unit, on a ventilator, or with multiple hospitalizations and emergency room visits (Smith et al., 2011).

Consider an eighty-three year old retired school principal with stage 4 lymphoma (a cancer of the immune system) and no advance directives (see Issue 3). He suffers severe respiratory distress, is admitted to an ICU, and is placed on a ventilator. His diagnosis was terminal with a prognosis of only weeks prior to the hospitalization. But because this was not clearly discussed, the patient had continued his treatments without knowledge that he was eligible for hospice. His ICU care will make no difference in his outcome; it is clearly overtreatment. His ICU stay adds $24,500 to his end-of-life care (much of this paid by Medicare) and adds considerable emotional distress to the family as they face the guilt of withdrawal of treatments. Hospital-based treatments at the end of life can also create problems. Patients are exposed to *iatrogenic events* in the hospital: unexpected drug interactions, avoidable medical errors, and side effects of treatment, which make the experience of end of life care much worse.

Compare this with a similar patient for whom the physician clearly identifies the poor prognosis of stage 4 lymphoma and recommends a hospice referral. The patient receives visits to her home by a hospice nurse and social worker and support for her family, costing less financially and emotionally and the patient dies quietly in her own home. Overtreatment of end-stage diseases can be considered *futile treatments*, when they provide no benefit, are medically ineffective, or are disproportionately burdensome at the end-of-life (President's Council, 2008, p. 91) (Issue 16).

Sometimes patients have experience with previous serious illness that they were able to treat and resolve. They bring this previous experience with an overly optimistic sense of how they will do with their current disease. However, the 45-year-old who survived cancer is far less likely to survive a completely different stage 4 cancer at the age of 80. Patients seeking hope for a cure often create *overutilization* of health services, that is, more visits, higher use of costly specialists, more hospitalizations, tests, procedures, and prescriptions than are otherwise appropriate for that disease (Emanuel & Fuchs, 2008).

Not all dying persons want ICU care. Many older adults prefer treatment focused on palliation rather than life-extension. But this can be quite different if the dying patient is only 13 or 30-years-old. Physicians and patients have difficulty acknowledging dying in young patients and miss the opportunity to refocus to a comfort approach. There are regional variations in end of life spending which are correlated with the number of specialists, hospital beds, and ICUs in that region (Barnato et al., 2007). Essentially, the places with the highest numbers of ICU beds have the highest numbers of ICU deaths, an indicator of inappropriate treatment of dying patients in the ICU (Wunsch et al., 2008). In regions with high ICU use, family members rate care as worse, not better. In one study, family members rate care for symptom control (pain, shortness of breath, and emotional needs) as worse in areas of the country that had high ICU use. They also had greater concerns about getting information from providers and rated respect for the patient as lower in those regions with high ICU use (Teno et al., 2005).

Overtreatment at the end of life is inhumane for several reasons. Overtreatment *dehumanizes* dying persons by disconnecting them from care-giving communities. Technologies medicalize natural dying. Overtreatment *depersonalizes* care by treating the patient as only a body and not addressing the emotional and spiritual needs that would otherwise be addressed in hospice. Viewing death as a medical failure rather than the normal part of the end of life discourages collaboration with caregivers and family members (Beckstrand, Moore, Callister, & Bond, 2009; Foucault, 1963; Risse, 1999; Sulmasy, 2006). Some claim overtreatment *consumerizes* dying patients by making dying patients the "clients," for whom dying processes are "coverable benefits." The pre-death technology, testing, and treatment are "billable events," but may be completely unnecessary for conquering the disease or changing the course of events (Callahan, 2008; Kaufman, 2006, 2009).

Others claim overtreatment *individualizes* dying by making decisions rationalistic. The focus on autonomy, doing what the patient chooses, means that patients (or family proxies) can demand or elect treatments that ignore logic, realistic outcomes, or resource limits (Barnato et al., 2007, p. 386; Randall & Downie, 2009). Family members may not have a clear picture of what care would be like if they do not use aggressive care approaches (Quill, Arnold, & Back, 2009). Occasionally, state courts are called in to address unrealistic family requests for futile treatments, and dying is prolonged while awaiting court decisions. Infant Emilio Lee Gonzales had a neurometabolic disorder and spent five months on a mechanical respirator awaiting the final court rulings (Texas, 2002; Truog, 2007).

In the NO article, Amanda Bennett relays the story of her husband's cancer treatment and argues that the treatments provided extra years of life that were priceless to her and her children. In the YES article, Shannon Brownlee raises questions about cost and quality of care at the end of life. She provides an experience of Dr. Peter Kibbe, who observed the end-of-life care for an elderly patient with severe dementia. The patient's implanted cardiac defibrillator frequently discharged, shocking the patient and causing severe pain and anxiety. The family insistence on heroic measures led to overtreatment that caused more pain and suffering at the end of life.

YES

Shannon Brownlee

Overtreated: Way Too Much Medicine Is Making Us Sicker and Poorer

Afterword: Sharing Decisions

Since *Overtreated* was first published, I've heard from hundreds of patients and their families, as well as from physicians, politicians, and policy makers. Many had personal anecdotes that echoed the themes I've laid out in this book: tales of the waste, mistreatment, and confusion that typify our fragmented health care system. One story in particular stood out to me, though—a story about those vulnerable last few months of life, when care rather than cure should be uppermost in the minds of our families and physicians. It attests to the size of the chasm that lies between the kind of care we hope for and the high-tech, often useless treatment we are likely to receive.

This story was related to me by Dr. Peter Kibbe, a physician who was working as a hospitalist in a medium-sized southern town. Kibbe's patient was a frail, elderly man who was suffering from heart failure, kidney failure, and complications from diabetes. The man had recently undergone surgery to have a battery-powered implantable cardiac defibrillator, or ICD, placed in his chest. The ICD is one of the wonders of modern medical technology. About the size of a very small cell phone, it is used in patients who are suffering from heart failure or other cardiac conditions that can cause the heart to fibrillate, or beat erratically. The ICD shocks the heart back into a proper rhythm, much like the external defibrillator paddles we recognize from television.

ICDs have been shown to be effective in preventing death from sudden cardiac arrest, and they can add as much as two to three years of life to a patient who would probably otherwise die from an advanced cardiac condition. On average, however, ICDs offer only a few months to the life of patients with advanced cardiac disease. Of course, there are drawbacks to the devices: They are hugely expensive, about $90,000 per year, and they deliver a powerful, often extremely unpleasant jolt whenever the device has to shock the heart. According to Kibbe, "It's like being kicked in the chest."

Here's the sad part of this story. Kibbe's patient was not only suffering from multiple organ failure, he was also severely demented—so demented, in fact, that he had no recollection of the surgery or that there was even a device implanted in his body. In light of the man's rapidly declining condition and his dementia, Kibbe said, "I was attempting to persuade the family to take a realistic attitude and choose a palliative course of care. They declined, intoxicated by the denial that the medical profession seems so willing to enable and encourage." One day, while Kibbe was on rounds, he stopped to sit with his patient when the man's device began to go off. "He was totally unaware of its presence or meaning," Kibbe told me. "He was stunned and screamed in pain from the discharge, and then accused me of doing this to him. He became frantic with pain and anxiety when it repeatedly discharged, clutched his chest and screamed at me to stop." A day or two later the man's heart finally failed completely and he died, but only after heroic efforts were made to revive him in accordance with the family's wishes.

This story, I think, embodies many of the most difficult and emotionally charged questions we must ask ourselves as patients, family members, physicians, and as a society. How can we best care for patients who are in the final stages of life? How do we stop thinking that failing to "do everything possible" for elderly, dying loved ones is tantamount to killing them? How can we as patients ensure that we get the care that we need and is likely to benefit us, and don't get care that endangers us or deprives us of the comfort and solace that we want? The answers to these questions are crucial not just at the end of life, but whenever we face serious illness and the possibility of being treated or hospitalized.

While deeply personal, these matters are also of urgent public concern, since we pay for health care collectively through taxes and our health insurance premiums. The number of Americans who lack health insurance is increasing each day, as more and more employers find themselves strapped by a looming recession and unable to pay the ever-rising cost of health insurance. The Democratic presidential primary debates continue to focus almost entirely on covering the uninsured, with scant mention of the problems of quality and cost. The plans put forward by Hillary Clinton and Barack Obama are virtually identical except that the Clinton plan calls for an individual mandate, which would require all Americans to carry health insurance, while the Obama plan does not. Absent from their discussion are the Congressional Budget Office's most recent projections that show that health care will consume 50 percent of the nation's gross domestic product by 2052. That's simply not a sustainable economy.

John McCain has been discussing the cost of health care, but his solutions revolve around deregulating insurance markets, a remedy that will do little to reduce unnecessary care. The McCain strategists are basing their remedies on the belief that the waste in our system results from a fragmented insurance market and from patients being insulated from the cost of the care they demand. Deregulating the insurance industry, along with giving patients a greater financial stake in their care and more information about their insurance companies, will push doctors and hospitals to do a better job—goes the thinking. There's a kernel of truth in the McCain analysis; patients and their families often demand care that offers little value, as the family of the man with the ICD did. But it is the supply of state-of-the-art medical resources, far more than uninformed patient demand, that drives up the use of expensive, unnecessary treatments.

With so little honest and clear discussion of the problems, perhaps it should come as no surprise that most Americans have an unrealistic opinion of our health care system. A recent poll conducted by Harvard and Harris Interactive found that nearly half of Americans still believe that we have the best health care in the world, with 68 percent of Republicans and 32 percent of Democrats polled saying it was the best. As I've described elsewhere in this book, this belief is simply not supported by the facts. We don't have the best health care in the world by a long shot—just the most expensive. Fixing our system requires remedying the factors that contribute to the extraordinary volume of unnecessary care.

Until then, there are things you can do as a family member or a patient to make sure you get the best care possible. If you are basically healthy and middle-aged or older, you will have to make choices about which screening tests you want and which drugs you are willing to take in order to prevent conditions you don't yet have. If you are seriously ill or suffering from a chronic condition like diabetes or heart disease, you have a host of decisions to make about tests, drugs, procedures, and surgeries. If you are in the hospital, you face all of these decisions and added dangers, such as potentially life-threatening infection, surgical error, and side effects from medications. Here are some suggestions for navigating these tricky waters:

Find a primary care doctor who communicates. Having a primary care doctor who knows you and who is willing to discuss your care in a way that you can understand is the single most important step you can take. A good doctor will listen carefully to you and will make sure you have all the information you need to make good decisions about your health. Once you find the right doctor, stick with him or her if you can, even if your employer changes insurance companies. Having a primary care doctor who watches over your care has been shown to lead to better outcomes than if you simply take yourself to multiple specialists.

Ask questions. Think of all doctors as guides, not gods, and ask questions whenever a physician prescribes a test, drug, or treatment. Many screening tests have not yet been shown to reduce your chances of dying from the condition for which they are screening. If your doctor recommends a screening test—such as the prostate-specific antigen test, which looks for possible signs of prostate cancer, or the calcium screening test, which looks for buildup in the coronary arteries—there are five questions you need to ask:

1. How good is the evidence that this screening test will reduce my risk of dying?
2. Is the test itself dangerous?
3. Could the test lead to my being treated unnecessarily?
4. Does the treatment I might face have side effects?
5. Can I make changes in my eating habits and lifestyle to reduce the risk of getting the disease?

Your doctor may not welcome such questions, or may feel that there isn't enough time in your appointment to answer them. Don't be deterred. Ask for another appointment that allows more time. If your doctor is dismissive, then maybe you need to find another doctor.

If your doctor prescribes a laboratory test, drug, procedure, or surgery, you should ask the following questions:

1. If it's a test, what does the doctor expect to learn from it? If it's a procedure, drug, or surgery, why do I need it? Drugs and procedures can relieve pain, reduce symptoms, and sometimes even cure a condition. Ask your doctor how the proposed drug or procedure is supposed to help you.
2. What is the drug or procedure? If you are facing surgery, ask your doctor to explain exactly how the surgery will be done. Ask if there is more than one way to do it. Some orthopedists use open surgery to replace a hip, while others may use "minimally invasive" laparoscopic techniques. Ask why your surgeon prefers one method over another. There may be multiple drugs for treating the same condition. Ask your doctor why he or she is prescribing one and not another.
3. What are the benefits of the drug or procedure? You need to know what you will gain. A hip replacement, for example, may allow you to walk again with greater ease, but it won't cure your arthritis.
4. How good is the evidence that I will benefit? Have there been clinical trials that show the treatment is better than other possible treatments or at least better than doing nothing? The Institute of Medicine estimates that only half of what doctors do is backed up by valid science. You need to know if the treatment your doctor is recommending is a proven therapy. If not, your doctor should explain to you why he or she thinks it's a good idea.
5. What are the potential risks? Every drug and every procedure has side effects, some more serious than others, and all major surgeries pose real and potentially significant harm. Simply being in the hospital exposes you to medical error or a hospital-acquired infection. You need to know the risks so you can decide if the danger or discomfort of your disease or condition seem more serious to you than the risks of the proposed treatment.
6. Is there an alternative to the drug or procedure? If you have high blood pressure, you may be able to bring it down with diet and exercise alone and avoid the side effects of blood pressure medicine. Before undergoing surgery for, say, shoulder pain, find out if most cases like yours resolve on their own, and how long it takes for the pain to go away.
7. What will happen if I don't take the drug or undergo the procedure or surgery? Your doctor may tell you your condition will worsen, or that it could get better on its own. You should be the one to decide if you prefer to wait and see what happens.
8. How much will it cost? Even if you have health insurance, you may have to pay out-of-pocket for part or even all of the treatment.

You can find more information about medical treatments on several authoritative Web sites, including one of the best online resources, the

Agency for Healthcare Research and Quality (www.ahrq.gov). Go to the "Consumer Health" section for information about a wide range of conditions and treatments. Also located on the AHRQ Web site is another excellent source of Information, the U.S. Preventive Services Task Force. The USPSTF consists of experts who convene on a regular basis to assess the scientific evidence available for many medical treatments and tests. While it is often more conservative than many physicians, the USPSTF and its Web site can help you weigh your options.

Ask for patient decision aids. Many medical decisions depend on your personal preferences and your values. If you have early stage breast cancer, for example, you will need to choose between a mastectomy, the removal of your breast, and a lumpectomy, the surgical removal of the tumor plus radiation. The two treatments are the same in terms of your chances of being cured of your cancer, but different women will prefer one over the other. To help you make this and many other medical decisions, you may need a patient decision aid, which may be a video you can take home or watch on the Web, written material, or a short film you watch in your doctor's office.

Decision aids now exist for a wide variety of treatments and tests, including: the PSA test for prostate cancer and other cancer screening tests, breast cancer treatment alternatives, treatment options for enlarged prostate, back surgery for low back pain, and others. A handful of hospitals around the country now offer patient decision aids, along with some physicians and insurers. If your doctor does not have an aid for you, ask your employer or your insurer.

Find yourself a palliative care doctor if you or a loved one is facing major surgery. Palliative care is a relatively new speciality in which physicians are highly trained in the control of pain. They can also coordinate your various physicians, a crucial step whenever you are hospitalized or about to undergo any major procedure for a life-threatening condition like cancer or end-stage heart failure. Why is coordination between doctors important? When several doctors are involved in your care, they are more likely to lose sight of necessary treatments and procedures, like making sure you get antibiotics within a few hours of being admitted to the hospital for pneumonia. Multiple doctors also mean multiple opportunities for error, duplication of tests, poor communication, and failure to make sure the patient receives the kind of care he or she wants. Most doctors do not call in a palliative care physician until the patient is already in dire straits. You can help yourself by asking for palliative care early.

Coordinate your own care. Talk to your primary care doctor about making sure he or she sees copies of your medical records from all of your various doctors. Somebody besides you needs to know what all of your doctors are doing—including all procedures, tests, and drugs they prescribe. This is especially important if you are on multiple drugs or have a chronic condition, like diabetes or an autoimmune disorder, that requires visits to multiple specialists.

If you take multiple medications or see more than one or two doctors who aren't sharing information about your health electronically, try to keep your own health records. There are Web-based records available to help you track your drugs, doctor visits, and the results of every test and every treatment, including www.revolutionhealth.com and www.mymedicalrecords.com. Keep hard copies of your records and take them with you on every visit to a doctor or the hospital. At the very least, you should keep all of your prescription and over-the-counter medications in one bag, along with any dietary supplements you are taking, and bring them with you when you visit your primary care physician.

If you have a chronic condition, help yourself stay out of the hospital. Find out from your doctor what leads to hospitalization among patients with your condition. Ask what you can do as a patient to avoid a crisis that might send you to the emergency room. For patients with heart failure, for example, you may want to find a nurse-coach who can help you learn to monitor your weight, which can indicate when you are retaining fluid and likely to wind up in the hospital. Some doctors and health plans employ nurses and nutritionists who can help you take care of yourself. Some health plans offer free advice over the phone.

Just imagine what would be possible if we could cut out the unnecessary care in our system. Eliminating unnecessary tests, hospitalizations, surgeries, and office visits would slash our national medical bill by a third. That would leave plenty of money to provide health insurance to every American. And, most important, it would improve the quality of our health. When the election is over, our politicians will eventually have to start discussing the rising cost of medicine, and if they are honest with us, they will address the problem of unnecessary care.

**Amanda Bennett and
Charles Babcock**

 **NO**

Lessons of a $618,616 Death

... **I**t was sometime after midnight on Dec. 8, 2007, when Dr. Eric Goren told me my husband might not live till morning. The kidney cancer that had metastasized almost six years earlier was growing in his lungs. He was in intensive care . . . and had begun to spit blood.

Terence Bryan Foley, 67 years old, my husband of 20 years, father of our two teenagers, a Chinese historian who earned his PhD in his sixties, a man who played more than 15 musical instruments and spoke six languages, a San Francisco cable car conductor and sports photographer, an expert on dairy cattle and swine nutrition, film noir, and Dixieland jazz, was confused. He knew his name, but not the year. He wanted a Coke.

Should Terence begin to hemorrhage, the doctor asked, what should he do?

This was our third end-of-life warning in seven years. We had fought off the others, so perhaps we could dodge this one, too. Terence's oncologist and I both believed that a new medicine he had just begun taking [Pfizer's kidney cancer drug] Sutent, would buy him more life.

Keep him alive if you can, I said.

Terence died six days later, on Friday, Dec. 14.

What I couldn't know then was that the thinking behind my request—along with hundreds of decisions we made over the years—was a window on the impossible calculus at the core of today's health-care dilemma. Terence and I were eager to beat his cancer. Backed by robust medical insurance provided by a succession of my corporate employers, we were able to wage a fierce battle. As we made our way through a series of expensive last chances, like the one I asked for that night, we didn't have to think about money, allocation of medical resources, the struggles of roughly 46 million uninsured Americans, or the impact on corporate bottom lines.

Terence's treatment was expensive. The bills for his seven years of medical care totaled $618,616, almost two-thirds of which was for his final 24 months. Still, no one can say for sure if the treatments helped extend his life.

Over the final four days before hospice—two in intensive care, two in a cancer ward—our insurance was billed $43,711 for doctors, medicines, monitors, X-rays, and scans. Two years later the only thing I can see that the money bought for certain was confirmation he was dying. Along with a colleague, Charles Babcock, I spent months poring over almost 5,000 pages of documents collected from six hospitals, four insurers, Medicare, three oncologists, and a surgeon. Those papers tell the story of a system filled with people doing their best. Stepping back and looking at that large stack through a different lens, a string of complex questions emerges.

31% for Paperwork

Health-care costs represent 17% of today's U.S. gross domestic product. Medicare devotes about a quarter of its budget to care in the last year of life, according to the policy journal *Health Affairs*. Yet as I fought to buy my husband more time, it didn't matter to me that the hospital charged more than 12 times what Medicare then reimbursed for a chest scan. It also didn't matter that UnitedHealthcare reimbursed the hospital for 80% of the $3,232 price of a scan, while a few months later our new insurer, Empire BlueCross & BlueShield, paid 24% for the same test. And I didn't have time to be thankful that the insurers negotiated the rates with the hospital so neither my employers nor I actually paid the difference between the sticker and discounted prices.

Looking at that stack of documents, it is easy to see why 31% of the money spent on health care went to paperwork and administration, according to research published in 2003 in the *New England Journal of Medicine*. . . . Often Terence's bills, with their blizzard of codes, took days to decipher.

The documents revealed an economic system in which the sellers don't set the prices and the buyers don't know what they are. Prices bear little relation to demand or how well goods and services work. "No other nation would allow a health system to be run the way we do it. It's completely insane," said Uwe E. Reinhardt, a political economy professor at Princeton University who has advised Congress, the Veteran's Administration, and other federal agencies on health-care economics.

In reviewing Terence's records, we found Presbyterian Medical Center in Philadelphia charged UnitedHealthcare $8,120 in 2006 for a 350 mg dose of the drug Avastin, which should have been free as part of a clinical trial. When my Bloomberg colleague inquired, the 80% insurance payment was refunded. A small mixup, but telling.

Some drugs Terence took probably did him no good. At least one helped fewer than 10% of patients. . . . These drugs are very expensive. Should every patient have the right to them?

Terence and I answered yes. Each drug potentially added life. Yet that, too, led me to a question I still can't answer. When is it time to quit? Congress dodged the question last year as it tried to craft a health-care bill. The mere hint of limiting the ability to choose care created a whirlwind of accusations of "death panels."

One thing I know is that I don't envy the policymakers. As the health-care debate heated up, I remembered the fat sheaf of insurance statements that had piled up after Terence's death. Our children, Terry, 21, and Georgia, 15, assented to my idea of gathering every record to examine what they would show about end-of-life care—its science, emotions, and costs. Terence would have approved.

Taking it all into account, the data showed we had made a bargain that hardly any economist looking solely at the numbers would say made sense.

Why did we do it? I was one big reason. Not me alone, of course. The system has a strong bias toward action. My husband, too, was unusual, said Keith Flaherty, his oncologist, in his passionate willingness to endure discomfort for a chance to see his daughter grow from a child to a young woman, and his son graduate from high school.

After Terence died, Flaherty drew me a picture of a bell curve, showing the range of survival times for people with kidney cancer. Terence was way off in the tail on the right-hand side, an indication he had beaten the odds. For many, an explosion of research and drug discoveries had made it possible to daisy-chain treatments and extend lives for years—enough time to keep our quest from having been total madness.

Terence used to tell a story, almost certainly apocryphal, about his Uncle Bob. Climbing aboard a landing craft before the invasion of Normandy, Bob's sergeant was said to have told the men that by the end of the day, 9 out of 10 of them would be dead. Said Bob: "Each one of us looked around and felt so sorry for those other nine poor sonsabitches."

For me, it was about pushing the bell curve. Knowing there was something to be done, we couldn't not do it. Believing beyond logic that we were going to escape the fate of those other poor sonsabitches.

It is hard to put a price on that kind of hope.

A Shadow but Good Odds

We found the cancer by accident, on Sunday, Nov. 5, 2000, in Portland, Ore. . . . Terence had been having stomach cramps for weeks. Suddenly he was lying on the bed, doubled over in pain. Our family doctor ordered him to the emergency room.

We were immediately triaged through. Not a good sign, I thought. The kids sat on the waiting-room floor, Barbies and X-Men around them, while Terence writhed in a curtained alcove. When he returned from a scan, the doctor said, almost as an aside: There's a shadow on his kidney. When he's feeling better, you should take a look at it. Both of us were annoyed. Why would we think about a shadow on his kidney? That wasn't the problem. He was in such pain he could barely breathe.

The cause of the pain turned out to be violent ulcerative colitis [a form of inflammatory bowel disease]. The damaged colon was removed on Dec. 13, in an operation that left Terence so weak that he spent three weeks, including Christmas morning, immobile in a chair. Colleagues delivered meals to the house. My sister wrapped presents. My boss sent over her husband to put up our lights. I felt so bad for Terence that I got him a cat, the pet he had long wanted. The orange kitten howled in a box under the tree.

And the shadow? We were so grateful he was out of pain that we would have ignored it had someone from the hospital not called to urge us to find out what it meant. Within a month, Terence was in surgery again. On Jan. 18, Dr. Craig Turner removed the diseased kidney. Emerging from the five-hour operation, Turner confirmed the worst: He believed the shadow was cancer. A week later, when Terence was well enough to walk into the doctor's office, Turner was reassuring.

"We got it all," he said.

Terence teared up. "Thank you for saving my life."

The bills from Regence BlueCross BlueShield of Oregon show the operation was relatively inexpensive, just over $25,000, about 4% of the eventual total charged to keep Terence alive. Our share was $209.87. I never looked at or thought about the total cost, or the $14,084 that our insurance—in reality, my employer—paid. We never had to consider who was actually shouldering the bills.

Kidney cancer is uncommon, accounting for about 3% of all cancers, or about 50,000 new cases in the U.S. last year, according to the Kidney Cancer Assn. Terence was a typical patient: an older man, overweight, and an ex-smoker. Asymptomatic [or unnoticeable] for a long time, most kidney cancers are discovered accidentally or too late. So we felt lucky. The first tool for fighting kidney cancer is usually the one used since medieval times: the knife, or its technological equivalent. If a tumor is removed early enough, before it flings microscopic cells into the bloodstream that can implant in other organs, surgery is close to a cure.

For Terence the odds looked good. His 7-centimeter tumor showed no signs of having spread. According to the traditional method of evaluating, or staging, the cancer, that meant he had an 85% chance of surviving five years. A lab report soon chilled our optimism. Tests on Terence's tumor showed that he had so-called collecting duct cancer. Named for the part of the kidney where it is thought to originate, collecting duct is the rarest and most aggressive form of kidney cancer. In my online research, almost everyone who had it died within months, sometimes weeks, of diagnosis.

Most kidney cancers don't respond well to chemotherapy. There was no accepted treatment after surgery. Almost nothing was known about collecting duct cancer. Only about 1% of kidney cancer patients receive that diagnosis. Dr. Turner and I could find just 50 cases documented in the medical literature worldwide, and nothing had proved effective in halting it. "Watchful waiting" was the recommended path.

Waiting for him to die was what we feared.

He didn't die. He got better. We didn't know why. We tried not to think about it.

By the spring of 2002, we had moved to Lexington, Ky., where I was the editor of the local newspaper and Terence was creating an Asia Center at the University of Kentucky. He seemed fine. He began moving Chinese and Japanese history books to his office. On Saturdays we drove through the bluegrass to take seven-year-old Georgia to riding lessons. We reluctantly let 13-year-old Terry crowd-surf at his first rock concert.

Then, on May 6, 2002, Terry called me at work, panic in his voice. "Mom, come home. Dad is very sick."

His father was in bed, his face flaming with fever, shaking with chills under a pile of blankets. He could barely speak. "The cancer is in my lungs," he said. "I've got six to nine months left."

Fear, and an Internet Plunge

He had been keeping that secret for months. In February, routine follow-up scans had spotted the cancer's spread. "The first thing Terence said was, 'Doc, do you have any female patients who have recently died? I need to find a widower so my wife can meet her next husband,' "his Lexington oncologist, Dr. Scott Pierce, later recalled. After more tests, Dr. Pierce prescribed Interleukin-2 because there were no other options. Injections of the protein, at $735 a dose, were intended to stimulate the immune response to help fight the cancer's invasion. The overall response rate was only about 10%. For most patients, Interleukin-2 did absolutely nothing.

Terence hadn't wanted to worry us. In his mind, if he recovered, we would never know how close he came; if he died, he would have spared us months of anguish. He started a diary and spent more time in the office so we would get used to his absence.

His secret was betrayed by his violent reaction to his first dose of IL-2. Suddenly his actions over the last several weeks made sense. He had been giving away musical instruments and pieces of art. "I have too much stuff," he had told me, a bizarrely improbable statement coming from him. I was amused, exasperated, and touched by his desire to protect us. Even under the strain of his disease, he was so much himself. "Did you think I wouldn't have noticed if you didn't come home one day?" I asked.

I spent that night awake in our dark living room. For the first and only time, I felt pure terror. A few days later I visited a therapist.

"I can't survive without him," I said.

"What does he say when you feel this way?" she asked.

"He says I can handle anything."

"You'll need to say that to yourself."

Terence stopped taking IL-2 after a few weeks of treatments, unable to stand the side effects.

I plunged into the Internet. If there were something out there that could save him, I was going to find it. . . . We could defeat this.

I downloaded papers, presentations to the Kidney Cancer Assn., abstracts from the National Library of Medicine. I called researchers and oncologists, pathologists and fellow journalists. When the research became overwhelming, I hired a retired nurse to help. My boss's wife, a nurse herself, dug in too. After I messaged one couple about a clinical trial in Texas, they offered us their spare bedroom. . . .

Awaiting Scans, Learning the Violin

The truth was we were both shaken by the dire prognosis.

"What would you regret dying without having seen?" I asked. He answered without hesitation: "Pompeii." We pulled Terry from his eighth-grade class, Georgia out of second, and flew to Italy to see the excavated remains of the city once buried under volcanic ash. We walked the cobbled streets, poked into frescoed houses, taverns, and baths, and took an eerie comfort from the 2,000-year-old shapes of families huddled together, trying to ward off disaster.

By then our research had led us to the Cleveland Clinic, where Dr. Ronald Bukowski had specialized in kidney cancer for over 20 years. At our first meeting, in August 2002, Terence explained that he had collecting duct cancer.

"No you don't," Bukowski said.

We were confused. How did he know?

"You're sitting here," he said. "If you had collecting duct, you would be dead."

Bukowski argued that the disease was growing so slowly that we should simply watch and wait. We did, for three years. Then, in December 2005, a scan showed that the cancer in his lungs had begun to grow.

By this time, research had progressed. New drugs designed to attack a tumor's blood supply were appearing to slow the growth of a wide range of cancers. Bukowski recommended we enter a clinical trial, pretty much the only way to get these targeted therapies. He referred us to Dr. Flaherty in Philadelphia, where we had moved in June 2003 when I changed jobs.

The drugs Flaherty was testing—a drug [that blocs the growth of new blood vessels by] Genentech called Avastin and [a kidney cancer drug by] Bayer called Nexavar—[that] had showed promise individually. The trial would find out how they worked together. In March 2006, Terence took his first intravenous dose of Avastin, an hour-long process, and swallowed his first Nexavar. The side effects were hard. There were rashes, sometimes debilitating stomach pains. But he continued teaching, picking up the kids at school, studying and writing. He worked on his book, a grammar text based on classical Chinese poetry. He started to learn to play the violin and to read and write Arabic. Every two weeks he went for an Avastin drip. And every month we anxiously awaited the results of a chest scan.

At first the cancer didn't budge. Then it began to retreat.

Because Terence was in a clinical trial, Genentech and Bayer provided their drugs free. I learned that over the years of Terence's battle with cancer, some insurers drove harder bargains than others. In December 2006, for example, United Healthcare paid $2,586 to University of Pennsylvania Hospital for a chest scan; in March 2007, after I switched employers, Empire BlueCross paid $776 for the same $3,232 bill.

When it came to the insurance companies, the sticker price meant little since they had negotiated their own deals with the hospital. Neither the hospital nor the insurance companies would elaborate. The entire medical bill for seven years, in fact, was steeply discounted. The $618,616 was lowered to $254,176 when the insurers paid their share and imposed their discounts. The portion of the charges that were not covered for the most part vaporized. Terence and I were responsible for and paid $9,468—less than 4%.

During the trial, Terence packed boxes for the troops in Iraq and Afghanistan, loading them in our kitchen with deodorant, wet wipes, Mars bars, Kool-Aid, beef jerky, batteries, and magazines. A veteran of Naval Intelligence and the U.S. Air Force reserves, he walked almost every day to the post office with a box addressed to "Any Soldier." Behind the counter, the smiling lady with the long red hair extensions became his friend, and every so often a soldier would drop him a thank-you note. . . .

Then, in August 2007, from half a world away, I heard the cancer return.

I was on a business trip to China when Terence coughed during one of our phone calls. By the time I got home, scans had confirmed growth of one of the lung's cancerous spots.

By now, more than six years had passed since we first saw the shadow, and I was used to the scares. Avastin's side effects—fatigue, stomach ailments, rashes—had been getting him down, and the doctor had agreed back in May to let him stop treatments. So we'll go back on the Avastin, I thought, or cut out or laser out the growth, add new treatments, and go on.

The records document our renewed fight. Terence resumed Avastin. Because he was no longer in a trial, our insurance company was billed $27,360 a dose, every two weeks, more than the cost of the kidney surgery in 2000. Empire BlueCross paid $6,566.40. We paid nothing. So who did the paying? The health insurance system depends on healthy people bearing the cost for sick ones like Terence. For all its incredible treatment benefits, the system is untenable. Should you have had a voice in Terence's final days? Would I make the same decision with my money for your loved ones? These are things I think about now but can't answer.

No Consensus

He coughed almost continuously. His weight plunged. He needed help on the stairs. He began to use a cane. When his friend Woody came to visit, Terence couldn't muster the breath to blow his cornet. He coughed and coughed and coughed. In the last week of October, he called me at work.

"I can't pick Georgia up at school," he said. "I can't get out of the chair." On Halloween, his Dracula costume stayed in the basement. We left the candy on the doorstep.

On Nov. 8 we saw Dr. Ali Musani, a pulmonologist specializing in cancer. We hoped that the growing tumor in Terence's chest could be removed. Unable to stand or sit unassisted, he lay on the floor and refused to get up. Alarmed, Musani admitted him to the hospital. He said there was nothing he could do about the tumor. He gently mentioned that it might be time to consider hospice. We brushed off the suggestion.

Terence stayed in the hospital four days. Meanwhile a quiet tension was building. Flaherty and I believed this episode to be a temporary setback. Other doctors and nurses saw a patient near the end.

On Nov. 11, before discharging him, a doctor propped one of Terence's scans on a light board so we could clearly see the blizzard of white spots, hundreds of tumors, covering his lungs.

Avastin wasn't stopping them.

Flaherty was not fazed by the growth, and pointed out that many of the doctors looking at the scans didn't understand the course of kidney cancer. He and I wanted to move on to the next link in the daisy chain of newly available drugs. Sutent, another targeted therapy, had been approved the year before. It worked as Avastin did, by stopping cancer's ability to build extra blood vessels to feed its growth, but in a different way. One $200 pill a day. A shot at more life. Sutent might have more serious side effects—rashes, fatigue, stomach distress, strokes—but Terence was game. He began taking it on Nov. 15.

At home, he drew a line down the middle of a piece of paper. On one side he wrote things to throw away. On the other, things to keep.

"Stop that!" I snapped. "You aren't going to die."

I prepared for what I expected would be a new phase of our life. I found protein drinks online and protein bars in a bodybuilding shop. I got forms for a handicapped license plate, looked into outfitting our row house with a stair lift.

Terence was no longer able to get in and out of bed alone, so I hired a health aide. Whatever he craved, I bought. I wrote down everything he ate. Cold grapefruit slices. Chicken noodle soup. Clam chowder. I counted the calories he consumed one day: 210.

On Friday, Dec. 7, just as the aide was packing to leave for the day, Terence looked up, startled, as the corners of his mouth foamed bright red with blood. It was a struggle to get him down our narrow stairs to the ambulance. In the emergency room it was clear something was seriously wrong. "What's your name?" asked the ER doctor. Terence responded correctly. "What's the date?" Terence gave the doctor what the kids and I recognized as "Daddy's 'Just how dumb are you?'" look. But he couldn't answer.

"Who's the President of the United States?" That triggered something. "That moron, Bush," he said.

Terence was admitted that night to a ward where Eric Goren was doing his last intensive-care overnight shift of a three-year residency. In a small break room, alongside vending machines selling soft drinks and chips, Goren told me that bleeding from the lungs might suddenly become uncontrollable. If that happened, what should he and his team do?

I wanted to see whether Flaherty still believed Sutent could make a difference, but I couldn't reach him. Goren and I settled on what the hospital called Code-A. Do everything possible to prevent a major bleed or anything life-threatening. But don't take heroic measures if death seems inevitable.

I called the children to the hospital.

My decision about Terence's treatment, so hard on Saturday, was easy by Monday. The scans now were showing signs of cancer in his brain, surrounded by a cascade of hundreds of tiny strokes. I had Terence's signed living will, but I didn't need it. I knew what this man who lived for books, music, and ideas would want.

When Flaherty arrived, he looked shaken. "I didn't expect this," he said.

That afternoon I signed the papers transferring Terence to hospice. The next day the hospital staff took away the machines and the monitors. The oncologists and radiologists and lab technicians disappeared. Hospice nurses, social workers, chaplains, and counselors for me and the children—began to arrive and the focus shifted from treatment to easing our transition.

Over the next three days we were charged $14,022 for the same hospital bed. Included were the pain and anxiety medications Ativan and Dialaudid, his monitoring, and counseling for a different kind of pain management for me and the children. The bill was less than a third of the previous four days' $43,711.

Terence drifted into a coma on Tuesday. I e-mailed his friends and read their goodbyes aloud, hoping he could hear and understand. I slept in a chair.

At about 2:30 a.m. Friday, a noise in the hall startled me. I awoke just in time to hold his hand as he died.

They gave me back his wedding ring the next day.

Ten days later, the kids hung Daddy's Christmas stocking alongside our three. I mailed the cards he had addressed months earlier, slipping in a black-bordered note. I threw away the protein bars, gave the energy drinks to a shelter, and flushed an opened bottle of Sutent down the drain.

Looking back, memories of my zeal to treat are tinged with sadness. Should I have given up earlier? Would earlier hospice care been kinder? I hadn't believed Terence was going to die so I had never confronted any of those dilemmas. And I never let us have the chance to say goodbye.

I think had he known the costs, Terence would have objected to spending an amount equivalent to the cost of vaccine for nearly a quarter million children in developing countries. That's how he would have thought about it.

But when I ask myself whether I would do it all again, the answer is—absolutely. I couldn't not do it again.

Second-Guessing

Late last year, I waded through a snowstorm to Keith Flaherty's office in Boston, where he had moved to a new job. Did we help Terence or harm him? There's a possibility, he said, that the treatment actually made the cancer worse, causing it to rage out of control at the end. Or, as another doctor suggested in passing at the time, the strokes were a side effect of the Sutent and not the cancer.

But neither Flaherty nor I believe that. The average patient on Flaherty's trial got 14 months of extra life. Without any treatment at all, Flaherty estimates that for someone with Terence's stage of the disease it was three months. Terence got 17 months—still within the realm of chance but on the far-right side of the bell curve.

There is another bell curve that Terence did not live to climb. It charts the survival times for patients treated not just with Sutent, Avastin, and Nexavar, but also [drugs for advanced kidney cancer like] Novartis' Afinitor and GlaxoSmithKline's Votrient—both made available since Terence's death. Doctors and patients now are doing what we dreamed of, staggering one drug after another and buying years more of life.

Slides on the results of Flaherty's clinical trial, presented at the 2008 meeting of the American Society of Clinical Oncology, showed that Avastin and Nexavar worked well on a wide variety of patients. Only Flaherty and I know that the solitary tick mark at 17 months was Terence.

Only I know that those months included an afternoon looking down at the Mediterranean with Georgia from a sunny balcony in southern Spain. Moving Terry into his college dorm. Celebrating our 20th anniversary with a carriage ride through Philadelphia's cobbled streets. A final Thanksgiving game of charades with cousins Margo and Glenn.

And one last chance for Terence to pave the way for all those other poor sonsabitches.

EXPLORING THE ISSUE

Does Too Much Treatment Result in an Inhumane Dying?

Critical Thinking and Reflection

1. Your elderly mother has severe heart disease and stage 4 colon cancer. The surgeon has indicated that he would like to try surgery, even though it is risky (because of her heart). You look up information and find out that "stage 4 colon cancer" means that it has spread to the lymph nodes and other parts of the body (liver or lungs). Discuss whether doing surgery for this patient would be "overtreatment."

2. Your father is in the late stages of a cancer called lymphoma. He has seen many different doctors. His new specialist describes transfusions and aggressive experimental therapies but has not mentioned hospice, or "death" or "dying." The new specialist is head of the overnight oncology unit that has six beds for just this type of treatment. How does insurance coverage for care influence treatment suggestions by specialists? Does the reimbursement system push more aggressive treatment to help pay for the beds available? How would you change this?

3. Your classmate has been fighting cancer for 6 years. She believes her oncologist will provide a miracle someday, but you can see she is wasting away and that she is dying. What do you say to her? What challenges are faced by the focus on autonomy and patient-centered decisions? Should physicians or society be allowed to simply stop futile treatments?

4. Because cancer registries have tracked treatments and outcomes for several decades, the prognosis for almost every type of cancer in the late stages is well established. Should patients and families be given these data tables with decision tools to better understand the full information on life expectancy to make decisions? Should patient and caregiver health literacy be tested before offering these end of life technologies?

5. Many of the cancer treatment are offered to patients in the late stages are experimental, and are unlikely to change the course of the late stage disease. These treatments would not be curative, but are often presented to families as a "new experimental treatment." Role play how you would explain the difference between a treatment that is curative and a treatment that is palliative.

Is There Common Ground?

Why limit end-of-life (EOL) treatment? *Five different ethical reasons* are given. Diverse treatments offer different thresholds for withholding or withdrawing medically futile treatments. Based on duties and obligation (*deontology*), relatives who are valid proxies make a "substituted judgment" for incapacitated dying based on patient self-determination (*autonomy*) or determine patient well-being called "bests interests" (*beneficence*; President's Commission, 1983). Others defend judgments of futility or scarce resources by competent providers using *caregiver paternalism* (Texas, 2002; Truog, 2007). Still others balance different kinds considerations based on outcomes (*beneficence*). Dying persons and caregivers can refuse treatments that are *medically ineffective, nonbeneficial, or disproportionately burdensome* at the end of life (Pellegrino, 2000, 2005; Pellegrino & Sulmasy, 2003; President's Council, 2008, p. 91).

Two new models are emerging. Autonomy is interpreted in two ways. Instead of focusing on noninterference with patients or surrogate sovereignty, some stress the *consciences of providers*, who are never obligated to provide "medically ineffective care or care contrary to applicable health-care standards" (1994 Health-Care Decisions Act; Wilkinson & Savulescu, 2011). Others argue for positive, authentic autonomy based on shared, *team based decision making* which includes care and character (Bernat, 2005; Taylor, Lillis, LeMone, & Lynn, 2010). Good communication prevents and resolves futility disputes; conflicts are better mediated than litigated. Some extrajudicial procedures such as ethics consultations avoid overtreatment or seeking protection in "safe harbors" to avoid litigation (Bernat, 2005; Texas, 2002; Truog, 2007). "Acrimony is beyond the scope of litigation to repair" (Meisel, 2005, S48).

Two kinds of *justice* arguments are made about end of life overtreatment. These weigh ICU resource macroallocation (rationing) and microallocation (access and triage). First, outcomes data shows overtreatment driven by providers including physician "enthusiasm" and "*supplier-induced demand*" with reduced hospice referrals (Barnato et al., 2007, p. 386). Secondly, an *egalitarian theory of justice* requires everyone to have a "fair opportunity" to benefit—or at least a community should not be placed at risk of harm by some treatment (nonmaleficence). "Even in the absence of limited resources, an ethical argument in favor of avoiding antibiotic therapy in patients with marginal benefit, or in those in whom therapy would be viewed as futile, can be made based on its collateral harm to other future patients" (Niederman & Berger, 2010, S520). Different models place health care professionals and patients in role conflicts. For example, allocation models require professionals to be patient advocates yet stewards of limited social resources for rationing and triage (Niederman & Berger, 2010). Consumer models shift professional providers and patient-clients from traditional trust based relations or fiduciary roles based on patient benefit called beneficence. Patients and health care professionals are now buyers and sellers of exchanged competent services, which demand vigilance on the part of either buyer (let the buyer beware, "caveat emptor") or seller (let seller beware, "caveat vendor").

Are emerging therapies changing death and dying? Is dying simply part of aging or a treatable medical condition? Is dying part of our natural life span, life expectancy, a condition without recovery, or a mere cause of death? Others ask whether new EOL treatments are creating a new medical literacy to distinguish terminal condition from care, imminent dying, futile condition from treatment, end-stage conditions and death as expected, foreseen, or anticipated.

Emerging technologies, diverse discretionary therapies, and plural ethical justifications assure us this debate will continue.

References

Barnato, A. E., Herndon, M. B., Anthony, D. L., Gallagher, P. M., Skinner, J. S., Bynum, J. P., et al. (2007). Are regional variations in end-of-life care intensity explained by patient preferences? A study of the US Medicare population. *Med Care, 45*(5), 386–393.

Beckstrand, R. L., Moore, J., Callister, L., & Bond, A. E. (2009). Oncology nurses' perceptions of obstacles and supportive behaviors at the end of life. *Oncology Nursing Forum, 36*(4), 446–453.

Beckstrand, R. L., Smith, M. D., Heaston, S., & Bond, A. E. (2008). Emergency nurses' perceptions of size, frequency and magnitude of obstacles and supportive behaviors in end of life care. *Journal of Emergency Nursing, 34*(4), 290–300.

Bennett, A. & Babcock, C. (2010, March 4). Lessons of a $618,616 death. *BusinessWeek (4170)*, 32–40.

Bernat, J. L. (2005). Medical futility: Definition, determination and disputes in critical care. *Neurocrit Care, 2*(2), 198–205.

Bradley, C. T. & Brasel, K. J. (2009). Developing guidelines that identify patients who would benefit from palliative care in the surgical intensive care unit. *Critical Care Medicine, 37*(3), 946–950. doi:10.1097/CCM.0b013e3181968f68

Brownlee, S. (2008). Afterward. In *Overtreated: Why too much medicine is making us sicker and poorer* (pp. 305–312). New York: Bloomsbury.

Callahan, D. (2008). Health care costs and medical technology. In M. Crowley (Ed.), *From birth to death and bench to clinic: The Hastings Center bioethics briefing book for journalists, policymakers, and campaigns* (pp. 79–82). Garrison, NY: The Hastings Center.

Committee for the National Conference of Commissioners on Uniform State Laws. (1994). *Uniform Health-Care Decisions Act.* Retrieved from www.law.upenn.edu/bll/archives/ulc/fnact99/1990s/uhcda93.htm

Crippen, D., Burrows, D., Stocchetti, N., Mayer, S. A., Andrews, P., Bleck, T., et al. (2010). Ethics roundtable: Open-ended ICU care: Can we afford it? *Critical Care, 14*(3), 222.

Curtis, J. & Vincent, J. (2010). Critical care 2: Ethics and end-of-life care for adults in the intensive care unit. *Lancet, 376*(9749), 1347–1353. doi:10.1016/S0140-6736(10)60143-2

DeLisser, H. M. (2009). A practical approach to the family that expects miracles. *Chest, 135*(6), doi:10.1378/chest.08-2805

Emanuel, E. J. & Fuchs, V. R. (2008). The perfect storm of overutilization. *Journal of the American Medical Association, 299*(23), 2789–2791.

Foucault, M. (1963). Naissance de la clinique—une archéologie du regard médical (Paris: 1963). The birth of the clinic: An archaeology of medical perception (London: 1973).

Hippocrates. (1995). The art. In G. B. Goold (Ed.), *The Loeb classical library, Hippocrates, Vol. II* (pp. 185–217). Cambridge, MA: Harvard University Press.

Jennings, B., Kaebnick, G., & Murray, T. (2005). *Improving end of life care: Why has it been so difficult?* Retrieved from www.thehastingscenter.org/Publications/SpecialReports/Detail.aspx?id=1344

Kaufman, S. (2006). *And a time to die: How American hospitals shape the end of life.* New York: University of Chicago Press.

Kaufman, S. (2009). Life-extending treatments for the oldest patients. *Health Cost Monitor.* Retrieved from http://healthcarecostmonitor.thehastingscenter.org/sharonkaufman/life-extending-treatments-for-the-oldest-patients/

Meisel, A. (2005). The role of litigation in end of life care: A reappraisal. In B. Jennings, G. Kaebnick, & T. Murray (Eds.), *Improving end of life care: Why has it been so difficult?* (pp. S47–S51). *Hastings Center Report Special Report, 35* (6), S47–S51.

Niederman, M. S. & Berger, J. T. (2010). The delivery of futile care is harmful to other patients. *Critical Care Medicine, 38*(10), S518–S522. doi:10.1097/CCM.0b013e3181f1cba5

Pellegrino, E. D. (2000). Decisions to withdraw life-sustaining treatment: A moral algorithm. *Journal of the American Medical Association, 283*(8), 1065–1067. doi:10.1001/jama.283.8.1065

Pellegrino, E. D. (2005). Futility in medical decisions: The word and the concept. *HEC Forum, 17*(4), 308–318.

Pellegrino, E. D. & Sulmasy, D. P. (2003). Medical ethics. In D. A. Warrell, T. M. Cox, & J. D. Firth (Eds.), *Oxford textbook of medicine.* New York: Oxford University Press.

President's Commission for the Study of Ethical Problems in Medicine and Biomedical and Behavioral Research. (1983). *Decision to forego life-sustaining treatment.* Washington, D.C.: U.S. Government Printing Office.

President's Council on Bioethics. (2008). A summary of the council's debate on the neurological standard for determining death. In Pellegrino, E., E., Bloom, F., Carson, B. et al. (Eds.), *Controversies in the determination of death: A white paper by the President's Council on Bioethics* (pp. 89–92). Washington, D.C.: The President's Council on Bioethics.

Quill, T. E., Arnold, R., & Back, A. L. (2009). Discussing treatment preferences with patients who want "everything." *Annals of Internal Medicine, 151*(5), 345–349.

Randall, F. & Downie, R. S. (2009). *End of life choices: Consensus and controversy.* New York: Oxford University Press.

Risse, G. (1999). *Mending bodies, saving souls: A history of hospitals.* New York: Oxford University Press.

Smith, T. J., Dow, L. A., Virago, E. A., Khatcheressian, J., Matsuyama, R., & Lyckholm, L. J. (2011). A pilot trial of decision aids to give truthful prognostic and treatment information to chemotherapy patients with advanced cancer. *Journal of Support Oncology, 9*(2), 79–86.

Sulmasy, D. P. (2006). *The rebirth of the clinic: An introduction to spirituality in health care.* Washington, D.C.: Georgetown University Press.

Taylor, C., Lillis, C., LeMone, P., & Lynn, P. (2010). *Fundamentals of nursing: The art and science of nursing care* (7th ed.). New York: Lippincott Williams & Wilkins.

Teno, J. M., Mor, V., Ward, N., Roy, J., Clarridge, B., Wennberg, J. E., et al. (2005). Bereaved family member perceptions of quality of end-of-life care in U.S. regions with high and low usage of intensive care unit care. *Journal of the American Geriatrics Society, 53*(11), 1905–1911. doi:10.1111/j.1532-5415.2005.53563.x

Texas Health and Safety Code. Chapter 166. Section 166.046. (2002). *Advance directives.* Retrieved from: www.statutes.legis.state.tx.us/SOTWDocs/HS/htm/HS.166.htm.

Truog, R. D. (2007). Tackling medical futility in Texas. *New England Journal of Medicine, 357*, 1–3. doi:10.1056/NEJMp078109

Wilkinson, D. & Savulescu, J. (2011). Knowing when to stop: Futility in the ICU. *Current Opinion in Anesthesiology, 24*(1), 160–165.

Wunsch, H., Angus, D. C., Harrison, D. A., Collange, O., Fowler, R., Hoste, E. J., et al. (2008). Variation in critical care services across North America and Western Europe. *Critical Care Medicine, 36*(10), 2787–2793. doi:10.1097/CCM.0b013e318186aec8

Additional Resources

Alpers, A. & Lo, B. (1999). Avoiding family feuds: Responding to surrogate demands for life-sustaining interventions. *Journal of Law, Medicine and Ethics, 27*(1), 74–80.

Armelagos, G. (2004). Emerging disease in the third epidemiological transition. In N. Mascie-Taylor, J. Peters, & S. T. McGarvey (Eds.), *The changing face of disease: Implications for society* (pp. 7–22). New York: Taylor & Francis.

Baker, C. D., Glaser, R. J., Claiborne, R., Tullock, G., & Bunker, J. (1985, June 13). Overtreatment: An exchange. *The New York Review of Books.* Retrieved from www.nybooks.com/articles/archives/1985/jun/13/overtreatment-an-exchange/

Battro, A., Bernat, J.L., Bousser, M.G. et al. (2006). Why the concept of brain death is valid as a definition of death: Statement by neurologists and others and response to objections (pp. 159–177)., in Working Group on Signs of Death, edited by Marcelo Sánchez Sorondo. Vatican City: Pontifical Academy of Sciences.

Carr, B. G., Addyson, D. K., & Kahn, J. M. (2010). Variation in critical care beds per capita in the United States: Implications for pandemic and disaster planning. *Journal of the American Medical Association, 303*(14), 1371–1372.

Daskivich, T., Chamie, K., Kwan, L., Labo, J., Palvolgyi, R., Dash, A., et al. (2011). Overtreatment of men with low-risk prostate cancer and significant comorbidity. *Cancer, 117*(10), 2058–2066.

Fry, S., Veatch, R. M., & Taylor, C. (2010). *Case studies in nursing ethics* (4th ed.). Sudbury, MA: Jones & Bartlett Publishers.

Gillick, M. R., Hesse, K., & Mazzapica, N. (1993). Medical technology at the end of life. What would physicians and nurses want for themselves? *Archives of Internal Medicine, 153*(22), 2542–2547.

Gries, C. J., Curtis, J., Wall, R. J., & Engelberg, R. A. (2008). Family member satisfaction with end-of-life decision making in the ICU. *CHEST, 133*(3), 704–712. doi:10.1378/chest.07-1773

Hofmann, B. (2002). Is there a technological imperative in health care? *International Journal of Technology Assessment in Health Care, 18*(3), 675–689.

Illich, I. (1974). *Medical nemesis.* London: Calder & Boyars.

Institute of Medicine. (2002). *Care without coverage: Too little, too late*. Washington, D.C.: National Academies Press.

Jonas, H. (1984). *The imperative of responsibility: In search of ethics for the technological age*. London: University of Chicago Press.

Kadiyala, S. (2009). Are U.S. cancer screening test patterns consistent with guideline recommendations with respect to the age of screening initiation? *BMC Health Services Research, 9*, 185–193.

Krakauer, E. L. (2007). To be freed from the infirmity of the age: Subjectivity, life-sustaining treatment, and palliative medicine. In J. Biehl, B. Good, & A. Kleinman (Eds.), *Subjectivity: Ethnographic investigations* (pp. 381–397). Berkeley, CA: University of California Press.

Lerner, B. H. (2008, March 25). When the disease eludes a diagnosis. *The New York Times*. Retrieved from www.nytimes.com/2008/03/25/health/views/25case.html

Lorenz, K., Lynn, J., Morton, S. C., Dy, S., Mularski, R., Shugarman, L., et al. (2004). End-of-life care and outcomes. Evidence report/technology assessment no. 110. (Prepared by the Southern California Evidence-based Practice Center, under Contract No. 290-02-0003.) AHRQ Publication No. 05-E004-2. Rockville, MD: Agency for Healthcare Research and Quality.

McCleane, G. J. (2008). *Pain management: Expanding the pharmacological options*. Singapore: Wiley-Blackwell.

Miller, K. (2008). *Choices in breast cancer treatment: Medical specialists and cancer survivors tell you what you need to know*. Baltimore, MD: Johns Hopkins University Press.

Murray, M., Fiset, V., Young, S., & Kryworuchko, J. (2009). Where the dying live: A systematic review of determinants of place of end-of-life cancer care. *Oncology Nursing Forum, 36*(1), 69–77. doi:10.1188/09.ONF.69-77

New York State Workgroup on Ventilator Allocation in an Influenza Pandemic NYS DOH/NYS Task Force on Life & the Law. (2007). *Allocation of ventilators in an influenza pandemic: Planning document*. Retrieved from www.health.state.ny.us/diseases/communicable/influenza/pandemic/ventilators/docs/ventilator_guidance.pdf

Paesman, M., Ameye, L., Moreau, M., & Rozenberg, S. (2010). Breast cancer screening in the older woman: An effective way to reduce mortality? *Maturitas, 66*(3), 263–267.

Powell, T., Christ, K. C., & Birkhead, G. S. (2008). Allocation of ventilators in a public health disaster. *Disaster Medicine Public Health Preparedness, 2*(1), 20–26.

Reisner-Sénélar, L. (2011). The birth of intensive care medicine: Björn Ibsen's records. *Intensive Care Medicine, 37*(7), 1084–1086. doi:10.1007/s00134-011-2235-z

Rieff, D. (2008). *Swimming in a sea of death: A son's memoirs*. New York: Simon and Schuster.

Rieff, P. (1987). *Triumph of the therapeutic: Uses of faith after Freud*. Chicago, IL: The University of Chicago Press.

Robert Wood Johnson Foundation ICU End-of-Life Peer Group. (2004). Use of intensive care at the end of life in the United States: An epidemiologic study. *Critical Care Medicine, 32*(3), 638–643.

Rubenstein, A. (2010). Judaism and nature: Reviewing the Jewish dimensions of Hans Jonas. *Religious Studies Review, 36*(1), 15–21. doi:10.1111/j.1748-0922. 2010.01396.x

Schneiderman, L. & Jecker, N. (2011). *Wrong medicine: Doctors, patients and futile treatment* (2nd ed.). Baltimore, MD: Johns Hopkins University Press.

Seymour J. (2003). Technology and "natural death": A study of older people. *Zeitschrift für Gerontologie und Geriatrie, 36*(5), 339–346.

Stone, J. (2007). Pascal's wager and persistent vegetative state. *Bioethics, 21*(2), 84–92. doi:10.1111/j.1467-8519.2007.00528.x

Strauss, G. M. & Dominioni, L. (2000). Perception, paradox, paradigm: Alice in the wonderland of lung cancer prevention and early detection. *Cancer, 89*(11), 2422–2431.

Taylor, R. (2007). *White coat tales: Medicine's heroes, heritage and misadventures.* New York: Springer.

Tinnelly, K., Kristjanson, L. J., McCallion, A., & Cousins, K. (2000). Technology in palliative care: Steering a new direction or accidental drift? *International Journal of Palliative Nursing, 6*(10), 495–500.

Tolstoy, L. (1869). *War and peace.* Reprint (1911). New York: E. P. Dutton.

Tu, M. S. & Chiou, C. P. (2007). Perceptual consistency of pain and quality of life between hospice cancer patients and family caregivers: A pilot study. *International Journal of Clinical Practice, 61*(10), 1689–1691.

Welch, H. G., Schwartz, L. M., & Woloshin, S. (2011). *Overdiagnosed: Making people sick in the pursuit of health.* Boston, MA: Beacon Press.

Wennberg, J. E., Bronner, K., Skinner, J. S., Fisher, E. S., & Goodman, D. C. (2009). Inpatient care intensity and patients' ratings of their hospital experiences: What could explain the fact that Americans with chronic illnesses who receive less hospital care report better hospital experiences? *Health Aff (Milwood), 28*(1), 103–112. doi:10.1377/hlthaff.28.1.103

Werko, L. (2000). Health technology assessment at the end of life: A realistic view of death and palliative care. *International Journal of Technology Assessment in Health Care, 16*(3), 903–906.

Whitmer, M., Hurst, S., Prins, M., Shepard, K., & McVey, D. (2009). Medical futility: A paradigm as old as Hippocrates. *Dimensions of Critical Care Nursing, 28*(2), 67–71.

Wolf, S. M. (2008). Confronting physician-assisted suicide and euthanasia: My father's death. *Hastings Center Report, 38*(5), 23–26.

Online Resources

American Hospital Association Statistics

www.aha.org/research/rc/stat-studies/fast-facts.shtml

Dartmouth Atlas of Health Care: End of Life Care

www.dartmouthatlas.org/keyissues/issue.aspx?con=2944

Dehumanization defined in Macmillan Encyclopedia of Death and Dying

www.encyclopedia.com/doc/1G2-3407200088.html

OECD Directorate for Employment, Labour and Social Affairs Health Data, 2011

www.oecd.org/document/16/0,3343,en_2649_34631_2085200_1_1_1_1,00.html

World Health Organization: Global Burden of Disease

www.who.int/healthinfo/global_burden_disease/en/

ISSUE 8

Are Feeding Tubes Obligatory?

YES: Allen G. Sandler, from "The Right to Nutrition and Hydration: A Need for Vigilance," *Intellectual and Developmental Disabilities* (vol. 47, no. 3, pp. 234–238, 2009)

NO: David Orentlicher and Christopher M. Callahan, from "Feeding Tubes, Slippery Slopes, and Physician-Assisted Suicide," *Journal of Legal Medicine* (vol. 25, no. 4, pp. 389–409, 2004)

Learning Outcomes

After reading this issue, you should be able to:

- Gain an understanding of the historical background of feeding tube use in patients.
- Describe the findings of studies on the use of PEG tubes in older adults with advanced dementia.
- Understand the importance of the symbolism of feeding patients at the end of life.
- Discuss the laws regarding the right to refuse feeding tubes or withdraw feeding tubes.
- Identify and debate the issues related to withholding or withdrawing tube feedings for disabled populations who may require tube feedings for years before they are considered terminally ill.
- Describe the benefit and the burden of feeding tubes in persons with terminal illnesses.

ISSUE SUMMARY

YES: Allen Sandler, an associate professor for special education, offers a case that demonstrates that nutrition and hydration were inappropriately viewed as futile treatment in a person with disabilities who was not truly terminal. He argues that persons with disabilities must have access to the same life-sustaining treatment as provided to those without a disability, including feeding tubes, and that decisions about futility must be carefully considered.

NO: David Orentlicher, professor of law, and Christopher Callahan, a physician, present the historical underpinnings of feeding tubes and how laws have allowed withholding or withdrawing feeding tubes in persons with serious or terminal illnesses. They provide evidence that allowing refusals of tube feedings has not led to the slippery slope of requiring tube feeding removals as once feared. Rather, there continues to be an overuse of feeding tubes in persons with terminal diseases.

Placement of feeding tubes has become common in persons with diseases that limit their ability to swallow. There are two main types of feeding tubes: nasogastric tubes are placed through the nose to the stomach, and are used for temporary feedings; and percutaneous endoscopic gastrostomy tubes (PEG tubes) placed directly through the abdominal wall into the stomach, which are used for more permanent feedings. Feeding tubes are often placed as a temporary measure for the provision of nutrition and medications when a patient has been hospitalized for a serious illness and the outlook for recovery is uncertain (Lynn & Harrold, 1999; Orentlicher & Callahan, 2004). The hope is that the patient will eventually recover his/her swallowing ability and return to normal eating (Lynn & Harrold, 1999). If the patient's condition worsens and there is no hope for recovery, families are often confronted with decisions to withdraw a feeding tube that has been put in place. In other cases, perhaps the majority of cases, feeding tubes are placed in patients with neurological diseases that impair swallowing, such as strokes, Parkinson's disease, Alzheimer's disease, multiple sclerosis (MS), amyotrophic lateral sclerosis (ALS), and other degenerative diseases. In these cases, placing a feeding tube near the end of life does nothing to change the course of the disease (Sampson, Candy, & Jones, 2009). Supporters of feeding tubes argue for the sanctity of life; feeding is essential to sustaining life and must be provided as a basic standard. From this point of view, any removal of feeding is considered morally wrong and is considered tantamount to killing the patients (Penner, 2005; Wick & Zanni, 2009). Naysayers identify that feeding tubes are not obligatory; patients who are in the process of dying are additionally burdened by food and fluids. Most medical professionals and the legal system have sided with those who believe that it is ethical to withhold or withdraw feeding tubes (Sulmasy, 2005, 2006). It is normal for patients to stop eating a few days prior to death, because the resulting dehydration makes their breathing less labored and congested and provides for a more comfortable death (Lynn & Harrold, 1999; Sulmasy, 2006).

The cases of Karen Quinlan, Nancy Cruzan, and Terri Schiavo highlighted the difficulty that families experience regarding the withdrawal of a feeding tube in a person in a persistent vegetative state (Ball, 2006; Sulmasy, 2005). Mrs. Schiavo was a victim of severe brain injury following a cardiac arrest. Her severe injury required total physical care in a nursing home. For 15 years, she was unable to communicate and was fed through a feeding tube. Her husband and her parents disagreed over whether her condition might improve and whether she would have wanted to be kept alive with the feeding tube. Mrs. Schiavo died after a long legal battle. The courts finally agreed that Mrs. Schiavo's previous statements provided compelling evidence that she would want the feeding tube removed, even though she did not have a written advance directive. Penner (2005) argues that Mrs. Schiavo was not truly terminally ill, she was simply severely disabled, and removal of the feeding tube threatens the disabled community. Similar to Sandler's argument in favor of tube feedings for disabled persons, Penner (2005) identifies that tube feedings are morally required for this group of vulnerable persons who cannot really be classified as terminally ill. However, in the Schiavo case the focus was on the previously expressed wishes of the patient, essentially, seeking an indication from the patient's family members what her wishes would be in this case. The case highlights the gray areas in ethical decisions, including "when is someone terminally ill or dying?"

Just as patients with persistent vegetative state could be thought of as "slowly terminal," someone with severe Alzheimer's disease or Parkinson's disease can have a long terminal phase to the disease. In the 1990s, researchers began to study outcomes of patients with neurological diseases or cancer who had feeding tubes placed. One study examined 288 hospitalized patients who received feeding tubes. The researchers explored family expectations of the outcomes of feeding tube placement. They found that even though 30 percent of these patients died within 6 months of feeding tube placement, families had very high expectations of outcomes. Families believed that the tube feeding would extend longevity and improve patient function. These high expectations were evident despite the fact that the patients had very little clinical improvement, 38 percent of the patients resided in nursing homes, and all were very dependent on others for care activities (Carey et al., 2006). Researchers have also identified poor outcomes of feeding tubes in persons with severe dementia. Sampson et al. (2009) found that enteral tube nutrition was not effective in prolonging survival for those with severe dementia, did not improve quality of life, and did not lead to better nourishment or prevent development of pressure sores. Some evidence indicated that for persons with severe dementia, feeding tubes may actually increase the risk of developing pneumonia (due to inhaling small quantities of the feed).

Even though this evidence is strong, other researchers found that most speech and language therapists routinely recommend feeding tubes in persons with severe dementia because they believe it is the "standard of care" for persons with swallowing problems regardless of how close to the end of life they may be (Sharp & Shega, 2009). If patient wishes aren't clearly stated on the record, health professionals may feel obligated to provide feeding tubes at the end of life. Some ethicists argue that despite what research shows about feeding tubes and outcomes, physicians and families continue to place feeding tubes in patients with advance dementia because they are uncertain how to show caring or concern if a feeding tube is not placed (Gillick & Volandes, 2008). When family members view feeding as a moral issue, they need examples of how best to demonstrate caring for someone who has difficulty eating at the end of life. They argue that a better approach to family members who want feeding tubes for persons with dementia is to acknowledge the symbolic value of nutrition for them and to seek an alternative means of satisfying the need to feed.

Sulmasy (2005) clarified the position of the Roman Catholic Church on tube feeding at the end of life after the death of Terri Schiavo. The church does not teach that all dying patients require feeding tubes or intravenous fluids, nor have Catholic teachings about life-sustaining treatments changed in any fundamental way. The church has never required people do everything possible to medically sustain life. *Catechism of the Catholic Church* states, "Discontinuing medical procedures that are burdensome, dangerous, extraordinary, or disproportionate to the expected outcome can be legitimate; it is the refusal of 'overzealous' treatment. Here one does not will to cause death; one's inability to impede it is merely accepted. The decisions should be made by the patient if he is competent and able or, if not, by those legally entitled to act for the patient, whose reasonable will and legitimate interests must always be respected" (U.S. Catholic Church, 2003). *Ethical and Religious Directives for Catholic Health Care Services* (Committee on Doctrine of the National Conference of Catholic Bishops, 2009) also states "Medically assisted nutrition and hydration become morally optional when they cannot reasonably be expected to prolong life or when they would be 'excessively burdensome for the patient or [would] cause significant physical discomfort. . . .'"

In summary, there have been several landmark legal cases regarding the use of feeding tubes, whether they are required for patients who are in persistent vegetative state, or for persons who had stated that they would not want feeding tubes if they were profoundly injured or suffering from an irreversible disease. A refusal can be made through a previously written advance directive or living will, or from a proxy who can clearly state the patient's wishes if they are incapacitated. Competent patients have the legal right to refuse tube feedings, just as they can refuse any medical treatment that they feel is against their personal beliefs or wishes.

In the YES article, Allen Sandler, an associate professor for special education, offers a case of a guardian of a disabled person making a decision about nutrition and hydration as futile treatment, even though the disabled patient was not truly terminal. He argues that persons with disabilities have access to the same life-sustaining treatment as provided to those without a disability, including feeding tubes, etc.

In the NO article, David Orentlicher, professor of law, and Christopher Callahan, a physician, present the historical underpinnings of feeding tubes and how laws have allowed withholding or withdrawing feeding tubes in persons with serious or terminal illnesses. They provide evidence that allowing refusals of tube feedings has not led to the slippery slope of fewer and fewer patients receiving tube feedings. Concerns that physicians would require tube feeding removals or would not allow feeding tubes in impaired patients (the slippery slope) has not happened as previously feared. Rather, there continues to be an overuse of feeding tubes in persons with terminal disease.

YES

Allen G. Sandler

The Right to Nutrition and Hydration: A Need for Vigilance

Recent public interest in legal cases related to the withdrawal of artificial nutrition and hydration at the end of life, such as the highly publicized Terri Schiavo case (Quill, 2005), have created a climate in which a potentially life-sustaining intervention, such as gastrostomy tube (G-tube) feeding, might be questioned as futile, and even cruel, when suggested for a person with a severe disability experiencing a health crisis. Lack of understanding exists among some in the health care community and among members of the general public (including some guardians and family members) concerning the distinction between managing medical challenges associated with a chronic disability and providing care at what might be mistakenly perceived to be the end of life (King, 2005). This can have potentially devastating consequences. As suggested by Pugh (2005), the distinction between living with a disability and a terminal illness may become "blurred" (p. 35), and [the] treatment routinely provided [to] individuals with a disability, such as G-tube feeding, might be denied as futile. The result may be an otherwise preventable death (Turnbull, 2005a).

The Case of Alice

Alice was a 49-year-old woman with congenital hydrocephalus and lifelong intellectual disability living in a state-funded community care facility. Her diagnoses included profound intellectual disability, bipolar disorder, seizure disorder, legal blindness, and scoliosis. Her strengths included the ability to feed herself with assistance, walk short distances with a walker, communicate using one- and two-word phrases, and sing songs she had learned as a child. Alice was described by her caregivers as a charming, outgoing woman with a good sense of humor who enjoyed singing, visits and phone calls from her family, animals (especially puppies), "swimming" at the community YWCA, and eating her favorite foods.

For unknown reasons, Alice became lethargic and unresponsive, stopped talking, and stopped eating and drinking. Medical tests failed to indicate a reason for her decline, and although there was no evidence of a terminal illness, her family believed she was dying. The nursing staff at the group home where she had lived for 13 years suggested that a G-tube be placed to provide

From *Intellectual and Developmental Disabilities*, June 2009, pp. 234–238. Copyright © 2009 by American Association on Intellectual and Developmental Disabilities AAIDD. Reprinted by permission via Copyright Clearance Center.

nutrition and hydration, but family members expressed their adamant opposition. They argued that a feeding tube not be placed because Alice's joy in life was from eating. Furthermore, they didn't want to prolong Alice's suffering and wanted to allow her a natural death. Her uncle, Alice's guardian, acknowledged that Alice "wasn't eating enough to sustain life" but justified his refusal of a G-tube through referencing recent literature (Gillick, 2000) indicating that feeding tubes are ineffective in prolonging life and that, rather than preventing suffering, they can actually bring it about through causing aspiration pneumonia. Alice's physicians, bound by the standards of their profession to generally accept the decision of a surrogate decision maker in such cases (American Medical Association, 2007) and privately expressing their own concerns regarding the quality of Alice's life, declared further treatment futile. The central venous line through which Alice received hydration and medication was disconnected; she was diagnosed with *failure-to-thrive*, a terminal diagnosis making her eligible for placement in a hospice; and she was moved to a hospice a short time later.

Analysis

This example is based upon an actual case. A brief review of its important elements may prove beneficial in clarifying the rights of people with disabilities to life-sustaining medical treatment and, thereby, enable others to more effectively advocate in support of these rights. The issues to be addressed include legal and professional guidelines related to withholding nutrition and hydration, determinations of futility, and recent research on the risks and benefits of G-tube feeding.

Legal and Professional Guidelines

Principles guiding health care decision making have been laid out in federal regulations implementing the Child Abuse Prevention and Treatment Act (42 U.S.C. Sec.5101; 45 C.F.R. Part 84, Section 84.55). These principles prohibit discrimination due to disability in health care and require that medically beneficial treatment be provided. A presumption in favor of treatment is articulated, although this presumption may be rebutted if (a) the individual is in an irreversible comatose state, (b) the treatment would be painful and not produce benefit, or (c) the treatment would not prevent death (Turnbull, 2005b). In Pennsylvania, where Alice resided, a state policy directive (MR Bulletin No. 00-98-08, 1998) consistent with these principles and referencing the Americans with Disabilities Act requires that people with intellectual disability have access to the same life-sustaining treatment as provided to those without a disability. Substitute decision makers may only terminate treatment if an individual has a terminal condition or is permanently unconscious.

Relevant professional guidelines are consistent with these legal standards. An American Association on Intellectual and Developmental Disabilities (AAIDD, 2005) position statement provides that nutrition and hydration may be withheld only if such treatment would prolong the process of dying, cause suffering, or if an individual is in an irreversible coma. An ARC policy statement (The Arc, 2002) asserts that surrogate decision makers have the authority to refuse nutrition and hydration only if a person's condition is terminal and death is imminent. Standards of the National Guardianship Association (National Guardianship Association, 2007) indicate that when making decisions regarding the withholding of medical treatment, including artificial nutrition and hydration, there should in all cases be a presumption in favor of continued treatment. This same presumption in favor of treatment is articulated in a position statement of Syracuse University's Center on Human Policy (2005), with the additional provisions that life-sustaining treatment, including the provision of food and liquids, should not be withheld unless death is genuinely imminent and the treatment is objectively futile. Because judgments of futility are sometimes based on subjective views regarding an individual's quality of life, the position statement's requirement that futility determinations be based on an objective appraisal of the chances that a treatment would be successful represents an important contribution to policy guidelines.

Because Alice was diagnosed with a condition that made her eligible for hospice placement (failure-to-thrive) and Alice's doctors stated that further treatment was futile, it appeared legally and professionally defensible to withhold nutrition and hydration. However, in Alice's case, failure-to-thrive occurred not in conjunction with a terminal illness but because she had, for unknown reasons, stopped eating. Failure-to-thrive is generally treatable in such cases (Bicket, 2004; Egbert, 1996), and temporary feeding via a G-tube may have helped Alice safely through her medical crisis.

Futility

It is likely that placement of a G-tube would have been successful in providing Alice with life-sustaining nourishment and hydration. That being the case, the statement by her physicians that a feeding tube would be futile was not based upon physiological or objective futility but on a conception of qualitative futility that has been questioned both in the fields of medicine and disability rights (Noble, 1999; Veatch, 1994; Weijer, 1999; Werth, 2005). Qualitative futility is assessed through asking questions such as, "Will the quality of life resulting from a medical intervention be so poor that the intervention does not actually benefit the person?" and "Will that person's life be worth living?"

In Alice's case, the relevant question was, "Is the quality of Alice's life sufficient to justify its preservation through providing artificial nutrition and hydration?" Despite caregivers' description of Alice as a charming woman who enjoyed many aspects of life, her family and physicians felt the quality of her life was so poor that efforts to keep her alive were not warranted. However, the use of subjective judgments based on quality of life to determine whether to withhold life-sustaining treatment is inconsistent with public policy (Syracuse University, Center on Human Policy, 2005), case law (Goldworth & Benitz, 1995; In the Matter of Baby K., 1993; Paris, Crone, & Reardon, 1990), as well as Pennsylvania state policy (MR Bulletin No. 00-98-08, 1998). Concern that citizens with disabilities in Pennsylvania might be discriminated against due to negative appraisals of the value of their lives is reflected in policy that prohibits determinations of futility based on value judgments regarding an individual's quality of life. Unfortunately, at the time Alice was denied a feeding tube, those advocating for her were not familiar with this state policy nor were they aware that determinations of futility could be based on questionable quality-of-life considerations.

Benefits and Risks of Feeding Tubes

Alice's guardian used recent research (Gillick, 2000) questioning the value of tube feeding to reject placement of a feeding tube. Although tube feeding in cases of advanced dementia and other terminal conditions is no longer recommended (Angus & Burakoff, 2003), feeding by G-tube is considered safe and effective for people with disabilities who have severe feeding difficulties (Borowitz, Sutphen, & Hutcheson, 1997; Heine, Reddihough, & Catto-Smith, 1995; Mathus-Vliegen, Koning, Taminiau, & Moorman-Voestermans, 2001; Samson-Fang, Butler, & O'Donnell, 2003). Especially pertinent to Alice's case is the indication for placement of a feeding tube in individuals who refuse to eat but show no evidence of a terminal illness (Angus & Burakoff, 2003). Feeding via G-tube has been shown to be of consistent benefit in bringing about weight gain and improving the quality of life of individuals with disabilities and their caregivers (McGrath, Splaingard, Alba, Kaufman, & Glicklick, 1992; Smith, Camfield, & Camfield, 1999; Sullivan et al., 2004; Tawfik, Dickson, Clarke, & Thomas, 1997).

There are complications associated with G-tubes: They may fall out, leak, or become blocked and bleeding or infection may occur at the ostomy site. However, the risks associated with these complications are outweighed by benefits in cases where this treatment is indicated (DeLegge et al., 2005). A concern that G-tube feeding might increase the risk of aspiration pneumonia (a fear expressed by Alice's guardian) was addressed in two recent studies involving individuals with severe disabilities. Both Gray and Kimmel (2006) and Sullivan et al. (2006) looked at rates of pneumonia and other chest infections prior to and 1 year following G-tube placement. They reported significant decreases following placement of feeding tubes. The fears expressed by Alice's guardian were not supported.

Conclusion

People with severe disabilities are at risk due to negative attitudes concerning the quality of their lives and the process through which physicians make judgments regarding futility of treatment. When questions arise concerning the provision of artificial nutrition and hydration, life-sustaining treatment may be withheld because of negative biases regarding the value of their lives. Misinformation regarding the risks and benefits of tube feeding in people with disabilities and confusion because this intervention has recently been noted to lack effectiveness in some other populations pose additional risk factors. Practitioners are urged to take care when explaining to surrogate decision makers the complex issues involved in decisions to withhold treatment, and they need to be aware that physicians give considerable weight to the decisions made by surrogates when making determinations of futility.

Back to Alice. Fortunately, a short time after her placement in a hospice, she began to eat again, and 3 weeks after she had been given a terminal diagnosis, the diagnosis was withdrawn. However, Alice's life had been put at risk due to fear and the lack of accurate information. Vigilance is needed to prevent others from experiencing similar risk.

References

American Association on Intellectual and Developmental Disabilities. (2005). *Caring at the end of life* [AAIDD position statement]. Retrieved February 12, 2008, from www.aaidd.org/content_170.cfm?navID531.

American Medical Association. (2007). *Code of medical ethics: Current opinions with annotations,* 2006–2007. E-2.20.

Angus, F., & Burakoff, R. (2003). The percutaneous endoscopic gastrostomy tube: Medical and ethical issues in placement. *The American Journal of Gastroenterology, 98,* 272–277.

Bicket, D. P. (2004). Common geriatric problems. In J. E. South-Paul, E. L. Lewis, & S. C. Matheny (Eds.), *Current diagnosis & treatment in family medicine* (pp. 494–505). New York: McGraw-Hill.

Borowitz, S. M., Sutphen, J. L., & Hutcheson, R. L. (1997). Percutaneous endoscopic gastrostomy without an antireflux procedure in neurologically disabled children. *Clinical Pediatrics, 36,* 25–29.

DeLegge, M. H., McClave, S. A., DiSario, J. A., Baskin, W. N., Brown, R. D., Fang, J. C., et al. (2005). Ethical and medicolegal aspects of PEG-tube placement and provision of artificial nutritional therapy. *Gastrointestinal Endoscopy, 62,* 952–959.

Egbert, A. M. (1996). The dwindles: Failure to thrive in older patients. *Nutrition Reviews, 54,* S25–S30.

Gillick, M. R. (2000). Rethinking the role of tube feeding in patients with advanced dementia. *New England Journal of Medicine, 342,* 206–210.

Goldworth, A., & Benitz, W.E. (1995). The case of Baby L revisited. *Clinical Pediatrics, 34,* 452–456.

Gray, D. S., & Kimmel, D. (2006). Enteral tube feeding and pneumonia. *American Journal on Mental Retardation, 111,* 113–120.

Heine, R. G., Reddihough, D. S., & Catto-Smith, A. G. (1995). Gastro-oesophageal reflux and feeding problems after gastrostomy in children with severe neurological impairment. *Developmental Medicine & Child Neurology, 37,* 320–329.

In the Matter of Baby K. (1993). 832 F.supp. 1022, E.D. Va.

King, A. (2005). What should we do for everyone? Response to "What should we do for Jay?" In W. C. Gaventa, & D. L. Coulter (Eds.) *End-of-life care: Bridging disability and aging with person-centered care* (pp. 27–32). New York: Haworth Pastoral Press.

Mathus-Vliegen, E. M. H., Koning, H., Taminiau, J. A. J. M., & Moorman-Voestermans, C. G. M. (2001). Percutaneous endoscopic gastrostomy and gastrojejunostomy in psychomotor retarded subjects: A follow-up covering 106 patient years. *Journal of Pediatric Gastroenterology and Nutrition, 33,* 488–494.

McGrath, S. J., Splaingard, M. L., Alba, H. M., Kaufman, B. H., & Glicklick, M. (1992). Survival and functional outcome of children with severe cerebral palsy following gastrostomy. *Archives of Physical Medicine & Rehabilitation, 73,* 133–137.

National Guardianship Association. (2007). *NGA Standard 15—Decision-making about withholding and withdrawal of medical treatment.* Retrieved February 12, 2008, from www.guardianship.org/pdf/standards.pdf

Noble, N. (1999, March). Do not resuscitate—Whose choice is it? *Tash Newsletter,* pp. 6–7.

Paris, J., Crone, R., & Reardon, F. (1990). Physicians' refusal of requested treatment: The case of Baby L. *New England Journal of Medicine, 322,* 1012–1015.

Pugh, G. (2005). The challenges of living and dying well: Response to "What should we do for Jay?" In W. C. Gaventa & D. L. Coulter (Eds.) *End-of-life care: Bridging disability and aging with person-centered care* (pp. 33–36). New York: Haworth Pastoral Press.

Quill, T. E. (2005). Terri Schiavo—A tragedy compounded. *New England Journal of Medicine, 352,* 1630–1633.

Samson-Fang, L., Butler, C., & O'Donnell, M. (2003). Effects of gastrostomy feeding in children with cerebral palsy: An AACPDM evidence report. *Developmental Medicine & Child Neurology, 45,* 415–426.

Smith, S. W., Camfield, C., & Camfield, P. (1999). Living with cerebral palsy and tube feeding: A population-based follow-up study. *Journal of Pediatrics, 135,* 307–310.

Sullivan, P. B., Juszczak, E., Bachlet, A. M. E., Thomas, A. G., Lambert, B., Vernon-Roberts, A., et al. (2004). Impact of gastrostomy tube feeding on the quality of life of carers of children with cerebral palsy. *Developmental Medicine & Child Neurology, 46,* 796–800.

Sullivan, P. B., Morrice, J. S., Vernon-Roberts, A., Grant, H., Eltumi, M., & Thomas, A. G. (2006). Does gastrostomy tube feeding in children with cerebral palsy increase the risk of respiratory morbidity? *Archives of Diseases in Children, 91,* 478–482.

Syracuse University, Center on Human Policy. (2005). *A statement of common principles on life-sustaining care and treatment of people with disabilities.* Retrieved November 11, 2008, from http://thechp.syr.edu/

Tawfik, R., Dickson, A., Clarke, M., & Thomas, A. G. (1997). Caregivers' perceptions following gastrostomy in severely disabled children with feeding problems. *Developmental Medicine & Child Neurology, 39,* 746–751.

The Arc. (2002). *Policy statement: Health care.* Retrieved February 12, 2008, from www.thearc.org/NetCommunity/Page.aspx?&pid-51372&srcid-5405

Turnbull, H. R. (2005a, May/June). One parent's perspective on Congress' intervention in end-of-life decision-making: Rud Turnbull's testimony before the U.S. Senate Committee on Health, Education, Labor and Pensions. *Tash Connections,* pp. 22–25.

Turnbull, H. R. (2005b). What should we do for Jay? In W. C. Gaventa, & D. L. Coulter (Eds.), *End-of-life care: Bridging disability and aging with person-centered care*. New York: Haworth Pastoral Press.

Veatch, R. M. (1994). Why physicians cannot determine if care is futile. *Journal of the American Geriatrics Society, 42,* 871–874.

Weijer, C. (1999). Medical futility. *Western Journal of Medicine, 170,* 254.

Werth, J. L. (2005). Concerns about decisions related to withholding/withdrawing life-sustaining treatment and futility for persons with disabilities. *Journal of Disability Policy Studies, 16,* 31–37.

David Orentlicher and
Christopher M. Callahan

Feeding Tubes, Slippery Slopes, and Physician-Assisted Suicide

Introduction

In the past few years, articles in the *New England Journal of Medicine*,[1] the *Journal of the American Medical Association*,[2] and the *Journal of the American Geriatrics Society*[3] have suggested that feeding tubes are substantially overused in patients with advanced dementia or other serious illnesses. Contrary to common understanding, artificial feeding often does not improve the patient's nutrition or ability to function.[4] The feeding tube, in fact, may not be providing any benefit to the patient in terms of length or quality of life.

Although the overuse of feeding tubes is troubling in some respects, it is reassuring in one important way. It indicates that slippery slope concerns about the "right to die" may be exaggerated. [Some commentators resisted recognizing the right for patients to forgo artificial nutrition, because they were concerned that, once this was legally allowed, it opened the door to a slippery slope of abuses. What would stop the laws from slipping from simply "allowing" discontinuation of nutrition, to "requiring" discontinuation of nutrition in vulnerable populations?] The legal option to refuse artificial nutrition and hydration would become a duty to refuse them.[5]

The overuse of feeding tubes provides important evidence for the view that extensions of the right to refuse life-sustaining treatment can occur without a slide down the slippery slope. Patients, families, and physicians apparently are reluctant to take action they think will hasten a patient's death, even if the action is permitted by law.[6] This reassuring finding is important for its own sake. Society needs to be alert to the possibility of premature terminations of life-sustaining treatment. Fortunately, it appears that feeding tubes are not being discontinued too soon. . . .

I. Feeding Tubes and Their Value for Patients

Perhaps because the value of artificial feeding seems intuitively obvious, the empirical literature is relatively sparse on the question of whether feeding tubes are beneficial for seriously and irreversibly ill patients. Most studies have involved retrospective chart reviews, and none of the prospective studies have involved a randomization of patients between tube feeding and oral feeding.[7]

From *Journal of Legal Medicine*, vol. 25, 2004, pp. 389–401. Copyright © 2004 by American College of Legal Medicine (ACLM). Reprinted by permission of Taylor & Francis Group via Rightslink.

At one time, tube feeding was provided exclusively by naso-gastric tubes that were inserted into the stomach by passing them through the nose, throat, and esophagus. While naso-gastric tubes are still used for short-term feeding, they have been replaced for long-term feeding by gastrostomy tubes. Gastrostomy tubes cause less discomfort for the patient, and they entail fewer complications than naso-gastric tubes (such as erosion of the nasal tissue and aspiration pneumonia).

Originally, gastrostomy tubes were inserted into the stomach during a surgical procedure that required the cutting of an opening into the abdominal wall. Dr. Michael Gauderer and his colleagues then developed the percutaneous endoscopic gastrostomy (PEG) procedure in 1979,[8] which requires only two small incisions into the abdominal wall (much like laparoscopic surgery now has supplanted open abdominal surgery for most gall bladder removals).

Gauderer reported that his experiences with high complication rates among children undergoing surgical gastrostomy motivated his research to find a safer alternative. Over the past 25 years, Gauderer and other scientists have demonstrated clearly that the PEG procedure is safer and associated with fewer complications than open gastrostomies. In reflecting on the success of this procedure, Gauderer notes that "in part because of its simplicity and low complication rate, this minimally invasive procedure also lends itself to overutilization."[9] He suggests that "much of our effort in the future needs to be directed toward the ethical aspects associated with long-term enteral feeding [because] . . . we as physicians must continuously strive to demonstrate that our interventions truly benefit the patient."[10]

One of the difficulties in understanding the benefits of PEG is the implicit assumption that, if the procedure provides nutrition and is safe, then it must be beneficial for those unable to eat because nutrition is so fundamental to health and recovery from illness. Over the past two decades, patients, clinicians, caregivers, and scientists have increasingly challenged this assumption. Most of the early research on PEG focused on short-term operative complication rates. Then, case reports and editorials began to surface about patients or patient groups who were harmed or endured prolonged suffering because of artificial feeding. These reports were followed by retrospective studies examining mortality and longer-term complication rates among older adults receiving PEG. Eventually, long-term prospective studies examining nutritional, functional, and quality of life outcomes were conducted. These studies demonstrated the limited beneficial effects of PEG among some older adults receiving the procedure, and particularly those with dementia. Here, we review the empirical evidence addressing the clinical outcomes of older adults receiving percutaneous endoscopic gastrostomy.

Until the mid-1990s, most studies reporting on the outcomes of PEG focused on the operative and peri-operative complications rates. This was understandable, given the clinical motivation for the early development of the procedure and the focus on decreasing the complication rate associated with open gastrostomies. Most of these studies relied on data from retrospective chart reviews of patients undergoing the procedure at major academic medical centers. In a review of 48 such studies, Wollman and colleagues reported a 95.7% success rate for PEG placement.[11] Major complications occurred in 9.4% of patients, minor complications in 5.9%, and tube-related complications in 16%.[12] Thus, the procedure clearly was safe in terms of peri-operative complications. However, Wollman also reported a 30-day mortality rate of 14.7% across all studies.[13] Although these deaths did not appear to be related to the procedure, this finding provided some early indications about the magnitude of competing morbidities among this patient population.

In 1997, Rabeneck and collaborators reported patient outcomes from a retrospective review of patients who received PEG in Veterans Affairs hospitals between 1990 and 1992.[14] The authors identified 7,369 veterans who had received a PEG for cerebrovascular disease, other neurologic disease, or cancer.[15] The complication rate was reported as low (4%), but the scientists reported 23.5% in-hospital mortality.[16] Furthermore, the median survival of the cohort receiving PEG was only 7.5 months.[17] The authors suggested that the high mortality rate was related to the patients' underlying disease rather than the procedure, but raised the question of the utility of the procedure among patients who were terminally ill.[18] In a similar study using claims data from hospitalized Medicare beneficiaries, Grant and colleagues reported mortality rates among 81,105 Medicare beneficiaries receiving gastrostomy in 1991.[19] The authors reported a 30-day mortality rate of 23.9%.[20] Mortality increased to 63% at one year and 81.3% at three years.[21] . . .

Callahan and colleagues conducted the first prospective study among all older adults receiving PEG in a defined community in order to identify a truly representative sample of older adults receiving the procedure.[22] Assembling the patient population in this manner provides greater assurance that all older adults receiving the procedure are included. Studies limited to outcomes among patients who survive the initial hospitalization may miss as many as 30% of the patients undergoing the procedure, because those patients die before they leave the hospital. Studies limited to a single academic medical center or hospital suffer from the selection biases that determine how patients come to receive the procedure at that particular site. For example, some tertiary medical centers may attract the most complicated patients and thus report higher mortality rates. Studies relying on national claims data are able to capture complication rates and mortality for a nationally representative sample, but typically cannot monitor nutritional parameters or functional status.

By monitoring the practice of all gastroenterologists in a small community in Indiana, Callahan and colleagues were able to identify 150 patients age 60 and older who had a PEG tube placed over a 15-month period. The mean age was 78.9 ± 8.1 (range 60–98), 56% were women, and 83.3% were white.[23] The mean Cumulative Illness Rating Scale score for this group of patients was higher than any other group reported in the literature, demonstrating the high burden of chronic illness among this cohort.[24] About half of the PEGs were placed during the course of care for an acute hospitalization and the other half were placed among chronically ill patients receiving care in the community. The most frequent indications for the PEG were stroke (40.7%), neurodegenerative disorders (34.7%), and cancer (13.3%). Among remaining patients (11.3%), the most frequent indication was prevention of aspiration pneumonia.[25]

There were 24 patients among the original 150 who could not undergo the detailed study assessment because they died precipitously following the procedure.[26] Among the patients surviving long enough to complete the baseline assessment, the majority reported severe impairment in their abilities to perform basic activities of daily living such as toileting, dressing, and bathing. Almost two-thirds of patients could not communicate verbally at the time of PEG. Among those capable of communication, the majority could not provide data for self-reported subjective health status measures because of severe cognitive impairment.[27] Thus, these data had to be collected from their caregivers. This finding highlights the limited capacity of many of these older adults to participate in their medical decision-making, including the decision to proceed with PEG.

The 30-day mortality among all patients undergoing the PEG procedure was 22% and 12-month mortality was 50%.[28] Among the 72 patients surviving at least 60 days, there were no changes in mean values of nutrition, physical function, cognitive function, mood, pain, or quality of life. Only rarely did patients experience improvement in functional or nutritional status.[29] The study also examined the process of care and found, perhaps surprisingly, that more than half of patients receiving PEG continued to receive food, liquids, or medications by mouth. One-third had to have the PEG tube replaced during the follow-up period. Nearly all patients reported PEG-related symptoms, such as vomiting and diarrhea, and many received treatment with sedative-hypnotics and narcotic analgesics.[30] In sum, the study findings depict older adults in the terminal stages of illness receiving the PEG in a perhaps desperate attempt to improve function and longevity or reverse the course of the illness. There clearly were patients in this cohort who did benefit from PEG, but the study was not large enough to begin to identify those patient characteristics that portend a favorable outcome. The definition of a favorable outcome can easily become a mercurial concept and some researchers have argued that PEG simply may provide for a more comfortable death. This does not, however, appear to be the reason that caregivers seek a PEG tube.

Callahan and colleagues reported patients' and caregivers' expectations for benefits from PEG tube feeding among the same cohort of patients described above.[31] Either patients or their surrogate decision-makers completed a semi-structured, face-to-face interview to map out the information-gathering process, expectations, and discussants involved in the decision to proceed with gastrostomy feeding.[32] Physicians completed a written questionnaire to determine their likelihood of recommending PEG tube placement, their involvement in the decision-making and recommendation process, and sources of perceived pressure in the decision-making.[33] Patients or their surrogate decision-makers reported that they discussed the decision to proceed with PEG with multiple people prior to accepting the procedure.[34] Often, these decision-makers sought the advice of family or friends who had a health care background. Decision-makers complained that they had to make their decisions based on incomplete information and reported considerable distress in arriving at the decision to proceed with artificial feeding. The decision for gastrostomy often appeared to be a "non-decision" in the sense that decision-makers perceived few, if any, alternatives.[35] Physicians also reported considerable distress in arriving at recommendations to proceed with PEG, including perceived pressures from families or other health care professionals. Providers whom the patient or caregiver identified as the primary care physician often reported that they were not intimately involved in the decision-making process.[36] These physicians had definable patterns of triage for PEG, but the assumptions underlying these patterns are not well supported by the medical literature (for instance, prevention of aspiration pneumonia).[37]

Decision-makers listed improved nutrition as the goal of PEG tube feeding in 70% of the cases. Other reasons included a desire to increase patient comfort (22%), extend life (18%), increase strength (14%), and help overcome an acute illness (10%).[38] Because data on these patients' long-term functional outcomes were lacking, decision-makers appeared to focus primarily on the short-term safety of the procedure and the potential for improved nutrition. Callahan and colleagues suggested that the interviews with decision-makers belied "a pervasive climate of 'inevitability' in the judgment to proceed with the artificial feeding."[39] Decision-makers simply saw no other reasonable alternatives.

Economic incentives also may play a role in medical decision-making about PEG tubes. Again using the cohort of older adults receiving PEG from the defined community, Callahan and colleagues estimated the economic costs of PEG tube feeding over one year.[40] Patients were interviewed at baseline and every two months for one year to obtain information on the use of enteral formula, complication rates, and health services. Inpatient charge data for all hospitalizations and PEG-related procedures for one year were obtained from the health care systems serving the defined community. Outpatient costs were estimated using volume data and customary charges for Medicare ambulatory visits.[41] Data collection was concluded at the time of the patient's death or one year post-PEG. The mean number of days of PEG tube feeding was 180 (range 5 to 365).[42] The average annual cost for PEG tube feeding for this cohort of patients was $7,488 (median $3,691) in 1997 dollars. The average daily cost of PEG tube feeding was $87.21 (median $33.50). The estimated cost of providing one year of feeding via PEG is $31,832 (median $12,227).[43]

The main components of these costs included the initial PEG procedure (accounting for 29.4% of total costs), enteral formula (24.9% of total costs), and hospital charges for major complications (33.4% of total costs). There was considerable variation in charges among patients due to the cost of rare but expensive major complications. Using cost estimates from the literature, the authors then compared the cost of PEG tube feeding to hand feeding and found little evidence that PEG tube feeding accounted for lower total costs. However, feeding patients via PEG resulted in cost shifts affecting the interests of the primary payer. Because PEG costs are primarily borne by third party payers such as Medicare and hand feeding is reimbursed only through the daily charges allowed for skilled facility care (or is provided by informal caregivers among those living in the community), there may be financial incentives for skilled facilities to favor PEG tube feeding.

In 2001, Dharmarajan and colleagues conducted a systematic review of the literature to summarize research on the outcomes of PEG in older patients with dementia.[44] They noted the absence of randomized trials of PEG tube feeding as compared to alternative methods such as hand feeding. Among 19 studies reporting patient outcomes, 11 studies had been published in the prior three years.[45] The Dharmarajan and colleagues review described the low rate of serious short-term complications, but a high 30-day mortality (~25%).[46] None of the reviewed studies demonstrated significant improvement in nutritional parameters, prevention of aspiration pneumonia, pressure sores, or infections, and some studies found the PEG tubes actually could increase the likelihood of these complications.[47] None of the reviewed studies demonstrated improvement in functional status, comfort, or quality of life.[48] Again, some studies suggested a decline in comfort with the use of PEG tubes. The authors concluded: "Although tube feeding may not be totally futile in all cases, an analysis of the benefits and risks seldom leads to a definite positive result in cognitively impaired individuals."[49]

In sum, the studies generally suggest that patients, families, and physicians misjudge the benefits derived from tube feeding. Recall, for example, the prospective PEG study in a small community. Researchers found that, of the patients who survived at least 60 days, more than two-thirds had no significant improvement in functional, nutritional, or subjective health status.[50] Other studies also have failed to detect improvements in functional or nutritional status, and they have not found any improvement in survival for patients with advanced dementia.[51] In the SUPPORT study, artificial feeding was associated with increased survival in coma patients but decreased survival in patients with acute kidney failure, multiple organ system failure, cirrhosis of the liver, or COPD.[52]

Tube feeding often is advocated to reduce the risk of aspiration pneumonia,[53] but studies in patients with advanced dementia have not shown that it reduces that risk.[54] Indeed, gastrostomy tube placement may increase the risk that the stomach contents will reflux into the esophagus, and some studies have found that tube feeding increases the risk of aspiration pneumonia.[55] Other purported benefits from artificial nutrition also have not materialized. Tube feeding has neither enhanced the healing of existing pressure sores nor prevented the formation of new sores. It also has not reduced the overall risk of infection.[56]

Although artificial feeding may be desired to ensure the comfort of a patient, that goal often is beyond the reach of feeding tubes. Patients often are restrained, either physically or with sedating drugs, to prevent them from pulling their tubes out, and this can be distressing to them.[57] Artificial feeding also can deprive patients of the pleasure they experience from eating.[58] In short, it appears that feeding tubes are being used in many patients without any real benefit to them.

II. The Absence of a Slippery Slope

Despite the questionable efficacy of artificial feeding, the use of feeding tubes is common. In 1995 alone, more than 120,000 PEG tubes were inserted into patients age 65 or older.[59] A study based on 1999 nationwide data found that more than a third of nursing home patients with advanced cognitive impairment had feeding tubes.[60] Concern with overuse of artificial feeding has spurred two recent, prominent discussions, with both authors concluding that tube feeding generally should not be used for patients with advanced dementia.[61] As one of the authors observed, difficulty with eating often is a sign of end-stage disease and tube feeding cannot stem the progression of illness at that point.[62] Hand feeding should be attempted, but artificial feeding generally cannot accomplish anything more for the patient than can hand feeding.

What is striking about the apparent overuse of feeding tubes is the extent to which it suggests that patients, families, and physicians have not succumbed to their freedom to withhold or withdraw artificial nutrition from irreversibly ill patients. In the 1980s, before courts clearly recognized a patient's right to forgo artificial feeding, ethicists, physicians, and other commentators engaged in a major debate about the morality of discontinuing nutrition and hydration in accordance with the patient's wishes. Many opponents of such a right warned that it would have serious consequences.

Daniel Callahan, for example, wrote that society can easily move from permitting the withdrawal of artificial nutrition to requiring its withdrawal. If patients never will regain their mental faculties, and medical care is very expensive, it is easy for society to conclude that there is no point in trying to prolong life with a feeding tube.[63] Mark Siegler, Alan Weisbard, and others also expressed concern that cost constraints would transform a right to die by withdrawal of artificial feeding into a duty to die that way.[64]

Yet, feeding tubes remain a mainstay of the care of patients whose ability to eat is compromised. The fundamental social ethic in favor of feeding those who are starving has not been eroded as feared.[65] As discussed above, feeding tubes are used even when they do not benefit the patients who receive them. In addition, other studies regularly show that physicians find it more difficult to stop feeding and hydration than to discontinue ventilators, dialysis, or other life-sustaining treatments[66] and also that physicians often are uncomfortable withholding or withdrawing nutrition, even when doing so is consistent with the patient's wishes.[67] . . .

The reluctance of physicians and families to discontinue feeding tubes parallels judicial behavior. Courts also have hesitated to authorize withdrawals of feeding tubes. Although judges have concluded that artificial nutrition and hydration are medical treatments in the same way as ventilators or dialysis and, therefore, have recognized an unqualified right of patients to have artificial nutrition discontinued, courts also have erected strict procedural rules to protect incompetent patients from premature withdrawals. When courts are asked whether feeding can be stopped for a patient who is neither terminally ill nor permanently unconscious, they consistently respond that feeding must be given in the absence of very clear evidence that the patient previously expressed a preference against tube feeding.

The Michigan Supreme Court's decision in *In re Martin*[68] is a good example. Michael Martin was injured in an automobile accident, leaving him with severe impairment of his intellectual and physical abilities. He could no longer walk or talk, and was dependent on a PEG tube for his nutrition. Although there was some disagreement among the medical experts who evaluated Mr. Martin, they generally concluded that he could understand some simple questions but he lacked an understanding of more complex matters like his physical capabilities and medical condition. They all agreed that his impairments were permanent.[69]

Mr. Martin's wife requested that the feeding tube be removed. In her opinion, he would not have wanted life-sustaining treatment given the severity of his injuries. In reaching her opinion, Ms. Martin drew on conversations that she had had with her husband. She testified:

> Discussions between Mike and me regarding what our wishes would be if either of us was ever involved in a serious accident, had a disabling or terminal illness or was dying of old age, began approximately eight years ago. These discussions occurred on many different occasions. As I indicate below, several were triggered by movies which we saw together. Mike's position was always the same: he did not want to be kept alive on machines and he made me promise that I would never permit it.
>
> Some of the conversations that we had about medical care in this context occurred after we watched movies about people who no longer were mentally competent either due to illness, accident, or old age; others involved people who could no longer do anything for themselves, such as persons who lived in a nursing home and could no longer feed or dress themselves and needed to wear diapers or have other measures taken to continue existing. Mike stated to me on several occasions: "That's bullshit, I would never want to live like that." He also said to me, "Please don't ever let me exist that way because those people don't even have their dignity.". . .
>
> Some movies that triggered our discussions were about accidents—car accidents, hunting accidents or other accidents near home or in water. Mike was an avid hunter and frequently expressed concerned [sic] about a hunting accident. Mike frequently told me that if he ever had an accident from which he would "not recover" and "could not be the same person," he did "not want to live that way." He would say, "Mary, promise me you wouldn't let me live like that if I can't be the person I am right now, because if you do, believe me I'll haunt you every day of your life." I stated my promise to him and made him promise me the same.[70]

The court held that the feeding tube could not be removed from Mr. Martin. According to the court, prior oral statements by the patient will be sufficient to justify withdrawal of treatment "[o]nly when the patient's prior statements clearly illustrate a serious, well thought out, consistent decision to refuse treatment under these exact circumstances or circumstances highly similar to the current situation."[71] Under this approach, a general refusal of artificial measures is not sufficient. Rather, patients must have spoken to the particular medical problem they have and possibly even to the specifics of artificial feeding. The California, New Jersey, and Wisconsin Supreme Courts also have adopted strict standards for withdrawing feeding tubes from incompetent patients who are neither terminally ill nor permanently unconscious.[72]

In the California case of *Wendland v. Wendland,*[73] Rose Wendland asked that a feeding tube be withdrawn from her husband, Michael Wendland, two years after an automobile accident left Mr. Wendland with severe and permanent brain damage.[74] He retained some ability to interact with others. As the court reported:

> At his highest level of function between February and July, 1995, Robert was able to do such things as throw and catch a ball, operate an electric wheelchair with assistance, turn pages, draw circles, draw an 'R' and perform two-step commands. For example, "[h]e was able to respond appropriately to the command 'close your eyes and open them when I say the number 3.' . . . He could choose a requested color block out of four color blocks. He could set the right peg in a pegboard. . . . He remained unable to vocalize. Eye blinking was successfully used as a communication mode for a while, however no consistent method of communication was developed."[75]

Despite this residual capacity to interact with people and his environment, Mr. Wendland's impairments were quite severe. The court also observed:

> The same medical report summarized his continuing impaiments as follows: "severe cognitive impairment that is not possible to fully appreciate due to the concurrent motor and communication impairments . . ."; "maladaptive behavior characterized by agitation, aggressiveness and non-compliance"; "severe paralysis on the right and moderate paralysis on the left"; "severely impaired communication, without compensatory augmentative communication system"; "severe swallowing dysfunction, dependent upon non-oral enteric tube feeding for nutrition and hydration"; "incontinence of bowel and bladder"; "moderate spasticity"; "mild to moderate contractures"; "general dysphoria"; "recurrent medical illnesses, including pneumonia, bladder infections, sinusitis"; and "dental issues."[76]

In rejecting the spouse's request that Mr. Wendland's feeding tube be discontinued, the court emphasized the need for clear and convincing evidence that Mr. Wendland "would have refused treatment *under the circumstances of this case.*"[77] Although Mr. Wendland had spoken about his desire not to live as a "vegetable," he had not disclosed his preferences for treatment when his medical condition would be superior to the condition of someone in a persistent vegetative state.[78] The New York Court of Appeals has adopted similarly strict standards for discontinuing feeding tubes, as well as ventilators and other treatments, from incompetent patients who are neither terminally ill nor permanently unconscious (or any incompetent patient).[79]

In sum, although the slippery slope was a real risk once courts recognized a right for patients to have artificial nutrition withheld or withdrawn, the evidence seems to suggest that, if anything, physicians, families, and judges have been too unwilling to discontinue the artificial feeding of patients. Indeed, one thing is clear—the freedom to refuse a feeding tube has not become a duty to do so.

References

1. Muriel R. Gillick, *Rethinking the Role of Tube Feeding in Patients with Advanced Dementia,* 342 New Eng. J. Med. 206 (2000).

2. Susan L. Mitchell et al., *Clinical and Organizational Factors Associated with Feeding Tube Use Among Nursing Home Residents with Advanced Cognitive Impairment,* 290 J.A.M.A. 73 (2003); Thomas E. Finucane et al., *Tube Feeding in Patients with Advanced Dementia: A Review of the Evidence,* 282 J.A.M.A. 1365(1999).

3. Christopher M. Callahan et al., *Outcomes of Percutaneous Endoscopic Gastrostomy Among Older Adults in a Community Setting,* 48 J. Am. Geriatr. Soc'y 1048 (2000); Thomas E. Finucane & Colleen Christmas, *More Caution About Tube Feeding,* 48 J. Am. Geriatr. Soc'y 1167 (2000).

4. Gillick, *supra* note 1; Mitchell et al., *supra* note 2; Finucane et al., *supra* note 2; Callahan et al., *supra* note 3.

5. Daniel Callahan, *On Feeding the Dying,* 13(5) Hastings Cen. Rep. 22 (1983); Mark Siegler & Alan J. Weisbard, *Against the Emerging Stream: Should Fluids and Nutritional Support Be Discontinued?,* 145 Arch. Intern. Med. 129 (1985).

6. Callahan et al., *supra* note 3.

7. Finucane et al., *supra* note 2; Callahan et al., *supra* note 3.

8. Michael L. Gauderer, *Twenty Years of Percutaneous Endoscopic Gastrostomy: Origin and Evolution of a Concept and Its Expanded Applications,* 50 Gastrointestinal Endoscopy 879 (1999); Michael L. Gauderer et al., *Gastrostomy Without Laparotomy: A Percutaneous Endoscopic Technique,* 15 J. Fed. Surg. 872 (1980).

9. Gauderer, *supra* note 8, at 882.

10. *Id.*

11. Bruce Wollman et al., *Radiologic, Endoscopic, and Surgical Gastrostomy: An Institutional Evaluation and Meta-Analysis of the Literature,* 197 Radiology 669, 701 (1995).

12. *Id.*

13. *Id.* at 702.

14. Linda Rabeneck et al., *Long-Term Outcomes of Patients Receiving Percutaneous Endoscopic Gastrostomy Tubes,* 11 J. Gen. Intern. Med. 287 (1996).

15. *Id.* at 288.

16. *Id.* at 289.

17. *Id.*

18. *Id.* at 291–92.

19. Mark D. Grant et al., *Gastrostomy Placement and Mortality Among Hospitalized Medicare Beneficiaries,* 279 J.A.M.A. 1973 (1998).

20. *Id.* at 1974, table 3.

21. *Id.*

22. Callahan et al., *supra* note 3; Christopher M. Callahan et al., *Decision-Making for Percutaneous Endoscopic Gastrostomy Among Older Adults in a Community Setting*, 47 J. Am. Geriatr. Soc'y 1105 (1999).

23. Callahan et al., *supra* note 3, at 1050.

24. *Id.*

25. *Id.*

26. *Id.*

27. *Id.*

28. *Id.*

29. *Id.* at 1050 & 1052, table 2.

30. *Id.* at 1050 & 1053, table 3.

31. Callahan et al., *supra* note 26.

32. *Id.* at 1106.

33. *Id.*

34. *Id.* at 1106–07.

35. *Id.* at 1107.

36. *Id.* at 1107 & 1108, table 1.

37. *Id.* at 1107.

38. Callahan et al., *supra* note 3, at 1052.

39. Callahan et al., *supra* note 26, at 1107.

40. Christopher M. Callahan et al., *Healthcare Costs Associated with Percutaneous Endoscopic Gastrostomy Among Older Adults in a Defined Community*, 49 J. Am. Geriatr. Soc'y 1525 (2001).

41. *Id.* at 1526–27.

42. *Id.* at 1527.

43. *Id.* at 1528, table 1.

44. Thiruvinvamalai S. Dharmarajan et al., *Percutaneous Endoscopic Gastrostomy and Outcome in Dementia*, 96 Am. J. Gastroenterology 2556 (2001).

45. *Id.* at 2557.

46. *Id.* at 2557–58.

47. *Id.* at 2559–60.

48. *Id.* at 2560.

49. *Id.* at 2561.

50. Callahan et al., *supra* note 3, at 1052, table 2.

51. Finucane et al., *supra* note 2.

52. Marie L. Borum et al., *The Effect of Nutritional Supplementation on Survival in Seriously Ill Hospitalized Adults: An Evaluation of the SUPPORT Data*, 48 J. Am. Geriat. Soc'y S33 (2000). COPD stands for chronic obstructive pulmonary (or lung) disease. Emphysema is a well-known type of COPD.

53. In aspiration pneumonia, the food and digestive secretions in the stomach are regurgitated up the esophagus and down the respiratory tract into the lungs.

54. Gillick, *supra* note 1, at 206–07; Finucane et al., *supra* note 2, at 1365–66.

55. Finucane et al., *supra* note 2, at 1365–66.

56. *Id.* at 1367.

57. Gillick, *supra* note 1, at 207–08.

58. *Id.* at 207; Finucane et al., *supra* note 2, at 1368.

59. Callahan et al., *supra* note 3, at 1048.

60. Mitchell et al., *supra* note 2.

61. Gillick, *supra* note 1; Finucane et al., *supra* note 2.

62. Gillick, *supra* note 1, at 207.

63. Callahan, *supra* note 5.

64. Siegler & Weisbard, *supra* note 5; William E. May et al., *Feeding and Hydrating the Permanently Unconscious and Other Vulnerable Persons*, 3 Issues L. & Med. 203 (1987).

65. Callahan, *supra* note 5; Gilbert Meilaender, *On Removing Food and Water: Against the Stream*, 14(6) Hastings Cen. Rep. 11 (1984).

66. David A. Asch et al., *The Sequence of Withdrawing Life-Sustaining Treatments from Patients*, 107 Am. J. Med. 153(1999).

67. Mildred Z.S. Solomon et al., *Decisions Near the End of Life: Professional Views on Life-Sustaining Treatments*, 83 Am. J. Pub. Health 14 (1999).

68. 538 N.W.2d 399 (Mich. 1995).

69. *Id.* at 402–04.

70. *Id.* at 411–12.

71. *Id.* at 411.

72. Spahn v. Eisenberg, 563 N.W.2d 485 (Wis. 1997); Wendland v. Wendland, 28 P.3d 151 (Cal. 2001); *In re* Conroy, 486 A.2d 1209 (N.J. 1985).

73. 28 P.3d 151 (Cal. 2001).

74. *Id.* at 154.

75. *Id.* at 154–55 (quoting from a medical evaluation submitted to the court).

76. *Id.* at 155 (quoting from a medical evaluation submitted to the court).

77. *Id.* at 173 (emphasis added).

78. *Id.*

79. *In re* Westchester County Med. Ctr., 531 N.E.2d 607, 613 (N.Y. 1988). When the patient is terminally ill or permanently unconsicious, the standards typically are more relaxed. *In re* Jobes, 529 A.2d 434 (N.J. 1987); Mark A. Hall et al., Health Care Law and Ethics 544–46 (6th ed. 2003).

EXPLORING THE ISSUE

Are Feeding Tubes Obligatory?

Critical Thinking and Reflection

1. What are the burdens of feeding tubes in dying patients? What do the writers identify as problems that occur in patients with feeding tubes?
2. Consider the situation of a family member who decides not to have a feeding tube (withholding) placed in an elderly parent who has suffered a massive stroke. The neurologist indicates that recovery is unlikely. How is this different than or similar to a family member (proxy) who elects to remove a feeding tube that has been in place (withdrawing) for 3 years because no recovery has occurred?
3. How are the issues of feeding tubes different for persons with disabilities as compared with persons who have advanced dementia? Does the degree of disability or the level of burden of the feeding make a difference?
4. What role does food and feeding others play within our culture or society? Do caregivers and family members lose an important nurturing ability when feeding is no longer possible? Are there other ways that families can demonstrate nurturing someone who is dying and is no longer interested in eating?

Is There Common Ground?

As the population ages there will likely be more and more families, patients, and caregivers facing decisions about whether or not to start a feeding tube. Most physicians, caregivers, and lawyers agree that withholding or withdrawing a feeding tube in a terminally ill patient is an acceptable approach to end-of-life care, and can prevent unnecessary suffering and burdens for dying patients. Although the law allows for withholding or withdrawing feeding tubes, the decision is almost always a difficult one for families (Wick & Zanni, 2009).

For many patients, tube feedings are placed at a time when the life expectancy or prognosis is not clear. Family members may hope for improvement or a miracle. Technological advances in health care have made feeding tube placement an easy outpatient procedure to perform, regardless of how realistic or unrealistic the outcomes for the patient may be. When a patient shows no sign of improvement, some family members are reluctant to remove a feeding tube because of a fear that they are actively "killing" the patient, rather than simply allowing them to die. Decisions are confounded in patients who left no advance directives about how they would want care to be handled if they had a terminal illness. These decisions might be less troubling if patients were encouraged or required to complete advance directive forms that identify their wishes for care if they become terminally ill, including a decision whether they would want tube feedings.

Sharing food and offering food to family members is an important nurturing gesture. But continuing to providing nutrition to a patient who is slowly losing his/her ability to digest and process food can increase suffering at the end of life. Discussions about whether or not to place a feeding tube should include information not only about the possible benefits of the feeding tube, but also the physiological burden of feedings in a dying patient, identification of the previously stated wishes of the patient, the prognosis of the illness, and the cultural and religious views of the family.

References

Ball, S. (2006). Nurse-patient advocacy and the right to die. *Journal of Psychosocial Nursing, 44*(12), 36–42.

Carey, T. S., Hanson, L., Garrett, J. M., Lewis, C., Phifer, N., Cox, C. E., et al. (2006). Expectations and outcomes of gastric feeding tubes. *American Journal of Medicine, 119*(6), 527.e11–527.e16. doi:10.1016/j.amjmed.2005.11.021

Committee on Doctrine of the National Conference of Catholic Bishops. (2009). *Ethical and religious directives for Catholic health care services* (5th ed.). Washington, D.C.: United States Conference of Catholic Bishops.

Gillick, M. R. & Volandes, A. E. (2008). The standard of caring: Why do we still use feeding tubes in patients with advanced dementia? *Journal of the American Medical Directors Association, 9*(5), 364–367.

Lynn, J. & Harrold, J. (1999). *Handbook for mortals: Guidance for people facing serious illness.* Retrieved from www.growthhouse.org/mortals/mor0.html

Orentlicher, D. & Callahan, C. M. (2004). Feeding tubes, slippery slopes and physician assisted suicide. *Journal of Legal Medicine, 25*(4), 389–409. doi:10.1080/01947640490887544

Penner, M. (2005). *End of life ethics: A primer.* Retrieved from www.str.org/site/News2?page=NewsArticle&id=5223

Sampson, E. L., Candy, B., & Jones, L. (2009). Enteral tube feeding for older people with advanced dementia. *The Cochrane Library, 2*, 1–25.

Sandler, A. G. (2009). A right to nutrition and hydration: A need for vigilance. *Intellectual and Developmental Disabilities, 47*(3), 234–238. doi:10.1352/1934-9556-47.3.234

Sharp, H. M. & Shega, J. W. (2009). Feeding tube placement in patients with advanced dementia: The beliefs and practice patterns of speech-language pathologists. *American Journal of Speech-Language Pathology, 18*(3), 222–230. doi:10.1044/1058-0360(2008/08-0013)

Sulmasy, D. P. (2005). Terri Schiavo and the Roman Catholic tradition of forgoing extraordinary means of care. *Journal of Law, Medicine & Ethics, 33*(2), 359–362.

Sulmasy, D. P. (2006). Are feeding tubes morally obligatory? *St. Anthony Messenger.* Retrieved from www.americancatholic.org/messenger/jan2006/feature1.asp

U.S. Catholic Church. (2003). *Catechism of the Catholic Church.* New York: Doubleday.

Wick, J. Y. & Zanni, G. R. (2009). Removing the feeding tube: A procedure with a contentious past. *Consulting Pharmacist, 24*(12), 874–883.

Additional Resources

Amella, E. J., Lawrence, J. F., & Gresle, S. O. (2005). Tube feeding: Prolonging life or death in vulnerable populations? *Mortality, 10*(1), 69–81. doi:10.1080/13576270500031089

American Nurses Association. (2010). *Position statement: Registered nurses' roles and responsibilities in providing expert care and counseling at the end of life.* Retrieved from www.nursingworld.org/MainMenuCategories/EthicsStandards/Ethics-Position-Statements/etpain14426.aspx

Detweiler, M., Kim, K., & Bass, J. (2004). Percutaneous endoscopic gastrostomy in cognitively impaired older adults: A geropsychiatric perspective. *American Journal of Alzheimer's Disease and Other Dementias, 19*(1), 24–30. doi:10.1177/153331750401900105

Freeman, C., Ricevuto, A., & DeLegge, M. (2010). Enteral nutrition in patients with dementia and stroke. *Current Opinion in Gastroenterology, 26*, 156–159. doi:10.1097/MOG.0b013e3283346fae

Jansen, L. A. & Sulmasy, D. P. (2002). Sedation, alimentation, hydration, and equivocation: Careful conversation about care at the end of life. *Annals of Internal Medicine, 136*(11), 845–849.

McNeil, D. (2003, October 26). In feeding-tube case, many neurologists back courts. *New York Times*, p. 18.

Teno, J. M., Mitchell, S. L., Skinner, J., Kuo, S., Fisher, E., Intrator, O., et al. (2009). Churning: The association between health care transitions and feeding tube insertion for nursing home residents with advanced cognitive impairment. *Journal of Palliative Medicine, 12*(4), 359–362. doi:10.1089/jpm.2008.0168

Torchia, J. (2003). Artificial hydration and nutrition for the PVS patient: Ordinary care or extraordinary intervention? *The National Catholic Bioethics Quarterly, 3*(4), 719–730.

Tucker, K. (2004). Medico-legal case report and commentary: Inadequate pain management in the context of terminal cancer. The case of Lester Tomlinson. *Pain Medicine, 5*(2), 214–228.

ISSUE 9

Does Withholding or Withdrawing Futile Treatment Kill People?

YES: Nathan E. Goldstein, Davendra Mehta, Ezra Teitelbaum, Elizabeth H. Bradley, and R. Sean Morrison, from "'It's Like Crossing a Bridge': Complexities Preventing Physicians from Discussing Deactivation of Implantable Defibrillators at the End of Life," *Journal of General Internal Medicine* (vol. 23, no. S1, pp. 2–6, 2008)

NO: Daniel P. Sulmasy, from "Within You/Without You: Biotechnology, Ontology, and Ethics," *Journal of General Internal Medicine* (vol. 23, no. S1, pp. 69–72, 2007)

Learning Outcomes

After reading this issue, you should be able to:

- Gain an understanding of the various treatments that might be withheld or withdrawn at the end of life.
- Describe the difference between withdrawing treatment and killing a patient who has a terminal illness.
- Understand the importance communication by health care professionals about outcomes of treatments when assisting patients in making decisions about end-of-life care.
- Discuss and describe the unique problem that implanted cardiac pacemakers and defibrillators can create in end-of-life decisions.

ISSUE SUMMARY

YES: According to Nathan Goldstein, Associate Professor of Geriatrics and Palliative Medicine at Mount Sinai Hospital in New York, and colleagues, physicians viewed deactivating implanted cardiac defibrillators (ICD) differently than withdrawal of other life-sustaining treatments; physicians also expressed discomfort in approaching this discussion with patients or family members.

NO: Daniel P. Sulmasy, a Franciscan friar, ethicist, and physician at the University of Chicago Medical Center, discusses the ethics of withdrawing futile treatments, and establishes the difference between forgoing a life-sustaining treatment (such as deactivating an ICD) and the intent implied in the word "killing."

Research on care in intensive care units indicates 50–70 percent of deaths occur after some type of treatment has been withdrawn or withheld (Melhado & Byers, 2011). In the United States, competent patients who are dying have the legal right to refuse treatment or have treatment withdrawn at any time based on their wishes. This legal grounding is based on the principle of autonomy, which is highly valued in Western cultures (Gilligan & Raffin, 1996). In order to demonstrate autonomous wishes, patients must be fully informed about the treatment, should not be coerced, and must have decisional capacity (see Issue 1). Advance directives which have been established to help guide families and clinicians about care can make difference in the kind of care patients receive at the end of life (see Issue 2). A presidential commission published a consensus document to support patient decisions to forego "futile" treatments, that is, treatments that are medically ineffective, nonbeneficial, or are disproportionately burdensome at the end of life (Pellegrino, 2000, 2005; Pellegrino & Sulmasy, 2003; President's Council on Bioethics, 2008, p. 91). However, treatments don't have to be "futile" to be refused by patients. Dying patients always have a right to refuse treatments that they do not want.

Regardless of patient views, a recent survey demonstrated that physicians may be reluctant to withdraw certain types of care (Farber, Simpson, Salam, Collier, Weiner, & Boyer, 2006; Rydvall & Lynöe, 2008). One study found that physicians were more likely to withhold or withdraw ventilators and hemodialysis than they were to withhold or withdraw artificial means of providing fluids and nutrition or antibiotic therapy (Farber et al., 2006). Although patients have the right to refuse, withdraw, or withhold any type of treatment at the end of life, researchers and ethicists have written more about the debate on tube feedings for dying patients (see Issue 10). In this issue, we discuss the withdrawing of implanted cardiac defibrillators (ICDs), a newer technology that patients may find complicates end-of-life care.

As our population ages, the daily decisions for dying patients may include simpler technologies (such as implanted cardiac devices) that advance directives rarely address (Goldstein, Mehta, Teitelbaum, Bradley, & Morrison, 2008; Mueller et al., 2010). Advance directives cannot specifically list each and every possible treatment given in the health care system. In order to understand the decisions to be made, one must understand the types of cardiac devices that can be implanted.

There are several different implanted cardiac devices that help patients to maintain heart rhythms and function. Simple pacemakers help the heart to maintain a sustainable heart beat; these are used when the heart's internal pacemaker fails to keep the pace that is normal (Kapa, Mueller, Hayes, & Asirvatham, 2010). When pacemakers are turned off, patients may experience slow heart rates, episodes of fainting, or blackouts. In their study almost one-third of physicians and one-quarter of patients surveyed believed that turning off a pacemaker in a patient who is pacemaker dependent was considered physician-assisted suicide (Kapa et al., 2010). Despite the knowledge of a patient's terminal illness and the focus on comfort, family members and health professionals are hesitant to turn off a cardiac regulating device.

Another device, implanted cardiac defibrillators (ICDs) work to correct deadly arrhythmias (irregular or unusual heart rhythms). These devices deliver a shock to the heart to bring it back to a normal rhythm (Kapa et al., 2010). Brownlee (2008) discusses the case of an elderly man with dementia, dying of renal failure, whose routine cardiac shocks frightened and alarmed him each time the device discharged (see Issue 9). A palliative care team helped the family in getting the device deactivated in order to allow the patient to die more comfortably. In one survey, patients, physicians, and lawyers were more likely to approve of deactivating an ICD device if it would provide comfort at the end of life (Kapa et al., 2010). Research on family decision making indicates that families fear making decisions that might be responsible for the patient's death, even though they are fully aware the patient is dying of some other disease (Melhado & Byers, 2011).

There are also more advanced devices for patients who are in heart failure (indicating a heart that is so diseased it does not pump effectively). A left ventricular assist device (LVAD) is a surgically implanted device that helps patients with heart failure by pulling blood from the left ventricle and pumping it into the aorta. This relatively newer technology is known as a *bridge to transplant* for patients in severe heart failure who are candidates for a heart transplant. If the patient is not a candidate for transplant or no transplantable heart is available, the LVAD is considered *destination therapy* (Mueller et al., 2010). However, this device is not without problems. Patients with this device can develop multiple strokes, risk infection, or develop multiorgan failure. Patients and families may find this treatment more burdensome than helpful and elect to turn off the device (Mueller et al., 2010). In the United States alone, over 5 million patients have heart failure and 250,000 of these have severe end stage heart failure, with a 1 year mortality rate of 50 percent. When presented with the option of extensive technology to "save their life," few patients or their family members grasp that because the life extension offered may be only another 5 months and could be filled with complications, hospitalizations, and further problems.

If the terminal illness is not cardiac related, family members may be focused on other care issues, unaware that there is an opportunity to turn off an implanted device. The simpler technologies of pacemakers and ICDs could have been implanted years, even decades before the patient develops the terminal illness. Researchers have found that physicians are reluctant to view a pacemaker or an ICD as an unnecessary or unwanted medical intervention (Kapa et al., 2010). Because of this, the decision to turn off the implanted device may not arise in conversations between families and physicians (Goldstein et al., 2008; Kapa et al., 2010).

If a patient is dying of cancer, families may mistakenly believe that refusals of treatment must be limited to only those treatments related to the terminal condition. This is not accurate. It is always within the patient's right to request stopping treatments of any kind at the end of life. If the device is interfering with death (from the cancer) or if it is prolonging suffering and protracting an intolerable burden of expense, the patient or family can amply justify deactivation (Ballentine, 2005; Kapa et al., 2010). Family members carry the burden of these decisions long after a patient's death, so it is important to help them understand that the disease is the underlying cause of death.

In the YES article, Goldstein and his colleagues interviewed physicians to determine whether conversations with family members included the possibility of deactivating the implanted cardiac defibrillator device. Although most physicians recognized that these conversations should occur, the reality was that they rarely occurred. Some physicians expressed concerns about permanence of turning off the ICD device. Others identified the advantage to turning off an ICD device was that it does not immediately cause the patient's death (Goldstein et al., 2008). Since there is a delay, family members may not link the discontinuation of the ICD to death as much as they might when a respirator is discontinued (Kapa et al., 2010).

In the NO article, Daniel Sulmasy reminds physicians that a treatment inside a patient does not make it exempt from discontinuing the treatment. He clarifies that killing is an intentional act that is nontherapeutic but specifically causes a human being's death (Sulmasy, 2008). By contrast, he argues, removing a treatment or refraining from initiating a treatment such that it allows a patient to die of his/her preexisting fatal disease does not carry the same intent. "Those actions that allow a patient to die are morally permissible when the physician's intentions are not to purposefully cause the death, but rather simply stopping the treatment" (Sulmasy, 2008).

YES

Nathan E. Goldstein et al.

"It's Like Crossing a Bridge": Complexities Preventing Physicians from Discussing Deactivation of Implantable Defibrillators at the End of Life

Introduction

There is a large body of evidence demonstrating that Implantable Cardioverter Defibrillators (ICDs) decrease the incidence of sudden cardiac death,[1–4] but little is known about the end-of-life care for these patients, most of whom die from either worsening of their underlying heart disease or other chronic illnesses. As a patient's condition deteriorates, physiologic changes (intrinsic and extrinsic to the heart) may affect the cardiac conduction system, leading to more arrhythmias and increasing the frequency of shocks. One study showed that up to 20% of family members of deceased patients reported that their loved one received a shock from their ICD in the last days to minutes of life.[5] Because ICD shocks can cause pain and anxiety and may not prolong a life of acceptable quality,[6–8] it is appropriate to consider ICD deactivation as a patient's clinical status worsens and death is near. Previous work has shown that clinicians and patients rarely engage in discussions about deactivating ICDs and most remain active until death.[5]

Given the expanding indications for ICD implantation,[1–4,9,10] the issue of device deactivation will become more relevant as the population ages. Under current Medicare criteria, approximately 3–4 million patients are currently eligible to receive these devices, with 400,000 new patients eligible each year.[3,11–13] Prior research has suggested that patients prefer physicians to initiate discussions about treatment options at the end of life. As most patients with an ICD will face a decision about deactivating the device near the end of their lives, we conducted this study to better understand barriers to clinician-initiated discussions about ICD deactivation. Because these conversations are infrequent and complex, it would be difficult to begin exploring the barriers impeding deactivation discussions using a traditional, closed-ended

From *Journal of General Internal Medicine*, vol. 23 (Supplement 1), 2008, pp. 2–6. Copyright © 2007 by Society of General Internal Medicine. Reprinted by permission of Springer Science and Business Media via Rightslink.

survey instrument. Instead, the qualitative method of using open-ended questions to conduct initial explorations[14-16] is more suited for understanding how physicians conceptualize the role of the device and determining barriers that impede engaging in conversations with patients about deactivating ICDs.

Methods

Study Design and Data Collection

We conducted a qualitative study using in-depth interviews[17,18] of physicians by means of open-ended questions from a predetermined discussion guide. . . . The guide begins with having physicians describe how they view their individual role in the overall care of patients with ICDs and how they explain to patients that they need an ICD. . . . Next, physicians are asked to describe a particularly memorable experience(s) relating to ICD deactivation discussions. (Of note, many ICDs are multifunctional devices that may also perform a pacing or resynchronization function. For purposes of this discussion, the term deactivation only refers to turning off the shocking function of a defibrillator.) During the course of describing this conversation, physicians were probed to determine what difficulties they encountered during these conversations. Finally, the interviewer described to the participants the medical literature revealing the low prevalence of these discussion in routine care[5] and asked clinicians why they thought these discussions happen so rarely.

Although many clinicians may care for patients near the end of life with ICDs, the investigators chose to focus on primary care physicians and those specialists who would be most involved with a patient's ICD. Therefore, we enrolled 4 groups of clinicians: general internists, geriatricians, cardiologists, and electrophysiologists. We believed that the most efficient way to determine barriers to these conversations was to interview clinicians who have had these discussions, so we only enrolled physicians who previously had a conversation about deactivation. In addition, physicians had to be in practice at least 1 year. . . .

Results

. . . When asked, almost every physician agreed that conversations about ICD deactivation should occur, but they all acknowledged that they rarely did this. Clinicians understood the importance of discussing ICD deactivation, but had difficulty translating the theoretical importance of these conversations to real-life scenarios. As described by a female Internist:

> It hadn't occurred to me to turn it off until [the cardiology fellow said] you could turn these things off and I'm like, 'oh, okay.' I mean it wasn't something that I had ever encountered, and it crossed my mind on a technical level, but not really, 'oh, I should have this conversation.'

When asked why they had such difficulty engaging in these conversations, participants postulated that there was something intrinsic to the nature and function of these devices that made it inherently difficult to think of them in the same context as other management decisions at the end of a patient's life. One physician described this as follows:

> People go on and off medications all the time; I put someone on Lasix, I increase their Lasix, I stop their Lasix, no big deal. You can change it again and again, but turning off a [defibrillator] is; it's like crossing a bridge to a certain extent. It's saying, 'you know, we have gone as far as we can go and you're not going to need this down the road you're traveling and we're going to shut it off.' There's a finality to turning it off that is not the same as just saying, well we'll stop this medication [and then later] we can restart it, because if you've made the decision to stop . . . the surveillance of a defibrillator, if you've made it for the right reasons, you're not going to be turning it back on. —male cardiologist

Another cardiologist suggested that these conversations are difficult to include in the context of other conversations because of the primary life-saving role of these devices. As she described:

> When you start talking about . . . turning it off, then you are sort of shutting off the hope.

In addition to its overall role, the small, unseen nature of the device makes it difficult for physicians to remember to include them as part of larger discussions about advance care planning, as characterized by a female cardiologist who stated:

> I think that one thing is that people don't think about [turning it off] because it's internalized.

Whereas some clinicians thought that the differences between ICDs and other technologies (e.g., ventilators, dialysis) used at the end of life make conversations about deactivation more difficult, other clinicians also believed that certain characteristics unique to the ICD make deactivation conversations easier.

> Well, I think it's different than a respirator, for example, because it's, you know, it's not like you turn [the ICD] off and the person dies. —female electrophysiologist

Another female electrophysiologist described this phenomenon similarly when she said,

> Well, I don't know, I think it makes it easier because it's sort of a random event in a sense. That, you know, by turning off the switch you're not killing the person.

Difficulties in including ICD deactivation discussions into other forms of care planning are not limited to the nature of the device itself. Another consistent theme was that physicians (both generalists and specialists) lacked the sense of rapport with patients to be able to discuss ICD deactivation. As a female electrophysiologist stated:

> I think you have to develop some sort of rapport with the patient before you can start to discuss [ICD deactivation]. For one thing, you don't want to scare the patient the first time you see them into thinking that they're dying.

Another clinician also described the importance of an established relationship by stating:

> I think most doctors don't do [ICD deactivation discussions] well. I think it is because they don't have the time . . . they don't know the patients well enough because of the way you practice now with insurance, you know, you don't develop the bond with patients now the way you used to. —female cardiologist

A final barrier to communicating about ICD deactivation was a feeling that deactivation was withdrawing life-sustaining care. As a clinician stated:

> I think that people just don't think of turning off things that were already started, even though it's like all technology, even though we say ethically and legally that there's no difference between withholding and withdrawing, I think for a lot of life-sustaining therapies, in practice it seems like it's different. —female internist

Discussion

Results from these qualitative interviews with clinicians from a variety of specialties in both academic and private practice settings demonstrate that although these physicians believe conversations about deactivating ICDs should happen as part of the other advance care planning discussions for patients with serious illness, this rarely occurs. Some of the reasons why these conversations do not occur seem to be similar to the larger literature on advance care planning (i.e., those discussions where patients' and their families' goals of care are elicited and treatment plans adjusted to be in line with those goals[19]), whereas others are unique to the ICD.

Many physicians in this study felt that because of a lack of time, they did not have a relationship with patients that would facilitate discussions about ICD deactivation—a finding other investigators have noted when examining barriers to advance care planning for patients with a variety of illnesses.[20,21] Clinicians also noted that they did not "do discussions well" and were concerned that they would either take away patients' hope or raise concerns about death; these are all concepts that have been found in other studies exploring barriers to advance care planning.[22–23] Physicians also discussed general concerns with withdrawing therapies. Whereas discussion about the withholding or withdrawing treatments are considered the same by ethicists,[24] it is known that physicians draw a distinction between these 2 treatments.[25-27]

There were issues relating to ICD deactivation, however, that were unique to the nature of the device itself. The majority of patients who have hemodialysis or ventilators withdrawn (the two most frequently studied technologies that are commonly withdrawn,[28-34]) will often die within hours to weeks. The interval between ICD deactivation and patient death may be much longer given the unpredictable nature of malignant arrhythmias. Because of this distinction between ICDs and other advanced technologies, clinicians who engage in conversations about deactivation are somehow insulated from feeling that they are "killing the person." Both hemodialysis and ventilator support also require large machinery, which creates a physical reminder that advanced technologies are being used to sustain life. In addition, these interventions have a large impact on the patient's overall quality of life. Because the ICD is so small and innocuous, its size does not create a daily interference with a patient's quality of life; therefore, discussions about their management at the end of life may not seem so pressing to clinicians. It would seem as though the nature of the device makes it less noticeable, but its small physical size seems to be not correlated to the large ethical dilemma it creates for physicians.

It is noteworthy that despite the difficulties added by the unique nature of the ICD, every clinician who participated in this study (whether in the role of primary care provider or specialist) felt they had a role in these conversations. Traditionally, one might assume that the job of having "difficult conversations" is that of the primary care provider, but there were no participants who expressed that they should be excluded from these conversations based on their medical subspecialty.

These data make it clear that clinicians believe they should engage in conversations about ICD deactivation, but the difficulty lies in creating effective future interventions to make these conversations easier. These conversations are made even more complex by the fact that in qualitative studies with patients (reported separately in this issue of the Journal) we found that relatively healthy community-dwelling outpatients with ICDs may not wish to engage in conversations regarding ICD deactivation. Although educational interventions have shown significant improvements in facilitating communication between clinicians and patients with advanced illness,[35-37] the data reported here demonstrate that there are unique barriers to communication about ICD deactivation, which might benefit from future interventions specifically designed for conversations about the management of these devices. These tools will need to take into account patients' reluctance to engage in these conversations, as well as the unique nature of the ICD and how this might hinder conversation.

As the number of implanted devices continues to expand in the future because of expanding eligibility and reimbursement, these conversations will be encountered with more frequency. Only by assuring that conversations about ICD deactivation routinely occur for all patients with advanced illness can we assure that patients and their families have the highest quality of care near the end of life.

References

1. Buxton AE, Lee KL, Fisher JD, Josephson ME, Prytowsky EN, Hafley GA. Randomized study of the prevention of sudden death in patients with coronary artery disease. N Engl J Med 1993;341(25):1882–90.

2. Moss AJ, Hall WJ, Cannom DS, et al. Improved survival with an implanted defibrillator in patients with coronary disease at high risk for ventricular arrhythmia. N Engl J Med. 1996;335(26):1933–40.

3. Moss AJ, Zareba W, Hall WJ, et al. Prophylactic implantation of a defibrillator in patients with myocardial infarction and reduced ejection fraction. N Engl J Med. 2002;346(12):877–83.

4. Bardy GH, Lee KL, Mark DB, et al. Amiodarone or an implantable cardioverter-defibrillator for congestive heart failure. N Engl J Med. 2005;352(3):225–37.

5. Goldstein NE, Lampert R, Bradley EH, Lynn J, Krumholz HM. Management of implantable cardioverter defibrillators in end-of-life care. Ann Intern Med. 2004;141:835–38.

6. Glikson M, Friedman PA. The implantable cardioverter defibrillator. Lancet. 2001;357:1107–17.

7. Eckert M, Jones T. How does an implantable cardioverter defibrillator (ICD) affect the lives of patients and their families? Int J Nurs Pract. 2002;8:152–57.

8. Sears SF, Conti J. Quality of life and psychological functioning of ICD patients. Heart. 2002;87:488–93.

9. Kadish A, Dyer A, Daubert JP, et al. Prophylactic defibrillator implantation in patients with nonischemic dilated cardiomyopathy. N Engl J Med. 2004;350(21):2151–8.

10. Bristow MR, Saxon LA, Boehmer J, et al. Cardiac-resynchronization therapy with or without an implantable defibrillator in advanced chronic heart failure. N Engl J Med. 2004;350(21):2140–50.

11. Gillick MR. Medicare coverage for technological innovations—time for new criteria? N Engl J Med. 2004;350(21):2199–203.

12. Brown D. Medicare to cover heart devices. The Washington Post 2003 June 7;A04.

13. Hlatky MA, Sanders GD, Owens DK. Evidence-based medicine and policy: the case of the implantable cardioverter defibrillator. Health Aff (Millwood). 2005;24(1):42–51.

14. Sofaer S. Qualitative methods: what are they and why use them? Health Serv Res. 1999;34(5 Pt 2):1101–18.

15. Sofaer S. Qualitative research methods. Int J Qual Health Care. 2002;14(4):329–36.

16. Strauss A, Corbin JM. Basics of Qualitative Research: Techniques and Procedures for Developing Grounded Theory. Thousand Oaks: SAGE Publications, Inc.; 1998.

17. McCracken G. The Long Interview. Thousand Oaks, CA: Sage Publications; 1988.

18. Strauss A, Corbin JM. Basics of Qualitative Research: Grounded Theory Procedures and Techniques. 2nd Edition. San Francisco: Sage Publications; 1990.

19. Lynn J, Goldstein NE. Advance care planning for fatal chronic illness: avoiding commonplace errors and unwarranted suffering. Ann Intern Med. 2003;138(10):812–8.

20. Morrison RS, Morrison EW, Glickman DF. Physician reluctance to discuss advance directives. An empiric investigation of potential barriers. Arch Intern Med. 1994;154(20):2311–8.

21. Curtis JR. Communicating about end-of-life care with patients and families in the intensive care unit. Crit Care Clin. 2004;20(3):363–80.

22. Weiner JS, Cole SA. Three principles to improve clinician communication for advance care planning: overcoming emotional, cognitive, and skill barriers. J Palliat Med. 2004;7(6):817–29.

23. Perry E, Swartz R, Smith-Wheelock L, Westbrook J, Buck C. Why is it difficult for staff to discuss advance directives with chronic dialysis patients? J Am Soc Nephrol. 1996;7(10):2160–8.

24. Luce JM, Alpers A. Legal aspects of withholding and withdrawing life support from critically ill patients in the United States and providing palliative care to them. Am J Respir Crit Care Med. 2000;162:2029–32.

25. Faber-Langendoen K, Bartels DM. Process of forgoing life-sustaining treatment in a university hospital: an empirical study. Crit Care Med. 1992;20(5):570–7.

26. Farber NJ, Simpson P, Salam T, Collier VU, Weiner J, Boyer EG. Physicians' decisions to withhold and withdraw life-sustaining treatment. Arch Intern Med. 2006;166(5):560–4.

27. Solomon MZ, O'Donnell L, Jennings B, et al. Decisions near the end of life: professional views on life-sustaining treatments. Am J Public Health. 1993;83(1):14–23.

28. Holley JL, Foulks CJ, Moss AH. Nephrologists' reported attitudes about factors influencing recommendations to initiate or withdraw dialysis. J Am Soc Nephrol. 1991;1(12):1284–8.

29. Hamel MB, Davis RB, Teno JM, et al. Older age, aggressiveness of care, and survival for seriously ill, hospitalized adults. SUPPORT Investigators. Study to Understand Prognoses and Preferences for Outcomes and Risks of Treatments. Ann Intern Med. 1999;131(10):721–8.

30. Cohen LM, Germain MJ, Poppel DM. Practical considerations in dialysis withdrawal: "to have that option is a blessing". JAMA. 2003;289(16):2113–9.

31. Phillips RS, Hamel MB, Teno JM, et al. Patient race and decisions to withhold or withdraw life-sustaining treatments for seriously ill hospitalized adults. SUPPORT investigators. study to understand prognoses and preferences for outcomes and risks of treatments. Am J Med. 2000;108(1):14–9.

32. Marr L, Weissman DE. Withdrawal of ventilatory support from the dying adult patient. J Support Oncol. 2004;2(3):283–8

33. Rubenfeld GD. Principles and practice of withdrawing life-sustaining treatments. Crit Care Clin. 2004;20(3):435–51, ix.

34. Cook D, Rocker G, Marshall J, et al. Withdrawal of mechanical ventilation in anticipation of death in the intensive care unit. N Engl J Med. 2003;349(12):1123–32.

35. Robinson K, Sutton S, von Gunten CF, et al. Assessment of the Education for Physicians on End-of-Life Care (EPEC) Project. J Palliat Med. 2004;7(5):637–45.

36. Weiner JS, Arnold RM, Curtis JR, Back AL, Rounsaville B, Tulsky JA. Manualized communication interventions to enhance palliative care research and training: rigorous, testable approaches. J Palliat Med. 2006;9(2):371–81.

37. Back AL, Arnold RM, Baile WF, Tulsky JA, Fryer-Edwards K. Approaching difficult communication tasks in oncology. CA Cancer J Clin. 2005;55(3):164–77.

Daniel P. Sulmasy

 **NO**

Within You/Without You: Biotechnology, Ontology, and Ethics

Implantable Cardioverter Defibrillators (ICDs) have proven very effective in preventing sudden cardiac death. Medicare's decision to pay for these devices all but assures that their use will soon become widespread.[1]

Yet, like any technological innovation, these devices are not an unalloyed good. Under certain circumstances it seems best to discontinue treatment. For example, some patients receive shocks so frequently that it becomes extremely burdensome. If a Do Not Resuscitate order is written, whether on the basis of the patient's underlying cardiac disease or some comorbid condition, it may be senseless to continue ICD use.

Several previously published ethical analyses of the discontinuation of ICD treatment have noted that some persons believe that discontinuing an ICD is ethically different from discontinuing other treatments. These analyses, by and large, have declared such misgivings to be misguided and have proceeded to analyze the discontinuation of ICD treatment using standard bioethical categories such as patients' rights, refusal of unwanted therapy, autonomy, futility, and non-maleficence.[2-6] Nonetheless, it seems that cardiologists and patients have not read the bioethics literature. Cardiologists and their patients view the deactivation of an ICD as something special, and they discuss the possibility very infrequently.

The 2 articles by Goldstein et al.[7,8] in this issue of *JGIM* are an important step toward understanding this discrepancy between ethical analysis and clinical reality. Broadly speaking, these articles demonstrate the significant contribution that qualitative studies can make to empirical research about ethics, delving more deeply into the meanings behind answers to survey questions. Specifically, these articles raise 2 important points for ethics. First, they show that issues long thought settled intellectually by ethicists, such as the difference between withholding and withdrawing life-sustaining treatments, still present lingering doubts for patients and practitioners. Patients and cardiologists alike seem to view implanting an ICD as a "bridge" that one crosses with no possibility of return. Second, these rich qualitative data suggest that there may be more going on here from a moral point of view than the ethics of the 1970s can handle. As technology progresses, ethics must keep pace.

From *Journal of General Internal Medicine*, vol. 23 (Suppl 1), 2007, pp. 69–72. Copyright © 2007 by Society of General Internal Medicine. Reprinted by permission of Springer Science and Business Media via Rightslink.

What may be different about an ICD? Paola and Walker[9] have suggested that the new wrinkle may be that the technology has been internalized—that an ICD may come to be viewed as having "become a part of the patient." Using the philosophical term for the study of being, ontology, they suggest that an external defibrillator is easier to forgo than one that is internal to the person, because the latter may be considered part of his or her being. Borrowing from the concepts of property law, they coin the term "biofixture" to describe technologies that have become part of a person. They accept the morality of the discontinuation of an ICD because they view this device as only partly a biofixture. They argue that a heart transplant, however, would be a real biofixture, and no one who is opposed to euthanasia would think it permissible to "deactivate" a transplanted heart.

This interesting foray into ontology and ethics raises many more questions than it answers, however. As biotechnological progress marches forward, new interventions are challenging our notions about the difference between killing and allowing to die. If one is opposed to euthanasia yet accepts the moral permissibility of discontinuing life-sustaining treatments under certain conditions, do new technologies, such as ICDs, require that the line between killing and allowing to die be redrawn? What is the "something intrinsic to the nature and function of these devices"[8] that causes some to consider them differently than other treatments?

Withholding vs. Withdrawing

The data from the articles by Goldstein et al. suggest that both cardiologists and their patients tend to think that once a device such as an ICD is in place, one ought not stop it. As a general rule, philosophers have suggested that the conditions under which one could justify withholding a treatment are those under which one could justify withdrawing a treatment. ICDs raise no new moral issues with respect to this question. For example, if the patient were irreversibly and imminently dying of a painful cancer and had recurrent ventricular tachycardia, one would be perfectly justified in not placing an ICD. Rationally, if the patient had an ICD implanted 2 years ago and now develops a painful cancer and death is imminent, deactivating the ICD seems just as justifiable as withholding it. What the studies of Goldstein at al. tell us, however, is that what seems equivalent according to the logic of ethics continues to feel psychologically different to both patients and practitioners. Clinicians must be sensitive to these feelings in dealing with concrete clinical cases.

Continuous vs. Intermittent?

Does the fact that the ICD is required intermittently rather than continuously mark a moral difference? Certainly it has not seemed so with respect to other life-sustaining treatments. The discontinuation of an intermittent treatment such as hemodialysis, should it become burdensome, has been judged morally acceptable by persons holding a wide variety of ethical viewpoints. In fact, as one of the cardiologists interviewed by Goldstein at al. reports, the very fact that it functions only intermittently might make it psychologically easier to deactivate an ICD than to deactivate the pacemaker of a patient with complete heart block. ICDs raise no new ethical issues in this regard.

Duration

Some might consider the duration of therapy morally important. But is this true? If the ICD in the case of the patient with cancer that I discussed above had been in place for 20 years instead of 2, with no changes except for batteries, would the duration alone make us think that it would be immoral to deactivate it if the patient were imminently dying, in great pain, and the device might only prolong that state? It seems to me this would not be the case. Consider a patient who has been ventilator-dependent for 30 years after contracting polio, is not depressed, and comes to the conclusion, "I've had enough." Might we not be more willing to accept his request to discontinue the ventilator as a well thought out and morally acceptable choice than if the same request were made by the patient after only 1 week of ventilator support? Duration of therapy does not seem to be the morally decisive factor.

Regulative vs. Constitutive?

All therapies are restorative in intent,[10] but different therapies restore patients in 2 broadly different ways. Some therapies are "regulative." That is to say they coax the body back toward its own homeostatic equilibrium. Antidysrhythmic drugs and antipyretics are regulative therapies in this sense. Other therapies are "constitutive." They take over a function that the body can no longer provide for itself. Pacemakers and insulin are constitutive therapies in this sense. Might this distinction mark a moral difference between killing patients and allowing them to die?

If anything, it would seem that the discontinuation of constitutive therapies would raise more questions than the discontinuation of regulative therapies. Mimicking physiology, doing what the body no longer can do for itself, seems closer to being "a part of the patient" than does a therapy that nudges the body into healing itself.

Despite the psychological differences that this distinction might raise, however, we still regularly accept the morality of discontinuing constitutive therapies such as ventilatory support. The fact that a treatment is constitutive does not seem to mark a moral difference between killing and allowing to die. Further, the fact that ICDs are regulative, not constitutive, suggests that this distinction cannot explain any special moral worries about deactivating an ICD.

Internal vs. External

Does the fact that a technology has become internal to the body mark the boundary between killing and allowing to die? This question seems to come closer to explaining the concerns raised by the patients and practitioners about deactivating ICDs, but does it stand up to ethical analysis? Does the fact that many new medical technologies are inside the body mean that they have thereby become part of the person so that deactivating an ICD or a pacemaker becomes morally equivalent to discontinuing the function of a natural heart by injecting KCl?

Elsewhere,[11] I have defined killing as an act in which an agent performs an action that creates a new, nontherapeutic, lethal pathophysiological state in a human being with the intention of thereby causing that human being's death. By contrast, I have defined allowing to die as an act in which an agent either performs an action to remove a treatment for a preexisting fatal disease or refrains from action that would treat a preexisting fatal disease, either intending that this person should die by way of that act or not so intending. The acts of allowing to die that have traditionally been thought morally permissible are those in which the physician's intentions are to aim not at making the patient dead, but simply at stopping the treatment.

These definitions make no reference to internal or external. By these definitions, deactivating an external pacemaker is morally equivalent to deactivating an internal pacemaker, and deactivating an external defibrillator is morally equivalent to discontinuing an ICD.

But is this correct? Does not having a device inside a patient make it a part of the patient, part of her physiology, so that stopping its function is killing? Certainly, this intuition seems correct if one is talking about a heart transplant. Stopping the function of a transplanted heart with an injection of KCl [potassium chloride] seems morally no different from stopping a native heart with an injection of KCl. And is not a heart transplant every bit as much a technological intervention as is an ICD?

Upon further reflection, the fact that a treatment is "inside" the body does not, of itself, seem to do the moral work some might think it does. Consider and compare the following technological interventions: an LHRH agonist implant for prostate cancer and a skin transplant after a severe burn. If one were to discontinue these therapies, however, the mere fact that one treatment is placed under the patient's skin, whereas the other is placed over the patient's skin does not constitute the difference between killing and allowing to die. If the patient with prostate cancer were experiencing hot flashes from the LHRH [luteinizing hormone-releasing hormone, a treatment for prostate cancer] action of the drug and having pain at the site of the implant, his request to have it removed should be honored. But what if the burn patient were to ask that the skin transplant be removed, saying that she had grown tired of the need to take anti-rejection medication? Without an intact integument, the patient would experience sepsis and die. Most plastic surgeons would refuse to do this on the grounds that they would be mutilating, if not killing, the patient, even if she were otherwise dying from some other comorbid disease. The mere fact that a technological intervention has been placed under the skin does not seem to mark the moral difference between killing and allowing to die.

Replacement vs. Substitute Therapy

So, then, perhaps those who have approached the question as a standard application of the principles typically used in bioethics are right after all. Perhaps there is nothing special about devices such as ICDs.

Such a conclusion would be overly hasty. Jansen has argued that the questions raised by advances in medical technology such as ICDs are challenging our notions about the boundaries of the self.[12] Particularly, as biotechnological treatments become more "bio" than "techno," we need to think clearly about the characteristics that render a treatment a part of the patient's self, so that its discontinuation is morally indistinguishable from killing. Jansen has offered 3 rules of thumb for helping to judge whether a particular technological intervention ought to be considered a part of the patient. She suggests that there are more serious grounds for considering the technological intervention a part of the patient if it is located inside the patient, has been in the patient for a long time, and plays something akin to what I have called a constitutive therapeutic role.

Certainly, none of these factors is, of itself, morally decisive. Jansen would not seem to disagree. I have explained above, however, why I believe none of these 3 factors can bear the weight of the distinction between killing and allowing to die. And, whereas Jansen's insight is correct—that some treatments must truly be considered within the ontological boundaries of the patient's "self"—I do not think the criteria she has suggested fully capture the distinction. And while I further agree with her that these will necessarily be rules of thumb and that a "bright line" will be hard to draw, I think we can press for greater clarity.

I would like to suggest 2 alternative guiding principles that, while provisional hypotheses, might advance the discussion.

First, interventions that are regulative are never "self." These interventions are distinct from the organism and extrinsic to its function, whether administered inside or outside the body. They function by attempting to regulate bodily functions, coaxing them back toward homeostasis. An ICD is regulative. It does not supply the heart rhythm. Rather, it shocks an abnormal cardiac rhythm back into normal sinus rhythm. Although it is internal to the body, it is still not "self." One of the patients quoted by Goldstein et al. illustrates the psychology of distinguishing between ICD and self nicely when she describes how she talks to her ICD, treating it as something other than her "self" although it is located within her.[7] Regulatory therapies, no matter how sophisticated, and whether located inside the body or not, can be thought about just as one would think about withholding or withdrawing more standard forms of therapy at the end of life. They may be forgone if they are futile or if the burdens of treatment become disproportionate to the benefits.

Second, some, but not all, constitutive therapies are distinct from the self. I am not certain how best to characterize this distinction, but my preliminary hypothesis is that we can distinguish between constitutive therapeutic interventions that have *replaced* the pathologically disordered function and those that are *substitutes* for the pathologically disordered function. The distinction between these 2 kinds of constitutive therapies will not always be clear, but I hope to make it clear enough that it can be clinically and morally useful. In my view, in the proper circumstances, it is morally permissible to withhold or withdraw substitutive therapies, but the more an intervention can be understood as a replacement therapy, the less it seems morally appropriate to withdraw it.

How Might Replacement and Substitutive Therapies Be Distinguished?

What I mean by a replacement therapy is a technological intervention that participates in the organic unity of the patient as an organism. This is what it really means to say that a technological intervention has become "a part of the patient." A replacement therapy is one that has become part of the patient's restored physiology. The most important feature of a replacement therapy is that it provides the function that has been pathologically lost, more or less in the same manner in which the patient was once able to provide this function when healthy. Thus, for instance, a renal transplant is a replacement therapy, whereas peritoneal dialysis (although it also takes place inside the body) is a substitutive therapy.

Additional signs suggestive of an intervention being a replacement therapy might include: (1) its responsiveness to changes in the organism or its environment, (2) properties such as growth and self-repair, (3) independence from external energy sources or supplies, (4) independence from external control by an expert, (5) immunologic compatibility, (6) physical integration into the patient's body. The paradigmatic replacement therapy is thus a well-functioning organ transplant from an identical twin. The more a technological intervention meets the conditions for being a replacement therapy, the harder it is to contend that it is extrinsic to the patient's identity.

This distinction between replacement and substitutive types of constitutive therapies might help us to say how far someone who is opposed to euthanasia could reasonably go in classifying certain cases as morally appropriate withdrawal of life-sustaining treatment rather than morally unacceptable cases of killing. Whereas there is no absolute standard for judging whether something is a replacement or a substitute, the more clearly a technology can be classified as a replacement therapy, the greater the case for judging that its discontinuation would constitute an immoral act of killing. Replacement therapies become part of the restored physiology of the patient, part of the integrated unity of the patient as an intact individual organism. To discontinue such therapies is better understood as introducing a new lethal pathophysiological state rather than discontinuing a treatment that is merely substituting for a preexisting lethal pathophysiological lack of that function. The discontinuation of a replacement therapy thus becomes an act of killing.

To illustrate, consider the fact that there are cases in which discontinuing insulin injections in a diabetic patient would be morally appropriate. If the patient were imminently dying of a malignancy, even the burdens of being injected with insulin or having finger-stick checks for blood glucose might be considered disproportionate to the benefits. We ought therefore to permit the discontinuation of insulin in some such cases. Insulin injections clearly represent a case of a constitutive rather than regulative therapy. The injections mimic the normal physiology. However, giving insulin by injection is a substitutive rather than replacement therapy. It provides the normal physiological function in an abnormal way and the treatment is not part of some new organic unity that has altered the identity of the patient.

Consider a slightly different case, however. If the same patient had previously undergone an islet cell transplant as a treatment for his diabetes, it would seem highly morally problematic to "discontinue" insulin therapy under these same end-of-life conditions by injecting streptozosin to kill the transplanted islet cells. Islet cell therapy is a replacement therapy and, as such, the injection of streptozocin would be mischaracterized if one were to describe it as the mere discontinuation of a life-sustaining therapy. The cells would have become part of the patient—an integrated aspect of her restored physiology—and to destroy these cells would be ethically indistinguishable from destroying the native islet cells of a healthy person.

Conclusions

Those who are opposed to euthanasia but supportive of the withholding and withdrawing disproportionately burdensome life-sustaining treatments need not demur at the idea of deactivating ICDs. The analysis I have presented shows that deactivating an ICD can be ethically distinguished from killing and considered a part of good palliative care. However, the argument necessary to reach this conclusion will doubtless prove challenging for persons unaccustomed to philosophical thinking. The data from Goldstein et al. describe in detail how much effort will be needed in making this argument clear for cardiologists and patients. It is critically important, however, that we begin thinking seriously and carefully about what makes an intervention a part of the patient, rather than a treatment that is extrinsic to the patient's self, even if it is located inside the patient's body. The rapid pace of technological progress assures us that these sorts of questions will continue to surface in clinical practice. Ethics, as the most practical branch of philosophy, must be prepared to keep pace with these challenges.

References

1. McClellan MB, Tunis SR. Medicare coverage of ICDs. N Engl J Med. 2005;352:222–4.

2. Lewis WR, Luebke DL, Johnson NJ, Harrington MD, Costantini O, Aulisio MP. Withdrawing implantable defibrillator shock therapy in terminally ill patients. Am J Med. 2006;119:892–6.

3. Braun TC, Hagen NA, Hatfield RE, Wyse DG. Cardiac pacemakers and implantable defibrillators in terminal care. J Pain Symptom Manage. 1999;18:126–31.

4. Berger JT. The ethics of deactivating implanted cardioverter defibrillators. Ann Intern Med. 2005;142:631–4.

5. Mueller PS, Hook CC, Hayes DL. Ethical analysis of withdrawal of pacemaker or implantable cardioverter-defibrillator support at the end of life. Mayo Clin Proc. 2003;78:959–63.

6. Pellegrino ED. Decisions to withdraw life-sustaining treatment: a moral algorithm. JAMA. 2000;283:1065–7.

7. Goldstein NE, Mehta D, Siddiqui S, et al. Sean Morrison RS. That's like an act of suicide: patients' attitudes toward deactivation of implantable defibrillators. J Gen Intern Med DOI 10.1007/s11606-007-0239-8.

8. Goldstein NE, Mehta D, Teitelbaum E, Bradley EH, Sean Morrison RS. It's like crossing a bridge: complexities preventing physicians from discussing deactivation of implantable defibrillators at the end of life. J Gen Intern Med 2007 DOI 10.1007/s11606-007-0237-x.

9. Paola FA, Walker RM. Deactivating the implantable cardioverter-defibrillator: a biofixture analysis. South Med J. 2000;93:20–3.

10. Jansen LA, Sulmasy DP. Proportionality, terminal suffering and the restorative goals of medicine. Theor Med Bioethics. 2002;23:321–37.

11. Sulmasy DP. Killing and allowing to die: another look. J Law Med Ethics. 1998;26:55–64.

12. Jansen LA. Hastening death and the boundaries of the self. Bioethics. 2006;20:105–11.

EXPLORING THE ISSUE

Does Withholding or Withdrawing Futile Treatment Kill People?

Critical Thinking and Reflection

1. Carl J. is a 15-year-old whose heart was seriously damaged by a viral infection. He has been in the hospital for several months awaiting a heart transplant and has had an LVAD device implanted to help circulate blood. Knowing that finding a heart for transplant is unlikely and the cost of his care is bankrupting his parents, he asks that the LVAD device be discontinued so that he can be allowed to die. Discuss and debate the ethical, legal, financial, and emotional implications of this request.

2. Imagine future technologies that might be used at the end of life. Why are the same ethical principles used as an approach to decision making, despite the changes in technology?

3. How could physicians improve conversations about end-of-life care with patients and families? Imagine computer programs that would help patients and families understand the prognosis (future outcome) of a disease with or without various treatments. Would this help or complicate decisions to withhold or withdraw treatment?

4. What is the difference between patients who request medications that would "help them die" and patients who make decisions to forego treatments and let nature take its course?

5. Find an older relative and give them this scenario. Imagine you had a pacemaker implanted to regulate your heart at the age of 70, and then you develop cancer at age 75. Ask if they would want to have a heart device stopped or deactivated when they were dying of cancer. Why or why not? Note their concerns and compare them to the readings.

Is There Common Ground?

Although the courts have clearly indicated that patients and their surrogates have the right to withhold or withdraw treatments that offer no benefit at the end of life, there is still some confusion about newer technologies. Most people indicate that they wish to die in their own home with a sense of dignity and comfort. They fear end-of-life care surrounded by technical devices (Schaller & Kessler, 2006). This wish raises questions as to *how* to approach treatment decisions regarding those who are hospitalized with a grave prognosis, and *when* it is correct to offer to stop treatments that are relatively unseen such as implanted cardiac devices (Kapa et al., 2010). Complicating these decisions is

247

the problem of physicians ignoring their patients' wishes or avoiding communication about these difficult decisions (Farber et al., 2006).

Patients or families may have false hopes or expectations of the technology or treatments that physicians are asking them to consider (Melhado & Byers, 2011). Improving end-of-life treatment discussions may help patients and surrogates redirect care practices to those that focus on comfort over technology.

References

Ballentine, J. M. (2005). Pacemaker and defibrillator deactivation in competent hospice patients: An ethical consideration. *American Journal of Hospice and Palliative Medicine, 22*(1), 14–19. doi:10.1177/104990910502200106

Brownlee, S. (2008). Afterword: Sharing decisions. In *Overtreated: Why too much medicine is making us sicker and poorer* (pp. 305–312). New York: Bloomsbury.

Farber, N. J., Simpson, P., Salam, T., Collier, V. U., Weiner, J., & Boyer, E. G. (2006). Physicians' decisions to withhold and withdraw life-sustaining treatment. *Archives of Internal Medicine, 166*(5), 560–564.

Gilligan, T. & Raffin, T. A. (1996). Whose death is it, anyway? *Annals of Internal Medicine, 125*(2), 137–141.

Goldstein, N. E., Mehta, D., Teitelbaum, E., Bradley, E., & Morrison, R. (2008). "It's like crossing a bridge:" Complexities preventing physicians from discussing deactivation of implantable defibrillators at the end of life. *Journal of General Internal Medicine, 23*(S1), 2–6. doi:10.1007/s11606-007-0237-x

Kapa, S., Mueller, P. S., Hayes, D. L., & Asirvatham, S. J. (2010). Perspectives on withdrawing pacemaker and implantable cardioverter-defibrillator therapies at end of life: Results of a survey of medical and legal professionals and patients. *Mayo Clinic Proceedings, 85*(11), 981–990. doi:10.4065/mcp.2010.0431

Melhado, L. W. & Byers, J. F. (2011). Patient's and surrogates decision making characteristics for withdrawing, withholding and continuing life sustaining treatments. *Journal of Hospice and Palliative Nursing, 13*(1), 16–28. doi:10.1097/NJH.0b013e3182018f09

Mueller, P. S., Swetz, K. M., Freeman, M. R., Carter, K. A., Crowley, M., Anderson Severson, C. J., et al. (2010). Ethical analysis of withdrawing ventricular assist device support. *Mayo Clinic Proceedings, 85*(9), 791–797. doi:10.4065/mcp.2010.0113

Pellegrino, E. D. (2000). Decisions to withdraw life-sustaining treatment: A moral algorithm. *Journal of the American Medical Association, 283*(8), 1065–1067. doi:10.1001/jama.283.8.1065

Pellegrino, E. D. (2005). Futility in medical decisions: The word and the concept. *HEC Forum, 17*(4), 308–318.

Pellegrino, E. D. & Sulmasy, D. P. (2003). Medical ethics. In D. A. Warrell, T. M. Cox, & J. D. Firth (Eds.), *Oxford textbook of medicine.* New York: Oxford University Press.

President's Council on Bioethics. (2008). A summary of the council's debate on the neurological standard for determining death. In Pellegrino, E., Bloom, F., Carson, B. et al. (Eds.), *Controversies in the determination of death: A white paper by the President's Council on Bioethics* (pp. 89–92). Washington, D.C.: The President's Council on Bioethics.

Rydvall, A. & Lynöe, N. (2008). Withholding and withdrawing life sustaining treatment: A comparative study of ethical reasoning of physicians and the general public. *Critical Care, 12*(1), R13. doi:10.1186/cc6786

Schaller, C. & Kessler, M. (2006). On the difficulty of neurosurgical end of life decisions. *Journal of Medical Ethics, 32*(2), 65–69. doi:10.1136/jme.2005.011767

Sulmasy, D. P. (2008). Within you/without you: Biotechnology, ontology, and ethics. *Journal of General Internal Medicine, 23*(S1), 69–72. doi:10.1007/s11606-007-0326-x

Additional Resources

American Medical Association. (1996). *Code of medical ethics opinion 2.20: Withholding or withdrawing life-sustaining medical treatment.* Retrieved from www.ama-assn.org/ama/pub/physician-resources/medical-ethics/code-medical-ethics/opinion220.page

Devictor, D., Latour, J. M., & Tissieres, P. (2008). Forgoing life-sustaining or death-prolonging therapy in the pediatric ICU. *Pediatric Clinics of North America, 55*(3), 791–804.

Downie, J. (2004). Unilateral withholding and withdrawal of potentially life-sustaining treatment: A violation of dignity under the law in Canada. *Journal of Palliative Care, 20*(3), 143–149.

Limerick, M. H. (2007). The process used by surrogate decision makers to withhold and withdraw life-sustaining measures in an intensive care environment. *Oncology Nursing Forum, 34*(2), 331–339. doi:10.1188/07.ONF.331-339

Meeker, M. & Jezewski, M. (2009). Metasynthesis: Withdrawing life-sustaining treatments: The experience of family decision-makers. *Journal of Clinical Nursing, 18*(2), 163–173. doi:10.1111/j.1365-2702.2008.02465.x

Mularski, R. A., Heine, C. E., Osborne, M. L., Ganzini, L., & Curtis, J. R. (2005). Quality of dying in the ICU: Ratings by family members. *CHEST, 128*(1), 280–287.

White, D. B., Curtis, J. R., Lo, B., & Luce, J. (2006). Decisions to limit life-sustaining treatment for critically ill patients who lack both decision-making capacity and surrogate decision-makers. *Critical Care Medicine, 34*(8), 2053–2059.

Internet References . . .

Death with Dignity National Center

www.deathwithdignity.org/

True Compassion Advocates

www.truecompassionadvocates.org/

The Washington State Death with Dignity Act

http://wei.secstate.wa.gov/osos/en/documents/i1000-text%20for%20web.pdf

The Oregon State Death with Dignity Report site

http://public.health.oregon.gov/ProviderPartnerResources/Evaluation
Research/DeathwithDignityAct/Pages/index.aspx

Assisted Suicide

*T*hree states in the United States have passed laws allowing patients who are dying to request lethal doses of medications from physicians. This unit explores three concerns regarding this practice. First, we discuss whether a patient should be allowed to take his/her own life prior to when they would have a natural death. In each of these states the patient must meet the criteria of being declared terminally ill, that is, expected to die within 6 months, and must be able to self-administer the medications. Second, we examine whether the states who have established the right to assisted death have been careful enough to provide legal safeguards against abuse of these laws. Researchers raise concerns that the physicians prescribing these terminal medications may not be screening the patients for depression or referring patients to counselors with enough frequency. Finally, the essays debate whether the practice of terminal sedation (providing strong sedatives and pain medications to terminally ill patients in the hospital) is simply a means for physicians to assist death in patients who cannot initiate it themselves. The writers of the essays identify the fine differences between terminal sedation and euthanasia.

- May a Dying Person Hasten Her Death?
- Can Legal Suicide Really Safeguard Against Abuse?
- Is Palliative Sedation Actually Euthanasia in Disguise?

ISSUE 10

May a Dying Person Hasten Her Death?

YES: Katrina Hedberg, David Hopkins, Richard Leman, and Melvin Kohn, from "The 10-Year Experience of Oregon's Death with Dignity Act: 1998–2007," *The Journal of Clinical Ethics* (vol. 20, no. 2, pp. 124–132, 2009)

NO: Susan M. Wolf, from "Confronting Physician-Assisted Suicide and Euthanasia: My Father's Death," *Hastings Center Report* (vol. 38, no. 5, pp. 23–26, 2008)

Learning Outcomes

After reading this issue, you should be able to:

- Describe the background and 10-year experience of the Oregon Death with Dignity Act.
- Learn about ethical and legal implications of ways to hasten death including forgoing treatment and nutrition-hydration, using painkillers, sedation, and legally safeguarded self-administration of lethal prescriptions.
- Identify and debate arguments of proponents and opponents to hastened death.
- Discuss and distinguish changed categories such as informed consent versus informed decision, physician-assisted suicide versus patient directed dying.

ISSUE SUMMARY

YES: Katrina Hedberg, the Oregon State Epidemiologist, Public Health Division, and colleagues discuss the characteristics of persons who have taken action under the Oregon Death with Dignity Act. These authors found that most of the dying patients who requested medications to end their lives felt a strong need for autonomy and control.

NO: Susan Wolf, the McKnight Presidential Professor of Law, Medicine & Public Policy at the University of Minnesota, discusses her long-standing opposition to physician-assisted suicide and reflects on how her father's death challenged that view.

This issue reviews four current practices of hastening death and their justifications. These include foregoing treatment and nutrition-hydration, using painkillers, sedation, and legal self-administration of lethal medication.

Two *concerns* come up again and again. Responsibilities called intergenerational justice weigh actual needs against future concerns. Is hastening death a poor private solution to unjust public health resource allocation? Hastened death should never come from inadequate pain or symptom management. Good palliation cares for pain, nausea, shortness of breath, spiritual needs, and other intolerable symptoms (Valente, 2004; Ganzini, Goy, Miller, Harvath, Jackson, & Delorit, 2003). Vulnerably dying should never misperceive themselves as burdens. Concrete help about goals at the end of life from dialogue engages negative attitudes and behaviors (Kelly, Burnett, Badger, Pelusi, Varghese, & Robertson, 2003; Valente, 2004).

This also avoids *myths*: not all terminally ill want to hasten death. Those in palliative programs tend not to—and reducing requests is worthwhile (Ganzini, Bronus, Mori, & Hsich, 2006; Battin, 2007). The rate of those terminally ill who want to hasten death varies from 17 to 43 percent. Psychological and social factors are more prevalent than physiological ones—such as a fear of pain rather than pain, comorbid depression, hopelessness, loss of dignity, the impact of spiritual beliefs and fears of being a burden (Coyle, 2004; Maytal & Stern, 2006: 301; Hudson et al., 2006).

Are documented *fears* well-founded among terminally ill of inappropriate treatment—overtreatment and undertreatment? Many fear "needless and prolonged suffering, uncontrolled pain, and expensive costs of dying. . . ." In industrialized societies, the most preventable suffering occurs among supervised dying. "By the year 2020, 2.5 million Americans older than 65 will die each year and approximately 40% of these deaths will occur in nursing homes. . . . About 1 in 3 residents die in the year after admission to an extended care facility" (Valente, 2004: 314).

Those nearest death request hastened dying. "1 in 5 physicians in the United States have received at least 1 request to assist a terminally ill patient to die, and approximately 3% to 18% accede to these requests." Almost half (47 percent) had a primary diagnosis of cancer, and more than a third with severe pain or discomfort, "dependent (53%), bedridden (42%), and expected to live less than 1 month (28%)." Most were lucid (90 percent) but experienced a recent deterioration in functional status (87 percent) and physicians believed almost half were depressed. Requests for hastened death came from "hopelessness, lack of social support, and sense of meaninglessness" (Meier, Emmons, Litke, Wallenstein, & Morrison, 2003: 1537).

Four different practices hasten death. Patients forego treatment and nutrition-hydration, use painkillers, sedation, and legally self-administer lethal medication in certain states (Schwartz, 2009).

With respect to nutrition and hydration and hastened death, two different practices distinguish patient conditions and intentions: *refusal of nutrition and hydration* (RNH) and *voluntarily stopping eating and drinking* (VSED). *Refusal of nutrition and hydration* is "a practice in which (1) the patient has an irreversible condition that interferes with normal appetite, digestion, or absorption of water and essential nutrients and (2) the patient has determined that the benefits of artificial nutrition are not proportionate to the burdens in this situation" (Jansen & Sulmasy, 2002; Miller, 2008). Advantages include disadvantages: a last resort that focuses on benefits and burdens requires vigilance to avoid requests based on poorly managed symptoms.

Voluntarily stopping eating and drinking (VSED) is a practice "in which (1) the patient has no underlying condition that interferes with normal appetite, digestion, or absorption of water and essential nutrients and (2) the patient nevertheless intends to end his or her own life by not eating or drinking" (Jansen & Sulmasy, 2002). Advantages include how it enables patients to discuss motives, reduces risks of implusivity, and enables symptom management. Disadvantages are its length of time—from one to three weeks (Berry, 2009). One-third of Oregon hospices nurses have reported VSED deaths as "good deaths." Twice the number of patients have died from VSED as those from self-administered lethal medication, chiefly among patients who were a decade older and more likely to have a neurological disease. Most important reasons include "a readiness to die, the belief that continuing to live was pointless, an assessment of the quality of life as poor, a desire to die at home, and a desire to control the circumstances of death" (Ganzini et al., 2003).

Clinical guidelines about *pain medicine* that hasten death emphasize different points. First, most end-of-life pain can be managed and there is "no convincing scientific evidence that *administering opioids*, even in very high doses, accelerates death" (HPNA, 2004). Second, caregivers need not condemn themselves for rare deaths from competent pain management. These are legitimate interventions to achieve reasonable outcomes (pain relief) with *foreseen but not intended risks* (hastened dying) (Ball, 2006). Commentators agree that such "double effects" include more than good caregiver intentions but also different conditions taken together or separately as justifying principles (Beauchamp & Childress, 2001), clinical rules (HPNA, 2004; Sulmasy & Pellegrino, 2000), or guidelines of prudence (Keenan, 1999). The Nurses Association's Code of Ethics for Nurses states, "The nurse should provide interventions to relieve pain and other symptoms in the dying patient even when those interventions entail risks of hastening death. However, nurses may not act with the sole intent of ending a patient's life. . . ."

Patient and caregiver use of palliative sedation describes two different kinds of *terminal sedation: sedation of the imminently dying* and *sedation towards death* (see Issue 14). *Sedation of the imminently dying* is "a practice in which (1) the patient is close to death (hours, days, or at most a few weeks); (2) the patient has one or more severe symptoms that are refractory (resistant) to standard palliative care; (3) the patient's physician vigorously treats these symptoms with therapy known to be efficacious; (4) this therapy has a dose-dependent side effect of sedation that is a foreseen but unintended consequence of trying to relieve the patient's symptoms; and (5) this therapy may be coupled with the withholding or withdrawing of life-sustaining treatments that are ineffective or disproportionately burdensome." *Sedation towards death* is a practice in which "(1) the patient need not be imminently dying; (2) the symptoms believed to be refractory to treatment are simply the consciousness that one is not yet dead; (3) the patient's physician selects therapy intended to render the patient unconscious as a means of treating the refractory symptoms; and (4) other life-sustaining treatments are withdrawn to hasten death" (Jansen & Sulmasy, 2002).

Anyone who is terminally ill and decisionally capable in Oregon (1997), Washington (2009), and Montana (2010) can receive a *prescription of lethal medicine*, provided specific safeguards are followed. Laws require self-administration. In Oregon, it accounts for about 1 in 1,000 deaths. One in 50 patients discuss it with doctors, as do 1 in 6 family members (Quill & Greenlaw, 2008). Concerns about loss of autonomy, ability to engage in enjoyable activities, loss of dignity, loss of bodily functions, family burden were more prominent than pain control (27 percent; Hedberg, 2010). Some 83 percent receive hospice care. "The quality of death experienced by those who received lethal prescriptions is no worse than those not pursuing physician-assisted death (PAD), and in some areas it is rated by family members as better" (Smith, Goy, Harvath, & Ganzini, 2011). However, some PAD requests change among patients with psychosocial treatments; current laws of discretionary psychiatric evaluation feature under-referrals (Rodriguez Davila, Vidal, Stewart, & Caserta, 2010; Hedberg, 2010).

"Hastened death" is one among *six debated changed terms*. Categories shift from prior "physician-centered terms" to "patient-centered" concepts such as aid in dying; and physician-assisted death. *Proponents* avoid negative past connotations such as voluntary "euthanasia" with its Nazi overtones. Words such as "suicide" psycho-pathologize "hastened dying" by linking it with mental dysfunctions (Daube, 1972). Laws state persons must make an "informed decision" rather than have "informed consent." Hastened death can be a "reasonable choice" based on "decision-making capacity" rather than "rational decision" based on (overly) cognitive "mental capacity" (Hotopf, 2010). Legislation precisely states physicians cannot assist death, but may assist dying; thus, state agencies deliberately renamed practices as death with dignity. *Opponents* charge such language masquerades objectionable practices by very few physicians; death with dignity is simply suicide and mercy killing (Marker & Smith, 1996; Tucker & Steele, 2007; Callahan, 2008; Muller, 2011).

In the YES article, Katrina Hedberg, and her colleagues discuss the characteristics of persons who have taken action under the Oregon Death with Dignity Act. These authors found that most of the dying patients who requested medications to end their lives felt a strong need for autonomy and control.

In the NO article, Susan Wolf, discusses her long-standing opposition to physician-assisted suicide and reflects on how her father's death challenged that view.

YES

Katrina Hedberg et al.

The 10-Year Experience of Oregon's Death with Dignity Act: 1998–2007

Background

On 27 October 1997, Oregon's Death with Dignity Act (DWDA) took effect, allowing physicians to prescribe a lethal dose of medication to be self-administered by terminally ill patients.[1] The law specifically prohibits euthanasia, in which a physician administers a lethal dose of medication to a patient (for example, through an injection). During the first 10 years the law was in effect, it was unique in the United States.

Whether jurisdictions should allow terminally ill patients to ingest lethal doses of medication as an option at the end of life continues to be heatedly debated. In the decade since implementation, the DWDA has been amended by the Oregon legislature, and its legality has been argued before the U.S. Supreme Court,[2] but the law remains in effect. Similar initiatives have been on the ballots in several states, and in November 2008, Washington State passed similar legislation, which took effect in the spring of 2009. A few countries (for example, the Netherlands, Belgium) have laws allowing physician-assisted suicide (similar to Oregon's law) as well as euthanasia (prohibited in Oregon); others have considered similar legislation (for example, Great Britain, Australia).

As the state agency responsible for monitoring participation in the act, the Oregon Department of Human Services believes that accurate data are important to parties on both sides of the policy debate, while we remain neutral about the law itself. During the past decade, annual reports and published articles have documented the number of participants, their demographic characteristics, and underlying medical conditions.[3] While trends in the Dutch experience with physician-assisted suicide and euthanasia have recently been published,[4] no studies have examined trends in DWDA participation in Oregon, which does not allow euthanasia, and has different cultural norms and medical care system than Europe. Trends in practice since implementation are important for other jurisdictions to take into account when considering legislation similar to Oregon's DWDA.

From *The Journal of Clinical Ethics,* vol. 20, no. 2, 2009, pp. 124–132. Copyright © 2009 by Journal of Clinical Ethics. Reprinted by permission.

Methods

Data Collection

To receive a DWDA prescription, a patient must be a terminally ill, adult Oregon resident expected to die within six months, capable of making and communicating healthcare decisions, and able to ingest oral medications. DWDA requires the prescribing and consulting physicians, psychiatrist or psychologist (when applicable), and dispensing pharmacist to report their compliance with the DWDA to the Oregon Department of Human Services once a prescription is written. Data collected from the documents include dates of request, type and dose of medication prescribed, and mental health evaluation referrals (when applicable) (find rules and forms at www.oregon.gov/DHS/ph/pas/index.shtml.)

After the patient's death certificate is received through standard procedures, we abstract demographic characteristics and underlying illness. The prescribing physician submits additional information about the deceased patient and the process on a standardized questionnaire. If the prescribing physician was not present during ingestion, we accept information from others who attended the patient's death. Data include end-of-life concerns, the process, and complications.

Analysis

For the purpose of this study, we included all deaths that occurred during the 10 years from 1 January 1998 to 31 December 2007 and resulted from ingesting a legally prescribed lethal dose of medication. Death rates were calculated using as the denominator all Oregon deaths during 1997 through 2006 (the most recent 10 years for which final mortality data were available). Using rate ratios, we compared the characteristics of participating patients to those of other Oregonians who died of the same underlying diseases, based on specific ICD-9 codes listed on death certificates. Although the data are population-based and not a sample, we performed statistical analyses using Mantel-Haenszel *chi*-square test and test for linear trend, and Fisher's exact test, on the assumption that the data are a sample in time.[5]

Results

During the years 1998 through 2007, physicians wrote 546 prescriptions, and 341 Oregonians died from ingesting a legally prescribed lethal dose of medication under the Death with Dignity Act. During this same time period, a total of 296,558 residents died of all causes (the total includes DWDA deaths), corresponding to an overall rate of 11.3 DWDA deaths per 10,000 total deaths. The numbers of DWDA patients and rates of participation increased from 16 patients (corresponding to 5.3 per 10,000 deaths) in 1998 to 49 patients (corresponding to 15.6 per 10,000 deaths) in 2007 (see figure 1).

Figure 1

Numbers of Death with Dignity Act Prescriptions and Deaths, 1998–2007

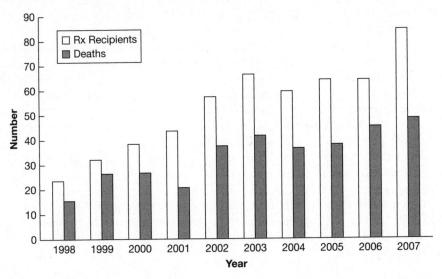

Patient Characteristics

The characteristics of participating patients are summarized in table 1. While most deaths (77 percent) occurred in those 55 to 84 years of age, rates (comparing DWDA patients to those who died of the same underlying diseases) were highest among those 18 to 34 years of age (65.0 per 10,000 deaths) and lowest in those ≥85 years (15.2). Most patients (97.4 percent) were White. Education level was associated with participation: those with post-baccalaureate education were 9.5 times more likely to use the DWDA than those lacking a high school education. Rates of participation for people living in rural Oregon east of the Cascade Mountains were lower than for those living in the Portland metropolitan area (rate ratio, or RR = 0.4; 95 percent confidence interval, or CI = 0.3, 0.6).

Patients with cancer accounted for 82.1 percent of the cases (see table 1). Rate ratios were elevated for all types of cancer (RR = 10.5; 95 percent; CI = 4.3, 25.3); with rates for ovarian cancer (82.7 per 10,000 deaths) and pancreatic cancer (76.6) being more than twice that for lung cancer (31.6). Although the absolute numbers of patients are small, the rate for those with amyotrophic lateral sclerosis (ALS) was 67 times higher, and the rate for patients with HIV/AIDS was 57 times higher than that for patients with heart disease.

Death with Dignity Act Process

Trends in the DWDA process are presented in table 2. As reported by physicians, the two most common factors that contributed to patients requesting prescriptions—a loss of autonomy and a decreasing ability to engage in enjoyable

Table 1

Characteristics of 341 DWDA Patients Who Died during 1998–2007 after Ingesting a Lethal Dose of Medication, Compared with 98,942 Oregonians Who Died from the Same Underlying Diseases[1]

Characteristics	DWDA Patients 1998–2007 (N = 341)[2]		Oregon Deaths, Same Diseases (N = 98,942)[3]		DWDA Deaths per 10,000 Oregon Deaths	Rate Ratio (95% CI)[4]	
Sex							
Male (%)	183	(53.7)	49,886	(50.4)	36.7	1.1	(0.9–1.4)
Female (%)	158	(46.3)	49,056	(49.6)	32.2	1.0	—
Age							
18–34 (%)	4	(1.2)	615	(0.6)	65.0	4.3	(1.5–12.1)
35–44 (%)	10	(2.9)	1,899	(1.9)	52.7	3.5	(1.7–7.0)
45–54 (%)	31	(9.1)	6,467	(6.5)	47.9	3.2	(1.9–5.2)
55–64 (%)	73	(21.4)	13,298	(13.4)	54.9	3.6	(2.4–5.5)
65–74 (%)	93	(27.3)	23,492	(23.7)	39.6	2.6	(1.7–3.9)
75–84 (%)	98	(28.7)	32,102	(32.4)	30.5	2.0	(1.4–3.0)
85+ (%)	32	(9.4)	21,069	(21.3)	15.2	1.0	—
Median years (range)	69	(25.0–96.0)	76	(18.0–112.0)	—	—	—
Race							
White (%)	332	(97.4)	95,047	(96.1)	34.9	1.0	—
Asian (%)	6	(1.8)	1,099	(1.1)	54.6	1.6	(0.7–3.5)
Native American (%)	1	(0.3)	702	(0.7)	14.2	0.4	(0.1–2.9)
Hispanic (%)	2	(0.6)	954	(1.0)	21.0	0.6	(0.2–2.4)
African-American (%)	0	(0.0)	1,070	(1.0)	0.0	0.0	—
Other (%)	0	(0.0)	43	(0.0)	0.0	0.0	—
Unknown	0	—	27	—	—	—	—
Marital status							
Married (%)	154	(45.2)	47,312	(47.9)	32.5	1.0	—
Widowed (%)	73	(21.4)	32,173	(32.6)	22.7	0.7	(0.5–0.9)
Divorced (%)	86	(25.2)	14,817	(15.0)	58.0	1.8	(1.4–2.3)
Never married (%)	28	(8.2)	4,381	(4.4)	63.9	2.0	(1.3–2.9)
Unknown	0	—	259	—	—	—	—
Education							
Less than high school (%)	27	(7.9)	22,170	(22.7)	12.2	1.0	—
High school graduate (%)	95	(27.9)	42,134	(43.2)	22.5	1.9	(1.2–2.8)
Some college (%)	79	(23.2)	18,578	(19.1)	42.5	3.5	(2.3–5.4)
Baccalaureate (%)	71	(20.8)	8,663	(8.9)	82.0	6.7	(4.3–10.5)
Post-baccalaureate (%)	69	(20.2)	5,967	(6.1)	115.6	9.5	(6.1–14.8)
Unknown	0	—	1,430	—	—	—	—
Residence							
Metro counties (%)	140	(41.1)	34,880	(35.3)	40.1	1.0	—
Coastal counties (%)	25	(7.3)	7,833	(7.9)	31.9	0.8	(0.5–1.2)
Other western counties (%)	151	(44.3)	41,150	(41.6)	36.7	0.9	(0.7–1.2)
East of the Cascades (%)	25	(7.3)	15,079	(15.2)	16.6	0.4	(0.3–0.6)

(Continued)

Table 1 (Continued)

Characteristics	DWDA Patients 1998–2007 (N = 341)[2]		Oregon Deaths, Same Diseases (N = 98,942)[3]		DWDA Deaths per 10,000 Oregon Deaths	Rate Ratio (95% CI)[4]
Underlying illnesses						
Neoplasms (%)	280	(82.1)	66,255	(67.0)	42.3	10.5 (4.3–25.3)
Lung and bronchus (%)	65	(19.1)	20,557	(20.8)	31.6	7.8 (3.2–19.4)
Pancreas (%)	30	(8.8)	3,914	(4.0)	76.6	19.0 (7.4–48.9)
Breast (%)	30	(8.8)	5,134	(5.2)	58.4	14.5 (5.6–37.2)
Colon (%)	23	(6.7)	5,315	(5.4)	43.3	10.7 (4.1–28.2)
Prostate (%)	20	(5.9)	4,365	(4.4)	45.8	11.3 (4.3–30.2)
Ovary (%)	17	(5.0)	2,055	(2.1)	82.7	20.5 (7.6–55.4)
Lymphoid/ hematopoietic (%)	10	(2.9)	5,728	(5.8)	17.5	4.3 (1.5–12.6)
Skin (%)	10	(2.9)	1,380	(1.4)	72.5	17.9 (6.1–52.4)
Brain (%)	8	(2.3)	1,751	(1.8)	45.7	11.3 (3.7–34.5)
Esophagus (%)	7	(2.1)	1,819	(1.8)	38.5	9.5 (3.0–30.0)
Oral Cavity (%)	6	(1.8)	521	(0.5)	115.2	28.5 (8.7–93.1)
Bladder & Ureter (%)	6	(1.8)	1,878	(1.9)	31.9	7.9 (2.4–25.9)
Liver (%)	6	(1.8)	1,470	(1.5)	40.8	10.1 (3.1–33.1)
Kidney (%)	5	(1.5)	1,471	(1.5)	34.0	8.4 (2.4–29.0)
Other (%)	37	(10.9)	8,897	(9.0)	41.6	10.3 (4.0–26.2)
Amyotrophic lateral sclerosis (%)	26	(7.6)	962	(1.0)	270.3	66.9 (25.7–173.8)
Chronic respiratory disease (%)	15	(4.4)	17,721	(17.9)	8.5	2.1 (0.8–5.8)
HIV/AIDS (%)	7	(2.1)	304	(0.3)	230.3	57.0 (18.2–178.6)
Heart disease (%)	5	(1.5)	12,375	(12.5)	4.0	1.0 —
Illnesses listed below[5] (%)	8	(2.3)	1,325	(1.3)	60.4	14.9 (4.9–45.6)

Notes

1. The same underlying disease is defined by specific ICD-9 code.

2. Unknowns were excluded when calculating percentages.

3. Ibid.

4. Confidence interval.

5. Includes alcoholic hepatic failure, corticobasal degeneration, diabetes mellitus with renal complications, hepatitis C, organ-limited amyloidosis, scleroderma, and Shy-Drager syndrome.

activities—increased over the 10-year period. In addition, reports of concerns about inadequate pain control (including fear of future pain) increased from 12.5 percent in 1998 to 32.7 percent in 2007 ($p < 0.02$), and reports about being a burden on family members or caregivers increased from 12.5 percent in 1998 to 44.9 percent in 2007 ($p = 0.01$).

The proportion of patients referred for a formal mental health evaluation declined, from 43.5 percent in 1999 to 0.0 percent in 2007 ($p < 0.001$); since 2003, the proportion has been 5.4 percent or less. Evaluations were more

Table 2

Ten-Year Trends in the Practice of the Oregon Death with Dignity Act, 1998–2007

Characteristic	Total	1998	1999	2000	2001	2002	2003	2004	2005	2006	2007	p value[1]
Number of deaths	341	16	27	27	21	38	42	37	38	46	49	—
End-of-life concerns (n)	337	16	27	27	17	38	42	37	38	46	49	—
Steady loss of autonomy (%)	89.0	75.0	77.8	92.6	94.1	84.2	92.9	86.5	78.9	95.7	100	0.007
Less able to engage in enjoyable activities (%)	86.6	68.8	81.5	77.8	76.5	84.2	92.9	91.9	89.5	95.7	85.7	0.007
Loss of dignity (%)	81.6	NA	NA	NA	NA	78.6	78.4	78.4	89.5	76.1	85.7	0.5
Losing control of bodily functions (%)	58.2	56.3	59.3	77.8	52.9	47.4	57.1	64.9	44.7	58.7	63.3	0.8
Burden on family, friends/caregivers (%)	39.2	12.5	25.9	63.0	23.5	36.8	38.1	37.8	42.1	43.5	44.9	0.01
Inadequate pain control or concern about it (%)	27.3	12.5	25.9	29.6	5.9	26.3	21.4	21.6	23.7	47.8	32.7	0.02
Financial implications of treatment (%)	2.7	0.0	0.0	3.7	5.9	2.6	2.4	5.4	2.6	0.0	4.1	0.1
Psychiatrist consulted (n)	335	16	23	25	21	38	42	37	38	46	49	—
Yes (%)	10.7	31.3	43.5	20.0	14.3	13.2	4.8	5.4	5.3	4.3	0.0	< 0.001
Receiving hospice care at time of death (n)	339	15	27	26	21	38	42	37	38	46	19	—
Yes (%)	85.8	73.3	77.8	88.5	76.2	92.1	92.9	89.2	92.1	76.1	87.8	0.4
Terminal diagnosis to prescription written (n)	244	6	9	11	16	24	37	33	26	41	41	—
≤ 10 weeks (%)	52.0	33.3	44.4	54.5	37.5	41.7	54.1	48.5	53.8	65.9	53.7	0.07
Prescription written to ingestion (n)	341	16	27	27	21	38	42	37	38	46	49	—
≤ 2 weeks (%)	61.9	81.3	55.6	81.5	52.4	60.5	71.4	73.0	60.5	47.8	51.0	0.02
Prescribing M.D. present at ingestion (n)	341	16	27	27	21	38	42	37	38	46	49	—
Yes (%)	32.8	50.0	59.3	51.9	42.9	34.2	28.6	16.2	21.1	32.6	22.4	< 0.001

Note

1. Chi-square test for trend.

likely among patients older than 75 years (14.3 percent) than those aged less than 65 years (4.3 percent; *p* for trend = 0.01). Hospice coverage remained high throughout the study period, and was 87.8 percent in 2007.

The interval between a terminal diagnosis and receiving a prescription shortened, although it was not statistically significant (*p* = 0.07), while the interval between receiving a prescription and ingesting medication lengthened (*p* = 0.02). Of 546 patients who received a prescription, 17 (5.0 percent) lived more than six months after receiving it. Of these, 11 (64 percent) lived six to 12 months, and six lived 12 to 23 months. While 106 participants (32 percent) had been patients of the prescribing physician for one year or more, 170 patients (51 percent) had known the prescribing physician for three months or less (median length of physician-patient relationship = 11 weeks). The percentage of prescribing physicians who were present at ingestion of the medication decreased from 59.3 percent in 1999 to 22.4 percent in 2007 (*p* < 0.001). The majority of patients (319; 93.5 percent) ingested their medications at home; this did not change over the study period.

Medications Prescribed

During the 10 years, secobarbital and pentobarbital were the primary medications prescribed, but the proportions varied by year (figure 2). Overall, 10 grams of pentobarbital most often led to death within one hour (91.6 percent of patients) compared to other barbiturate and dose combinations (table 3). Of the 316 patients with known time until death, 61 (19.3 percent) lived longer than

Figure 2

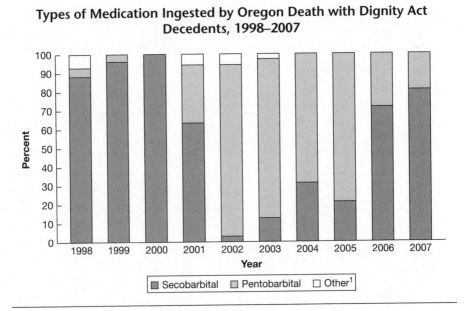

Types of Medication Ingested by Oregon Death with Dignity Act Decedents, 1998–2007

■ Secobarbital   ■ Pentobarbital   □ Other[1]

Note

1. Includes secobarbital and pentobarbital prescribed in combination, or with morphine.

Table 3

Interval between Ingestion and Unconsciousness/Death by Medication Type and Dose[1]

	Total[2]		Secobarbital, 9 g.		Secobarbital, 10 g.		Pentobarbital, 9 g.		Pentobarbital, 10g	
	n	%	*n*	%	*n*	%	*n*	%	*n*	%
Total	341	100	113	33.3	58	17.0	36	10.6	123	36.1
Unconsciousness										
0–10 minutes	273	88.9	78	83.0	52	92.9	26	89.7	110	92.4
11+ minutes	34	11.1	16	17.0	4	7.1	3	10.3	9	7.6
Unknown	34	—	19	—	2	—	7	—	4	—
Death[3]										
0–60 minutes	255	80.7	72	73.5	45	80.4	22	68.8	109	91.6
61 minutes–6 hours	39	12.3	17	17.3	8	14.3	8	25.0	5	4.2
>6 hours	22	7.0	9	9.2	3	5.4	2	6.3	5	4.2
Unknown	25	—	15	—	2	—	4	—	4	—

Notes

1. Other combinations ofmedications and doses were taken by *n* = 11.

2. Ibid.

3. In addition, one patient ingested 10 grams of secobarbital, remained unconscious for 65 hours, awakened, and died from his illness two weeks later. He is not included in this report.

one hour after ingestion; 22 (7.0 percent) lived longer than six hours. In addition, in 2005 one person ingested 10 grams of secobarbital, remained unconscious for two and one-half days before re-awakening, and died two weeks later from his underlying illness. Patients who ingested a partial dose before becoming unconscious (5.8 percent of patients) were more likely to live longer than six hours compared to those who ingested the entire dose (22.2 percent versus 6.2 percent $p = 0.03$). Patients who experienced partial emesis (5.7 percent) were more likely to live longer than six hours than those who did not (21.1 percent versus 6.1 percent; $p = 0.04$).

Physicians' Characteristics

From 2001 through 2007, 109 different physicians wrote one or more DWDA prescriptions for medications that were ingested by their patients. (Physician identifier codes are not available for 1998 through 2000.) Of these physicians, 72 (66.1 percent) wrote one prescription; 17 (15.6 percent) wrote two; while three physicians (2.0 percent) wrote more than 10. These three physicians wrote 62 (22.8 percent) of 271 prescriptions written during 2001 through 2007. Medical specialties of the 109 physicians included family practice (41.3 percent), internal medicine (27.5 percent), and oncology (20.2 percent). Most physicians (57.8 percent) had been in practice for 20 or more years.

From 1998 through 2007, the Oregon Department of Human Services filed 18 reports with the Oregon Medical Board for physicians failing to adhere to the requirements of the DWDA, most commonly for improper completion of the patient's written request (for example, the patient and witnesses did not sign at the same time). Other reasons included failure to file required documentation in a timely manner (one report was filed more than a year after the patient's death), incomplete documentation, and failure to wait 48 hours after the written request before writing the prescription. The Oregon Medical Board's investigations did not find that any physicians had violated good faith compliance with the act.

Discussion

Oregon's DWDA law remains controversial 10 years after its implementation. Proponents and opponents disagree even on what terminology should be used; because of the connotations of the language, proponents prefer the terms "physician aid in dying," "hastened death," and "death with dignity," and opponents prefer the term "physician-assisted suicide." The terms "suicide" and "dignity" have political implications, in that they can influence acceptance or rejection of proposed legislation similar to Oregon's DWDA. We continue to struggle to find a term to describe what is permitted under Oregon's law that is widely understandable and maintains our neutrality.

While the number and rate of patients who participate in DWDA increased in the decade that the law has been in effect, the number of participants remains small compared to the number of all deaths in Oregon, corresponding to 0.1 percent. Jurisdictions that allow euthanasia have higher rates than Oregon does: from 1990 through 2005, the rate of euthanasia in the Netherlands fluctuated between 1.7 percent and 2.4 percent, and physician-assisted suicide fluctuated from 0.1 percent to 0.2 percent of all deaths.[6] This likely reflects different cultural norms and end-of-life medical care practices in the Netherlands and Oregon.

The demographic characteristics and medical diagnoses of patients remained stable over the 10 years. Participation rates remained highest among persons younger than 85 years, who were White or Asian, had more formal education, and had a diagnosis of cancer. When the DWDA was first enacted in Oregon, considerable debate focused on whether or not vulnerable populations, such as persons of color or patients who were poor or uneducated would be coerced into participating in the DWDA. The Oregon data demonstrate that this has not materialized, a finding similar to that in the Netherlands.[7]

The reported primary concerns of patients that led to a request for medication have also remained stable. The two most common concerns of patients that were reported by physicians during the first years—a loss of autonomy and a decreasing ability to engage in enjoyable activities—continued to be the most common in the tenth year. These findings are consistent with those of other studies based on interviews with patients and family members that examine Oregon patients' motivations for using the DWDA, which include wanting control over the circumstances surrounding death and concerns about loss of function, dignity, and independence.[8]

Several worrisome trends, however, have emerged over the decade. The increase in reported concern about inadequate (current or future) pain control is noteworthy, as is the concern about being a burden on caregivers. The DWDA specifically requires the prescribing physician to review alternatives to DWDA, including comfort care, hospice care, and pain control. During the 10-year study period, enrollment in hospice among patients remained consistently high, with 73 percent to 93 percent of patients receiving hospice care at the time of death (mean = 86 percent). Nonetheless, patients' reported concerns about inadequate pain control underscore the need for physicians to address the pain of terminally ill patients, which is supported by a recent requirement for physicians to take training in pain control for licensure in Oregon. The increase in reported concerns about inadequate pain control in DWDA patients merits further study, as does the concern about being a burden.

Another worrisome trend is a decline in requests for formal psychiatric evaluation: evaluations decreased from approximately one-third of the patients in the first two years after implementation of the act, to none in 2007. Psycho-social evaluation is part of hospice intake, and physicians may not have thought a more formal evaluation was necessary. Nonetheless, a recent study of terminally ill patients in Oregon who requested a prescription under the act found that three of 18 patients who received prescriptions met clinical criteria for depression.[9] Although the act expressly requires evaluation by a licensed psychiatrist or psychologist if a condition causing impaired judgment is suspected, the decline in formal evaluations raises concerns that depression remains undiagnosed in some patients who request and receive a prescription under the DWDA.

Changes in the DWDA medication prescribed over time appear to have been driven not by evidence of efficacy or risk of complications, but by availability and cost. In May 2001, Eli Lilly Company reported that it stopped producing secobarbital due to lack of raw materials, leading to a decline in its use. Physicians then began prescribing oral ingestion of the available liquid (injectable) form of pentobarbital, which costs approximately $1,500 for 10 grams, compared to approximately $100 for 10 grams of oral secobarbital.[10] In September 2003, Ranbaxy Pharmaceuticals began producing secobarbital, coinciding with an increase in its use. While both medications led to unconsciousness within 10 minutes for most patients (89 percent), the time until death was less consistent; these findings are similar to the Dutch experience, where 12 percent of patients had prolonged time until death and 2 percent awakened.[11]

Most participating physicians wrote one or two prescriptions from 2001 through 2007 (years for which data are available); however, three physicians wrote more than 10 prescriptions each, and wrote nearly one-fourth of all of the prescriptions written. Previous studies indicate that as many as half of Oregon physicians may not be willing to write a prescription under the DWDA.[12] Thus, patients may be referred to physicians within larger health systems who have more experience with DWDA, or physicians who are known to be advocates of the act. This may account for why half of patients knew the prescribing physician for three months or less.

Issues not addressed in Oregon's law have been a source of controversy since DWDA implementation. The act outlines requirements prior to a prescription being written, but not procedures after the medication is dispensed. For example, it does not require a prescribing physician to follow a patient, nor to reassess a patient for decline in cognitive function that might develop and lead to impaired judgment. Several studies have found that a patient's interest in acquiring a DWDA prescription fluctuates over time.[13] Thus, it may be prudent for prescribing physicians to have an ongoing dialog with patients to assure that end-of-life concerns are met. The act also does not require a physician to be present when a patient ingests the prescribed medication. In addition, while the act assigns to the Oregon Department of Human Services responsibility for monitoring participation in the DWDA, it does not assign enforcement authority nor does it provide resources to support regulatory activities, which has left us open to charges of bias.[14]

Data regarding Oregon's experience with DWDA in the past decade are important for the ongoing policy debate. While our experience might not be directly applicable to other jurisdictions with different population characteristics (Oregon's residents are mostly White) and end-of-life care practices (Oregon has high levels of hospice coverage and advanced care planning),[15] Oregon's experience provides an important perspective as a jurisdiction that allows self-ingestion of lethal doses of medication, but not euthanasia. This option continues to be used by only a small number of terminally ill Oregonians.

Notes

1. Oregon Death with Dignity Act, Oregon Revised Statute 127.800–127.995, http://oregon.gov/DHS/ph/pas/index.shtml, accessed 18 February 2008.

2. United States Supreme Court, *Syllabus: Gonzalez Attorney General, et al. vs. Oregon, et al.*, argued 5 October 2005, decided 17 January 2006, www.supremecourtus.gov/opinions/05pdf/04-623.pdf, accessed 18 February 2008.

3. A.E. Chin et al., "Legalized physician-assisted suicide in Oregon—The first year's experience," *New England Journal of Medicine* 340 (1999): 577–83; A.D. Sullivan, K. Hedberg, and D.W. Fleming, "Legalized physician-assisted suicide in Oregon—The second year," *New England Journal of Medicine* 342 (2000): 598–604; A.D. Sullivan, K. Hedberg, and D. Hopkins, "Legalized physician-assisted suicide in Oregon, 1998–2000," *New England Journal of Medicine* 344 (2001): 605–7; K. Hedberg, D. Hopkins, and K.N. Southwick, "Legalized physician-assisted suicide in Oregon, 2001," *New England Journal of Medicine* 346 (2002): 450–2; K. Hedberg, D. Hopkins, and M. Kohn, "Five years of legal physician-assisted suicide in Oregon," *New England Journal of Medicine* 348 (2003): 961–4.

4. A. van der Heide et al., "End-of-life practices in the Netherlands under the Euthanasia Act," *New England Journal of Medicine* 356 (2007): 1957–65; R.L. Marquet et al., "Twenty five years of requests for euthanasia and physician assisted suicide in Dutch general practice: Trend analysis," *British Medical Journal* 327 (2003): 201–2.

5. SPSS Version 15.0.0. SPSS Inc, Chicago, Illinois; J.H. Abramson, "WINPEPI (PEPI-for-Windows): Computer programs for epidemiologists," *Epidemiologic Perspectives & Innovations* 1, article 6 (2004).

6. Van der Heide et al., "End-of-life practices in the Netherlands," see note 4 above.

7. M.P. Battin et al., "Legal physician-assisted dying in Oregon and the Netherlands: Evidence concerning the impact on patients in 'vulnerable' groups," *Journal of Medical Ethics* 33 (2007): 591–7.

8. Sullivan, Hedberg, and Fleming, "Legalized physician-assisted suicide in Oregon—The second year," see note 3 above; L. Ganzini, E.R Goy, and S.K. Dobscha, "Why Oregon patients request assisted death: Family members' views," *Journal of General Internal Medicine* 23 (2008): 154–7; R.A. Pearlman et al., "Motivations for physician-assisted suicide: Patient and family voices," *Journal of General Internal Medicine* 20 (2005): 234–9.

9. L. Ganzini, E.R. Goy, S.K. Dobscha, "Prevalence of depression and anxiety in patients requesting physicians' aid in dying: Cross sectional survey," *British Medical Journal* 337 (2008): a1682.

10. Gary Schnabel, Oregon Board of Pharmacy, personal communication with the authors, February 2008.

11. J.H. Groenewoud et al., "Clinical problems with the performance of euthanasia and physician assisted suicide in the Netherlands," *New England Journal of Medicine* 342 (2000): 551–6.

12. L. Ganzini et al., "Oregon physicians' attitudes about and experiences with end-of-life care since passage of the Oregon Death with Dignity Act," *Journal of the American Medical Association* 285 (2001): 2363–9.

13. L. Ganzini et al., "Interest in physician-assisted suicide among Oregon cancer patients," *The Journal of Clinical Ethics* 17, no. 1 (Spring 2006): 27–38; E.J. Emanuel, D.L. Fairclough; and L.L. Emanuel, "Attitudes and desires related to euthanasia and physician assisted suicide among terminally-ill patients and their care givers," *Journal of the American Medical Association* 284 (2000): 2460–8.

14. K. Foley and H. Hendin, "The Oregon report: Don't ask, don't tell," *Hastings Center Report* 29 (May–June 1999): 37–42.

15. V.P. Tilden et al., "Out-of-hospital death: Advance care planning, decedent symptoms, and caregiver burden," *Journal of the American Geriatric Society* 52 (2004): 532–9; B. Han et al., "National trends in adult hospice use: 1991–1992 to 1999–2000," *Health Affairs* 25 (2006): 792–9.

Susan M. Wolf

 **NO**

Confronting Physician-Assisted Suicide and Euthanasia: My Father's Death

Duty: An act . . . required of one by position, social custom, law, or religion. . . . Moral obligation.

—American Heritage Dictionary of the English Language, 4th ed.

My father's death forced me to rethink all I had written over two decades opposing legalization of physician-assisted suicide and euthanasia.[1] That should not have surprised me. Years ago, when I started working on end-of-life care, he challenged my views on advance directives by insisting that he would want "everything," even in a persistent vegetative state. "I made the money, so I can spend it." More deeply, he argued that the Holocaust was incompatible with the existence of God. There is no afterlife, he claimed. This is it, and he wanted every last bit of "it" on any terms.

My father was a smart, savvy lawyer, the family patriarch. He was forceful, even intimidating at times. We had fought over the years, especially as I neared college. That was probably necessary—my separating and our disengaging. When I was a child, it was a family joke how often he and I said the same thing at the same time. We were alike in many ways.

My father was diagnosed with a metastatic head and neck cancer in 2002. His predictable view was "spare no effort." A top head and neck surgeon worked through conflicting pathology reports to locate the primary tumor in the thyroid and excise the gland. Metastases would crop up from time to time, but radiation and then CyberKnife radiosurgery kept them in check. For five years he did well.

Things changed in June of 2007. The last CyberKnife treatment was billed as the worst, with significant pain likely to follow. Sure enough, ten days later, my father's pain on swallowing became severe. He began losing weight—a lot of it. He weakened. He fell twice in his apartment. His regular internist was out of town, so he went to the emergency room of a local hospital. Doctors did little for this seventy-nine-year-old man with a five-year history of metastatic thyroid cancer plus emphysema and chronic obstructive pulmonary disease.

He was briefly discharged to home but finally made it to the head and neck surgeon who had found the primary tumor in 2002. One look at my father and the surgeon admitted him, ordering a gastrostomy tube to deliver nutrition. Now my father was in an excellent hospital, with the head and neck, pulmonology, and gastroenterology services working him up. The mood brightened and the family gathered around him. I spent days in his sunny hospital room reminiscing, plowing through the *New York Times* with him, singing the college fight songs he offered as lullabies when I was little.

With multiple services focusing on my father's condition, I hoped the picture would soon come clear. I waited for a single physician to put the pieces together. And the medical picture was becoming worse. A surgical procedure revealed cancer in the liver. Pulmonology added pneumonia to the roster of lung ailments. Meanwhile, dipping oxygen saturation numbers drove a trip to the intensive care unit. Attempted endoscopy revealed a tumor between the esophagus and trachea, narrowing the esophagus. But no physician was putting the whole picture together. What treatment and palliative options remained, if any? What pathways should he—and we—be considering at this point?

He Said He Wanted to Stop

My father was becoming increasingly weak. He was finding it difficult to "focus," as he put it. He could not read, do the *New York Times* crossword puzzles he used to knock off in an hour, or even watch TV. Fortunately, he could talk, and we spent hours on trips he had taken around the world, family history, his adventures as a litigator. But he was confined to bed and did little when he was alone.

Then one morning he said he wanted to stop. No more tube feeding. No one was prepared for this switch from a lifetime of "spare no effort." He told me he feared he was now a terrible burden. I protested, knowing that I would willingly bear the "burden" of his illness. I suspect that what others said was more powerful, though. I was later told that the doctor urged him not to stop, warning that he would suffer a painful death, that morphine would be required to control the discomfort, and that my father would lose consciousness before the day was out. Instead of assuring my father that health professionals know how to maintain comfort after termination of artificial nutrition and hydration, my father was scared away from this option. Weeks later, my father would wish aloud that he had carried through with this decision.

Convinced now that he had no choice, my father soldiered on. But hospital personnel announced that it was time for him to leave the hospital. We were incredulous. He could not stand, walk, or eat. He had bedsores. Even transferring him from bed to a chair was difficult. And the rigors of transporting him in the early August heat were worrisome. But they urged transfer to a rehabilitation facility. My father was assured that with continued tube feeding and rehab, he could be walking into the surgeon's office in October.

It seemed to me my father was being abandoned. His prognosis was clearly bad and he himself had now raised the prospect of stopping tube feeding and dying, but it shocked me to see the hospital try to get rid of him. Yes, the hospital said he could return (somehow) in late September to see the ENT oncologist. But as far as I knew, that physician had never even met my father. And I doubted my father would make it to September. Still, no one was integrating the big picture. There seemed to be little choice. My father was successfully transported by ambulance to another hospital with a well-regarded rehabilitation unit.

The transfer provided brief respite. My father was delighted that he was now only blocks from his apartment, and the enticing possibility of actually going home beckoned. But the rehab unit demanded hours per day of rigorous work from each patient. My father was too weak. And his pneumonia was an issue. He was moved off rehab to the medical floor. A compassionate and attentive hospitalist appeared, trying to put together the big picture. She set about collecting the reports from the prior two hospitals and integrating them. Again, many teams were on board, including rheumatology now for flaring gout.

I requested the palliative care team. Even though my father could be lucid and "himself," I listened painfully as he faltered through the questions on their minimental exam. It was hard to accept that this paragon of analytic and verbal precision was failing. I alerted a member of the palliative care team that my father had evidently been misinformed at the prior hospital about the consequences of stopping artificial nutrition and hydration. I urged her to find a time to reassure him that he indeed had choices, could refuse treatments if he wanted to, and could be confident that his comfort would be maintained. I made clear to her that I hoped he would choose to stay the course for now and remain with us, but that he deserved to know that he had the choice. My father had designated his two proxy decision-makers (one of them me), but could still participate in the medical decision-making. His values and his subjective experience—whether he wanted more interventions or had reached his limit—were key.

Still unresolved, though, was the question of where we were headed. Could tube feeding and rehab bring him home and even walking into the surgeon's office in October? Was there treatment that could slow the growth of the newly discovered cancer in his lung? Should we instead pursue hospice care? At times, my father's illness seemed like *Rashomon,* a story with conflicting versions and possible trajectories. But soon my father was back in the ICU, with oxygen saturation percentages dipping into the seventies. Tube feeding was so uncomfortable that it was administered slowly through the night. Pain medication was a constant. Despite this, he held court in his room, enjoying the banter, and offering his own with that wry smile and cocked eyebrow.

He was briefly transferred to the pulmonary care unit, as the most pressing issues at this point were actually not cancer but lung mucus and secretions, as well as pneumonia. I arrived one morning to find him upset. His nurse was not answering his calls, and his immobility left him at her mercy. I summoned the highly experienced and empathetic supervisor, but even behind closed doors with her he was afraid to speak plainly. I saw this tough-as-nails litigator reduced to fearful dependence.

"Can We Accelerate?"

By morning there was a new problem. My father had developed a massive bleed. Nursing had found him in a pool of his own blood, lying among the clots. The gastroenterologists took him in for a procedure, spending hours trying to find the source of the bleed. They never found it. My father required transfusion of most of his blood volume. The bleeding abated, but we knew it could resume any time.

That was it—the final blow. My father was back in the ICU now, but the bleed and the hours spent searching for its source were too much. He waited until we gathered at his bedside. His speech was halting now, but his determination obvious. "Tell me my choices." We went through each option—you can keep going like this, or you can go back to the floor if the ICU is bothering you, or you can halt the tube feeding and IV hydration. You also can wait, rather than deciding right now.

For close to an hour we stayed in a tight circle around his bed, straining to hear his every word, crying, responding to each question. At one point, I thought he wanted to wait, but he called us back. "It could happen again. At 2 a.m.," he said. He wanted a decision now. "That's what I want. To terminate." He made it clear he wanted to stop tube feeding and IV hydration. But that wasn't enough. He wanted consensus.

With the decision made, we set about communicating it to the caregivers and getting new orders written. It was then that he uttered three words that shook me. "Can we accelerate?" It seemed he was asking for more—a fast death, by assisted suicide or euthanasia. Reflexively, I said no, but with a promise—we can make absolutely certain they keep you comfortable. Even if you can't talk, even if you appear comatose, if you merely furrow your brow, we'll know you need more pain medication.

I knew right away that I needed to think through my "no." In reality, we were in the ICU of a major hospital in a jurisdiction that allowed neither assisted suicide nor euthanasia. Indeed, no jurisdiction in the United States allows euthanasia, and my father was beyond assisted suicide by swallowing prescribed lethal medication, as he couldn't swallow anything. But I still needed to think this through.

I knew that in some ways, my father presented what proponents of assisted suicide and euthanasia would regard as a strong case. He was clearly dying of physical causes, unlike the controversial 1991 *Chabot* case in the Netherlands involving a patient who was merely depressed. He certainly had less than six months to live. He was probably depressed by his illness, but in a way that was appropriate to his situation. His decisional capacity had surely declined, but he was able to express definite treatment preferences.

Moreover, he wasn't asking for a change in policy or law. Statewide or national changes in policy require considering a huge range of patients, anticipating the predictable errors and abuses. The Dutch have bravely documented all of this through empirical study of their practice of legalized euthanasia—violations of the requirement for a contemporaneous request by a competent patient, doctors failing to report the practice as required, and practice falling down the slippery slope to euthanasia of newborns.[2] Oregon has documented its experience with legalized assisted suicide, too, but only the cases reported as required, leaving great uncertainty about cases not reported.[3] My father wasn't asking for societal change, though, only whether he himself could "accelerate." I faced the highly individual question of how to do right by my own father.

We Kept Vigil, Around the Clock

In truth, it was life that answered the question, not logic. In some ways, it would have been psychologically easier, or at least faster, to bring the ordeal we all were experiencing to a quick end. I was in a city far from my husband and children, doing shifts at my father's bedside at all hours, fearful of more looming medical disasters increasing his discomfort. But instead of ending all of this and fleeing, we stayed, redoubling our attention to him. I stroked his thick white hair. He and I reminisced. He was always a great raconteur. We talked and talked over the next days. The decision to stop tube feeding actually seemed to lighten his load. A decision. In a way, it was a relief.

And executing the decision took work, itself a devotion. It was around 6 p.m. when the decision was made. The ICU doctor came to the bedside to confirm the new plan and assure my father that he would be kept comfortable. But the palliative care professional, about to go off-duty, insisted that my father would need to leave the hospital. I was astonished. Was she saying he could not terminate treatment here? That the hospital had no in-patient hospice care? That you could accept invasive treatment at this hospital, but not refuse it? After years of working on end-of-life issues, I knew better. I confronted her: "You know that my father has a constitutional and common law right to refuse invasive treatment, including in this hospital." She acceded, but insisted that he would no longer meet the criteria for hospitalization; he would need to leave, to a hospice facility or home. The hospital evidently had no hospice to offer. Fine, we would set about arranging admission to hospice.

There was more—concerns over whether the fluid flowing through a remaining line would wrongly prolong his life and whether giving morphine by pump rather than through his line would do the same. I reached out by cell phone and e-mail to colleagues who were expert in maintaining comfort when artificial nutrition and hydration are stopped. We signed the papers requesting transfer to hospice. At one point, my father asked, "Will I see the end coming or fade away?" No one in the hospital was counseling my father. I worked my cell phone for answers and carried them to my father's bedside. To a man who could hold no faith after the Holocaust, I even brought the words and experience of my rabbi.

We kept vigil, around the clock. He was out of the ICU now, in a hospital room awaiting transfer to hospice. As he began to doze more and talk less, we watched carefully for the slightest sign of discomfort. We had promised we would assure his comfort. That meant constant vigilance.

The last time I saw my father, he was motionless. His eyes were closed. He had stopped speaking. He appeared unresponsive. His breathing was quieter, rasps gone with dehydration. I took his hand. I told him I loved him. I stroked his hair, still full and silvered. I spoke to him from the heart, words that remain between him and me. Then I heard myself say, "If I am a good mother, it's because you were a great father." And to my surprise, he moved his jaw. Not his lips or his mouth. But he opened his jaw three times. It was our signal, the one we'd worked out in the ICU. Three means "I-love-you." Tears streamed down my face. I struggled, remembering the rabbi's caution that the ones we love most may need permission to leave us, to die. "I know you may have to leave before I get back. That's okay." It felt nearly impossible to let him go. My chest was bursting. The pain was crushing.

When I finally left, I was working to breathe. Taking one step then another. Breaking down, collecting myself, breaking down again. He died not long after.

In the End

I will not pretend—there was a price to be paid for going the longer way, not the shorter. My father died slowly. He had to trust that we would keep a ferocious vigil, demanding whatever palliative care he needed. It was he who traveled that road, not me. I paid my own price, though. I felt the heavy weight of his trust and the obligation to fight for him. I was scared I might fail. I felt very close to the jaws of death.

But with every memory we shared while he could speak, every lilt of his eyebrow and wry smile, we basked together in life, reveled in a bit more of fifty-four years together and his nearly eighty on this earth. Family and caregivers did manage to keep him comfortable. He died loved and loving.

I grieve still. I reread the letters he wrote home from Oxford in his twenties, I pore over the genealogy charts he painstakingly constructed over decades, I finger the abacus he kept in his law office. I go to e-mail him, then remember. I would not want to bear the burden of having "accelerated," of causing his death by euthanasia or assisted suicide; this is hard enough. My father's death made me rethink my objections to legalizing assisted suicide and euthanasia, but in the end it left me at ease with what I've written. Staying, keeping vigil, fighting to secure a comfortable death, stroking his hair, standing guard as death approached was my duty. It was the final ripening of my love. We both changed, even closer at the end.

Notes

1. In the mid-1980s, I had led the Hastings Center project that developed *Guidelines on the Termination of Life-Sustaining Treatment and the Care of the Dying* (Indianapolis: Indiana University Press, 1987). For a sample of my subsequent work on physician-assisted suicide, see "Gender, Feminism, and Death: Physician-Assisted Suicide and Euthanasia," in *Feminism and Bioethics: Beyond Reproduction,* ed. S.M. Wolf (New York: Oxford University Press, 1996), 282–317; "Physician-Assisted Suicide in the Context of Managed Care," *Duquesne Law Review* 35 (1996): 455–79; "Physician-Assisted

Suicide, Abortion, and Treatment Refusal: Using Gender to Analyze the Difference," in *Physician-Assisted Suicide,* ed. R. Weir (Indianapolis: Indiana University Press, 1997), 167–201; "Facing Assisted Suicide and Euthanasia in Children and Adolescents," in *Regulating How We Die: The Ethical, Medical, and Legal Issues Surrounding Physician-Assisted Suicide,* ed. L.L. Emanuel (Cambridge, Mass.: Harvard University Press, 1998), 92–119, 274–94; "Pragmatism in the Face of Death: The Role of Facts in the Assisted Suicide Debate," *Minnesota Law Review* 82 (1998): 1063–1101; and "Assessing Physician Compliance with the Rules for Euthanasia and Assisted Suicide," *Archives of Internal Medicine* 165 (2005): 1677–79.

2. I discuss all of this in my work cited above. See also P.J. van der Maas et al., "Euthanasia and Other Medical Decisions Concerning the End of Life," *Lancet* 338 (1991): 669–74; L. Pijnenborg et al., "Life-Terminating Acts without Explicit Request of Patient," *Lancet* 341 (1993): 1196–99; P.J. van der Maas et al., "Euthanasia, Physician-Assisted Suicide, and Other Medical Practices Involving the End of Life in the Netherlands, 1990–1995," *New England Journal of Medicine* 335 (1996): 1699–1705; G. van der Wal et al., "Evaluation of the Notification Procedure for Physician-Assisted Death in the Netherlands," *New England Journal of Medicine* 335 (1996): 1706–11; A. van der Heide and P.J. van der Maas, "Medical End-of-life Decisions Made for Neonates and Infants in the Netherlands," *Lancet* 350 (1997): 251–55; B.D. Onwuteaka-Philipsen et al., "Euthanasia and Other End-of-life Decisions in the Netherlands in 1990, 1995, and 2001," *Lancet* 362 (2003): 395–99; T. Sheldon, "Only Half of Dutch Doctors Report Euthanasia, Report Says," *British Medical Journal* 326 (2003): 1164; T. Sheldon, "Dutch Reporting of Euthanasia Cases Falls—Despite Legal Reporting Requirements," 328 (2004): 1336; B.D. Onwuteaka-Philipsen et al., "Dutch Experience of Monitoring Euthanasia," *British Medical Journal* 331 (2005): 691–93; E. Verhagen and P.J.J. Sauer, "The Groningen Protocol: Euthanasia in Severely Ill Newborns," *New England Journal of Medicine* 352 (2005): 959–62; A. van der Heide et al., "End-of-Life Practices in the Netherlands Under the Euthanasia Act," *New England Journal of Medicine* 356 (2007): 1957–65.

3. See K. Foley and H. Hendin, "The Oregon Report: Don't Ask, Don't Tell," *Hastings Center Report* 29, no. 3 (1999): 37–42; E.J. Emanuel, "Oregon's Physician-Assisted Suicide Law: Provisions and Problems," *Archives of Internal Medicine* 156 (1996): 825–29.

EXPLORING THE ISSUE

May a Dying Person Hasten Her Death?

Critical Thinking and Reflection

1. Why do most people seek to hasten their deaths? With regard to the Oregon Death with Dignity Act, what are its key features, worrisome trends, and circumstances unique to Oregon?
2. Consider the situation of your sister with ALS who wants help from you and your family to stop eating and drinking. What would you discuss with her about her choices, hopes, and fears?
3. Consider the situation of your cousin from Oregon who is dying from cancer and has asked you to be with him when he dies from self-termination. He is conflicted because his strict religious family is opposed to this. Discuss what you think and say.
4. *Discuss*: Compare stories that show how "hastening death" for dying is different in three places: where assisted death is decriminalized (Netherlands), assisted suicide is legalized (Switzerland), and self-termination is regulated (Oregon, Washington, Montana).
5. *Discuss*: Your newborn's condition means she will not live long; in addition she has intense pain in the NICU (Newborn Intensive Care Unit), where her treatment makes her cry constantly. Your spouse wants them to "put her to sleep." What do you do? Is palliative sedation to unconsciousness (PSU) the same as sedation to death (SD) (Sulmasy, Daniel, & Jansen, 2002 exchange with Quill)?

Is There Common Ground?

A punishment to some, to some a gift, and to many a favor.

Seneca

Because I could not stop for death, He kindly stopped for me; The carriage held but just ourselves and immortality.

Emily Dickinson

May one hasten her death? Choices to hasten death blend *autonomy* and *mercy-compassion* but face three rebuttals including the *wrongness of killing, threats to professional integrity,* and *slippery slope abuses* (Battin, 2005; Quill, 2008). Some argue that a wish to hasten death is a reasonable decision to conclude a life, perhaps even an heroic act of self-relinquishment. Other are concerned that a wish to hasten death is a communication of distress and possibly a desire for self-harm. Side by side with diverse efforts to debate *justifications* for hastening death are parallel cultural traditions that *explain* hastened death as *exceptionally loving sacrifice* or *pathologically self-inflicted harm*. Hastened deaths are interpreted as three kinds of exceptional circumstances: as ideally heroic relinquishments in the face of adversity called *merciful self-denial* (Grisez, 1997; Thomasma, 1998) or *excusing conditions* due to disabling features of personal life such as *personality disorders* (DSM IV) or caused by *social burdens* (Droge & Tabor, 1992; altruistic and anomic suicide in Durkheim, 1997 [1897]). Three public health goals criss-cross: *democratizing the idea and practice of painless death* while *limiting practices of self-caused death* because of vital understandings about how effective management *reduces requests and suicide risks* from personality disorders and social stressors.

Even when a person cannot foresee her own future misery, few defend hastened death by another against the consent of the dying (*involuntary euthanasia*) (Schwarts, 2007). Mercy killing that is without the consent of (unconscious) dying (*nonvoluntary*) based on suffering has some defenders on grounds that are *utilitarian* or even *caregiver paternalism* (Singer, 2011; Netherlands Law, 2002). Some help dying but resist hastened death with a Hippocratic tradition of accompanied trust-filled *patient beneficence* (Kass, 1989; Pellegrino, 1992; Sugarman & Sulmasy, 2010); others defend it as either reasonable to assist or perform (Battin, 2007; Quill, 2008).

Three kinds of *duty and obligation arguments* are made about hastening death. The Supreme Court has determined that persons have a *civil liberty to refuse* life-sustaining treatment but not a constitutional right to assisted death to "determine the time and manner of one's death." Yet three state legislatures permit hastened death as a right to *safeguarded lethal self-administration for terminally ill* (Quinlan, 1976; Cruzan, 1990; *Washington v. Glucksberg*, 1997a; *Vacco v. Quill*, 1997; Sabatino, 2007). Some debate whether hastened death opposes responsibilities for *self-preservation, to others or the divine* (Aristotle, Augustine, Kant, Hume, Paton, 1979, Sandel, 2010). Others defend hastened death where prolonged, medicalized dying directly *threatens* such responsibilities (Cahill, 1977, 1991; Küng, 1982, 1995; Farley, 1995). Some argue that very specific positive duties for a hastened death are based upon obligations to lessen overwhelming burdens on the specific family caregiving networks. Critics object this rejects responsibilities to vulnerable relatives (*communitarianism* in Harvey, 1997; Ackerman, 2000). Some argue a duty to hastened death is based on a *globally allocated resources* that unjustly favor medicalized longevity among wealthy. Critics rebut resource transfers would not lead to fair redistribution (Unger, 1996; Battin, 2000). Three positions about hastening death interpret *remaining life as having worth or utilitarian value*. *Vitalists* argue that life has nearly an absolute value which should (almost) never be sacrificed and that complete life support should never be withdrawn or withheld early. *Instrumentalists* argue that life has functional value that can be relinquished for a greater good such that persons can determine the timing and manner of death either for themselves or others. *Proportionate caregivers* argue that life has an intrinsic but nonetheless relative value and that under conditions of clinical futility, when there is a disproportionate relationship between the burdens and the effectiveness of treatment, life support may be withdrawn (Pellegrino, 2000, 2003; German Protestant and Catholic Bishops, 1975–2010). Most who reject any intention to directly hasten death are especially clear about limits to sustain life in explaining that some treatments are extraordinary (nonobligatory; Grisez, 1990, 1997; Sulmasy et al., 2002) or disproportionate to expected outcomes (Grisez, 1990, Pellegrino, 2003).

Additional Resources

Ackerman, F. (2000). "For now I have my death": The duty to die vs. the duty to help the ill stay alive. *Midwest Studies in Philosophy, 24*, 172–185.

Aquinas, S. T. II, 64, 5, *Is it legitimate to kill oneself?* from II/2. Volume 38. Injustice, trans. M. Lefebure. New York: McGraw-Hill and Blackfriars, 1975, 63–79.

Aquinas. Commentary on Aristotle's Nichomachean Ethics, trans. C.I. Litzinger. New York: Henry Regnery Company, 1964; Notre Dame, IN: Dumb Ox Books, 1993, 347–351.

Augustine, Contra Gaudentium Donatistarum Episcopum. Ed. M. Petschenig 1910, vol. 53, (CSEL) Corpus Scriptorum Ecclesiasticorum Latinorum. Contra Gaudentium Donatistarum episcopum libri duo. Ed. M. Petschenig, G. Finaert, E. Lamirande, Biblioteque Augustinienne 32: Paris, Desclee de Brouwer, 1965, 510–685; PL = Migne, Patrologia Latina, 43:707–758.

Ball, S. C. (2006). Nurse-patient advocacy and the right to die. *Journal of Psychosocial Nursing 44*(12), 36–46.

Battin, M. (2000). Global life expectancies and the duty to dies. In J. Humber & R. Almeder (Eds.), *Is there a duty to die*. Totawa, NJ: Humana Press.

Battin, M. (2005). *Ending life: Ethics and the way we die*. Oxford: Oxford University Press.

Beauchamp, T. L. & Childress, J. (2001). *Principles of biomedical ethics*. Oxford: Oxford University Press.

Berry, Z. (2009). Responding to suffering: Providing options and respecting choice. *Journal of Pain and Symptom Management, 38*(3), 797–800.

Breitbart, W., Rosenfeld, B., Pessin, H., Kaim, M., Funesti-Esch, J., Galietta, M., et al. (2000). Depression, hopelessness, and desire for hastened death in terminally ill patients with cancer. *JAMA, 284*, 2907–2911.

Buiting, H., van Delden, J., Onwuteaka-Philpsen, B., Rietjens, J., van Tol, D., Gevers, J., et al. (2009). Reporting of euthanasia and physician-assisted suicide in the Netherlands: Descriptive study. *BMC Medical Ethics, 10*, 18. doi:10.1186/1472-6939-10-18.

Cahill, L. (1977). A natural law reconsideration of euthanasia. *Linacre Quarterly, 44*(February (1)), 47–63.

Cahill, L. (1991). Bioethical decisions to end life. *Theological Studies, 52*, 107–127.

Callahan, D. (2008). Organized obfuscation: Advocacy for physician assisted suicide. *Hastings Center Report, 38*(5), 30–32.

Cholbi, M. (2008). "Suicide." *Stanford Encyclopedia of philosophy*. Retrieved from http://plato.stanford.edu/entries/suicide/

Coyle, N. & Sculco, L. (2004). Expressed desire for hastened death in seven patients living with advanced cancer: A phenomenologic inquiry. *Oncology Nursing Forum, 31*(4), 699–709.

Daube, D. (1972). The linguistics of suicide. *Philosophy and Public Affairs, 1*(4), 387–437.

Droge, A. J. & Tabor, J. D. (1992). *A noble death: Suicide and martyrdom among christians and jews in antiquity*. New York: HarperCollins and HarperSanFrancisco.

Durkheim, E. (1997) [1897]. *Suicide: A study in sociology*. New York NY: The Free Press.

Dworkin, R. (1993). *Life's dominion: An argument about abortion, euthanasia, and individual freedom*. New York: Alfred A. Knopf.

Editor. (March 29, 1984). Gov. Lamm asserts elderly, if very ill, have "duty to die." *New York Times*. Retrieved from www.nytimes.com/1984/03/29/us/gov-lamm-asserts-elderly-if-very-ill-have-dutyto-die.html

Farley, M. (1995). Issues in contemporary Christian ethics: The choice of death in a medical context. *The Santa Clara Lectures, 1*(3), 1–19.

Ganzini, L., Beer, T. M., Brouns, M., Mori, M., & Hsieh, Y. C. (2006). Interest in physician-assisted suicide among Oregon cancer patients. *The Journal of Clinical Ethics, 17*(1), 27–38.

Ganzini, L., Goy, E. R., Miller, L. L., Harvath, T. A., Jackson, A., & Delorit, M. A. (2003). Nurses' experiences with hospice patients who refuse food and fluids to hasten death. *New England Journal of Medicine, 349*, 359–365.

Ganzini, L., Silveira, M. J., & Johnston, W. S. (2002). Predictors and correlates of interest in assisted suicide in the final month of life among ALS patients in Oregon and Washington. *Journal of Pain and Symptom Management, 24*(3), 312–317.

German Protestant and Catholic Bishops. (1975–2010). Gemeinsame Texte 17: Sterbebegleitung statt aktiver Sterbehilfe, Eine Textsammlung kirchlicher Erklärungen mit einer Einführung des Vorsitzenden der Deutschen Bischofskonferenz und des Vorsitzenden des Rates der Evangelischen Kirche in Deutschland.

Goedicke, H. (1970). *The report about the dispute of a man with his Ba: Papyrus Berlin 3024*. Baltimore, MD/London: The Johns Hopkins Press.

Grisez, G. (1990). Should nutrition and hydration be provided to *permanently-unconscious* and other mentally disabled persons? *Linacre Quarterly, 57*, 30–43.

Grisez, G. (1997). Q43, is it wrong to wish for death? And Q47: May a husband consent to stopping feeding his permanently unconscious wife? In *Difficult moral questions: Way of the Lord Jesus*. Vol III. (pp. 196–202; 218–225). Steubenville, Ohio: Franciscan Press.

Gunderson, M. (2004). A Kantian view of suicide and end-of-life treatment. *Journal of Social Philosophy, 35*(2), 277–287.

Hardwig, J. (2000). *Is there a duty to die and other essays in medical ethics*. New York: Routledge.

Hospice and Palliative Nurses Association. (2004). *The ethics of opiate use within palliative care.* HPNA position statement. Retrieved from www.hpna.org/PicView .aspx?ID=709

Hotopf, M., Lee, W., & Price, A. (2011). Assisted suicide: Why psychiatrists should engage in the debate. *The British Journal of Psychiatry, 198,* 83–84.

Hudson, P. L., Kristjanson, L. J., Ashby, M., Kelly, B., Schofield, P., Hudson, R., et al. (2006). Desire for hastened death in patients with advanced disease and the evidence base of clinical guidelines: A systematic review. *Palliative Medicine, 20*(7), 693–701.

Hume, D. (2001) [1756]. *Four dissertations and essays on suicide and the immortality of the soul.* South Bend: IN; St. Augustine's Press.

Jacobs, S. (2003). Behind the research: Death by voluntary dehydration: What the caregivers say. *The New England Journal of Medicine, 349,* 325–326.

Jansen, L. (2004). No safe harbor: The principle of complicity and the practice of voluntary stopping of eating and drinking. *Journal of Medicine and Philosophy, 29*(1), 61–74.

Kant, I. (1950). *Foundations of the metaphysics of morals,* trans. L. W. Beck. New York: Macmillan, 1990, 50.

Kant, I. (1952). Grundlegung zur Metaphysik der Sitten, ed. K. Vorländer, Hamburg: Felix Meiner, 57, Royal Prussian Academy edition page 433.

Kant, I. (1991) [1785]. *Grundlegung zur Metaphysik der Sitten/The moral law: Kant's groundwork of the metaphysic of morals.* Translated by Herbert James Paton (1887–1969). London/New York: Routledge.

Kass, L. R. (1989). Neither for love nor money: Why doctors must not kill. *Public Interest,* (94), 25.

Keenan, J. F. (1993). The function of the principle of double effect. *Theological Studies, 54,* 294–315.

Kelly, B., Burnett, P., Badger, S., Pelusi, D., Varghese, F. T., & Robertson, M. (2003). Doctors and their patients: A context for understanding the wish to hasten death. *Psychooncology, 12*(4), 375–384.

Küng, H. & Jens, W. (Eds.). (1998). Menschenwürdig Sterben. Ein Plädoyer Für Selbstverantwortung. Piper; Auflage: 2. Aufl., 36. Tsd (1995), Translated as *Dying with dignity: A plea for personal responsibility.* New York: Continuum Publishing Group.

Kung, H. (1982). Ewiges leben? (Piper; Auflage: Neuauflage, Nachdruck. 1982, 2007). *Eternal life? Life after death as a medical, philosophical and theological problem.* Wipf and Stock Publishers, 2003.

Marker, R. L. & Smith, W. J. (1996). The art of verbal engineering. *Dusquesne Law Review, 81,* 81–107.

Maytal, G. & Stern, T. A. (2006). The desire for death in the setting of terminal illness. *Journal of Clinical Psychiatry, 8*(5), 299–305.

Meier, C., Emmons, C., Litke, A., Wallenstein, S., & Morrison, R. S. (2003). Characteristics of patients requesting and receiving physician-assisted death. *Archives of Internal Medicine, 163,* 1537–1542.

Miller, Michael, Dr. (2008). *Dying wish.* Film. Retrieved from http://74.220.215.84/ ~goinpeac/dyingwishmedia/

Mueller, D. (1973). Review of Goedicke, Hans. (1970). *The report about the dispute of a man with his Ba: Papyrus Berlin 3024*. Baltimore, MD/London: The Johns Hopkins Press. *Journal of Near Eastern Studies, 32*(3), 353–354.

Muller, D. (2011). Attention to language in a request for physician aid in dying. *The American Journal of Hospice & Palliative Care, 28*, 63–64.

Netherlands Law. (2002). Wet toetsing levensbeëindiging op verzoek en hulp bij zelfdoding (Termination of Life on Request and Assisted Suicide Law). See "uitzichtloos en ondraaglijk lijden van de patiënt" ("the unbearable and hopeless suffering of the patient"). Retrieved from www.nvve.nl/nvve2/pagina.asp?pagkey=71892#staatsblad.

Novak, D. (1975). *Suicide and morality: The theories of Plato, Aquinas and Kant and their relevance for suicidology*. Atlanta, GA: Scholars Studies Press.

Paton, J. (1971). *The categorical imperative: A study in Kant's moral phihlosophy*. University of Pennsylvania.

Pellegrino, E. D. & Sulmasy, D. P. (2003). Medical ethics. In D. A. Warrell, T. M. Cox, & J. D. Firth (Eds.), *Oxford textbook of medicine*. New York: Oxford University Press.

Pellegrino, E. D. (1992). Why doctors must not kill. *Journal of Clinical Ethics, 3*(2), 95–102.

Pellegrino, E. D. (2000). Decisions to withdraw life-sustaining treatment: A moral algorithm. *Journal of the American Medical Association, 283*(8), 1065–1067. doi:10.1001/jama.283.8.1065

Pence, G. E. (2007). Is there a duty to die. In G. Pence (Ed.), *The elements of bioethics* (pp. 233–262). Dubuque, IA: McGraw-Hill.

Pope, T. M. & Anderson, L. E. (2011). Voluntarily stopping eating and drinking: A legal treatment option at the end of life. *Widener Law Review, 17*(2), 363–427.

Quill, T. & Greenlaw, J. (2008). Physician-assisted death. In M. Crowley (Ed.), *From birth to death and bench to clinic: The Hastings Center bioethics briefing book for journalists, policymakers, and campaigns* (pp. 137–142). Garrison, NY: The Hastings Center.

Robinson, J. (2010). Baxter and the return of physician assisted suicide. *Hastings Center Report, 40*(6), 15–17.

Rodriguez Davila, S. L., Vidal, E., Stewart, J. T., & Caserta, M. T. (2010). Management of a request for physician-assisted suicide. *American Journal of Hospice and Palliative Care, 27*, 63–65.

Sabatino, C. (2007). Advance directives and advance care planning: Legal and policy issues. Retrieved from http://aspe.hhs.gov/daltcp/reports/2007/adacplpi.htm

Sandel, M. (2010). *Justice: What's the right thing to do?* New York, NY: Farrar, Straus and Giroux.

Schwartz, J. K. (2007). Death by voluntary dehydration: Suicide or the right to refuse a life-prolonging measure? *Widener Law Review, 17*, 351–361.

Schwartz, J. K. (2009). Stopping eating and drinking. *American Journal of Nursing, 109*(9), 52–61.

Singer, P. (2011). *Practical ethics*. Cambridge: Cambridge University Press, 1979; second edition, 1993; third edition, 2011.

Smith, K. A., Goy, E. R., Harvath, T. A., & Ganzini, L. (2011). Quality of death and dying in patients who request physician-assisted death. *Journal of Palliative Medicine, 14*(4), 445–450.

Sugarman, J. & Sulmasy, D. (2010). *Methods in medical ethics*. Washington, DC: Georgetown University Press.

Sulmasy, D. & Pellegrino, E. (1999). Double effect: Clearing up the double talk. *Annals of Internal Medicine, 159*, 545–550.

Sulmasy, D. P. & Jansen, L. A. (2002). Sedation, alimentation, hydration, and equivocation: Careful conversation about care at the end of life. *Annals of Internal Medicine, 136*, 845–849.

Sulmasy, D. P., Ury, W. A., Ahronheim, J. C., Siegler, M., Kass, L., Lantos, J., et al. (2000a). Responding to intractable terminal suffering. *Annals of Internal Medicine; 133*, 560–562.

Sulmasy, D. P., Ury, W. A., Ahronheim, J. C., Siegler, M., Kass, L., Lantos, J., et al. (2000b). Palliative treatment of last resort and assisted suicide. *Annals of Internal Medicine, 133*, 562–563.

Thomas, C. (1980). First suicide note? *British Medical Journal, 281*(6235), 284–285 (Later as Discourse of a Man with his Ba, by Wim van den Dungen). Retrieved from www.sofiatopia.org/maat/ba.htm

Thomasma, D. (1998). Assisted death and martyrdom. Christian *Bioethics, 4*(2), 122–142.

Tucker, K. & Steele, F. B. (2007). Patient choice at the end of life getting the language right. *The Journal of Legal Medicine, 28*, 305–325.

Unger, T. (1996). *Living high and letting die*. New York: Oxford.

United States Conference of Catholic Bishops. (2011). *To live each day with dignity*. Retrieved from www.usccb.org/issues-and-action/human-life-and-dignity/assisted-suicide/to-live-each-day/

Vacco v. Quill, 521 U.S. 793 (1997). Retrieved from http://supreme.justia.com/us/521/793/case.html

Valente, S. K. (2004). End of life challenges: Honoring autonomy. *Cancer Nursing, 27*, 314–319.

Vetter, P. (2008). "Dying wish" documents death of Dr. Michael Miller with conscious choice to stop eating and drinking. *American Chronicle*, July. Retrieved from www.americanchronicle.com/articles/view/69683

Washington State Catholic Conference. (2006). *A guide to making good decisions for the end of life: Living will and durable power of attorney for health care*. Retrieved from http://thewscc.org/

Washington v. Glucksberg. (1997a). 521 U.S. 702 (1997). Retrieved from http://supreme.justia.com/us/521/702/case.html

Washington v. Glucksberg. (1997b). Supreme Court. Retrieved from http://law2.umkc.edu/faculty/projects/ftrials/conlaw/glucksberg.html

ISSUE 11

Can Legal Suicide Really Safeguard Against Abuse?

YES: **Ronald A. Lindsay**, from "Oregon's Experience: Evaluating the Record," *The American Journal of Bioethics* (vol. 9, no. 3, pp. 19–27, 2009)

NO: **Daniel Callahan**, from "Organized Obfuscation: Advocacy for Physician-Assisted Suicide," *Hastings Center Report* (vol. 38, no. 5, pp. 30–32, 2008)

Learning Outcomes

After reading this issue, you should be able to:

- Gain an understanding of seven recurrent charges of abuse in legally safeguarded, lethal self-administration for terminally ill with decisional capacity: inadequate safeguards in compliance and reporting; false autonomy; misplaced compassion; wrongful killing; bad medicine, slippery slopes, and risks to vulnerable populations.
- Describe different legal safeguards of eligibility (residency, decisional capacity, terminal status) and procedures (physicians consults, waiting periods).
- Understand empirical, ethical, and legal concerns about safeguards regarding different vulnerable populations.
- Identify and debate misuse or abuse best described in different terms that are ethical, criminal, and civil law.

ISSUE SUMMARY

YES: Ronald Lindsay, a lawyer and CEO of the Center for Inquiry, reviews the first decade of the Oregon Death with Dignity Act and identifies that key ethical and legal concerns raised by opponents are addressed with legal protections put into place.

NO: Cofounder of the Hastings Research Center, Daniel Callahan argues that advocates for physician-assisted suicide describe what they do in confusing terms and prescribe regulations without adequate public scrutiny.

For seven centuries Anglo-American common law has punished or disapproved of suicide and assisting suicide. In 1997 the U.S. Supreme Court determined that neither the due process clause nor the equal protection clause of the 14th Amendment includes a right to assisted suicide (*Vacco v. Quill*, 1997; *Washington v. Glucksberg*, 1997). This issue surveys *seven different charges of abuse and rebuttals* regarding legal *regulation* of lethal self-administration for terminally ill with decisional capacity: *inadequate safeguards in compliance and reporting; false autonomy; misplaced compassion; wrongful killing; bad medicine, slippery slopes, and risks to vulnerable populations* (Battin, 2008). From 1999 to 2007, American pathologist and euthanasia activist Dr. Jack Kevorkian served 8 years of his 10–25 year prison sentence of *second degree murder* for helping ALS patient Thomas Youk die, after having assisted more than 130 others.

But physician-assisted dying, or what opponents call physician-assisted suicide and proponents call aid in dying, is legally evolving. "Death with dignity" by lethal self-administration has become legal in three states (Oregon, Washington, Montana). Safeguards protect and restrain; they *substantively constrain who is eligible* with restrictions such as residency, competency-decisional capacity, and terminal status with *procedurally required* steps such as two physician consultations, waiting periods, third party co-signers, voluntary family notification, and options to rescind.

Arguments about abuse face several common *myths*. Claims about *abuse* incorrectly assume *cultural consensus* about appropriate *uses* ("legal, lethal self-administration") or disproportionate *mis-uses* ("over-utilization"). Does abuse refer to *actual cases* (influence or pressure), *patterns* (Kevorkian's "back alley suicides"), *policies* (encouraging overutilization), or *laws* (self-administration versus assistance) (Tucker, 2008)? Nor is there agreement about how wide the category is of those *who are at risk*; those with terminal diagnoses, imminently dying, in end stage illnesses, facing futile treatments, expected to die, vulnerable populations, disabled, nonprivileged without healthcare access, competent, incompetent, unduly influenced, or abused by others (Clarke, 1996, n71). Some debate whether "safeguards" should eliminate or effectively *reduce* risks.

Arguments about abuse share common *concerns* to keep self-termination rare. *Is* what is *legally permitted* becoming typically *expected*, or morally *required*? Are public health concerns to reduce self-killing and improve symptom management *displaced* by permitted self-termination?

Charges of abuse operate alone and together. Some charges of abuse refer to specific *laws*, some to *reporting systems*, some to documented *patterns of practices*, and some to *design flaws* in different analyses (Netherlands Reports, Oregon Reports, Battin, 2008). Critics charge *compliance and surveillance of data* is unverifiable (Drake, 2007), is inadequate (Grogan, 2007), is insufficient (Hendin & Foley, 2008), masks widespread euthanasia (Callahan, 2008), and insufficiently screens for depression (Schadenburg, 2004; Hicks, 2007; Ganzini in Battin, 2008). Defenders rebut that reports *generate adequate information* ("population based") (Battin, 2008; Lindsay, 2009).

Autonomy and Abuse: End-of-life choices feature different kinds of autonomy. Proponents judge *nonmaleficence* is owed to *decisions* authorized by dying persons to have "control over the timing and manner" of *imminent death events* (Bioethicist Amicus Brief, Baxter, 2009). A chief risk is premature choices. A liberty right of self-determination based on *decision-making capacity* permits self-death provided that choices don't harm others (Battin, 2008). Opponents argue more effective palliative care for *dying processes* is experienced as *benificent* by enabling autonomy to be more *self-governing* through better symptom management that reduces death requests (State and Amici Briefs, Baxter, 2009). "Rescue" jeopardizes focus: goals are not lengthening survivability but improving comfort that varies with different terminal conditions.

Mercy, Compassion, and Abuse: Proponents argue a compassionate state must defend an individual's right to end life based on *resilient self-control over death events* (Battin, 2008; Tucker, 2008). Opponents counter such control is misplaced mercy because true compassion requires the *state to widen accessibility for resilient pain control for all in dying processes* (including palliation). Hence political and religious communities owe dying persons *solidarity* in seeking comfort for persons to die a death of her own as accompanied in vulnerability as dignified (German Pastors, Washington State Catholic Conference, 2006).

Wrongful Killing as Abuse: Opponents say (a law permitting) assistance in death is objectively or theoretically an *in-principled kind of abuse* based on the wrongness of killing because it violates the sanctity of life, respect for life, the wrongness of suicide, or the wrongness of murder (Kass, 1989; Pellegrino, 1992; Sulmasy, 2002; Battin, 2005, 2008). Proponents counter with *principled* and *empirical* arguments: most patients who seek assisted death are not inflicting self-harm prematurely but concluding a life on their own terms (Tucker, 2008). Empirically, sanctity of life seems overstated; safeguards warrantee that only the terminally ill may use the law; only one in six requests are granted; the median wait time is 43 days (Battin, 2008).

Bad Medicine as Abuse: Opponents argue assisted death undercuts the *integrity of the medical profession* by violating a historic oath not to kill (Hippocratic Oath, Nightingale Pledge) and inappropriately use medicines (e.g., Battin, 2005, 2008; Pellegrino, 1992). In practice, the required safeguard of a second medical opinion is circumvented by "doctor shopping." Neither doctor need be qualified nor have training in palliative medicine, nor ability to recognize frequent comorbid depression—data show under-referrals (Battin, 2008; Dore, 2010, 2011). Because "self-administration" is limited to "ingesting," this can include "absorbing" (in nutritional bag) or implied administration by another (Tucker, 2008; Dore, 2010, 2011). Proponents counter that *Hippocrates historically resisted overtreatment*; and in an age of end stage dying, it is appropriate for patients themselves to decide (Seay, 2001). Choice demonstrably has improved public health with better end-of-life patient palliation.

Slippery Slope as Abuse from Inadequate Safeguards or Underground Practices: Opponents and proponents debate how assisted death does have or will have *different kinds of slippery slopes*—whether personal, domestic, institutional, or social—or must weigh underground practices (Battin, 2005, 2008; Mitchell, 2007; Dore, 2010, 2011). Some argue *usage is not from a vulnerable* population because most users are white, well-educated, and insured.

Vulnerable Groups and Abuse: *Opponents* argue two kinds of expansions will occur—more will become vulnerable and gradually dying will also include suffering (as in Netherlands, 2002). Those already demonstrated at risk (HIV/AIDS) will widen to others heretofore protected who demonstrably suffer in dying—such as children, developmentally disabled, mentally dysfunctional, uninsured, ethnic minorities (Byock, 1998; Foley & Hendin, 2002; Battin, 2008). *Defenders* counter that legitimate concerns about abuse have been empirically demonstrated to be nearly nonexistent in practice. Research suggests that persons with HIV/AIDS are at risk, but not others (Battin 2008).

Opponents charge that safeguards either are inadequate or principally protect the legal security of caregivers. *Defenders* rebut that safeguards are not failsafe but are meant to reduce risks. For example, Washington State safeguards restrict those eligible to adults (18 years of age and older), residents, and terminally ill who can voluntarily request assistance. Nothing guarantees—but *merely warrantees against* temporaries, incompetents, or incapacitated, nonterminal, or coerced referrals. That a patient must be informed of a palliative hospice option and have two waiting periods—15 days between oral and written requests and 48 hours between written request and prescription—*warrantees against* a "rushed" decision, but doesn't guarantee the quality of care received. Noncoercion or confidentiality is *warranteed* by witnesses who are not relatives, inheritors, or employed caregivers—as well as optional kinship disclosure. However, these safeguards cannot guarantee that end-of-life decisions will optimally involve concerned family members. The patient's option to rescind—and the fact that more than a third don't take medicine—*warrantees respect for a patient* to change her mind, but neglects social momentum in processes favoring expectations to self-terminate.

Ronald Lindsay, a lawyer and CEO of the Center for Inquiry, reviews the first decade of the Oregon Death with Dignity Act. He identifies data from Oregon's decade-long experience that refute predictions that the quality and availability of palliative care declined, and suggest risks of abuse are outweighed by benefits of legalization.

Senior Research Scholar, President Emeritus, and Cofounder of the Hastings Research Center, Daniel Callahan argues that advocates for physician-assisted suicide do two things. First, they *describe* what they are doing in unclear, evasive, or confusing terms ("obfuscate"). Second, they recommend or *prescribe* such practices as good in principles, regulatory policies, and law. Historically, Dutch reports in the 1980's—later confirmed in 1990, 1995, and 2005—contained undocumented euthanasia without informed consent of patients (nonvoluntary euthanasia), then reasoned that unreported euthanasia was based on appropriate caregiver paternalism (judging "quality of life") not abuse. American advocates shifted from "suicide" to "physician aid in dying" to please voters with term "death with dignity" that claims dignity depends upon control. As evident in the support for Washington state's measure by former Governor Booth who had Parkinson's, what began as a quest for control of pain, really medicalizes autonomy by controlling death events. State regulations in Washington and Oregon do not collect or disclose needed data from public scrutiny and debate.

YES

Ronald A. Lindsay

Oregon's Experience: Evaluating the Record

Since November 1997, Oregon has had in place a statute that authorizes physicians, under certain conditions, to provide terminally ill patients with a prescription for medication the patients can take to hasten their deaths. Prior to implementation of the Oregon Death with Dignity Act (ODWDA), opponents of assisted dying vigorously opposed the new law. In fact, implementation of the ODWDA—initially approved by voters in 1994—was delayed for 3 years by litigation that sought to prevent the law from going into effect, and opponents successfully campaigned to place a repeal measure on the ballot in 1997. Voters decisively rejected the proposed repeal (60% to 40%).

Those who opposed the ODWDA offered arguments similar to the arguments advanced by opponents of assisted dying elsewhere. These arguments included both ethical objections not amenable to factual refutation and predictions of various harmful consequences. For example, in addition to invoking the sanctity-of-life principle, opponents claimed that assisted dying could not be regulated properly and would result in a large number of patients being coerced or pressured into requesting assistance in dying. In their 1996 article, Callahan and White unqualifiedly proclaimed that "it is impossible in principle and in practice to regulate . . . [physician-assisted suicide] successfully" (2). Opponents also argued that following legalization the quality of palliative care would decline, that the "vulnerable"—variously defined as women, racial and ethnic minorities, the disabled, the poor, or some combination of these groups—would be adversely affected in disproportionate numbers by legalization, and that once assisted dying was legalized, inevitably we would begin our fall down the slippery slope to legalizing assisted suicide on demand or nonvoluntary euthanasia.

A decade after implementation of the ODWDA, the weight of the evidence suggests that these predictions of dire consequences were incorrect. The records compiled under the ODWDA, the investigations by researchers, and the diligent but largely fruitless efforts of opponents of legal assistance in dying to generate evidence of abuse have all failed to establish the existence of widespread abuses. Moreover, the overwhelming number of persons receiving assistance under the ODWDA are white, well-educated, and financially

From *The American Journal of Bioethics,* March 2009, pp. 19–26. Copyright © 2009 by Routledge/Taylor & Francis Group. Reprinted by permission via Rightslink.

secure, and their gender approximates that of the general population. With respect to palliative care, there is evidence that the quality of palliative care has actually improved in Oregon since adoption of the ODWDA. With respect to the dreaded slippery slope, there has been scant effort to expand the classes of persons eligible for assistance in dying or to loosen the regulations physicians and patients must follow in order for legal assistance to be provided. The wording of the ODWDA remains virtually unchanged. Moreover, there is not a scintilla of evidence to suggest the ODWDA has caused physicians, patients, or Oregonians in general to value life less.

Nonetheless, some who have evaluated Oregon's record maintain that it is too ambiguous to justify legalization of assistance in dying in other states, while others contend the evidence actually argues against legalization. Such conclusions confront us with an important methodological question: How are we to evaluate the evidence from Oregon? As argued below, the assessments of Oregon's experience by opponents of legalization are flawed, in part because they utilize improper criteria for evaluating Oregon's record.

The remainder of this article will first provide a brief argument about the benefits of legalization, and, in particular, will explain why the option of physician assistance in dying is so important for the terminally ill. Some may think this is well-trod territory, but the argument provided here draws attention to considerations that are sometimes overlooked. Moreover, we cannot properly evaluate the harms from legalization without weighing them against the benefits. The article will then expand on its analysis of Oregon's experience, discussing four major concerns that have been presented by opponents, namely the supposed negative effects on palliative care, the alleged disparate impact on the vulnerable, the initiation of the slide down the slippery slope, and the problem of abuse, understood to mean the problem of persons receiving assistance improperly (for example, because they were coerced or not competent to request assistance). The problem of abuse will receive more attention because it is the strongest argument against legalization. The article's last section will propose an appropriate framework for analyzing the record from Oregon.

Before proceeding to my argument, a brief word about terminology. This article uses the terms *assistance in dying* or *assisted dying* rather than *assisted suicide*. . . . The term *physician-assisted suicide* connotes an action in which the physician intentionally participates in bringing about the patient's death. Under the ODWDA, not only must the patient be terminally ill before requesting a prescription for a lethal dose of medication from his physician, but also the patient maintains control of the process throughout and decides when, if at all, the patient will ingest the medication. More than one-third of the patients who obtain a prescription under the ODWDA never take the drug; others ingest the drug months after it is prescribed. Under these circumstances, it seems more accurate to describe the practice as *physician-assisted dying* than *physician-assisted suicide*.

Let us now turn now to a summary of reasons why physician assistance in dying provides an important benefit to some patients.

The Importance of Physician Assistance in Dying for the Terminally Ill

It is sometimes forgotten in the debate over assistance in dying that the ODWDA and similar proposed statutes apply only to the terminally ill and require physician consultation. Both of these factors are critical in assessing both the morality of the practice and the wisdom of legalizing assistance in dying.

Respect for autonomy is one reason for supporting legalization of assistance in dying, but it is not a sufficient reason. To begin, no state currently prohibits anyone from ending his own life, so it is unclear why a general prohibition on assistance in dying constitutes a substantial infringement of autonomy. In the classic 1958 article against the legalization of assisted dying, Yale Kamisar made a similar point. . . .

Kamisar's contention has some merit if one focuses only on the physically robust. Indeed, offering assistance to those truly capable of doing "the job themselves" may improperly circumvent an important psychological barrier to hasty, ill-considered decisions—leaving aside any moral problems that may be raised by the offer of such assistance.

However, the issue being debated is *physician* assistance in dying for the *terminally ill*. Let us first consider the importance of terminal illness. Ending one's life without assistance is an option only for those with access to the proper means and the ability to use them. One crucial fact acknowledged only infrequently by the opponents of assistance in dying is that the State and its licensed agents control access to medications that are efficient in bringing about a peaceful death. Because the State maintains control of the dispensation of barbiturates and similar medications, a person must have access to firearms, knives, or other such means of death *and* possess the ability to use these means effectively to commit suicide without assistance. In the last stages of a terminal illness "the patient is likely to lack the capacity to commit suicide on his own." Many of the terminally ill are physically frail and have impaired mobility. One survey found that approximately 75% of those Oregonians who obtained assistance in dying were confined most of the time to a bed or chair. For someone in such a situation, being denied assistance effectively results in that person being kept alive against the person's will. The terminally ill have a much stronger liberty interest in assistance in dying because, unlike the physically healthy, they need assistance to die.

A person's terminal illness also provides some assurance that a request for assistance in dying is not the product of some hasty, irrational decision. A person who is dying is beyond the hope of any cure and is in an objectively verifiable condition. . . . These patients are not volatile individuals reacting to serious but passing problems, such as rejection by a lover or taunting from schoolmates. Instead, they face an inevitable death. The statistics collected in Oregon confirm that virtually all those who have sought assistance have been in the terminal stages of cancer, amyotrophic lateral sclerosis, AIDS, or some other terminal, distressing condition. Simply put, for those requesting assistance in dying, their choice is between dying peacefully now or dying within a short time after what they regard as pointless suffering.

Some may question my claim that the terminally ill cannot 'do the job themselves,' provided they act quickly. . . . However, if we want the terminally ill both to live as long as possible *and* to consult with their physicians about alternatives to a hastened death, then legalizing assistance in dying is the best way to accomplish these objectives . . . . Assuming we desire a regulatory scheme that encourages persons to live as long as they find their lives worthwhile, a policy of permitting physician assistance in dying for the terminally ill is much more likely to accomplish this objective than banning assistance in dying (Posner 1995, 247–248).

The claim that legalizing assistance in dying actually encourages many to live longer, and some to forego hastening their death altogether, is not mere speculation. Oregon's experience confirms this. Although approximately 15 in 100 dying Oregonians seriously consider hastening their deaths, and although many of these discuss this option with their physicians, only approximately 1 in 100 decide to request assistance, and only approximately 1 in 700 actually use prescribed medication to hasten their deaths, with rates of death under the ODWDA in recent years ranging from approximately 13 to 15 per 10,000 deaths. Significantly, research surveys suggest that the rate of legal physician-assisted dying in Oregon may be significantly less that the rate of *illegal* physician-assisted dying in other states, and there is evidence that illegal assistance in Oregon is extremely rare. Knowledge that escape from intolerable suffering is always available can diminish the felt need to hasten one's death, and allowing physicians to discuss all options with their patients promotes a thorough consideration of all these options, including alternatives to hastened death such as hospice care. . . .

Let us now consider the significance of the physician's role, and why it is important not just to allow assistance in dying, but to authorize *physician* assistance in dying. The role of a treating physician is crucial in the context of end-of-life care. Legalizing physician assistance in dying allows the terminally ill to discuss all aspects of their condition and treatment, including their anxieties and fears, with a knowledgeable and—one would hope—caring expert. Legalization encourages a frank exploration of options, permitting a patient to make an informed decision. Sensitive physicians will use the full extent of their training and experience in assessing the patient's condition and the prospects for effective alternatives to hastening death, such as palliative care. The physician's expertise is important in evaluating, in consultation with the patient, which alternatives might be feasible. Similarly, the physician's expertise is important for determining whether the patient is competent to make a decision concerning the course of treatment. Surveys indicate that Oregon physicians take seriously their responsibility of screening patients for signs of depression or impaired judgment. Forbidding physicians to discuss the option of a hastened death will not stop some patients from hastening their deaths; it will prevent them from receiving appropriate professional care.

In sum, legalizing physician assistance in dying shows both compassion and respect for the desire of the terminally ill to make critical decisions about the course of their own lives, whereas denying them the possibility of this assistance compels them to live in suffering. Moreover, legalizing this option brings added benefits, including increasing the likelihood that patients' decisions about end-of-life options will be informed and deliberate as opposed to uninformed and precipitous.

Of course, individual rights always must be balanced against the common good. It is both legally advisable and morally permissible, if not obligatory, to restrict the actions of some individuals if these actions pose a significant threat of harm to others. . . . It is time now to consider in more detail the experience under Oregon's statute to determine whether Oregon's record confirms or refutes the claims that legal assistance in dying inevitably results in serious harmful consequences.

The Experience in Oregon: A Beneficial Impact on Palliative Care

Directly contrary to the predictions of opponents of legal assistance in dying, who argued that post-legalization physicians and other healthcare workers would expend little effort to alleviate the symptoms of the terminally ill—because these patients could just 'go ahead' and die—there has been no evidence to indicate the quality of palliative care in Oregon has diminished. To the contrary, there is evidence that the quality of palliative care has actually improved in Oregon since implementation of the ODWDA. Many physicians have made a conscious effort to improve their knowledge of palliative care so they can offer appropriate treatment options to their patients. The reality is that in a state where assistance in dying is legal, physicians and other healthcare workers are motivated to spend more time with patients in discussions about end-of-life choices, carefully exploring options and arranging for palliative care as an alternative to hastening death. Few treating physicians want their patients to choose hastened death as the first option.

Opponents of legal assistance in dying often try to frame the debate as a choice between effective palliative care and assistance in dying. This is misleading to say the least. No responsible advocate of assistance in dying has ever suggested we should de-emphasize palliative care. Furthermore, the evidence indicates that inadequate palliative care is not a significant motivation for requesting assistance in dying. It is striking that more than 85% of the patients who have availed themselves of assistance in dying under the ODWDA were enrolled in hospice, usually considered the gold standard for palliative care. Patients are electing to hasten their deaths not because they are receiving inadequate care, but because the care they receive cannot remedy their anxiety, frustration, hopelessness, and anguish.

The Experience in Oregon: No Disparate Impact on the Vulnerable

The argument that we should not legalize assistance in dying because of the disproportionately adverse, or "disparate," impact the practice allegedly will have on various vulnerable groups has a very questionable moral premise—one that remains largely unexamined despite the frequency with which this argument is advanced. To consider this an important argument against legalization one must believe that it somehow makes a difference whether proportionally more Blacks than Whites, more women than men, more poor than wealthy, for example, are pressured into choosing assistance in dying. When one thinks about this proposition, one should be able to see that it is not morally sound. What matters is whether someone has been coerced or pressured into requesting assistance in dying, *not* the race, sex, ethnicity, etc. of that person. Coercing a rich White male into requesting assistance in dying is just as morally repugnant as coercing a poor African American woman into making such a request.

In any event, we do not have to debate at any length the normative portion of the disparate impact argument because Oregon demonstrates it lacks empirical support. The persons who have received assistance in Oregon are overwhelmingly White (in fact, not one African American has received assistance); most are financially secure; most are men; and they are better educated than the population as a whole. Even those who are doubtful about legalization have acknowledged that fears about abuse of the vulnerable have not materialized. In fact, if there is any disparate impact, the impact may be felt by those patients who want assistance but who lack the education and confidence to assert their rights forcefully enough to obtain assistance. That is regrettable, but it may be the unavoidable price of having adequate procedural safeguards in place.

The Experience in Oregon: No Slippery Slope

Many predicted that once the practice of physician assistance in dying was legalized, neither Oregon nor any other state would be able to contain the practice of hastening death to competent, terminally ill patients. Instead, the practice inevitably would be broadened to include anyone who wants to die for any reason, or perhaps Oregon would legalize nonvoluntary euthanasia—the mercy killing of someone not presently capable of making her desires known—or even involuntary euthanasia.

It is beyond dispute that the tumble down the slippery slope has not occurred in Oregon. The same classes of patients are eligible for assistance in dying that were eligible in 1997. The law has not been broadened, nor has there been any serious effort to do so.

Of course, the slippery slope argument is itself very slippery. Its advocate can always resort to the excuse that although the predicted fall into the abyss has not happened yet, it is just a matter of time. But no one has offered a persuasive argument why expansion of the practice to morally dubious cases is inevitable.

Some have tried. Consider this statement from the oft-cited report of the New York State Task Force on Life and the Law:

> A policy of allowing assisted suicide or euthanasia only when a patient voluntarily requests an assisted death, and a physician also judges that assisted suicide or euthanasia are appropriate to relieve suffering, is inherently unstable. The reasons for allowing these practices when

supported by *both* a patient's request and a physician's judgment would lead to allowing the practices when *either* condition is met. . . .

This reasoning is not sound. If legislation stipulates that two conditions are necessary for a certain action, why is the conjunction of these two conditions "inherently unstable"? . . . [T]here is no compelling reason to abandon either the ODWDA's requirement that the patient's request be voluntary or the ODWDA's requirement that a physician certify the patient as competent and terminally ill.

The argument of the New York State Task Force used a version of the slippery slope argument often called the *conceptual slope;* in other words, legalization for terminally ill patients will serve as precedent for offering legal assistance to other categories of individuals. There is also the *causal slope* version, which maintains that legalizing assistance in dying will bring about a material change in our attitudes, in particular by corroding our respect for life. One of the unnoticed flaws of the causal slippery slope argument is the implicit assumption that allowing assistance in dying necessarily shows less respect for life. But what is the justification for assuming that the operative attitude of those who favor assistance in dying for the terminally ill is a diminished respect for life? No empirical study suggests that those who favor assistance in dying have less respect for life. At least arguably, the primary operative attitudes are respect for self-determination, compassion for the plight of someone who is suffering, and a desire by (some) physicians to provide appropriate end-of-life care. Respecting the right of a terminally ill person to make his own decision about the course of his remaining days hardly seems to evince an attitude of diminished respect for life. Thus, a key element of the causal slippery slope argument is missing. The projected progressive erosion of respect for life can hardly take place if it has not even started. Certainly, there is nothing to suggest that Oregonians have a diminished respect for life.

The Experience in Oregon: Effective Prevention of Abuse

We have disposed of three of the consequentialist arguments against legalization. . . . The next argument has more weight. This is the argument that persons will obtain prescriptions even though they should not be receiving assistance, because they are not competent, they are being coerced or manipulated, etc.

In examining the evidence from Oregon, we should first remind ourselves of the procedural requirements that must be satisfied before patients receive assistance. To be eligible for assistance, patients must have received a diagnosis from their attending physician that they have a terminal illness that will cause their death within 6 months and they must be capable of making their own healthcare decisions. A second physician must confirm both the diagnosis of a terminal illness and the patient's competence. As a prerequisite to receiving assistance, patients must make a series of voluntary, verifiable requests that confirm the desire for assistance is durable: The patient must make two oral requests for assistance, separated by at least fifteen days, and one written request, signed in the presence of two witnesses. To help ensure the patient's decision is an informed one, treating physicians are required to inform the patient of alternatives to a hastened death, such as comfort care, hospice care, and enhanced pain control. Moreover, a patient must be referred to counseling if either the prescribing or the consulting physician believes she might be suffering from a psychological disorder that can cause impaired judgment. Provided these safeguards are followed conscientiously, the possibility that an incompetent or coerced individual will receive assistance is small.

The procedural hurdles a patient must surmount prior to receiving assistance are not the only safeguards. The eligible patient maintains control of the process throughout. The patient may rescind her request, decline to fill the prescription she receives from her physician, and decide not to take the medication once she fills the prescription. As already indicated, many who receive a prescription never take the medication. As an additional safeguard, the patient must ingest the prescribed drug; the physician may not administer it.

The procedural requirements and safeguards of the ODWDA cannot, of course, guarantee that all requests for assistance are truly voluntary and informed. Nonetheless, it is striking that despite the microscope under which the Oregon practice has been examined, there is not one undisputed example of a coerced request for assistance or similar serious abuses. . . .

In addition to complying with the foregoing procedural requirements, physicians must maintain records of the process leading to the prescription and these records are shared with the Oregon Department of Human Services. These records provide the basis for an annual, public report. . . . The mandated records have been supplemented by interviews and empirical research. . . .

These records and research results are important for assessing some aspects of the abuse argument. Prior to legalization, opponents of legal assistance in dying predicted physicians would place thousands of patients on a fast track to death, with the implication that many patients would be receiving assistance improperly. However, from the inception of the ODWDA through 2007, only approximately 570 patients received a prescription for medication that would assist them to die and—strikingly—only approximately 340 patients actually ingested the lethal dose of medication that was prescribed for them. Oregon has not become a suicide mill.

In addition, there is no substantial evidence that someone who was incompetent or not in a terminal condition received assistance (although a few patients have lived significantly longer than 6 months following their diagnosis). No physician or relative of the patient has been charged with improperly providing assistance or coercing the patient into hastening his death. With respect to data that might indirectly reflect pressure to request assistance, the state's reports reveal that only three of the patients who have ingested the prescribed medication, or less than 1%, were uninsured and only nine, or approximately 3%, mentioned financial concerns as a motivation for seeking assistance in dying. (From the reports, it is not clear what these concerns might be; it may simply be that some patients believe any further treatment would be a waste of money, even when insurance covers most of the costs.)

Critics of the ODWDA have focused on a couple of cases that supposedly illustrate how easily the ODWDA's safeguards can be circumvented, namely the notorious cases of "Helen" (not her real name) and Kate Cheney. . . . An objective appraisal of these cases indicates that they do not provide convincing evidence of abuse. This article will not discuss all the details of these cases because the reader can readily access other works that provide this information. But suffice it to say that the case of Helen is often cited as an example of 'doctor-shopping' and hurried decision-making among other problems. However, although Helen did switch physicians at least in part to find a physician who would be willing to help her hasten her death, the physician who refused to help her had not known her for very long; he was treating her only because her previous primary physician had recently left the practice. As to the alleged rush to die (Helen was still mobile), the timelines set forth in the ODWDA were followed and there is nothing to indicate Helen was not terminal or that her decisions to request and to ingest the medication were not voluntary. . . .

With respect to Cheney, some claim that her relatives, in particular, her daughter, were eager to see her die and that Cheney may have been unduly influenced by her daughter. Again, a closer look at the facts reveals these concerns are based on suppositions and a tendentious interpretation of events. . . .

As to the alleged "eagerness" of Cheney's daughter to see her die, this is a claim that lacks any support apart from the perceptions of those making this claim. . . . Foley and Hendin also make the interesting assertion that: "Sending Kate to the nursing home was sending her a message that she was a burden." The millions of families who send their beloved relatives to nursing homes so they can receive better care might take issue with that assertion. The cases of Helen and Ms. Cheney are more revealing of the fierceness of the opposition to legalization of assistance in dying than they are of flaws in the regulatory framework.

In sum, what evidence there is does not indicate that abuse is common. Arguably, the evidence suggests there has not been any case of abuse, but no definitive conclusion about the complete absence of abuse can be drawn. First, there may be abuses of which we are not aware. Second, as the cases of Helen and Ms. Cheney indicate, the inferences to be made from some cases are disputed. In light of the residual uncertainty about the existence of abuses, we need to consider how the evidence from Oregon should be evaluated.

Weighing the Evidence

Three of the four anti-legalization arguments based on harmful consequences can be refuted with confidence based on the data from Oregon. The "disparate impact on the vulnerable" argument is an argument based on numbers, so numbers suffice to refute it. It's undeniable that the ODWDA has not been broadened, so the slippery slope argument also has been refuted. Refutation of the palliative care argument is not quite as straightforward, but there is no evidence that the quality or availability of palliative care has declined, some evidence that its availability and quality have improved, and substantial evidence that most patients are not motivated to request assistance because of inadequate palliative care.

This leaves the abuse argument. As indicated, there remains some uncertainty about the level of abuse, but that does not imply we cannot make reasonable conclusions based on the available evidence. Opponents commonly make four mistakes in evaluating the evidence.

Improper Reliance on Individual Cases

It is commonplace in the debates over assistance in dying for opponents to claim that no matter how compelling an individual's suffering may be, that does not imply we should legalize assistance in dying; we need to consider the effects of legalization on the public as a whole. This is a valid point. . . . Even assuming the safeguards of the ODWDA were circumvented in the cases of Helen and Kate Cheney, this does not indicate that the safeguards have been circumvented in a large number of cases, much less that the ODWDA should be repealed and legalization resisted in other states. If we required perfection in any regulatory scheme that exposed persons to a risk of serious harm, we would not allow trucks on the road, meat in the stores, imported toys, or trial by jury.

Improper Skepticism About the Data and the Statute's Safeguards

Some opponents argue that scattered information about individual cases is all that can be used in evaluating the ODWDA because there is no reliable summary information. Furthermore, there is no reliable mechanism in place to report or control abuses because the Oregon Department of Human Services has no investigatory authority, there is no express requirement in the ODWDA to report abuses, and no identifying information is made public.

First, it is worth noting that opponents sometimes forget that the information complied under the ODWDA has been supplemented by a number of empirical studies and surveys across several disciplines, including medicine, nursing, and social work. Obviously . . . they can provide us with sufficient information to draw some reasonable conclusions, including the conclusion that most physicians are conscientious in screening patients and the rate of legal assistance in dying in Oregon is remarkably low. If Oregon has created a culture of death and the safeguards of the ODWDA can be easily circumvented, this last statistic is inexplicable. If a physician can achieve immunity by marching a patient through steps that opponents maintain do little to control a physician's conduct, then the physician will utilize the ODWDA's procedures rather than risk prosecution. Frequent abuses would produce a much higher rate of assisted dying.

With respect to the alleged deficiencies in the statute regarding reporting of abuses, these criticisms ignore both the relevant social and legal background. That there is no express statutory requirement to report abuses does not in any way suggest that Oregonians should not report abuses to the proper authorities. Assisting a suicide remains a crime in Oregon; specifi-cally, it is categorized as second degree manslaughter (Oregon Rev. Stat., sec. 163.125). A physician who assists a patient to die can avoid criminal liability and administrative discipline if and only if she complies fully with the pro-cedural requirements of the ODWDA. There is no need for a separate report-ing requirement of abuses under the ODWDA, nor is there a need to invest the Department of Human Services with investigatory authority because Oregon's criminal justice system and professional discipline system remain in place. Those concerned about abuses can report to the police, the local prosecutor, or the Oregon Board of Medical Examiners (BME) any physician who coerces a patient, who provides assistance to an incompetent, who does not engage a second, consulting physician, etc. The BME maintains a website that permits concerned persons to submit complaints about physicians elec-tronically. Given the diligent monitoring of practice under the ODWDA by opponents, it strains credulity to claim that abuses have not been reported or investigated simply because the ODWDA relies on existing state agencies to do their job. . . .

Finally, the operating assumption of opponents appears to be that because the safeguards of the ODWDA *could* be circumvented by the unscru-pulous or uncaring, this means they inevitably *will* be circumvented in a sub-stantial number of cases. Typically, this is not the assumption on which we base our regulation of the work of healthcare professionals. To the contrary, we assume most will adhere to established standards of conduct with little direct oversight. The supposition that many Oregon physicians will be less than conscientious in the context of assistance in dying lacks any support beyond rhetoric.

Failure to Consider the Benefits of Legalization

Weighing the advantages and disadvantages of a proposed course of action requires one to take account of the advantages. . . . [T]he availability of assis-tance in dying is important for a substantial portion of the terminally ill, whether or not they actually decide to hasten their deaths.

Granted, there is no universally accepted metric for measuring and bal-ancing the benefits to be gained from legalization against the risks to some resulting from possible abuses. . . . [B]ecause we do not know exactly where to draw a line does not mean that there are no situations that clearly fall on one side of the line or the other. How many cases of coerced or nonvoluntary requests should result in reconsideration of the wisdom of legalization? A few cases of abuse should not require us to block or repeal legislation that provides a substantial benefit. In another regard, scores of coerced or nonvoluntary requests each year should produce doubts about whether assistance in dying can be appropriately regulated.

Fortunately, the record in Oregon is clear enough that we do not have to engage in a difficult balancing between the harms caused by abuses and the benefits provided to patients by the ODWDA. One cannot state with cer-tainty that there have been no abuses under the ODWDA. But one can state with some assurance that the ODWDA's safeguards have prevented the level of abuses that opponents predicted and that would counsel against legalization.

Failure to Utilize an Appropriate Baseline for Evaluating the Risks of Abuse

I have already alluded . . . to our practice of allowing patients to forego life-preserving treatment. It is useful to compare this practice to legal assistance in dying and the alleged harms that result from legalization. In particular, in thinking about the tolerable level of abuses from legal assistance in dying, it is helpful to bear in mind the fact that competent patients have virtually an absolute right to refuse treatment, even when this refusal will hasten their deaths. Moreover, compared to the regulation of requests for assistance in dying under the ODWDA, there is negligible regulation of the withdrawal or withholding of life-sustaining treatment for competent patients. No law requires the patient refusing treatment to make a series of oral and written requests over a set period of time. No one is required to probe the patient's reasoning or to suggest alternatives to having the treatment stopped. And, typically, no investigation is carried out to determine whether the patient is being improperly influenced by relatives who are concerned about long-term care obligations or financial burdens. Because there is little oversight over this process, we can only guess at the number of deaths that have been improperly hastened, yet we have determined that the freedom to decide on a course of treatment is important enough that patients should be allowed this choice even though the availability of this option probably results in some abuses, with fatal consequences.

Some may argue that the practices of assistance in dying and foregoing life-sustaining treatment are morally distinguishable, but if they are, they are distinguishable for reasons unrelated to the risks of harm attendant on the practice. One cannot consistently argue that assistance in dying is too risky, but concede that allowing patients to forego life-preserving treatment is not. This is especially true given that we have at least some reliable data indicating abuses are infrequent under the ODWDA, but nothing comparable with respect to the nationwide practice of allowing patients to forego life-sustaining treatment. Opponents of legalizing assistance in dying often seem to suggest that the risks of harm from legalization are unique. They are not. We already allow patients to incur the risks of a coerced or nonvoluntary death so some might have the freedom to avoid the suffering associated with a prolonged death. Any appropriate analysis of the risks of legalized assistance in dying must take into consideration analogous practices we deem acceptable.

Conclusion

There are, of course, reasons for opposing legalization of assistance in dying other than the supposed harmful consequences of legalization. But to the extent public policy on this issue is supposed to be informed by evidence regarding these alleged harmful consequences, the Oregon experience argues for legalization of assisted dying in other states, provided these states follow a regulatory scheme similar to Oregon's. . . .

Admittedly, the fact that the ODWDA has been in effect for ten years without causing the dreadful consequences opponents predicted does not guarantee that other states will have similar experiences. However, Oregon's record is more relevant for determining public policy on this issue than the armchair speculation of philosophers. The Supreme Court in *Washington v. Glucksberg* urged that the debate over assistance in dying be conducted and resolved in the "laboratory of the states." Oregon's experiment has provided us with results that, while not definitive or free of all ambiguity, are sufficiently clear to provide guidance. It is time to apply these results to other states.

Daniel Callahan  **NO**

Organized Obfuscation: Advocacy for Physician-Assisted Suicide

An ancient but evergreen practice with controversial political and ethical issues is to manipulate ideas and language, spinning them to serve one's ends. My example will be the current physician-assisted suicide debate, now being played out with a ballot initiative in the state of Washington. The advocates for physician-assisted suicide make use of a favorite method from the spin tool box, that of obfuscation, defined in dictionaries as an effort to render something unclear, evasive, or confusing. I believe that in recent years, many (though hardly all) advocates of euthanasia and physician-assisted suicide have used organized obfuscation as a political tactic, and Washington is no exception.

The seeds of this interpretation were planted in my mind in the late 1980s. In the January–February 1989 issue of the *Hastings Center Report,* we published an article by a Dutch cardiologist, Richard Fenigsen, titled "A Case against Dutch Euthanasia."[1] We did so with considerable trepidation. The article seemed extreme in its accusations, the only available footnotes were in Dutch, and we had no good way of independently verifying his critique. In brief, he charged that there were far more instances of euthanasia than reported, that regulations promulgated by Dutch courts to control the practice were widely ignored, and that euthanasia without informed consent of patients (called "nonvoluntary euthanasia") was common. We decided to take a chance and published the article.

We were almost instantly assaulted with a remarkable (and obviously orchestrated) deluge of complaints from Dutch health authorities and organizations, as well as euthanasia advocacy groups. They included, among others, the Dutch Society of Health Law, twenty-five prominent medical and health care figures who joined to send us a letter, and the Dutch Society for Voluntary Euthanasia.[2] Their message was uniform and unsparing: we should not have published such an irresponsible article, filled with unverifiable charges and baseless accusations and displaying a gross misunderstanding of the practice of euthanasia in the Netherlands. (We Americans just didn't get it!)

A few lines from those letters became memorable. One of them was that the Dutch meaning of euthanasia was that of "a deliberate life-ending action

From *Hastings Center Report,* vol. 38, no. 5, 2008, pp. 30–32. Copyright © 2008 by The Hastings Center. Reprinted by permission of Wiley-Blackwell.

. . . [as the result of] an enduring [patient] request. 'Euthanasia,' therefore, is by necessity, *voluntary.*"[3] Another letter asserted that "it is impossible for people who do not want euthanasia to be forced or maneuvered into it because that would violate the definition of euthanasia."[4] The notion that one could not be forced into something because it would violate a definition is surely imaginative (and philosophers of language should take note). The letters evaded the question of whether nonvoluntary euthanasia (now turned into an oxymoron) actually took place.

As it turned out, however, Fenigsen was shortly proved strikingly right, even if not in all details. In a series of confidential interviews with physicians and an examination of death certificates, three surveys in 1990, 1995, and 2001 found that approximately two percent of all Dutch deaths (3,500 or so) came from euthanasia and physician-assisted suicide, about 1,000 of which were without the patient's explicit request.[5] Fewer than 45 percent were reported, as required by law.

But the apologists were not giving up on spin. Yes, those figures are probably correct, they seemed to say, but they did not mean what they seemed (to outsiders) to mean. Foreigners just don't understand that the Dutch doctor–patient relationship is far more intimate than in other countries. Their doctors know what their patients would want even if they have never said anything; and, besides, it is a physician's ethical duty to judge the patient's quality of life and to act accordingly, even without consent. In sum, to call the survey results evidence of "abuse" was to misunderstand the special and compassionate culture of Dutch medicine.

If the Dutch advocates cut the template for organized obscurantism, many American euthanasia/physician-assisted suicide advocates were quick to make use of it. Consider the phrase "death with dignity," the title of the Oregon physician-assisted suicide legislation in 1997, and now the title of the proposed Washington state legislation, which closely follows the Oregon model. The implication of the phrase is that physician-assisted suicide is the only route to a death with dignity. Since just about everyone of any advanced age knows of friends and family members who died peaceful, dignified deaths—and good hospice care can provide just that ending to life—the use of the phrase to legitimate physician-assisted suicide is a flagrant cooptation of wording widely used to describe a peaceful death. Why does suicide endow a death with dignity? Does dignity depend upon control?

If the use of "death with dignity" is entirely misleading, it is noteworthy that many supporters of the Washington ballot initiative couple that move with a deliberate attempt to avoid calling the proposed legislation "physician-assisted suicide." They have apparently concluded that the word "suicide" is what one newspaper reporter called "a killer at the ballot box."[6] Some more acceptable phrases are "medically assisted death," "hastened death," and "patient-directed aid-in-dying." Most amusing (in the black humor department) is the fact that, after the failure of an outright euthanasia 1988 ballot initiative in California, Oregon advocates decided that physician-assisted suicide was a better bet, and so it turned out to be. Now even that concept is being jettisoned, no doubt too clear and accurate for political use.

A notable feature of the Washington initiative is the role of a former governor, Booth Gardner, a voluble and tireless advocate of the proposed legislation.[7] A victim of Parkinson disease, he has attracted special attention because of a son who opposes the legislation. But there are some other features of Gardner's advocacy that merit attention. One of them is that he knows his medical condition would not qualify for physician-assisted suicide (because it is not terminal). His declared long-term aim is a law that would only require "unbearable suffering," whether from a terminal disease or not. The history of euthanasia in the Netherlands has over the years moved exactly in that direction.

The other feature of his stance is that it is "My life, my death, my control," which he calls "my impeccable logic."[8] The proposed Washington legislation requires no claim of pain or other forms of distress, only that a person "be suffering from a terminal disease." An important outcome of the Oregon law over the years is that a "loss of autonomy" has been a leading reason (around 85 percent) given by those requesting physician-assisted suicide. Gardner's assertion of "control" perfectly fits that pattern. While I can offer no evidence, my guess is that the public thinks the aim of the legislation is relief of pain, not the pursuit of a final control of one's life.

The latter I take to be a lifestyle choice—a medicalization of autonomy having little to do with the historical goals of medicine or the professional ethic of physicians. Hippocrates understood that some 2,500 years ago. Moreover, since suicide is not illegal and Gardner is perfectly capable of taking his own life (as are many if not most of those who have made use of physician-assisted suicide in Oregon), the real aim seems to be to confer medical legitimation on a particular and hardly universal way of ending one's life. Does the public in Washington understand that, and would they in any case care if they did?

The final form of obfuscation I would single out has been in the proposed regulation of physician-assisted suicide. When Oregon initiated its law, it was widely presented as a potential model for other states, an instance of the "laboratory of the states" as a testing ground for innovative policies. But it is a laboratory lacking all transparency and accountability, with no information other than of a statistical kind made available to the public. The proposed Washington law is no less blunt in its denial of public information: "the department of health shall adopt rules to facilitate the collection of information. . . . Except as otherwise required by law, the information . . . may not be made available for inspection by the public."[9]

In the case of Oregon, we have been assured that all is well, that no abuses are occurring. In their confidence and firmness, those assurances are the equal of those expressed in the Netherlands prior to its confidential surveys. But Oregon has never sponsored a confidential survey, and probably never will. If you know, just *know*, there are no abuses, why bother? The flavor of the proposed law in Washington does not suggest a survey will ever be carried out there either.

Regulations of that kind, protected from public scrutiny, but with the ring of authority and oversight, are a Potemkin-village form of regulatory obfuscation. They look good, sound good, feel good, but have nothing behind them. But they are as good a token as any of the story of euthanasia and physician-assisted suicide from the Netherlands forward. I do not count my skepticism as a direct ethical argument against them, which I have made elsewhere, but only as an example of the way single-minded advocates can foul the waters of public debate. Stirring up some verbal muck can work wonders for a bad cause.

References

1. R. Fenigsen, "A Case Against Dutch Euthanasia," *Hastings Center Report* Special Supplement 19, no. 1 (1989): 22–30.

2. "Mercy, Murder, and Morality" (letters), *Hastings Center Report* 19, no. 6 (1989): 47–52.

3. Ibid., 47.

4. Ibid., 48.

5. P.J. Maas et al., "Euthanasia, Physician-Assisted Suicide, and Other Medical Practices Involving the End of Life in the Netherlands," *New England Journal of Medicine* 335 (1996): 1699; N. Gorsuch, *The Future of Assisted Suicide and Euthanasia* (Princeton, N.J.: Princeton University Press, 2006), 102–41.

6. C. Ostrom, "Just Don't Call It Suicide, Initiative Backers Say," *Seattle Times,* January 10, 2008.

7. D. Borgner, "Death in the Family," *New York Times Magazine,* December 2, 2007.

8. Ibid.

9. "The Washington Death with Dignity Act," Section 15 (2).

EXPLORING THE ISSUE

Can Legal Suicide Really Safeguard Against Abuse?

Critical Thinking and Reflection

1. Which abuse most concerns you and why—an individual case, cases, patterns, trends? Should abuse be subject to ethics, regulations, criminal, or civil law? Which safeguard is best/worst in response to this abuse? Why?

2. *Consider* the situation of a mother living in Montana in her final months with "terminal cancer." Oncologists focused on treatment not palliation; hence, her pain management has been poor. Because she was caregiver to her mother who suffered terribly from cancer, she seeks a referral to self-terminate; estranged children won't help. You disagree with PAD, but as her social worker, she asks you to be one of her witnesses. What do you discuss with her about her choices, hopes, and fears?

3. *Discuss:* Is self-termination for ALS patients who may not be able to ingest "regularized" by permitting assistance; does this frustrate good palliation? Is the Oregon Public Health Department the best organization for taxpayers to reasonably expect to defend the law, monitor compliance, collect and share data, and protect the welfare of a vulnerable patient (Hendin & Foley, 2008, Lindsay, 2009)?

4. *Discuss:* Increasing numbers of patients request, receive, and don't use lethal medications. Should a person who has gone through the process and legally received medications to self-terminate—but refuses to take them—be regarded as unstable or intransigent by caregivers? Should she continue to receive more than comfort care—that is publically supported?

5. *Discuss:* You are a nurse in a Washington State Hospital rotation. You discover better reporting of self-termination is possible: reliable data about nonvoluntary coercion can help establish a baseline for what counts as abuse. Widened data collection could come by nondisclosure of physicians from whom requested self-killing is sought (e.g., as in Netherlands). But one advisor cautions: "No! Don't document answers that risk unwanted legal scrutiny of medical records." What information would you like to know from someone who wishes to die—that is now lacking?

Is There Common Ground?

My Life, My Death, My Choice

Final Exit

It's the ultimate form of discrimination to offer people with disabilities help to die without having offered real options to live.

Diane Coleman, *Not Dead Yet*

A *personal decision* is part of a *public policy* about lethal self-termination—both involve ethics (what justifies), administration (procedures of what, how, when, and where), and private and civic practices (legislative, executive, judicial). Few seriously *defend* abuses—but meanings, extents, and remedies for disputed practices remain contested. Although most states have *decriminalized suicide* due to changed views of social shame and presumptions of personal affliction—many wrestle with notions of "sound mind" for insurance claims (Simon, Levenson, & Shuman, 2005). Prior criminal penalties have been abolished which included forfeiting property. Suicide has not been completely *legalized*—which is to remove all or most legal obstacles–prohibitions. In Europe, public debates concern *decriminalization* (Netherlands, Belgium, Germany) and *legalization of assistance* in suicide (Switzerland). *Physician performed voluntary euthanasia* is not legal in the United States, but under certain circumstances, it is not prosecuted in the Netherlands or Belgium. Likewise, under certain conditions, *non-physician assisted suicide* is not prosecuted in Switzerland or Germany.

In the United States, a *right to refuse life-sustaining treatment* is well-established—debates have shifted from *legalization* to *regulation* of safeguarded lethal self-administration (Tucker, 2008). *Legalization* became *regulation* as social advocacy movements re-invented their self-identity from negative "Euthanasia" titles; some mobilized public opinion and coordinated 75 percent of Oregon's individual cases as "Compassion in Choices" but are opposed by "True Compassion Advocates" (Dowbiggin, 2005; Hendin & Foley, 2008).

Do substantive and procedural safeguards help public health legitimately restrict self-killing (Langford, 2008)? In 2008, some 36,000 persons committed suicide nationwide; one out of six were over 65, 80 percent were white men, although only one of eight are in the general population; most were by firearms; most suffered from a diagnosable depressive condition. When older adults attempt suicide they normally succeed; one out of four in contrast to one out of every 100–200 attempts by younger adults. Many elderly are off the radar screen of media and society (Conwell & Duberstein, 2001; Harwood, Hawton, Hope, Harriss, & Jacoby, 2006).

Defenders rebut that those who use DWDA are *not* impulsive, pathological suicides but typically acts of terminally ill involving family support and control (Lieberman, 2006; Tucker, 2008). Who choose DWDA? Some argue data show usage is not from a vulnerable population because most are white, well-educated, and insured. More than 80 percent have some kind of cancer with typically intact cognitive awareness. "People who died with a physician's assistance were more likely to be members of groups enjoying comparative social, economic, educational, professional, and other privileges. . . . Ninety-four percent died at home, with the median time between medication and unconsciousness being 5 minutes, and between ingestion and death being 25 minutes, with no complications in 95 percent of cases . . ." (Battin, 2008). The most important reasons for requesting PAD were "wanting to control the circumstances of death and die at home; loss of independence; and concerns about future pain, poor quality of life, and inability to care for one's self" (Ganzini, Goy, & Dobscha, 2009). Negatively, those who choose DWDA have cited loss of autonomy (89.9) and loss of dignity (83.8) and an ability to engage in enjoyable activities and loss of body functions (87.4) and being a burden (38.3).

Critics charge that safeguards are chiefly concerned to protect insurance claims and give immunity from criminal and civil liability to health care professionals for a patient's suicide. "Actions taken in accordance with this chapter do not, for any purpose, constitute suicide, assisted suicide, mercy killing, or homicide, under the law" (Washington State Death with Dignity Act). This leaves open for discussion how well and by what means safeguards enable palliation and counseling for dying—or uphold interests of stakeholders such as family or others (inheritors or creditors). For some, reporting constraints and the shift from informed consent to decisionally capable have not clarified concerns about financial abuse that convert patients in control to citizens as burdens (Dore, 2010, 2011).

Defenders counter that experience shows why legalizing PAD reduces abuse for four demonstrable reasons; the number of individuals has remained small; concerns that this would displace palliative care are not true (it arguably increases it); the scope has remained limited to terminal patients with physician cooperation (Lewey, 2010). "Patients are able to remain rational longer when they do not fear losing control over the timing and manner of their death (recall that more patients request and receive lethal barbiturates than actually use them); because the stricter oversight reduces the potential for abuses, and because doctors respond to requests for PAS by improving end of life care" (Dahl & Levy, 2006). About such important, autonomous decisions as death events, some argue that outsiders must demonstrate great respect and forbearance (Preston in Baxter Amicus).

Debates over 10 years of data remain contested. *Defenders* cite the *small absolute number* of deaths and that nearly a third of requests remain unused as evidence for the good use by dying persons of *legal decisional capacity* (Quill & Greenlaw, 2008; Tucker, 2008; Battin, 2008). Even infrequent and atypical cases of abuse in regulatory schemes lack a baseline to adequately compare them to risks from withholding or withdrawing life preserving treatment (Lindsay, 2009). *Critics* charge that cases of abuse reflect *increasing trendlines* of requests and misuse among small numbers of health care professionals who have shifted from being consultants to facilitators (Hendin, 1999). These professionals have abandoned a (pathologizing) *medical model wherein suicide requests involve treatable depression*. These cases demonstrate both minimal standards (screening "decisionally incapacitated") resulting in psychiatric under-referrals and inadequate end-of-life palliation (Foley & Hendin 2002, 2008).

Additional References

Ackerman, F. (2000). For now I have my death: The duty to die vs. the duty to help the ill stay alive. *Midwest Studies in Philosophy, 24*.

American Association of Suicidology. (2009). *2006 official final data: Rates, numbers, and rankings of each state. Statistics.* Retrieved May 14, 2009, from www.suicidology.org/web/guest/stats-and-tools/statistics

American Foundation for Suicide Prevention. Retrieved from www.afsp.org/index .cfm?fuseaction=home.viewPage&page_id=1

Ball, S. C. (2006). Nurse–patient advocacy and the right to die. *Journal of Psychosocial Nursing, 44*(12), 36–46.

Battin, M. (2000). Global life expectancies and the duty to dies. In J. Humber & R. Almeder (Eds.). *Is There a duty to die.* Totawa, NJ: Humana Press.

Battin, M. (2005). *Ending life: Ethics and the way we die.* Oxford: Oxford University Press.

Battin, M. (2008). Physician-assisted dying and the slippery slope: The challenge of empirical evidence. *Willamette Law Review, 45*(1), 91–136.

Baxter vs. Montana. (2009). *Related Legal Documents and Friend of the Court Amicus Briefs.* Retrieved from www.compassionandchoices.org/sslpage.aspx?pid=416

Berry, Z. (2009). Responding to suffering: Providing options and respecting choice. *Journal of Pain and Symptom Management, 38*(3), 797–800.

Beauchamp, T. L. & James, F. C. (2001). *Principles of Biomedical Ethics.* Oxford.

Breitbart, W., Rosenfeld, B., Pessin, H., Kaim, M., Funesti-Esch, J., Galietta, M., et. al. (2000). Depression, hopelessness, and desire for hastened death in terminally ill patients with cancer. *Journal of the American Medical Association, 284,* 2907–2911.

Buiting, H., van Delden, J., Onwuteaka-Philpsen, B., Rietjens, J., van Tol, D., Gevers, J., et al. (2009). Reporting of euthanasia and physician-assisted suicide in the Netherlands: Descriptive study. *BMC Medical Ethics, 10*(18). doi: 10.1186/1472-6939-10-18

Byock, I. (1998). *Dying well: Peace and possibilities at the end of life.* New York: Penguin-Riverhead Books.

Callahan, D. (2008). Organized obfuscation: Advocacy for physician assisted suicide. *Hastings Center Report, 38*(5), 30–32.

Campbell, C. (2008). Ten years of death with dignity. *The New Atlantis, 22,* 33–46.

Centers for Disease Control. WISQARS. Retrieved from www.cdc.gov/injury/ wisqars/index.html/

Cholbi, M. (2008). "Suicide." *Stanford Encyclopedia of Philosophy.* Retrieved from http://plato.stanford.edu/entries/suicide/

Clarke, A. E. (1996). Autonomy and death. *Tulane Law Review, 71*(1), 45–137.

Clayton, P. (2009). *Suicide and the elderly.* Medical Director, American Society for Suicide Presentation. www.afsp.org/files/Misc_//standardizedpresentation3 .ppt.

Conwell, Y. & Duberstein, P. (2001). Suicide in elders. *Annals NY Academy of Science, 932,* 132–147.

Coyle, N., Sculco, L. (2004). Expressed desire for hastened death in seven patients living with advanced cancer: A phenomenologic inquiry. *Oncology Nursing Forum, 31*(4), 699–709.

Dahl, E. & Levy, N. (2006). The case for physician assisted suicide: How can it possibly be proved? *Journal of Medical Ethics, 32,* 335–338.

Daube, D. (1972). The linguistics of suicide. *Philosophy and Public Affairs, 1*(4), 387–437.

Department of Health and Human Services (DHHS), Public Health Service. (2001). National strategy for suicide prevention: Goals and objectives for action. Retrieved May 14, 2009, from http://mentalhealth.samhsa.gov/publications/allpubs/SMA01-3517/default.asp#toc

Dore, M. (2010). "Death with Dignity": A recipe for elder abuse and homicide (albeit not by name). *Marquette Elder's Advisor, 11*(2), Spring 2010.

Dore, M. (2011). Physician-assisted suicide: A recipe for elder abuse and the illusion of personal choice. *Vermont Bar Journal.*

Dore, M. (2011). Report to the 62nd legislature for the State of Montana LC 0041—The Montana Elder Abuse Prevention Act. Presented by Senator Greg Hinkle. A bill for an Act entitled: "An Act Prohibiting Aid in Dying."

Dowbiggin, I. (2005). *A concise history of Euthanasia: Life, death, God and medicine.* Lanham, MD: Rowan and Littlefield.

Drake, S. (2007). Latest Pro-Euthanasia Research Redefines "Slippery Slope" and Uses "Soft" Data, 79 Newsl. Euthanasia Prevention Coal., Oct. 2007, at 3, available at www.euthanasiaprevention.on.ca/Newsletters/newsletter79.pdf.

Droge, A. J. & James D. T. (1992). *A noble death: Suicide and martyrdom among Christians and Jews in antiquity.* New York: HarperCollins/HarperSanFrancisco.

Durkheim, E. (1997) [1897]. *Suicide: A study in sociology.* The Free Press.

Dworkin, R. (1993). *Life's dominion: An argument about abortion, euthanasia, and individual freedom.* New York: Alfred A. Knopf.

Editor. (March 29, 1984), Gov. Lamm Asserts Elderly, If Very Ill, Have 'Duty To Die' New York Times. Retrieved from www.nytimes.com/1984/03/29/us/gov-lamm-asserts-elderly-if-very-ill-have-duty-to-die.html

Farley, M. (1995). Issues in contemporary Christian ethics: The choice of death in a medical context. *The Santa Clara Lectures, 1*(3), 1–19.

Foley, K. & Herbert H. (2002). *The case against assisted suicide and for the right to end of life care.* Baltimore: Johns Hopkins.

Ganzini, L., Silveira, M. J., & Johnson, W. S. (2002). Predictors and correlates of interest in assisted suicide in the final month of life among ALS patients in Oregon and Washington. *Journal of Pain and Symptom Management, 24*(3), 312–317.

Ganzini, L., Goy, E. R., Miller, L. L., Harvath, T., Jackson, A., & Delorit, M. A. (2003). Nurses' experiences with hospice patients who refuse food and fluids to hasten death. *New England Journal of Medicine, 349*, 359–365

Ganzini, L., Beer, T. M., Brouns, M., Mori, M., Hsieh, Y. C. (2006). Interest in physician-assisted suicide among Oregon cancer patients. *Journal of Clinical Ethics, 17*(1), 27–38.

Ganzini, L., Goy, E. R., & Dobscha, S. K. (2009). Oregonians' reasons for requesting physician aid in dying. *Archives of Internal Medicine, 169*(5), 489–492.

German Protestant and Catholic Bishops. (1975–2010). Gemeinsame Texte 17: Sterbebegleitung statt aktiver Sterbehilfe, Eine Textsammlung kirchlicher Erklärungen mit einer Einführung des Vorsitzenden der Deutschen Bischofskonferenz und des Vorsitzenden des Rates der Evangelischen Kirche in Deutschland.

Goedicke, H. (1970). *The report about the dispute of a man with his Ba: Papyrus Berlin 3024.* Baltimore and London: The Johns Hopkins Press.

Grisez, G. (1990). Should nutrition and hydration be provided to permanently unconscious and other mentally disabled persons? *Linacre Quarterly, 57,* 30–43.

Grisez, G. (1997). Question 43, Is it wrong to wish for death? and Q47: May a husband consent to stopping feeding his permanently unconscious wife? In *Difficult moral questions: Way of the Lord Jesus.* Vol. III. Steubenville, Ohio: Franciscan Press.

Grogan, E., Thorns, A., Campbell, C., Stark-Toller, C., Oliver, D., Harlow, T., et. al. (2007). Are vulnerable groups no more likely to receive physician-assisted dying? *Journal of Medical Ethics,* Retrieved November 8, 2007, from http://jme.bmj.com/cgi/eletters/33/10/591

Gunderson, M. (2004). A Kantian view of suicide and end-of-life treatment. *Journal of Social Philosophy, 35*(2), 277–287.

Hardwig, J. (2000). *Is there a duty to die and other essays in medical ethics.* New York: Routledge.

Hedberg, K., Hopkins, D., Kohn, M. (2003). Five years of legal physician-assisted suicide in Oregon. *The New England Journal of Medicine, 348,* 961–964.

Hedberg, K. & Tolle, S. (2009). Putting Oregon's Death with Dignity Act in perspective: Characteristics of decedents who did not participate. *The Journal of Clinical Ethics, 20*(2), 133–135.

Hedberg, K., Hopkins, D., Leman, R., & Kohn, M. (2009). The 10-year experience of Oregon's death with dignity act: 1998–2007. *The Journal of Clinical Ethics, 20*(2), 124–132.

Hotopf, M., Lee, W., & Price, A. (2011). Assisted suicide: Why psychiatrists should engage in the debate. *The British Journal of Psychiatry, 198,* 83–84.

Hume, D. [1756] (2001). *Four dissertations and essays on suicide and the immortality of the soul.* Chicago, IL: St. Augustine's Press.

Jacobs, S. (2003). Behind the research: Death by voluntary dehydration: What the caregivers say. *The New England Journal of Medicine, 349,* 325–326.

Jansen, L. A. (2004). No safe harbor: The principle of complicity and the practice of voluntary stopping of eating and drinking. *Journal of Medicine and Philosophy, 29*(1), 61–74.

Harwood, D. M. J., Hawton, K., Hope, T., Harriss, L., & Jacoby, R. (2006). Life problems and physical illness as risk factors for suicide in older people: A descriptive and case–control study. *Psychological Medicine, 36*(9), 1265–1274.

Hawton, K. & Harriss, L. (2006). Deliberate self-harm in people aged 60 years and over: Characteristics and outcome of a 20-yer cohort. *International Journal of Geriatric Psychiatry, 21,* 572–581.

Hendin, H. (1999). Euthanasia consultants or facilitators? Few euthanasia consultants in the Netherlands act as independent evaluaters of the patient's situation. *Medical Journal of Australia, 170,* 351–352.

Hendin, H. & Foley, K. M. (Eds.) (2002). *The case against assisted suicide: For the right to end of life care.* Baltimore: Johns Hopkins.

Hendin, H. & Kathleen M. Foley (2008). Physician-assisted suicide in Oregon: A medical perspective. *Michigan Law Review, 106*(8), 1613, 1636–1637.

Hicks, M. H. (2007). Rapid response to timothy quill editorial, mentally ill given short shrift. *British Medical Journal, 10*, 2007. Retrieved from www.bmj .com/cgi/eletters/335/7621/625#177848

Hospice and Palliative Nurses Association, HPNA Position Statement (2004). The ethics of opiate use within palliative care. Retrieved from www.hpna .org/PicView.aspx?ID=709

Hudson, P. L., Kristjanson, L. J., Ashby, M., Kelly, B., Schofield, P., Hudson, R., et al. (2006). Desire for hastened death in patients with advanced disease and the evidence base of clinical guidelines: A systematic review. *Palliative Medicine, 20*(7), 693–701.

Kass, L. R., (1989). Neither for love nor money: Why doctors must not kill. *Public Interest, 94*, 25.

Keenan, J. F. (1993). The function of the principle of double effect. *Theological Studies, 54*, 294–315.

Kelly, B., Burnett, P., Badger, S., Pelusi, D., Varghese, F. T., Robertson, M. (2003). Doctors and their patients: A context for understanding the wish to hasten death. *Psychooncology, 12*(4), 375–384.

Kung, H. (1982, 2007). Ewiges Leben? (Munich: Piper Verlag, Auflage: Neuauflage, Nachdruck. 1982, 2007). *Eternal life? Life after death as a medical, philosophical and theological problem.* Eugene OR: Wipf and Stock Publishers.

Küng, H. & Walter, J. (Eds.) (1998). Menschenwürdig Sterben. Ein Plädoyer Für Selbstverantwortung. Piper; Auflage: 2. Aufl., 36. Tsd (1995), Translated as *Dying with dignity: A plea for personal responsibility.* New York: Continuum Publishing Group.

Langford, L. (2008, October). *Framework for mental health promotion and suicide prevention in senior living communities.* Working draft for the meeting. It takes a community: A summit on opportunities for mental health promotion and suicide prevention efforts in senior living communities. Gaithersburg, MD: Suicide Prevention Resource Center.

Lewey, G. (2010). *Assisted death in Europe and America: Four regimes and their lessons.* Oxford: Oxford University Press.

Lieberman, E. J. (2006). Letter to the Editor, Death with Dignity. *Psychiatric News*, August 4, 2006.

Margaret P. B., van der Heide, A., Ganzini, L., van der Wal, G., & Onwuteaka-Philipsen, B. D., et al. (2007). Legal physician-assisted dying in Oregon and the Netherlands: Evidence concerning the impact on patients in "Vulnerable" Groups. *Journal of Medical Ethics, 33*.

Marker, R. L. & Smith, W. J. (1996). The art of verbal engineering. *Dusquesne Law Review, 81*, 81–107.

Marker, R. Prescription death—Suicide as a medical treatment (12/18/2007). Retrieved from www.catholicity.com/commentary/marker/01941.html

Meier, C., Emmons, C.-A., Litke, A., Wallenstein, S., Sean Morrison, R. (2003). Characteristics of patients requesting and receiving physician-assisted death. *Archives of Internal Medicine, 163*, 1537–1542.

Miller, M. (2008). *Dying wish* Film. Retrieved from http://74.220.215.84/ ~goinpeac/dyingwishmedia/

Mitchell, J. B. (2007). *Understanding assisted suicide: Nine issues to consider.* Ann Arbor, MI: University of Michigan.

Mueller, D. (1973). Review of Goedicke, Hans. (1970). *The report about the dispute of a man with his Ba: Papyrus Berlin 3024.* Baltimore and London: The Johns Hopkins Press, 1970. *Journal of Near Eastern Studies, 32*(3), 353–354.

Muller, D. (2011). Attention to language in a request for physician aid in dying. *The American Journal of Hospice & Palliative Care, 28,* 63–64.

Maytal, G. & Stern, T. A. (2006). The desire for death in the setting of terminal illness. *Journal of Clinical Psychiatry, 8*(5), 299–305.

Netherlands Law. (2002). Wet toetsing levensbeëindiging op verzoek en hulp bij zelfdoding (Termination of Life on Request and Assisted Suicide Law) See "uitzichtloos en ondraaglijk lijden van de patiënt" ("the unbearable and hopeless suffering of the patient") Retrieved from: www.nvve.nl/nvve2/pagina.asp?pagkey=71892#staatsblad

Novak, D. (1975). *Suicide and morality: The theories of Plato, Aquinas and Kant and their relevance for suicidology.* Atlanta, GA: Scholars Studies Press.

Oregon Death with Dignity Act. (2009). ORS 127.800 ff. Retrieved from http://public.health.oregon.gov/ProviderPartnerResources/EvaluationResearch/DeathwithDignityAct/Pages/index.aspx

Orfali, R. (2011). *Death with dignity: The case for legalizing physician-assisted dying and euthanasia.* Minneapolis, MN: Mill City Press.

Paton, J. (1971). *The categorical imperative: A study in kant's moral philosophy.* USA: University of Pennsylvania.

Pellegrino, E. D. (1992, Summer). Why doctors must not kill. *The Journal of Clinical Ethics, 3*(2), 95–102.

Pellegrino, E. D. (2000). Decisions to withdraw life-sustaining treatment: A moral algorithm. *Journal of the American Medical Association, 283*(8), 1065–1067. doi:10.1001/jama.283.8.1065

Pellegrino, E. D. & Sulmasy, D. P. (2003). Medical ethics. In D. A. Warrell, T. M. Cox, & J. D. Firth (Eds.), *Oxford textbook of medicine.* New York: Oxford University Press.

Pence, G. E. (2007). Is there a duty to die. In G. E. Pence (Ed.), *The elements of bioethics* (pp. 233–262). Dubuque, IA, USA: McGraw-Hill.

Pickett, J. (2009). Can legalization improve end of life care? An empirical analysis of the results of the legalization of euthanasia and physician assisted suicide in the Netherlands and Oregon. *Elder Law Journal, 16,* 332.

Pope, T. M. & Anderson, L. E. (2011). Voluntarily stopping eating and drinking: A legal treatment option at the end of life. *Widener Law Review, 17*(2), 363–427.

Quill, T. & Greenlaw, J. (2008). Physician-assisted death. In M. Crowley (Ed.), *From birth to death and bench to clinic: The Hastings Center bioethics briefing book for journalists, policymakers, and campaigns.* (pp. 137–142). Garrison, NY: The Hastings Center.

Robinson, J. (2010). Baxter and the return of physician assisted suicide. *Hastings Center Report, 40*(6), 15–17.

Rodriguez Davila, S. L., Vidal, E., Stewart, J. T., & Caserta, M. T. (2010). Management of a request for physician-assisted suicide. *The American Journal of Hospice & Palliative Care, 27,* 63–65.

Sabatino, C. (2007). *Advance directives and advance care planning: Legal and policy issues.* Retrieved from http://aspe.hhs.gov/daltcp/reports/2007/adacplpi.htm

Sandel, M. (2010). *Justice: What's the right thing to do?* New York, NY: Farrar, Straus and Giroux.

Schadenberg, A. (2004). *Assisted suicide in Oregon: Lessons learned and unanswered questions.* Retrieved from May 20, 2004, www.lifenews.com/bio276.html

Schneiderman, L. J. (2005). "Book Review" Physician-assisted dying: The case for palliative care and patient choice. In T. E. Quill & M. P. Battin (Eds.). *JAMA, 293,* 501.

Schwartz, J. K. (2009). Stopping eating and drinking. *American Journal of Nursing, 109*(9), 52–61.

Schwartz, J. K. (2007). Death by voluntary dehydration: Suicide or the right to refuse a life-prolonging measure? *Widener Law Review, 17,* 351–361.

Seay, G. (2001). Do physicians have an inviolable duty not to kill? *The Journal of Medicine and Philosophy, 26*(1), 75–91.

Simon, R. I., Levenson, J. L., & Shuman, D. W. (2005, June). On sound and unsound mind: The role of suicide in tort and insurance litigation. *The Journal of the American Academy of Psychiatry and the Law, 33*(2), 176–182.

Singer, P. (2011). *Practical ethics.* Cambridge: Cambridge University Press, 1979; second edition, 1993; third edition, 2011.

Smith, K. A., Goy, E. R., Harvath, T. A., & Ganzini, L. (2011). Quality of death and dying in patients who request physician-assisted death. *Journal of Palliative Medicine, 14*(4), 445–450.

Substance Abuse and Mental Health Services Administration. (2011). *Promoting emotional health and preventing suicide: A toolkit for senior living communities.* HHS Publication No. SMA 4515, CMHS-NSPL-0197. Rockville, MD: Center for Mental Health Services. Retrieved from http://store.samhsa.gov/product/SMA10-4515

Sugarman, J. & Sulmasy, D. P. (2010). *Methods in Medical Ethics.* Georgetown.

Sulmasy, D. P. & L. A. Jansen (2002). Sedation, alimentation, hydration, and equivocation: Careful conversation about care at the end of life. *Annals of Internal Medicine, 136,* 845–849.

Sulmasy, D. P., Ury, W. A., Ahronheim, J. C., Siegler, M., Kass, L., Lantos, J., et. al. (2000a). Responding to intractable terminal suffering. *Archives of Internal Medicine, 133,* 560–562.

Sulmasy, D. P., Ury, W. A., Ahronheim, J. C., Siegler, M., Kass, L., Lantos, J., et al. (2000b). Palliative treatment of last resort and assisted suicide. *Archives of Internal Medicine, 133,* 562–563.

Sulmasy, D. & Pellegrino, E. (1999). Double effect: Clearing up the double talk. *Archives of Internal Medicine, 159,* 545–550.

Thomas, C. (1980). First suicide note? *British Medical Journal, 281*(6235), 284–285 (later as Discourse of a Man with his Ba, by Wim van den Dungen). Retrieved from www.sofiatopia.org/maat/ba.htm

Thomasma, D. (1998). Assisted death and martyrdom. *Christian Bioethics, 4*(2), 122–142.

Tucker, K. (2008). In the laboratory of the states: The progress of Glucksberg's invitation to states to address end-of-life choice. *Michigan Law Review, 106,* 1593–1612.

Tucker, K. (2009). At the very end of life: The emergence of policy supporting aid in dying among mainstream medical and health policy associations. *Harvard Health Policy Review, 10*(1), 45–47.

Tucker, K. & Steele, F. B. (2007). Patient choice at the end of life getting the language right. *The Journal of Legal Medicine, 28,* 305–325.

Tucker, K. L., Harper, M., & Spiers, P. A. (2007). The sky is not falling: Disability and aid-in-dying. In T. H. Lillie & J. L. Werth (Eds.), *End of life issues and persons with disabilities.* Austin, TX: PRO-ED.

Unger, T. (1996). *Living high and letting die.* New York: Oxford.

United States Conference of Catholic Bishops. (2011). *To live each day with dignity.* Retrieved from www.usccb.org/issues-and-action/human-life-and-dignity/assisted-suicide/to-live-each-day/

Vacco v. Quill, 521 U.S. 793 (1997). Retrieved from http://supreme.justia.com/us/521/793/case.html

Valente, S. K. (2004). End of life challenges: Honoring autonomy. *Cancer Nursing, 27,* 314–319.

Varghese, F. T., Leigh, R., Turner, M. J., Vamos, M., Kelly, B. J., & Cook, D. (2000, September 3–7). Psychiatric issues surrounding assisted suicide & euthanasia among terminally ill patients. In J. C. Holland, & M. Watson (Eds.), *Psychooncology; Proceedings 5th World Congress of Psycho-Oncology. 5th World Congress of Psycho-Oncology.* Melbourne, Australia (S26).

Vetter, P. (2008, July 28). "Dying wish" documents death of Dr. Michael Miller with conscious choice to stop eating and drinking. *American Chronicle.* Retrieved from www.americanchronicle.com/articles/view/69683

Washington v. Glucksberg. (1997). 521 U.S. 702 (1997) http://supreme.justia.com/us/521/702/case.html

Washington v. Glucksberg (1997b). Supreme Court. Retrieved from http://law2.umkc.edu/faculty/projects/ftrials/conlaw/glucksberg.html

Washington State Catholic Conference (2006). *A guide to making good decisions for the end of life: Living will and durable power of attorney for health care.* Retrieved from www.thewscc.org/

Washington State Death with Dignity Act. (2008). RC70.245. www.doh.wa.gov/dwda/

Online Resources

Oregon Death with Dignity Act ORS 127.800 ff

http://public.health.oregon.gov/ProviderPartnerResources/EvaluationResearch/DeathwithDignityAct/Pages/index.aspx

Washington State Death with Dignity Act (2008) RC70.245

www.doh.wa.gov/dwda/

Montana (*Baxter v. Montana,* 2009) Related Legal Documents and Friend of the Court Amicus Briefs

www.compassionandchoices.org/sslpage.aspx?pid=416

The Continuing Challenge of Assisted Death: The Nursing Role in Assisted Death, Mary Ersek

www.medscape.com/viewarticle/468566_5

Ethical Arguments for and Against Assisted Death, Mary Ersek

www.medscape.com/viewarticle/468566_4

National Reference Center for Bioethics Literature

http://bioethics.georgetown.edu/

Bioethics Resources on the Web

http://bioethics.od.nih.gov/

PRO
Compassion in Choices

https://compassionandchoices.org/sslpage.aspx

Death with Dignity

www.deathwithdignity.org/

ANTI
True Compassion Advocates

www.truecompassionadvocates.org/

Not Dead Yet

www.mcil.org/mcil/mcil/ndy.htm

ISSUE 12

Is Palliative Sedation Actually Euthanasia in Disguise?

YES: **Margaret P. Battin**, from "Terminal Sedation: Pulling the Sheet over Our Eyes," *Hastings Center Report* (vol. 38, no. 5, pp. 27–30, 2008)

NO: **National Ethics Committee, Veterans Health Administration**, from "The Ethics of Palliative Sedation as a Therapy of Last Resort," *American Journal of Hospice and Palliative Care* (vol. 23, no. 6, pp. 483–491, 2007)

Learning Outcomes

After reading this issue, you should be able to:

- Gain an understanding of five ethical differences that distinguish PS from euthanasia, including foreseen but unintended outcomes, imminently dying, life-sustaining treatment, existential suffering, and decisional capacity.
- Describe differences between sedation until death of imminently dying and sedation toward death.
- Understand the importance of knowing why decisions about palliative sedation are separate from choices to forgo life-sustaining treatment.
- Discuss and distinguish whether PS is appropriate for "existential" suffering without physical symptoms.
- Identify and debate whether PS can be provided to patients without decisional capacity.

ISSUE SUMMARY

YES: Margaret Battin, a philosopher and ethicist from the University of Utah, argues that clinical practices of palliative sedation and euthanasia are conceptually alike yet different in ways that generate public debates concerning distinctions between misuses and abuses of palliative sedation.

NO: The National Ethics Committee of the Veterans Health Administration outlines guidelines for palliative sedation as an approach of last resort for dying patients with intolerable symptoms.

$\mathbf{I}$s "palliative sedation" concealed "euthanasia"? This issue distinguishes these practices surveys an emerging professional consensus and reviews recommendations for institutional policy. *Five key ethical concerns* have driven questions about palliative sedation (PS). These ask about how PS is different than euthanasia; whether one must be imminently dying; whether one must be willing to forgo life-sustaining treatment as a condition of PS; whether PS is appropriate to "existential" suffering without physical symptoms; and whether PS can be provided to patients without decisional capacity.

Palliative Sedation

What is *palliative sedation* (PS)? In general terms, it means "sedating a patient to the point of unconsciousness to relieve one or more symptoms that are intractable and unrelieved despite aggressive symptom-specific treatments, and maintaining that condition until the patient dies" (Taylor, 2003).

Palliative sedation is *different* than sedating side effects of surgery with anticipated recovery, or pain relief, or time-limited (respite) therapy. *Cultural consensus is evolving* about key terms for personal decisions (consent or capacity), policy (effective pain relief), and clinical guidelines (team-based help). For example, modern "hospice" was invented in 1967 as a philosophy not a place of care. Some of the first guidelines (algorithms) for "palliative sedation" were developed in 1994 regarding candidate selection, medicines, overseeing practitioners, continuous versus intermittent sedation, nonphysical suffering, ideal practice settings, and ethical issues (Cherny & Portenoy, 1994; Olsen, Swetz, & Mueller, 2010). The term *terminal sedation* was first used in 1991 (Enck, 1991). "Terminal sedation" refers to a class of patients who are dying and an outcome of therapy. But maintaining a terminal patient under sedation *until* she dies—sedation of the imminently dying—is different than sedating a terminal patient *toward* death (Sulmasy and Jansen, 2002; Cellarius, 2008) (Issue 12).

Palliative Sedation and Euthanasia

For two and half millennia in western cultures, "euthanasia" has minimally meant, "a good death"—considered worthwhile in different terms for different audiences. When *voluntary*, some call killing by another *mercy death*; *mercy killing* occurs against consent (*involuntarily*) or without consent (*nonvoluntarily*, for one who is unconscious).

There are *common concerns*. Health care and community services are *not organized* to meet needs of large numbers of those who experience prolonged and progressive illness before death (Lynn, 2004). In Europe and the United States, there are *more patients, fewer caregivers*, yet terminal designations vary (1 year in the United Kingdom, 6 months in the United States). Hospice and palliative care have *different origins and funding* (more public support in Europe) that affect different locations and experiences of delivery. Since the 1980s in the United States, a Hospice movement has grown from volunteerism to organizational affiliations; professionalizations of palliative care subspecialties have decisively improved symptom management (AAHPM). Best practices in both include team-based multidisciplinary approaches, yet hospice is a philosophy of end-of-life care and palliative care is not restricted to terminal illness. Why do so many still die in alienating environments of "hospitals," with *undertreated pain*?

Myths ignore widespread *practical consensus* about pain relief with foreseen but not intended risks (hastened dying). *Proponents And Opponents Agree About Ethically Easy Cases of legitimate uses of lethally risky pain relief.* For example, actions with multiple effects should (1) *not be intrinsically wrong* (e.g., morphine used for pain). These (2) may *foresee a bad effect* while intending a good effect; morphine relieves pain, depresses respiratory drive, and potentially hastens death. (3) But a *bad effect doesn't cause a good effect*; that is, respiratory depression and death don't cause pain relief. (4) Using morphine is *a means proportionate to an end* in which an expected good outweighs a particular bad. Morphine is proportionate and suitable to pain; pain is significant and death is imminent (Battin, 2008; National Ethics Committee, 2007; Quill, Lo, Brock, & Meisel, 2009; Sulmasy, 1999, Sulmasy, Curlin, Brungardt, & Cavanaugh, 2010; Sulmasy in Buckley, 2012).

Opponents to terminal sedation argue that palliative sedation is ethically different from physician-assisted suicide and euthanasia based on intention and proportionality. PS can be appropriate when its primary intent is to relieve the patient's suffering (double effect #2 above), death results from the disease (DE #3), and the risk of harm is proportionate to the expected benefit of comfort (DE #4, HPNA, 2004; National Ethics Committee, 2007; ANA, Olsen et al., 2010). Some *proponents* of terminal sedation argue that various versions of "double effect" over-rely on clinical intentions that exclude hastening death (DE #2) and oversimplify interactions among multiple therapies. Opponents and proponents of terminal sedation disagree about how to interpret sedation to unconsciousness.

Intolerable Suffering or Exclusively Imminently Dying

Some seek to extend permission for PS to those with *intolerable suffering* (Netherlands Law, 2002; Singer, 1979, 2011). Others argue that sedation for the imminently dying is not euthanasia (Russell, Williams, & Drogan, 2010). Some argue different kinds of *slippery slope* considerations make it ethically appropriate to limit palliative sedation to patients who are imminently dying (Cellarius, 2008). These include concerns that expansions of PS to intolerable suffering could liken PS to physician-assisted suicide/death (PAS/PAD) and/or shift it from a therapy of last resort to a replacement for palliation (National Ethics Committee, 2007).

Mandatory Forgoing of Life-Sustaining Treatment

Should willingness to forgo life-sustaining treatment be a condition for administering/receiving palliative sedation? Because PS provides relief, there is professional *consensus* that all PS candidates should have a *Do Not Resuscitate* (DNR) and all DNR patients should be candidates. There is *disagreement* over whether *other life-sustaining treatments* must be relinquished (e.g., ventilator support, dialysis, ANH). Proponents argue that most patients who are candidates for PS are near death and—as a separate decision—will (and should) have already decided to forgo life-sustaining treatments to avoid prolonged dying. Opponents argue that some want both pain relief and prolongation of life-sustaining treatment; hence, both choices should be honored on grounds of autonomy.

Palliative Sedation for Existential Suffering

Is palliative sedation an ethically appropriate response to "existential" suffering—as distinct from physical symptoms that resist treatment (called refractory)? The debate has struggled to *define and clinically distinguish* existential suffering from psychiatric conditions (depression); to *determine whether relief is a proportionate goal*; and to *decide whether such relief is a goal of medicine* provided through pharmacological intervention by health care professionals. Arguments exist on all sides—even among professional organizations (National Ethics Committee, 2007). For example, *proponents* argue that in rare circumstances, "terminal sedation" can be appropriate for "existential distress" (anxiety) (Morita, Tsunoda, Inoue, & Chihara, 2000; Rousseau, 2000; Berger, 2010). *Opponents* argue that palliative sedation is not an appropriate remedy for forms of affliction without physical symptoms (pharmacological parsimony in Sulmasy et al., 2000a, 2000b, 2002; Sulmasy & Jansen, 2002; Levy & Cohen, 2005; Olsen et al., 2010).

Palliative Sedation for Those Without Decisional Capacity

May palliative sedation be provided to patients who lack decision-making capacity? Laws in Oregon, Washington State, and Montana shift from informed consent to "decisional capacity." Practices in the Netherlands have been criticized for permitting assisted death of persons who were unconscious; hence, charges are that nonvoluntary killings amount to active euthanasia without request or *mercy killings* (Battin, 2008; Ganzini, 2009; Singer, 1979, 2011 edition). Physicians report that use of sedation includes an intention to hasten death (Rietjens, van der Heide, Vrakking, Onwuteaka-Philipsen, van der Maas, & van der Wal, 2004). Many central European systems of public health (still) rely on *caregiver paternalism*; in the United States "care" ethics is competency and skill based in response to *patient autonomy*. North American defenses of "difficult" nonvoluntary euthanasia require valid proxies to use a "best interest standard" (Dombrowski, 2007). Rather than rely on health care professionals, a national American committee recommended that a valid surrogate can also make a decision for a patient regarding palliative sedation—but such PS must be a therapy of last resort that does not deliberately terminate patients (National Ethics Committee, 2007).

YES

Margaret P. Battin

Terminal Sedation: Pulling the Sheet over Our Eyes

T erminal sedation—also called "palliative sedation," "continuous deep sedation," or "primary deep continuous sedation"—has become a new favorite in end-of-life care, a seeming compromise in the debate over physician-assisted dying. Like all compromises, it offers something to each side of a dispute. But it is not a real down-the-middle compromise. It sells out on most of the things that may be important—to both sides. To corrupt an already awkward metaphor, terminal sedation pulls the sheet over our eyes. Terminal sedation may still be an important option in end-of-life care, but we should not present it as the only option in difficult deaths.

Proponents of assisted dying point to autonomy and mercy. The principle of autonomy holds that people are entitled to be the architects, as much as possible, of how they die. (Of course, autonomy has limits—one cannot inflict harm on others—and when one is no longer competent, values and interests may be expressed only indirectly; advance directives or surrogate decisionmakers must be brought into play. But the principle itself is clear enough.) The principle of mercy requires that pain and suffering be relieved to the extent possible. These two principles operate in tandem to underwrite physician-assisted dying: physician assistance in bringing about death is to be provided just when the person voluntarily seeks it and just when it serves to avoid pain and suffering or the prospect of them. *Both* requirements must be met.

Opponents base their objections to physician-assisted dying on two other concerns. One is the sanctity of life, a religious or secular absolute respect for life that is held to entail the wrongness of killing, suicide, and murder. This principled objection holds regardless of whether a patient seeks assistance in dying in the face of pain and suffering. The second objection is that physician-assisted dying might lead to abuse. This concern is often spelled out in two ways: physician-assisted dying risks undercutting the integrity of the medical profession, and institutional or social pressures might make people victims of assisted dying they did not want.

These latter objections operate independently. One could be opposed to aid in dying on sanctity-of-life grounds even without fearing the slippery slope, and one could worry about the slippery slope without accepting the sanctity-of-life concerns. Often, however, these two concerns are fused in a general objection—a joint claim that it is wrong for doctors to kill and that if

From *Hastings Center Report*, September/October 2008, pp. 27–30. Copyright © 2008 by The Hastings Center. Reprinted by permission of the publisher via Copyright Clearance Center.

doctors *do* kill, even in sympathetic cases like that of the seriously suffering and already dying patient who begs for help, then they might start killing in other, more worrisome cases as well. In short, it's autonomy *and* mercy on the one side, sanctity of life *and/or* the possibility of abuse on the other. That's the standoff over physician-assisted dying, argued in a kaleidoscope of ways over the past several decades.

Terminal sedation is often proffered as an alternative last resort measure that can overcome these practical and ideological disputes. In the 1997 cases *Washington v. Glucksberg* and *Vacco v. Quill*, the Supreme Court recognized the legality of providing pain relief in palliative care even if doing so might shorten life, provided the intention was to relieve pain. But careful scrutiny of terminal sedation—particularly sedation to unconsciousness, in which nutrition and hydration are withheld—suggests that it is not much of a compromise after all.

An Inadequate Compromise

Consider how terminal sedation fails to meet the concerns that underlie the dispute.

Autonomy. Consent of the person affected is central to the concept of autonomy, but it is not and—as a consequence of some political interpretations—*cannot* be honored in decisions to use terminal sedation. First, terminal sedation is often used for patients suffering from severe pain, for whom pain management has failed, but if pain is severe enough, reflective, unimpaired consent may no longer be possible. Decision-making must be deflected to a second party. (Of course, voluntary, informed consent is often challenged by pain: consider women in the throes of labor consenting to an epidural or a caesarean, or trauma victims consenting to surgery.)

More importantly, even when the decision is made in advance of the onset of intense pain, the focus of consent is obscured. Terminal sedation may end pain, but it also ends life. It does so in two ways: it immediately ends sentient life and the possibility for social interaction, and then, because artificial nutrition and hydration are usually withheld, it also ends biological life. But because the assumption is that sedation is used just to end pain, without the *intention* of ending life, the patient cannot be asked for consent to end his or her life, but only to relieve his or her pain. Of course, the consent process could include some mention of the possibility that relieving pain might inadvertently shorten life, but if the acknowledgment that life will be ended is stronger than that, the question of what is intended will arise. Thus, the focus of consent is on avoiding pain, but it should be on causing death.

The new euphemism, "palliative sedation," now often used instead of the more distressing "terminal sedation," only reinforces this problem. By avoiding the word "terminal" and hence any suggestion that death may be coming, the most important feature of this practice is obscured and terminal sedation is confused with "palliative care." Thus, the patient cannot consent to the really significant decision—whether his or her life shall be ended now. Autonomy is therefore undercut whether the patient's capacity for reflection is impaired by severe pain or not.

Mercy. Terminal sedation is typically used only at the very end of the downhill course, and only when the patient's pain has become extreme and other palliative measures are not effective. A broad study of pooled data over the last forty years on pain in cancer found that 59 percent of patients on anticancer treatment and 64 percent of patients with advanced metastatic disease experience pain.[1] Agitation, delirium, dyspnea, seizures, urinary and fecal retention, and nausea and protracted vomiting are also problems. Bernard Lo and Gordon Rubenfeld, writing in the *Journal of the American Medical Association,* discuss a forty-nine-year-old cancer patient given very high doses of morphine who developed myclonus: seizures in the extremities and eventually in the whole body, producing intense pain.[2] As they say of palliative sedation for her and other dying patients: "We turn to it when everything else hasn't worked."

Terminal sedation to unconsciousness can certainly provide relief from such suffering, but some patients wish to avoid this long downhill course—especially the last stages of it. The use of terminal sedation "to relieve pain" presupposes that the patient is *already* experiencing pain. It provides no rationale for sedating a patient who is not currently in pain. Thus, the rationale for the use of terminal sedation in effect *requires* that the patient suffer.

The sanctity of life. The dispute over the principle of the wrongness of killing, or the sanctity of life, has focused mainly on ending a person's life before it would "naturally" end. Terminal sedation does not honor this principle. Rather, it unarguably causes death, and it does so in a way that is not "natural."

It is important to be perfectly clear about the process. Terminal sedation commonly involves two components: 1) inducing sedation, and 2) withholding the administration of fluids and nutrition. The first is not intrinsically lethal,[3] but the second is, if pursued long enough. Patients who are sedated to the degree involved in terminal sedation cannot eat or drink, and without "artificial" nutrition and hydration will necessarily die, virtually always before they would have died otherwise. Patients are sometimes sedated to unconsciousness with food and fluids continued—a practice that extends the dying period (and the cost), but this is not the usual form.

The death itself is not "natural," either. The airy, rather romantic notion of "natural" death usually refers to death that results from an underlying disease, but in terminal sedation death typically results from or is accelerated by dehydration. This is not "natural" dehydration; it is induced by a physician. If respect for the sanctity of life means that a patient's life should not be caused to end, but rather that death must occur only as the result of the underlying disease process, then terminal sedation does not honor this principle.

The possibility of abuse. This concern takes two general forms: 1) concern that the integrity of the medical profession will be undercut, and 2) concern that various familial, institutional, or social pressures will maneuver the patient into death when that would have been neither her choice nor in accord with her interests. Yet there is nothing in the practice of terminal sedation that offers greater protection against the possibility of abuse in either of these forms than does direct physician-assisted dying. Is the integrity of the medical

profession likely to be undercut? There are many vivid forms of this charge lev-
eled against direct physician-assisted dying—that physicians are overworked,
anxious to cover their mistakes, unwilling to work with patients they dislike,
biased against patients of certain class or racial backgrounds, beholden to
cost pressures from their HMOs, and so on—but there is no reason to assume
that terminal sedation would be less subject to these abuses than direct aid in
dying. Indeed, direct aid in dying, at least as it is legally practiced in Oregon,
requires a series of safeguards—confirmation of a terminal diagnosis, oral and
written consent, a waiting period, and more—that do not come into play in
terminal sedation. Terminal sedation has no institutional safeguards built in.

What about the sorts of familial, institutional, or social pressures that
opponents claim would maneuver a patient into choosing death when
that would not have been his choice? In terminal sedation, the choice a patient
faces is already obscured: it is not framed as a choice of death versus life, but
only as pain versus the relief of pain—a seemingly far easier choice to make,
and hence one presumably far more easily shaped by external pressures from
greedy family members, overworked or intolerant physicians, or the agents
of cost-conscious institutions. *You don't need to suffer like this* is all they need
to say.

In short, terminal sedation offers no greater protection against abuse
than do the institutional safeguards established for (direct) physician aid in
dying.

The Case in Favor of Terminal Sedation

Several writers in the field have argued, as I have, that terminal sedation fails
to satisfy fully any of the major principles on either side of the aid in dying
disputes. Timothy Quill, describing in close detail the "ambiguity of clinical
intentions," has pointed out that it is virtually impossible for the clinician
administering terminal sedation to intend palliation but not intend that death
occur.[4] David Orentlicher lambasted the 1997 Supreme Court decision in
Washington v. Glucksberg and *Vacco v. Quill* for "rejecting physician-assisted suicide, embracing euthanasia."[5] Tim Quill, Rebecca Dresser, and Dan Brock have
skewered the Court's tortuous use of double-effect reasoning in supporting
the practice of terminal sedation while rejecting voluntary, patient-requested
physician-assisted suicide.[6]

Just the same, a case may be made for terminal sedation. It offers a definitive response to uncontrollable suffering. The gradual induction of death over
the several days or more that terminal sedation takes may appeal to some
patients and their families, especially if this slow process is perceived as gentler
and easier for the patient, and as permitting the family more time to absorb
the reality of their loss. It may also be perceived as less final than physician-
assisted death: some forms of palliative sedation involve lightening up on the
level of sedation periodically—for example, once a day—to see if the patient
is still suffering.

The argument in favor of terminal sedation is one of perceptions: it may
feel natural (even if it is not), it may *feel* safer (even if it offers less protection

from abuse), it may *feel* like something the patient can openly choose (even if the choice is constructed in a way that obscures its real nature), and it may *feel* to the physician as if it is more in keeping with medical codes that prohibit killing (even if it still brings about death). We live in a society that tolerates many obfuscations and hypocrisies, and this may be another one we ought to embrace.

The Need for Guidelines

But we should do so with caution, and with a measure of skepticism about efforts to promote it. Some months before the November ballot that would include the state of Washington's measure I-1000, which is modeled on Oregon's Death with Dignity Act, the American Medical Association Council on Ethical and Judicial Affairs issued a report on "Sedation to Unconsciousness in End-of-Life Care."[7] This report makes an earnest effort to try to preclude many of the practical and ethical difficulties with palliative sedation. For example, the report acknowledges the importance of patient or surrogate consent. It insists that the patient's symptoms really warrant this measure. It emphasizes the importance of interdisciplinary consultation and careful monitoring. And it distinguishes between physical and existential suffering, insisting that palliative sedation may be appropriate in the former but that measures like social supports are to be used for the latter.

However, in its effort to distinguish palliative sedation (it avoids the expression "terminal sedation") from euthanasia, the report undercuts its own courage in addressing these difficult issues by trying to argue that palliative sedation (the permissible strategy) has nothing in common with euthanasia (the impermissible strategy). It does not distinguish between voluntary euthanasia (legal in the Netherlands and Belgium), nonvoluntary euthanasia (of a patient no longer capable of expressing his wishes or of giving legal consent), and involuntary euthanasia (against the patient's wishes). It fails to notice that the Dutch and the Nazi senses of "euthanasia" are entirely different, and that one could welcome the former while reviling the latter.

The AMA report distinguishes palliative sedation from euthanasia (or physician-assisted suicide or aid in dying) on the basis of intention—an application of the well-worn principle of double effect—and then attempts to infer intent from the pattern of practice. "One large dose" or "rapidly accelerating doses" of morphine may signify a bad intention—seeking to cause death—whereas "repeated doses or continuous infusions" are benign. This is naive in the extreme. It's the slyest courtier who poisons the emperor gradually; what could equally well be inferred from repeated doses and continuous infusions is a clever attempt to cover one's tracks. Nor is it clear what counts as "large doses" or other treatment measures in this simplistic dichotomy.

Is a fentanyl patch in a fentanyl-naive patient "rapidly accelerating" or "continuously infusing" when opioid tolerance may be in question? If a hydromorphone infusion for a patient with myoclonus is increased overnight from forty milligrams per hour to one hundred, does the increase count as "rapidly accelerating"? Are one hundred milligram boluses of hydromorphone given every fifteen to thirty minutes on top of a one hundred milligram/hour infusion considered to be "large doses," or are they merely "repeated" doses? What about the doses involved in initiating palliative sedation for this patient: a loading dose of phenobarbital and maintenance on a continuous phenobarbital infusion, together with intravenous dantrolene to lessen the myoclonus? In the case of the forty-nine-year-old cancer patient discussed by Lo and Rubenfeld, the patient died within approximately four hours of the initiation of palliative sedation. Indeed, the average survival in terminal sedation cases is just 1.5 to 3.1 days.[8]

What is astonishing is the AMA's attempt to try to differentiate between different sorts of clinical intentions on the basis of observed practice, when it is simply not possible—nor morally defensible—to draw this false bright line between them. These unworkable distinctions can only exacerbate the unease and legal dread in physicians who work to ease their patients' dying.

It's not that palliative sedation/sedation to unconsciousness/terminal sedation is wrong. It's that it can be practiced hypocritically, as the AMA report seems to ensure. Because there is so much anxiety that it might be confused with euthanasia, the features that it shares with euthanasia are obscured or sanitized. This is where the sheet is pulled over our eyes. The implausible effort to draw a completely bright line between continuous terminal sedation and euthanasia makes the practice of terminal sedation both more dangerous and more dishonest than it should be—and makes what can be a decent and humane practice morally problematic.

Another factor that hasn't been adequately explored is where terminal sedation ought to fit on a spectrum of end-of life options: much of the "compromise" discussion seems to suggest that terminal sedation is the one and only way to deal with difficult deaths. But there are many last resort options, including patient-elected cessation of eating and drinking and direct physician-assisted dying. Terminal sedation is not an acceptable "compromise" if it overshadows these alternatives.

There is no reason why everyone facing a predictable, potentially difficult death should die in the same way. Knowing that pain is likely in some diseases and that even with the best palliative care not all pain can be relieved, some patients will prefer to avoid the worst, so to speak, and choose an earlier, gentler way out. Some will want to hang on as long as possible, in spite of everything. There is no reason that terminal sedation should not be recognized as an option, but there are excellent reasons why it should not be seen as the *only* option—or even the best option—for easing a bad death.

References

1. M.H. van den Beuken-van Everdingen et al., "Prevalence of Pain in Patients with Cancer: A Systematic Review of the Last 40 Years," *Annals of Oncology* 18, no. 9 (2007): 1437–49.
2. B. Lo and G. Rubenfeld, "Palliative Sedation in Dying Patients: 'We Turn to It When Everything Else Hasn't Worked,'" *Journal of the American Medical Association* 294 (2005): 1810–16.

3. For an analysis of data from the National Hospice Outcomes Project concerning whether opioids used in terminal illness cause death, see R.K. Portenoy et al., "Opioid Use and Survival at the End of Life: A Survey of a Hospice Population," *Journal of Pain and Symptom Management* 32, no. 6 (2006): 532–40.

4. T.E. Quill, "The Ambiguity of Clinical Intentions," *New England Journal of Medicine* 329 (1993): 1039–40.

5. D. Orentlicher, "The Supreme Court and Terminal Sedation: Rejecting Assisted Suicide, Embracing Euthanasia," *Hastings Constitutional Law Quarterly* 24, no. 4 (1997): 947–68.

6. T.E. Quill, R. Dresser, and D.W. Brock, "The Rule of Double Effect: A Critique of Its Role in End-of-Life Decision Making," *New England Journal of Medicine* 227 (1997): 1768–71.

7. American Medical Association Council on Ethical and Judicial Affairs, CEJA Report 5-A-08, "Sedation to Unconsciousness in End-of-Life Care."

8. C. Vena, K. Kuebler and S.E. Schrader, "The Dying Process," in K. Kuebler, M.P. David, and C.C. Moore, eds., *Palliative Practices* (St. Louis, Mo.: Elsevier Mosby, 2005), 346, citing data from 1998 and 2000. See also Veterans Affairs National Ethics Teleconference, Terminal Sedation, August 27, 2002, online at www.ethics.va.gov/ ETHICS/docs/net/NET_Topic_20020827_Terminal_ Sedation.doc.

**National Ethics Committee,
Veterans Health Administration**

 **NO**

The Ethics of Palliative Sedation as a Therapy of Last Resort

For most patients nearing the end of life, there comes a point at which the goals of care evolve from an emphasis on prolonging life and optimizing function to maximizing the quality of remaining life, and palliative care becomes the priority. Providing adequate relief of symptoms for dying patients is one of the hallmarks of good palliative care.[1] Yet for some patients, even aggressive, high-quality palliative care fails to provide relief. For patients who suffer from severe pain, dyspnea, vomiting, or other symptoms that prove refractory to treatment, there is consensus that deep sedation—so-called palliative sedation—is an appropriate intervention of last resort.[2-5] The National Hospice and Palliative Care Organization[6] and the American Academy of Hospice and Palliative Medicine[7] support the use of sedation to treat otherwise unrelievable suffering at the end of life, and the practice has been endorsed by the End-of-Life Care Consensus Panel of the American College of Physicians (ACP)–American Society of Internal Medicine (ASIM),[8] and the American Medical Association.[9]

This report by the National Ethics Committee (NEC), Veteran Health Administration (VHA) examines what is meant by palliative sedation, explores ethical concerns about the practice, reviews the emerging professional consensus regarding the use of palliative sedation for managing severe, refractory symptoms at the end of life, and offers recommendations for ethical practice within the VHA.

What Do We Mean by "Palliative Sedation?"

The literature describes several uses of sedation as a palliative intervention at the end of life, variously referred to as *total*, *palliative*, or *terminal* sedation.[3,6,8,10-13] Broadly, the practice involves "sedating a patient to the point of unconsciousness to relieve one or more symptoms that are intractable and unrelieved despite aggressive symptom-specific treatments, and maintaining that condition until the patient dies."[14] The intent, thus, is to provide symptom relief for a dying patient when all other efforts have failed.

From *American Journal of Hospice and Palliative Medicine*, December/January 2007, pp. 483–491.
Copyright © 2007 by American Journal of Hospice and Palliative Medicine. Reprinted by permission of Sage Publications via Rightslink.

Palliative sedation is distinct from sedation that normally accompanies therapeutic interventions, such as intubation or treatment of severe burns, when recovery is expected or more likely to occur.[15–17] Intentionally sedating the patient as a palliative intervention is also distinct from the unintended and variable sedative effects of medications administered for pain relief.[18,19] Some scholars and practitioners further distinguish palliative sedation from "respite sedation" for terminally ill patients; that is, time-limited therapy (e.g., 24 to 48 hours) offered in the hope that temporary sedation will break a cycle of pain, anxiety, and distress.[17]

For purposes of this analysis, the NEC defines palliative sedation as:

> The administration of nonopioid drugs to sedate a terminally ill patient to unconsciousness as an intervention of last resort to treat severe, refractory pain or other clinical symptoms that have not been relieved by aggressive, symptom-specific palliation.

There is broad professional agreement that palliative sedation is a clinically and ethically appropriate response when patients who are near death suffer severe, unremitting symptoms.[7,8,10,11,19–22] The following algorithm has been proposed to help clinicians determine when a symptom is truly refractory:

1. Are further interventions capable of providing further relief?
2. Is the anticipated acute or chronic morbidity of the intervention tolerable to the patient?
3. Are the interventions likely to provide relief within a tolerable time frame?[15,23]

If the answer to any of these three questions is "no," then these are refractory symptoms for which palliative sedation may be considered.

Palliative sedation is provided for a wide range of symptoms. One recent review of published studies, for example, found that the primary indications for this intervention included pain, nausea and vomiting, shortness of breath, and agitated delirium.[13,20,24–26] Other indications for which palliative sedation has been reported include urinary retention due to clot formation,[24] gastrointestinal pain, uncontrolled bleeding,[13] and myoclonus.[27] Many also support palliative sedation to relieve severe psychologic distress in a dying patient,[15,20,28] with the important caveat that potentially treatable mental health conditions first be ruled out.[29]

Ethical Concerns About Palliative Sedation

Ethical debate about palliative sedation has been framed largely in terms of 5 key questions:

1. Is palliative sedation ethically different from physician-assisted suicide and euthanasia?
2. Is palliative sedation ever ethically appropriate for patients who are not imminently dying?

3. Should willingness to forgo life-sustaining treatment be a condition for administering/receiving palliative sedation?
4. Is palliative sedation an ethically appropriate response to "existential" suffering?
5. May palliative sedation be provided to patients who lack decision-making capacity?

1. Is Palliative Sedation Different from Physician-Assisted Suicide and Euthanasia?

Palliative sedation has been widely discussed in the context of debates about physician-assisted suicide and euthanasia.[11,30,31] Indeed, palliative sedation has been proposed as an ethically acceptable alternative to physician aid in dying.[10,11] Yet despite considerable attention to these questions during the past decade, many clinicians remain uncertain or confused about the ethical differences among these practices.[27]

Although debate continues in some quarters, the dominant view in the professional medical and bioethics communities holds that palliative sedation is ethically different from physician-assisted suicide or euthanasia. These analyses focus on intention and proportionality.[8,10,11,31,32] With respect to intention, the primary intention in both physician-assisted suicide and euthanasia is to cause the patient's death; the patient's suffering ends as a result. In contrast, the primary intention in palliative sedation is to relieve the patient's suffering; death occurs as a result of the underlying disease process. (Note that because death occurs as a result of the disease process, palliative sedation shares a critical feature with established ethically accepted practice of forgoing life-sustaining treatment.) Medication is used only in sufficient doses to achieve unconsciousness (not a lethal dose).[10] The limited evidence currently available suggests that deep sedation is unlikely to hasten death.[19,20,33,34] In response to concerns that it is difficult to assess practitioners' intentions objectively,[35] it has been argued that those intentions can be evaluated indirectly in a general way; for example, by observing practitioners' choice and usage of sedating medications.[4]

Proportionality is a second ethically significant factor in distinguishing palliative sedation from physician assisted suicide and euthanasia. In medicine, the principle of proportionality requires that "the risk of causing harm must bear a direct relationship to the danger and immediacy of the patient's clinical situation and the expected benefit of the intervention."[11] Practitioners are permitted to perform, and patients to undergo, treatments and procedures that carry grave risks when there are commensurate benefits to be gained. Think of the example of surgery for a patient who is seriously injured in a car accident: Administering general anesthesia carries a foreseeable risk of death. Yet the good intended—for example, saving the patient's leg or minimizing brain damage—is usually held to be significant enough to justify taking a substantial risk to obtain it. In palliative sedation, although the means—deep, continuous sedation for a dying patient—are grave, they are proportional to the goal to be achieved: relieving severe, unremitting suffering when all other interventions acceptable to the patient have failed.[8,11,15,36,37]

The distinction between palliative sedation and either physician-assisted suicide or euthanasia recognized in the emerging medical and ethical consensus is also supported in case law. In its 1997 decisions in *Vacco v. Quill* and *Washington v. Glucksberg*,[38] 2 cases that dealt with physician-assisted suicide, the US Supreme Court seemed to distinguish palliative sedation from assisted suicide as legally acceptable practice.[21,39] The court did not explicitly address palliative sedation as such, but did indicate strong support for aggressive symptom relief for dying patients, even to the point of rendering the patient unconscious.

> *The Committee concludes that there is a meaningful difference between palliative sedation and physician-assisted suicide or euthanasia.*

2. Is Palliative Sedation Ever Ethically Appropriate for Patients Who Are Not Imminently Dying?

The professional community is also divided about whether palliative sedation is ethically appropriate for a patient who experiences intolerable, irremediable suffering but who is not imminently dying. If palliative sedation is an ethically appropriate response to severe, intractable suffering, the argument goes, why should it be available only to patients who are on the verge of death? To withhold palliative sedation from patients whose symptoms are severe and refractory to aggressive care solely because they are not expected to die very soon, or because their condition makes it extremely difficult to predict likely time to death with any confidence, imposes an arbitrary constraint and condemns these individuals to endure unrelieved suffering for a potentially long period of time.[6,8,30]

We recognize the ethical salience of this position. In our judgment, however, more compelling concerns are raised by the prospect of permitting palliative sedation for a patient who is expected to survive for months or years. Sedating a patient to unconsciousness carries significant risks, and palliative sedation is understood to be literally an intervention of *last* resort at the end of life.

Allowing palliative sedation when the patient can reasonably be expected to live for months (or longer) risks eroding the distinction between palliative sedation and physician-assisted suicide or euthanasia. Sedating such a patient to relieve suffering while respecting his or her right to forgo artificially administered nutrition and hydration or other indicated life-sustaining treatment will directly and predictably shorten the patient's life, a result clearly contrary to the goal of palliative sedation.[40]

Providing palliative sedation to patients who are not imminently dying also raises slippery slope concerns. Palliative sedation is generally considered appropriate only for patients who are terminally ill, but if not at the threshold of imminent death, at what other point in the trajectory of terminal illness can we draw a sufficiently bright line to distinguish when palliative sedation is and when it is not ethically permissible? Moreover, accepting "terminally ill" alone as a sufficient criterion for palliative sedation instead of the more restrictive "imminently dying" may increase the risk that the practice would some day be extended to individuals who are not terminally ill.[41]

Furthermore, intentionally sedating a patient and maintaining continuous deep sedation while providing life-sustaining treatment for an indefinite, but possibly prolonged span poses its own challenges. Such scenarios are likely to be emotionally distressing for the patient's intimates, and indeed, for staff.[42]

A further concern, originally raised in reference to physician-assisted suicide,[43] may also be cogent with respect to palliative sedation for patients who are not imminently dying; that is, that deep sedation will come to be seen as an alternative to providing appropriate palliative care. High-quality palliative care is an essential condition for the ethical practice of palliative sedation.

We recognize that it is not possible to predict with certainty how long a patient will live. Patients with terminal cancer follow a relatively predictable course to death,[44] but even for these patients, physicians' predictions about the timing of death are not very accurate.[45,46] For patients with other types of life-limiting illness, such as end-stage lung or heart disease, prognostication is even more challenging.[44] Ultimately, the determination that a patient has entered the final phase of dying rests not on precise predictions of survival but on well-considered, informed professional judgment, which argues for the involvement of practitioners with appropriate expertise, including palliative care specialists, in decision-making about palliative sedation.

The Committee concludes that it is ethically appropriate to restrict palliative sedation to patients who are imminently dying.

3. Should Willingness to Forgo Life-Sustaining Treatment Be a Condition for Administering and Receiving Palliative Sedation?

Professional consensus about best practice for palliative sedation clearly establishes that patients who do not have a do-not-resuscitate (DNR) order should not be considered appropriate candidates for palliative sedation.[12,15,16,20,22,23,47–49] The Committee believes this is an appropriate standard consistent with the overall goals of palliative sedation. However, debate continues within the medical community about whether it is ethically appropriate to provide other life-sustaining interventions, such as ventilator support, dialysis, or artificially administered nutrition and hydration to patients who receive palliative sedation.[30,31,40,49]

For most patients who are appropriate candidates for palliative sedation, the question of life-sustaining treatment is not likely to arise. These are patients near death, for whom the overriding goal of care is no longer to optimize function or prolong survival but to provide comfort and symptom relief. Most such patients will already have stopped eating and drinking.[19,33] As a practical matter, most patients who are candidates for palliative sedation will have already decided to forgo all life-sustaining interventions. When this is not the case, the decision to forgo life-sustaining treatment should be clearly distinguished from and made independently of the decision to provide palliative sedation.[50]

Some dying patients who are appropriate candidates for palliative sedation will, however, want *both* palliative sedation *and* life-sustaining treatment. For these patients, the goal of care is 2-fold: to relieve suffering *and* to prolong life. Many cultural and religious traditions place high moral value on prolonging life and practitioners have a prima facie obligation to respect these views, an obligation that also resonates with core values of medicine as a profession.

Consensus in the professional community is that candidates for palliative sedation should have a DNR order. However, we find no compelling argument to limit other concurrent life-sustaining interventions, such as artificially administered nutrition and hydration or ventilator support, for patients who receive palliative sedation, so long as those interventions are clinically indicated. To require that a patient consent to forgo *all* life-sustaining treatments as a condition for receiving the only intervention that will relieve the patient's intolerable suffering (ie, palliative sedation) seems to us ethically and professionally insupportable.

We recognize that views are divided on the question. Most members of the Committee would argue that first and foremost, continuing to provide life-sustaining treatment to a patient who receives palliative sedation and who wants life-sustaining treatment(s) other than cardiopulmonary resuscitation upholds the value of respect for patients as moral agents and autonomous decision makers. Some members, however, see it as unnecessarily prolonging dying, a view we realize others may share. We acknowledge that for both family members and health care professionals who hold this latter view, providing life-sustaining treatment concurrent with palliative sedation may create significant distress.

These considerations carry significant implications for decision making about palliative sedation. Practitioners have an obligation to describe as clearly as possible the likely clinical scenarios for a patient who is considering palliative sedation, and should work with patients and families to establish a clear plan of care before sedation is initiated. This should include discussion of what life-sustaining treatments will be withdrawn, continued, or initiated (if clinically indicated) after the patient has been sedated. This will help patients, their surrogates, other family members, and, indeed, the treatment team understand what is expected to happen once the patient has been sedated and better prepare them for the decisions that may need to be made when the patient is no longer conscious.

As potential sources of conflict, diverging views on the question of life-sustaining treatments for patients who receive palliative sedation also highlight the importance of assuring that appropriate mechanisms are in place to assist stakeholders in resolving disagreements if they arise, including ethics consultation.

The Committee concludes that willingness to forgo life-sustaining treatment should not be a condition for the administration of palliative sedation.

4. Is Palliative Sedation Ethically Appropriate when Suffering Is "Existential"?

One of the most deeply contested questions about palliative sedation is whether the practice is ethically appropriate as a response to existential suffering, as distinct from pain or other clinically defined physical or psychiatric symptoms. The debate about existential suffering has evolved around three basic concerns: (1) the difficulty of clearly defining existential suffering and of distinguishing it clinically from treatable psychiatric conditions such as depression; (2) whether relief of existential suffering represents a "proportionate" goal; and (3) whether relief of existential suffering as such is within the goals of medicine, and thus whether providing a pharmacologic intervention for such suffering is appropriate for health care professionals.

Distinguishing existential suffering from psychologic distress. One difficulty is that there is no single, agreed on definition of existential suffering that is sufficiently clear and concrete to offer guidance in clinical contexts. "Making a diagnosis of suffering," it has been argued, "differs from the usual diagnostic process that internists are familiar with because suffering is an affliction of the person, not the body."[51] The suffering experienced by patients near death may reflect concerns about a prolonged dying process, retaining control, the burden their dying imposes on others, and strengthening personal relationships.[51]

It can, moreover, be extremely difficult to draw bright lines among physical, psychologic, and existential suffering.[29,50] Psychologic distress often contributes to pain, dyspnea, and other symptoms, for example, as well as the reverse. Nor is it always easy for practitioners to determine with confidence whether a patient's distress represents a normal, "appropriate" reaction to the prospect of impending death or indicates the presence of a potentially treatable mental health condition.[52] It is even more challenging to assess whether the patient's distress reflects the kind of response to the irremediable losses imposed by illness and assaults to the sense of self that we would call existential suffering.

"Proportionality" and relief of existential suffering. A further concern can be framed as the following question: Is the goal of relieving severe, refractory existential suffering sufficiently grave or "proportionate" to justify sedating the patient into unconsciousness for the time remaining to him or her? Some answer in the affirmative, arguing that existential suffering "can be just as distressful and refractory as physical suffering,"[36] but acknowledge that practitioners may find it difficult to consider palliative sedation when a patient's existential suffering is not associated with significant physiologic deterioration.[29,47] Opponents of palliative sedation for existential suffering argue that permitting practitioners to make necessarily subjective judgments about the

existential well-being of patients risks placing health care professionals and patients on a slippery slope at the bottom of which lies abuse of palliative sedation and danger to patients.[37]

Relief of existential suffering and the goals of medicine. Undeniably, for some patients, suffering at the end of life cannot be attributed solely or primarily to refractory clinical symptoms.[53] But although relieving suffering is one of the core goals of medicine,[51,54] questions have been raised about whether attempting to relieve existential suffering through a specifically clinical intervention, such as palliative sedation, is an appropriate activity for health care professionals.[55] Essentially the same concern has been raised with respect to physician-assisted suicide and euthanasia. As the ACP-ASIM noted in its position statement opposing physician-assisted suicide, "one can raise serious questions about whether medicine should arrogate to itself the task of alleviating all human suffering, even at the end of life."[56]

Despite these concerns, there is some degree of support for palliative sedation in response to existential suffering within the professional hospice and palliative care community in the United States. For example, the Hospice and Palliative Care Federation of Massachusetts has provided guidelines for providers, although it has not formally endorsed palliative sedation,[49] and the National Hospice and Palliative Care Organization has cautiously supported the practice in principle.[6]

These are challenging issues on which the Committee finds that as individuals we do not share a uniform perspective. This lack of consensus within the Committee itself recommends to us the wisdom of taking a conservative stance with respect to palliative sedation for existential suffering. Further, in our view, VA's mission and its unique patient population create a special risk that permitting VA practitioners to offer palliative sedation when the patient's suffering cannot be defined in reference to clinical criteria could erode public trust in the agency; therefore, as a committee, we do not endorse this practice. We acknowledge that restricting the availability of palliative sedation in this way may fail to address the needs of some patients whose suffering cannot be relieved by other means. We commend the commitment of health care professionals and other staff throughout VHA to provide open, empathic support even as clinical interventions fall short of alleviating the individual's suffering. We find the conclusion reached by the ACP-ASIM in its position paper on physician-assisted suicide cogent in our context:

> [W]hen the patient's suffering is interpersonal, existential, or spiritual, the tasks of the physician are to remain present, to "suffer with" the patient in compassion, and to enlist the support of clergy, social workers, family, and friends in healing the aspects of suffering that are beyond the legitimate scope of medical care.[56]

> *The Committee concludes that palliative sedation should not be used to treat existential suffering in the absence of severe, refractory clinical symptoms.*

5. May Palliative Sedation Be Provided to Patients Who Lack Decision-Making Capacity?

Because the decision to sedate a patient to unconsciousness and maintain that state until he or she dies is a serious one, some might argue that palliative sedation should be considered only for patients who can consent to it themselves. However, confining palliative sedation to patients who have decision-making capacity risks excluding many patients whose suffering cannot be relieved by other means for whom surrogates are empowered to make all other treatment decisions. Indeed, many patients for whom palliative sedation would be considered will already have lost the capacity to participate in shared decision making because of the progression of their underlying condition, the effects of treatment, or unmanageable symptoms. To deny a patient's surrogate the possibility of consenting to palliative sedation undermines the surrogate's role in shared decision making and in effect undermines the patient's right to choose this intervention.

> *The Committee concludes that palliative sedation may be provided to patients who lack decision-making capacity with the informed consent of the authorized surrogate decision-maker.*

Conditions for Ethically Sound Practice

At various points throughout the foregoing discussion we have noted the important role in palliative sedation of professionals from multiple disciplines. We have also stressed that providing high quality palliative care is a prerequisite to decisions about palliative sedation. These fundamental conditions for ethically appropriate practice of palliative sedation are well recognized in the professional community.[11,12,15,19,22,23,47,48] Consultation with practitioners expert in pain and symptom management is essential to assure that a patient's symptoms truly are refractory before palliative sedation is considered,[11,12,15,22,23,48] and to initiate and monitor sedation.[12] Likewise patients must be assured access to expert psychologic and spiritual assessment and support.[11,15,23,47,48,57]

The decision to sedate a dying patient to unconsciousness for the duration of his or her life should be made only after careful clinical evaluation and thoughtful deliberation, and must be implemented with appropriate monitoring and supervision.

Recommendations

Although debate continues about how broadly to define the range of circumstances in which palliative sedation is appropriate, the emerging professional and ethical consensus is clear: Palliative sedation is an ethically appropriate therapy of last resort for patients who are experiencing severe, unremitting, refractory clinical symptoms at the end of life. The National Ethics Committee therefore recommends that VA adopt policy that:

1. Permits the administration of palliative sedation (by definition, as a last resort) only:
    a) when severe pain or other clinical symptoms (e.g., dyspnea, nausea and vomiting, agitated delirium) is/are not ameliorated by aggressive symptom-specific interventions that are tolerable to the patient;
    b) for patients who have entered the final stages of the dying process and who have a DNR order;
    c) with the signed informed consent of the patient, or surrogate if the patient lacks decision-making capacity, as required by VA policy for treatments or procedures involving general anesthesia.[58]

2. Establishes safeguards to protect patients' interests and assure consistent, high quality care by:
    a) providing for consultation with experts in palliative medicine, psychiatry or clinical psychology, and spiritual care as appropriate in the decision-making process;
    b) clarifying with the patient and/or surrogate the plan of care regarding:
        i. concurrent life-sustaining treatment (including, but not limited to, artificially administered nutrition and hydration),
        ii. regular assessment of the patient's clinical status and ongoing eligibility for palliative sedation, and
        iii. health care professionals' obligation to discontinue deep sedation in the event the patient's status improves;
    c) assuring the participation of a health care professional with appropriate expertise in palliative care and the administration of palliative sedation;
    d) assuring that the patient continues to receive appropriate care and hygiene;
    e) monitoring sedation to assure adequate and continuous unconsciousness while avoiding inappropriate or unnecessary untoward drug effects;
    f) documenting the rationale for palliative sedation and the informed consent conversation appropriately in the patient's health record; and
    g) establishing clear procedures for resolving disagreements about treatment plans or specific treatment decisions, including ethics consultation when appropriate.

References

1. National Consensus Project for Quality Palliative Care. *Clinical Practice Guidelines for Quality Palliative Care*, 2004. Available at www.nationalconsensusproject.org. Accessed December 3, 2004.

2. Chiu TY, Hu WY, Lue BH, Cheng SY, Chen CY. Sedation for refractory symptoms of terminal cancer patients in Taiwan. *J Pain Symptom Manage.* 2001;21:467–472.

3. Morita T, Tsuneto S, Shima Y. Definition of sedation for symptom relief: a systematic literature review and a proposal of operational criteria. *J Pain Symptom Manage.* 2002;24:447–453.

4. Morita T, Chinone Y, Ikenaga M, et al, for the Japan Pain, Palliative Medicine, Rehabilitation, and Psycho-Oncology Study Group. Ethical validity of palliative sedation therapy: A multicenter, prospective, observational study conducted on specialized palliative care units in Japan. *J Pain Symptom Manage.* 2005;30:308–319.

5. Kaldjian LC, Jekel JF, Bernene JL, Rosenthal GE, Vaughan-Sarrazin M, Duffy TP. Internists' attitudes towards terminal sedation in end of life care. *J Med Ethics.* 2004;30:499–503.

6. National Hospice and Palliative Care Organization. *Total Sedation: A Hospice and Palliative Care Resource Guide.* Alexandria, VA: NHPCO; 2000.

7. American Academy of Hospice and Palliative Medicine. *Statement on Sedation at the End-of-Life.* American Academy of Hospice and Palliative Medicine, September 13, 2002. Available at www.aahpm.org/positions/sedation.html. Accessed August 30, 2005.

8. Quill TE, Byock IR, for the ACP-ASIM End-of-Life Care Consensus Panel. Responding to intractable terminal suffering: the role of terminal sedation and voluntary refusal of food and fluids. *Ann Intern Med.* 2000;132: 408–414.

9. American Medical Association. Brief of the American Medical Association, the American Nurses Association, and the American Psychiatric Association, et al. as *Amici Curiae* in Support of Petitioners. *Vacco v. Quill et al.* (US S. Ct. No. 95-1858 November 12, 1996).

10. Quill TE, Coombs Lee B, Nunn S. Palliative treatments of last resort: choosing the least harmful alternative. *Ann Intern Med.* 2000;132:488–493.

11. Quill TE, Lo B, Brock DW. Palliative options of last resort: a comparison of voluntarily stopping eating and drinking, terminal sedation, physician-assisted suicide, and voluntary active euthanasia [health law and ethics]. *JAMA.* 1997;278:2099–2104.

12. Braun TC, Hagen NA, Clark T. Development of a clinical practice guideline for palliative sedation. *J Palliat Med.* 2003;6:345–350.

13. Muller-Busch HC, Andres I, Jehser T. Sedation in palliative care—a critical analysis of 7 years experience. *BMC Palliat Care.* 2003;2. Available at www.biomedcentral.com/1472-584X2/2. Accessed August 30, 2005.

14. Taylor RM. Is terminal sedation really euthanasia? *Med Ethics (Burlingt, Mass).* 2003;10:3, 8.

15. Cherny NI, Portenoy RK. Sedation in the management of refractory symptoms: guidelines for evaluation and treatment. *J Palliat Care.* 1994;10:31–38.

16. Hospice and Palliative Nurses Association. *Palliative Sedation at End of Life.* Hospice and Palliative Nurses Association, June 2003. Available at www.hpna.org/pdf/Palliative_Sedation_Position_Statement_PDF.pdf. Accessed August 30, 2005.

17. Rousseau P. Palliative sedation [guest editorial]. *Am J Hosp Palliat Care.* 2002;19:295–297.

18. Goldstein-Shirley J, Jennings B, Rosen E. Total sedation in hospice and palliative care. Unpublished discussion paper prepared for the Ethics Committee of the National Hospice Association, November 23, 1999.

19. Hallenbeck JL. Terminal sedation for intractable distress: not slow euthanasia but a prompt response to suffering. *West J Med.* 1999;171:222–223.

20. Cowan JD, Palmer TW. Practical guide to palliative sedation. *Curr Oncol Rep.* 2002;4:242–249.

21. Burt RA. The Supreme Court speaks—not assisted suicide but a constitutional right to palliative care. *N Engl J Med.* 1997;337:1234–1236.

22. Schuman Z, Lynch M, Abrahm JL. Implementing institutional change: an institutional case study of palliative sedation. *J Palliat Med.* 2005;8:666–676.

23. Salacz M, Weissman DE. *Fast Fact and Concept #106: Controlled Sedation for Refractory Suffering—Part I.* End-of-Life Physician Education Resource Center, 2004. Available at www.eperc.mcw.edu. Accessed January 27, 2005.

24. Greene WR, Davis WH. Titrated intravenous barbiturates in the control of symptoms in patients with terminal cancer. *South Med J.* 1991;84:332–7.

25. Fainsinger RL, Waller A, Bercovici M, et al. A multicentre international study of sedation for uncontrolled symptoms in terminally ill patients. *Palliative Med.* 2000;14: 257–265.

26. Kohara H, Ueoka H, Takeyama H, et al. Sedation for terminally ill patients with cancer with uncontrollable physical distress. *J Palliat Med.* 2005;8:20–25.

27. Lo B, Rubenfeld G. Palliative sedation in dying patients: "We turn to it when everything else hasn't worked" [Perspectives on care at the close of life]. *JAMA.* 2005;294:1810–16.

28. Rousseau P. Palliative sedation and sleeping before death: a need for clinical guidelines? *J Palliat Med.* 2003;6:425–427.

29. Cherny NI. Commentary: sedation in response to refractory existential distress: walking the fine line. *J Pain Symptom Manage.* 1998;16:404–406.

30. Billings JA, Block SD. Slow euthanasia. *J Palliat Care.* 1996;12:21–30.

31. Kingsbury RJ, Ducharme HM. The debate over total/terminal/palliative sedation. The Center for Bioethics and Human Dignity, January 24, 2002. Available at www.cbhd.org/resources/endoflife/kinsbury-ducharme_2002-01-24.htm. Accessed September 26, 2005.

32. Sulmasy DP, Pellegrino ED. The rule of double effect: clearing up the double talk. *Arch Intern Med.* 1999;159:545–549.

33. Lynn J. Terminal sedation [letter to the editor]. *New Engl J Med.* 1998;338:1230.

34. Sykes N, Thorn A. Sedative use in the last week of life and the implications for end-of-life decision making. *Arch Intern Med.* 2003;163:341–344.

35. Quill TE, Dresser R, Brock DW. The rule of double effect—a critique of its role in end-of-life decision making [sounding board]. *N Engl J Med.* 1997;337:1764–1771.

36. Rousseau P. The ethical validity and clinical experience of palliative sedation. *Mayo Clin Proc.* 2000;75:1064–1069.

37. Jansen LA, Sulmasy DP. Sedation, alimentation, hydration, and equivocation: careful conversation about care at the end of life. *Ann Intern Med.* 2002;136:845–849.

38. Vacco v. Quill, 521 U.S. 793 (1997); Washington v. Glucksberg, 521 US 702 (1997).

39. Terminal sedation vs PAS: difference just semantics? *Med Ethics Advis.* 2005;8:91–93.

40. Gillick MR. Terminal sedation: an acceptable exit strategy? *Ann Intern Med.* 2004;141:236–237.

41. Sheldon T. Dutch euthanasia law should apply to patients "suffering through living," report says. *BMJ.* 2005;330:61.

42. Morita T, Ikenaga M, Adachi I, et al; Japan Pain, Rehabilitation, Palliative Medicine, and Psycho-Oncology Study Group. Family experience with palliative sedation therapy for terminally ill cancer patients. *J Pain Symptom Manage.* 2004 28:557–565.

43. Foley KM. Competent care for the dying instead of physician-assisted suicide [editorial]. *N Engl J Med.* 1997;336:53–58.

44. Lunney JR, Lynn J, Foley DJ, Lipson S, Guralnik JM. Patterns of functional decline at the end of life. *JAMA.* 2003;289:2387–2392.

45. Glare P, Virik K, Jones M, et al. A systematic review of physicians' survival predictions in terminally ill cancer patients. *BMJ.* 2003;327:195–200.

46. Lamont EB, Christakis NA. Complexities in prognostication in advanced cancer: "to help them live their lives the way they want to" [Perspectives on care at the close of life]. *JAMA.* 2003;290:98–104.

47. Rousseau P. Existential suffering and palliative sedation: a brief commentary with a proposal for clinical guidelines. *Am J Hosp Palliat Care.* 2001;18:151–53.

48. Salacz ME, Weissman DE. *Fast Fact and Concept #107: Controlled Sedation for Refractory Suffering—Part II.* End-of-Life Physician Education Resource Center, 2004. Available at www.eperc.mcw.edu. Accessed January 27, 2005.

49. Hospice and Palliative Care Federation of Massachusetts. *Palliative Sedation Protocol: A Report of the Standards and Best Practices Committee.* Norwood, MA: Hospice and Palliative Care Federation of Massachusetts; 2004. Available at www.hospicefed.org/hospice_pages/reports/pal_sed_protocol.pdf. Accessed August 30, 2005.

49. Orentilecher D. The Supreme Court and physician-assisted suicide-rejecting assisted suicide but embracing euthanasia. *N Engl J Med.* 1997;337:1236–39.

50. Hallenbeck JL. Terminal sedation: ethical implications in different situations. *J Palliat Med.* 2000;3:313–320.

51. Cassell EJ. Diagnosing suffering: a perspective. *Ann Intern Med.* 1999;131:531–534.

52. Block SD. Assessing and managing depression in the terminally ill patient. *Ann Intern Med.* 2000;132:210–218.

53. Morita T, Tsunoda J, Inoue S, Chihara S. Terminal sedation for existential distress. *Am J Hosp Palliat Care.* 2000;17:189–195.

54. Jonsen AR, Siegler M, Winslade WJ. *Clinical Ethics.* 2nd ed. New York, NY: Macmillan Publishing Co; 1986.

55. Callahan D. When self-determination runs amok. *Hastings Center Rep.* 1992;22:52–55.

56. Snyder L, Sulmasy DP, for the Ethics and Human Rights Committee, ACP-ASIM. Physician-assisted suicide [position paper]. *Ann Intern Med.* 2001;135:209–216.

57. Block SD. Psychological considerations, growth, and transcendence at the end of life: the art of the possible. *JAMA.* 2001;285:2898–2905.

58. U.S. Department of Veterans Affairs. VHA Handbook 1004.1: *Informed Consent for Clinical Treatments and Procedures.* January 2003.

EXPLORING THE ISSUE

Is Palliative Sedation Actually Euthanasia in Disguise?

Critical Thinking and Reflection

1. Can you name or cite a case of palliative sedation that to you seems a clear case of actual "euthanasia" that was "disguised"? Which safeguard is best/worst in response to this nondisclosure (capacity, consent, last resort, etc.)? Should this be a matter of ethics, professional monitoring, public policy, criminal or civil law?
2. Consider the situation of your elderly grandfather whose death from cancer is imminent and is in hospice treatment. He has decisional capacity. He does not live in Oregon, Washington, or Montana; he wants to say goodbye and be sedated "into oblivion." What do you discuss with him about his memories, expectations, hopes, and choices?
3. Your gifted and distinguished elderly aunt is terminally ill and is in hospice care with new friends. She was an accomplished nurse-educator. She has a DNR but wants to continue ANH and ventilator support in addition to receiving palliative sedation. What do you ask her to share about her goals at the end of life?
4. A young student who has been living with HIV for years is especially distressed at its transition to AIDS amidst a family breakup; assistance is sought for termination owing to "existential" suffering about a grim demise. What advice do you offer?
5. Retired parents were caregivers for decades of a Downs-syndrome adult daughter Martha; they ask your advice. They brought Martha home for care for end stage cancer hospice care; they must decide for palliative sedation for Martha who is not decisionally capable.

Is There Common Ground?

> To die, to sleep—
> To sleep—perchance to dream. Ay, there's the rub!
> (William Shakespeare, *Hamlet* III, I, 65–68)

> . . . a person doesn't die when he should but when he can.
> (. . . *uno no se muere cuando debe sino cuando puede.*)
> (Gabriel García Márquez, 1967, 100, 2006, 241)

Euthanasia has always had *advocates*, but its eugenic forms and scale became culturally sinister in the nineteenth and especially twentieth centuries. In the midst of genocide, organized criminal state policies of National Socialist eugenic euthanasia selected and murdered tens of thousands of persons for "life unworthy of life" (*Lebensunwertes Leben*). Many defeated in war committed mass suicides (Lifton, 2000; Faulstich, 2000; Battin, 1994, 2005; Walters, 2007; Goeschel, 2009; Black, 2010). Some attack certain PS practices but none are defended based on these memories; current debates are about end-of-life decisions that are voluntary—albeit debatably influenced.

There is near unanimous *consensus* about who decides about palliative sedation—the patient or valid proxy (National Ethics Committee, 2007; Battin, 2008)—which medications are lethal, and that a patient should be terminal (6 months in the United States, 1 year in the United Kingdom). There is practical consensus about side effects of specific medications (sedation and lethal risks), and emerging consensus about how to best diagnose end life symptoms (e.g., Edmonton Symptoms Assessment Scale [ESAS]), that a patient's symptoms should warrant PS, and the importance of consultation and monitoring (National Ethics Committee, 2007; American Medical Association Council on Ethical and Judicial Affairs, 2008).

Proponents lump or equate "palliative sedation" with "continuous deep sedation," "primary deep continuous sedation" (Battin, 2008), "total sedation," "controlled sedation," and "sedation for intractable distress in the dying" (Rady & Verheijde, 2010). Some proponents argue voluntary terminal sedation is compatible with good nursing or clinical practice at the end of life (Woods, 2004; Tännsjö, 2004; Quill & Greenlaw, 2008, Quill et al., 2009). *Proponents and opponents* agree that *"disguised" practices* of terminal sedation are in fact euthanasia that risks being back-alley, un(der)regulated, and underreported; nondisclosed practices remain contested on different grounds. Are patients and caregivers adequately involved? What professional standards are observed? What kind of legal accountability exists (criminal, civil due care)? Practices of terminal sedation should be either *restricted* where life is intentionally taken against the sanctity of life (Gormally), or be *granted very limited permissions* based on informed consent (Kuhse), rights-based voluntary autonomy (Brock), or caregiver paternalism with due care (van Delden, all in Tännsjö, 2004). Furthermore, some who misinterpret terminal sedation as *maltreatment* actually poorly understand contested boundaries of palliative *mistreatments* (Battin, 2008). *Opponents* charge that such "continuous deep sedation" or "slow euthanasia" is sedation to death; they tend to be *splitters* who claim that clinicians intend to assist dying by comforting patients ("palliate") using therapies with side effects ("sedation")—sometimes with foreseen but *unintended* lethal consequences (Sulmasy & Pellegrino, 1999; Loewy, 2001; Matersveldt, 2009; Rady & Verheijde, 2010; Claessens et al., 2011). Some claim terminal sedation either cannot or should not be a regulated practice (Eckerdal and Callahan in Tännsjö, 2004).

Hence *proponents of terminal sedation avoid* the category "suicide," because it suggests mental instability (DSM IV, Durkheim); proponents likewise either avoid "euthanasia," because it suggests state-sponsored criminal murder, or rename euthanasia as a defensible practice under certain conditions (Singer, 2010). Palliative sedation and safeguarded lethal self-administration require patient consent. *Opponents counter* that historically "suicide" and "euthanasia" have remained *negative risks*. Those who choose self-termination—and some who seek palliative sedation for those who are not dying but have intolerable suffering—feature under-referrals for effective palliation or counseling. Hence, argue opponents, the lack of screening for psychiatric comorbid depression can encourage dysfunctional self-killing historically called suicide in psychological or sociological senses (DSM IV, Durkheim). Second, opponents claim that state practices, which "permit" by "safeguarding" and "regulating" self-termination, end up effectively normalizing assisted death (euthanasia). In a health care system controlled by fees, paying clients, and beneficiaries, a legal option to end a life of complex dying places a cultural burden on dying to perceive themselves as burdensome to caregivers. The question is not will others directly kill me, rather—given legal options and cultural presumptions of self-control—why don't I control the timing and manner of my own death events with assisted help? *Proponents* counter that such "slippery slope" concerns are real, but empirical research shows them to be minimal (Battin, 2005, 2008; Hendin & Foley, 2008; Lindsay, 2009, Issue 13).

Additional Resources

American Board of Medical Specialties. (2006). *ABMS establishes new subspecialty certificate in hospice and palliative medicine.* ABMS Guide to Physician Specialties.

American Medical Association Council on Ethical and Judicial Affairs. (2008). Report, CEJA Report 5-A-08. "Sedation to Unconsciousness in End-of-Life Care."

Ball, S. C. (2006). Nurse-patient advocacy and the right to die. *Journal of Psychosocial Nursing, 44*(12), 36–46.

Battin, M. (2000). Global life expectancies and the duty to dies. In: J. Humber & R. Almeder (Eds.) *Is there a duty to die.* Totawa, NJ: Humana Press.

Battin, M. (2005). *Ending life: Ethics and the way we die.* New York: Oxford University Press.

Battin, M. (2008). Physician assisted dying and the slippery slope: The challenge of empirical evidence. *Willamette Law Review, 45,* 91.

Battin M. P. (1994). *The least worst death: Essays in bioethics on the end of life.* New York: Oxford University Press.

Battin, M. P. (2008). Terminal sedation: Pulling the sheet over our eyes. *Hastings Center Report, 38*(5), 27–30.

Battin M. P., van der Heide, A., Ganzini, L., van der Wal, G. & Onwuteaka-Philipsen, B. D. (2007). Legal physician-assisted dying in Oregon and the Netherlands: Evidence concerning the impact on patients in "vulnerable" groups. *Journal of Medical Ethics, 37*(3), 171–174.

Baxter v. Montana. (2009). Related legal documents and friend of the court amicus briefs. Retrieved from www.compassionandchoices.org/sslpage.aspx?pid=416

Beauchamp, T. L. & Childress, J. F. (2001). *Principles of biomedical ethics.* Oxford: Oxford University Press.

Berger, J. (2010). Re-thinking guidelines for the use of palliative sedation. *Hastings Center Report, 40*(3), 33–38.

Berry, Z. (2009). Responding to suffering: Providing options and respecting choice. *Journal of Pain and Symptom Management, 38*(3), 797–800.

Black, M. (2010). *Death in Berlin: From Weimar to divided German.* Cambridge: Cambridge University Press.

Breitbart, W. S., Rosenfeld, B., Pessin, H, Kaim, M., Funesti-Esch, J., & Galietta, M., et al. (2000). Depression, hopelessness, and desire for hastened death in terminally ill patients with cancer. *Journal of the American Medical Association, 284,* 2907–2911.

Buckley, W. J., Daniel, P. S., Mackler, A., & Sachedina, A. (2012, February). Ethics of palliative sedation and medical disasters: Four traditions advance public consensus on three issues. *Ethics and Medicine: An International Journal of Bioethics, 28*(1), 35–63.

Buiting, H., van Delden, J., Onwuteaka-Philpsen, B., Rietjens, J., van Tol, D., Gevers, J., et al. (2009). Reporting of euthanasia and physician-assisted suicide in the Netherlands: Descriptive study. *BMC Medical Ethics, 10,* 18. doi: 10.1186/1472-6939-10-18.

Byock, I. (1998). *Dying well: Peace and possibilities at the end of life.* New York City: Penguin-Riverhead Trade.

Callahan, D. (2008). Organized obfuscation: Advocacy for physician assisted suicide. *Hastings Center Report, 38*(5), 30–32.

Campbell, C. (2008). Ten years of death with dignity. *The New Atlantis, 22,* 33–46.

Cellarius, V. (2008). Terminal sedation and the "imminence condition." *Journal of Medical Ethics*, 2008, 34, 69–72.

Cellarius, V. & Henry, B. (2010, March 2). Justifying different levels of palliative sedation. *Annals of Internal Medicine, 152,* 332.

Cherny, N. I. & Portenoy, R. K. (1994). Sedation in the management of refractory symptoms: Guidelines for evaluation and treatment. *Journal of Palliative Care, 10,* 31–38.

Claessens, P., Genbrugge, E, Vannuffelen, R., Broeckaert, B, Schotsmans, P., & Menten, J. (2007). Palliative sedation and nursing the place of palliative sedation within palliative nursing care. *Journal of Hospice and Palliative Nursing, 9*(2), 100–106.

Claessens, P., Menten, J., Schotsmans, P., & Broeckaert, B. (2011). Palliative sedation, not slow euthanasia: A prospective, longitudinal study of sedation in flemish palliative care units. *Journal of Pain and Symptom Management, 41*(1), 14–24.

Coyle, N. & Sculco, L. (2004). Expressed desire for hastened death in seven patients living with advanced cancer: A phenomenologic inquiry. *Oncology Nursing Forum, 31*(4), 699–709.

Dahl, E. & Levy, N. (2006). The case for physician assisted suicide: How can it possibly be proved? *Journal of Medical Ethics, 32,* 335–338.

Daube, D. (1972). The linguistics of suicide. *Philosophy and Public Affairs, 1*(4), 387–437.

Department of Health and Human Services (DHHS), Public Health Service. (2001).

Dombrowski, D. (2007, Autumn). Personhood and life issues: A Catholic view conscience. Washington, DC: Catholics for Choice.

Dowbiggin, I. (2005). *A concise history of euthanasia: Life, death, god and medicine.* Lanham, MD: Rowan and Littlefield.

Droge, A. J. & Tabor, J. D. (1992). *A noble death: Suicide and martyrdom among Christians and Jews in antiquity.* New York: HarperCollins.

Durkheim, E. (1997 [1897]). *Suicide: A study in sociology.* New York: The Free Press.

Dworkin, R. (1993). *Life's dominion: An argument about abortion, euthanasia, and individual freedom.* New York: Alfred A. Knopf.

Enck, R. E. (1991). Drug-induced terminal sedation for symptom control. *American Journal of Hospic Palliative Care, 8*(5), 3–5.

Farley, M. (1995). Issues in contemporary christian ethics: The choice of death in a medical context. *The Santa Clara Lectures, 1*(3), 1–19.

Faulstich, H. (2000). Die zahl der "uthanasie"-opfer. In: A. Frewer & C. Eickhoff (Eds.), *"Euthanasie" und die aktuelle, sterbehilfe-debatte* (pp. 218–234). Frankfurt: Campus.

Foley, K. & Herbert H. (2002). *The case against assisted suicide and for the right to end of life care.* Baltimore: Johns Hopkins.

Gabriel, G. M. (1967/2006). *Cien años de soledad.* Buenos Aires: Editorial sudamericanos, 1967. *One hundred years of solitude.* New York: Harper.

Ganzini, L., Beer, T. M., Brouns, M., Mori, M., Hsieh, Y. C. (2006). Interest in physician-assisted suicide among Oregon cancer patients. *Journal of Clinical Ethics, 17*(1), 27–38.

Ganzini, L., Goy, E. R., & Dobscha, S. K. (2009). Oregonians' reasons for requesting physician aid in dying. *Archives of Internal Medicine, 169*(5), 489–492.

Ganzini, L., Goy, E. R., Miller, L. L., T. A. Harvath, T. A., Jackson, A., & Delorit, M. A. (2003). Nurses' experiences with hospice patients who refuse food and fluids to hasten death. *New England Journal of Medicine, 349,* 359–365.

Ganzini, L., Silveira, M. J., & Johnston, W. S. (2002). Predictors and correlates of interest in assisted suicide in the final month of life among ALS patients in Oregon and Washington. *Neurology, 24*(3), 312–317.

German Protestant and Catholic Bishops. (1975–2010). Gemeinsame Texte 17: Sterbebegleitung statt aktiver Sterbehilfe, Eine Textsammlung kirchlicher Erklärungen mit einer Einführung des Vorsitzenden der Deutschen Bischofskonferenz und des Vorsitzenden des Rates der Evangelischen Kirche in Deutschland.

Gillick, M. R. (2004). Terminal sedation: An acceptable exit strategy? *Annals of Internal Medicine, 141*(3), 236–237.

Goedicke, H. (1970). *The report about the dispute of a man with his Ba: Papyrus Berlin 3024.* Baltimore and London: The Johns Hopkins Press.

Goeschel, C. (2009). *Suicide in Nazi Germany.* New York: Oxford University Press.

Grisez, G. (1990). Should nutrition and hydration be provided to permanently unconscious and other mentally disabled persons? *Linacre Quarterly, 57,* 30–43.

Grisez, G. (1997). Is it wrong to wish for death? May a husband consent to stopping feeding his permanently unconscious wife? In: G. Grisez (Ed.), *Difficult moral questions: Way of the lord jesus* (Vol. III). Steubenville, OH: Franciscan Press.

Grogan, E., Thorns, A., Campbell, C., Starke-Toller, C., Oliver, D., Harlow, T. Beattie, R. George, R. (2007, November 8). Are vulnerable groups no more likely to receive physician-assisted dying? *Journal of Medical Ethics.* Retrieved from: http://jme.bmj.com/cgi/eletters/33/10/591.

Gunderman, R. B. (2002). Is suffering the enemy? *Hastings Center Report 32*(2), 40–44.

Gunderson, M. (2004). A Kantian view of suicide and end-of-life treatment. *Journal of Social Philosophy, 35*(2), pp. 277–287.

Hartocollis, A. (2009). *Hard choices for a comfortable death: Sedation. New York Times.*

Hedberg, K. & Susan, T. (2009) Putting Oregon's Death with Dignity Act in perspective: Characteristics of decedents who did not participate. *The Journal of Clinical Ethics, 20*(2), 133–135.

Hedberg, K., Hopkins, D., & Kohn, M. (2003). Five years of legal physician-assisted suicide in Oregon. *New England Journal of Medicine, 348,* 961–964. Correspondence

Hedberg, K., Hopkins, D., Leman, R., & Kohn, M. (2009). The 10-year experience of Oregon's Death with Dignity Act: 1998–2007. *The Journal of Clinical Ethics, 20*(2), 124–132.

Hegel, G. W. F. (2005) [1807]. *Hegel's preface to the phenomenology of spirit, translation and running commentary by Yirmiyahu Yovel.* Princeton: Princeton University Press.

Hendin, H. (1999). Euthanasia consultants or facilitators? Few euthanasia consultants in the Netherlands act as independent evaluators of the patient's situation. *Medical Journal of Australia, 170,* 351–352.

Hendin, H. & Foley, K. (Eds.) (2002). *The case against assisted suicde: For the right to end of life care.* Baltimore: Johns Hopkins.

Hendin, H. & Foley, K. (2008). Physician-assisted suicide in Oregon: A medical perspective. *Issues in Law & Medicine, 24*(2), 121–145.

Hicks, M. H. (2007, October 10). Rapid response to timothy quill editorial, mentally ill given short shrift. *British Medical Journal.* Retrieved from: www.bmj.com/cgi/eletters/335/7621/625#177848.

Hospice and Palliative Nurses Association. (2004). *HPNA position statement.* Providing Opioids at the End of Life. Pittsburgh, PA: National Office. Retrieved from: www.hpna.org/DisplayPage.aspx?Title=Position.

Hotopf, M., Lee, W., & Price, A. (2011). Assisted suicide: Why psychiatrists should engage in the debate. *The British Journal of Psychiatry, 198,* 83–84.

Hudson, P. L., Kristjanson, L. J., Ashby, M., Kelly, B., Schofield, P., Hudson, R., et al. (2006). Desire for hastened death in patients with advanced disease and the evidence base of clinical guidelines: A systematic review. *Palliative Medicine 20*(7), 693–701.

Hume, D. ([1756], 2001). *Four dissertations and essays on suicide and the immortality of the soul.* Chicago, IL: St. Augustine's Press.

Jacobs, S. (2003). Behind the research: Death by voluntary dehydration: What the caregivers say. *New England Journal of Medicine, 349,* 325–326.

Jansen, L. (2004). No safe harbor: The principle of complicity and the practice of voluntary stopping of eating and drinking. *Journal of Medicine and Philosophy, 29*(1), 61–74.

Kass, L. R. (1989, Winter). Neither for love nor money: Why doctors must not kill. *Public Interest, 94,* 25.

Keenan, J. F. (1993). The function of the principle of double effect. *Theological Studies, 54,* 294–315.

Kelly, B., Burnett, P., Badger, S., Pelusi, D., Varghese, F. T., & Robertson, M. (2003). Doctors and their patients: A context for understanding the wish to hasten death. *Psychooncology, 12*(4), 375–384.

Kon, A. A. (2011, June). Palliative sedation: It's not a panacea. *American Journal of Bioethics, 11*(6), 41–42.

Levy, M. H. & Cohen, S. D. (2005). Sedation for the relief of refractory symptoms in the imminently dying: A fine intentional line. *Seminars in Oncology, 32,* 237–246.

Lewey, G. (2010). *Assisted death in Europe and America: Four regimes and their lessons.* New York, NY: Oxford University Press.

Lieberman, E. J. (2006, August 4). Letter to the editor, death with dignity. *Psychiatric News, 41*(15): 29.

Lifton, R. J. (1986, 2000). *The Nazi doctors: Medical killing and the psychology of genocide.* New York: Basic Books.

Lindsay, R. A. (2009). Oregon's experience: Evaluating the record. *The American Journal of Bioethics, 9*(3), 19–27.

Loewy, E. H. (2001). Terminal sedation, self-starvation and orchestrating the end of life. *Archives of Internal Medicine, 161,* 329–332.

Lynn, J. (2004). *Sick to death and not going to take it anymore!: Reforming health care for the last years of life.* Berkeley: University of California Press.

Matersveldt, L. J. (2009). Deep and continuous palliative sedation (terminal sedation): Clinical-ethical and philosophical aspects. *Lancet Oncology, 10,* 622–627.

Meier, C., Emmons, C.-A., Litke, A., Wallenstein, S., & Morrison, R. S. (2003). Characteristics of patients requesting and receiving physician-assisted death. *Archives of Internal Medicine, 163,* 1537–1542.

Mitchell, J. B. (2007). *Understanding assisted suicide: Nine issues to consider.* Ann Arbor, MI: University of Michigan.

Morita, T., Tsunoda, J., Inoue, S., & Chihara, S. (2000). Terminal sedation for existential distress. *American Journal of Hospice and Palliative Care, 17*(3), 189–195.

Mueller, D. (1973). Review of Goedicke, H. (1970). The report about the dispute of a man with his Ba: Papyrus Berlin 3024. *Journal of Near Eastern Studies, 32*(3), 353–354.

Muller, D. (2011). Attention to language in a request for physician aid in dying. *The American Journal of Hospice Palliative Care, 28,* 63–64.

Myrtal, G. & Stern, T. A. (2006). The desire for death in the setting of terminal illness. *Journal of Clinical Psychiatry, 8*(5), 299–305.

National Ethics Committee, Veterans Health Administration. (2007). Ethics of palliative sedation as a therapy of last resort. *American Journal of Hospic Palliative Care, 23*(6), 483–491.

National Public Radio. (1997). Critique of the double effect with Dr. Timothy Quill and Dr. Daniel Sulmasy. Retrieved from www.npr.org/programs/ death/971211.death.html. Accessed on July 12, 1997.

Netherlands Law. (2002). Wet toetsing levensbeëindiging op verzoek en hulp bij zelfdoding (Termination of Life on Request and Assisted Suicide Law) See "uitzichtloos en ondraaglijk lijden van de patiënt" ("the unbearable and hopeless suffering of the patient") Retrieved from: www.nvve.nl/nvve2/pagina .asp?pagkey=71892#staatsblad

Novak, D. (1975). *Suicide and morality: The theories of Plato, Aquinas and Kant and their relevance for suicidology.* Scholars Studies Press.

Olsen, M., Swetz, K. M., & Mueller, P. S. (2010). Ethical decision making with end-of-life care: Palliative sedation and withholding or withdrawing life-sustaining treatments. *Mayo Clinic Proceedings, 85*(10), 949–954.

Oregon Death with Dignity Act ORS 127.800 ff. Retrieved from: http://public.health .oregon.gov/ProviderPartnerResources/EvaluationResearch/DeathwithDignityAct/ Pages/index.aspx

Orfali, R. (2011). *Death with dignity: The case for legalizing physician-assisted dying and euthanasia.* Minneapolis, MN: Mill City Press.

Pellegrino, E. D. (1992, Summer). Why doctors must not kill. *Journal of Clinical Ethics, 3*(2), 95–102.

Pellegrino, E. D. (2000). Decisions to withdraw life-sustaining treatment: A moral algorithm. *Journal of the American Medical Association, 283*(8), 1065–1067. doi:10.1001/jama.283.8.1065

Pellegrino, E. D. & Sulmasy, D. P. (2003). Medical ethics. In: D. A. Warrell, T. M. Cox, & J. D. Firth (Eds.), *Oxford textbook of medicine.* New York: Oxford University Press.

Pickett, J. (2009). Can legalization improve end of life care? An empirical analysis of the results of the legalization of euthanasia and physician assisted suicide in the Netherlands and Oregon, *Elder Law Journal, 16,* 332.

Quill, T. & Greenlaw, J. (2008). Physician-assisted death. In: M. Crowley (Ed.), *From birth to death and bench to clinic: The Hastings Center bioethics briefing book for journalists, policymakers, and campaigns* (pp. 137–142). Garrison, NY: The Hastings Center.

Quill, T., Lo, B., Brock, D. W., & Meisel, A. (2009). Last-resort options for palliative sedation. *Annals of Internal Medicine, 151*(6), 421–424.

Quill, T., Rebecca Dresser, J. D., & Brock, D. W. (1997). The rule of double effect— a critique of its role in end-of-life decision making. *New England Journal of Medicine, 337,* 1768–1771.

Rady, M. Y. & Verheijde, J. L. (2010). Continuous deep sedation until death: Palliation or physician-assisted death? *American Journal of Hospice Palliative Care, 27*(3), 205–214.

Rietjens, J. A. C., van der Heide, A., Vrakking, A. M., Onwuteaka-Philipsen, B. D., van der Maas, P. J., & van der Wal, G. (2004). Physician reports of terminal sedation without hydration or nutrition for patients nearing death in the Netherlands. *Archives of Internal Medicine, 141,* 178–185.

Risse, G. (1999). *Mending bodes, saving souls: A history of hospitals.* New York, NY: Oxford University Press.

Robinson, J. (2010). Baxter and the return of physician assisted suicide. *Hastings Center Report, 40*(6): 15–17.

Rodriguez Davila, S. L., Vidal, E., Stewart, J. T., & Caserta, M. T. (2010). Management of a request for physician-assisted suicide. *American Journal of Hospice and Palliative Care, 27,* 63–65.

Rousseau, P. (2001). Existential suffering and palliative sedation: A brief commentary with a proposal for clinical guidelines. *American Journal of Hospice and Palliative Care, 18*(3), 151–153.

Russell, J., Williams, M., & Drogan, O. (2010). Sedation for the imminently dying. *Neurology, 74,* 1303–1309.

Sabatino, C. (2007). Advance directives and advance care planning: Legal and policy issues. Retrieved from: http://aspe.hhs.gov/daltcp/reports/2007/adacplpi.htm.

Sandel, M. (2010) *Justice: What's the right thing to do?* New York: Farrar, Straus and Giroux.

Schadenberg, A. (2004). Assisted suicide in Oregon: Lessons learned and unanswered questions. Retrieved from: www.lifenews.com/bio276.html.

Schneiderman, L. J. (2005). Book review of physician-assisted dying: The case for palliative care and patient choice. In: T. E. Quill & M. P. Battin (Eds.), *JAMA 293*(4), 501

Schwartz, J. K. (2007). Death by voluntary dehydration: Suicide or the right to refuse a life-prolonging measure? *Widener Law Review, 17,* 351–361.

Schwartz, J. K. (2009). Stopping eating and drinking. *American Journal of Nursing, 109*(9), 52–61.

Seay, G. (2001). Do physicians have an inviolable duty not to kill? *Journal of Medicine and Philosophy, 26*(1), 75–91.

Simon, R. I., Levenson, J. L., & Shuman, D. W. (2005, June). On sound and unsound mind: The role of suicide in tort and insurance litigation. *Journal of American Academy Psychiatry Law, 33*(2), 176–182.

Singer, P. (1979). *Practical ethics.* Cambridge: Cambridge University Press, 1979; 2nd ed., 1993; 3rd ed, 2011.

Smith, G. P. II (2011). Refractory pain, existential suffering, and palliative care: Releasing an unbearable lightness of being. *Cornell Journal of Law And Public Policy, 20,* 469–532.

Smith, K. A., Goy, E. R., Harvath, T. A., & Ganzini, L. (2011). Quality of death and dying in patients who request physician-assisted death. *Journal of Palliative Medicine, 14*(4), 445–450.

Substance Abuse and Mental Health Services Administration. (2011). Promoting emotional health and preventing suicide: A toolkit for senior living communities. HHS Publication No. SMA 4515, CMHS-NSPL-0197. Rockville, MD: Center for Mental Health Services. Retrieved from: http://store.samhsa.gov/product/SMA10-4515.

Sugarman, J. & Sulmasy, D. (2010). Methods in medical ethics. Washington, DC: Georgetown University Press.

Sulmasy, D. & Pellegrino, E. (1999). Double effect: Clearing up the double talk. *Archives of Internal Medicine, 159,* 545–550.

Sulmasy, D., Curlin, F., Brungardt, G. S., & Cavanaugh, T. (2010, March 2). Justifying different levels of palliative sedation. *Annals of Internal Medicine, 152,* 332–333.

Sulmasy, D. P. & Jansen, L. A. (2002). Sedation, alimentation, hydration, and equivocation: Careful conversation about care at the end of life. *Annals of Internal Medicine. 136*, 845–849.

Sulmasy, D. P., Ury, W. A., Ahronheim, J. C., Siegler, M., Kass, L., Lantos, J., et al. (2000a). Responding to intractable terminal suffering. *Annals of Internal Medicine, 133*, 560–562.

Sulmasy, D. P., Ury, W. A., Ahronheim, J. C., Siegler, M., Kass, L., Lantos, J., et al. (2000b). Palliative treatment of last resort and assisted suicide. *Annals of Internal Medicine, 133*, 562–563.

Tännsjö, T. (Ed.) (2004). *Terminal sedation: euthanasia in disguise? Developments in Hydrobiology*. Berlin: Springer.

Taylor, R. M. (2003). Is terminal sedation really euthanasia? *Medical Ethics, 10*(3), 8.

Thomas, C. (1980). First suicide note? *British Medical Journal, 281*(6235), 284–285 (Later as Discourse of a Man with his Ba, by Wim van den Dungen. Retrieved from: www.sofiatopia.org/maat/ba.htm.

Thomasma, D. (1998). Assisted death and martyrdom Christian. *Bioethics, 4*(2), 122–142.

Tucker, K. (2008). In the laboratory of the states: The progress of Glucksberg's invitation to states to address end-of-life choice. *Michigan Law Review, 106,* 1593–1612.

Tucker, K. (2009). At the very end of life: The emergence of policy supporting aid in dying among mainstream medical and health policy associations. *Harvard Health Policy Review, 10*(1), 45–47.

Tucker, K. & Steele, F. B. (2007). Patient choice at the end of life getting the language right. *The Journal of Legal Medicine, 28,* 305–325.

Tucker, K. L., Harper, M., Spiers, P. A. (2007). The sky is not falling: Disability and aid-in-dying. In: T. H. Lillie & J. L. Werth (Eds.), *End of life issues and persons with disabilities*. Austin, TX: PRO-ED.

Unger, T. (1996). *Living high and letting die*. New York: Oxford.

Uniform Rights of the Terminally Ill Act. (1989). Retrieved from: www.law.upenn.edu/bll/archives/ulc/fnact99/1980s/urtia89.pdf

United States Conference of Catholic Bishops. (2011). To live each day with dignity. Washington, DC: United States Conference of Catholic Bishops. Retrieved from: www.usccb.org/toliveeachday.

Vacco v. Quill, 521 U.S. 793. (1997). Retrieved from: http://supreme.justia.com/us/521/793/case.html

Valente, S. K. (2004). End of life challenges: Honoring autonomy. *Cancer Nursing, 27,* 314–319.

Van Delden, J. J. M. (2007). Terminal sedation: Sources of a restless ethical debate. *Journal of Medical Ethics, 33,* 187–188.

Varghese, F. T., Leigh, R., Turner, M. J., Vamos, M., Kelly, B. J., & Cook, D. (2000, September). Psychiatric issues surrounding assisted suicide & euthanasia among terminally ill patients. In: J. C. Holland & M. Watson (Eds.), *Psychooncology; Proceedings 5th World Congress of Psycho-Oncology* (pp. 3–7). Melbourne, Australia.

Vetter, P. (2008, July 28). "Dying wish" documents death of Dr. Michael Miller with conscious choice to stop eating and drinking. *American Chronicle*. Retrieved from: www.americanchronicle.com/ articles/view/69683.

Walters, L. (2007). Paul Braune confronts the National Socialists' "euthanasia" program. *Walters Holocaust Genocide Studies, 21*, 454–487.

Washington State Catholic Conference. (2006). A guide to making good decisions for the end of life: Living will and durable power of attorney for health care. Seattle, WA: Washington State Catholic Conference. Retrieved from: www.thewscc.org/

Washington State Death with Dignity Act. (2008). RC70.245. Retrieved from: www.doh.wa.gov/dwda/

Washington v. Glucksberg. (1997). 521 U.S. 702 (1997). Retrieved from: http://supreme.justia.com/us/521/702/case.html

Washington v. Glucksberg. (1997). Supreme Court. Retrieved from: http://law2.umkc.edu/faculty/projects/ftrials/conlaw/glucksberg.html

Williams, G. (2001). The principle of double effect and terminal sedation. *Medical Law Review, 9*, 41–53.

Woods, S. Is terminal sedation compatible with good nursing care at the end of life? *International Journal of Palliative Nursing, 10*(5), 244–247.

Online Resources

American Academy of Hospice and Palliative Medicine (AAHPM)

www.aahpm.org/

American Hospice Foundation

www.americanhospice.org/

American Medical Association Council on Ethical and Judicial Affairs (2008), CEJA Report 5-A-08, "Sedation to Unconsciousness in End-of-Life Care."

www.ama-assn.org/ama/pub/physician-resources/medical-ethics/code-medical-ethics/opinion2201.page

American Society of Pain Management Nursing

www.aspmn.org/

American Association of Colleges of Nursing—Peaceful Death: Recommended Competencies and Curricular Guidelines for End-of-Life Nursing Care

www.aacn.nche.edu/faculty/curriculum-guidelines

Cicely Saunders International

www.cicelysaundersfoundation.org/

End-of-Life Nursing Education Consortium (ELNEC) Project

www.aacn.nche.edu/elnec

National Hospice and Palliative Care Organization

www.nhpco.org/templates/1/homepage.cfm

Hospice and Palliative Nurses Association

www.hpna.org/

St. Christopher's Hospice

www.stchristophers.org.uk/

Oregon Death with Dignity Act ORS 127.800 ff

http://public.health.oregon.gov/ProviderPartnerResources/Evaluation Research/DeathwithDignityAct/Pages/index.aspx

Washington State Death with Dignity Act (2008) RC70.245

www.doh.wa.gov/dwda/

Montana (Baxter vs. Montana, 2009) Related Legal Documents and Friend of the Court Amicus Briefs

www.compassionandchoices.org/sslpage.aspx?pid=416

Uniform Rights of the Terminally Ill Act (1989)

www.law.upenn.edu/bll/archives/ulc/fnact99/1980s/urtia89.pdf

National Reference Center for Bioethics Literature

http://bioethics.georgetown.edu/

Bioethics Resources on the Web

http://bioethics.od.nih.gov/

International Association for the Study of Pain: Pain Terms Defined

www.iasp-pain.org/AM/Template.cfm?Section=Pain_Defi...isplay .cfm&ContentID=1728

Internet References . . .

American Medical Association Council on Ethical and Judicial Affairs

www.ama-assn.org/ama/pub/about-ama/our-people/ama-councils/
council-ethical-judicial-affairs.page

Presidential Commission for the Study of Bioethical Issues

http://bioethics.gov/

President's Commission on Bioethics—Controversies in the Determination of Death

http://bioethics.georgetown.edu/pcbe/reports/death/Controversies_in_the_
Determination_of_Death_for_the_web_(2).pdf

Uniform Determination of Death Act

http://people.bu.edu/wwildman/WeirdWildWeb/courses/thth/projects/thth_
projects_2003_lewis/udda.pdf

"Wither Thou Goes" from *The Doctor Stories* by Richard Selzer

Manucci, M. (2008). *The Moment of Death* (DVD, Documentary). National Geographic.

http://bioethics.georgetown.edu/pcbe/background/selzer.html

Determining Definitions
of Death

*T*his unit identifies concerns about how we define death. Before the advent of respirators and technology that can sustain a physical body for great lengths of time, death was declared when the patient had no pulse or respirations. Defining death became much more complicated when machines were able to make a body "look like" it was alive, but the personhood within that body had died. The essays explain the different definitions for death that are acceptable in different states or countries. There are criteria for death, physical exam findings, that also vary from hospital to hospital. In addition, the interpretation of the findings of specific tests to determine death is not standardized in this country. Conflicting information is confusing for family members and loved ones who want to make the right decision about discontinuing technology. The very use of the term "life support" is confusing when the patient already meets the criteria for death.

- Is Brain Death Dead Enough?

ISSUE 13

Is Brain Death Dead Enough?

YES: Eun-Kyoung Choi, Valita Fredland, Carla Zachodni, J. Eugene Lammers, Patricia Bledsoe, and Paul R. Helft, from "Brain Death Revisited: The Case for a National Standard," *Journal of Law, Medicine & Ethics* (vol. 36, no. 4, pp. 824–836, 2008)

NO: Kristin Zeiler, from "Deadly Pluralism? Why Death-Concept, Death-Definition, Death-Criterion and Death-Test Pluralism Should Be Allowed, Even Though It Creates Some Problems," *Bioethics* (vol. 23, no. 8, pp. 450–459, 2009)

Learning Outcomes

After reading this issue, you should be able to:

- Gain an understanding of importance of a clear definition of when someone is dead.
- Distinguish between the *definition* of death, the *operational criteria* for death, and *tests for* death.
- Discuss the Uniform Determination of Death Act and whether this should be revised to include broader definitions of death.
- Describe the meaning of "death-test pluralism" in everyday language.
- Identify and debate which vulnerable populations would be harmed by definitions of death that are too broad or vague.

ISSUE SUMMARY

YES: Eun-Kyoung Choi and colleagues at the Charles Warren Fairbanks Center for Medical Ethics in Indianapolis review the current definitions and call for national standard for brain death that would eliminate uncertainty across hospitals, states, and jurisdictions.

NO: Kristin Zeiler, a medical ethicist, argues that the definitions of whole brain death as the irreversible cessation of "all" functions of the brain is limiting, because it doesn't embrace other biological possibilities of death. She discusses the need to link death definitions with operational criteria and the specific tests that can measure those criteria when someone has died.

"**I**s he dead?" The media portrayal of death and the determination of death have changed dramatically over the past 75 years. Movies from the 1940s portrayed death as a dramatic event where someone (maybe not even a doctor) checked the patient for a pulse and breathing, then shook his head grimly indicating there was none. However, movies from the 2000s show frantic efforts at resuscitation and life saving before a final scene at a hospital where a physician pronounces death. This issue presents the challenges of death definitions, the issues of establishing criteria for death, and the difficulty of establishing which tests or examination findings that physicians must use to support those definitions and criteria.

Before the 1950s, it was clear that death occurred when a person's heart and circulatory system had permanently and irreversibly ceased to function. Death was defined as someone for whom no pulse or respirations were present and the body was cold to the touch (Choi et al., 2008; Shah & Miller, 2010). However, the first kidney transplantation in 1954 and the development of intensive care units in the 1960s changed this definition (Choi et al., 2008; President's Council on Bioethics, 2008). Physicians had an interest in saving lives through organ transplants, but the ruling requires that a donor must be declared dead. If the physicians waited until the patient met the heart and lung (cardiopulmonary) definition of death, the organ tissues would begin to die because of the loss of oxygen, and be unacceptable for transplantation. If there were no brain death criteria, the organs of persons with massive head injuries would not be able to be used for transplantation, because their organs would be unusable by the time they met the cardiopulmonary criteria. If, however, a definition of brain death was established, then living (viable) tissue could be removed from patients whose brain had ceased functioning, but whose circulation was being supported artificially (Choi et al., 2008; Shah & Miller, 2010).

The first documents to define brain death were developed in 1968 by the Ad Hoc Committee of the Harvard Medical School to Examine the Definition of Brain Death. The Harvard Committee defined death as a loss of function of the brain and spinal cord. State legislatures adopted versions of this "brain death" definition into state statutes. In 1980, the Uniform Determination of Death Act was published. The UDDA defines death as "[a]n individual who has sustained *either* (1) irreversible cessation of circulatory and respiratory functions, *or* (2) irreversible cessation of all functions of the entire brain, including the brain stem, is dead."

There is a difference between the *definition* of death and *the criteria* or standards that are used to declare death. Although the UDDA definition seems quite clear, whole brain death is really not the case of every severely brain injured person who is seen in the hospital. Hospitals needed to establish *criteria* that would be used to make sure that patients meet the definition of the "cessation of function of the entire brain and brain stem." Initially, the Harvard Committee recommended the following criteria: unreceptivity, unresponsiveness, no movement or breathing, no brainstem reflexes, flat electroencephalogram (EEG), irreversibility during at least 24 hours. The criteria excluded persons with hypothermia (body temperature < 90°F or 32.2°C), and excluded persons who were maintained on central nervous system depressants (Ad Hoc Committee, 1968). These criteria were only the beginning. By 1978, thirty different diagnostic criteria for establishing death had been published (Shewmon, 2009).

In 1995, the American Academy of Neurology (AAN) established prerequisite criteria, clinical examination requirements, and testing to be conducted to determine brain death (Quality Standards Subcommittee of AAN, 1995). Their prerequisite criteria established that the cause of the brain damage must be known and must not be reversible. The practice parameters included specific directions and criteria for a complete physical and neurological examination that must have certain findings to determine brain death. These guidelines note that brain death is a *clinical* diagnosis, which means that it can be determined by the physician's complete neurological physical exam. The tests that are done to confirm clinical findings (such as EEGs, ultrasounds, or brain scans) are not mandatory by these guidelines, but are recommended for further confirmation and documentation (Quality Standards Subcommittee of AAN, 1995).

Although these criteria and tests appear straightforward, the findings and difficulties with brain death definitions, criteria, and testing are enormous. Physicians and physiologists have argued that, for example, even in "brain dead" patients, the pituitary gland (in the brain) continues to secrete hormones involved in bodily functions (Choi et al., 2008). Does this mean that the patient does not meet the criteria of whole brain death? Others argue that the term "brain death" should be replaced with the term "brain-based determination of death," since brain dead patients may still show traditional signs of life (warm moist skin, a pulse, breathing) (Capron, 2001; President's Council on Bioethics, 2008; Shewmon, 2009). These signs of life are really "a mask that hides from plain sight the fact that the biological organism has ceased to function" (President's Council on Bioethics, 2008, p. 3). Complicating the issue are the media reports that *life* support is being removed from a brain dead patient, when it may be more accurate to state that the patient had died, and then the machines were removed (Capron, 2001; Shaner, Orr, Drought, Miller, & Siegel, 2004).

Not all patients who have profound neurological damage meet every criterion established by the AAN for "whole brain death," although these patients will never be able to meaningfully interact with the world. Many patients with severe brain damage require nursing home care for the remainder of their lives. One could argue that the "personhood" of patients is in their higher brain function (thinking, talking, understanding) and that brain death could be defined based on these higher functions. However, if loss of higher brain function was allowed as criteria for brain death, it would mean that patients in persistent vegetative state or profoundly demented patients or anencephalic infants (absence of a major portion of the brain) could be considered dead. It is unlikely that definitions of death or criteria would be expanded to include this (Capron, 2001; President's Council on Bioethics, 2008; Shah & Miller, 2010).

Finally, the debate about differing death definitions, criteria, and tests is complicated by variations in state laws. Although most jurisdictions have adopted the language of the Uniform Definition of Death Act, not all have (President's Council on Bioethics, 2008). However, all states do include a statute that defines death and that includes brain death. Some states allow for more than one concept of death, and some allow individuals to apply some alternative death criteria based on religious or cultural beliefs (Zeiler, 2009). Having more than one definition or criteria or testing is referred to as *pluralism*. This means that any one of several criteria or tests might be allowed in the determination of death. Having more than one definition can open up any clear diagnosis to scrutiny by those who do not support that definition (Capron, 2001).

Shaner, et al., (2004) provides clear and specific policies and procedures of identifying brain death. He reviews the Council on Ethical Affairs of the California Medical Association (CEA) set of policies and procedures for determining neurological death. He emphasizes the need for consistency in using these procedures so that family members understand the certainty that brain death has occurred.

In the YES article, Eun-Kyoung Choi and colleagues at the Charles Warren Fairbanks Center for Medical Ethics in Indianapolis review the current definitions and call for national standard for brain death that would eliminate uncertainty across hospitals, states, and jurisdictions.

In the NO article, Kristen Zeiler, a medical ethicist, argues that the definitions of whole brain death as the irreversible cessation of "all" functions of the brain is limiting, because it doesn't embrace other biological possibilities of death. She argues for death definition, criteria, and testing "pluralism." She discusses the need to consider more than one death definitions, operational criteria, and specific testings to accommodate the religious and cultural beliefs that also define death.

YES

Eun-Kyoung Choi et al.

Brain Death Revisited: The Case for a National Standard

The concept of brain death evolved because advancements in medical science permitted unprecedented artificial maintenance of vital body functions by external means.[1] Although the concept of brain death is accepted clinically, ethically, and legally in the United States, there is no national standard for the determination of brain death.[2] There is evidence that variability and inconsistency in the process of determining brain death exist both in clinical settings and in State statutes.[3] Several studies demonstrate that medical personnel determine brain death in variable ways,[4] and have variable understandings of the definition of brain death.[5] The declaration of death has significant legal consequences such as probate proceedings and liability issues for wrongful death.[6] Inconsistencies in the determination of death may therefore be medically, ethically, and legally problematic.[7]

After the first organ transplantation surgery was successfully conducted in 1954,[8] individuals dying neurological deaths have become an important source of potential organ donors.[9] However, the demand for organs for transplantation has rapidly increased, outpacing the organ supply.[10] As of March 2008, there were more than 98,270 people waiting for organ transplants in the United States.[11] However, only 28,350 patients received organ transplants in 2007.[12] Public concern regarding premature determination of brain death still exists, and such concern may contribute to the public's reluctance to donate organs of their loved ones after the declaration of brain death.[13] In this context, the lack of a uniform standard for determining brain death may increase public suspicion about the determination of brain death, thereby negatively affecting the organ supply.

... In this paper, we examine the barriers to the establishment of a national brain death standard, the theoretical and the practical advantages of a national brain death standard, and the complexities of enforcement of such a standard policy, if one could be arrived at. We end by proposing that a federal brain death policy—aimed at improving the consistency of brain death determinations among clinicians and hospitals, based on accepted clinical standards such as those provided by the American Academy of Neurology, and residing in the regulations of the Joint Commission—be implemented as a unified national standard.

Development of Definition of Brain Death

Traditionally, death was defined as the irreversible cessation of cardiopulmonary function.[14] This traditional definition of death, however, was challenged by advances in medical technology. Because cardiac and respiratory function could be artificially maintained by using life support technology, another clinical definition of death began to focus on the cessation of brain function.[15] In *Smith*, in which a husband and a wife suffered fatal injuries in the same accident and the wife died 17 days later after the husband's death, the Supreme Court of Arkansas ruled that although the wife lost consciousness at the time of the accident and did not regain consciousness, eventually dying 17 days later, the Simultaneous Death Act relating to the disposition of property was inapplicable.[16]

As time progressed, despite the early courts' reluctance to accept the idea of death by neurological criteria, the increased demand for organ donors accelerated the development of the concept of brain death. After the first kidney transplantation was conducted in 1954, the demand for viable organs increased.[17] However, ethical issues arose because the cardiopulmonary definition of death did not permit timely harvesting of donor organs.[18] Clinicians agreed that, ethically, patients must be pronounced dead before unpaired vital organ harvesting may begin,[19] so the declaration of death based on neurological criteria permitted transplant teams to procure donor organs from patients even when a heartbeat was still present. From a legal perspective, there had been pressure to create legislation articulating that brain dead patients should be pronounced legally dead to be considered dead donors.

As a response to these issues, in 1968, the Ad Hoc Committee of the Harvard Medical School to Examine the Definition of Brain Death (hereafter Harvard Committee) published a report which was the first formal attempt to establish the definition of brain death.[20] The Harvard Committee defined brain death as the loss of function of the brain and spinal cord.[21] It provided the basis of the brain death concept in the United States. After this report, in 1970, Kansas was the first state in the United States to write the brain death concept into law. Afterwards, other states began to adopt brain death into law or to accept it judicially.[22]

The efforts to reach a consensus on the definition of brain death from the legal perspective led to the drafting of the Uniform Determination of Death Act (UDDA) in 1980, which was published the following year in the President's Commission for the Study of Ethical Problems in Medicine and Biomedical and Behavioral Research report "Defining Death: A Report on the Medical, Legal and Ethical Issues in the Determination of Death."[23] The UDDA was approved by the National Conference of Commissioners on Uniform State Laws, in cooperation with the American Medical Association, the American Bar Association, and the President's Commission on Medical Ethics. It acknowledged neurological criteria as the basis for determining death in the United States.[24] The UDDA states that "[a]n individual who has sustained either (1) irreversible cessation of circulatory and respiratory functions, or (2) irreversible cessation of all functions of the entire brain, including the brain stem, is dead. A determination of death must be made in accordance with accepted medical standards."[25] Although the UDDA does not specify any test or measures for determining brain death, it provides the national legal framework for defining death, and has been adopted by all 50 states and the District of Columbia.[26] The majority of states have adopted the language of the UDDA in their statutes, with some minor variations.[27] Arizona, Massachusetts, and Washington adopted the brain death concept judicially.[28]

Because the UDDA does not provide uniform clinical standards for the determination of brain death, in practice, clinicians and researchers have developed varying guidelines for determining brain death. In July, 1981 the President's Commission report provided expert medical guidelines for the determination of death, including brain death.[29] . . . In 1995, the American Academy of Neurology (AAN) published guidelines for determining brain death in adults, setting prerequisites and defining confounding factors in determining brain death and stating that the clinical examination is the primary mechanism for determining brain death.[30] Afterwards, the process for determining brain death has been further clarified.[31]

Remaining Controversies in the Definition of Brain Death

[Authors have questioned the current definition of brain death because it is logically inconsistent.] . . . For example, some features of brain function remain intact after brain death (e.g., posterior pituitary secretion of anti-diuretic hormone and thermoregulation).[32] This raises an inconsistency with the definition of brain death in the UDDA: "irreversible cessation of all functions of the entire brain, including the brain stem." Chiong has argued convincingly that the concept of brain death has irresolvable philosophical fuzziness, and that brain death merely serves to clarify, though not to resolve, the inconsistencies inherent in the definition.[33] We have chosen to put aside this interesting and ongoing debate for the moment, since for all practical purposes, the concept of brain death has achieved sufficient acceptance by the medical, legal, and ethical communities that it is used by clinicians every day. . . .

Historical Evolution of Guidelines for Brain Death Determination

The first guidelines promulgated by the Harvard Committee in 1968 defined brain death using the following clinical criteria: "unreceptivity, unresponsiveness, no movement or breathing, no brainstem reflexes, flat electroencephalogram, irreversibility during at least 24 hours and exclusion of hypothermia (body temperature < 90°F or 32.2°C) or central nervous system depressants."[34] The Harvard Committee defined brain death as the loss of function of the whole central nervous system. However, the guideline was changed later, eliminating parts of the guidelines referring to the spinal cord from the definition because the function of the spinal cord can continue without the function of the brain.[35] In 1981, the guidelines offered by the President's Commission for the Study of Ethical Problems in Medicine and Biomedical and Behavioral Research confirmed the definition of brain death which was made at the report by the Harvard Committee above.[36] The Commission's guidelines also addressed the use of confirmatory tests to reduce the duration of the required period of observation time.[37] However, when a patient has anoxic damage [loss of oxygen], a 24-hour observation period was recommended by the President's Commission guidelines.[38]

In 1995, the AAN published its consensus view derived from clinical evidence for determining brain death in adults.[39] The AAN guidelines specify prerequisite criteria, clinical examinations, and confirmatory tests.[40] First, the prerequisite criteria require that the cause of brain death be established with certainty and that reversible conditions be excluded. Second, the guidelines specify that the clinical examination is the basis for the determination of brain death. The examination includes assessment of coma, absent motor response, absent brainstem reflexes, and apnea. In addition, the AAN guidelines specify that the clinical examination should be repeated within a six-hour interval. Third, although the clinical examination is the basis for the determination of brain death, confirmatory tests are desirable in patients whose circumstances make a full clinical examination difficult. For instance, confirmatory tests are recommended when a patient's condition impedes the clinical examination.

In 2001, Wijdicks summarized work describing the foundations and implementation of brain death tests, providing a clinically useful summary of the AAN guidelines.[41] In this discussion, Wijdicks specified steps in the clinical examinations, enumerated the neurologic states which mimic brain death, provided explanations for the role of confirmatory tests, specified confounding factors, and suggested some guidelines for the determination of brain death in children.[42] In particular, he provided a detailed description for the proper conduct of the apnea test.[43]

Because neither the Harvard Committee nor the AAN guidelines addressed the determination of brain death in children, a task force for the determination of brain death in children was formed by representatives from relevant groups such as the American Bar Association, the American Academy of Neurology, the American Neurological Association, the American Academy of Pediatrics, and the Child Neurology Society in 1987.[44] The task force published standards for the determination of brain death in infants and children.[45] The guidelines, called the Guidelines for the Determination of Brain Death in Children, are stringent, specifying a period of more extensive observation depending on the age of children and requiring confirmatory tests in some circumstances.[46]

In summary, although several guidelines have been suggested over times, there seems to be consensus on essential components necessary for determining brain death, and these essential components have not radically evolved since the Harvard criteria of the late 1960s. These include: (1) prerequisite conditions should be met; an etiology of the unresponsive coma should be known and potentially reversible causes of coma, such as intoxication or hypothermia, should be excluded,[47] (2) the clinical examination should be the basis of the diagnosis of brain death and should include the following: unresponsiveness, unreceptivity, no spontaneous movements, no brainstem reflexes and apnea. Those conditions should be persistent when the examinations are repeated,[48] and (3) confirmatory tests are necessary when clinical examination is impossible to apply.[49] Valid confirmatory tests include cerebral angiography, electroencephalography, transcranial doppler ultrasonography, evoked potentials, and nuclear imaging.[50]

Although these essential components are well established, there remain several unresolved issues in relation to the clinical determination of brain death. A lack of uniformity in performing the required clinical assessment, misunderstanding of the concept of brain death, legal issues pertinent to brain death, and public concern about premature death determination remain troubling issues which might be improved through the establishment of a national standard. We examine each of these in turn.

Variability in Guidelines Across State Statutes and Clinical Practice

Variability and inconsistency in the procedures specified for determining brain death have been found both in State statutes[51] and in some surveys of health institution policies.[52]

Variability Across the Jurisdictions

The majority of states which have a brain death statute adopt language similar to the UDDA. However, there are notable differences among statutes in the specific requirements for brain death determination.[53] Those differences include, for example, the qualifications of the clinician responsible for determining brain death and the number of determiners required.[54] . . . Table 1 shows the States which have specific requirements for determiners.

Table 1

Variations in Qualifications and Number of Brain Death Determiners

States	Qualification of Determiner	Number of Determiners	Other Requirement
Alaska	Physician or Registered Nurse	–	
Connecticut	Physicians	2	
Florida[*]	Physicians	2	
Georgia	Physician or Registered Nurse	–	
Iowa	Physicians	2	
Kentucky	Physicians	2	
Michigan	Physician or Registered Nurse	–	
New Jersey[†]	–	–	Religious Accommodation
New York[†]	–	–	Religious Accommodation
Virginia[‡]	Physicians	2	

[*]One physician shall be the treating physician and the other physician shall be a board-eligible or board-certified neurologist, neurosurgeon, internist, pediatrician, surgeon, or anesthesiologist.[55]

[†]Required physician to honor religious objection to brain death.[56]

[‡]A physician who shall be duly licensed and a specialist in the field of neurology, neurosurgeon, or electroencephalography, and another physician.[57]

Concerning the qualifications of the determiner, while the statutes of Alabama, Hawaii, Delaware, Missouri, and Ohio require that the determination of death be made by a physician, the statutes of Alaska, Georgia, and Michigan specify that a physician or registered nurse may pronounce the death of a person in accordance with the Act.[58]

Regarding the number of determiners, in most states one physician can diagnose brain death, but in some states, independent confirmation by a second physician is required.[59] Among the states which require a second physician, Florida specifically mandates that "one physician shall be the treating physician and the other physician shall be board-eligible or board-certified neurologist, neurosurgeon, internist, pediatrician, surgeon or anesthesiologist."[60] The Virginia statute specifically calls for a specialist in neurology, neurosurgery, or electroencephalography.[61]

There are also differences in how state statutes treat withdrawing of mechanical life support from patients who have been declared brain dead. In general, once the patient is pronounced brain dead, either by a proper medical diagnosis or by judicial determination, mechanical life support can be removed.[62] In other words, after a patient is determined to be brain dead, no civil or criminal liability will result from removing the body from life sustaining equipment.[63] . . . Most states have adopted similar positions, so that pronouncement of brain death is sufficient cause for removing patients from positive pressure ventilator treatment. Nevertheless, New York and New Jersey have changed their statutes to accommodate religious objections. These amendments require physicians to consider requests to continue medical care on religious grounds despite a diagnosis of brain death.[64]

Inconsistencies and Misunderstanding in the Definition of Brain Death

The current lack of a specific nationally accepted standard for the determination of brain death probably leads to inconsistencies and misunderstandings in the definition of brain death. Several studies have suggested that inconsistencies or errors may occur in conducting tests intended to confirm brain death.[65] In one survey in 1989, among 195 physicians and nurses who were likely involved in the process of organ procurement for transplantation, only 35% of them correctly answered to the questions regarding the brain death criteria which were adopted in the UDDA.[66]

Furthermore, several subtleties in the determination of brain death may lead to confusion during the clinical assessment.[67] In some cases, although the clinical criteria for brain death are met, spontaneous and reflex movements may be observed in brain dead patients.[68] Those movements do not preclude the diagnosis of brain death when they result from spinal reflexes.[69] In one study, 39% of brain dead patients demonstrated spontaneous or reflex movements.[70] The most common reflex movements were finger jerks, the undulating toe flexion sign, the triple flexion response, the Lazarus sign, and facial myokymia.[71] These movements are usually seen within the first 24 hours following whole brain death.[72] The Harvard Committee criteria stipulated that the presence of spinal or cephalic reflexes precluded brain death.[73] In 1995, however, when the AAN recommendations for diagnosing brain death were published, the presence of spinal reflexes were considered to be consistent with brain death.[74] In addition to spinal movements, other confounding situations exist. A review of published reports contends that, even when the clinical examination meets the criteria of brain death, some brain functions such as posterior pituitary function, cortical function, and brain stem function may still remain.[75] However, such findings are not consistent with the definition of brain death in the UDDA which defines the cessation of all functions of the entire brain as brain death. A national standard could serve to eliminate such inconsistencies and improve understanding and assessment of brain death by making it clear that, although medical evidence acquired since the introduction and refinement of the brain death concept has suggested that some functions of the brain can persist (e.g., neuroendocrine and thermoregulatory function) even when the essential criteria for brain death have been fulfilled, such functions do not preclude or rule out brain death. In this way, a national standard would serve to clarify through consensus such apparent inconsistencies in clinical findings with the language of the UDDA.

Variability in Clinical Practice

In the earliest study of its kind that we identified, wide variations among individual physicians were found.[76] One survey was conducted among 112 neurosurgeons and neurologists asking about their practices in determination of brain death.[77] This study found significant variability in the criteria used by individual practitioners.[78] The criteria most frequently used by the clinicians in this study included the absence of a pupillary reflex (88%), the absence of a corneal reflex (85%), a lack of ventilatory effort with disconnection of the ventilator (84%), and the absence of eye movements with head turning (80%).[79] On the other hand, fewer clinicians included an absent gag reflex (69%) or cough reflex (61%), dilated pupils (59%), a body temperature over 90°F (56%), or a blood barbiturate level of zero (43%).[80] Regarding isoelectric electroencephalogram, 29% required only one and 36% required two electroencephalograms 24 hours apart.[81] The time interval between brain death evaluations varied from 6 to 24 hours.[82] There were wide variations in responses to a hypothetical situation in which the family of a patient satisfying brain death criteria did not want death to be declared:[83] 47% of the physicians would continue the ventilator without declaring the patient dead, but 29% of them would declare the patient dead while continuing ventilator support.[84] Only 6% would stop the ventilator despite the family's wishes.[85]

. . . In determining brain death, many hospitals have developed or used policies referring to the guideline of AAN in 1995 as a basis for the determination.[86] Some hospitals do not have any policy on determination of brain death.[87] Several studies suggest that variability in the determination of brain death exists between institutions[88] and within a single hospital.[89]

One study surveyed 600 randomly selected hospitals in the United States with respect to their policies and practices regarding brain death and obtained responses from 140 hospitals.[90] This study found substantive variability among hospital policies for the determination of brain death.[91] According to this study, significant differences were found between examined hospital policies and the AAN and other guidelines.[92] Differences were found in how policies specified prerequisite conditions, testing methods during the clinical examinations, the kinds of acceptable confirmatory tests, and whether or not those confirmatory tests were required.[93] In this survey, 12% of respondents did not identify any confounding conditions or factors in order to avoid errors in determination.[94] Most hospitals (88%) set specific core temperatures for clinical determination of brain death, but differences were found in threshold temperatures specified.[95] The thresholds ranged from 32.2°C to 36.0°C.[96] As for exclusion of elevated levels of blood alcohol, only 14% of the respondents specified this exclusion in the policy.[97]

Second, differences were found in individual hospitals'requirements regarding the qualifications of determiners, the number of determiners needed, the performance of the apnea test, repetition of clinical examinations and time interval.[98] In all of the policies examined, only physicians could declare brain death.[99] However, 25% of the respondents required or recommended that a neurologist or neurosurgeon be the determiner of brain death.[100] Regarding the number of determiners, two physicians were required by 46% of the hospitals and one physician was required in 42%.[101] Apnea testing was required in most hospitals (96%), but the endpoints for evaluations were inconsistent.[102] It is important for physicians to allow a patient's $PaCO_2$ to rise above a threshold before conducting the apnea test to ascertain that breathing centers in the brain stem have been maximally stimulated before a positive test is declared. The majority of policies specify a $PaCO_2$ r 60 mmHg as a threshold, as suggested by the AAN guidelines.[103] Most hospitals required or recommended two clinical examinations within a certain period of time, however, the time interval specified varied from 2 to 24 hours.[104]

Third, as for confirmatory tests, 8% required confirmatory tests and 74% recommended them.[105] Most hospitals listed more than one option and considered them equivalent.[106] The confirmatory tests specified in policies included electroencephalograms, nuclear cerebral blood flow studies, angiogram, transcranial doppler, and evoked potentials test.[107]

In another recent survey, Greer et al. asked the *U.S. News and World Report* top 50 neurology and neurosurgery programs in the United States in 2006 to provide their guidelines for brain death determination.[108] They reviewed the responses from 41 institutions and found that 3 institutions from this list did not have official guidelines.[109] After examining the guidelines with comparison to the AAN guidelines, they found variations in the qualification of determiners, procedures for testing, and apnea testing.[110]

Another study which reviewed the records of brain death determinations examined internal variations within individual hospitals and found poor compliance with brain death guidelines.[111] The authors found that, in the clinical documentation analyzed, single-step clinical examinations were documented comparatively well, but multi-step examinations and confounding factors were documented with less frequency.[112] Among the clinical examinations, while pupillary (86%) and gag reflexes (78%) were relatively frequently (though not universally) documented, corneal reflexes (57%) and motor responses (66%) were less frequently noted.[113] This study also suggested that documentation by the neurosurgeons was generally more complete than documentation by nonneurosurgeons, such as general surgeons and trauma surgeons.[114]

Regarding variability in the practice of determining brain death in pediatric patients, according to data collected between December 1989 and December 1992 from 16 pediatric intensive care units (PICUs) in the United States, substantial variability was found in the criteria, specifically in the methods of apnea testing and in the use of confirmatory tests for the diagnosis of brain death.[115] Moreover, some practices were contradictory to the Guidelines for the Determination of Brain Death in Children and to recommendations for apnea testing.[116] For instance, apnea testing was not conducted in 25% of patients and even if the apnea testing was done, PCO_2 did not reach 60 mmHg at the end of the test in 8% of the brain dead patients.[117] In another survey which attempted to determine whether the American Academy of Pediatrics Guidelines for the Determination of Brain Death in Children were truly used by clinicians, particularly in instances of brain death secondary to head trauma, the results demonstrated that the majority of pediatric hospitals and pediatric neurosurgeons did not follow the guidelines exactly.[118]

In the absence of specific statutory guidelines specifying the procedures to be used in the determination of brain death, guidelines are determined by individual hospital policy or practice. . . . Variability in policies or guidelines contributes to inconsistencies in the practice of determining brain death. Such variability can lead to inequities.[119] For instance, a patient might be pronounced brain dead in State A or hospital A under their statutes or policies, but he or she could be considered to be alive in State B or hospital B based on their differing statutes or policies. Moreover, such variability probably contributes to doubt about the reliability and objectivity of the determination among lay family members. The lack of accepted national standards for determination of brain death contributes to the variability in the process of determining brain death both by virtue of existing state statute and by variability in hospital policies and physician practices. Although a national standard would not directly impact the documented variability in clinicians' practices with respect to brain death determination, it would minimize the variability seen in state statutes and hospital policies. . . .

Legal Issues

The law considers death to be an event,[120] and the timing of death has significant implications regarding rights and obligations. Once a patient is pronounced dead, legal issues such as probate proceedings, organ donations, insurance claims,[121] or actions for wrongful death and criminal prosecution may be initiated.[122]

One legal question that arose early following the definition of the concept of brain death was whether a physician is liable for the death of a patient when he or she removes a patient from life support following a brain death determination. Now, both statutes and judicial decisions on brain death provide legal immunity for any clinician who removes patients from positive pressure ventilator treatment following the determination of brain death[123] and protect physicians from civil or criminal liability.[124] In *Nethery*, the Texas criminal court ruled that testimony of medical examiner that victim was dead and had died from bullet wound in the head was sufficient to establish cause of death, despite the allegation that the victim was on life support systems prior to death.[125] Actions against physicians attempting to make removal of life support the proximate cause of death have not been successful.[126]

The Appellate Court of Illinois concluded that it would not establish criteria for determining brain death because it acknowledged that the new technologies would continue to change the tests used for determining cessation of brain function and that it deferred to evolving clinical standards used for such determination.[127] For this reason, the UDDA and other statutes do not articulate the specific standards for the determination of brain death.

Because the UDDA and state' statutes do not specify the practical clinical standard for the determination of brain death, there is no uniform, medically accepted standard for determining brain death. This issue has arisen in criminal cases, for example, in which it has been argued as a defense for the alleged perpetrator that, because a physician did not follow a medically accepted standard, his determination of brain death was premature, and that the withdrawal of life support was the proximate cause of victim's death. In *United States v. Gomez*, the United States Army Court of Military Review held that the military judge properly instructed the jury on brain death as the correct standard for determining death.[128] In *Gomez*, the military judge instructed that "[t]he determination of brain death must be made in accordance with accepted medical standards, such as the Harvard Brain Death tests."[129] Considering the fact that this decision was made in 1983 when the guidelines for determination of brain death were not as well developed, it would be far more meaningful to refer to the Harvard Committee criteria as the accepted medical standard. After the guidelines by the Harvard Committee published in 1968, however, several subsequent guidelines, which were slightly different from one another, have been published and some variations have existed in guidelines used in the hospitals. . . . Without clinical agreement and consistency regarding a medically accepted standard of brain death determination, courts are left without common principles to apply and determination remains legally contentious.

Similarly, conflicting state statutes may lead to inequitable treatment under the law. Because, as discussed earlier in this paper, state statutes vary with respect to such issues as the qualifications of and the number of determiners, the resulting brain death determinations may be different. The fundamental legal inequity herein can be demonstrated by this example: if a victim of a crime were to be suspected of being brain dead, the accused perpetrator of the crime could be subject to severe penalties under a state's provision with more liberal brain death criteria and penalized less severely under a less liberal state's provisions. As a result, the decision about the physician's liability could be made differently depending on the jurisdiction.

Public Suspicion and Misunderstanding of Brain Death

The concept of brain death is accepted worldwide[130] including the United States.[131] Nevertheless, many lay people remain suspicious of the concept of brain death,[132] fearing that premature determination of death may be prompted by the need for donor organs.[133] In a recent survey examining public' attitude and beliefs about the determination of death and its relationship to organ transplantation, over 98% of the respondents had heard of the term brain death, but only 33.7% of them believed that brain dead patients were legally and clinically dead.[134] Because brain dead patients may still be perceived to be alive and because spinal reflexive movements can be observed,[135] many people remain confused about the validity of brain death. In addition, the act of withdrawing positive pressure ventilator treatment from patients who have been declared brain dead can be easily misunderstood and may be accompanied by emotional turmoil if family members still believe that a patient is alive.[136]

The concept of brain death provided the ethical, medical, and legal justification for the procurement of vital organs. Considering the current shortage of organ supply, various efforts, such as the use of extended criteria donor organs, aggressive donor management, and the Massachusetts Organ Donation Initiative, have been used to increase the pool of potential organ donors.[137] Along with such efforts, however, public concern about premature determination of brain death continues to be an obstacle. Simmoff et al. interviewed 420 families who made decisions on the matter of donation and found that 25% of the families chose not to donate based on their mistrust of the health care system.[138]

Given the results of such findings, it is reasonable to conclude that the lack of standard procedures for the determination of brain death and the variability in guidelines among hospitals and states continues to reduce the credibility of brain death determination and may contribute to public concerns that physicians are using brain death to hasten patients' death determination solely for the purpose of organ donation. Such mistrust may contribute to the current shortage of donor organs.

A National Standard for the Determination of Brain Death Is Needed

We believe that a national medical and legal standard for the determination of brain death is needed to resolve the challenges identified above. We also believe that there exists sufficient expert consensus on the standard to make this feasible. First, a nationally unified standard will provide clinical and procedural consistency, reducing variations in brain death determinations by requiring all hospitals and physicians to follow the nationally unified standard. All potential brain dead patients would be more likely to be treated equally. Second, a unified and consistent standard would provide potential determiners of brain death with a consistent set of procedures to use in the process of determining brain death, making determination more legitimate. All hospitals could feel comfortable adopting the nationally accepted policies, reducing variability of institutional policies. Third, a unified and consistent standard would minimize the potential for inconsistent legal outcomes. Fourth, if the standard for determination of brain death is accurate and consistent, public concern that brain death is only a surreptitious means of prematurely declaring death would likely decrease. Thus, a unified and consistent standard would help to increase the credibility of the determination of brain death, and the resulting increase in trust should lead to improved opportunities for organ harvesting. Finally, although it may be argued that it is not reasonable to include specific clinical standards in federal policy because, presumably, the clinical criteria will change over time with advances in medical science and technology, there is no reason that provisions for updating the standards could not also be codified.

Considerations in Establishing a Nationally Unified Standard

Since the guidelines set forth by the AAN are commonly referenced by clinicians or hospitals, despite variations in individual hospital policies,[139] we believe that the AAN guidelines should be the basic model for a national standard provided. The following points need to be addressed by such a standard.

First, regarding prerequisite conditions, how to determine whether the prerequisite conditions exist and what should be done if the prerequisite conditions preclude further clinical testing should be addressed. For instance, Baron et al. suggest that, if the patient is suspected to be intoxicated by certain drugs, their pharmacokinetic profiles should be considered in determining the timing of assessments.[140] These prerequisite conditions should include those specified by the AAN criteria, including exclusion of complications, drug intoxication, and poisoning.[141] Second, for the performance of the clinical examination, minimum core temperature and the number of and time intervals between examinations should be unambiguously specified. The AAN sets 32°C or higher temperature as a minimum temperature for the diagnosis of brain death, but some clinicians argue that apnea tests cannot be conducted below 36.5°C.[142] Therefore, the difference in temperature threshold leads to ambiguity that would best be resolved by consensus.[143] The repetition of the clinical examination is meant to minimize the technical errors in examinations and to assure irreversibility of the clinical conditions. In this regard, the time interval for multiple examinations is important. However, there is little evidence as to the basis of minimum recommended time interval.[144] Thus, an appropriate time interval should be determined by consensus until more research arrives at a better clinical understanding.

Third, as for confirmatory tests, when confirmatory tests should be done is comparatively well established.[145] That is, when clinical examinations cannot be completed because confounding factors exist, confirmatory tests are recommended or required. However, which confirmatory tests should be done is not widely agreed upon.[146] Young et al. suggested some criteria to determine which confirmatory tests should be done:[147]

(1) there should be no false positives: when the test confirms brain death, there should be none who recover or who have the potential to recover, (2) the test should be sufficient on its own to establish that brain death is or is not present, (3) the test should not be susceptible to confounders such as drug effects or metabolic disturbances, (4) the test should be standardized in technology, technique, and classification of results, (5) the test should be available, safe and readily applied.

These criteria are a useful guide for determining which test should be conducted. Young et al. have suggested that brain bloodflow studies meet these criteria.[148] The AAN guidelines rank order confirmatory tests from most to least specific.[149] Table 2 is the AAN list, in order.[150] Consensus criteria are identified by individual tests.[151]

Fourth, as addressed in several studies[152] and in the AAN guidelines,[153] confounding factors, if not appropriately accounted for, may lead to an incorrect diagnosis of brain death. Considering the profound meaning and consequences of death, therefore, the confounding factors should be specified in detail in a national standard. In addition, the method for determining whether confounding factors exist and, if they exist, what should be done about them should be addressed.

Fifth, the qualification and number of determiners should be explicit in a unified national standard with consideration given to the following: Flowers and Patel concluded in their study in which 71 patients were examined retrospectively, that the clinical diagnosis of brain death is highly reliable when the experienced examiners determined based on the established criteria.[154] The authors emphasized the importance of the examiner's qualification.[155] In addition, considering the fact that the accurate and infallible diagnosis of death is crucial, the examinations should be conducted by specialists such

Table 2

Ordered List of Confirmatory Tests

A. Conventional angiography. No intracerebral filling at the level of the carotid bifurcation or circle of Willis. The external carotid circulation is patent, and filling of the superior longitudinal sinus may be delayed.

B. Electroencephalography. No electrical activity during at least 30 minutes of recording that adheres to the minimal technical criteria for EEG recording in suspected brain death as adopted by the American Electroencephalographic Society, including 16-channel EEG instruments.

C. Transcranial Doppler ultrasonography

 1. Ten percent of patients may not have temporal insonation windows. Therefore, the initial absence of Doppler signals cannot be interpreted as consistent with brain death.

 2. Small systolic peaks in early systole without diastolic flow or reverberating flow, indicating very high vascular resistance associated with greatly increased intracranial pressure.

D. Technetium-99m hexamethylpropyleneamineoxime brain scan. No uptake of isotope in brain parenchyma ("hollow skull phenomenon").

E. Somatosensory evoked potentials. Bilateral absence of N20-P22 response with median nerve stimulation. The recordings should adhere to the minimal technical criteria for somatosensory evoked potential recording in suspected brain death as adopted by the American Electroencephalographic Society

---

as neurologists, neurosurgeons, or intensive care unit physicians in order to prevent potential errors. However, in the light of the capacity of smaller hospitals that are less likely to have round-the-clock access to such specialists,[156] the uniform standard should pragmatically allow a single clinician of any type *so long as that clinician has expertise in the proper procedures for determining brain death* to make the determinations. According to the Uniform Anatomical Gift Act Section 8, physicians who participate in the process of the organ transplantation should not serve as brain death determiners.[157] This stipulation should be included in the standard. There are few data to support requiring a specific number of determiners. In the United States, the number of determiners is one or two physicians and in other countries, it varies from one up to four.[158] Whether one or two individuals must separately arrive at the determination of brain death should be arrived upon by consensus. We suggest that, given constraints such as hospital size and access to specialists, one accurate and meticulous determination by a single, experienced clinician should be considered sufficient.

Finally, important concerns about the accuracy of the documentation surrounding brain death determination have been raised.[159] This issue would be solved substantially if a unified standard stipulated what brain death documentation should include, and required that it be done accurately and carefully. In this regard, how to document the process of brain death determination should be incorporated into the standard, which could minimize potential error in the determination process.

Forum for Enforcement of Standard

A nationally unified brain death standard would necessitate that the standards be enforced. Such an enforcing body would need to be a national organization or institution which has the authority to impose its standard on hospitals or perhaps allow a private right of action for individuals harmed by its misapplication. A group charged with enforcing brain death determination criteria would need to have a well-balanced view and would need to be invested in improving the quality and safety of care provided by hospitals.

We suggest that, considering those factors, the Joint Commission (formerly the Joint Commission for the Accreditation of Healthcare Organizations— JCAHO), an organization that already certifies compliance with various clinical criteria and measures, seems a logical forum to create and enforce standards for determination of brain death. The Joint Commission is an independent and non-profit organization and the nation's standards-setting and accrediting body for health care organizations. The Joint Commission has developed a certification program for transplant centers.[160] This new program provides the standards for organ procurement, selection of patients, and protection of donor rights. . . . The modified AAN guidelines could be suggested as the basis for national standards and in order to enforce the established standards in hospital or institutions, the Joint Commission would be an appropriate forum to implement and to enforce the standards without necessitating the change of the state statutes.

Conclusion

Although the brain death concept is generally accepted throughout the world including in the United States, there is no unified standard for all hospitals and medical personnel or for courts for determining brain death at a practical level. The absence of such a unified standard contributes to variations in determination of brain death and has raised other issues. Those issues include equity problems, errors in the process of determining brain death, misunderstanding of brain death, legal issues, and public concerns about premature determination of brain death. In order to resolve those issues, a nationally unified standard should be established. In doing so, all hospitals or institutions and health professionals involved in brain death determination would be able to rely on the standards, thereby resolving issues identified here associated with disparate guidelines and standards, and reducing public concern about premature determinations of death by improving the credibility of determination of brain death and, therefore of organ procurement.

References

1. D. B. Hoch, "Brain Death: A Diagnostic Dilemma," The Journal of Nuclear Medicine 33, no. 12 (1992): 2211–2213, at 2212; A. Halevy and B. Brody, "Brain Death: Reconciling Definitions, Criteria, and Trusts," Annals of Internal Medicine 119, no. 6 (1993): 519–525, at 519; T. Randell, "Medical and Legal Considerations of Brain Death," Acta Anesthesiologica Scandinavica 48 (2004): 139–144, at 139; L. Baron, S. D. Shemie, J. Teitelbaum, C. J. Doig, "Brief Review: History, Concept and Controversies in the Neurological Determination of Death," *Canadian Journal of Anesthesia* 53, no. 6 (2006): 602–608, at 603.

2. E. F. M. Wijdicks, "The Clinical Criteria of Brain Death Throughout the World: Why Has It Come to This?" *Canadian Journal of Anesthesia* 53, no. 6 (2006): 540–543, at 540 [hereinafter Clinical Criteria]; D. J. Powner, M. Hernandez, T. E. Rives, "Variability among Hospital Policies for Determining Brain Death in Adults," *Critical Care Medicine* 32, no. 6 (2004): 1284–1288; E. F. M. Wijdicks, "Brain Death Worldwide: Accepted Fact but No Global Consensus in Diagnostic Criteria," *Neurology* 58, no. 1 (2002): 20–25, at 24 [hereinafter Brain Death Worldwide].

3. See Wijdicks (Clinical Criteria), *supra* note 2, at 540; Wijdicks, (Brain Death Worldwide), *supra* note 2, at 23; M. Y. Wang, P. Wallace, and P. J. Gruen, "Brain Death Documentation: Analysis and Issues," *Neurosurgery* 51, no. 3 (2002): 731–736, at 732–3; Alabama: Ala. Code 1975 § 22-31-1 (2000); Alaska: Alaska Stat. § 09.68.120 (West 1995); Arizona: *State v. Fierro*, 603 P.2d 74 (Ariz. 1979); Arkansas: Ark. Code. Ann. § 20-17-101 (West 1985); California: Cal. Health & Safety Code § 7180 (West 1982); Colorado: Colo. Rev. Stat. Ann. § 12-36-136 (West 1981); Connecticut: Conn. Gen. Stat. Ann. § 19a-279h (West 1988); Delaware: 24 Del. C. § 1760 (West 2005); District of Columbia: D.C. Code § 7-601 (1982); Florida: Fla. Stat. Ann. § 382.009 (West 1987); Georgia: Ga. Code Ann., § 31-10-16 (West 1992); Hawaii: Haw. Rev. Stat. § 327C-1 (West 1998); Idaho: Idaho Code § 54-1819 (West 1981); Illinois: 755 Ill. Comp. Stat. Ann. 50/1–10

(West 2004); Indiana: Ind. Code Ann. 1-1-4-3 (West 1986); Iowa: Iowa Code Ann. § 702.8 (West 2001); Kansas: Kan. Stat. Ann. § 77–205 (West 1984); Kentucky: Ky. Rev. Stat. Ann. § 446.400 (West 1986); Louisiana: La. Rev. Stat. Ann. 9:111 (2001); Maine: Me. Rev. Stat. Ann. tit. 22, § 2811 (1983); Massachusetts: *Commonwealth v. Golston*, 366 N.E.2d 744; Maryland: MD. Code Ann., Code, Health—Gen. § 5-202 (West 1998); Michigan: Mich. Comp. Laws. Ann. § 333.1033 (West 1992); Minnesota: Minn. Stat. Ann. § 145.135 (West 1989); Mississippi: Miss. Code Ann. § 41-36-3 (West 1981); Missouri: Mo. Ann. Stat. § 194.005 (West 1982); Montana: Mont. Code Ann. § 50-22-101 (1983); Nebraska: Neb. Rev. Stat. § 71-7202 (1992); Nevada: Nev. Rev. Stat. Ann. § 451.007 (West 1985); New Hampshire: N. H. Rev. Stat. Ann. § 141-D:2 (1987); New Jersey: N. J. Stat. Ann. § 26:6A-3 (West 1991); New Mexico: N. M. Stat. Ann. § 12-2-4 (West 2007): New York: N. Y. Comp. Codes R. & Regs. tit. 10, § 400.16 (1987); North Carolina: N. C. Gen. Stat. Ann. § 90-323 (West 1979); North Dakota: N. D. Cent. Code § 23-06.3-01 (West 1989); Ohio: Ohio Rev. Code Ann. § 2108.30 (West 1981); Oklahoma: Okla. Stat. Ann. tit. 63, § 3122 (West 1986); Oregon: OR. Rev. Stat. Ann. § 432.300 (West 1997); Pennsylvania: 35 Pa. Stat. Ann. § 10203 (West 1982); Rhode Island: R.I. Gen. Laws 1956, § 23-4-16 (1982); South Carolina: S. C. Code Ann. § 44-43-460 (2006); South Dakota: S.D. Codified Laws § 34-25-18.1(1990); Tennessee: Tenn. Code Ann. § 68-3-501 (West 1982); Texas: Tex. Health & Safety Code Ann. § 671.001 (Vernon 1995); Utah: Utah. Code Ann. § 26-34-2 (West 2007); Vermont: Vt. Stat. Ann. tit. 18, § 5218 (West 1981); Virginia: Va. Code Ann. § 54.1-2972 (West 2004); Washington: *In re Welfare of Bowman*, 617 P. 2d 731 (Wash. 1980); West Virginia: W.Va. Code Ann. § 16-10-1 (West 1989); Wisconsin: Wis. Stat. Ann. § 146.71 (Wet 1982); Wyoming: Wyo. Stat. Ann. § 35-19-101 (1985) [hereafter State's statute and cases, State statutes if only referring to the statutes, State cases if only referring to the cases].

4. R. E. Mejia and M. M. Pollack, "Variability in Brain Death Determination Practices in Children," *JAMA* 274, no. 7 (1995): 550–553, at 551–552; S. J. Youngner, C. S. Landefeld, and C. J. Coulton, B. W. Juknialis, and M. Leary, "'Brain Death' and Organ Retrieval: A Cross-sectional Survey of Knowledge and Concepts among Health Professionals," *JAMA* 261, no. 15 (1989): 2205–2210, at 2208–2209; see Wang et al., *supra* note 3, at 732–733.

5. S. Jeffrey, "Brain Death Guidelines Vary Widely at Top US Neurological Hospitals," *available at* <www.medscape. com/viewarticle/564125> (last visited October 6, 2008); see Youngner et al., *supra* note 4, at 2208-2209.

6. See Baron et al., *supra* note 1, at 607.

7. *Id.*

8. S. Kulkarni and D. C. Cronin II, "Ethical Tensions in Solid Organtransplantation: The Price of Success," *World Journal of Gastroenterology* 12, no. 20 (2006): 3259–3264, at 3261.

9. The Organ Procurement and Transplantation Network, *available at* <www .optn.org/about/donation/whoCanBeADonor.asp> (last visited October 6, 2008).

10. See Kulkarni and Cronin, *supra* note 8, at 3259.

11. The United Network for Organ Sharing, *available at* <www.unos.org> (last visited October 6, 2008).

12. The Organ Procurement and Transplantation Network, *available at* <www
.optn.org/latestData/rptData.asp> (last visited October 6, 2008).

13. N. M. Lazar, S. Shemie, G. C. Webster, and B. M. Dickens, "Bioethics for
Clinicians: 24 Brain Deaths," *Canadian Medical Association Journal* 164
no. 6 (2001): 833–836, at 834.

14. *In re Quinlan*, 355 A.2d 647 (N. J. 1976).

15. See Halevy and Brody, *supra* note 1, at 519.

16. *Smith v. Smith*, 317 S.W.2d 275 (Ark. 1958).

17. R. D. Truog and W. M. Robinson, "Role of Brain Death and The Dead-
Donor Rule in the Ethics of Organ Transplantation," *Critical Care Medicine*
31, no. 9 (2003): 2391–2396, at 2391.

18. *Id.*

19. See Randell, *supra* note 1, at 140.

20. *Id.*

21. See State statutes and cases, *supra* note 3.

22. See Wang et al., *supra* note 3 at 732.

23. Uniform Determination of Death Act 1980, prefatory note. (West 1980)

24. Uniform Determination of Death Act 1980. (West 1980)

25. See Wang et al., *supra* note 3, at 732.

26. See State's statutes, *supra* note 3.

27. See State's cases, *supra* note 3.

28. E. F. M. Wijdicks, "The Diagnosis of Brain Death," *New England Journal of
Medicine* 344, no. 16 (2001): 1215-1221, at 1215.

29. The Quality Standards Subcommittee of the American Academy of Neu-
rology, "Practice Parameters for Determining Brain Death in Adults,"
Neurology 45, no. 5 (1995): 1012-1014 [hereafter Quality Standards
Subcommittee].

30. See Wijdicks, *supra* note 29, at 1216.

31. See Wijdicks, *Clinical Criteria, supra* note 2, at 540.

32. D. A. Shewmom, "Chronic 'Brain Death': Meta-analysis and Conceptiual
Consequences," *Neurology* 51 (1998): 1538–1545; A. Halevy and B. Brody,
"Brain Death: Reconciling Definitions, Criteria, and Tests," *Annals of In-
ternal Medicine* 119 (1993): 519–255; R. D. Truog, "Is It Time to Abandon
Brain Death?" *Hastings Center Report* 27, no. 1 (1997): 29–37.

33. W. Chiong, "Brain Death without Definitions," Hastings Center Report
35, no. 6 (2005): 20–30.

34. See Randell, *supra* note 1, at 140.

35. See Baron et al., *supra* note 1, at 603.

36. See Wijdicks, *supra* note 29, at 1215.

37. *Id.*

38. See Quality Standards Subcommittee, *supra* note 32.

39. *Id.*

40. See Wijdicks, *supra* note 29.

41. *Id.*

42. *Id.*, at 1216.

43. See Mejia and Pollack, *supra* note 4, at 550.

44. See Randell, *supra* note 1, at 142; Mejia and Pollack, *supra* note 4, at 550.

45. See Mejia and Pollack, *supra* note 4, at 550.

46. See Randell, *supra* note 1, at 140; Quality Standards Subcommittee, *supra* note 32, at 1012; Canadian Neurocritical Care Group, "Guidelines for The Diagnosis for Brain Death," *Canadian Journal of Neurological Sciences* 26, no. 1 (1999): 64–66, at 64.

47. See Quality Standards Subcommittee, *supra* note 31, at 1012–1013; Canadian Neurocritical Care Group, *supra* note 46, at 65.

48. See Wijdicks, *supra* note 29, at 1220; Quality Standards Subcommittee, *supra* note 32, at 1013.

49. *Id.*

50. See State's statutes, *supra* note 3.

51. See Wijdicks, *Clinical Criteria, supra* note 2, at 540; Wijdicks (Brain Death Worldwide), *supra* note 2, at 23; Powner et al., *supra* note 2, at 1285; Mejia and Pollack, *supra* note 4, at 551; Wang et al., *supra* note 3, at 732–733; Jeffrey, *supra* note 5, at 1; M. Y. Chang, L. A. McBride, and M. A. Ferguson, "Variability in Brain Death Declaration Practices in Pediatric Head Trauma Patients," *Pediatric Neurosurgery* 39 (2003): 7–9, at 9.

52. See Wijdicks (Brain Death Worldwide), *supra* note 2, at 21.

53. See State's statutes, *supra* note 3.

54. *Id.*

55. Fla. Stat. Ann. § 382.009 (West 1987)

56. N. Y. Comp. Codes R. & Regs. tit. 10, § 400.16 (e)(3) (1987); *Matter of Long Island Jewish Medical Center*, 641 N.Y.S.2d 989 (N. Y. App. Div. 1996); *Matter of Conroy*, 486 A.2d 1209 (N. J. 1985).

57. Va. Code Ann. § 54.1-2972 (West 2004)

58. Alaska Stat. § 09.68.120 (West 1995); Ga. Code Ann., § 31-10-16 (West 1992); Mich. Comp. Laws. Ann. § 333.1033 (West 1992)

59. Conn. Gen. Stat. Ann. § 19a-279h (West 1988); Fla. Stat. Ann. § 382.009 (West 1987); Iowa Code Ann. § 702.8 (West 2001); Kentucky: Ky. Rev. Stat. Ann. § 446.400 (West 1986); Va. Code Ann. § 54.1-2972 (West 2004)

60. Fla. Stat. Ann. § 382.009 (West 1987)

61. Va. Code Ann. § 54.1-2972 (West 2004)

62. *Lovato v. Dist.Court of Tenth Judicial Dist*, 601 P.2d 1072 (Colo. 1979); *Dority v. Superior Court*, 145 Cal. App. 3d 273 (Cal. Ct. App. 1983); *In Re Haymer*, 450 N.E.2d 940 (Ill. App. Ct. 1983)

63. A. M. Capron, "Brain Death: Well Settled Yet Still Unresolved," *New England Journal of Medicine* 344, no. 16 (2001): 1244–1246, at 1244–1245 ("The term 'brain death' has become so familiar that it is not likely to be replaced by a more precise and less confusing term, such as 'brain-based determination of death.' Nonetheless, physicians who rely on diagnostic criteria of the sort set forth by Wijdicks ought to recognize that the language they use not only reflects but also sows confusion. Since 'brain dead' patients show such traditional signs of life warn, moist skin, a pulse,

and breathing, it is not surprising that many people seem to think that 'brain dead' is a separate type of death that occurs before 'real' death. This confusion is reinforced when hospital personnel state—and journalists repeat—that 'life support' is being removed from such patients.")

64. N. J. Statues Ann. 52:17B-88.1 through 88.6; N.Y. Public Health Law 4210-c(1) et seq.

65. See Wang et al., *supra* note 3, at 732–733; Mejia and Pollack, *supra* note 4, at 551–552; Youngner et al., *supra* note 4, at 2208–2209; R. Burck, L. Anderson-Shaw, M. Sheldon, and E. A. Egan, "The Clinical Response to Brain Death: A Policy Proposal," *JONA's Healthcare Law, Ethics, and Regulation* 8, no. 2 (2006): 53–59, at 55.

66. See Youngner et al., *supra* note 4 at 2208.

67. See Halevy and Brody, *supra* note 1, at 520–521; T. A. Ala, "A Case Meeting Clinical Brain Death Criteria with Residual Cerebral Perfusion," *American Journal of Neuroradiology* 27 (2006): 1805–1806, at 1805; G. Saposnik, J. A. Bueri, J. Maurino, R. Saizar, and N. S. Garretto, "Spontaneous and Reflex Movements in Brain Death," *Neurology* 54 (2000): 221–224, at 221.

68. See Ala, *supra* note 69, at 1806, 1882; Saposnik et al., *supra* note 69, at 221.

69. *Id.*

70. See Saposnik et al., *supra* note 69, at 222.

71. *Id.*

72. *Id.*

73. G. Saposnik, J. Maurino, and J. Bueri, "Movements in Brain Death," *European Journal of Neurology* 8 (2001): 209–213, at 209.

74. See Quality Standards Subcommittee, *supra* note 30, at 1013; Saposnik et al., *supra* note 75, at 212.

75. See Halevy and Brody, *supra* note 1, at 520.

76. P. M. Black and N. T. Zervas, "Declaration of Brain Death in Neurosurgical and Neurological Practice," *Neurosurgery* 15 (1984): 170–174, at 170.

77. *Id.*

78. *Id.*

79. *Id.*, at 171.

80. *Id.*, at 171–172.

81. *Id.*, at 172.

82. *Id.*, at 173.

83. *Id.*, at 171.

84. *Id.*

85. *Id.*

86. See Powner et al, *supra* note 2, at 1284.

87. *Id.*, at 1285.

88. See Powner et al, *supra* note 2, at 1285; Mejia and Pollack, *supra* note 4, at 551; Jeffrey, *supra* note 5, at 1.

89. See Wang et al., *supra* note 3, at 732–733.

90. See Powner et al, *supra* note 2, at 1284–1285.

91. *Id.*, at 1285.

92. *Id.*, at 1285–1287.

93. *Id.*

94. *Id.*, at 1285.

95. *Id.*

96. *Id.*

97. *Id.*

98. *Id.*

99. *Id.*, at 1285–1287.

100. *Id.*, at 1285.

101. *Id.*, at 1286.

102. *Id.*

103. *Id.*

104. *Id.*

105. *Id.*

106. *Id.*, at 1287.

107. *Id.*

108. See Jeffrey, *supra* note 5, at 1.

109. *Id.*

110. *Id.*, at 1–2.

111. See Wang et al., *supra* note 3, at 732.

112. *Id.*, at 732–733.

113. *Id.*, at 734.

114. *Id.*

115. See Mejia and Pollack, *supra* note 4, at 550–552.

116. *Id.*, at 551–552.

117. *Id.*

118. See Chang et al., *supra* note 52, at 8.

119. S. M. Izac, "Quality Assurance in Determinations of Brain Death," *American Journal of Electroneurodiagnostic Technology* 44, no. 3 (2004): 159–171, at 161.

120. See Lazar et al., *supra* note 12, at 834.

121. *Janus v. Metro. Life Ins. Co.*, 482 N.E.2d 418 (Ill. App. 1985).

122. See Baron et al., *supra* note 1, at 607.

123. *Lovato*, 601 P.2d 1072; *In re Haymer*, 450 N.E.2d 940.

124. *Dority*, 145 Cal. App. 3d 273.

125. *Nethery v. State*, 692 S.W.2d 686 (Tex. Crim. App. 1985).

126. *Ewing v. State*, 719 N.E.2d 1221 (Ind. 1999); *People v. Lai*, 131 A.D.2d 592 (N.Y. App. Div. 1987); *State v. Guess*, 715 A.2d 643 (Conn. 1998); *State v. Olson*, 435 N.W.2d 530 (Minn. 1989); *United State v. Market*, 65 M.J. 677 (N-M. Ct. Crim. App. 2007)

127. *In re Haymer*, 450 N.E.2d at 945 n. 9.

128. *United States v. Gomez*, 15 M.J. 954 (A.C.M.R. 1983)

129. *Id.*, at 959.

130. See Wijdicks, *Clinical Criteria, supra* note 2 at 540.

131. See State's statutes, *supra* note 3.

132. See Burke et al., *supra* note 67, at 55.

133. See Kulkarni and Cronin, *supra* note 8, at 3261; Lazar et al., *supra* note 12 at 834; see also J. McKinley, "Surgeon Accused of Speeding a Death to Get Organs," *New York Times*, February 27, 2008, *available at* <www.nytimes.com/2008/02/27/us/27transplant.html?_r=1&oref=slogin> (last visited October 6, 2008).

134. L. A. Siminoff, C. Burant, and S. Younger, "Death and Organ Procurement: Public Beliefs and Attitudes," *Social Science & Medicine* 59, no. 11 (2004): 2325–2334, at 2330.

135. See Saposnik et al., *supra* note 75, at 210.

136. A. M. Capron, "Brain Death—Well Settled Yet Still Unresolved," *New England Journal of Medicine* 344, no. 16 (2001): 1244–1246, at 1245.

137. See Kulkarni and Cronin, *supra* note 8, at 3260 (Extended criteria for organ donor include the donors whose characteristics are not considered to be ideal or standard.); Howard Koh et al., "A Statewide Public Health Approach to Improving Organ Donation: The Massachusetts Organ Donation Initiative," *American Journal of Public Health* 97, no. 1 (2007): 30–36 (Massachusetts Organ Donation Initiative is to form a unique partnership among organ procurement organizations, major teaching hospitals, and the state's department of public health to increase organ supply by focusing on reaching families during a time of critical decision-making.); A. Salim, "The Effect of a Protocol of Aggressive Donor Management: Implications for the National Organ Donor Shortage," *Journal of Trauma, Injury, Infection and Critical Care* 61, no. 2 (2006): 429–435 (In other words, the characteristics include advanced age, hypertension, and abnormal organ donor function. Aggressive donor management intends to increase organ supply by identifying potential donors in early stage.)

138. L. A. Siminoff, M. B. Mercer, G. Graham, and C. Burant, "The Reasons Families Donate Organs for Transplantation: Implications for Policy and Practice," *The Journal of Trauma, Injury, Infection, and Critical Care* 62, no. 4 (2006): 969–978, at 973.

139. See Powner et al., *supra* note 2, at 1284.

140. See Baron et al., *supra* note 1, at 606.

141. Quality Standards Subcommittee, *supra* note 30, at 1012.

142. See Randell, *supra* note 1, at 140.

143. *Id.*, at 143.

144. *Id.*, at 141.

145. *Id.*, at 141; see Wijdicks, *supra* note 29, at 1220; Quality Standards Subcommittee, *supra* note 30, at 1013.

146. Quality Standards Subcommittee, *supra* note 30, at 1013.

147. G. Bryan Young, S. D. Shemie, C. J. Doig, and J. Teitelbaum, "Brief Review: The Role of Ancillary Tests in the Neurological Determination of Death," *Canadian Journal of Anesthesia* 53, no. 6 (2006): 620–627 at 621.

148. *Id.*, at 625.

149. See Quality Standards Subcommittee, *supra* note 30, at 1013.

150. *Id.*

151. *Id.*

152. See Halevy and Brody, *supra* note 1, at 520–521; Ala, *supra* note 69, at 1806; Saposnik et al., *supra* note 69, at 221; E. F. M. Wijdicks, E. M. Manno, and S. R. Holets, "Ventilator Self-Cycling May Falsely Suggest Patient Effort during Brain Death Determination," *Neurology* 65, no. 5 (2005): 774.

153. See Quality Standards Subcommittee, *supra* note 30, at 1013.

154. W. M. Flowers and B. R. Patel, "Accuracy of Clinical Evaluation in the Determination of Brain Death," *Southern Medical Journal* 93 no. 2 (2000): 203–206, at 206.

155. *Id.*

156. See Powner et al, *supra* note 2, at 1285.

157. Uniform Anatomical Gift Act (West 1987).

158. See Wijdicks (Brain Death Worldwide), *supra* note 2, at 21.

159. See Wijdicks (Clinical Criteria), *supra* note 2, at 541; Wang et al., *supra* note 3, at 736.

160. The Joint Commission on Accreditation of Healthcare Organizations, *available at* <www.jointcommission.org/CertificationPrograms/TransplantCenter Certification/> (last visited October 6, 2008).

Kristin Zeiler

Deadly Pluralism? Why Death-Concept, Death-Definition, Death-Criterion and Death-Test Pluralism Should Be Allowed, Even Though It Creates Some Problems

Introduction

During the 1980s in the West, there has been a consensus regarding the accuracy of the whole-brain death criterion, i.e. 'the irreversible cessation of all functions of the brain, including the brain stem.'[1] While consensus on this issue can still be found at the level of national policies, the whole-brain death concept and its implications[2] have been criticized for being theoretically incoherent, internally inconsistent[3] and biologically implausible.[4]

Alternative concepts of death have been suggested, such as the higher-brain death concept. Others have argued for the heart-lung death concept. A number of policies and laws have also been established regarding concepts of death, death definitions, corresponding death criteria and tests for death.[5] In these cases, it has often been assumed that there should be *one* legal concept of death. This, however, is not the case in the New Jersey Death Definition Law and in the Japanese Transplantation Law. Both of these laws allow for more than one death concept within a single legal system. Both of them allow individuals who do not share particular death criteria to apply alternative death criteria to their *own* deaths. Furthermore, both of them relate preference for a particular concept of death to religious and/or cultural beliefs. It has been said these laws signal 'a new direction' for policies and laws in this area.[6]

This article argues for pluralism regarding death concepts, death definitions, death criteria and death tests—i.e. pluralism regarding death concepts and their implications—within certain limits. . . .

The Debate: Death Concepts and Their Implications

In Western history, death has been assumed to occur at the moment of irreversible cessation of respiration and circulation.[7] This is the heart-lung death criterion, consonant with the heart-lung definition of death as the 'permanent

From *Bioethics*, vol. 23, no. 8, 2009, pp. 450–456, 457–459. Copyright © 2009 by Blackwell Publishing, Ltd. Reprinted by permission via Rightslink.

cessation of the flow of vital bodily fluids.'[8] By the 1950s, however, new medical technology made it possible for machines to regulate a patient's heartbeat and breathing, even though the patient had irreversibly lost the capacity to breathe naturally. It was then argued that when the functions of the whole brain had been irreversibly lost, the patient was dead—and should be declared dead—even if medical technology could maintain heartbeat and breathing. The first steps towards a general acceptance of the whole-brain death concept were taken by the Harvard Medical School Committee when they developed a set of neurological criteria for determining death.[9]

The concept of whole-brain death is often defined as the irreversible cessation of 'the integrated functioning of the organism as a whole'[10] and the corresponding criterion for death is 'the irreversible cessation of all functions of the brain, including the brain stem.'[11] When the concept and its implications were introduced, it was argued that it was primarily the brain that was 'responsible for the functioning of the organism as a whole.'[12] When the whole brain was destroyed, the organism had 'ceased functioning.' This, it was claimed, proved the biological accuracy of the concept and its implications.

The definition of the concept whole-brain death and the corresponding criterion and tests have been criticized, however, for being theoretically incoherent and internally inconsistent. In order to understand the death debate, it is important to distinguish between concepts of death, which should involve definitions of death; operational criteria for death, which make it possible to determine when the definition has been fulfilled; and tests for death, which make it possible to evaluate whether the criteria have been satisfied.[13] Specific criteria for death must correspond to a given definition.[14] The problem in discussions of brain-death, some have stated, is that not all those patients who satisfy the criteria also satisfy the definition. Nor is it the case that all those patients who fulfil the necessary tests also fulfil the criteria.[15] As one example, it has been shown that about 20% of those patients who fulfil the tests for whole-brain death still demonstrate cerebral electrical activity on electroencephalograms, i.e. they do not fulfil the standard criterion for whole-brain death.[16] . . .

The whole-brain death criterion has also been criticized as being biologically implausible. When the criterion was introduced, it was based on the assumption that death of the brain stem implied the (more or less) imminent death of the whole organism. This is no longer the case, since advanced technology can replace brain stem function and bodies belonging to brain-dead patients can be kept alive for long periods of time. Furthermore, in the early discussions of brain-death it was assumed that the brain stem was the supreme regulator of the body; this is no longer—critics state—assumed to be the case. Regulation of immunity, haematopoesis and glucose metabolism, as three examples, take place independent of the brain stem.[17] For these reasons, it has been said, the whole-brain death criterion is problematic.[18]

The controversies about the concept of whole-brain death and its implications have led some to argue for a return to the heart-lung death concept. Others have argued for a higher-brain death concept and higher-brain death has been defined as the irreversible loss of the human being's consciousness.

The core of the matter is the irreversible loss of the patient's conscious life, her/his capacity for remembering, judging, reasoning, and acting.[19] The concept of higher-brain death has also been criticized by those who consider it to be counter-intuitive. It has been criticized for equating death with the irreversible loss of certain mental functions, which, if strictly applied to patients in persistent vegetative states, would mean that these would in fact be dead, as would anencephalic neonatal children.[20]

There is another group of arguments in the discussion on the death concept, death definition, death criteria and death test: religious and/or cultural arguments. Such arguments have been put forward by orthodox Jews, certain Buddhists as well as some groups of Native Americans, and by Malay people on the island of Langkawi—as some examples. . . . The New Jersey Death Definition Law gives 'religious beliefs' as a reason why individuals should be allowed to choose between being declared dead upon the basis of heart-lung death criteria or whole-brain death criteria.[21] Religious and/or cultural understandings of death also play a role in the Japanese Transplantation Law.[22] These two laws are particularly relevant in exploring reasons why legal pluralism as regards death concepts and their implications is positive and also problematic. Therefore, they will be presented in some length.

Two Examples: The New Jersey Law and the Japanese Law

When the New Jersey state adopted its death declaration law, it was acknowledged that certain religious groups would not endorse the whole-brain death concept, the whole-brain death definition or the corresponding criteria and tests for death. Orthodox Jews were one such group, who argued against the concept of whole-brain brain death, based on a certain understanding of Genesis 7:22. This text describes the story of Noah, his family and the animals that were with them in the Ark when the floodwaters destroyed 'every living thing' in the region: 'everything on dry land in whose nostrils was the breath of life died.'[23] This has been interpreted as an argument for the heart-lung death concept, the heart-lung death definition and the heart-lung death criteria and tests.[24] As long as one can breathe, as long as the body is warm, and as long as the heart is beating, one is alive.

. . . The New Jersey Death Declaration Law has an exemption clause stating that people who reject the whole-brain death neurological criteria on religious grounds will not be declared dead on the basis of these criteria. This is an 'opt-out' approach, according to which individuals who do not share these criteria for a particular kind of reasons—i.e. religious reasons—should not be declared dead on the basis of criteria that they do not accept. It is explicitly stated that the

> death of an individual shall not be declared upon the basis of neuro-logical criteria [. . .] when the licensed physician authorized to declare death, has reason to believe, on the basis of information in the individual's available medical records, or information provided by a member of the individual's family or any other person knowledgeable about the individual's personal religious beliefs, that such a declaration would

violate the personal religious beliefs of the individual. In this case, death shall be declared, and the time of death fixed, solely upon the basis of cardio-respiratory criteria.[25]

Consider also the example of the Japanese Transplantation Law. The Japanese discussion of brain death started in 1968, when a heart from a brain dead patient was transplanted. The physician in charge of the transplantation was accused of illegal human experimentation. Criticisms were directed at the whole brain-death concept and its implications. Seventeen years later, the Japanese committee on brain death and transplantation made a distinction between 'medical criteria for brain death' and 'the concept of human death.' The latter issue, it was stated, should be decided on the basis of a consensus among Japanese citizens.[26] In the debate that followed, three major arguments were put forward. It was argued that it would be difficult for people to accept brain death since the whole-brain dead person's body would still be warm, i.e. a psychological argument.[27] It was also argued that the tests for determining whether the brain-death criteria were satisfied would not test the cessation of the function of all brain cells, only the observable functions of the brain, i.e. it was an argument against the internal consistency of the criteria and the tests.[28] Furthermore, it was argued that the Japanese understanding of body and soul is different from the one in the West. In the West, the soul is thought to exist primarily in relation to the mind, whereas the Japanese understanding of the soul implies that the soul is dispersed throughout the body.[29] In line with this reasoning, it was argued that the essence of human beings lies not only in one's rationality and self-consciousness, but also in one's body.[30] . . .

The final report by the Japanese committee was published in 1992. It stated the majority view according to which brain death implied human death. It also contained the opinion, by the minority in the committee, that brain death should not be considered as human death. The resulting Japanese Transplantation Law, enacted in 1997, allows for two alternative death concepts. The law gives the patient the opportunity to choose to be declared dead either on the basis of the heart-lung death criteria or on the basis of the whole-brain death criteria. It allows organ donation under certain restricted circumstances from bodies declared dead in accordance with the criteria for whole-brain death or heart-lung death. If nothing is known about the patient's views on death, the patient should be declared dead on the basis of the heart-lung death criterion. In this sense, Japanese transplantation law takes the heart-lung death criteria as the default criterion.[31]

Why Pluralism? Which Kind of Pluralism?

. . . There are obvious difficulties in determining exactly when a human person dies. Whereas medicine can tell when certain biological functions are irreversibly lost, and whereas death is a biological phenomenon, the question as to when a human person is dead is not a biological, medical question. Here, an important distinction is the one between questions such as 'which are the necessary criteria for making sure that all the functions of the whole brain or the higher brain functions has been irreversible lost?' and questions such as 'when is person P dead?' 'should a brain-dead individual be treated as a dead person?' or 'what are the conditions for our ceasing to exist?'[32] Some have suggested that the latter questions can be reduced to a set of moral questions as regards when it is acceptable to terminate life supporting medical technology or when it is acceptable to bury someone's body. However, . . . it is not a moral question whether a particular person who was alive yesterday is also alive today.[33] Certain moral questions may be *evoked* depending on the situation in which someone dies, but this does not imply that the question of when a particular person has ceased to exist is moral. Instead, . . . the question of when a certain person is dead is a metaphysical question, and a philosophical and/ or religious question.

Consider the following examples. Some will claim that the human person dies when soul and body are separated, when there is a total loss of the somatic integrated unity of bodily functions.[34] Others, such as the Malay people on the island of Langkawi, for whom blood has a central place in ideas about life as well as death, will claim that for humans death occurs when all the blood leaves the body.[35] Still others may hold the view that a person's time of death is qualified by the relatives' sense of 'that person's continuity in the body of another.'[36] This is also the logic behind the view that organ donation can be seen as a way to live on 'through another person.'[37] These are not examples to frown upon with the claim that some people may have these views simply because they do not know any better. Those who have these views, or other views, may have an inaccurate understanding of death but the important point, which these examples highlight, is that *we need to address metaphysical issues concerning the nature of reality and the self in order to analyse the issue of death adequately.*[38]

Metaphysics and Comprehensive Doctrines

Metaphysical issues as regards the nature or reality, the self and death may be labelled background beliefs, part of what Rawls has called 'comprehensive doctrines' or what others have labelled 'deep values.'[39] Regardless of how we label them, these issues do matter to the kind of understanding of death that we consider plausible. It is important to analyse these metaphysical issues not only in order to understand the arguments for or against a certain concept of death in the cultures of orthodox Jews, Buddhists, Japanese groups or the Malay people on the island of Langkawi. It is also important to examine them in order to understand other arguments, possibly more common in the West, for or against different concepts of death.

It should be noted that my aim here is not to argue for or against a particular concept of death, a particular definition of death or particular criteria of or tests for death. My aim is to make it plausible that the question 'when is a human person dead?' is partly a metaphysical question and a philosophical and/or religious question. My aim is also to make it plausible that metaphysical views matter for which view of death we consider convincing.[40] *If* the exact time of the death of the human person is a metaphysical, philosophical and/or religious question, variations in views on the issue should not come as a surprise. Furthermore, I claim, if this is the case, a certain kind of pluralism as regards death concepts and their implications is not only unsurprising but something that modern democratic pluralistic societies need to accept. . . .

What Pluralism?

Rawls states that a pluralism of 'incompatible yet reasonable comprehensive doctrines' should be expected within modern societies. A comprehensive doctrine is a doctrine that includes conceptions of what is of value in human life or in ideals of personal virtue, such as exemplified by Christianity, Buddhism, different forms of Kantianism or Utilitarianism, or some kind of philosophical naturalism. A comprehensive doctrine may be religious as well as secular. Arguably, comprehensive doctrines also include concepts of when human, personal life begins and when a human person dies.

As citizens of a modern democracy, Rawls explains, we should not expect any comprehensive doctrines to be affirmed by all or even nearly all citizens. Indeed, the consequence of the reasonable pluralism of irreconcilable comprehensive doctrines is that we never can reach a non-oppressive agreement about comprehensive philosophical, moral or religious principles. This being the case, we need to find strategies to live with a reasonable pluralism of such doctrines. . . .

In the face of deep disagreement, we need first to examine whether it is necessary to have a uniform policy or law on the particular issue. According to Rawls, the state should try, as far as possible, 'to avoid disputed philosophical, as well as disputed moral and religious, questions.'[41] This examination of whether a uniform law or policy is necessary should be based on what Rawls labels public reason, i.e. reason not based on the comprehensive doctrines, and the aim of the examination is to reach an overlapping consensus as to whether a policy or law is necessary or not. If the particular issue under discussion is considered to be one where a uniform law or policy is needed, arguments for and against the particular issue discussed need to be brought forward. . . . Finally, in discussions of disputed questions where public policy and laws are considered necessary, and where public reason fails to arrive at any decision, citizens must vote on the question according to their 'complete ordering of political values.' The outcome of the vote is to be seen as 'legitimate provided all government officials, supported by other reasonable citizens, of reasonably just constitutional regime sincerely vote in accordance with the idea of public reason.' Rawls concludes that this means not that the outcome is true but that it is 'reasonable and legitimate law, binding on citizens by the majority principle.'

Each of these steps will now be discussed in relation to the death concept debate. I take it to be evident that a deep disagreement exists on this issue. There are different understandings of what the death of the human person means and when it takes place. Furthermore, I will allow myself to assume that the questions of what the death of the human person means and when death takes place are philosophical, religious and partly metaphysical questions.

As a first step, if we follow Rawls, we need to determine whether a uniform law or regulative policy is necessary. A pragmatic reason can be given for the need for a law or policy. If medical professionals have no law or policy to rely on, patients may be declared dead on different grounds and according to different views on death. This could result in an unfortunate arbitrariness, which would probably be experienced as frustrating for the professionals, the relatives and the patients. How will I, as a relative, know that the particular physician in charge does not declare my loved one dead in accordance with her personal death concept, death definition and the corresponding criteria and tests (that I may consider unreasonable)? . . .

How uniform does the law or policy need to be? I will certainly not argue for the desirability of separate laws for different communities within one and the same country. Difficulties with such approaches have been highlighted elsewhere.[42] However, a uniform law, i.e. a law that applies to all citizens of a particular country, can still be a law that accepts three different kinds of death concepts as legal. As long as all citizens are bound by this law, it qualifies as uniform.

For our next step, we need to ask what uniform law or policy is needed, and what characterizes a desirable procedure for arriving at this law or policy. . . .

The Role of Metaphysics, a Modified Version

Why is it important that metaphysical issues are also discussed in the public political forum if the reasons brought forward are based only on comprehensive doctrines? Metaphysical issues are, typically, issues where citizens hold different beliefs. Although arguments for a particular metaphysical view can and should be brought forward, we do not know (yet) which view is the accurate one. We may argue that some views are less rational than others, that some views are based on inaccurate or bad metaphysics, and/or that some arguments just don't lead to the assumed conclusion. Still, there is uncertainty as to which metaphysically-based understanding of death is the accurate one, and this uncertainty calls for humility.

Consider, as an example, the Japanese citizen who claims that the soul is dispersed throughout the body and that essence of the human being lies not only in one's rationality and self-consciousness, but also in one's body. He may be asked to give reasons for these views, as may all of us. He may answer that this builds on a certain holistic understanding of what it means to be a human being; he may cite religious texts for holding this view. Of course, someone may tell him that he needs to find public reasons to back up his religious views, in due time, but could it really be argued that that this is a good way or, possibly, even one of the best ways to respect his views? I think this is, at least, unclear.[43] I suggest that not only respect, but also understanding, can be better enabled if metaphysical issues and reasons based only on comprehensive doctrines are welcomed, discussed and (to a certain extent, to be clarified below) allowed to influence policy- and law-making. This could be a way to enhance the understanding and critical examination of different views that exist side by side in a pluralistic society.

Consider also the issue of voting. Voting on metaphysical issues would result in the majority's view becoming the legal one. Again, I will suggest another route, in order better to respect citizens' different beliefs—but without jeopardizing the possibility of a law or policy. What is needed, I shall suggest, is a reasonable legal pluralism as regards death concepts and their implications.

Reasonable Pluralism as Regards Death Concepts and Their Implications

A certain kind of reasonable legal pluralism in areas of disputed metaphysical, philosophical and/or religious questions should be allowed. This view needs also to be qualified: pluralism in areas of disputed metaphysical, philosophical and/or religious questions should prevail as long as the disputed questions concern the individual and the resulting policy or law or acts based on the policy/law do not harm the lives of other individuals to an intolerable extent. As noted by Robert M. Veatch, this is also the view that has been taken in discussions of religious dissent. This pluralism as regards death concepts and their implications allows individuals who do not share a particular concept of death to apply an alternative death concept to their own deaths. A reasonable legal pluralism allows people to have different views on metaphysical questions. Still, there are limits to this pluralism. I do not claim that *any* view of death should be legally acceptable.

Solves Some Problems, Creates Others

Allowing pluralism as regards concepts of death, death definitions, corresponding criteria and tests solves the problem of different people having different concepts of death. . . . This is important in modern, pluralistic societies. The New Jersey law and the Japanese Law should not be looked upon as odd examples, but as positive ways forward. Pluralism is acknowledged regarding the question of what death means and when someone is dead—within certain limits. . . .

At stake here is reciprocity with other citizens. This need not imply that everyone shares a particular view; nor does it imply that only one concept of death is legal. Fair terms of cooperation may well take place if it is argued that those who do not share the heart-lung death criterion need not be declared dead in accordance with it. I suggest, however, that reasonable concepts of death, definitions of death, criteria and tests for death should also be internally coherent and/or logically consistent given the particular world view that they may be based upon. Furthermore, reasonable concepts of death and their implications should not contradict accepted contemporary medical knowledge. I suggest that either the heart-lung death concept, or the whole-brain, or the higher-brain death concepts are acceptable.

Second, what are 'intolerably' harmful consequences? I suggest that the feeling of discomfort that some may have at the thought of the death concept, death definition, death criterion and death test pluralism does not qualify as intolerable. Although this pluralism evokes practical problems, these practical problems cannot be seen as intolerably harmful. Still, such practical problems need to be addressed. The pluralism as regards death concepts and their implications implies that potential donors/relatives of the donors should discuss not only whether donation should take place, but also which concept of death the potential donor prefers. This would, in some cases, render the situation more complex. Many people prefer not to talk or think about death, which is problematic for those relatives who will face the question of which concept of death their father/mother/spouse/child etc. had. This may be not only psychologically problematic but also ethically questionable. On the one hand, it needs to be asked if it is ethically acceptable that these complex questions should be directed at the relatives, at a time when their world may just have been turned upside down. On the other hand, not giving the relatives the opportunity to explain and discuss what death concept, death definition and death criteria should be used is undesirably paternalistic.

If some people prefer not to contemplate alternative concepts of death, definitions of death and criteria and tests for death, should their interest override the interest of those persons who do not want to be declared dead on the basis of a concept they reject? For the sake of respecting reasonable pluralism in modern societies, an opt-out scheme could be used. Those who have not contemplated alternative concepts of death and their implications when alive, for different reasons, will be declared dead in accordance with the default version. The default version should be the concept that most people in the particular country share. This is a sociological reason for a particular death concept and its implications: the default version should be the one that most people can be assumed to have preferred, provided that it meets the previous criteria for reasonableness. This sociological reason says nothing about whether the default version is the most accurate one.

Some may also consider the lack of global consensus as a major difficulty. Consider, therefore, a second, rather far-fetched scenario. Someone is declared dead in accordance with the definition of the higher-brain death concept and the corresponding criteria, in a particular country that allows no pluralism as regards death concepts and their implications and in which the higher-brain death concept is the accepted version. Imagine also that, for some reason, this person is driven by ambulance to a nearby hospital in another country; this country allows death-concept, death-definition, death-criterion and death-test pluralism. Since it is known that the person hold a heart-lung death concept, he is now not dead. Is that not too problematic? This is certainly not an easy situation. The fact that countries already differ as regards death concepts, death definitions, death criteria and death tests does not make it easier. Still, it could be argued that this scenario is an argument for harmonizing policies and laws—globally—but it is *not* an argument against death-concept, death-definition, death-criterion and death-test pluralism as such.

There at present is no culture-independent version of death that can be taken as a gold standard . . . and there are variations in views not only between but also within societies. For this reason, the New Jersey Law and the Japanese Law, as regards allowing pluralism in modern states, are ways forward.

Notes

1. *Uniform Determination of Death Act.* 12 Uniform Laws Annotated 320 (1990 Supp.)

2. It is important to distinguish between *concepts* of death, which must involve *definitions* of death, corresponding *criteria* for death and *tests* for death. When I discuss death concepts, death definitions, death criteria and tests for death, however, I will allow myself to refer to these as 'death concepts and their implications.'

3. R.D. Truog. 1998. Is It Time to Abandon Brain Death? In *The Ethics of Organ Transplantation.* A.L Caplan and D.H. Coelho, eds. New York: Prometheus Books.

4. A. Shewmon. The Brain and Somatic Integration: Insights into the Standard Rationale for Equating 'Brain Death' with Death. *JMed Philos* 2001; 26: 457–478; Kerridge, I.H. et al. Death, Dying and Donation: Organ Transplantation and the Diagnosis of Death. *J Med Ethics* 2002; 28: 89–94.

5. See for example the Swedish Committee on Defining Death. 1984. *The Concept of Death.* Stockholm: Swedish Ministry of Health and Social Affairs; President's Commission for the Study of Ethical Problems in Medicine and Biomedical and Behavioural Research. 1981. *Defining Death: Medical, Legal and Ethical Issues in the Definition of Death.* Washington, DC: US Government Printing Office; Goldbeck-Wood. S. Germany Passes New Transplant Law. *BMJ* 1997; 315: 7.

6. R.S. Olick. Brain Death, Religious Freedom, and Public Policy: New Jersey's Landmark Legislative Initiative. *Kennedy Inst Ethics J* 1991; 1: 285.

7. This is the secular version of the traditional understanding of death in the West. In the religious (i.e. Christian) version, death is thought to occur when the soul is separated from the body. Of course, this phenomenon cannot be empirically observed but it was, historically, assumed to take place at the moment of irreversible cessation of breathing and/or irreversible cessation of cardiac activity. Compare the Jewish tradition, discussed in footnote 24.

8. A. Halevy & B. Brody. Brain Death: Reconciling Definitions, Criteria, and Tests. *Ann Intern Med* 1993; 119: 519–523.

9. Ad Hoc Committee of the Harvard Medical School to examine the definition of death. A Definition of Irreversible Coma. *JAMA* 1968; 205: 337–340.

10. Halevy & Brody, *op. cit.* note 8. There are also slightly different formulations, such as death being 'the permanent cessation of function-ing of the organism as a whole.' J. Bernat, C. Culver & B. Gert. On the Definition and Criterion of Death. *Ann Intern Med* 1981; 94: 389–394. For discussions of these whole-brain death definitions, see E.T. Bartlett & S.J. Younger. 1988. Human Death and Destruction of NeoCortex. In *Death: Beyond Whole-Brain Criteria.* R.M. Zaner, ed. Dordrecht: Kluwer Academic Publishers.

11. *Uniform Determination of Death Act, op. cit.* note 1.

12. J.L. Bernat. The Definition, Criterion, and Statute of death. *Semin Neurol* 1984; 4: 45–51.

13. Truog, *op. cit.* note 3.

14. This may sound straight-forward, but it should be noted that the same physiological indicators are sometimes used as criterion and sometimes as parts of definitions. As an example, the ability to experience consciousness can be seen as a marker indicating that someone is alive *or* as the essence of life. M.S. Pernick. 1999. Brain Death in a Cultural Context. In *The Definition of Death. Contemporary Controversies.* S.J. Younger, R.M. Arnold & R. Shapiro, eds. Baltimore and London: The John Hopkins University Press. It should also be noted that in the early discussion of the concept of whole-brain death, whole-brain death criteria were more discussed than whole-brain death definitions. For a discussion of some of such definitions, see Bartlett & Younger, *op. cit.* note 10.

15. Truog, *op. cit.* note 3.

16. M.M. Grigg et al. Electroencephalographic Activity after Brain Death. *Arch Neurol* 1987; 44: 948–954; Halevy & Brody *op. cit.* note 8; A. Halevy. Beyond Brain Death? *J Med Philos* 2001; 26: 493–501.

17. Kerridge et al., *op. cit.* note 4.

18. It has also been argued that if one equates death with the irreversible loss of the 'somatic integrative unity of the organism as a whole,' one cannot equate the death of the human person with the death of the same human being's whole brain, since many somatic integrative functions are not brain-mediated. Shewmon, *op. cit.* note 4. For further discussion of the whole-brain definition, see *J Med Philos* 2001; 26 and *J Med Ethics* 1991; 17. However, a distinction can also be made between death defined as the irreversible cessation of all functions of the entire brain, including the brain stem, and death defined as the irreversible cessation of all functions of the entire brain, not including the brain stem.

19. S.J. Younger & R.M. Arnold. Philosophical Debates about the Definition of Death: Who Cares? *J Med Philos* 2001; 26: 527–537. For a discussion of the higher-brain death criteria and the view that death takes place when the integration of bodily and (higher) mental functions are irreversibly lost, see Veatch, R.M. Brain death and slippery slopes. *J Clin Ethics* 1992; 3: 181–187.

20. Shewmon, *op. cit.* note 4. Here, it should be noted that some proponents for higher-death definition(s) claim that the irreversible loss of certain mental functions is a necessary but not sufficient criterion for death.

21. New Jersey Statutes. Annotated. *Declaration of Death.* 26:6A-5. St Louis, Mo: West Publishing; 1991:232–235.

22. *Zoki no Ishoku nikansuru Horitsu* [The Law concerning Organ Transplantation], July 16th, 1997, Law no. 104 of 1997.

23. Genesis 7:22. *Bible. New Revised Standard Version.* 1989. For an overview of Jewish discussion on the Death Definition, see F. Rosner. 1999. The Definition of Death in Jewish Law. In *The Definition of Death. Contemporary Controversies.* S.J. Younger, R.M. Arnold & R. Shapiro, eds. Baltimore, Md. and London: The John Hopkins University Press. See also J.D. Bleich. 1999. *Time of Death in Jewish Law.* New York: Z Berman.

24. The traditional view of Judaism is that death occurs upon the separation of the soul from the body. The question *when* this takes place is debated. The Babylonic Talmud (tractate Yoma) states that in order to determine

whether someone is dead one should examine the person's respiration ('his nose'). The Babylonic Talmud also adds that examination of cardiac activity may be necessary ('some say: Up to his heart.') (See F. Rosner, *op. cit.* note 23, pp. 210–221). In modern time, some rabbis accept the whole-brain death definition and the whole-brain death criterion, whereas others hold that death occurs when there is an irreversible cessation of respiration (i.e. a heart-lung death criterion). Still others argue that in Medieval Jewish thought, cessation of respiration was regarded as indicative of prior cessation of cardiac activity. Indeed, respiration without cardiac activity was thought to be impossible. In line with this reasoning, the irreversible cessation of both cardiac activity and respiration are necessary criteria for death. Rabbis who have this view do not accept the whole-brain death definition or the whole-brain death criterion. See J.D. Bleich. Establishing criteria for death. *Contemporary Halakhic Problems.* New York: Ktav & Yeshiva University Press, 1977: 372–393; F. Rosner & M.D. Tendler. Definition of Death in Judaism. *J Halacha Contemp Soc* 1989; 17: 14–31.

25. New Jersey Statutes, *op. cit.* note 21, 22: 6A-4.

26. M. Morioka. Reconsidering Brain Death: A Lesson from Japan's Fifteen Years of Experience. *Hastings Cent Rep* 2001; 31: 44.

27. M. Nakajima. *Mienai Shi [Invisible Death].* Bungei Shunju, 1985, cited in Morioka, *op. cit.* note 26.

28. T. Tachibana. *Noshi [Brain death].* Chuo Koron Sha, 1986, cited in Morioka, *op. cit.* note 26.

29. A Bagheri. Organ Transplantation Laws in Asian Countries: A Comparative Study. *Transplant Proc* 2005; 37.

30. E. Ohnuki-Tierney. Brain Death and Organ Donation. Cultural Bases of Medical Technology. *Current Anthropology* 1994; 35: 233–254; M. Lock. 2002. *Twice Dead. Organ Transplants and the Reinvention of Death.* Berkeley: University of California Press.

31. *Zoki no Ishoku nikansuru Horitsu, op cit.* note 22; Morioko, *op. cit.* note 26; Baghieri, *op. cit.* note 29. See also M. Lock. Deadly Disputes; Hybrid Selves and the Calculation of Death in Japan and North America. *Osiris* 1998; 13. If organ donation should be allowed to take place, however, the donor must have expressed which death concept and criteria she or he wanted to be used, the wish to donate organs must have been written beforehand, and the family must agree on both the death concept and organ donation.

32. J. McMahan. 1998. Brain Death, Cortical Death, Persistent Vegetative State. In *A Companion to Bioethics.* H. Kuhse & P. Singer, eds. Oxford: Blackwell Publishing: 255.

33. Ibid.

34. John Paul II. 2000. *Address to the XVIII International Congress of the Transplantation Society,* Aug 29, 2000. It should be noted that one can accept changed criteria for death without altering one's comprehensive doctrine.

35. J. Carsten. 2004. *After Kinship.* Cambridge: Cambridge University Press.

36. Ibid: 102.

37. M. Crowley-Matoka & M. Lock. Organ Transplantation in a Globalised World. *Mortality* 2006; 11: 173.

38. See also G. Khushf. Owning up to our Agendas: On the Role and Limits of Science in Debates about Embryos and Brain Death. *J Law Med Ethics* 2006: 58–75.

39. R. Veatch. Abandoning Informed Consent. *J Med Ethics* 1995; 25: 5–12.

40. Consider one example. Assume, as suggested by Georg Khushf, that I consider that the 'the subjectively perceived unity of experience has no status beyond the experience itself, and [that] when the biographical continuity integral to perceived self-unity is lost, then nothing of the person remains' (Khushf, *op. cit.* note 39, p. 60). This is a philosophical stand-point, not a medical one. Certainly, I may combine this understanding of the self with different understandings of death, but it will suit some understandings of death better than others. This particular understanding can effectively underpin the view that the death of the human person, 'occurs at a certain stage of brain disintegration, when neuronal traces of experience can no longer be united with the self-resonant dynamic associated with the "I"' (Khushf, *op. cit.* note 39, p. 61). Then some version of brain-death becomes plausible—more so than the traditional heart-lung death definition.

41. J. Rawls. 1999b. Justice as Fairness: Political Not Metaphysical. In *Collected Papers*. S. Feeman, ed. Harvard: Harvard University Press: 394.

42. For example, it needs to be asked who defines the distinct communities, how dynamic they are and, in mixed marriages, should different laws apply to the different individuals if they belong to different communities, and if two individuals belonging to different communities with contradictory laws are in conflict on a matter regulated differently in these two laws, how should this conflict be solved? For a discussion of different kinds of legal pluralism, see for example A-J. Arnaud, From Limited Realism to Plural Law. Normative Approach versus Cultural Perspective. *Ratio Juris*, 1998; 11: 246–258 and M. Chiba. Other Phases of Legal Pluralism in the Contemporary World. *Ratio Juris* 1998; 11: 228–245.

43. R. Bellamy's criticism of Rawls' views is noteworthy. Bellamy claims that at the heart of Rawls' theory lies a certain concept of citizenship that mainly those already devoted to this political liberalism may endorse: a concept of citizens as individuals who do not consider certain religious or philosophical convictions as crucial to their way of living, or even to their identity, and who therefore may find it comparably easy not to bring in comprehensive doctrines in public political debates. See R. Bellamy. 1999. *Liberalism and Pluralism. Towards a Politics of Compromise*. London and New York: Routledge.

EXPLORING THE ISSUE

Is Brain Death Dead Enough?

Critical Thinking and Reflection

1. What is "whole brain death"? How do clinicians determine that such a condition is present in a given patient?
2. Imagine that you are a nurse at the bedside of a patient that has been declared dead, but is still connected to a respirator and other tubes and machines. The family asks, "If he is still warm and his heart is still beating, how could he be dead?" Discuss your response and identify the difficulties this creates?
3. Why is the issue of organ donation linked to the definition of death? Identify how the dead donor rule plays an important part in being able to retrieve organs for transplant.
4. Are there psychological, spiritual, or emotional definitions of death? If yes, how do they fit with the clinical definitions of death?
5. Are there patients who were declared dead but later found to be alive? Discuss the problems that occur when health professionals are lax about the criteria that they use in establishing death. What patients are most vulnerable to this happening?

Is There Common Ground?

In the recent white paper by the President's Council on Bioethics (2008), the group of physicians, ethicists, and lawyers agreed that the controversy over the death definitions and criteria is complicated by the limited understanding of the general public. Families are more likely to challenge physicians when they have misunderstandings of what might be expected for a patient with whole brain death. Rather than broadening the definitions or the criteria for death determination, physicians need to consistently apply the criteria established, and clearly communicate the findings in a way that helps survivors understand that death has occurred.

Even patients who are positively and reliably diagnosed with "brain death" (total brain failure) can continue to exhibit *many* functions that are simply not controlled by the brain—examples include maintaining some degree of blood pressure and body temperature, eliminating wastes, providing a cellular immune response to infection, or exhibiting a stress response to an incision. Good communication, explanations of findings, and providing emotional comfort to family members can help them, as the face these clinical realities of a loved one who has died (Applebaum, Tilburt, Collins, & Wendler, 2008; President's Council on Bioethics, 2008; Shaner et al., 2004; Shewmon, 2009).

References

Ad Hoc Committee of the Harvard Medical School. (1968). A definition of irreversible coma: Report from the ad hoc committee of the Harvard Medical School to examine the definition of brain death. *Journal of the American Medical Association, 205*(6), 337–340.

Applbaum, A., Tilburt, J. C., Collins, M. T., & Wendler, D. (2008). A family's request for complementary medicine after patient brain death. *Journal of the American Medical Association, 299*(18), 2188–2193. doi:10.1001/jama.299.18.2188

Capron, A. (2001). Brain death-well settled yet still unresolved (editorial). *New England Journal of Medicine, 344*(16), 1244–1246. doi:10.1056/NEJM200104193441611

Choi, E., Fredland, V., Zachodni, C., Lammers, J., Bledsoe, P., & Helft, P. R. (2008). Brain death revisited: The case for a national standard. *Journal of Law, Medicine & Ethics, 36*(4), 824–836. doi:10.1111/j.1748-720X.2008.00340.x

President's Council on Bioethics. (2008). *Controversies in the determination of death.* Washington, DC: President's Council on Bioethics. Retrieved from http://bioethics.georgetown.edu/pcbe/reports/death/Controversies%20in%20the%20Determination%20of%20Death%20for%20the%20Web%20(2).pdf

Report of the Quality Standards Subcommittee of the American Academy of Neurology. (1995). Practice parameters for determining brain death in adults. *Neurology, 45,* 1012–1014.

Shah, S. K. & Miller, F. J. (2010). Can we handle the truth? Legal fictions in the determinations of death. *American Journal of Law & Medicine, 36,* 540–585.

Shaner, D. M., Orr, R. D., Drought, T., Miller, R. B., & Siegel, M. (2004). Really most sincerely dead. *Neurology, 62,* 1683–1686.

Shewmon, D. A. (2009). Brain death: Can it be resuscitated? *Issues in Law & Medicine, 25*(1), 3–14.

Zeiler, K. (2009). Deadly pluralism? Why death-concept, death-definition, death-criterion and death-test pluralism should be allowed, even though it creates some problems. *Bioethics, 23*(8), 450–459. doi:10.1111/j.1467-8519.2008.00669.x

Additional Resources

Beach, P., Hallett, A. M., & Zaruca, K. (2011). Organ donation after circulatory death: Vital partnerships. *American Journal of Nursing, 111*(5), 32–40.

Bresnahan, M. J. & Mahler, K. (2010). Ethical debate over organ donation in the context of brain death. *Bioethics, 24*(2), 54–60. doi:10.1111/j.1467-8519.2008.00690.x

Campbell, C. S. (2004). Harvesting the living? Separating "brain death" and organ transplantation. *Kennedy Institute of Ethics Journal, 14*(3), 301–318. doi:10.1353/ken.2004.0027

Domínguez-Gil, B., Delmonico, F. L., Shaheen, F. M., Matesanz, R., O'Connor, K., Minina, M., et al. (2011). The critical pathway for deceased donation: Reportable uniformity in the approach to deceased donation. *Transplant International, 24*(4), 373–378. doi:10.1111/j.1432-2277.2011.01243.x

Koppelman, E. R. (2003). The dead donor rule and the concept of death: Severing the ties that bind them. *American Journal of Bioethics, 3*(1), 1–9. doi:10.1162/152651603321611782

Lock, M. (2004). Living cadavers and the calculation of death. *Body & Society, 10*(2/3), 135–152. doi:10.1177/1357034X04042940

Miller, F. G. & Truog, R. D. (2009). The incoherence of determining death by neurological criteria: A commentary on controversies in the determination of death, a white paper by the President's Council on Bioethics. *Kennedy Institute of Ethics Journal, 19*(2), 185–193.

Nair-Collins, M. (2010). Death, brain death, and the limits of science: Why the whole-brain concept of death is a flawed public policy. *Journal of Law, Medicine & Ethics, 38*(3), 667–683. doi:10.1111/j.1748-720X.2010.00520.x

Spielman, B. (2003). Surrogates and respect for donors. *American Journal of Bioethics, 3*(1), 18–19.

Valeo, T. (2010). Neurological criteria for organ donation after cardiac death. *Neurology Today, 10*(9), 30–31.

Zielinski, P. B. (2011). Brain death, the pediatric patient, and the nurse. *Pediatric Nursing, 37*(1), 17–22.

Online Resources

American Medical Association Council on Ethical and Judicial Affairs

www.ama-assn.org/ama/pub/about-ama/our-people/
ama-councils/council-ethical-judicial-affairs.page

Presidential Commission for the Study of Bioethical Issues

http://bioethics.gov/

President's Commission on Bioethics—Controversies in the Determination of Death

http://bioethics.georgetown.edu/pcbe/reports/death/Controversies%20in%20
the%20Determination%20of%20Death%20for%20the%20Web%20(2).pdf

Uniform Determination of Death Act

http://people.bu.edu/wwildman/WeirdWildWeb/courses/thth/
projects/thth_projects_2003_lewis/udda.pdf

"Wither Thou Goes" from *The Doctor Stories* by Richard Selzer

http://bioethics.georgetown.edu/pcbe/background/selzer.html

Internet References . . .

Hospice Foundation of America

These sites provide information on hospice, how to find a hospice, and what hospice care is for, and also have information for professionals.

www.hospicefoundation.org/
www.hospicenet.org/

Dartmouth Atlas of Health Care: End-of-Life Care

This Web site provides information on how end-of-life care is different in different areas of the country. It also provides maps and information showing areas with high ratios of hospitals and providers that have high end-of-life costs compared with other areas of the country.

www.dartmouthatlas.org/keyissues/issue.aspx?con=2944

The Cost of Dying—CBC News Report

This is a great documentary on the high costs of care at the end of life. It discusses how families struggle with decisions for continuing care.

www.cbsnews.com/stories/2009/11/19/60minutes/main5711689.shtml

The High Cost of Dying—MSN Money Report

This is another great documentary on the high costs of care at the end of life. It discusses how families struggle with decisions for continuing care.

http://money.msn.com/retirement-plan/the-high-cost-of-dying-thestreet.aspx

Hospice, Policy, and Costs of Dying

Hospice is a philosophy of care that provides physical, emotional, and spiritual care for patients and their families when a patient is dying. This unit discusses the hospice model of care and the criteria that need to be met to enroll a patient in hospice. However, the majority of patients die in the hospital, not in their own home or hospice. The roundtable discussion of physicians from around the world provides some insight into why dying patients in America are more likely to continue to receive care in intensive care units; even the physicians in other countries would refer the patient to palliative care or hospice. The costs for care as patients approach the end of life can be very high. The essays for Issue 15 discuss financial research on the out of pocket costs for hospital and nursing home care at the end of life. Even though elders have some subsidized medical care through Medicare, these costs are substantial. Others identify that sub-sidized care only adds to the costs of care in the last year of life. Older adults were more likely to want expensive end-of-life treatments if they were subsidized by Medicare, but less likely to want treatments if survival chances were poor or their spouse would be impoverished by their care.

- Is It Better to Die in Hospice Than Hospitals?
- Should Eldercare at the End of Life Be Subsidized?

ISSUE 14

Is It Better to Die in Hospice Than Hospitals?

YES: Maryjo Prince-Paul, from "When Hospice Is the Best Option: An Opportunity to Redefine Goals," *Oncology Nurse* (vol. 23, no. 4, pp. 13–17, 2009)

NO: David Crippen, Dick Burrows, Nino Stocchetti, Stephan A. Mayer, Peter Andrews, Tom Bleck, and Leslie Whetstine, from "Ethics Roundtable: 'Open-Ended ICU Care: Can We Afford It?'," *Critical Care* (vol. 14, p. 222, 2010)

Learning Outcomes

After reading this issue, you should be able to:

- Gain an understanding of the criteria patients must meet to be eligible for hospice.
- Describe the barriers to hospice referrals (physician barriers, patient barriers, family barriers).
- Understand the importance of communication about prognosis in the use of hospice or palliative care.
- Discuss and identify the challenges in identifying ICU patients that could transition to hospice.

ISSUE SUMMARY

YES: Maryjo Prince-Paul of the Francis Payne Bolton School of Nursing at Case Western discusses the hospice model of care and the criteria that need to be met to enroll in hospice.

NO: David Crippen, a physician in the Department of Critical Care at the University of Pittsburgh Medical Center, presents a roundtable discussion with physicians around the world who have very different views about how to approach the care of a dying patient who is using an expensive intensive care resource at the end of life.

When asked, most Americans indicate that they would prefer a symptom-free, pain-free death at home, surrounded by family and friends. However, most Americans (60 percent) actually die in the hospital and 20 percent of these die in intensive care units (ICUs) (Pantilat, 2008; Lusardi et al., 2011). There are many factors that prevent patients from dying at home. For example, patients who suffer sudden, traumatic, life threatening injuries from a fall, car accident, or work injury would immediately be transported to the hospital for life saving attempts before being pronounced dead. Patients who have chronic diseases (heart disease, lung disease) may be hospitalized during an unstable episode and may be unable to be weaned from a respirator, or die from an overwhelming infection or from their underlying disease (Lusardi et al., 2011). In this issue we discuss the advantages and disadvantages of deaths at home with hospice and deaths in hospitals or ICUs.

Hospice care is a philosophy of care, not a place of care as many believe (Rogers, 2009). Although there are some inpatient hospice units, usually when a patient "goes on hospice" they are cared for at home by family members. The goal of hospice is the provision of comfort (physical and emotional) to dying patients in the last 6 months of life. Although originally designed as a care approach for cancer patients, patients can meet criteria for hospice if they have a 6-month life expectancy with other end stage diseases (congestive heart failure, COPD, Parkinson's disease, dementia) (Rogers, 2009; Prince-Paul, 2009). Hospice care can occur in many different places, in the patient's home (if they have a caregiver), in an assisted living or nursing home, or in a hospice facility.

Generally, hospice does not provide 24 hour caregivers to patients. When patients enroll in hospice, they must identify a family member(s) or hired caregiver(s) that will provide the actual day-to-day care. Hospice provides weekly visits from a registered nurse (sometimes more frequently) to supervise care and answer questions that patients or their family caregiver might have. Patients who require 24 hour care from skilled professionals are generally referred to nursing homes for hospice, or to special hospice units. Hospice services also have social workers, psychologists, and chaplains that can visit a patient as needed. Hospice care services do not include any measures that are meant to aggressively reverse the terminal illness (Douglas, 2007; Prince-Paul, 2009; Pantilat, 2008; Rogers, 2009).

There are downsides to receiving care on hospice. Some family members become overwhelmed providing care at home to a dying patient. They become worried about getting the medications wrong, or overdosing the patient, or they become concerned about symptoms that they don't understand. Although hospice nurses are available by telephone 24 hours a day, they are not physically present all of the time to provide care support.

In contrast, patients who are critically ill often die in the hospital (Lusardi et al., 2011). Health care professionals may know that patients prefer to die at home, but have difficulty recognizing when someone is close to dying or meets criteria for hospice (Crippen, Burrows, et al., 2010). Sometimes critically ill patients unexpectedly recover. Making a clear prognosis about which patients are dying is not always easy. Plans for discharging critically ill patients from the hospital are also challenging. One hospital established a "going home initiative" to assist patients as they transition from the ICU to hospice care at home (Lusardi et al., 2011). Instability of the patient condition and disagreements among family members were barriers to these transitions. Sometimes the palliative comfort care would have been too complex for family caregivers to handle, or the family had limited resources in managing care at home (Lusardi et al., 2011).

There are marked regional differences in referrals to hospice. The Dartmouth Atlas of Health (2010) compared deaths in hospitals versus hospice in different regions of the country for Medicare recipients. More than half of Medicare recipients getting cancer treatment at Westchester Medical Center in Valhalla, NY (57.3 percent) ended up dying in the hospital. This compares with only 18.7 percent of cancer patients who died in the hospital at Evanston Northwestern Healthcare in Evanston, IL (Dartmouth Atlas of Health Care, 2010; Rau, 2010). The Dartmouth study implies that the difference in where a patient may die is linked to the physician prognosis and willingness to refer to hospice. The outcome for both groups in each region is the same; these are dying patients after all. But in some parts of the country, similar patients are sent home for hospice care which is more comforting and less expensive for Medicare. One survey of oncologists reported that one in five oncology physicians would wait to have a conversation about do-not-resuscitate (DNR) orders until a few days or few hours before the patient's death (Baile, Lenzi, Parker, Buckman, & Cohen, 2002, p. 2189). Both families and physicians may be reluctant to give up on aggressive treatments. In either case, these families are more likely to have patients die in the hospital, surrounded by technology. It would be helpful to better understand why families and physicians in other areas of the country appear to be more amenable to hospice.

Critical care physicians are aware that the highly technical world of the ICU is not an ideal place to die. In 2008, the American Academy of Critical Care Medicine issued a consensus statement of recommendations for end-of-life care in the ICU (Truog et al., 2008). Their recommendations include: provide training on communication skills to physicians; initiate a family conference early in the ICU stay to discuss and establish goals, values, and directives; conduct interdisciplinary team rounds so that families are not faced with different specialists giving different messages; refer dying patients to a palliative care team or provide an ethics consult when families are demanding futile care; and develop a supportive culture for staff and families of patients dying in the ICU (Truog et al., 2008). They provide guidelines for clinical approaches on how to help families cope with the patient's clinical symptoms as the technology is removed.

In the YES article, Maryjo Prince-Paul of the Francis Payne Bolton School of Nursing at Case Western discusses the hospice model of care and the criteria that need to be met to enroll in hospice. She discusses the eligibility criteria for hospice and offers a case presentation as an example of a hospice referral.

In the NO article, David Crippen, a physician in the Department of Critical Care at the University of Pittsburgh Medical Center, presents a roundtable discussion with physicians around the world who have very different views about how to approach the case of a dying patient who is using an expensive intensive care resource at the end of life. He notes the differences in the aggressive approaches by the U.S. physicians, who question the diagnoses, want to order more tests, or wait a longer time to determine possible outcomes. He compares these with intensive care physicians from European countries, who approach the same case more conservatively and refer the patient to palliative care (hospice).

YES

Maryjo Prince-Paul

When Hospice Is the Best Option: An Opportunity to Redefine Goals

Ms. D is a 45-year-old woman with ovarian cancer and hepatic metastatic disease. She has received multimodal treatment over the past 5 years. Ms. D lives in her own home, is divorced, and is a single parent of two adolescent children. Her mother is her primary caregiver and also has a deteriorating health condition.

Ms. D's functional status is very poor. She was enrolled in a phase I clinical trial, however a further decline in functional status, coupled with increased symptoms and diminished renal function, required that she withdraw from participation in the trial.

Her cancer has progressed with extensive peritoneal involvement and increased ascites that are managed with a peritoneal catheter. She and her children have stopped talking to one another and there is increased tension between Ms. D and her mother. Ms. D has begun to question her spirituality and feels that God is punishing her.

She does not want her health care providers to think that she is "giving up and throwing in the towel." She was admitted to the hospital with intractable nausea and vomiting and a possible malignant bowel obstruction. She has no advanced care planning and is a full code. . . . [W]e need to assess the situation and ask ourselves, "Is this patient appropriate for referral to hospice care?"

Introduction

As Americans, we live in a death-denying society, surrounded by expansive, advanced technology and interventions that can extend and prolong life at all costs. We have made great strides in cancer care through early detection, prevention, and treatment, yet a significant number of patients still do not survive their disease. In 2008, for example, the American Cancer Society estimated 1,437,180 new cancer cases (all sites) and 565,650 deaths.[1] Most people who have survived cancer and completed their course of treatment live with the underlying fear and uncertainty that their cancers may return. While some people with advanced cancer are living longer and with improved quality of life, hospice care is a choice that provides a unique set of benefits, services, and support.[2]

From *Oncology (Nurse Edition)*, April 2009, pp. 13–17. Copyright © 2009 by UBM Medica Ltd. Reprinted by permission via Wright's Media.

Although patients and families report that they are satisfied once enrolled in hospice level of care, many patients are referred too late or not at all.[3] Less than one-third of patients receive hospice care near the end of life and those who are referred die within days.[4] The transition to hospice care, including the establishment of a trusting relationship with the inter-disciplinary team, takes some time, and patients with very short lengths of stay cannot reap all of the benefits of hospice care.[5] Because oncology nurses are typically the mainstay during patients' and families' course of cancer care, they stand at the forefront in assisting patients with complex end-of-life care decisions and in facilitating end-of-life care discussions.

What Is Hospice?

The Hospice Foundation of America defines hospice as comfort and supportive care given to patients and their loved ones when illness does not respond to treatments that have curative intent.[6] The philosophy of hospice is to provide the total care of patients who have a life-limiting illness. This includes meeting patients' physical, social, spiritual, and psychological needs. The goal of hospice is neither to prolong life nor hasten death, but rather to maximize quality of life for patients as they travel along this last journey.

Patients, regardless of age, are eligible to receive hospice care if their physicians certify them as having a life expectancy of 6 months or less, should the disease follow its expected course. While it is the role of the physician to recommend hospice care, it is the patient's right and decision to determine when hospice is appropriate and which program suits his needs. Although insurance coverage for hospice is available through Medicare, most private insurance plans, including HMOs and other managed care organizations, include hospice level of care as a benefit. Forty-four states in the US have a Medicaid Hospice Benefit. Also, through community contributions, memorial donations, and foundation gifts, many hospices can provide free services to patients unable to pay for them. Other programs charge in accordance with ability to pay.

The Medicare Hospice Benefit

In 1982, the Tax Equity and Fiscal Responsibility Act authorized Medicare to reimburse for hospice services. Due to the passage of this bill, hospice became publicly funded under the Medicare Hospice Benefit.[7] The Medicare and Medicaid hospice benefits include the same services: skilled nursing care, medical social service, hospice physician services, and counselor/spiritual care. (These services/team members are considered "core" and are required by all hospice programs.) Depending on program size, a variety of other services may be provided by the hospice interdisciplinary team. These may include nursing assistants; homemaker services; physical, occupational, and speech therapies; expressive therapies (e.g., art, music, horticultural); durable medical equipment; and medications.

Three of the most distinguishing characteristics of the hospice care delivery model include trained volunteers, 24-hour on-call availability, and bereavement support for 1 year after the death of the loved one. Trained volunteers can offer companionship, provide necessary respite time for the primary caregiver, and help with everyday tasks such as grocery shopping and babysitting. A hallmark of hospice care is the 24-hour, 7-day-a-week availability of a hospice team member. Patients and caregivers are often relieved to know that someone can be telephoned in the middle of the night if a problem arises, and that a visit will be made to the patient's residence if needed. As hospice care is patient-family–centered care, surviving family members will be attended to for 1 year through a bereavement support program. The hospice care team and designated bereavement support professionals will visit them at specific time points, contact them by telephone and/or mail, or provide information about other bereavement support groups.

Most hospice care is provided in the home, but it is sometimes necessary for the patient to be admitted to an acute care, extended care, or hospice inpatient facility. Should a patient's needs exceed that which a family can provide, and if deemed medically necessary, continuous care in the home can be provided for 8- to 24-hour periods on a short-term basis.

Why Hospice?

Hospice provides an alternative to what many perceive as overuse of technology and poor symptom control for dying patients, a perception confirmed by the 1995 Study to Understand Prognosis and Preferences of Outcomes and Risks of Treatment (SUPPORT).[8] This study, the largest research project examining end-of-life care in the US, found people die in pain, isolation, and perhaps with unnecessarily increased health care costs. Also, families of patients who died in hospitals reported insufficient information about existing community resources such as hospice care.

Furthermore, a US Institute of Medicine report concluded that "people have come to both bear a technologically overtreated and protracted death and dread the prospect of abandonment and untreated physical and emotional stress."[9] Casarett et al. suggest that a variety of other factors may have a greater influence on hospice use, including a lack of communication about patients' preferences for treatment and care.[4]

Health care providers are often unaware of patients' preference regarding life-sustaining treatment or interventions.[10,11] Too often, in the absence of forethought, healthcare providers become involved in futile interventions, with patients' wishes and preferences for care unknown and family members burdened by questions about choices. These concerns may be diminished with the help and support of a hospice team.

Hospice Care: Barriers and Misconceptions

Many barriers to and misconceptions about hospice care remain embedded in our society. As oncology nurses, it is important to understand these issues and recognize how to resolve these barriers to the utilization of hospice care. The following communication strategies may be helpful in responding to feelings commonly expressed by patients when healthcare providers initiate discussions about hospice.

- *"This means I'm giving up!"* The benefit of treatment must always be weighed against the burden of treatment and the patient's prognosis. Health providers should always consider the patient's performance status, symptom burden, psychological distress, and personal preferences. *A possible response:* "Some people may actually have improved quality of life when involved in hospice care because symptoms are being effectively managed. If, in the future, you want to have an intervention that hospice does not provide, you can withdraw from hospice care. We will not abandon you. We will assess how you are feeling overall and make decisions that are consistent with your wishes."
- *"I can't be that sick; I really don't need that yet!"* As discussed, an adequate period of time is necessary for patients to develop a trusting relationship with the hospice interdisciplinary team. *A possible response:* "In the past months, we focused on treating your disease. Recently, the goals of care have shifted. Now, we are trying to help you live as fully as possible by treating your symptoms and helping you obtain your goals. The time to reap the full benefits of hospice care is now. Hospice care can also provide support for your family."
- *"There's no hope left."* Hope is a necessary element of survival and is essential for most patients with a life-limiting illness. Oncology nurses should respect a patient's desire to maintain hope but must be able to balance that hope with the obligation to provide accurate information. This allows for reorganization of priorities and for adaptations in coping with the disease process. *A possible response:* "Sometimes we have to redefine what we hope for . . . it may be an opportunity to heal past hurts, to leave a legacy, or to attend an upcoming family event."

Effective communication is the cornerstone of end-of-life care and sets the tone for all aspects of care in the advanced cancer experience. Communication among the oncology nurse, patient, family, and other healthcare team members is a continuous process as patient management shifts from attempts at cure to a focus on comfort.

The Case Scenario (Ms. D): A Hospice Referral

Metastatic ovarian cancer with poor functional status and malignant bowel obstruction is associated with a poor prognosis.[12] Owing to Ms. D's rapid physical decline, increased physical and psychological symptoms, and her challenged personal relationships with her children, her mother, and God, discussions about hospice level of care should be initiated immediately. No further options for curative treatment are available for Ms. D. After clarifying Ms. D's understanding of her disease and expectations, the oncology nurse can facilitate discussion about her goals of care. This can include other members of the healthcare team (e.g., physicians and social workers). Optimally, a collaborative meeting between the family and hospice provider should be planned.

In this forum, there would be adequate time to respond to patient and family concerns, to have the hospice provide information, and to develop an individualized plan of care to meet the needs of Ms. D and her family.

Performing advanced care planning discussions now and attending to Ms. D's wishes may help to relieve the burden of care from her mother later. Ms. D will also benefit from a meeting with her children. The importance of family increases with the diagnosis of cancer and the threat of death heightens involvement with close, important relationships. Cancer patients also have been found to show less psychological distress if they seek control through a partnership with God or higher power.[13] Patients had more depression, poorer quality of life, and exhibited anger toward others if they perceived their illness as a punishment from God.[14] Spiritual counseling provided by a hospice team would provide Ms. D with an opportunity to discuss her relationships with God and her children.

Implications for . . . Nurses

The most important focus of end-of-life care is to identify ways to improve the dying experience. Because of the intimate contact and close proximity of the . . . nurse to the patient and family through day-to-day observation and care, patients are in a pivotal position to affect quality of life at the end of life for themselves and their families. The American Nurses Association states that nurses have a duty and responsibility to educate patients and families about end-of-life care issues, to communicate relevant information about complex decision-making processes, and to advocate for patients. The diagnosis of advanced cancer carries with it the element of time, and as death nears, time becomes more critical. Having a sense of life completion, by being able to help others, saying and sharing important things, finding a sense of meaning and peace within oneself, and making a positive difference in the lives of others may allow people with advanced illness to reflect on a life well-lived.[15] Support, guidance, and facilitation by . . . nurses have the potential to make a significant difference in the extent to which advanced cancer patients die well and at peace.

References

1. American Cancer Society: Cancer Facts and Figures, 2008. Atlanta, GA, 2008. Available at: http://seer.cancer.gov/csr/1975_2005/results_single/sect_01_table.01 .pdf. Accessed on February 22, 2009.

2. Casarett D, Pickard A, Bailey FA, et al: Do palliative consultations improve patient outcomes? *J Am Geriatr Soc* 56(4):593–599, 2008.

3. Casarett DJ, Crowley R, Hirschman K, et al: Caregivers' satisfaction with hospice care in the last 24 hours of life. *Am J Hosp Palliat Care* 20(3):205–210, 2003.

4. Casarett D, Van Ness PH, O'Leary JR, et al: Are patient preferences for life-sustaining treatment really a barrier to hospice enrollment for older adults with serious illness? *J Am Geriatr Soc* 54(3):472–478, 2006.

5. Lynn J: End-of-life care listed as a national research priority. *Am J Hosp Palliat Care* 18(2):85–86, 2001.

6. Hospice Foundation of America: What Is Hospice? Available at: www .hospicefoundation.org/hospiceInfo/. Accessed on February 22, 2009.

7. Carlson MD, Morrison RS, Bradley EH: Improving access to hospice care: Informing the debate. *J Palliat Med* 11(3):438–443, 2008.

8. Knaus WA, Harrell FE Jr, Lynn J, et al: The SUPPORT prognostic model. Objective estimates of survival for seriously ill hospitalized adults. Study to understand prognoses and preferences for outcomes and risks of treatments. *Ann Intern Med* 122(3):191–203, 1995.

9. Field MJC: Approaching Death: Improving Care at the End of Life. Field MJ, Cassel CK (eds). Washington DC, National Academy Press, 1997.

10. Wenger NS, Phillips RS, Teno JM, et al: Physician understanding of patient resuscitation preferences: Insights and clinical implications. *J Am Geriatr Soc* 48(5 suppl):S44–S51, 2000.

11. Wenger NS, Kanouse DE, Collins RL, et al: End-of-life discussions and preferences among persons with HIV. *JAMA* 285(22):2880–2887, 2001.

12. Ripamonti C, Bruera E: Palliative management of malignant bowel obstruction. *Int J Gynecol Cancer* 12(2):135–143, 2002.

13. Breitbart W, Rosenfeld B, Pessin H, et al: Depression, hopelessness, and desire for hastened death in terminally ill patients with cancer. *JAMA* 284(22):2907–2911, 2000.

14. Pargament K, Smith B, Koenig H, et al: Patterns of positive and negative religious coping with major life stressors. *J Sci Study Religion* 37:717–724, 1998.

15. Steinhauser KE, Bosworth HB, Clipp EC, et al: Initial assessment of a new instrument to measure quality of life at the end of life. *J Palliat Med* 5(6):829–841, 2002.

David Crippen et al.

Ethics Roundtable: "Open-Ended ICU Care: Can We Afford It?"

The Case

The patient is a 27-year-old previously healthy male with a diagnosis of viral encephalitis. . . . For 3 months, he has been in status epilepticus (SE) [having continuous seizures] on high doses of barbiturates, benzodiazepines, and ketamine and a ketogenic feeding-tube formula. He remains in burst suppression on continuous electroencephalography (EEG). He is trached [has a breathing tube] and has a percutaneous endoscopic gastrostomy (PEG) feeding tube. He has been treated several times for pneumonia, and he is on a warming blanket and is on [medications] to maintain his blood pressure. His vitals are stable and his lab work is within limits. The sedation is decreased under EEG guidance every 72 hours, after which he goes back into [seizures] and heavy sedation is resumed. The latest magnetic resonance imaging (MRI) shows edema but otherwise no obvious permanent cortical damage. The family wants a realistic assessment of the likely outcome. The neurologist tells them the literature suggests the outlook is poor but not 100% fatal. As long as all of his other organs are functioning on life support, there is always a chance the seizures will stop at some time in the future, and so the neurologist recommends an open-ended intensive care unit (ICU) plan and hopes for that outcome.

David Crippen

A fundamental tenet of legal justice is that it is better to let ten guilty men go free than convict one innocent man. The reciprocal in medicine is that it is better to artificially maintain life in ten death spirals than miss one expected survivor. Physicians are famous for ignoring impediments to the care of their individual patients. No long-shot treatment is shelved and no expense is spared no matter how dim the potential outcome. A righteous contempt is shown toward administrative pleas to consider cost.

In the past, this strategy worked only as well as the ability of the resource allocation system providing for it: an open-ended credit card with an unclear path to replete funds. Now we are seeing strong evidence of a new health care allocation system that will create a closed system whereby excising some portions of the pie directly affects the size of the other portions. The bigger some portions get, the fewer are available.

The amount of money spent on end-of-life care, specifically dying at the end of life, dwarfs other expenditures. And the unique situation of critical care will create a double dip for each patient maintained on artificial life support. If we are willing to maintain 100 moribund patients in ICUs for a prolonged period to yield one long-shot survivor, we do not pay for just the survivor. We pay also to warehouse the other 99 failures not quite dead or alive but with stable vital signs.

Since it is difficult to know on admission which patients will benefit from life-supporting organ failure reversal, we admit all comers for a trial. Now comes a logical extension of that policy. At any time in the course of treatment, it is equally difficult to predict outcome, so we should maintain most if not all moribund patients indefinitely to avoid killing the occasional unexpectedly survivor.

In the case presented here, we have a long-term ICU patient with a small but potentially survivable prognosis on a seemingly endless course of life support. Ten years ago, most physicians would have buckled down and maintained such a patient simply until he died of something else. As in a poker game, the winning card was still in the deck but could appear at any time.

Physicians are looking at anecdotal evidence that we should wait longer before declaring unsalvageability, but we are facing health care reform that will expect physicians to care for more patients more cheaply. That pie can be cut only so many ways. Every day a long-term patient lies in an ICU is a day that resources for other patients diminish commensurately. How long is long enough? How long is too long? How many moribund patients are we willing to warehouse to find one outlier? The question then becomes how will our intrepid concern for our individual patients be affected by real-time competition for others desiring their pieces of the pie?

Dick Burrows

Can we afford open-ended ICU care? No, the resources are inadequate.

There can be no argument that improved technology has revolutionized medical treatment. There is improved survival in many conditions that previously would have been fatal.

The downside is an assumption that a technical (ICU) solution can solve an adaptive sociocultural problem;[1] death and dying are not the result of a failure of technology. So far, death remains undefeated,[2] resulting in questionable costs that are greatest in the last few weeks of life. Death occurs in 100% of people, but dying is a process, and the exact time of death is seldom definable, making individual decisions to stop resuscitation extremely difficult, especially in cases in which technology has delayed death, and there are always those who 'beat the odds'. The failure of medical school curricula to address the topic of death and dying[2] means that clinicians are ill equipped to deal with the subject. The pressure to apply the technology, irrespectively of costs, is considerable.

Medicine has changed to accommodate the cost of the technology. The days in which the patient approached the doctor and paid for the service (when the patient could) are long gone. A third party, either the state or insurance of some sort, has taken responsibility for payment, but the relationship is complex, and ultimately the individual or (more likely) the family remains responsible for medical care. This is reflected in the fact that 62% of bankruptcies in the US are for medical reasons.[3]

As a result, the right of the physician to treat as he or she sees fit has been curtailed by the third party on the basis of the economic costs of treatment. It is difficult to ascertain the number of (adult) intensive care beds that should be provided for the population. One paper indicates six beds per 100,000 persons.[4] In 2004, in KwaZulu-Natal, South Africa, there was less than one ICU bed per 100,000 persons and this has not increased substantially. This meant that, in 2004, ICU clinicians at two hospitals in Durban denied entry to as many as half of the critically ill patients. The most common reason to refuse admission was that the unit was full. Another reason was that, in the view of the ICU staff, the admission would achieve no benefit to the patient. Consequently, the patient in the case above would not have been admitted. A mechanism did exist in some hospitals to refer patients as an interim measure to a private unit but this was often curtailed for budget reasons. If a patient was insured, he or she would be admitted to a private hospital but a call to transfer him or her to the state sector would be inevitable when the insurance coverage was exhausted. At that time, the prognosis would be reviewed and a decision to admit or not to admit would be made.

The distinction between patient autonomy and economic issues is unclear as the clinician has a duty not to waste resources[5] and is forced to make decisions short of a point of certainty.[6] The availability of resources simply shifts that point away from certainty, and it serves no purpose to walk away from the problem, insisting that someone else deal with it.

In this part of the world (Ireland), the patient in the case above would be admitted, but the economic realities of the moment indicate that this will likely change precipitously over the coming months as there is a progressive failure to service demands. At some point, treatment will have to stop, the state will ration care, and the insurance company will limit coverage or initiate proceedings against the estate if treatment continues in the absence of continuing funds. Negotiation and conciliation will be the order of the day. It will be difficult.

Nino Stocchetti

I think that the care plan in this case should be changed after 3 months or perhaps before. Three aspects should be considered:

1. The benefit for the patient. It looks very doubtful after such long treatment, and iatrogenic damage due to high-dose barbiturates and so on is obvious. My experience with high-dose barbiturates . . . is that severe cardiac, hemodynamic, and infectious complications are the rule after the first days. I never used them for more than 7 to 10 days.
2. The benefit for the family. Family stress can reach unbearable levels in months of never-ending tension.
3. The benefit for society. My unit has 6 beds, 4 during summertime. This shortage and the costs related to every ICU bed make the responsible

use of resources essential.[7] Keeping a highly specialized bed occupied for months denies this resource to others.

What makes this case especially difficult is the lack of strong evidence concerning the expected outcome. In traumatic brain injury, we base our prognosis on several thousands of cases,[8] whereas for encephalitis, there is no database of comparable size. In fact, there is no large database at all. Anecdotal cases and even small series are of limited use, and different opinions and doubts are respectable.

However, an SE [status epilepticus—continuous seizures] refractory to maximal treatment for 3 months indicates extremely severe brain damage and does confirm that we do not have an effective treatment. Having confirmed the inefficacy of maximum treatment for 3 months, I would conclude that it is rather futile. Then the difficult choice is to justify a protracted unuseful treatment rather than its withdrawal.

Due to the admitted limited knowledge, I would ask colleagues from outside the department, with an international reputation, for a collegial expert opinion. If they confirmed my assessment, I would proceed; otherwise, I would wait further. Then I would offer the family the option of external consultation in order to dispel the notion that the reason the therapy plan is being pursued is that the treating doctors are bored or mistaken. The family has the right to call other experts.

Having collected the (presumed homogeneous) opinions of various colleagues (including, eventually, someone nominated by the family) about the futility of further insistence, I would talk again with the family, hoping to obtain their consensus. My proposal would be to stop [sedating medications], aiming at spontaneous breathing, not restarting high-dose sedation even if SE [status epilepticus—continuous seizures] re-appeared. I would give the family the option of transferring the patient to another institution, if required.

Stephan A. Mayer

I would absolutely continue to offer long-term aggressive care and support to this patient. Tremendous and unexpected recoveries can happen only if you let them.

If there is one condition that can defy expectations and from which patients can emerge after months and months in coma, it is SE [status epilepticus—continuous seizures] in a young patient with normal brain imaging and a clinical diagnosis of encephalitis. The literature, in fact, is replete with reports of similar patients recovering from coma after several months on pentobarbital.

One of our more memorable patients at Columbia [University, College of Physicians and Surgeons] was a Taiwanese woman in her early 20s with highly refractory SE [status epilepticus—continuous seizures] whom we diagnosed with an ovarian tum[or] and . . . encephalitis. It took several months to terminate the seizures, which came back relentlessly every time the pentobarbital was lifted, just like in the patient described above. Thereafter, she was in a seizure-free vegetative state for over 6 months. Finally, New York Presbyterian Hospital paid over $100,000 for an air ambulance to fly her back to a hospital in Taiwan. It was that or provide a lifetime of care to an undocumented alien in a persistent vegetative state.

Imagine our shock when, 6 months later, the accepting neurologist sent us a photograph of her, smiling and apparently intact. It took a year for her to start to follow commands, then she entered rehabilitation, and now she has a second chance on life, with minimal disability. We never in our wildest dreams expected her to recover after we sent her back to Taiwan. And she would never have had that chance if we had pushed the family to pull the plug when she was in our ICU.

Of course, patients have the right to be treated the way they want to and that includes the right to refuse unwanted life support. We all believe that, as physicians, we should not play God—it is not our role to make these decisions, and the patient has the final say. But the ideal of free will in medical decision-making is just that: an ideal. In real life, the decisions that family members make are a direct consequence of what they hear from us.

In the scenario above, I would provide a realistic estimate of the likely spectrum of outcomes in 1 year with continued full-court aggressive support. I would estimate that four possible outcomes have an equal likelihood of occurring: (a) dead of a fatal medical complication, (b) vegetative, (c) conscious and severely disabled, or (d) walking and talking and working on a good recovery. I would remind the family that as long as the goal is survival to discharge, our team would collectively focus on complete recovery as the goal of our efforts. Given that information, I then would provide three potential goals of action: (a) full medical support until discharge, (b) full medical support with a do-not-resuscitate (DNR) order, and (c) DNR and terminal extubation. These are the 'three paths,' and they can pick only one path. I do not allow families (or ourselves) to pursue prolonged life support combined with ambivalent and half-hearted medical or neurological intervention.

Finally, I always give the family the option of changing the plan, cutting their losses, and opting for comfort at any point down the road if they feel that their loved one has been through enough. I call it our 'money back guarantee.'

Peter Andrews

This illustrative case has some unusual features that require further clarification. But the question 'what management plan is in the best interests of this previously healthy young man, who is now requiring multiple-organ support for intractable SE [status epilepticus—continuous seizures] and requiring barbiturate coma because of recurrent seizures?' is important. I believe that the prognosis after 3 months on intractable SE [status epilepticus—continuous seizures] as a complication of presumed viral encephalitis is poor in the extreme.

Before we can conclude that withdrawal of organ support is appropriate, a number of actions are required:

1. A multi-disciplinary team (MDT) discussion about this very difficult case should occur between neurology, critical care, neurophysiology, and infectious diseases. Possibly, a consult from a national expert on the encephalitis in question would also help establish the likely

prognosis with more certainty. Neurophysiology should be involved, monitoring the seizures on a daily basis.

2. The serum levels of anticonvulsants (those in addition to barbiturates) should be measured to establish that they are in their 'therapeutic range.' . . . Once these agents are optimized and after at least 24 hours of burst suppression induced by barbiturates, the anesthetic agent should be reduced. Recurrence of seizures (assessed by EEG and clinical exam and ideally with video EEG for both) mandates action to suppress this activity. This is the sequence of events described in this case.

3. After such a long period of seizures, it is likely that severe cerebral injury has occurred. However, I would consider the use of hypothermia to see whether this intervention could improve the situation.[10] There are reports of success in SE [status epilepticus—continuous seizures] with this intervention.

After 3 months of intractable SE [status epilepticus—continuous seizures] still requiring barbiturate-induced burst suppression, the outlook is very poor. Further MRI sequences may be helpful to document the extent of neurological damage (that is, diffusion-weighted imaging, diffusion tensor imaging, and so on). The neurologist has stated to the family that the outlook is poor but not 100% fatal. The literature that this prognosis is based upon is likely to come from papers relating to the particular viral encephalitis. I would suggest, however, that when the situation is complicated by such a long period of SE [status epilepticus—continuous seizures], the outlook is considerably worse.

If the patient were comatose but not in SE [status epilepticus—continuous seizures] and not requiring advanced organ support, I would recommend discharge to an acute neurology ward with a tracheostomy and PEG or RIG (radiologically inserted gastrostomy) feeding. The situation could then be monitored over a number of weeks or months. However, in this case, the MDT should agree on this prognosis and then meet with the family to discuss changing the emphasis of care to palliation and comfort care.

Tom Bleck

The data available from studies of SE [status epilepticus—continuous seizures] in the literature really provide no guidance in dealing with a case such as this. There are published cases of recovery after long durations of SE [status epilepticus—continuous seizures] refractory to treatments other than suppression by barbiturates (weeks to months), but there are no population-based or even hospital-based analyses with denominators to provide an estimate of the likelihood of functional recovery. My practice in this circumstance is to pay attention to the MRI results; if the MRI does not show evidence of progressive tissue destruction, then I continue to support the patients aggressively. I am aware of several patients who were in SE [status epilepticus—continuous seizures] suppressed with high-dose barbiturates for over 3 months and who eventually awakened and returned to reasonably normal function. In my experience, about 1 patient out of 5 in this patient's circumstances returns to work or school after prolonged treatment for refractory SE [status epilepticus—continuous seizures] and almost all of the remainder die in the ICU. So I agree with the neurologist in this case.

In the absence of demonstrated brain destruction, withdrawing aggressive therapy for SE [status epilepticus—continuous seizures] because the staff or family is exhausted by the strain of prolonged treatment would likely result in another example of self-fulfilling prophecy. This phenomenon is being recognized with increasing frequency in neurocritical care. As a resident, I was trained to appear wise by hanging crepe and counseling an early transition to comfort care. As I get older, I sometimes ponder how many potentially functional survivors I consigned to an early grave. This is an area that cries out for a multi-center outcome analysis based on quality of life-years. . . .

Leslie Whetstine

Conclusions

This case highlights, among other things, the remarkable differences in health care resource allocation throughout the world. Both Bleck and Mayer, neurologists practicing in the US, are reluctant to withdraw an enormous expenditure of time and resources if there is a marginal chance for survival.[11] Both conclude that there are insufficient data to accurately prognosticate long-term outcome and so continuing open-ended aggressive treatment is appropriate. Their approach contrasts markedly with that of Burrows and Stocchetti, intensivists practicing in Europe. Both Burrows and Stocchetti must consider the investment of time and resources because expending resources on one patient impacts the care of others. While the Americans do not discuss the issue of cost as a determinant factor in their analyses, the Europeans clearly regard it as a key component to the issue.

Andrews does not address cost but instead recommends an MDT [multidisciplinary team] approach to assess the patient as well as additional tests and therapies to ensure that all possibilities for improvement have been exhausted. He concludes that if such an alternative care plan showed no further change, intractable SE [status epilepticus—continuous seizures] described in the clinical scenario would indicate moving to a palliative care plan. Crippen, an American with a utilitarian mindset, unveils the iniquities inherent in a private practice system by asking difficult questions that run contrary to American sensibilities. Although he does not go so far as to invoke the concept of rationing as prioritization, it is the logical conclusion to his argument.

This case illustrates the need for resource allocation policies at the macro level. Before this can be done, however, established guidelines that are grounded in evidence-based medicine are necessary. Otherwise, the inflammatory rhetoric commonly heard in the current health care reform debate in the US (that government or some other regulatory body will be 'killing grandma') will paralyze discussion. Moreover, it is worth noting that Burrows and Stocchetti are not individual physicians flouting the rules; they are acting within constraints that their countries have implemented. Mayer and Bleck cannot be expected to ameliorate the shortcomings of an unfair and moribund system on their own.

Ethically, this case emphasizes the need for taking resource allocation policies to a level away from individuals making isolated anecdotal decisions at the bedside. Taking the debate to a level of authoritative data erases the potential for capricious decision making. Once those data are transparently obtained, a rational discussion as to what level is appropriate to stop treatment can proceed.

The public needs assurance that they are not deprived of treatment based on an arbitrary or mercenary economic model. Within the past 6 months, an authoritative figure, Sanjay Gupta, published a book[12] that chronicled recovery from near death; a patient diagnosed in persistent vegetative state is now allegedly using assistive communication devices, and a poorly managed recommendation regarding mammogram protocols reinforced societal disdain for bureaucratic regulation. These cases as well as the one presented here should be viewed through the lens of objective data rather than the bias of individual physicians.[13] When this occurs, the care of these patients will be standardized for the most benefit, the most reasonable cost, and the most equity for all.

References

1. Bosk CL, Dixon-Woods M, Goeschel CA, Pronovost PJ: Reality check for checklists. *Lancet* 2009, 374:444–445.

2. Illich I: Death undefeated. *BMJ* 1995, 311:1652–1653.

3. Himmelstein DU, Thorne D, Warren E, Woolhandler S: Medical bankruptcy in the United States, 2007: results of a national study. *Am J Med* 2009, 122:741–746.

4. Lyons RA, Wareham K, Hutchings HA, Major E, Ferguson B: Population requirement for adult critical-care beds: a prospective study. *Lancet* 2000, 355:595–598.

5. Levinsky NG: The doctor's master. *N Engl J Med* 1984, 311:1573–1575.

6. Shaw GB: Prologue. In *The Doctor's Dilemma*. 1906.

7. Doig C, Murray H, Bellomo R, Kuiper M, Costa R, Azoulay E, Crippen D: Ethics roundtable debate: patients and surrogates want 'everything done'—what does 'everything' mean? *Crit Care* 2006, 10:231.

8. Murray GD, Butcher I, McHugh GS, Lu J, Mushkudiani NA, Maas AI, Marmarou A, Steyerberg EW: Multivariable prognostic analysis in traumatic brain injury: results from the IMPACT study. *J Neurotrauma* 2007, 24:329–337.

9. Knake S, Gruener J, Hattemer K, Klein KM, Bauer S, Oertel WH, Hamer HM, Rosenow F: Intravenous levetiracetam in the treatment of benzodiazepine refractory status epilepticus. *J Neurol Neurosurg Psychiatry* 2008, 795:588–589.

10. Corry JJ, Dhar R, Murphy T, Diringer MN: Hypothermia for refractory status epilepticus. *Neurocrit Care* 2008, 9:189–197.

11. Robakis TK, Hirsch LJ: Literature review, case report, and expert discussion of prolonged refractory status epilepticus. *Neurocrit Care* 2006, 4:35–46.

12. Gupta S: *Cheating Death: The Doctors and Medical Miracles that Are Saving Lives Against All Odds*. New York: Wellness Central; 2009.

13. Rosenhek R, Binder T, Porenta G, Lang I, Christ G, Schemper M, Maurer G, Baumgartner H: Predictors of outcome in severe, asymptomatic aortic stenosis. *N Engl J Med* 2000, 343:611–617.

EXPLORING THE ISSUE

Is It Better to Die in Hospice Than Hospitals?

Critical Thinking and Reflection

1. If you were in a motor vehicle accident and had sustained injuries that were life threatening, would you want family members to take you out of the ICU home to die? Why or why not? What would be the barriers for doing this?
2. Consider the difficulties physicians face as they try to determine whether someone has 6 months to live or not (the criteria for hospice). What are the risks of them declaring a patient fit for hospice too soon?
3. Why do you think some families continue to demand care, seek second opinions, and want additional testing done when physicians have explained that their loved one is dying in the ICU? What would be better ways to approach this conversation?
4. You are the ICU nurse caring for a patient who has been in the ICU for 3 weeks with no improvement. You know that she has no hope for survival, and that each day in the ICU is costing $4,500. The patient's wife is worried that she will go bankrupt with the copay, but the son and daughter believe there could be a miracle. What would you do? (see additional resources on when families believe in miracles).
5. Discuss whether costs should ever be considered in the care of dying patients? Is every second of life (even if tethered to respirators and tubes) worth it? Why or why not?

Is There Common Ground?

The National Coalition on Health Care (2009) identified the costs of health care in 2009 at approximately $2.5 trillion or 17.6 percent of the 2009 gross domestic product of the United States. Caring for patients in ICUs in the United States makes up 15–25 percent of total hospital costs, and has been estimated as 1–2 percent of the gross national product (Halpern, Pastores, & Greenstein, 2004). Given these numbers, a clearer vision of appropriate care at the end of life that respects patients and families both physically and fiscally needs to be established. Health care providers need to develop skills for conducting clear conversations about expected outcomes of care and make appropriate referrals to hospice and palliative care.

Families also need to develop realistic expectations of technology. If not, the U.S. health care system will bankrupt the country by continuing to provide very aggressive care in the last days and last hours of life. Despite major efforts to have patients prepare advance directives for end-of-life care, most families and patients cannot anticipate when a hospitalization, illness, or injury will result in a terminal condition. Programs like the "Going Home Initiative" can help with discharge from the ICU to a more homelike setting. But these programs require good planning and interdisciplinary cooperation as they identify and approach appropriate patients and their family members. Health care professionals who are well informed about hospice can guide patients and family members so that the patient can be in the environment that they prefer when they die.

References

Baile, W. F., Lenzi, R., Parker, P. A., Buckman R., & Cohen, L. (2002). Oncologists' attitudes toward and practices in giving bad news: An exploratory study. *Journal of Clinical Oncology: Official Journal of the American Society of Clinical Oncology, 20*, 2189.

Connor, S. R., Pyenson, B., Fitch, K., Spence, C., & Iwasaki, K. (2007). Comparing hospice and nonhospice patient survival among patients who die within a three-year window. *Journal of Pain and Symptom Management, 33*, 238–246.

Douglas, A. (2007). Quality of life in hospice versus non-hospice terminally ill adults. *Journal of Hospice and Palliative Nursing, 9*(4), 182–189.

Finley, E. & Casserette, D. (2009). Making difficult decisions easier: Using prognosis to facilitate transition to hospice. *CA: A Cancer Journal for Clinicians, 59*, 250–263. doi:10.3322/caac.20022

Gaeta, S. & Price, K. (2010). End of life issues in critically ill cancer patients. *Critical Care Clinics, 26*, 219–227. doi:10.1016/j.ccc.2009.10.002

Halpern, N. A., Pastores, S. M., & Greenstein, R. J. (2004). Critical care medicine in the United States 1985–2000: An analysis of bed numbers, use, and costs. *Critical Care Medicine, 32*, 1254–1259.

Lusardi, P., Jodka, P., Stambovsky, M., Stadnicki B., Babb B., Plouffe D., et al. (2011). The going home initiative: Getting critical care patients home with hospice. *Critical Care Nurse, 31*(5), 46–57.

National Coalition on Health Care. (2009). Containing costs and avoiding tax increases while improving quality: Affordable coverage and high value care. Retrieved from http://nchc.org/blog/nchc-white-paper. Accessed October 25, 2011.

Pantilat, S. (2008). End-of-life care for the hospitalized patient. *The Medical Clinics of North America, 92*, 349–370.

Prince-Paul, M. (2009). When hospice is the best option. *Oncology Nurse, 23*(4), 13–17.

Rau, J. (2010). Where you die depends on where you live. *Kaiser Health Newsletter*. Retrieved from: www.kaiserhealthnews.org/Stories/2010/November/17/dartmouth-cancer-death.aspx.

Rogers, T. (2009). Hospice Myths: what is hospice really about? *Pennsylvania Nurse, 64*(4), 4–8.

Ryder-Lewis, M. (2007). Going home from the ICU to die: A celebration of life. *Nursing in Critical Care, 10*(3), 116–121.

Truog, R. D., Campbell, M. L., Curtis, J. R., Haas, C. E., Luce, J. M., Rubenfeld, G. D., et al. (2008). Recommendations for end-of-life care in the intensive care unit: A consensus statement by the American Academy of Critical Care Medicine. *Critical Care Medicine, 36,* 953–963.

Additional Resources

Delisser, H. M. (2009). A practical approach to the family that expects miracles. *Chest, 135*(6). doi:10.1378/chest.08-2805

Quill, T., Arnold, R., & Back, A. L. (2009). Discussing treatment preferences with patients who want "everything." *Annals of Internal Medicine, 151,* 345–349.

Online Resources

American Cancer Society Website, information on hospice

**www.cancer.org/Treatment/FindingandPayingforTreatment/
ChoosingYourTreatmentTeam/HospiceCare/index**

answers questions on what is hospice, who pays for hospice, questions to ask.

The National Hospice and Palliative Care Organization

www.nhpco.org/templates/1/homepage.cfm

American Hospice Foundation

www.americanhospice.org/

ISSUE 15

Should Eldercare at the End of Life Be Subsidized?

YES: National Bureau of Economic Research, from "Out-of-Pocket Health Care Expenditures at the End of Life," www.nber.org/aginghealth/2010no2/w16170.html

NO: Li-Wei Chao, José A. Pagán, and Beth J. Soldo, from "End-of-Life Medical Treatment Choices: Do Survival Chances and Out-of-Pocket Costs Matter?" *Medical Decision Making* (vol. 28, no. 4, 2008)

Learning Outcomes

After reading this issue, you should be able to:

- Gain an understanding of the limitations of financing of health care through Medicare.
- Understand the importance of full disclosure of treatment outcomes and treatment costs in making decisions at the end of life.
- Discuss and distinguish the difference between insurance-paid costs and out-of-pocket costs.
- Identify and debate whether reducing the costs spent by Medicare at the end of life would actually be used for important health care for other persons.

ISSUE SUMMARY

YES: In a National Bureau of Economic Research paper, researchers Samuel Marshall and Jonathan Skinner of the Department of Economics at Dartmouth College and Kathleen McGarry of the Department of Economics at UCLA discuss the out-of-pocket costs for hospital and nursing home care at the end of life and how these can be a drain on households even though elders have some subsidized medical care through Medicare.

NO: Li-Wei Chao and José A. Pagán of the University of Pennsylvania and Beth J. Soldo of the University of Texas Pan Am identify that older adults were more likely to want expensive end-of-life treatments if they were subsidized by Medicare, but less likely to want treatments if survival chances were poor or their spouse would be impoverished by their care.

Prior to the 1960s, 34 percent of the older adult population lived in poverty because of health care costs that were privately paid. It was difficult for persons over age 65 to get private health insurance coverage at that time (National Academy of Social Insurance, 2011). In 1965, Medicare was created as a national health insurance policy under the Social Security Act. While this insurance has helped to improve the health and longevity of older Americans, it has also created some problems. Since virtually everyone over the age of 65 has health insurance, tests and procedures that might not otherwise have been done in the past are done today because these procedures produce revenue for doctors and hospitals. This issue will discuss the advantages and disadvantages of providing subsidized health care for older adults at the end of life and examine the out-of-pocket costs that are still incurred by older Americans.

The cost of health care at the end of life accounts for a high proportion of total health care costs in the United States. The percentage of Medicare payments attributable to patients in their last year of life was 28.3 percent in 1978 and has remained about the same at 25.1 percent in 2006 (Donley & Danis, 2011). In order to really address the question of whether end-of-life care for older adults should be subsized, one might imagine what care for older adults would be like without any Medicare entitlement program. The thousands of Americans without health insurance can attest to the problems this would create. If there were no Medicare entitlement program, older adults or their family members would have to cover their own health-related costs after retirement and at the end of life. Our society could easily slip back into the pre-Medicare situation of more than one-third of older adults living below poverty because all of life savings are spent on health-related costs.

Perhaps a better question is how can we reduce the costs of the existing subsidized care for older adults at the end of life? When researchers examine possible ways of reducing health care costs at the end of life, they look at two areas: how to reduce costs that society bears collectively through insurance premiums and how to reduce the individual out-of-pocket costs related to care at the end of life that are not covered by insurance (Donley & Danis, 2011).

Several efforts have been made to reduce the costs of end-of-life care that are incurred by society. One study found that Medicare beneficiaries enrolled in a Medicare Healthcare Management Organization (HMO) used 51 percent fewer hospital days in the last two years of life when compared with fee-for-service enrollees (Fonkych, O'Leary, Melnick, & Keeler, 2008). Because HMOs have financial incentives to manage care, they make coordinated efforts to better communicate patient goals and eliminate unnecessary or undesired care. Patients who are seen as approaching the end of life are referred to skilled nursing facilities and hospices rather than continuing to incur higher hospital costs (Fonkych et al., 2008). Fee-for-service Medicare (i.e., Medicare that simply pays for each bill submitted) lacks incentives to manage these dollars. Sixteen different specialists can order multiple kinds of the same types of testing for end-of-life patients, and each of these are simply paid under fee-for-service Medicare. Since there are no incentives to manage or monitor spending at the end of life for these patients, costs increase as physicians and hospitals bill for each treatment.

Another approach to reducing costs to society is to reduce the aggressive and unnecessary treatments and tests at the end of life by having physicians include discussions of personal out-of-pocket costs with discussions of proposed treatment approaches (Baily, 2011; Donly & Denis, 2011). Although discussing costs of care prior to making clinical decisions has been controversial, some argue that leaving costs out of the discussion does not fully respect the patient's autonomy either (Baily, 2011; Epstein, 2007). If a patient or their family must pay for a treatment they can't afford, then it seems unethical for a physician to leave costs out of the conversation. Although older adults have insurance, one study reported that terminally ill patients with moderate or high care needs are more likely to rate costs of their terminal illness and medical care as a moderate or great economic hardship on their family (Emanuel, Fairclough, Slutsman, & Emanuel, 2000). In a study of patients with cancer, 19 percent had used up all or most of their personal savings, 21 percent were unable to pay for their basic necessities, and 9 percent had declared bankruptcy (Blendon, Brodie, Benson, Altman, & Buhr, 2006).

Some countries facing a burgeoning population of older adults discuss the issues of the economic burden of care in other ways, raising the possibility of *rationing* health care to older adults, or debating whether certain persons over the age of 80 should be admitted to intensive care units (ICUs) (Boumendil, Somme, Garrouste-Orgeas, & Guidet, 2011; Epstein, 2007; Russell, Greenhalgh, Burnett, & Montgomery, 2011). Clinicians argue that if studies on intensive care for older patients could predict and determine which subsets of elderly patients have good outcomes from ICU, costs could be reduced. They cite research that has helped pediatricians to identify the survival and quality-of-life issues for premature babies in neonatal ICUs. There are studies that show subpopulations of babies for whom neonatal intensive care is so demonstrably ineffective or so costly that it should not be provided (Lantos & Meadow, 2011). Because of the accuracy of these prognoses, neonatal intensive care has become increasingly cost efficient. If similar data could help predict outcomes for subpopulations of elders for whom ICU care offers no benefit, Medicare costs could be curtailed. These groups of older adults could be referred more appropriately to palliative care or hospice rather than spending precious federal funds on ICU care before death (Lantos & Meadow, 2011).

Currently, one of the few successful approaches to reducing end-of-life costs is to ensure that patients have a clear sense of their prognosis and that patients have established advance directives for their care (see Issue 2) (Pope, Arnold, & Barnato, 2011). End-of-life care is less costly and more likely to reflect patients' wishes when advance directives are in place (Silveira, Kim, & Langa, 2010).

In the argument for the YES position, Marshall, Skinner, and McGarry (2010) provide evidence that the out-of-pocket costs for hospital and nursing home care at the end of life can be a drain on households even though elders have some subsidized medical care through Medicare. Their argument supports subsidized care because elders are still incurring substantial costs that are not covered.

In the argument for the NO position, Chao, Pagán, and Soldo (2008) identify that older adults were more likely to want expensive end-of-life treatments if they were subsidized by Medicare, but less likely to want treatments if survival chances were poor or their spouse would be impoverished by their care. This data supports the need to discuss costs as part of the decision-making process for end-of-life care choices.

Out-of-Pocket Health Care Expenditures at the End of Life

While virtually all Americans age 65 and above are covered by Medicare, they may nonetheless face significant out-of-pocket health care expenditures. Medicare includes numerous deductibles and copayments, and many people do not have a "medigap" policy to cover these costs. Home health care and nursing home expenditures must be paid for out-of-pocket, unless individuals are poor enough to qualify for Medicaid or have purchased an expensive long-term care insurance policy. Even those with generous insurance coverage may face the costs of specialized food or medical equipment to manage their health conditions.

As health generally declines with age, these out-of-pocket expenditures may be particularly high towards the end of life. High out-of-pocket medical expenditures may strain the finances of older households, for example by draining a couple's assets when one spouse gets sick and leaving little for the other spouse later in life. The risk of high expenditures may also be an important factor in household decisions regarding how much to save and how quickly to spend assets in retirement.

In *The Risk of Out-of-Pocket Health Care Expenditures at End of Life* (NBER Working Paper 16170), researchers Samuel Marshall, Kathleen McGarry, and Jonathan Skinner estimate the magnitude of these expenditures. They focus not only on the average amount but also on the distribution of expenditures, to better understand the risks that older households face.

The authors use the Health and Retirement Study (HRS) for their analysis, a data set which includes detailed information on the health care expenditures of older individuals. Notably, the HRS conducts an "exit interview" after the death of a survey respondent in order to collect data on the period up to the person's death from a surviving spouse or other family member.

Despite the rich data available in the HRS, the authors nonetheless face a number of challenges in estimating these costs. First, individuals may not answer questions about some expenditure categories or may only be able to provide a range rather than an exact amount. Second, as the survey is administered at fixed two-year intervals but respondents may die at any time, information on spending since the last survey will cover different periods of time for different individuals. Third, some respondents report expenditure amounts that appear to be implausibly large. The authors may overstate the risk of

From *NBER Reporter*, no. 2, 2010. Published by the National Bureau of Economic Research.

medical expenditures if they use this data but may understate the risk if they do not. Much of their analysis focuses on their strategies for dealing with these challenges.

The authors find that out-of-pocket expenditures toward the end of life are large—the average amount is $11,618 in the last year of life. There is also considerable variation in end-of-life expenditures, with ten percent of respondents spending more than $29,000 per year and the top one percent of respondents spending more than $94,000 per year. These values are large relative to the non-housing wealth of a typical older household, which is about $25,000.

The authors find that the largest single category of spending is nursing home and hospital expenditures, which average $4,731 in the last year of life; roughly two-thirds of that amount is for nursing home care. Here too the distribution is skewed, with the top one percent spending more than $75,000 per year in this category. Other big expenditure categories include insurance ($1,746 on average), prescription drugs ($1,496), home health care and helpers ($1,966) and spending to make houses accessible ($721).

The authors also explore whether out-of-pocket health care expenditures vary with the respondent's income or wealth. They find that they do, particularly with respect to wealth—the richest 20 percent of households spend an average of $18,232, versus $7,173 for the poorest 20 percent of households. These differences appear to be driven mostly by greater spending for nursing homes, home health care, and items related to making houses accessible. The greater spending by wealthier households in these categories may reflect their ability to "buy" both the ability to stay at home longer and more comfortable living arrangements once they move to nursing home care, but could also indicate that low-wealth individuals do not receive needed health care.

In short, the authors find that out-of-pocket health care expenditures "represent a numerically large and potentially important drain on financial resources, particularly for households as time of death nears." They note that their results are "thus consistent with the view that many elderly may continue to hold (or even accumulate) wealth as a hedge against uninsured costs surrounding expensive end of life care-giving for themselves or their spouse."

Li-Wei Chao, José A. Pagán, and
Beth J. Soldo

 **NO**

End-of-Life Medical Treatment Choices: Do Survival Chances and Out-of-Pocket Costs Matter?

Introduction

Over the last four decades, the poverty rate of the U.S. elderly population has fallen by more than 60%, and the most recent data (2005) show that only about one of every ten people aged 65 and older (3.6 million) earned less than the poverty level.[1] Yet, the poverty rate of elderly widows is three times higher than that of elderly married women.[2] Recent studies provide convincing evidence that out-of-pocket health care expenditures incurred prior to the death of a spouse are partially responsible for the impoverishment of the surviving spouse.[3,4] As much as one fourth of the increase in elderly poverty after widowhood has been attributed to end-of-life (EOL) out-of-pocket health care expenditures.[2] This added financial burden may also be related to major depression and poorer health outcomes for elderly spousal caregivers.[5,6,7]

Although out-of-pocket medical expenditures prior to the death of a spouse can drive the surviving spouse into poverty, it is unclear from the literature whether people would and should forego expensive late-life medical care to prevent asset depletion. For example, an altruistic spouse may choose to forego expensive EOL medical care to protect assets in order to shield the widowed spouse from impoverishment or from a decline in living standards after widowhood.

There is also limited research on how individuals respond to changes in prognosis of life-threatening health conditions under different health care financing mechanisms, and on their views as to whether policy choices for various treatment options should depend on prognosis and financing. For example, when would a terminally-ill person agree to forego medical treatment that prolongs survival, and how is this decision modified under different survival probabilities and diverse cost scenarios? Would the same terminally-ill person opt for treatment despite low probability of success just because health insurance coverage results in low out-of-pocket cost?

From *Medical Decision Making,* vol. 28, no. 4, 2008, pp. 511–523. Copyright © 2008 by Sage Publications. Reprinted by permission via Rightslink.

The purpose of this study is to analyze the various EOL medical treatment choices that elderly and near elderly adults would recommend for a hypothetical elderly woman with cancer, when the treatment choices have varying probabilities of success and substantially different financial implications. To the extent that the recommendations are for a hypothetical person, the choices reflect the respondents' policy choices, rather than choices for themselves.

Methods

Data Source and Study Population

We used survey data from the Asset and Health Dynamics Among the Oldest Old Study (AHEAD) and the Health and Retirement Study (HRS)—which include identical experimental modules with various vignettes on EOL medical treatment—to study the AHEAD and HRS respondents' expressed recommendations for various hypothetical treatments for cancer. . . .

The original HRS included non-institutionalized adults born from 1931 to 1941, who were selected from a nationally representative sample of U.S. households that included oversamples of blacks, Hispanics, and Florida residents, using a multi-stage area probability sample design. The HRS was designed to follow age-eligible individuals and their spouses as they transition from active worker into retirement. Data collection through in-home, face-to-face interviews began in 1992 with a panel of 12,654 participants, with subsequent telephone re-interviews every two years thereafter.[8] The AHEAD study was designed as a supplementary sample to the HRS to examine health, family, and economic variables in the post-retirement period and at the end of life. The first wave of AHEAD began in 1993 with a sample of 8,222 participants, who were selected from the same nationally representative sample of U.S. households as the original HRS, but by selecting participants who were born in 1923 or before. . . . HRS and AHEAD both contain detailed information on demographics, health status, housing, family structure, employment, work history, disability, retirement plans, net worth, income, and health and life insurance. . . .

[The AHEAD and HRS surveys] included a set of experimental questions that were asked to 605 and 556 randomly-selected respondents of each study, respectively. Respondents listened to a vignette that asked them to consider the treatment choice for a hypothetical married woman in her eighties of unspecified race or ethnicity with a life-threatening form of cancer. Respondents were told that this woman would die within a few months if she did not undergo a treatment plan that could delay the spread of cancer. The treatment would make her dependent on personal care help during the treatment period. The treatment's probability of success was either low or high (20% or 60%), and the out-of-pocket treatment costs were also either low (with Medicare covering the costs) or high (with near depletion of household savings because Medicare would not cover the costs). All four combinations of success probabilities (low vs. high) and out-of-pocket costs (low vs. high) were presented in four different vignettes to the respondents. . . .

Results

From the original 1161 respondents that were randomized into the cancer treatment experimental module, we excluded 18 that had missing values for our core set of explanatory variables, leaving us with 1143 observations (with 554 from HRS and 589 from AHEAD). No respondent was excluded based on answers to the cancer treatment experimental module because everyone assigned to the module gave some form of response to these questions. . . .

To simplify our discussion below, the verbatim transcripts of the four vignettes are reproduced at the bottom of Table 1. Although most respondents gave answers of "yes" or "no" to the vignettes, some respondents answered "don't know" or "depends" or "refused to answer" some of the vignettes. . . .

The top panel of Table 1 summarizes the decisions made by the respondents in the four different groups. Each group had a different sequence of how the treatment vignettes were presented, with the four possible combinations

Table 1

Percentage Agreeing to Hypothetical Cancer Treatment, Grouped by Vignette Sequence

(1)	(2)	(3)	(4)
Treatment Vignettes	**Financing Mechanism**	**Survival Probability**	**Full Sample**
M20	Medicare	20%	37.10
M60	Medicare	60%	58.01
S20	Savings	20%	26.51
S60	Savings	60%	42.17
Percentage of Sample			100

Note: Number in brackets denotes the sequence of vignettes for each group; p-value by Kruskal-Wallis test

Descriptions of Vignettes:

M20: "Now I'd like to describe a specific situation and get your opinion about it. Here is the situation: A married woman in her 80s is told by her doctor that she has a life-threatening form of cancer. The doctor tells her that without any treatment she is likely to die within the next few months. He describes a 4-month treatment plan aimed at delaying the spread of the cancer. The treatment itself would make her fairly uncomfortable, and she would have to rely on others for personal care during the treatment. The treatment costs are fairly high but Medicare will pay most of the costs. The doctor tells her that, with the treatment, she stands a 20% chance of living 2 or 3 good years after completing the treatment. Do you think she should agree to the treatment?"

M60: "What if the doctor had, instead, told her that with the treatment, she stood a 60% chance of living 2 or 3 good years? Do you think she should agree to the treatment then?"

S20: "Now let's say the situation is a bit different. The same woman faces the same decision whether to agree to the same 4-month treatment for her cancer, but this time instead of Medicare paying most of the costs, she and her husband will have to pay most of the costs. They could afford to do so but it would take almost all of their savings. The doctor tells her that, with the treatment, she stands a 20% chance of living 2 or 3 good years after completing the treatment. Do you think she should agree to the treatment?"

S60: "What if the doctor had, instead, told her that with the treatment, she stood a 60% chance of living 2 or 3 good years? Do you think she should agree to the treatment then?"

of financing source (Medicare vs. savings) and treatment success (20% vs. 60%) making up the four groups. Column 1 presents the codes we used for each of the four possible vignettes to indicate the financing mechanism (Column 2) and the survival probability (Column 3). In Column 1, "M" denotes Medicare financed, "S" denotes savings financed, "20" denotes 20% treatment success, and "60" denotes 60% treatment success.

. . . The rankings of the percentages of respondents in favor of treatment for the four vignettes were consistent with a priori expectations. The percentage of respondents that would recommend accepting S20, the vignette when the treatment had to be financed out of the patient's own savings and had only a 20% survival chance, was far lower than the percentage that would favor M60, the vignette where the treatment was financed by Medicare and the survival chance was 60%, with the acceptance rates for the other two vignettes falling between the two extremes.

[T]he recommendation to accept or reject the hypothetical treatment was related to the sequence with which the vignettes were presented.

The four vignettes varied on two dimensions: financing and survival probability. Because the respondents were given discrete choices (yes or no) to the treatment in the vignettes, we do not observe the true underlying latent variables that form the decision basis for the respondents. Instead, we observe the various cut off points that actually could serve as bounds (or thresholds) for the latent variables. The cut off points for financing are near depletion of the patient's savings vs. low financial cost, and for survival, 20% and 60%. Under the two vignettes when Medicare covers the treatment costs, the financing variable is fixed (low financial cost) but the survival probability variable is varied. Therefore, *conditional on Medicare paying for the treatment*, the respondents' recommendations under the two survival probabilities essentially reflect the respondents' latent "reservation" survival probability or, equivalently, the minimum survival probability the respondents feel that the treatment must provide the patient in order for the respondents to recommend that the patient accept the treatment. When the respondents recommend accepting treatment at 20% survival probability, the respondents' reservation survival probability is less than or equal to 20%; when the respondents reject treatment at 20% but accept when survival is 60%, the respondents' reservation survival probability is between 20% and 60%. . . . The first kind of respondents has a latent reservation survival probability for the patient (*conditional on* Medicare coverage) that is less than 20%, because they would recommend that the patient accept treatment with a 20% survival. The second kind of respondents has a latent reservation survival probability for the patient between 20% and 60%. The third kind of respondents has a latent reservation survival probability for the patient that is higher than 60%, because they would recommend that the patient reject the treatment even when it offered 60% survival for the patient.

. . . When Medicare covers for the treatment costs, a total of 424 respondents have a less than 20% reservation survival probability for the patient. They would recommend that the patient accept the treatment when survival is 20%. However, when treatment has to be financed by the patient's own savings, these same respondents' reservation survival probability for the patient shifts higher, so that some respondents require the treatment to have a higher survival probability before they would recommend that the patient in the vignette accept the treatment. Thus, when the patient had to pay for the treatment, 303 respondents still had a reservation survival probability for the patient of less than 20%, 62 respondents required a higher reservation survival probability of between 20% to 60%, and 59 respondents had a reservation survival probability greater than 60%. Similarly, when Medicare covers the costs, a total of 239 respondents had a reservation survival probability between 20% to 60%. However, when the treatment costs had to be covered by the patient's own savings, 122 out of the original 239 respondents would recommend rejecting treatment with a 60% survival, suggesting that their reservation survival probability for the patient was higher than 60%. Therefore, when financing changed from Medicare to the patient's own savings, some respondents would continue to recommend the same treatment, but other respondents would recommend rejecting the same treatment, because such treatment no longer met their higher reservation survival probability for the patient. Thus, a total of 243 or 21% of the respondents rejected the same treatment when financing changed from Medicare to savings-depletion.

　　. . . [T]he respondents could recommend to (i) accept treatment when it is financed by the patient's own savings, (ii) reject treatment when savings-financed but accept if Medicare-financed, or (iii) reject treatment even when Medicare financed. The first type of respondents has a very low reservation wealth for the patient, since they would rather see that the patient deplete savings and opt for the treatment at 60% survival than to have the patient maintain her current wealth but receive no treatment. The second type has a reservation wealth level for the patient that is between asset depletion and the patient's current wealth. The third type has a reservation wealth level for the patient that is more than the patient's current wealth; these respondents feel that the patient must be *paid* before the respondents would recommend that the patient accept treatment with a 60% survival probability.

　　. . . [M]ale and black respondents stood out as having a much lower odds of having a high reservation threshold for the patient, suggesting that they had low reservation levels for both the survival and wealth variables. In other words, they are more likely to recommend that the patient accept treatment, regardless of survival probability or financing source. Under Medicare financing (Column 2), married respondents (whose spouses were not in poor health) were more likely than those not married to recommend that the patient accept treatment, although such a differential effect was not significant when the treatment entailed depletion of the patient's savings (Column 3). The respondent's health or prior history of cancer did not seem to matter in the treatment recommendations; however, married respondents with spouses in poor health were far more likely to recommend accepting treatment than those who were married but whose spouses were not in poor health.[9] Respondent's age, household wealth, education, and religion did not seem to matter. . . .

　　One question we set out to answer was whether people would recommend as part of health policy that the hypothetical woman in the vignettes forego cancer treatment that potentially entailed impoverishing herself or her spouse. A corollary question, then, is whether those who recommended that the patient accept treatment under Medicare financing would recommend that the patient forego treatment when the treatment had to be financed by the patient's own savings. The answer is a resounding yes, among many of the respondents. . . .

One relevant question is who would be more likely to switch recommendations when the financing switched from Medicare to the patient's own savings. . . .

The results of this [analysis] show that male and black respondents were far less likely to switch treatment recommendations even if it meant depleting the patient's own savings. Interestingly, Hispanic respondents were far more likely to change their minds (than whites and blacks) and to recommend that the patient opt out of treatment when financing for the treatment changed from Medicare to the patient's own savings. Respondents in the AHEAD cohort were more likely to opt out as well, having controlled for age. Finally, marital status, health status, spouse's health status, cancer history, education, and household wealth were not significant determinants of switches in treatment recommendations when financing changed from Medicare to the patient's savings. . . .

Discussion

With a unique data set that included elderly and near-elderly respondents in the U.S. and their answers to a set of vignettes about end-of-life health care treatment decisions on behalf of a hypothetical elderly woman, we explored how elderly and near elderly adults assess EOL medical treatment choices with varying probabilities of success and with substantially different financial implications. Before we discuss some of the main results and implications, we shall first highlight the limitations of our study, so that the results could be interpreted in light of these limitations.

Our study suffers from two main limitations. First, the respondents were asked about their opinion on cancer treatment choices for an anonymous, *hypothetical* woman in her 80's of unknown race or ethnicity. While the answers should reflect the respondents' health policy choices, it is unclear whether some respondents also answered these vignettes taking the perspective of making the treatment choices for themselves or their spouse, rather than for a hypothetical person. Decisions based on the respondent's own life versus that of a hypothetical person will likely depend on the emotional context, financial status, or other personal factors. We have controlled for some of these effects by including a set of demographic covariates, but our statistical analyses have not fully accounted for all the factors related to actual versus hypothetical answers that would bias our results.

Another important limitation to our study is that the respondents may have had difficulty in fully understanding the rather complex vignettes used to collect the data. For instance, the vignettes used 20% and 60% as survival probabilities, and some respondents may have had trouble interpreting probabilities. The way the vignettes were presented to the respondents also does not necessarily reflect how physicians normally convey information for treatment choices. In fact, physicians do not have uniform methods of presenting outcomes and uncertainty. Differences in the framing of outcomes (survival vs. mortality, for instance) and the level of uncertainty (relative risk reduction, number of people needed to treat, probabilities) have both been shown to result in different treatment choices.[10] Although the literature recommends presenting information using multiple modalities, using charts, graphs, and simple heuristics (such as using 1-in-10 instead of 10% probability), there is no consensus about how best to present these kinds of information even during the "informed consent" process.[11] Clearly, more research is needed in this important part of physician-patient clinical decision making, especially when physicians themselves are also influenced by framing and the way risk and uncertainty are presented.[12]

In view of these limitations, our study does have some interesting although sometimes perplexing findings. We found that many respondents would recommend foregoing costly EOL treatments for a hypothetical woman in a set of vignettes, when the treatment cost would wipe out the patient's savings. Among the total of 663 respondents that would recommend opting for care when it was financed by Medicare, 243 (or 36.7% of them) would not recommend accepting the same treatment if the woman in the vignette had to deplete savings to pay for the treatment. These numbers indicate that when treatment cost is not covered by Medicare, the respondents feel that the patient must be "compensated" with a higher treatment survival probability for them to recommend accepting treatment. Viewing this from an alternative angle, when treatment cost is covered by Medicare, respondents would recommend opting for care that had even a low survival probability. This latter phenomenon is the well-studied and well-documented moral hazard,[13] which essentially says that people will consume more care when the out of pocket cost is low.

While it seems self-evident that people would be more likely to recommend opting for treatment if the patient's out-of-pocket costs were low, it is interesting that many of the respondents would recommend against treatment even when it entailed a low financial cost to the patient. This may reflect concerns about various direct, indirect, and intangible costs related to the treatment. The vignettes state that Medicare will pay *most* of the costs and, as such, respondents may believe that the patient's out-of-pocket costs would still be significant even under the Medicare financing option because it does not cover *all* of the costs. The vignettes also indicated that the subject "would have to rely on others for personal care during the treatment." Non-monetary costs associated with caregiving and the monetary costs of hiring a caregiver may be important in actual treatment decisions.[14] In addition to these direct medical and non-medical costs, there is also the pain and suffering associated with the treatment. However, it is difficult to assess how these costs induced any type of response bias. For instance, in terms of the pain and suffering, respondents with a history of cancer did not differ in their recommendations than those who have never had cancer.

Our study also found that black respondents were far more likely to recommend opting for treatment regardless of survival probability or payment source, a finding consistent with many prior studies.[15] White respondents were more likely to recommend opting out of care if that care meant depletion of the patient's savings. Interestingly, Hispanics were even more likely than whites to recommend opting out of such care; their treatment recommendations were the most sensitive to change in how the treatment would be financed. This finding needs to be further explored in other datasets, because as far as we know, this has not been documented in the literature.

We also found that females were far more likely than males to switch out of treatment that they had recommended accepting under Medicare financing but now had to be paid out of the patient's pocket. [T]his gender differential was significant only among married respondents; i.e., married women were much more likely to recommend switching out of treatment when Medicare no longer paid, but women that were not married were not significantly more likely than unmarried men to recommend switching out of treatment. Many reasons are possible why there is this strong gender differential in recommendations. The vignettes asked about an elderly married woman with a threatening form of cancer needing treatment, and it is possible that the respondents were more altruistic than selfish: married male respondents might have identified more with the husband in the vignettes and felt that the wife should get care even if it meant impoverishing the patient's husband, but married female respondents might have identified more with the woman in the vignette and felt that the patient herself should forego care to prevent impoverishing her spouse. Willingness-to-pay studies among couples where one spouse has mild to moderate dementia and the other spouse is a caretaker have found evidence of altruism motives between the dyad.[16] One way to further study this treatment recommender vs. treatment recipient gender effect would be to randomize the gender of the cancer patient in the hypothetical vignettes in future research. Another possible reason for the gender differential is that men might be more aggressive than women in opting for medical treatments, as in treatments for coronary artery disease.[17] . . . Given that women and men differed in their recommendations in these vignettes, the use of spouses as durable powers of attorney to make EOL care decisions should be further examined, since women and men clearly had different preferences. This is an additional piece of evidence that discordant decisions could be likely even with advance directives.[18]

Finally, we found that the order in which the various treatment options were presented had an effect on the recommendation of uptake for the treatment. The ordering effect could be due to starting point bias in that the respondents latched onto their first answer as the framework to answer the subsequent vignettes. The respondents could also have been affected by framing. Each vignette was framed with both gain and loss: the survival probability was framed as a gain and the financing was framed as a loss. Prior research has found that framing had an impact on patient's decisions.[19] Moreover, in going from one vignette to the next, the sequence of vignettes was presented as gains, losses, or some combination of the two. Prior studies have documented ordering effects in willingness-to-pay for medical care for the public, but starting point bias and framing were found not to be dominant explanations.[20]

The vignettes in our data were much more personal and asked the respondents to make a specific treatment choice for a woman in the vignette. Some of our findings do suggest that framing (in terms of whether the sequence of vignettes was presented as losses or gains across the vignettes) was a potential explanation for some of the ordering effect. The complexity of the vignettes and of their sequences of presentation, however, prevented us from further exploring the reasons for the ordering effect. Nevertheless, future research on ordering effects and their clinical relevance is warranted.

References

1. DeNavas-Walt, C.; Proctor, BD.; Lee, CH. Income, poverty, and health insurance coverage in the United States: 2005. U.S. Government Printing Office; Washington, DC: 2006. U.S. Census Bureau, Current Population Reports, P60–231.

2. McGarry K, Schoeni RF. Widow(er) poverty and out-of-pocket medical expenditures near the end of life. J Gerontol B Psychol Sci Soc Sci May;2005 60(3):S160–8.

3. Fan JX, Zick CD. The economic burden of health care, funeral, and burial expenditures at the end of life. J Consum Aff 2004;38:35–55.

4. Zick CD, Fan JX, Chang K. Impending widowhood and health care spending. Soc Sci Res 2004;33:538–55.

5. Morrison RS. Health care system factors affecting end-of-life care. J Palliat Med 2005;8(Suppl 1):S79–87.

6. Rabow MW, Hauser JM, Adams J. Supporting family caregivers at the end of life: "they don't know what they don't know". JAMA Jan 28;2004 291(4):483–91.

7. Schulz R, Beach SR. Caregiving as a risk factor for mortality: the Caregiver Health Effects Study. JAMA Dec 15;1999 282(23):2215–9.

8. Heeringa, SG.; Connor, JH. Technical Description of the Health and Retirement Survey Sample Design. Institute for Social Research, University of Michigan; Ann Arbor, MI: May. 1995

9. Ai C, Norton EC. Interaction terms in logit and probit models. Economics Letters 2003;80:123–129.

10. Wills CE, Holmes-Rovner M. Patient comprehension of information for shared treatment decision making: state of the art and future directions. Patient Education and Counseling 2003;50:285–290.

11. Moxey A, O'Connell D, McGettigan P, Henry D. Describing treatment effects to patients: How they are expressed makes a difference. Journal of General Internal Medicine 2003;18:948–959.

12. McGettigan P, Sly K, O'Connell D, Hill S, Henry D. The effects of information framing on the practices of physicians. Journal of General Internal Medicine 1999;14:633–642.

13. Pauly MV. The economics of moral hazard: comment. American Economic Review 1968;58:531–537.

14. Byock IR. End-of-life care: a public health crisis and an opportunity for managed care. Am J Manag Care 2001;7:1123–32.

15. Searight HR, Gafford J. Cultural diversity at the end of life: Issues and guidelines for family physicians. American Family Physician 2005;71: 515–522.

16. Konig, M.; Zweifel, P. Willingness-to-pay against dementia: Effects of altruism between patients and their spouse caregivers. University of Zurich Working Paper; Sep. 2004.

17. Heidenreich PA, Shlipak MG, Geppert J, McClellan M. Racial and sex differences in refusal of coronary angiography. The American Journal of Medicine August 15;2002 113(3):200–207.

18. Fagerlin A, Ditto PH, Hawkins NA, Schneider CE, Smucker WD. The use of advance directives in end-of-life decision making. American Behavioral Scientist 2002;46(2):268–283.

19. Armstrong K, Schwartz JS, Fitzgerald G, Putt M, Ubel PA. Effect of framing as gain versus loss on understanding and hypothetical treatment choices: Survival and mortality curves. Medical Decision Making 2002;22:76–83.

20. Stewart JM, O'Shea E, Donaldson C, Shackley P. Do ordering effects matter in willingness-to-pay studies of health care? Journal of Health Economics 2002;21:585–599.

EXPLORING THE ISSUE

Should Eldercare at the End of Life Be Subsidized?

Critical Thinking and Reflection

1. Discuss the scenario as described in the NO article by Chao, Pagán, and Soldo: A married woman in her 80s is told by her doctor that she has a life-threatening form of cancer. The doctor tells her that without any treatment she is likely to die within the next few months. He describes a 4-month treatment plan aimed at delaying the spread of the cancer. Even if she gets this treatment, she only has a 20 percent chance of living 2 or 3 years. The treatment itself would make her fairly uncomfortable, and she would have to rely on others for personal care during the treatment. The treatment costs are fairly high, but Medicare will pay most of the costs. Do you think she should agree to the treatment? If Medicare didn't cover the treatment and it took almost all of their savings, should she agree to the treatment? What if the physician added that even with the treatment 98 percent of patients have died within 5 years?

2. How do insurance companies meet financial obligations if some patients have very high end-of-life costs that are well beyond the amounts that they paid into the insurance pool? Why is there a problem if people use insurance for unnecessary treatments?

3. Identify the difference between collective costs of insurance and out-of-pocket personal costs. Give examples of each.

4. Does society have an obligation to provide health care at the end of life for older patients? Is this different than obligations to younger or poor dying patients?

5. Is it ethical to ration health care to older adults simply because of their age? Would it be ethical to ration health care to older adults in the last year of life? Why or why not?

Is There Common Ground?

As the number of Medicare enrollees grows from 46 million in 2010 to 76 million in 2030, demographers warn that the amount of money spent on prolonging lives of old people may become unsustainable. Efforts could be made to change the fee-for-service model of health care, so that the financial incentives to hospitals and physician groups require them to step back and ask "what are we doing here?" and "are we being good stewards of the federal/societal dollars to provide appropriate care at the end of life?" Clinicians need to have clear, honest, and understandable discussions with patients about the prognosis of their condition. These discussions should include whether the treatments available will actually make any difference in the course of the patient's end-of-life care. Patients make very different decisions about aggressiveness of health care when costs or impoverishment are added to the equation (Chao, Pagán, & Soldo, 2008).

Outcome-based studies could help clinicians identify the appropriateness of admission to ICU or continuation of ICU support for older adults. All intensive treatments for frail older adults should be revisited periodically and discussions should clearly include prognoses and cost implications. Older patients who do not respond well to treatments could be redirected to palliative care options. Changing eldercare to this focus could save money and suffering while allocating resources toward those who would most benefit (Lantos & Meadow, 2011).

References

Baily, M. A. (2011). Futility, autonomy and the cost of end of life care. *Journal of Law, Medicine & Ethics, 39*(2): 172–182.

Blendon, R. J., Brodie, M., Benson, J. M., Altman, D. E., & Buhr, T. (2006). Americans' views of health care costs, access, and quality. *Milbank Quarterly, 84*(4), 623–657. doi:10.1111/j.1468-0009.2006.00463.x

Boumendil, A., Somme, D., Garrouste-Orgeas, M., & Guidet, B. (2011). Should elderly patients be admitted to the intensive care unit? *Intensive Care Medicine, 33*(7), 1252–1262. doi:10.1007/s00134-007-0621-3

Donley, G. & Danis, M. (2011). Making the case for talking to patients about the costs of end of life care. *Journal of Law, Medicine & Ethics, 39*(2), 183–193.

Emanuel, E. J., Fairclough, D. L., Slutsman, J., & Emanuel, L. (2000). Understanding the economic and other burdens of terminal illnesses: The experience of patients and their caregivers. *Annals of Internal Medicine, 132*, 451–459.

Epstein, M. (2007). Legitimizing the shameful: End-of-life ethics and the political economy of death. *Bioethics, 21*(1), 23–31

Fonkych, K., O'Leary, J. F., Melnick, G. A., & Keeler, E. B. (2008). Medicare HMO impact on utilization at the end of life. *The American Journal of Managed Care,14*(8), 505–512

Lantos, J. D. & Meadow, W. L. (2011). Costs and end of life care in the NICU: Lessons for the MICU? *Journal of Law, Medicine & Ethics, 39*(2), 184–200.

National Academy of Social Insurance. (2011). What is the history of Medicare? Retrieved from www.nasi.org/learn/medicare/history. Accessed on October 29, 2011.

Pope, T. M., Arnold, R. M., & Barnato, A. E. (2011). Caring for the seriously ill: Cost and public policy. *Journal of Law, Medicine, and Ethics, 39*(2), 183–193.

Russell, J., Greenhalgh, T., Burnett, A., & Montgomery, J. (2011). "No decisions about us without us"? Individual healthcare rationing in a fiscal ice age. *British Medical Journal, 342*, d3279.

Silveira, M., Kim, S. K., & Langa, K. M. (2010). Advance directives and outcomes of surrogate decision making before death. *The New England Journal of Medicine, 362*, 13.

Additional Resources

Lakdawalla, D., Goldman, D., Jena, A. B., & Agus, D. B. (2011). Medicare end-of-life counseling: A matter of choice. *Health Policy Outlook, No. 7,* August. Retrieved from www.aei.org/docLib/HPO-2011-08-No-7-g.pdf

Moon, M. & Bocutti, C. (2002). *Medicare and end of life care.* Robert Wood Johnson Foundation: The Urban Institute. Retrieved from www.urban.org/uploadedPDF/1000442_Medicare.pdf

The Dartmouth Atlas of Health Care. Retrieved from www.dartmouthatlas.org/

Internet References . . .

Dartmouth Atlas of Health Care: End-of-Life Care

www.dartmouthatlas.org/keyissues/issue.aspx?con=2944

Understanding Cultural Issues and Death: Information for Schools and Crisis Response Teams

www.nasponline.org/resources/principals/culture_death.aspx

Duke Institute on Care at the End of Life

http://divinity.duke.edu/initiatives-centers/iceol

PBS, Death, and Dying

www.pbs.org/wnet/religionandethics/lessons/death-and-dying/
procedures-for-teachers/344/

Transcultural Competency in End-of-Life Care

www.topsy.org/culturalcompetency.html
www.culturediversity.org/links.htm

Death and Dying in World Religions

www.wabashcenter.wabash.edu/resources/guide-headings.aspx
www.wabashcenter.wabash.edu/resources/result-browse
.aspx?topic=429&pid=427

Religion and Euthanasia

www.bbc.co.uk/ethics/euthanasia/religion/religion.shtml

Chaplaincy Web Sites

Web links of interest to chaplains and other related sites can be found here.

www.professionalchaplains.org/index.aspx?id=127#chaplaincy_prof_orgs

Dying and Death as Cultural Performances

*C*ultural *including religious practices related to dying are widely varied around the world. Although many persons may find comfort in religious beliefs as they are dying, this unit also raises the issue of* religious pain *in dying patients. Depending on the person, religion may provide comforting rituals and community support or it may be the source of unresolved issues, of guilt or fear. Dying patients who are worried about some previous behavior or breaking the moral codes of religion may spend dying days worrying rather than comforted by faith. This unit also explores cultural differences of patients that must be considered when approaching end-of-life decision making. Support of cultural rituals is important in end-of-life care. However, one of the essays raises the issue that supporting end-of-life care preferences of some racial groups may cost society huge sums in expensive futile treatments. Cultural groups who prefer life-sustaining treatments can make their end-of-life care more traumatic and uncomfortable. Finally, this unit discusses the historic and current reasons why the rituals of funerals are important to those who mourn. Another essay challenges the long-standing view of Kubler-Ross's five stages of grieving, and provides data from newer research by George Bonnano, which indicates that grieving is unique to each individual.*

- Is Dying Improved by Belonging to a Religious Community Rather Than Simply Being a Spiritual Person?
- Is Dying Made Better by Culturally Competent End-of-Life Care?
- Do Funeral Rituals Help Grief?

ISSUE 16

Is Dying Improved by Belonging to a Religious Community Rather Than Simply Being a Spiritual Person?

YES: Carolyn F. Pevey, Thomas J. Jones, and Annice Yarber, from "How Religion Comforts the Dying: A Qualitative Inquiry," *OMEGA* (vol. 58, no. 1, pp. 41–59, 2008)

NO: Lamont Satterly, from "Guilt, Shame, and Religious and Spiritual Pain," *Holistic Nursing Practice* (vol. 15, no. 2, pp. 30–39, 2001)

Learning Outcomes
After reading this issue, you should be able to: • Gain an understanding of how religious practices and personal spiritual quests improve dying.   • Understand how spiritual well-being at the end of life is measured differently in stories, social functions, and symbolic connections.   • Discuss and distinguish trust in cosmic order; prayers; accompanied friendship; guilt and shame; anger with God; hope in afterlife; belief in miraculous cure.   • Describe different impacts on dying well between belonging to a religious community and personal spiritual quests.   • Identify and debate how religious belonging and spiritual quests help or harm one's quality of dying.

ISSUE SUMMARY

YES: Carolyn Pevey and her colleagues at Auburn University Montgomery report findings of a qualitative study which identified several ways in which some Christian religions were linked to better coping with dying. Religious faith provided a source of strength and an avenue of social support through the dying process.

NO: Lamont Satterly, Master of Divinity and founder of the SEARCH foundation, raises the issue of religious pain in dying patients. He describes patients who have unresolved issues because of guilt or fear of breaking moral codes of their religion.

*I*s *prayer medicine?* What spiritual quests or communal religious practices improve or worsen dying? Trust in cosmic order (Pevey, Jones, & Yarber, 2008–2009)? Prayer (Taylor & Outlaw, 2002; Jantos & Kiat, 2007; Balboni et al., 2011)? Accompanied friendship (Fitzgerald, 2006; Reinis, 2007)? Guilt and Shame (Satterly, 2008); Anger with God (Exline, Park, Smyth, & Carey, 2011)? Hope in Afterlife (Dezutter et al., 2009)? Belief in miraculous cure (Sulmasy, 2006)? This issue examines *three different kinds* of religious social practices and quests for personal spiritualities. It surveys how spiritual well-being is measured by dozens of instruments in *story-needs*, *social functions*, and *symbolic interconnections*. These influence religious coping, and patient vulnerability.

Spirituality, Religion, and Dying: Story-Needs, Social Functions, Deep Interconnections

In addition to physical and psychosocial aspects, *spirituality* has been defined as a key dimension of palliative care (Puchalski, 2006; Puchalski et al., 2009; Gijsberts et al., 2011). Personal spirituality is contrasted with religion interpreted as shared texts, practices, and beliefs (Sulmasy, 2006). The psychological value of communal support ("religion") and spiritual well-being on dying persons are increasingly well-documented, as well as the negative impact of spiritual distress on the quality of dying (National Cancer Institute). There is *cultural consensus* that spiritual and religious care at the end of life *cannot be reduced* to categories that are *only biomedical* ("metastatic pancreatic cancer"), *ethical* ("code status," "futility"), *psychosocial* ("denial," "disposition") nor merely subjective, unquestionable delusions that are *psychopathologies*. Not every futile treatment request based on a belief in miracles is necessarily pathological (Sulmasy, 2006).

Spiritual but Not Religious

How are your spirits? Why might a question about the *personal* well-being of a dying person come from a chaplain *usually* trained to recognize *different* religious affiliations? The United States is one of the most religiously diverse locales in the world. More than 90 percent believe in "God," 80 percent in an "afterlife," 76 percent hold religion as significant, and religious attendance hovers at about 50 percent. Increasingly Americans change religions (44 percent), are unaffiliated (16 percent), or mix religious traditions; self-identified Protestants are less than one-half of the population. One-quarter of adults connect with certain aspects of eastern religions. Dying persons expect caregivers to address complex spiritual and religious needs (Fuller, 2001; Balboni et al., 2007; Pew Forum, 2008, 2009; Ai & McCormick, 2010). Some chaplaincy departments have been renamed from "Departments of Pastoral Care" to "Departments of Spiritual Care" (Hunter, 2004; Ai & McCormick, 2010).

Is Spirituality One or Many Measurable Outcomes?

In 1998, the Association of American Medical Colleges (AAMC) studied spirituality and medicine at medical schools (Puchalski, 2006). Nurses and social workers have done likewise—and the National Cancer Institute has published a "Study of Spirituality in Cancer Care." In the past century, "care ethics" has become professionalized in Anglo-American worlds of demand-based health care that distinguish care as personal affect, solicitude, skilled competence, and personal regard (Reich, 2004; Jecker & Reich, 2004; Fry, 2004). Health care chaplaincy began in the 1920s; in 2002, a national association of clinical pastoral education listed 350 accredited training programs and 600 trained supervisors (Hunter, 2004).

Yet why is there still "not widespread acceptance of a [single] standardized method to assess, plan, intervene and evaluate spiritual care in nursing" (Puchalski, 2006)? From 1978 through 2009, more than 230 research articles have measured and applied "spirituality" according to more than two dozen assessment instruments (Gijsberts et al., 2011).

Measuring Story-Needs, Social Functions, Symbolic Interconnections

Dying and death are improved, according to how well religious practices or personal spiritualities express *story-needs*, enhance *social functions*, or promote *symbolic interconnections* among social and natural worlds.

Why is pancreatic cancer ending my life? For some the chief religious challenge of dying is personal *existential meaning*. Positive religious coping "existentially" has been shown to improve quality of life for cancer patients (NCI). Different scales measure "Spiritual Well-Being" (JAREL Spiritual Well-Being Scale in Gijsberts et al., 2011). Here questions connect compelling stories (narratives) with striking images such as metaphors of transcendence. These *express* comparatively rich experiences and suggest optimal *coping* behaviors such as effective pain relief and avoiding punishment images, interpreted with *phenomenologies* (Puchalski, 2006; Phelps et al., 2009; Dezutter et al., 2009). At the end of life, many believers, atheists, and agnostics interpersonally cope or blame in similar terms: the same being or higher power who helps is accused in *anger to God* (Smith-Stoner, 2007; Exline et al., 2011).

Will heart surgery help cure my doubts about God's love (Mother Theresa)? For some the main religious challenge of dying is a surrounding *secular* culture. Confessional *belonging* and nonbelonging social practices are described in terms of how well they *functionally* assist or resist individual *belief* and unbelief (Lustig, 2003; Bradley, 2009; Dezutter et al., 2009). Some instruments measure communal relationships, activities, and behaviors (RCOPE in Gijsberts et al., 2011). Religious identity is linked to a willingness to use aggressive end-of-life treatments (Balboni et al., 2007). Certain religious activities improve the quality of end of life such as perceived group support, interventions, and types of prayer (Taylor, NCI).

Can my incurable cancer make a more just, sustainable, and humane world? For those for whom the chief religious challenge of dying in plural cultures is *diversity*, issues become which cultural competencies best interpret our social and natural *connectedness*. Personal *embodied identity* is represented and assessed by different communities with interpretive frameworks some call *structuralisms* (Bell, 1992, 1997; Grimes, 2002; Holloway, 2006; Smith-Stoner, 2007; Pui-Lan, Compier, & Rieger, 2007; Ai & McCormick, 2010; Krishna, 2011).

Common questions about death and dying are related to stories that speak to meaning. Social roles affirm dignity and cultural symbols reconnect healing relationships. Persons use stories to express *meanings*. The end of cure is not the end of *healing*; sometimes *relationships need reconciliation* through real or symbolic reconnections (Sulmasy, 2006).

Religions and Spiritualities Based on Story-Needs

Am I at peace? Patient-centered approaches to spiritual care ask questions about stories based on *perceptions*. Religion and spirituality assess "quality of life" in terms of perceived *human needs*: religious needs, spiritual concerns, religious convictions, spiritual well-being, *existential meaning*, peace, harmony, and trust. How do we measure religious or spiritual needs? None are reduced to "satisfaction with spiritual care" but "spirituality" is defined differently. These include Spiritual Well-being (meaning and purpose in *relation to self* such as "peace," self-connectedness), Spiritual Cognitive Behavioral Context (*relationships with others*, beliefs), and Spiritual Coping (seek and express, Gijsberts et al., 2011).

Religions and Spiritualities Based on Social Functions

Who cares for me in my vulnerable dependence? Best caregiving practices take some kind of diagnostic spiritual history; they use some *biopsychosocial-spiritual model of care* to delegate skills that are clinical or spiritual to meet such needs (Puchalski, 2006; Sulmasy, 2006; Gijsberts et al., 2011). Dying persons *use* certain religious practices or personal spiritualities to *socially function* through norms, customs, traditions, institutions, and roles. How does such dying express spiritual aspirations or respond to religious belonging? Are dying persons merely "patients" or also agents who create meanings?

From Dwelling-Focused Religiousness to Spiritual-Seeking Interconnectedness

How does my dying connect me with wider natural and social transformations? Wholistic-relational spiritual care asks wider questions: Am I master of my destiny, in tune with the infinite or sheer recipient (Marty, 2005)? American religious landscapes have dramatically changed since the 1960s with more and more persons self-identifying as "spiritual but not religious" (Wuthnow, 1998; Fuller, 2001; Hout & Fisher, 2002; Greeley, 2003; Wink & Scott, 2005; Ai & McCormick, 2010). An evolution of American faiths has occurred—especially among Baby Boomers (1943–1960)—from dwelling-focused religiousness of traditional affiliations to spirituality-seeking and more recently "practice-seeking." Both are moved by needs for deep interconnectedness among nature and society that emphasize nontraditional ways of interpreting transcendence and life transitions (Wuthnow, 1998; Killen & Silk, 2004; Ai & McCormick, 2010).

YES Carolyn F. Pevey, Thomas J. Jones, and Annice Yarber

How Religion Comforts the Dying: A Qualitative Inquiry

Abstract

Although considerable social science research has explored religiosity and death anxiety, and many have theorized that religion comforts the dying, with speculations on the mechanisms by which religion comforts, very little research has asked people who were actually dying to discuss religion. This article reports on answers given by 38 hospice patients to the questions: Is religion a comfort to you? How does religion comfort you? This study found that religion, when it comforted these dying people, did so by offering a relationship to the dying, by giving the hope of life after death, through identifications, and through the assurance of cosmic order. The authors suggest theoretical perspectives accounting for these functions.

Literature Review

Because of its promise of an afterlife, it seems reasonable to think that religion can comfort people who are dying. This assumption has been explored in the important theoretical works of Berger (1967) and Becker (1973), who indicate that religion is an important resource to which dying people may look for comfort or meaning.

Unfortunately, there is very little empirical data testing these theories. . . .

Yet little research exists which directly studies people who know they are dying, or who may, as Black puts it, feel the "press of finitude" (2006, p. 69) more intensely than those who are elderly or ill, but not terminally ill.

Religion and Death-Coping

Pargament's (1997) exploration of the various ways in which religion assists people in coping indicates how flexible people can be in maintaining religiosity even in the face of events which hold the possibility of posing challenges to faith. He suggests that religion can assist people who are faced with life-threatening illnesses by enabling a surrender (p. 252) to something sacred or superior in some way to the individual (see Becker, 1973, for a detailed

From *Omega: Journal of Death and Dying*, February 2010, pp. 41–59. Copyright © 2010 by Baywood Publishing Co., Inc. Reprinted by permission via the Copyright Clearance Center.

discussion of the dynamics of this), and also that people can be remarkably resilient when teasing out religions' meanings in the midst of crises. He suggests further that among the religious, the spontaneous reporting of religious comfort when asked what helps in coping may be an attempt to "conserve" meaning; that is, to maintain religious belief through affirmation, rather than a true indicator of the source of each person's comfort (p. 278). While personal mastery is associated with better health outcomes (Mirowsky & Ross, 1986), the issue has been particularly difficult for those who study the effects of religion on coping, because in religious coping, it is precisely personal mastery which is often surrendered to a higher and/or divine power. Ellison and Levin (1998) remark that religious people may feel as though they retain control via relinquishing control to an all powerful and caring deity. Additionally, Ellison and Levin are careful to note that although religious belief is often associated with positive health, it may also have adverse effects on mental health.

Religion and Bereavement: Reunion, Social Support, and Meaning

. . . Although many studies of religion and coping with bereavement find religion helpful, at least one (Sherkat & Reed, 1992) found that religious participation does not significantly affect depression among people who are suddenly bereaved.

When religion does help, it does so by helping us to structure our grief (Warner, 1959) and providing social support and meaning (McIntosh, Silver, & Wortman, 1993). Religious coping may include the idea of a later reunion with a loved one. Cook and Wimberly (1983) note that the idea of "larger purpose" in death is a type of meaning construction with which religion is helpful and add that some religious coping may include the idea of a later reunion with loved ones.

Not only can religion help the bereaved cope, and by extension should help those experiencing anticipatory grief, but research also points to the effectiveness of religiosity in coping with illness in particular. Among the elderly, whose two major stressors are conflict and loss, prayer is the most often used coping strategy (Manfredi & Pickett, 1987). Chalfant, Heller, Roberts, Briones, Aguirre-Hochsbaum, and Fau (1990) write that clergy are used as a source of coping for psychological distress more frequently than are medical doctors. The optimistic outlook of religious people and their feelings of personal control (Gorush & Smith, 1983) may also be a factor in lower rates of depression among religious people. But whether religion promotes or inhibits feelings of personal control is not a settled issue (Ellison & Levin, 1998).

Religion is a source of strength and help in stressful situations (Griffeth, Young, & Smith, 1984). The spiritual support offered by religion may be most helpful for depression and self-esteem among those experiencing high life stress rather than low stress situations (Hathaway & Pargament, 1991; Maton, 1989) and although the first author has observed many peaceful deaths, the dying process is often perceived as perhaps the most stressful of all life events. Although belief in God may intensify just before a dangerous event and then decline to pre-event levels after people realize they are recovering (Shrimali & Broota in Pargament, 1997), those using hospice services rarely recover. Religion may allow us to re-frame a situation in a positive light (Pargament, Ensing, Falgout, Olsen, Reilly, Hartsman, & Warren, 1990), but even when used for the same situations, religion is more powerful and "consistently more palliative" in coping than is positive reappraisal alone (Matlin, Wethington, & Kessler, 1990, p. 117). People who know that they are dying may suffer from depression, and Koenig, Kvale, and Ferrel (1988) report that the negative relationship between religion and depression is so strong, that only health accounts for more good morale than religion.

Lin, Woelfel, and Light (1985) suggest that part of the reason for the beneficial effects of religion on depression may be the social support which religion offers. However, Koenig, George, and Seigler (1988) say that two-thirds of the people that they studied who claim religious coping used only personal or private behaviors, which indicates that it is not the social function of religion alone which is helpful. Further, Pollner (1989) has argued that even without other human beings, or what we normally consider to be support, religion can be beneficial in offering the social support of a *perceived* other. Additionally, Ellison (1994) notes that embeddedness in a religious community can lower stress, but adds that religious communities can also be sources of stress via social control in myriad ways. Generally speaking, and with few exceptions, religion and/or spirituality (because these terms do not yet have widely accepted precise distinctions, both are used in this article) has been shown a source of effective coping in life crises. But there is also some evidence that religion may not always be important to the dying.

. . . Levy, Dupras, and Samson (1985) also found no significant correlation between religiosity and death anxiety in general, but within religious groups found that the very religious are less anxious than the moderately religious or the not very religious. They found no significant difference in death anxiety between the very and the not-at-all religious.

In the main, the studies to date suggest that although death anxiety and religiosity may be negatively correlated in the general population, we know very little about people who are nearing death. Since very little research has directly explored the link between death proximity and religious belief, it is too early to conclusively report an effect of religiosity on death anxiety in the dying. . . .

This study attempts to further our understanding of the function of religion for the dying by reporting on interviews of patients at Cedar Hospice, a not-for-profit hospice in Central Texas, about their religious beliefs (pseudonyms are used for all proper names in this report to protect confidentiality). Hospice patients are unique, because unlike most people, they are told when they enter the program that their doctors do not expect them to live more than 6 months. In other words, they aren't just "very sick" or "gravely ill"—they are *dying*, and they have been informed of this, even if they may not have accepted it.

During the course of interviews, three themes of religious comfort (cosmic order, divine relationship, and afterlife) arose. The importance of others also emerged as a theme in three ways, two already suggested by prior research—that is, physical others with whom respondents communicated, also known as social support; the noumenal other, or god; and finally, the other with whom respondents identified. These are discussed in greater detail below.

Method

The 38 interviews on which this article reports were obtained over a period of 2.5 years, and ranged from 45 minutes to 5 hours in length, with an average length of 1.5 hours. . . .

This sample was overwhelmingly Christian, with 35 respondents identifying as Christian, one agnostic, and two in Alcoholics Anonymous (AA). . . . Eleven were divorced, 16 married, three were single, and eight widowed. Four had AIDS, two ALS, 21 were diagnosed with cancer, eight had lung disease excluding cancer, and four had cardiovascular conditions. One patient had lung disease as well as cancer.

These interviews were guided by a set of questions (Appendix A) and prompts about religion. . . . Smith writes of a "shift away from the social as order or as rules or as meaning to the social as actually happening" (Smith, 1992, p. 92). The question in this research was whether the "social as actually happening" as regards religion and death could be found in the social as has been theorized.

Religious Comfort

. . . Many, when asked directly whether religion comforted them, said that it did. Since "comfort" is not a sociologically precise term, the interview participants themselves were asked to explain what it meant to them in their detailed discussions of how religion comforted them.

Cosmic Order

Two respondents emphasized that they were comforted by their religious belief that God is in control. Beth B. (a 74-year-old Protestant dying from cancer) cited religion as important to her comfort because it gave her the knowledge that someone was in charge and taking care of matters. She said that God is loving and caring, and, "what he has charge of, he takes care of." Walter F. (age 54, Catholic, with cancer) also mentioned that it comforted him to know that "God is in control."

It would come as no surprise to Berger that order or rationality is important to people who knew they were dying. His fecund work (1967) on the function of religion to make sense of things when the forces of marginality overwhelm (or what psychologists might consider a threat to the "assumptive world") predicts some of the responses to this question. The sense that there is a god and that God has a plan for everything to work out provided a sense of comfort, or perhaps reassurance, to some of the respondents. In this way, the assumptive world may remain intact, in spite of what at first seems threatening.

Researchers Pargament (1997) and Mirowsky and Ross (1986) have discussed the importance of feelings of control in people faced with crises, and although he doesn't discuss the mechanisms by which giving up can be beneficial in terminal illness, Pargament notes that surrender is sometimes an appropriate response to negative life events (p. 252). The belief that an ultimately powerful other is in control of one's life may make such surrender easier.

Divine Relations

Some respondents reported feeling comfort from the idea that someone else was in control of their lives, as though they experienced god as an extant "other." Their reports bolster Pollner's (1989) compelling evidence that relationships with "divine others" can be as beneficial to health as relationships with tangible humans. Most of the respondents in this study, when asked how religion comforted them, referred to their having a personal relationship with God. Betty S. (a 55-year-old Baptist with heart disease) said that God was her very good friend, as did Happy F. (age 65, Church of Christ, with COPD), who said that she carries on conversations with God just as she does with any other person. Louise F. (a Baptist cancer patient of 75 years) said that she is comforted by the assurance that she has a good relationship and has communication with God. . . .

Edith P.'s response was particularly poignant, given her situation:

'Cause you know, you can talk in prayers what you can't say to people, 'cause you know, God's going to be listening to you. (Edith P.)

This 78-year-old divorced woman had two daughters; one lived nearby and visited often, but the other lived far away and had visited for about 2 weeks at a time, totaling four times in the previous year. One of her daughters said to her about her illness "you're born, you live and you die and it's part of living and there's not much you can do about it." Edith P. (Finnish Congregationalist with ovarian cancer) expressed sadness at her daughter's attitude and cried often during the interview, particularly when talking about having to miss future involvement in the lives of her grandchildren. Her relationship with God may have comforted her by allowing her to freely express all that she is feeling to a perceived other, particularly when corporeal others may have seemed less than sympathetic. Pargament et al. (1990) have shown that understanding God as a supportive partner is associated with positive mental health, and Edith P.'s remarks, though very sad, seemed to support their findings.

Afterlife

The traditional Christian depiction of heaven as a place of rest, plenty, and comfort is often understood as a driving force behind religious sentiments. Marx ([1844] 1964), for example, argued that the belief in reward after death for all the suffering in life was the primary tool used by elites to prevent the majority of society from insisting on economic justice.

Two respondents reported obtaining religious comfort through the positive sanctions, or strict assurance of the state of grace that religion offered them. For example, Mrs. W. (a 95-year-old Catholic reporting "old age") said that it comforted her because the priest will give last rites.

Similarly, Bevvy C. (aged 41, with ALS), a Catholic all her life, was comforted by having received an annulment. . . .

Of the 38 people in this interview study, 23 reported a belief in an afterlife, although most of them were unable to describe it. For example, one woman said:

> I don't know very much about it except I believe in God and I believe in Jesus and I believe in the hereafter. (Wanda M., 80-year-old Methodist with lung cancer)

Those who did have an idea of what an afterlife would be like imagined a tranquil place: "I think it's going to be beautiful in a very peaceful serene atmosphere" (Sadie L.). It is important to note, however, that belief in an afterlife in itself is not necessarily a religious comfort (Ellison, 1994).

Sadie L. believed in heaven, and that it was a beautiful place; however, she also believed in hell, and had concerns that she may not be able to enjoy serenity in an afterlife. Indeed, she thought that her illness gave her some insight into how bad hell could be:

> I think there is definitely a hell. It, I have no knowledge of how it will be but I know that this, feeling I have (her sickness) would be a very miserable eternal life. (Sadie Lee)

Thus, although several respondents agreed on what heaven would be like, the uncertainty of where each would spend eternity was not terribly comforting. . . .

Of particular note in these responses was the number of Christians who didn't believe in an afterlife at all. Seven Christian respondents reported that either they didn't believe, or they didn't have a sure opinion about whether or not there was an afterlife. One of these, Alfred B. (a 52-year-old Baptist ALS patient), referred to song lyrics to explain that he didn't know about an afterlife but would "swear there ain't no heaven, and pray there ain't no hell." Another, Daisy C., an 83-year-old Methodist dying of cancer, said that she just couldn't see an afterlife:

> I don't see it as being all people that I used to know and everything . . . to me when you're gone, you're gone. You're completely dead . . . I just feel like once I'm put in the ground I'm put in the ground, that's it. My life has ended.

While these comments could suggest that Mrs. C. is loosely attached to her religion/church; this is not the case. She prayed daily, reported feeling very close to God, and said, "If I couldn't turn to God with everything I don't know what I would do."

The fact that a large percentage of Christian respondents were without firm beliefs in an afterlife is interesting because they call into question the habit among many people of understanding members of congregational categories as sharing the same belief sets. This is especially surprising in light of the fact that this group would have fairly high religiosity scores, based on their accounts of their prayer practices. This finding may suggest an avenue for further research enhancing that of Donohue (1993) and McGuire (1988 reported in McGuire, 2002). Belief in an afterlife was not necessarily the most comforting aspect of religious comfort for the dying people interviewed here, even though many found comfort in their religion.

Identifications

Sunden has suggested that people identify with certain religious or spiritual figures, and that one way to understand how a respondent perceives her relationship with a divine other is to ask her with whom, in her religious texts, she identifies, and then follow up with questions about that identified person's relationship with God. Sunden's role theory claims that understanding the roles people take in relation to God via the inspirational stories can reveal the sort of relationship with God that the subject experiences (Kallstad, 1987; Pollner, 1989; Wikstrom, 1987).

Interested in the participants' perceptions of their relationships with a divine other, Sunden's suggestion was adopted in this study. Specifically, I asked each respondent whether they consumed religious or spiritual literature or television/radio programming, and if so, whether there was anyone to whom they felt especially close in those texts. If there was, follow up questions about the identified person's relationship with God were asked. The results were mixed. It is possible that a lack of familiarity with the religious or spiritual literature could be the reason that more people didn't report feeling particularly close to any individual therein, or perhaps they were merely not accustomed to considering their own psychological processes, but for whatever reason, only eight reported such a feeling, and of those, only six gave a rationale. Such a lack of familiarity could also be a result of the particular religions with which the respondents were familiar not having emphasized particular stories as a major component of faith and/or practice. The literary responses are examined here as well as the responses of those who cited living persons. On the one hand, only 11 people suggested that they had any sort of identification with the characters of religious stories; but on the other hand, when the respondents did note such an identification, Sunden's ideas were supported.

These others, falling somewhere between those who offer social support and the noumenal other, also offer comfort through identification, and the themes of afterlife arise again here as well for those who professed belief in it.

Lynn S., a 41-year-old male dying of AIDS, was one of four people who indicated a living person in response to this question, rather than a person in one of the stories. Mr. S., a recovering alcoholic and drug abuser, said that he felt especially close to John Bradshaw, public speaker and author of many self-help books for people in recovery. Mr. S. said that Bradshaw has a personal relationship with God and is in recovery. . . .

Betty S. said that her relationship with her pastor most closely paralleled her relationship with God and that this relationship was one in which "he understands my feelings and he's quite an extraordinary man."

In addition, Abel Z., 32 years old and dying from AIDS, said that his relationship with God is like the one that he has with his mother. He mentioned his mother, a Methodist minister, and her attention and concern many times throughout the interview. . . .

Hank W. mentioned a living person, when he said that he identified with Billy Graham, whom he said was a powerful speaker. . . .

Bevvy C. said that Jesus was the person from the literature to whom she felt especially close, and that "he is salvation and he died for us, for our sins, because of the sin of Adam and Eve we're all born with sin and Jesus died for us, to save us from the sin of Adam and Eve." When Mrs. C. discussed talking about her illness with her family, the idea of savior is reiterated, but in her own experience. . . .

Similarly, Sadie L. may have liked St. Paul because she felt that his life had been somehow like her own:

> [He] was a very bad person at one time, very bad . . . murdered a lot of people and, it was in prison, I'm sure I can relate to that. But when he, because (he was), Jesus' follower, he was very faithful and he was a preacher so, he never gave up. (Sadie L.)

. . . Identifications were not reported by every respondent, but when they were, Sunden's thesis fit very well: those who identified with religious or spiritual characters also had circumstances explaining the identification. Bevvy C. identified with the suffering Christ, as she taught her family valuable lessons through her own suffering; Mr. E. identified with Paul, revealing zeal like Paul's for spreading the gospel; and Mr. Y., a soldier, identified with another soldier, David. Very few people reported such identifications, however.

Mr. F.'s responses deserve special attention, however. He identified with John the Baptist, who

> . . . tried to explain to people that what was going on was not right but, there would be somebody coming that would make it right.

. . . Not only did Mr. F. express regrets about the way that he had lived his life, some of his remarks suggested that he hoped his religious conversion might result in a physical cure for his cancer. Mr. F. was a self-described "baby Catholic," as he had converted only 2½ months prior to our interview, 2 weeks after he received his terminal prognosis. This suggested that he had "found" a revitalized faith in an effort to save himself either from the flames of hell or the cancer itself, but perhaps from both. In his final words he suggested that hope for a cure may have been part of the reason for his conversion:

> But I'm not going to go for nothing that would be putting it in my head that I'm cured miraculously or anything. Every day I wake up I always ask, you know, I've always got that thought, you know, could you

have taken this all away from me Jesus and one day everybody's saying when's that old guy gonna croak so we can get this funeral over with or something why, then I'm gonna say maybe Jesus has just decided you know, he ain't ready for it, it ain't gonna happen. . . .

It is difficult to say whether Mr. F. found comfort or distress in his religion and his remarks are also suggestive that he may have been in some denial, even though he had stated that he realized he was terminally ill. Kübler-Ross (1971) might have called this the "bargaining stage," during which the ill person tries to make a deal with God in hopes of living longer. The preponderance of sociological studies in religion have found that religiosity is positively associated with well-being, such as lower rates of depression, more optimism, and even better health. But like Mr. E., who would not recognize his loved ones in heaven, Mr. F. is an example of someone not reaping all the positive benefits of religiosity which so many studies have found.

Social Support

There is some evidence that one of the mechanisms by which religion can improve our health and sense of well-being is by social support (Cohen & Wills, 1985; Pollner, 1989). This social support is most effective when people perceive their social networks ready and able to provide aid (Wethington & Kessler, 1986), and this is considered an "instrumental" type of social support (Cohen & Wills, 1985).

Past studies suggest that religion may have beneficial effects on depression, thereby providing comfort, because it offers social support, which people may experience even without the benefit of corporeal others. The fact that living humans are not required in order for people to experience religion's benefits may explain why religious coping helps people even when they only use personal or private religious behaviors. Indeed, religious communities made up of corporeal others can lower stress, but they can also be sources of stress by their function as agents of social control (Ellison, 1994; Koenig, George, and Seigler, 1988; Lin, Woelfel, & Light, 1985; Pollner, 1989).

Although the social support effects of religiosity have been widely cited as promoting positive mental health states, respondents in this study did not discuss this aspect of religious coping. Although several people mentioned their friends at church, no one suggested that their religious organizations' instrumental support had been a factor in their religious social support. This could be because the participants were already receiving adequate services from hospice personnel, because the primary recipients of this sort of religious support are the caregivers, rather than the patients, or for some other reason which another investigation may be able to decipher.

Discussion

The present study sought to explore the manner in which religion may function to comfort the dying. We find evidence that participants found comfort from religion by its ability to provide order to life (as Berger, 1967, suggested), a relationship with a divine other (Pollner, 1989), and the belief in an afterlife. Participants reported finding comfort in relinquishing control of their present circumstances to a higher being or purpose (Becker, 1973), believing that God is in control, and that God will take care of them and their circumstances. Although others (e.g., Mirowsky & Ross, 1986; Pargament, 1997) have argued that feeling in control is important to people faced with crises, these findings suggest, following Pargament (1997), that when faced with the inevitability of death, relinquishing control can offer comfort. The meanings of giving up, or surrender are thus a promising focus for future research.

Distinct from tangible human relationships, religion offered comfort to some respondents by providing a personal relationship with a divine other. Those reporting such a relationship characterized it as one in which they could freely express their thoughts and feelings, especially when family and friends do not understand or lack empathy with the participants' emotional states. Thus, the ability to communicate openly and have a close personal relationship with an understanding partner—in this case, God—seems to offer relief and comfort to those who are faced with terminal illnesses. While this finding lends support to the contention of Pargament et al. (1990) and Pollner (1989), that understanding God as a supportive partner is associated with positive mental health outcomes, it also argues for the value of the spiritual component in hospice services. At the same time, it suggests that close and candid personal relationships with understanding humans might provide richer support and comfort for those dying without an expressed religiosity, and this is also an area for possible further research.

Particularly surprising was the relatively small importance that many of the respondents seemed to place on an afterlife, especially given that this sample was quite religious in the Christian faith. While those who believed in an afterlife were often unable to describe what that afterlife would encompass, those who did describe it seemed to anticipate the traditional Christian conception of tranquility and beauty. On the other hand, some afterlife believers seemed to have mixed feelings regarding their place or position in that afterlife. For instance, a few respondents had concerns that their behaviors might have prohibited them from gaining a comfortable place in that afterlife, which may have elicited a bit of distress.

Lastly, of the aspects of religion explored in this study, religious social support was discussed least often; that is, it appeared less influential in the lives of these terminally ill. We contend that this lack of reported influence may be due to the fact that hospice patients receive a majority of their services from hospice personnel and that it is their caregivers who may reap the benefits of religious social support. In other words, the argument of institutional differentiation, that we no longer have the social need for the religious institutions we once did (McGuire & Spickard, 2002) because other institutions are shouldering the care once offered by religious organizations, may be reflected by our respondents' replies to the questions about religious comfort as social support.

Limitations

As with all research, there are limitations in this study. . . .

This study is limited most by the small, non-random nature of the sample. Because of this, the results are not generalizable to the population . . . hospice in general . . .

There may be better ways to study religion and the dying; however, in order to find people with the most certain "press of finitude," it seems reasonable to seek people in hospice settings. . . .

As one reviewer has suggested, in-depth, longitudinal case studies would be one method which might be more useful in studying religion and death. Grounded theory would be more practical using longitudinal case studies, as there would be ample time to code and revise during the interviewing process as themes emerged. If possible, such case studies could employ interviews, common religiosity surveys, as well as attendance and participation records. . . . Further, interviews of loved ones could help the researcher learn to what extent religious matters have figured into the lives of the people studied. . . .

Conclusion

The findings of this study may have implications for end of life programs, as well as education and research. Hospice teams . . . Religious laity and professionals alike must eventually realize, when they render spiritual care, that those they serve may or may not share orthodox beliefs.

Moreover, to expand on the multidimensionality of religion as articulated by the participants in this study, we may rethink notions of religion in the context of life stages and shifts in life circumstances, especially related to life-threatening illnesses. In other words, it is possible that religiosity for the well is distinct from the religiosity of the very ill or dying.

In future research, religious comfort as described in personal life stories could have important implications for developing measures of religious comfort across life circumstances. Although we recognize that our small and non-random sample prevents generalizations from our findings to the population, we also realize that the rich qualitative data we have uncovered in this unique and difficult to access sample may help other researchers to investigate the confluence of religion and death.

Appendix A

Interview Questions: How important is religion/spirituality in your life? Is it a comfort to you and how? What do you believe about God? (If subject believes in God, explore imagery. Ask how subject pictures God or would explain God to another person, and what their relationship to God is like.) What do you believe about an afterlife? Type of religion, length of religious affiliation, church attendance, involvement with religious group. *Religious behavior:* whether the person reads or enjoys hearing devotional and/or inspirational stories (if subject does enjoy this, ask if there is any person in that literature to whom they feel especially close, if there is, ask who it is, what that person is like, and what their relationship to God is like), and whether they engage in private prayer and its frequency. Have you ever felt alienated from your religious or spiritual community?

References

Becker, E. (1973). *The denial of death.* New York: The Free Press.

Berger, P. L. (1967). *The sacred canopy: Elements of a sociological theory of religion.* Garden City, NY: Doubleday and Company.

Black, H. K. (2006). The sacred self: Suffering narratives in old age. *Omega, 53* (1–2), 69–85.

Chalfant, H. P., Heller, P. L., Roberts, A., Briones, D., Aguirre-Hochsbaum, S., & Fau, W. (1990). The clergy as a resource for those encountering psychological distress. *Review of Religious Research, 31,* 305–313.

Cohen, S., & Wills, T. A. (1985). Stress, social support, and the buffering hypothesis. *Psychological Bulletin, 98,* 310–357.

Cook, J. A., & Wimberly, D. W. (1983). If I should die before I wake: Religious commitment and adjustment to the death of a child. *Journal for the Scientific Study of Religion, 22,* 222–238.

Donohue, M. J. (1993). Prevalence and correlates of new age beliefs in six protestant denominations. *Journal for the Scientific Study of Religion, 32*(2), 177–184.

Ellison, C. G. (1994). Religion, the life stress paradigm, and the study of depression. In J. S. Levin (Ed.), *Religion in aging and health: Theoretical foundations and methodological frontiers* (pp. 78–121). Thousand Oaks, CA: Sage.

Ellison, C. G., & Levin, J. S. (1998). The religion-health connection: Evidence, theory, and future directions. *Health Education & Behavior, 25,* 700–720.

Gorush, R. L., & Smith, C. S. (1983). Attributions of responsibility to God: An interaction of religious beliefs and outcomes. *Journal for the Scientific Study of Religion, 22,* 340–352.

Griffeth, E. H., Young, J. L., & Smith, D. L. (1984). An analysis of the therapeutic elements in a black church service. *Hospital and Community Psychiatry, 35,* 464–469.

Hathaway, W. L., & Pargament, K. I. (1991). The religious dimensions of coping: Implications for prevention and promotion. *Prevention in Human Services, 9*(2), 65–92.

Kallstad, T. (1987). The application of the religio-psychological role theory. *Journal for the Scientific Study of Religion, 26,* 183–201.

Koenig, H. G., George, L. K., & Seigler, I. C. (1988). The use of religion and other emotion-regulating coping strategies among older adults. *The Gerontologist, 28,* 303–310.

Koenig, H. G., Kvale, J. N., & Ferrel, C. (1988). Religion and well-being in later life. *The Gerontologist, 28*(1), 18–28.

Kübler-Ross, E. (1971). *Stages of dying.* Paper presented at the Gerontology Center of the University of Southern California in Los Angeles (70007) 12-10-71.

Levy, J. J., Dupras, A., & Samson, J. M. (1985). Religion, death and sexuality in Quebec: Research note. *Les Cahiers de Recherches en Sciences de la Religion, 6,* 25–34.

Lin, N., Woelfel, M. W., & Light, S. C. (1985). The buffering effect of social support subsequent to an important life event. *Journal of Health and Social Behavior, 26,* 247–263.

Manfredi, C., & Pickett, M. (1987). Perceived stressful situations and coping strategies used by the elderly. *Journal of Community Health Nursing, 4*(2), 99–110.

Marx, K. ([1844] 1964). Contribution to the critique of Hegel's philosophy of right. In *On religion.* New York: Schocken.

Matlin, J. A., Wethington, E., & Kessler, R. C. (1990). Situational determinants of coping and coping effectiveness. *Journal of Health and Social Behavior, 31,* 103–122.

Maton, K. I. (1989). The stress-buffering role of spiritual support: Cross-sectional and prospective investigations. *Journal for the Scientific Study of Religion, 28,* 310–323.

McGuire, M. (2002). *Religion: The social context.* Belmont, CA: Wadsworth.

McGuire, M., & Spickard, J. (2002). Religion in the modern world. In M. McGuire, *Religion: The social context* (pp. 283–325). Belmont, CA: Wadsworth.

McIntosh, D. N., Silver, R. C., & Wortman, C. B. (1993). Religion's role in adjustment to a negative life event: Coping with the loss of a child. *Journal of Personality and Social Psychology, 65*(4), 812–821.

Mirowsky, J., & Ross, C. E. (1986). Social patterns of distress. *Annual Review of Sociology, 12,* 23–45.

Pargament, K. I. (1997). *The psychology of religion and coping: Theory, research, practice.* New York: The Guilford Press.

Pargament, K. I., Ensing, D. S., Falgout, K., Olsen, H., Reilly, B., Van Hartsma, K., & Warren, R. (1990). God help me: Religious coping efforts as predictors of the outcomes to significant negative life events. *American Journal of Community Psychology, 18,* 793–824.

Pollner, M. (1989). Divine relations, social relations, and well-being. *Journal of Health and Social Behavior, 30,* 92–104.

Schmitt, R. (2005). Systematic metaphor analysis as a method of qualitative research. *The Qualitative Report, 10*(2), 358–394.

Sherkat, D. E., & Reed, M. D. (1992). The effects of religion and social support on self-esteem and depression among the suddenly bereaved. *Social Indicators Research, 26,* 259–275.

Smith, D. (1992). Sociology from women's experience: A reaffirmation. *Sociological Theory, 10,* 88–98.

Warner, W. L. (1959). *The living and the dead.* New Haven: Yale University Press.

Wethington, E., & Kessler, R. C. (1986). Perceived support, received support, and adjustment to stressful life events. *Journal of Health and Social Behavior, 27,* 78–89.

Wikstrom, O. (1987). Attribution, roles and religion: A theoretical analysis of Sunden's role theory of religion and the attributional approach to religious experience. *Journal for the Scientific Study of Religion, 26,* 212–227.

Guilt, Shame, and Religious and Spiritual Pain

Hospice care is dedicated to alleviating the pain of dying people. In addition to physical, social, and psychological pain, religious or spiritual pain can add to the struggles of many patients. Religious pain is rooted in guilt leading toward punishment and experienced as fear. It is resourced through the positive teachings of the patient's religious legacy. Spiritual pain is rooted in shame leading a patient to abandon hope in God's love. It is resourced through bringing unconditional love to the patient's sense of self-hatred and inner criticism.

Dying is first and foremost a spiritual experience. While this statement is an obvious opinion, it nevertheless appears to hold among those who provide daily care for the dying. Nurses, nursing assistants, volunteers, and family members all can testify to the important role that religion plays among dying patients. In my years of work as a hospice chaplain, it certainly stands true.

Since the earliest years of the hospice movement in the United States, interdisciplinary teams have been dedicated to a holistic approach to patient care. Along with alleviating physical, emotional, and spiritual pain, hospice teams have stood together in addressing religious and spiritual pain. Unfortunately, there has been a profound lack of clarity in understanding this concern.

When I first began dialoging over the job description of a hospice chaplain, I found myself unclear about the role. It was apparent that the chaplain was an important addition to the interdisciplinary team, however, it was equally certain that no one was quite sure about what was to be done. Medicare had placed a requirement in its conditions for certification, and a chaplain was necessary. What he or she did was a bit more confusing.

In one of my earliest team meetings, the hospice director asked me if I felt a patient was in "religious pain." I remember thinking that I had no idea what religious pain was, to say nothing of knowing if a patient was "in" it or not. Following that meeting I raced to the library to learn all I could about religious pain, only to discover that if anything was written about the subject, it must be a secret document. Religious pain remained a mystery to me. Obviously I had my own ideas, but most of them focused on the problems an individual has with God. Perhaps religious pain meant a patient was

From *Holistic Nursing Practice*, January 2001, pp. 30–39. Copyright © 2001 by Aspen Publishers, Inc. Reprinted by permission of Wolters Kluwer Health via Rightslink.

angry with God, or had difficulty praying. I wondered if family members felt cheated by the potential loss of a husband or father, blaming their powerlessness on God.

Several weeks into my investigation of religious pain, the hospice director again approached me to discuss a patient's emotional struggles. This time the question was worded differently, "Do you think this patient is in 'spiritual pain'?" Scurrying to the library, I discovered as little information on spiritual pain as I had previously found on religious pain. This presented me with two terms with two different dynamics.

Over the next few years, I spoke with many religious professionals regarding their definitions of religious and spiritual pain. The common denominator I soon discovered was that the terms were used frequently with little comprehension of what they meant. The "condition" of religious or spiritual pain was as vague as a conversation about the meaning of forgiveness. Helping people in religious pain was somewhat akin to helping someone learn how to love. It sounded positive and important; the problem was that religious and spiritual pain remained a mystery.

After struggling with this issue for some time, I received a telephone call from the husband of a patient. He asked me to visit his wife, an 83-year-old woman with ovarian cancer. I was somewhat surprised since I knew that her pastor visited with her at least two times a week, and she had dismissed me in our earlier meetings.

"I guess you're wondering why I asked to see you," she said to me from her hospital bed.

"Oh I supposed you had just been missing me," I told her.

She smiled and then said, "Well the reason I wanted to talk to you was that I have a question to ask you, and I'm too embarrassed to ask my pastor." I kept still, and she continued. "Putting it simply, I guess I wanted to know if you think I'm going to go to heaven?"

I'm not sure if my face showed my surprise but I quickly said, "Where did that question come from?"

She was silent for a moment and then said, "I was looking at my old family scrapbook yesterday and came across some photos of my Aunt Ellen. She was my mother's sister. Well, anyway, I was thinking back to a time when I was a girl and we went to visit Aunt Ellen, my mother and me."

She stopped talking for another minute and then went on, "I guess this is where some of the embarrassment comes in. While my mother and Aunt Ellen were having coffee in the kitchen, I went into Aunt Ellen's bedroom and was looking through her drawers in her nightstand." She took one or two deep breaths. "And I took a fifty-cent piece out of her bottom drawer." She looked at me for my reaction. "There were five or six of them laying in the bottom of the drawer and I took one." She started to cry, "I stole money from my aunt."

"You must have been very young," I offered.

"Well, I was around 7, I think," she said, "but that doesn't change the fact that I stole money. It's one of the Ten Commandments you know."

"Yes, I know," I replied.

"That's why I was wondering about heaven." She started to cry again. "God must be terribly disappointed in me, and I wonder what He'll do to me after I die. My grandmother was a seamstress and she told me that if you sew on Sunday, you have to take the stitches out with your nose after you die. If that's what happens when you sew on Sunday, what do they do to you if you're a thief? I'm so afraid!"

Religious Pain

It was after this conversation that I began to see a pattern in many of my patients. A connection seemed to emerge between guilt and fear, and a patient's religious dogmas or creeds. Most definitions of religion incorporate phrases such as a "set of values," or a "moral code," indicating some type of guidance system for life. It is against these codes, dogmas, or creeds that patients tend to measure their lives. Since many patients have an enormous amount of time for thinking, it is not unusual for a life review to occur that considers past decisions, actions, and behaviors. Seldom does a patient emerge from such self-evaluations unscathed.

In the above example, the patient was examining a childhood event against the moral code of her religious tradition. Unfortunately, once a patient starts to travel down that road, guilt and fear quickly surface. Rarely does an interior court get called to order where the defendant is found innocent. Coupled with the power of family and religious legacies, patients find themselves sinking into a pit of guilt from which there seems little hope of escape.

Religious pain, then, is a condition in which a patient is feeling guilty over the violation of the moral codes and values of his or her religious tradition. Sometimes this condition rests with perceived major transgressions such as abortion, adultery, or overt cruelty. Other times, religious pain emerges from much "lighter" infractions such as not seeking a second opinion, or failing to take better care of one's self. Regardless, patients in religious pain believe that God is keenly disappointed in their past or present behaviors, actions, or thoughts.

It is important for health care professionals to recognize that religious pain does not have to make sense in order for a patient to experience it. Religious pain is highly personal and deeply subjective. Although it springs from the patient's religious traditions and values, religious pain is always an interpretation of that belief. It is the patient's personal judgments weighed against the dogmas and creeds of his or her religious history and legacy.

Sadly, guilt is not content to stand alone within the mind of the patient. In most people, guilt asks for, and therefore always receives, punishment. Such a fact is well known by patients everywhere. It has been experienced throughout life and especially during childhood days. "Wait until your father comes home and then you'll get it," gets translated into "Wait until you die and God gets His hands on you for your transgression, then you'll really get it." Is it any wonder that the primary emotion of religious pain is fear? In anticipation of punishment, and rooted in guilt, the patient lies in deep anxiety for the moment of reckoning.

While this may smack of fundamentalism and its teaching on the fear of hell for sins untold, religious pain in most patients is far subtler. It roots in unexplored early childhood teachings attributed to issues of authority. Faced with death and all of its ramifications and fears, the notion of religious pain only adds to the mandate of the interdisciplinary team.

In my experience, some patients foster a belief that future punishment can be avoided if enough self-pain is administered in the here and now. Many people believe that it is better to suffer in the present before God gets His hands on them. I have worked with patients who refused pain medication with the belief that suffering now will make a difference with God in the future.

The Resourcing of Religious Pain

During the dying process, many patients return to the religious legacies of their childhood. A 70-year-old man may be a current member of an Episcopal parish. However, when his religious trail is followed, one finds that he was raised in a Presbyterian family, but attended a United Church of Christ parish while in college. After marriage he joined his wife's Baptist church, but the family started visiting an Episcopal parish since it was the closest to their suburban home. Faced with dying, he may find himself returning to the religious legacies of his Presbyterian roots.

Perhaps people return to their childhood religious legacies at the time of dying since for many it was the first time they heard about death. In their childhood, a pet or grandparent may have died, and the religious teachings regarding death and afterlife were presented. In the Christian tradition, it may have been the first time they heard about resurrection or heaven. For many, the first concept of a funeral, with all of its mysteries and values, appeared in childhood. These early experiences impact with a depth at an emotional level, often emerging during the dying process.

In the resourcing of religious pain, the examination of the patient's religious legacy becomes critical. Since guilt is central to the patient's religious pain, the concept of forgiveness as experienced in his or her tradition is a central theme to be explored. Every major religion of the world has a formula for "cleansing"; therefore, when a patient expresses guilt for past violations of dogmas or moral codes, the religious professional needs to bring the teachings of the childhood legacies to address the issue. In particular, the patient's own beliefs regarding guilt and forgiveness need to be fully explored, searching for the ways in which redemption can be brought to the presenting difficulty.

It needs to be said here that each helper must constantly be aware of keeping his or her own religious concepts aside. Patients do not need to be confused with myriad theologies regarding forgiveness. The simplest and most helpful way to lead a patient away from guilt and punishment is with his or her own religious legacies. For a patient with childhood legacies in the Methodist religion, for example, seek the assistance of a trained professional with a background in the teachings of that denomination. In Judaism, have a clear understanding of the patient's roots and then call for assistance.

When met with the rituals, teachings, and creeds of each individual's religious legacies, religious pain diminishes greatly. It is not through conversions or evangelical fervor that most patients receive relief; instead, a simple process of forgiveness leads them out of the pit of punishment and into a more positive, hopeful view of the transition into death.

Spiritual Pain

In contrast to religious pain, spiritual pain is a much more complicated issue to explore in the light of the struggles of the dying patient. Even the attempt at defining spiritual pain is difficult. While religion tends to focus on a person's set of moral codes and creeds, centering on the behavior of an individual, spirituality is about the business of a person's relationship with the source (God) of his or her life. Obviously there is a vast difference between behavior and relationship. In religious pain, behavior is measured, found lacking, and potentially leading to future punishment. Healed by forgiveness, religious tradition suggests a "way out" for this immoral or unacceptable behavior. However, when the relationship is damaged or suspect, how does a patient find a way through such pain?

To understand spiritual pain, one must explore the nature of relationship, particularly the concepts of love. Since most traditions allow for the hopeful belief in the unconditional love of God, patients may find themselves in an unfamiliar place. Although desired in every fiber of their being, patients have little or no historic experience with unconditional love. The world does not operate in an unconditional fashion, and most people are strangers to love without strings.

Children tend to grow up accompanied by two major needs. One is the wish to do whatever they want, whenever they so choose. The other is the desire to be absolutely loved by parents and other authority figures in their lives. It does not take long in childhood development for these two forces to clash. One cannot always do what he or she wishes and still receive the needed approval of mom and dad. It is at this point that tradeoffs occur, and children decide daily whether to risk the approval of parents in exchange for their latest desire or whim. When the desire wins out, the chastisement begins. Unfortunately, when children feel this disapproval of parents they leap to certain powerful conclusions about themselves, the most prevalent being "I am a bad person," or "Something is wrong with me."

Children with such legacy conclusions form false images about themselves, out of which a certain "mask" self gets born. An "idealized self-image" becomes the personality presented to the world in an intense attempt to receive approval by showing others what the child believes needs to be seen. Love is sought through pretense, and over a period of years a natural confusion emerges as the child struggles to determine his or her "real" self in contrast to the mask self. Sadly, even though confused, the child is keenly aware of his or her falseness in certain areas of life.

It is in this area that one can begin to understand the power of shame in life. Throughout life, many people hide their true feelings and thoughts in a frantic attempt to be loved. Many times these pretenses are successful, and no one uncovers the hidden self. However, from time to time, the mask drops, either through life's circumstances or a careless mistake, and the real self is seen, if only for a moment. It is during such unmasking that shame is born, a condition in which a person feels fully seen and exposed. As the idealized self-image presented to the world in exchange for love is dropped, shame rushes in with a force and power all of its own. Shamed individuals speak of feeling "found out" or "exposed," praying for the ground to open and swallow them whole. The need to hide is intense. . . .

An exploration of shame is critical in an understanding of spiritual pain. Since shame is born out of an exposed, apparently unworthy and damaged self, people in shame hide from attempts to love and provide nurturing and hope. The word *apparently* is used since shame had little to do with the truthfulness of conclusions about the self, and everything to do with the perceptions of the individual in his or her self-judgments.

Religious pain is rooted in guilt leading to potential punishment while spiritual pain is grounded in the emotion of shame, with all of its potentially harmful consequences. Patients in spiritual pain are those who have concluded, through their own self-judgments, that there is something wrong with them at their core. Often words like "damaged goods" or "a mistake" are used in the patient's description of the self. While guilt often says, "I made a mistake," shame suggests that, "I *am* a mistake."

Having struggled a lifetime in an attempt to hide the damage, patients in spiritual pain, now approaching death and a possible day of reckoning, find themselves terrified of divine exposure. The fear is that God will not see what has been so successfully hidden from all other relationships for decades. Obviously the results of being exposed to God's eyes will be horrendous.

Bill was a 62-year-old man with lung cancer. Along with the anticipated difficulties in breathing, he struggled with enormous anxiety, seemingly unrelated to his prognosis. At times he would say, "I can't wait to escape this world." His nurse reported to the hospice team his emotional difficulties, and psychiatric drugs were prescribed. Although they tended to mask his fear somewhat, he still expressed great anxiety over "something" he could not name.

As I met with him for the first time, we began to explore his childhood religious legacies. Born in the Midwest, Bill had been raised in a Baptist church. His record indicated that he was not a member of any particular tradition at this time, although he had been exploring Buddhism. In my first conversation with him he spoke of his homosexuality, sharing that he had lived with the same partner for over a quarter of a century. Bill talked tenderly of his love for his partner, often sharing stories of how he was now caring for Bill's physical needs.

In future meetings, it became apparent that although Bill had been quite comfortable in his gay lifestyle, he had avoided "coming out" with his own family throughout his life. Over the years, when his parents came to visit from the Midwest, his partner would move out for 1 or 2 weeks, successfully hiding Bill's homosexuality. When going back "home," Bill had always traveled by himself. No one in his legacy history knew of his orientation. In one session,

Bill told me that in his childhood church, homosexuality was one sin below murder but just an inch above child abuse. "I wouldn't be welcome back in my home church," he told me.

It was obvious from our conversations that Bill carried a great deal of guilt for his homosexual lifestyle. While emotionally coming to grips with it at one level, he had never been able to stand up and be who he truly was. He was, in psychological terms, unable to individuate. As we explored his guilt, Bill wrestled with an enormous demon. If he asked God to forgive him for his "sin," as identified in his childhood religious teachings, would such a confession obliterate all of the love and joy of his relationship of the past 25 years? Could he ask forgiveness for a "sin" which he did not identify as sinful?

Eventually we were able to explore the possibility of asking God to forgive him for any ways in which he had abandoned his faith, realizing that there were many different meanings to such a prayer. Bill held on to the notion that he would be forgiven *any* sin if he offered a general confession. It seemed to work for him, and he prayed daily for forgiveness.

While there was some relief, Bill soon became more anxious. One day he told me, "You know, I know that God forgives sins and loves everyone—it says so in the Bible—but if God knew me the way I know me, it would be a different story." At that moment Bill was putting into words the concept of spiritual pain. He was expressing the fact that his attempt to hide his "sins" from others had been extended to a successful deception of God. With his impending death, Bill's mask would be torn off and God would see him in all of his "nakedness." This concept sent Bill into a renewed sense of terror. The fear of being found out by his parents, hometown people, pastors, and teachers was now extended to God.

The following day when I visited with Bill, he turned his face away from me toward the wall. "I don't need any help from anybody," he said. His partner told me that Bill would not allow him to rub his back or even to hold his hand. Bill was in the early stages of "hiding" from Love for the fear of being seen as "damaged" or "bad." He was in spiritual pain. Several days later Bill died, sitting up in his favorite chair with his eyes open. He had told his partner that he believed if he did not shut his eyes, he would not die. Sadly, his fear overpowered him toward the end of his life.

Meeting Spiritual Pain

Unlike religious pain, spiritual pain is not responsive to a formula, creed, or doctrine. There is no mandate within tradition for the releasing of spiritual pain. It is a self-imposed exile from divine love and emerges from legacies of self-criticism and harsh judgments. Rooted in shame, spiritual pain sees only an unmasking by God, an occurrence that coincides with death. While Bill was somewhat successful in his attempt to feel forgiven by God for the "sins" of his life, he was unable to feel acceptable to God since he was unacceptable to himself, a fact given power by his unwillingness to be authentic within his family system.

It is virtually impossible to accept the unconditional love of God while at the same time imposing self-judgments of the most severe kind. When the inner critic of a patient's life claims that he or she is unlovable, as evidenced by living a "hidden" life, opening to the love of God seems incredulous. The old statement "If you don't love yourself, you will not be able to love others," is only partially accurate. The fact is that if one does not love oneself, one will never trust the love of another. Since Bill *knew* that he was damaged goods, and testified to that belief each time he hid his true self from his family, how could he possibly believe that God would think otherwise? We assume that God thinks the same thing we do.

Resourcing spiritual pain thus becomes a matter of convincing a patient that he or she is a lovable person, despite any and all inner thoughts to the contrary. The healing only can occur when unconditional love is allowed to enter into a self that had previously wallowed in self-criticism or self-hatred. Obviously this is a difficult task, both for the patient and the health care professional. To bring love and acceptance into a life that has previously felt unlovable is a major challenge. In the truest sense, it is my conviction that everyone is in spiritual pain to a greater or lesser degree. Healing, unfortunately, is the work of decades for most people. The average length of enrollment before death, for most hospice patients, is a little less than a month.

The question remains: How can one bring unconditional love to patients who are living, and dying, in shame? As I have worked with this issue over many years, I have discovered that love is suspect for many patients. I get paid to visit and offer my words of help and solace. The nurse is a salaried professional, paid to visit and provide care, as is the nursing assistant. On the other hand, the volunteer is visiting out of desire. There are no strings attached, no monies paid, and most volunteers are in the home, or at the hospital bedside, because they choose to be present. This, in itself, can feel miraculous to a patient. Someone sees enough worth in the patient to stand beside him or her without coercion or salary. The hospital orderly who stops his or her busy tasks to genuinely inquire about the patient's condition brings worth to the patient. A newspaper delivery person who stops on the porch and says, "How are you doing today, Mr. Smith?" means more than a dozen visits from a paid professional.

Bringing unconditional love to a patient who believes only in conditional acceptance is the major way to break down the walls of spiritual pain. While it is only a start, it can make a profound difference nevertheless. Most patients have found their way into spiritual pain decades earlier through harsh inner criticism. Hospice workers know that the dysfunction of years cannot be turned around in a few short weeks; however, love can be brought to each patient with the hope of offering some relief to the fears that focus on God's disappointment.

I often define spiritual pain as "the felt absence of the ever-present God." Patients, in their attempts to hide from God's disapproving eyes, obviously feel His absence. It is impossible to hide from God in one area and not feel His absence everywhere. Spiritual pain, then, leads to an absence of joy, hope, and future possibility of divine union. It is always self-imposed, making it extremely difficult to heal. Nevertheless, the hospice worker has no choice but to bring unconditional love to the patient and family in every possible way. Each time a patient wonders about the possibility of his or her self-worth, love will push the potential of healing one step further toward hope and joy.

A Final Word

In this brief article I have tried to divide religious pain from spiritual pain. While I am very much aware that many religious traditions do not separate religion from spirituality, for the purpose of clarity I have found it helpful. Religious and spiritual pain both point to the powerful realization that one's personal psychology cannot be separated from one's religious and spiritual path. Self-esteem does indeed affect the ways people experience God. Guilt, from a psychological perspective, is a block to freedom. It calls forth the need for a doctrine of forgiveness, mostly available from a spiritual dimension.

Also, I am painfully aware that journal articles are generally scholarly pieces filled with footnotes and quotations. This article is not. Certainly the years of study, conferences, books, and personal experience have brought me to the conclusions in these few pages. Therefore, I have listed some suggested reading of works that have helped me grow in my understanding of spiritual and religious pain.

Ultimately both religious and spiritual pain leave a patient in enormous fear. It is my hope that the easy road of psychiatric drugs will only be taken as a last resort. Masking a patient's religious pain prior to his or her opportunity to attempt to work through the many painful issues of guilt leaves a patient to die without the healing for which hospice stands. Attempting to use words to reassure a patient dying in self-hatred will never be successful. Along with the dedication to alleviate pain, the interdisciplinary team needs to proclaim love to all as the deepest gift they have to offer.

Suggested Reading

Anderson AC. *The Problem Is God—The Selection and Care of Your Personal God.* Walpole, NH: Stillpoint Publishing; 1984.

Barks C, trans. *The Essential Rumi.* New York: Harper Collins; 1995.

Bertman S. *Facing Death—Images, Insights, and Interventions.* New York: Hemisphere Publishing Corp; 1991.

Bly R. *What Have I Ever Lost by Dying?* New York: Harper Collins; 1992.

Cohen A. *The Dragon Doesn't Live Here Anymore—Loving Fully, Loving Freely.* Somerset, NJ: Alan Cohen Publications; 1990.

Colegrave S. *By Way of Pain—A Passage into Self.* Rochester, VT: Park Street Press; 1988.

Dass R. *Journey of Awakening—A Meditator's Guidebook.* New York: Bantam Books; 1985.

Fleming U, ed. *Meister Eckhart—The Man from Whom God Nothing Hid.* Springfield, IL: Templegate Publishers; 1988.

Fremantle F, Trungpa C, trans. *The Tibetan Book of the Dead*. Boston: Shambhala Publications; 1975.

Guntzelman J. *Blessed Grieving—Reflections of Life's Losses*. Winona, MN: Saint Mary's Press, Christian Brothers Publications; 1992.

Jampolsky L. *The Art of Trust—Healing Your Heart and Opening Your Mind*. Berkeley, CA: Celestial Arts; 1994.

Kornfield J. *A Path with Heart*. New York: Bantam Books; 1993.

Kubler-Ross E. *On Life after Death*. Berkeley, CA: Celestial Arts; 1991.

Levine S. *Heating into Life and Death*. Garden City, NY: Anchor Press Doubleday; 1987.

Levine S. *Who Dies?* Garden City, NY: Anchor Press Doubleday; 1984.

Menten T. *Gentle Closings—How to Say Goodbye to Someone You Love*. Philadelphia: Running Press; 1991.

Mitchell S. *The Enlightened Heart—An Anthology of Sacred Poetry*. New York: Harper & Row; 1989.

Nisker W. *Crazy Wisdom*. Berkeley, CA: Ten Speed Press; 1990.

Rajneesh B. *The Book of the Secrets*. New York: Harper & Row; 1976.

Rinpoche S. *The Tibetan Book of Living and Dying*. San Francisco, CA: Harper; 1992.

Rodegast P, Stanton J, compilers. *Emmanuel's Book*. New York: Bantam Books; 1987.

Satterly L. *Tattooed in the Cradle—The Healing Journey from Family to Spiritual Wholeness*. Maple Glen, PA: The SEARCH Foundation; 1993.

Starr J, ed. *Two Suns Rising—An Anthology of Eastern and Western Mystical Writings*. New York: Bantam Books; 1992.

Yancey P. *Where Is God When It Hurts?* Grand Rapids, MI: Zondervan Publishing House; 1977.

Zukav G. *The Seat of the Soul*. New York: Simon & Schuster; 1989.

EXPLORING THE ISSUE

Is Dying Improved by Belonging to a Religious Community Rather Than Simply Being a Spiritual Person?

Critical Thinking and Reflection

1. *Discuss*: What have you heard? What key positive and negative religious images guide spiritual/religious coping with death? For example: father, mother, journey, destination, enlightenment, compassion, Zion, household, temple/kingdom/Jerusalem, the communion of the saints, ummah, "in Abraham's arms . . ." versus Judge, punishment, cross-crucifixion, hell, scapegoat, affliction, emptiness, annihilation, etc.

2. *Consider*: Your Chinese speaking uncle from Hong Kong became a Buddhist monk after the death of your aunt. He has metastasized pancreatic cancer, was referred to a small Lutheran hospital near you for pain treatment during his final days. He clearly needs but refuses pain relief to avoid sedation because of Buddhist belief about dying with a clear mind. What is a role for a non-Chinese speaking chaplain (Keown, 2005; Ai & McCormick, 2010)?

3. *Discuss*: Having been baptized and attended a Catholic grade school, your aunt became a Methodist in high school and a Quaker in college while doing volunteer work as a journalist in New York City. She married a nonpracticing Jew, and both attended a Buddhist temple for years in California before he died. Diagnosed with end stage heart disease, she describes herself as a "recovering Christian" who is drawn to ritual symbols of Eastern Orthodox Christianity. You are her niece-caregiver. What do you ask her chaplain to help her and you understand about her journeys and end-of-life decisions (e.g., Kazantzakis, 1961)?

4. *Discuss*: You have 6 months to live and your insurance coverage is poor. What are some of the key factors that distinguish positive and negative religious coping? For example, how does the unjustness of global health-care access make it difficult to trust a cosmic order, or increase anger to God?

5. *Discuss*: Your brother has strong religious belief in a miraculous cure of his spreading leukemia (metastatic cancer). He wants chemotherapy. Does a belief in miraculous obligate a health-care team to offer futile (nonbeneficial) treatment (Sulmasy, 2006)? What do you discuss with him about his expectations and hopes?

Is There Common Ground?

Death is before me today
As a man longs to see his house
When he has spent years in captivity.

(Egypt, Discourse of a Man with his Ba [1991–1802 bce],
Goedicke, 1970; Mueller, 1973; Thomas, 1980)

I hope for nothing. I fear nothing. I am free.

(Δεν ελπίζω τίποτα. Δε φοβούμαι τίποτα. Είμαι λεύτερος.
Gravestone Epitaph, Nikos Kazantzakis, 1883–1957)

*I know I have a believing customer who shifts from saying "If I die" to "When
I die . . ."*

(Life Insurance Sales Agent)

A shared history discloses *five cultural myths* about current dying as spiritual quests and religious processes. *Practical barriers* to good religious and spiritual care at the end of life are *overcome with best practices* regarding afterlife anticipations, religious coping, and patient-centered models.

A Shared History of Dying Together

Are religiosity and spirituality for the well different than for the very ill or dying (Pevey et al., 2008–2009)? Death and dying are deeply rooted in social lives and global living. Magic, religions, and sciences diverged across 150,000 years since *Homo sapiens* arose and 60,000 years since living descendants continued from their first dispersal from Africa. Deliberate burials show care for the sick that differently re-connect ("re-ligio") with embodied and unembodied selves or others (spiritus, "breath"). Through education of urban elites, religions in India, China, and the west emerged in pivotal ages ("axial") between 800 BCE and 200 CE. In every era since, care for sick and dying recalibrated relationships among individuals and urban communities (Risse, 1999; Lambert, 1999). Some who separate end-of-life choices as religious social practices from personal spiritual quests demonstrate that individuals who feel cutoff from communities seek more aggressive end-of-life care (Balboni et al., 2007; Daaleman, 2008; Puchalski et al., 2009). Others who connect personal spirituality to religious communal practices give evidence that interdisciplinary, team-based care helps integrate personal with public, and practices with beliefs (Sulmasy, 2006; Gijsberts et al., 2011)

Five Cultural Myths About Spiritual Quests and Religious Processes for Dying

Despite acknowledged importance in end-of-life care, why are there still basic *disagreements* about what constitutes religion and spirituality (King & Koenig, 2009)? Arguments about how to improve dying intersect with lively debates about how personal meanings (beliefs) relate to social practices (cultural performances). Recent retrievals of roles for spirituality and religion at the end of life *lack cultural consensus* due to contested meanings about *five key counter-posed categories*: communal–personal; theistic–Eurocentric; dynamic–conformity; autonomy versus process; and role conflicts.

Linking religion to *institutional affiliation* with a historic communal tradition, by contrasting it to spirituality as an *individual dimension* of personal life quest, is widespread but oversimplified. Historic religions are not merely public; belief and meaning are never completely private (Killen & Silk, 2004). Many understandings focus upon beliefs (divine) or practices (rituals) that presuppose Western *theistic models* for increasingly, geographically *diverse diaspora cultural* populations (Orthodox, Muslim, Latino/a, Asian). In addition, plural traditions that are global are frankly *nontheist*, atheist, or understand theistic socialization as a belief in an empathic relational partner as a Eurocentric cultural bias (Hinduism, Buddhism, Daoism—Bell, 1992, 1997; Killen & Silk, 2004; Keown, 2005; Pui-Lan et al., 2007). Many measures of religious coping need to be recalibrated (Exline et al., 2011). Among plural cultures and diverse traditions do wide-ranging prayer practices as communication improve dying according to how well they express story-needs, function socially, or symbolize interconnections (Taylor & Outlaw, 2002; Jantos & Kiat, 2007; Balboni et al., 2011)?

Third, false dilemmas counterpose choices for dying persons as either–or. In fact, dying persons *dynamically*, culturally perform constructive meanings and renegotiate conformity to *perceived static* structural systems of meaning (social roles as patients, clinical–procedural rules, Grimes, 1992, 2002; Daaleman, 2008a, 2008b). Fourth, many support programs for care of the dying interpret religion and spirituality in terms of how they encourage *choice, patient preferences, and health care literacy*. Yet, some *autonomy-based models* presuppose that individual decisions about meaning and transformation are ultimately significant in cultures of demand-based health care. When *spiritual well-being* is understood as chiefly a managed *private preference, religion* has become *functionally* secularized according to a Western model of global *consumerism* (Koenig, 2002; Miller, 2005; Marty, 2005).

Fifth, caregivers of dying persons (including chaplains) face tensions in *role conflicts* regarding commitments to be: patient advocates; members of historic helping professions (nurses, physicians, historic traditions of faith); maintainers of appropriate institutional policy neutrality; and agents of change for a more just world defined variously in terms that are egalitarian, need, merit, contribution, productivity, justice as fairness, or functional capacity. Focusing on *processes rather than content* in moral decision making is wise; historically chaplains helped organize hospital ethics committees in the 1970s and 1980s (Hunter, 2004; Pesut, 2009).

Dying: Personal Quests and Social Processes

Dying persons, therapeutic styles of ministry, and spiritual caregivers measure good dying as different kinds of process or quest. What *critics* reject as *too passive, defenders* counter as social interpretations of dying and death, which are *socially resilient*, because they negotiate *this worldly meanings*. Some measure the decisions of dying persons by how well they reflect *processes* of trustworthy decisions ("openness") or circumstantially appropriate responses ("situation ethics") or seem responsible ("nondefensive") (Hunter, 2004). Others ask about dying regarding aspirations in *moral–spiritual* terms: do they seek ideally exceptionally loving, heroic relinquishments in the face of adversity called *merciful self-denial* (Grisez, 1997; Thomasma, 1998), *sin-avoidance* (safer "tutiorism" such as "Don't kill yourself"), *feasible benefits* (either "seek biomedical goods of stable functioning" or form character through training for ascetic virtuosi), or *"accept transformative wholeness"* such as contemporary versions of mysticism that urge "relinquish control to great beings" (Marty, 2005). Why? Some believers hold "My dying is *religiously accompanied* and my post-mortal destiny is *shared"* (Keown, 2005; Fitzgerald, 2006; Reinis, 2007).

Overcoming Practical Barriers

Hesitancies and *barriers* to good religious and spiritual care at the end of life are more practical than theoretical. Historically in the United States, until the mid-1980s, spirituality and religion were virtual synonyms. In the United States; physicians are "less likely than the general population to believe in God (76 percent vs 83 percent), and report that they are less likely to try to incorporate their religious beliefs into all aspects of their lives (58 percent vs 73 percent)" (Sulmasy, 2006). Most physicians and nurses face pressures to spend less time with patients—and few have specialized training in theology, spirituality, or pastoral counseling of the sick. It is presumptuous, at best, for a health care professional to try to convince a patient that his theology of miracles lacks sophistication (Curlin et al., 2005; Sulmasy, 2006). "The focus [for nurses] on aggressive technological treatment for acute physical conditions relegates caring and compassionate presence to a nonessential, unsupported aspect of healthcare" (Puchalski, 2006). Patients demanding futile care in expectation of a miracle may fear abandonment, suspect unjust undertreatment for financial reasons, or fear giving up prematurely (Sulmasy, 2006).

Practical Maxims

Practical cultural consensus has generated maxims about afterlife anticipations, religious coping, and patient-centered models.

Afterlife, Post-Mortal Existence, Post-Mortem Judgment

Afterlife hopes and fears influence the quality of dying in coping, practices, and symbols. Dying persons experience paradoxical hopes based on trust in cosmic order or accompanied friendship—and some believers fear punishing judgment and nonbelievers fear final annihilation. Among cancer survivors, short-term negative images of God predict distress (NCI). Most traditions around the world agree dying persons are not alone and death is not the end; even if death is not all there is to dying, many conceptualize this "otherness" differently than the empathic, relational partner of theism used in many measurement instruments (Marty, 2005; Exline et al., 2011).

Religious Coping Is Twofold

By relying on faith and healthy adaptation, positive religious coping helps deal with stress of illness and end of life. Among patients with advanced cancer, some research demonstrates that positive religious coping is associated with (1) spiritual well-being as meaningfulness and peace (NCI) and (2) elsewhere as receipt of more intensive life-prolonging medical care at the end of life (Phelps et al., 2009). Such religious copers might feel their extra efforts either collaborate with God, or resist palliative care because it prematurely abandons a spiritual calling not to "giv[e] up on God [before he has] given up on them." Such persons may believe that God knows "when it is time to die" or have "religiously informed moral positions that place high value on prolonging life" (Sulmasy, 2006; Phelps et al., 2009).

Overly aggressive end-of-life care has been associated with poor quality of death and poses risks of negative outcomes for religious copers and caregiver bereavement (Phelps et al., 2009). Negative religious coping ("anger at God," "illness is punishment") is associated with guilt, anxiety, fear, spiritual shame, denial, spiritual distress, and poorer overall quality of life among end-stage cancer patients. It should be referred to pastoral care or clergy (Satterly, 2001; Sulmasy, 2006; NCI; Exline et al., 2011; Gijsberts et al., 2011).

Toward Patient-Centered Interdisciplinary Models

There is *cultural consensus* that good end-of-life care should be formed by *best practices* of patient-centered, team-based, interdisciplinary approaches with outcome-based information drawn from measures of spiritual well-being sensitive to plural cultural and diverse spiritual traditions. Patient vulnerability requires caregivers to have empathy to the ultimate concerns of patients, not merely proselytize (Sulmasy, 2006; Puchalski, 2006). Many assessment tools and interdisciplinary teams interact with patient, family, and community.

Historically, spiritual quests and religious practices can help improve dying and sustain living caregivers.

Additional Resources

Ai, A. L., & McCormick, T. R. (2010). Increasing diversity of Americans' faiths alongside baby boomers' aging: Implications for chaplain intervention in health settings. *Journal of Health Care Chaplaincy, 16*, 24–41.

Balboni, M. J., Babar, A., Dillinger, J., Phelps, A. C., George, E., Block, S. D., et al. (2011). "It Depends": Viewpoints of patients, physicians, and nurses on patient-practitioner prayer in the setting of advanced cancer. *Journal of Pain & Symptom Management, 41*(5), 836–847.

Balboni, T. A., Vanderwerker, L. C., Block, S. D., Paulk, M. E., Lathan, C. S., Peteet, J. R., et al. (2007). Religiousness and spiritual support among advanced cancer patients and associations with end-of-life treatment preferences and quality of life. *Journal of Clinical Oncology, 25*(5), 555–560.

Bell, K. (1992). *Ritual theory, ritual practice.* Oxford: Oxford University Press.

Bell, K. (1997). *Ritual: Perspectives and dimensions.* Oxford: Oxford University Press.

Bradley, C. T. (2009). Roman Catholic doctrine guiding end-of-life care: A summary of the recent discourse. *Journal of Palliative Medicine, 12*(4), 373–377.

Center for Health Care Ethics, Religious Traditions and Health Care. (1999–2002) *Decisions Handbook Series.* 18 Vols. Park Ridge, IL: Center for Health, Faith, and Ethics.

Corsentino, E. A., Collins, N., Sachs-Ericsson, N., & Blazer, D. G. (2009). Religious attendance reduces cognitive decline among older women with high levels of depressive symptoms. *The Journals of Gerontology: Series A: Biological Sciences and Medical Sciences, 64A*(12), 1283.

Curlin, F. A., Lantos, J. D., Roach, C. J., Sellergren, S. A., & Chin, M. H. (2005). Religious characteristics of US physicians: A national survey. *Journal of General Internal Medicine, 20,* 629–634.

Daaleman, T. P., Usher, B. M., Williams, S. W., Rawlings, J., & Hanson, L. C. (2008a). An exploratory study of spiritual care at the end of life. *Annals of Family Medicine, 6,* 406–411.

Daaleman, T. P., Williams, C. S., Hamilton, V. L., & Zimmerman, S. (2008b). Spiritual care at the end of life in long term care. *Medical Care, 46*(1), 85–91.

Dezutter, J., Soenens, B., Luyckx, K., Bruyneel, S., Vansteenkiste, M., Duriez, B., et al. (2009). The role of religion in death attitudes: Distinguishing between religious belief and style of processing religious contents. *Death Studies, 33,* 73–92.

Exline, J. E., Park, C. L., Smvth, J. M., & Carev, M. P. (2011). Anger to god, cognitive predictors prevalence and links with adjust to bereavement and cancer. *Journal of Personality and Social Psychology, 100*(1), 129–148.

Fetzer Institute/National Institute on Aging Working Group. (1999). *Multidimensional measurement of religiousness/spirituality for use in health research.* Kalamazoo, MI: Fetzer Institute.

Fitzgerald, P. J. (2006, Winter). Into the hands of the father: The invention of ministry to the dying. *Santa Clara Magazine,* pp. 20–23.

Fry, S. (2004). Nursing ethics. In S. Post (Ed.), *Encyclopedia of bioethics* (Revised edition). (3rd ed., Vol. IV, pp. 1898–1903). New York, NY: Thompson-Gale.

Fuller, R. C. (2001). *Spiritual, but not religious.* New York, NY: Oxford University Press.

German Protestant and Catholic Bishops. (1975–2010). Gemeinsame Texte 17: Sterbebegleitung statt aktiver Sterbehilfe, Eine Textsammlung kirchlicher Erklärungen mit einer Einführung des Vorsitzenden der Deutschen Bischofskonferenz und des Vorsitzenden des Rates der Evangelischen Kirche in Deutschland.

Gijsberts, M.-J., H. E, Echteld, M. A., van der Steen, J. T., Muller, M. T., Otten, R. H. J., Ribbe, M. W., et al. (2011). Spirituality at the end of life: Conceptualization of measurable aspects—A systematic review. *Journal of Palliative Medicine, 14*(7), 852–863.

Gillick, M. R. (2004). Terminal sedation: An acceptable exit strategy? *Annals of Internal Medicine, 141*(3), 236–237.

Goedicke, H. (1970). *The report about the dispute of a man with his Ba: Papyrus Berlin 3024.* Baltimore, MD: The Johns Hopkins Press.

Greeley, A. M. (2003). *Religion in Europe at the end of the second millennium: A sociological profile.* New Brunswick, NJ: Transaction Publishers.

Grimes, R. (1992). *Readings in ritual studies.* Upper Saddle River, NJ: Prentice Hall.

Grimes, R. (2002). *Deeply into the bone: Re-inventing rites of passage.* Berkeley, CA: University of California Press.

Grisez, G. (1990). Should nutrition and hydration be provided to permanently unconscious and other mentally disabled persons? *Linacre Quarterly, 57,* 30–43.

Grisez, G. (1997). Q43, "Is it wrong to wish for death?" and "Q 47: May a husband consent to stopping feeding his permanently unconscious wife?" In *Difficult moral questions: Way of the Lord Jesus* (Vol. III). Steubenville, OH: Franciscan Press.

Grogan, E., Andrew, T., Colin, C., Claire, S.-T., David, O., Tim, H., Rosaleen, B., & Rob, G. (2007). Are vulnerable groups no more likely to receive physician-assisted dying?, *Journal of Medical Ethics.* Retrieved from http://jme.bmj .com/cgi/eletters/33/10/591. Accessed on November 8, 2007.

Holloway, M, (2006). Death the great leveller? Towards a transcultural spirituality of dying and bereavement. *Journal of Clinical Nursing, 15,* 833–839.

Hout, M. & Fisher, C. (2002). Why more Americans have no religious preference: Politics and generations. *American Sociological Review, 67,* 165–190.

Hunter, R. J. (2004). Pastoral care and healthcare chaplaincy. In S. Post (Ed.), *Encyclopedia of bioethics* (Revised edition). (3rd ed., Vol. IV, pp. 1975–1980). New York, NY: Thompson-Gale.

Jantos, M. & Kiat, H. (2007). Prayer as medicine: How much have we learned? *The Medical Journal of Australia, 186*(10 Suppl), S51–S53.

Jecker, N. & Reich, W. (2004). Contemporary ethics of care. In S. Post (Ed.), *Encyclopedia of bioethics.* (Revised edition). (3rd Ed., Vol. I, pp. 367–374). New York, NY: Thompson-Gale.

Kazantzakis, N. (1961). *Report to Greco,* translated by Peter A. Bien, New York, NY: Simon and Schuster, 1965; Oxford: Bruno Cassirer, 1965; London: Faber and Faber, 1965; New York, NY: Bantam Books, 1971.

Kearney, M. (1996). *Mortally wounded: Stories of soul pain, death, and healing.* New York, NY: Touchstone.

Keown, D. (2005). End of life: The Buddhist view. *Lancet, 366*(9489), 952–955.

King, M. B. & Koenig, H. G. (2009). Conceptualising spirituality for medical research and health service provision. *BMC Health Services Research, 9,* 116.

Koenig, B. (2002). "Choice" in end-of-life decision making: Researching a fact or a fiction? *The Gerontologist, 42*(Special Issue III), 114–128.

Krishna, L. K. R. (2011). Decision-making at the end of life: A Singaporean perspective. *Asian Bioethics Review, 3*(2), 118–126.

Kuhl, D. (2002). *What dying people want: Practical wisdom for the end of life.* New York, NY: Public Affairs.

Lambert, Y. (1999). Religion in modernity as a new axial age: Secularization or new religious forms? *Sociology of Religion, 60*(3), 303–333.

Lustig, A. (2003, May 23). End of life decisions: Does faith make a difference? *Commonweal, 130,* 7.

Marty, M. (2005). Religion and healing: The four expectations. In L. L. Barnes & S. S. Sered (Eds.), *Religion and healing in America* (pp. 487–504). Oxford: Oxford University Press.

Mathers, C. D. & Loncar, D. (2006). Projections of global mortality and burden of disease from 2002 to 2030. *PloS Medicine, 3*(11), e442.

Metcalf, P. & Huntington, R. (1991). *Celebrations of death: The anthropology of mortuary ritual.* Cambridge: Cambridge University Press.

Miller, V. J. (2005). *Consuming religion: Christian faith and practice in a consumer culture.* New York, NY: Continuum.

Mueller, D. (1973). Review of Goedicke, Hans. (1970). *The report about the dispute of a man with his Ba: Papyrus Berlin 3024.* Baltimore, MD: Johns Hopkins Press, 1970. *Journal of Near Eastern Studies, 32*(3), 353–354.

National Cancer Institute. *Spirituality in cancer care.* Retrieved from www.nci.nih .gov/cancertopics/pdq/supportivecare/spirituality/

National Consensus Project. *The development of clinical practice guidelines for quality palliative care.* Retrieved from www.nationalconsensusproject.org/

O'Connell, Killen, P., & Silk, M. (Eds.) (2004). *Religion and public life in the pacific Northwest: The "None" zone.* Lanham, MD: Altamira Press.

Oshansky, S. & Ault, A. B. (1986). The fourth stage of the epidemiologic transition: The age of delayed degenerative diseases. *Milbank Quarterly, 64*(3), 355–91.

Pesut, B. (2009). Incorporating patients' spirituality into care using Gadow's ethical framework. *Nursing Ethics, 4,* 418–428.

Pevey, C. F., Jones, T. J., & Yarber, A. (2008–2009). How religion comforts the dying: A qualitative inquiry. *OMEGA, 58*(1), 41–59.

Pew Forum. (2008). *U.S. religious landscape survey.* Retrieved from http://religions .pewforum.org. Accessed on November 27, 2011.

Pew Forum. (2009). *Many Americans mix multiple faiths: Eastern, new age beliefs widespread.* Retrieved from http://pewforum.org/docs/?DocID=490. Accessed on November 27, 2011.

Phelps, A. C., Paul, K. M., Matthew, N., Tracy, A. B., Alexi, A. W., Elizabeth, M. P., Elizabeth, T., Deborah S., John, R. P., Susan, D. B., & Holly, G. P., (2009). Religious coping and use of intensive life-prolonging care near death in patients with advanced cancer. *JAMA, 301*(11), 1140–1147.

Puchalski, C. (Ed.) (2006). A time for listening and caring: Spirituality and the care of the chronically ill and dying. New York, NY: Oxford University Press.

Puchalski, C., Ferrell, B., Virani, R., Otis-Green, S., Baird, P., Bull, J., et al. (2009). Improving the quality of spiritual care as a dimension of palliative care: The report of the consensus conference. *Journal of Palliative Medicine, 12,* 885–904.

Puchalski, C. M., Lunsford, B., Harris, M. H., & Miller, T. (2006). Interdisciplinary spiritual care for seriously ill and dying patients: A collaborative model. *The Cancer Journal, 12*(5), 398–416.

Pui-Lan, K. (2005). *Post-colonial imagination and feminist theology.* Westminister, UK: John Knox.

Pui-Lan, K., Compier, D. H., & Rieger, J. (2007). *Empire and the Christian tradition: New readings of classical theologians.* Minneapolis, MI: Augsburg-Fortress.

Rainbird, K. J., Perkins, J. J., & Sanson-Fisher, R. W. (2005). The needs assessment for advanced cancer patients (NA-ACP): A measure of the perceived needs of patients with advanced, incurable cancer. A study of validity, reliability and acceptability. *Psychooncology, 14,* 297–306.

Reich, W. (2004). Care, history of the notion of care and historical dimensions of an ethic of care in healthcare. In S. Post (Ed.), *Encyclopedia of bioethics*. (Revised edition). (3rd Ed., Vol. I, pp. 349–367). New York, NY: Thompson-Gale.

Reinis, A. (2007). *Reforming the art of dying: The ars moriendi in the German Reformation (1519–1528)*. Farnham, UK: Ashgate.

Risse, G. B. (1999). *Mending bodes, saving souls: A history of hospitals*. Oxford: Oxford University Press.

Rubinstein, R. L., Black, H. K., Doyle, P. J., Moss, M., & Moss, S. Z. (2011). Faith and end of life in nursing homes. *Journal of Aging Research, 2011*, 1–7.

Satterly, J. (2001). Guilt, shame, and religious and spiritual pain. *Holistic Nursing Practice, 15*(2), 30–39.

Smith-Stoner, M. (2007). End-of-life preferences for atheists. *Journal of Palliative Medicine, 10*(4), 923–928.

Sugarman, J. & Sulmasy, D. (2010). *Methods in medical ethics*. Washington, DC: Georgetown University Press.

Sulmasy, D., Curlin, F., Brungardt, G. S., & Cavanaugh, T. (2010, March 2). Justifying different levels of palliative sedation. *Annals of Internal Medicine, 152*, 332–333.

Sulmasy, D. & Pellegrino, E. (1999). Double effect: Clearing up the double talk. *Archives of Internal Medicine, 159*, 545–550.

Sulmasy, D. P. (2006). Spiritual issues in the care of dying patients: "It's okay between me and God." *JAMA, 296*(11), 1385.

Sulmasy, D. P. & Jansen, L. A. (2002). Sedation, alimentation, hydration, and equivocation: Careful conversation about care at the end of life. *Annals of Internal Medicine, 136*, 845–849.

Sulmasy, D. P., Ury, W. A., Ahronheim, J. C., Siegler, M., Kass, L., Lantos, J., et al. (2000a). Responding to intractable terminal suffering. *Annals of Internal Medicine, 133*, 560–562.

Sulmasy, D. P., Ury, W. A., Ahronheim, J. C., Siegler, M., Kass, L., Lantos, J., et al. (2000b). Palliative treatment of last resort and assisted suicide. *Annals of Internal Medicine, 133*, 562–563.

Taylor, E. J. & Outlaw, F. H. (2002). Use of prayer among persons with cancer. *Holistic Nursing Practice, 16*(3), 46–60.

Thomas, C. (1980). First suicide note? *British Medical Journal, 281*(6235), 284–285; (Later as Discourse of a Man with his Ba, by Wim van den Dungen. Retrieved from www.sofiatopia.org/maat/ba.htm.)

Thomasma, D. (1998). Assisted death and martyrdom. *Christian Bioethics, 4*(2), 122–142.

Ufema, J. (2004). Religious beliefs: Are you saved? *Nursing, 34*(9), 29.

United States Conference of Catholic Bishops (2011). *To live each day with dignity*. Retrieved from www.usccb.org/issues-and-action/human-life-and-dignity/assisted-suicide/to-live-each-day/

Washington State Catholic Conference (2006). *A guide to making good decisions for the end of life: Living will and durable power of attorney for health care*. Retrieved from http://thewscc.org/.

Wink, P. & Scott, J. (2005). Does religiousness buffer against the fear of death and dying in late adulthood? Findings from a longitudinal study. *Journal of Gerontology: Psychological Sciences, 60B*, P207–P214.

Wuthnow, R. (1998). *After heaven: Spirituality in America since the 1950s.* Berkeley, CA: University of California Press.

Online Resources

The Association for Clinical Pastoral Education

www.acpe.edu

Duke Institute on Care at the End of Life

http://divinity.duke.edu/initiatives-centers/iceol

George Washington Institute for Spirituality and Health (GWISH)

www.gwish.org

The Healthcare Chaplaincy

www.healthcarechaplaincy.org/index.asp

Spirituality, Religious Wisdom, and the Care of the Patient, *Yale Journal for Humanities in Medicine*

http://info.med.yale.edu/intmed/hummed/yjhm/spirit2004/spiritintro2004.htm

University of Virginia Health System, Chaplaincy Services and Pastoral Education. "Religious Beliefs and Practices Affecting Health Care"

www.healthsystem.virginia.edu/internet/chaplaincy/rbpahc.cfm

National Cancer Institute: Spirituality in Cancercare

www.nci.nih.gov/cancertopics/pdq/supportivecare/spirituality/

National Consensus Project: The Development of Clinical Practice Guidelines for Quality Palliative Care

www.nationalconsensusproject.org/

American Association of Pastoral Counsellors

http://aapc.org/

International Council on Pastoral Care and Counselling

www.icpcc.net/

Association of Professional Chaplains

www.professionalchaplains.org/

The Canadian Association for Pastoral Practice and Education

www.cappe.org/

National Association of Catholic Chaplains

www.nacc.org/

National Association of Jewish Chaplains

www.najc.org/about/mission

Muslim Chaplains Association

www.muslimchaplains.org/

Hindu Chaplaincy

www.hinduchaplaincy.com/

Buddhist Chaplaincy

www.upaya.org/index.php

ISSUE 17

Is Dying Made Better by Culturally Competent End-of-Life Care?

YES: H. Russell Searight and Jennifer Gafford, from "Cultural Diversity at the End of Life: Issues and Guidelines for Family Physicians," *American Family Physician* (vol. 71, no. 3, pp. 515–522, 2005)

NO: Amber E. Barnato, Denise L. Anthony, Jonathan Skinner, Patricia M. Gallagher, and Elliott S. Fisher, from "Racial and Ethnic Differences in Preferences for End-of-Life Treatment," *Journal of General Internal Medicine* (vol. 24, no. 6, pp. 695–701, 2010)

Learning Outcomes

After reading this issue, you should be able to:

- Gain an understanding of the cultural differences in end-of-life care.
- Describe the difference between cultural preferences and preferences that may be limited by understanding of treatments available (health literacy).
- Debate the implications of restricting futile care to persons of other cultures.
- Discuss the underpinning socioeconomic and religious differences that may impact differences in choices for aggressive care at the end of life.
- Identify and debate whether the cultural background of the health care provider could influence end-of-life care choices offered to patients.

ISSUE SUMMARY

YES: Professor H. Russell Searight, of Lake Superior State University, and Jennifer Gafford, a psychologist, write about the cultural differences of patients that must be considered when approaching end-of-life decision making and how these approaches can improve care.

NO: Amber Barnato, a physician at the Center for Health Research at the University of Pittsburgh, and colleagues describe a study of end-of-life care preferences which found some cultural/racial groups prefer life-sustaining treatments that make their care at the end of life more likely to be in the hospital with aggressive treatments.

Cultural beliefs, values, and rituals influence choices throughout one's lifetime. Health care choices are also influenced by cultural beliefs and values. Understanding the cultural underpinnings of patient choices becomes essential when patients are facing end-of-life care (Johnson, Kuchibhatla, & Tulsky, 2010). Researchers have demonstrated that end-of-life preferences vary significantly between different races or ethnicities (Duffy, Jackson, Schim, Ronis, & Fowler, 2006). For example, researchers have found that blacks and Hispanics are reluctant to use hospice, are less likely to complete advance directives, and are less likely to want life-sustaining treatment withdrawn, even if it is futile (Duffy et al., 2006).

Race and ethnicity predict end-of-life decisions even when researchers adjusted data for socioeconomic and educational status. For example, given equal educational levels, black physicians remained more likely than their non-Hispanic white counterparts to choose aggressive treatment options (Curlin, Nwodim, Vance, Chin, & Lantos, 2008). Physicians' perspectives on end of life appear to be linked to ethnicity, geographic region, experience caring for the dying, and the religious characteristics. Physicians from minority ethnicities were more likely to be opposed to physician assisted suicide, terminal sedation, and withdrawal of life support. Catholic physicians were more likely than Protestant physicians to be opposed to withdrawal of artificial life support. This research suggests that deep rooted cultural and religious beliefs and values influence physicians as well as patients in the choices that they make for end-of-life care (Curlin et al., 2008).

One researcher conducted a series of focus groups to examine cultural beliefs about end-of-life care. Research subjects included Arab Muslim, Arab Christian, Hispanic, and black men and women, and compared interview findings from all ethnicities (Duffy et al., 2006). These researchers found that some end-of-life care wishes were important to all groups, including: wanting to be kept comfortable at the end of life; having good physician communication about diagnosis, prognosis, and treatment; having responsibilities taken care of; being offered hope and optimism; and having spiritual beliefs honored. Her findings indicated that most subjects also identified having love and compassion, being cared for, expressing feelings, fixing relationships, being able to say good-bye, being given choices, making plans, not being in pain, and being "ready to go" as very important (Duffy et al., 2006).

Several studies have particularly noted racial disparities in aggressiveness of care at the end of life. This is thought to be linked to the fact that African Americans have lower rates of advance directives and are less likely to choose hospice as compared with whites. However Hanchate, Kronman, Young-Xu,

Ash, and Emanuel (2009) dispute this, suggesting choosing hospice would do little to reduce the costs of end-of-life care for minorities, especially if the choice was made after all other avenues for were exhausted. They studied the records of 160,000 Medicare patients who died, examining Medicare costs in the last 6 months of life. They found substantial differences by race, ethnicity, and geographical location of the death. The three minority groups died of similar causes when compared with white patients, but black Medicare decedents (especially those living in high cost urban areas) were significantly more likely to receive resuscitation, mechanical ventilation, and gastrostomy for artificial feedings than white decedents living in the same area. They also noted that Hispanics were even more likely than blacks to receive ICU care, mechanical ventilation, dialysis, and cardiac catheterization. These researchers speculated that if nonwhites received timely, effective care throughout their lives may find it easier to reject futile cardiac resuscitation, mechanical ventilation, and artificial nutrition at the end (Hanchate et al., 2009). Other researchers have noted preferences for life-sustaining therapies make be linked to African American spirituality or beliefs about death and dying, or could be linked to a general mistrust of the health care system which offered years of unequal care access (Johnson et al., 2010; Hanchate et al., 2009).

Others suggest that choices for aggressive care at the end of life are linked to poor health literacy, not understanding the full implication of the outcome of care, or not completely understanding that the aggressive care will be futile (Volandes et al., 2008). Physicians and researchers have raised concerns about the need to continue to offer aggressive care and give everything to the demanding families of minority patients who are dying, even when that care is known to be futile. If our health care providers must provide very aggressive care to be "culturally competent," then health care costs at the end of life will remain high. However, some researchers argue that there is a better way to approach end-of-life discussions with cultural competence.

Volandes et al. (2008) wondered if health literacy issues (i.e., understanding of health-related information) for minority patients might affect end-of-life decisions. To test their question, they conducted interviews of 144 clinic patients and measured their health literacy ability and placed subjects in low, moderate, and high levels of health literacy. Afterwards, a physician simply described the situation of an advanced dementia patient and asked subjects if they were in this condition, what would they prefer related to tube feeding, resuscitation, and other end-of-life choices. Finally, they showed the person a video of what someone with advanced dementia looks like, and again asked the preferences for end-of-life care. They found that even subjects with low health literacy were more likely to change preferences for aggressive care after viewing the video. Their understanding of the verbal description of late stage dementia was limited. However, some subjects with low health literacy continued with their decision for aggressive care.

Another way of helping to support cultural preferences in end-of-life care is to understand the importance of including family members, community members, or religious leaders to support patients and families in their decisions. In one study, white families who discussed placing a dying person on life support wanted to do so to sustain them temporarily until other family members could be assembled; African American families in the same study requested life support to sustain life at all costs and hope for a miracle (Shrank et al., 2005). Understanding the need for respectful communication regarding the patient's condition and establishing trust with African American families may improve decision making at the end of life. Researchers in this study noted the strong emphasis on faith in the African American families and their request for hope in conversations focused on end-of-life decisions. Gerdner, Cha, Yang, and Tripp-Reimer (2007) provide a rich insight into the views on dying and rituals related to death and burial for the Hmong population. She notes that in the Hmong community, clan leaders play a large role in decisions that are made for community members who are at the end of life.

In the YES article, Searight and Gafford identify the cultural differences of patients that must be considered when approaching end-of-life decision making. They offer guidance for working with translators, guides to cross cultural conversations, and ideas for how to present bad news to patient families who are facing critical end-of-life decisions.

Barnato, Anthony, Skinner, Gallegher, and Fisher provide an opposing view. Their study of end-of-life care preferences has found that some cultural/racial groups prefer life-sustaining treatments that make their care at the end of life more likely to be in the hospital with very aggressive treatments. This study indicates that always following cultural views would mean that minority patients would be more likely to die uncomfortable deaths tethered to machines in an intensive care unit.

YES

H. Russell Searight and
Jennifer Gafford

Cultural Diversity at the End of Life: Issues and Guidelines for Family Physicians

Ethnic minorities currently compose approximately one third of the population of the United States. The U.S. model of health care, which values autonomy in medical decision making, is not easily applied to members of some racial or ethnic groups. Cultural factors strongly influence patients' reactions to serious illness and decisions about end-of-life care. Research has identified three basic dimensions in end-of-life treatment that vary culturally: communication of "bad news"; locus of decision making; and attitudes toward advance directives and end-of-life care. In contrast to the emphasis on "truth telling" in the United States, it is not uncommon for health care professionals outside the United States to conceal serious diagnoses from patients, because disclosure of serious illness may be viewed as disrespectful, impolite, or even harmful to the patient. Similarly, with regard to decision making, the U.S. emphasis on patient autonomy may contrast with preferences for more family-based, physician-based, or shared physician- and family-based decision making among some cultures. Finally, survey data suggest lower rates of advance directive completion among patients of specific ethnic backgrounds, which may reflect distrust of the U.S. health care system, current health care disparities, cultural perspectives on death and suffering, and family dynamics. By paying attention to the patient's values, spirituality, and relationship dynamics, the family physician can elicit and follow cultural preferences.

Ethnic minorities compose an increasingly large proportion of the population of the United States. In the 2000 census, about 65 percent of the U.S. population identified themselves as white, with the remaining percentage representing the following ethnic groups: black (13 percent); Hispanic (13 percent); Asian-Pacific Islander (4.5 percent); and American-Indian/Alaskan native (1.5 percent). About 2.5 percent of the population identify themselves as bi-ethnic, and this figure is likely to continue to grow.[1]

The challenge for family physicians in an increasingly diverse society is to learn how cultural factors influence patients' responses to medical issues such as healing and suffering, as well as the physician-patient relationship. The American Academy of Family Physicians (AAFP) has published cultural

From *American Family Physician*, February 1, 2005, pp. 515–522. Copyright © 2005 by American Academy of Family Physicians. Reprinted by permission.

Strength of Recommendations

Key clinical recommendation	Label	References
Many ethnic groups prefer not to be directly informed of a life-threatening diagnosis.	C	6
In cultural groups in which patients are not directly informed about a serious prognosis, family members may want the physician to discuss the patient's condition with family members only.	C	6, 34
When considering therapeutic options, physicians should consider that members of many cultural groups prefer that family members, rather than patients, make treatment decisions.	C	6, 34
Direct discussion of advance directives and therapeutic support levels may be undesirable in situations in which they are viewed as potentially harmful to patients' well being.	C	14
When physician-patient communication occurs through a translator, trained health care translators make fewer errors than untrained translators.	C	35

A = consistent, good-quality patient-oriented evidence; B = inconsistent or limited-quality patient-oriented evidence; C = consensus, disease-oriented evidence, usual practice, opinion, or case series.

proficiency guidelines[2] and policy and advocacy statements about diversity in AAFP educational activities.[3] In addition, sensitivity to cultural diversity is integrated within the AAFP's policy statement on ethical principles for end-of-life care.[4] Specifically, principle 5 states: "Care at the end of life should recognize, assess, and address the psychological, social, spiritual/religious issues, and cultural taboos realizing that different cultures may require significantly different approaches."

Although cultural proficiency guidelines exist,[5] few resources are available to family physicians regarding ways to apply these guidelines to direct patient care. Many physicians are unfamiliar with common cultural variations regarding physician-patient communication, medical decision making, and attitudes about formal documents such as code status guidelines and advance directives. End-of-life discussions are particularly challenging because of their emotional and interpersonal intensity.

Physicians also are challenged by the tremendous diversity within specific ethnic minority groups (Table 1).[6,7] In fact, research suggests that when compared with whites of European descent, ethnic minorities exhibit greater variability in their preferences.[8] Therefore, while certain styles of communication and decision making may be more common in some cultures, stereotyping should be avoided. Generalizations about specific cultures are not always applicable to specific patients.

Principlism, a well-established ethical framework for medical decisions in the United States and Western Europe, highlights cross-cultural differences

Table 1

Points of Cultural Diversity in Health Care

Emphasis on individualism versus collectivism

Definition of family (extended, nuclear, nonblood kinship)

Common views of gender roles, child-rearing practices, and care of older adults

Views of marriage and relationships

Communication patterns (direct versus indirect; relative emphasis on nonverbal communication; meanings of nonverbal gestures)

Common religious and spiritual-belief systems

Views of physicians

Views of suffering

Views of afterlife

Information from references 6 and 7.

that occur along four dimensions: autonomy, beneficence, nonmaleficence, and justice.[9,10] Although many patients in the United States value autonomy, other cultures emphasize beneficence. In the United States, legal documents such as advance directives and durable powers of attorney are strategies to prolong autonomy in situations in which patients can no longer represent themselves. Other cultures, however, de-emphasize autonomy, perceiving it as isolating rather than empowering. These non-Western cultures believe that communities and families, not individuals alone, are affected by life-threatening illnesses and the accompanying medical decisions.[11] Cultures valuing nonmaleficence (doing no harm) protect patients from the emotional and physical harm caused by directly addressing death and end-of-life care. Many Asian and Native American cultures value beneficence (physicians' obligation to promote patient welfare) by encouraging patient hope, even in the face of terminal illness.

Cultural influences in late-life care became particularly evident with the passing of the 1990 Federal Patient Self Determination Act (PSDA).[12] Case studies appeared that highlighted unforeseen dilemmas in the PSDA's implementation among some ethnic and cultural groups.[13,14] Subsequent research and case studies identified three basic dimensions in end-of-life treatment that may vary culturally: communication of "bad news," locus of decision making, and attitudes toward advance directives and end-of-life care.

Communicating Bad News

The consumer movement, legal requirements, an emphasis on patient informed consent, and reduced physician authority have contributed to health-related "truth telling" in the United States. Outside the United States,

Table 2

Guidelines for Medical Interviews with Translators

Ideally, the translator should not be a family member.

Translators should be trained to respect patient confidentiality.

Physicians should orient the translator to the process of the medical encounter.

Physicians should request a literal, word-for-word translation.

Physicians should request the translator to ask the physician to restate or clarify unfamiliar terms.

After making a complete statement, the physician should pause for translation.

The physician should look directly at the patient, rather than at the translator, when either the physician or patient is speaking.

The physician should speak in the second person. For example, he or she might ask, "Where is your pain?" rather than "Can you ask him where he hurts?"

Information from references 17 and 18.

health care professionals often conceal serious diagnoses from patients. Physician strategies commonly employed to minimize direct disclosure include using terminology that obscures the seriousness of a condition or communicating diagnostic and treatment information only to the patient's family members. Many African and Japanese physicians, when discussing cancer with patients or family members, choose terms such as "growth," "mass," "blood disease," or "unclean tissue,"[15] rather than specifically describing a potentially terminal condition. In Hispanic, Chinese, and Pakistani communities, family members actively protect terminally ill patients from knowledge of their condition. In the United States, this protection may include deliberately not translating diagnosis and treatment information to patients,[16] a situation that is less likely to arise with appropriate use of a translator (Table 2).[17,18]

There are four primary reasons for nondisclosure: (1) certain cultures specifically view discussion of serious illness and death as disrespectful or impolite[5,19,20]; (2) some cultures believe that open discussion of serious illness may provoke unnecessary depression or anxiety in the patient; (3) some cultures believe that direct disclosure may eliminate hope; and (4) some cultures believe that speaking aloud about a condition, even in a hypothetic sense, makes death or terminal illness real because of the power of the spoken word.

In many Asian cultures, it is perceived as unnecessarily cruel to directly inform a patient of a cancer diagnosis.[15,21] Even among people of European background, Bosnian-Americans and Italian-Americans perceive direct disclosure of illness as, at minimum, disrespectful, and more significantly, inhumane.[15,22] Recent immigrants to the United States described Bosnian physicians as "going around" the diagnosis and being indirect about serious illness in contrast to American physicians, whose directness they described as hurtful.[22]

Emotional reaction to news of serious illness is also considered directly harmful to health. It is thought that a patient who is already in pain should not have to grapple with feelings of depression as well.[21] This negative emotional impact on health also appears to be one of the primary reasons that Chinese patients are less likely to sign their own do-not-resuscitate (DNR) orders.[23] This concern, together with Asian values of reverence for aging family members,[7] may be especially pronounced in elderly patients who, because of their frailty, are perceived as more vulnerable to being upset by bad news. In addition, the special status of the elderly in Asian culture includes a value that they should not be burdened unnecessarily when they are ill.[11,15,24]

Direct disclosure of bad health news may eliminate patient hope. Bosnian respondents indicated that they expected physicians to maintain patients' optimism by not revealing terminal diagnoses.[22] Among other ethnic groups emphasizing this perspective of hope, there is the notion that factors outside of medical technology, such as a divine plan and personal coping skills, may be more important for survival than physician intervention.[5] Filipino patients may not want to discuss end-of-life care because these exchanges demonstrate a lack of respect for the belief that individual fate is determined by God.[24] If their hope is shattered, patients are no longer able to enjoy their daily lives and may feel they are ". . . among the dead while still alive."[11(p213)]

Finally, Native American, Filipino, and Bosnian cultures emphasize that words should be carefully chosen because once spoken, they may become a reality. For example, a commonly held Navajo belief is that negative words and thoughts about health become self-fulfilling. Carrese and Rhodes[14] noted that Navajo informants place a particularly prominent value on thinking and speaking in a "positive way." About one half of their Navajo informants would not even discuss advance directives or anticipated therapeutic support status with patients because these verbal exchanges were considered potentially injurious. Similarly, the reluctance of Chinese patients and their families to discuss possible death is based on the belief that direct acknowledgement of mortality may be self-fulfilling.[23]

Locus of Decision Making

In the past 30 years, the U.S. system of medical ethics has de-emphasized physician beneficence and increasingly emphasized patient autonomy. A patient's capacity for making independent decisions is questioned only if cognitive function or patient judgment appears to be impaired by medical or psychiatric illness. In contrast, many ethnic communities view it as appropriate to withhold potentially distressing information from cognitively intact, competent patients. Therefore, the North American cultural norm of individual decision making about medical care may have to be altered when physicians care for ethnically diverse patients. Alternate models of decision making include family-based, physician-based, and shared physician-family decision making (Table 3).[5,19,25]

Cultures that place a higher value on beneficence and nonmaleficence relative to autonomy have a long tradition of family-centered health care

Table 3

Cross-Cultural Interview Questions
Regarding Serious Illness and End-of-Life Care

"Some people want to know everything about their medical condition, and others do not. What is your preference?"

"Do you prefer to make medical decisions about future tests or treatments for yourself, or would you prefer that someone else make them for you?"

To patients who request that the physician discuss their condition with family members: "Would you be more comfortable if I spoke with your (brother, son, daughter) alone, or would you like to be present? " *If the patient chooses not to be present:* "If you change your mind at any point and would like more information, please let me know. I will answer any questions you have." *(This exchange should be documented in the medical record.)*

When discussing medical issues with family members, particularly through a translator, it is often helpful to confirm their understanding: "I want to be sure that I am explaining your mother's treatment options accurately. Could you explain to me what you understand about your mother's condition and the treatment that we are recommending?"

"Is there anything that would be helpful for me to know about how your family/community/ religious faith views serious illness and treatment?"

"Sometimes people are uncomfortable discussing these issues with a doctor who is of a different race or cultural background. Are you comfortable with me treating you? Will you please let me know if there is anything about your background that would be helpful for me to know in working with you or your (mother, father, sister, brother)?"

Information from references 5, 19, and 25.

decisions. In this collective decision process, relatives receive information about the patient's diagnosis and prognosis and make treatment choices, often without the patient's input. Compared with persons of black and European descent, Koreans and Mexican-Americans were more likely to consider family members, rather than the patient alone, as holding the decision-making power regarding life support.[9] With acculturation, Mexican-Americans were more likely to agree that patients should be directly informed of their conditions. However, acculturated Mexican-Americans continued to view decision making as a family-centered process.[5,8] Blacks may view an overly individualistic focus as disrespectful to their family heritage.[5,26,27]

Among Asian cultures, family-based medical decisions are a function of filial piety—an orientation toward the extended family as opposed to individual patient self-interest.[24] Illness is considered a family event rather than an individual occurrence.[11] Interests in Asian families are often bi-directional—there is an equivalent concern about the impact of the elderly person's death on the family.

Many societies attribute a high degree of authority, respect, and deference to physicians.[28-30] Patients and families defer end-of-life decisions to the physician, who is seen as an expert. Eastern European medicine has had a long tradition of physician-centered, paternalistic decision making. In

Russian medicine, the physician rather than the patient or patient's family often unilaterally determines a patient's level of life support.[29] Recent Bosnian immigrants to the United States reported that they would prefer that physicians, because of their expert knowledge, make independent decisions to reduce the burden on patients and their families.[22]

In Asian, Indian, and Pakistani cultures, family members and physicians may share decisional duties. Family care of the terminally ill in Asian and Indian cultures is a shared responsibility for cognitively intact and incapacitated relatives. Physicians in Pakistan may be adopted into the family unit and addressed as parent, aunt, uncle, or sibling.[30] This family status provides the physician with a role sanctioning his or her involvement in intimate discussions.[30]

Advance Directives and End-of-Life Care

Survey data suggest that about 20 percent of the U.S. population has advance directives.[31,32] Most investigators find significantly lower rates of advance directive completion among Asians, Hispanics, and blacks.[31,32] For example, about 40 percent of elderly white patients indicated that they had an advance directive, compared with only 16 percent of elderly blacks.[33] In one study,[8] none of the Korean respondents had advance directives, and relatively few of the Hispanics had completed these documents. The low rates of advance directive completion among non-whites may reflect distrust of the health care system, health care disparities, cultural perspectives on death and suffering, and family dynamics such as parent-child relationships (Tables 3[5,19,25] and 4[34,35]).

Among blacks, nonacceptance of advance directives appears to be part of a much broader pattern of values regarding quality of life, as well as a historical legacy of segregation. DNR orders may be viewed as a way of limiting expensive health care or as cutting costs by ceasing care prematurely.[11] Historically, this perspective may stem from a long history of distrust of the white-dominated health care system. The Tuskegee syphilis study,[36] in which infected black men were followed for 40 years but were not informed of the availability of penicillin treatment, is well known in the black community.

The reluctance of blacks to formally address end-of-life care also may stem from a history of health care discrimination. Although individual studies vary, the preponderance of evidence indicates that nonwhites, even after controlling for income, insurance status, and age, are less likely to receive a range of common medical interventions such as cardiac catheterization, immunizations, and analgesics for acute pain.[37,38] Although issues such as geographic patterns of medical care play some role in these disparities,[39] mistrust of the health care system is likely to be a factor in the lower rates of organ donation among blacks, as well as a reduced acceptance of hospice care.[40,41] Blacks with colon cancer were more likely than comparably ill white patients to want artificial nutrition, mechanical ventilation, and cardiopulmonary resuscitation.[41] Similarly, black patients overall are about one half as likely to accept DNR status and are more likely than whites to later change DNR orders to more aggressive levels of care.[42] These attitudes also carry over to black physicians, who are significantly more likely than their white colleagues to recommend aggressive treatment to patients with brain damage and known terminal illness.[43] Similarly, black physicians are less likely to accept physician-assisted suicide as an acceptable intervention.[43]

In addition to a historical legacy of unequal care, black patients also appear to view suffering somewhat differently than whites of European background. While whites may be concerned about dying patients undergoing needless suffering, black physicians and patients are more likely to think of suffering as spiritually meaningful, and life as always having some value.[11,44] Survival alone, even if it involves significant pain, may be an important demonstration of religious faith.[5]

Among Hispanics, the lack of acceptance of advance directives may stem from a view of collective family responsibility.[45] Hispanic patients may be reluctant to formally appoint a specific family member to be in charge because of concerns about isolating these persons or offending other relatives. Instead, a consensually oriented decision-making approach appears to be more acceptable in this population. Formalization of this process is seen as unnecessary and potentially harmful, because it may lead to increased and extended family conflict.[45]

Finally, among Asians, aggressive treatment for elderly family members is likely to be guided by filial piety. Asian adults feel a responsibility to reverently care for aging parents. This sense of obligation makes it difficult for relatives to request other than extraordinary measures.[20] Similarly, elderly Asian parents may experience a reciprocal obligation to continue living for the emotional well-being of their adult children.[20]

Guidelines for Cross-Cultural Communication

Physicians can actively develop rapport with ethnically diverse patients simply by demonstrating an interest in their cultural heritage. Attention to dimensions such as those listed in Table 1[6,7] should help physicians develop a more detailed understanding of important cultural issues. The power imbalance of physician-patient interaction may make it particularly difficult for ethnic minority patients to directly request culturally sensitive care. Through skillful use of patient-centered questions (Table 3)[5,19,25] and by including interpreters as necessary (Table 2),[17,18] physicians can develop a richer understanding of patients' health care preferences.

Patient preferences for nondisclosure of medical information and family-centered decision making may be disorienting initially to American-trained physicians. When treating patients from cultures with norms of nondisclosure, physicians might describe the dimensions of informed consent and offer to provide diagnostic and treatment information (Table 4).[34,35] By offering autonomy to patients, cultural norms are respected while rights to independent decisions are simultaneously acknowledged.[46,47] A patient who refuses diagnostic information and prefers family- or physician-centered decision making has made a clear, voluntary choice. Physicians should also appreciate that, in certain cultures, while communication about serious illness and death may not be overt,

Table 4

Cross-Cultural Communication for Serious Illnesses and End-of-Life Care

Issue	Potential solution
Ethnic minorities, which compose about one third of the U.S. population, often have distinct norms for physician-patient communication and decision making for seriously ill patients.	Physicians can become knowledgeable about cultural norms in patients they commonly treat. They can describe the dimensions as they apply to specific ethnic groups (see Table 1). Physicians should ask patients directly about cultural issues that may affect communication patterns and treatment.
Up to 17 percent of the U.S. population speaks a primary language other than English.	Physicians must find accessible, trained translators. Untrained translators should be briefly oriented to their role (see Table 2).
Some cultures view directly informing patients of a serious diagnosis as harmful.	Physicians can ask patients if they would like to be directly informed of the results of medical investigations. Physicians can let patients know that they will discuss the patient's condition with the patient at any time. These exchanges should be documented in the medical record (see Table 3).
Patients may prefer that their family members be the recipients of diagnostic and treatment information.	If a patient prefers that family members receive information, find out which family member(s).
Treatment decisions may be made by an informally appointed family member, family-wide consensus, or physician-family collaboration.	Physicians should ask patients how they would like treatment decisions to be made. At this point, the physician can determine the extent to which patients/family members wish to be involved in treatment decisions.
When compared with whites of Northern European background, patients who belong to other ethnic groups are less likely to complete formal advance directives.	Physicians should inform patients and/or family members about the availability of written advance directives and durable powers-of-attorney. They can ask the patient or family if there is a preferred approach for making decisions on the patient's behalf.
Patients from some cultures, particularly those with histories of health care discrimination, may not trust physicians who are of a different ethnic background.	In this situation, it is good to ask patients directly if they are comfortable working with a physician of a different ethnic background. When appropriate, physicians can acknowledge that members of a particular ethnicity have had histories of less than optimal care. Patients and family members can be encouraged to inform the physician immediately if they have quality-of-care concerns.

Information from references 34 and 35.

information may be conveyed with subtlety. Facial expressions, voice tone, and other nonverbal cues may convey the seriousness of a patient's status without the necessity for explicit statements. In addition, stories about "good" deaths of family and community members may be shared with seriously ill patients.[14]

The physician's partnership with his or her patients and their families provides unique insight into their values, spirituality, and relationship dynamics, and may be especially helpful at the end of life. By eliciting and following cultural preferences regarding disclosure, advance planning, and decisional processes that relate to seriously ill patients, family physicians can provide culturally sensitive end-of-life care.

References

1. United States Census Bureau. U.S. Census, 2000. Washington, D.C.: 2001.

2. American Academy of Family Physicians. Positions and policies: cultural proficiency guidelines (2001, 2003). Accessed online December 16, 2004, at: www.aafp.org/x6701.xml.

3. American Academy of Family Physicians. Positions and policies: diversity-assuring sensitivity to diversity in AAFP education (2000). Accessed online December 16, 2004, at: www.aafp.org/x6711.xml.

4. American Academy of Family Physicians. Position and policies: ethics, core principles for end-of-life care, principle 5 (2000, 2002). Accessed online December 16, 2004, at: www.aafp.org/x6791.xml.

5. Kagawa-Singer M, Blackhall LJ. Negotiating cross-cultural issues at the end of life: "You got to go where he lives." JAMA 2001;286:2993–3001.

6. McGoldrick M, Giordano J, Pearce JK, eds. Ethnicity and family therapy. 2d ed. New York: Guilford, 1996.

7. Searight HR. Family-of-origin therapy and diversity. Washington, D.C.: Taylor & Francis, 1997.

8. Blackhall LJ, Murphy ST, Frank G, Michel V, Azen S. Ethnicity and attitudes toward patient autonomy. JAMA 1995;274:820–5.

9. Beauchamp TL, Childress JF. Principles of biomedical ethics. 4th ed. New York: Oxford University Press, 1994.

10. Sugarman J, ed. 20 common problems: ethics in primary care. New York: McGraw-Hill, 2000.

11. Candib LM. Truth telling and advance planning at the end of life: problems with autonomy in a multicultural world. Fam Syst Health 2002;20:213–28.

12. Federal patient self-determination act 19090, 42 U.S.C. 1395 cc(a).

13. Braun KL, Nichols R. Cultural issues in death and dying. Hawaii Med J 1996:55:260–64.

14. Carrese JA, Rhodes LA. Western bioethics on the Navajo reservation. Benefit or harm? JAMA 1995;274:826–9.

15. Holland JL, Geary N, Marchini A, Tross S. An international survey of physician attitudes and practice in regard to revealing the diagnosis of cancer. Cancer Invest 1987;5:151–4.

16. Kaufert JM, Putsch RW. Communication through interpreters in health-care: ethical dilemmas arising from differences in class, culture, language, and power. J Clin Ethics 1997;8:71–87.

17. Herndon E, Joyce L. Getting the most from language interpreters. Fam Pract Manag 2004;11:37–40.

18. Flores G, Abreu M, Schwartz I, Hill M. The importance of language and culture in pediatric care: case studies from the Latino community. J Pediatr 2000;137:842–8.

19. Hern HE Jr, Koenig BA, Moore LJ, Marshall PA. The difference that culture can make in end-of-life decision-making. Camb Q Healthc Ethics 1998;7:27–40.

20. Frank G, Blackhall LJ, Michel V, Murphy ST, Azen SP, Park K. A discourse of relationships in bioethics: patient autonomy and end-of-life decision making among elderly Korean Americans. Med Anthropol Q 1998;12:403–23.

21. Matsumura S, Bito S, Liu H, Kahn K, Fukuhara S, Kagawa-Singer M, et al. Acculturation of attitudes toward end-of-life care: a cross-cultural survey of Japanese Americans and Japanese. J Gen Intern Med 2002;17:531–9.

22. Searight HR, Gafford J. "It's like playing with your destiny": Bosnian immigrants' views of advance directives and end-of-life decision-making. J Immigr Health. [In press]

23. Liu JM, Lin WC, Chen YM, Wu HW, Yao NS, Chen LT, et al. The status of the do-not-resuscitate order in Chinese clinical trial patients in a cancer centre. J Med Ethics 1999;25:309–14.

24. Yeo G, Hikuyeda N. Cultural issues in end-of-life decision making among Asians and Pacific Islanders in the United States. In: Braun K, Pietsch JH, Blanchette PL, eds. Cultural issues in end-of-life decision making. Thousand Oaks, Calif: Sage, 2000:101–25.

25. Ersek M, Kagawa-Singer M, Barnes D, Blackhall L, Koenig BA. Multicultural considerations in use of advance directives. Oncol Nurs Forum 1998;25:1683–90.

26. Waters CM. Understanding and supporting African Americans' perspectives of end-of-life care planning and decision making. Qual Health Res 2001;11:385–98.

27. Berger JT. Cultural discrimination in mechanisms for health decisions: a view from New York. J Clin Ethics 1998;9:127–31.

28. Schlesinger M. A loss of faith: the sources of reduced political legitimacy for the American medical profession. Milbank Q 2002;80:185–235.

29. Karakuzon M. Russia. In: Crippen D, Kilcullen JK, Kelly DF, eds. Three patients: international perspectives on intensive care at the end-of-life. Boston: Kluwer, 2002:67–72.

30. Moazam F. Families, patients, and physicians in medical decision-making: a Pakistani perspective. Hastings Cent Rep 2000;30:28–37.

31. Pietch JH, Braun KL. Autonomy, advance directives, and the patient self-determination act. In: Braun K, Pietsch JH, Blanchette PL, eds. Cultural issues in end-of-life decision making. Thousand Oaks, Calif: Sage, 2000:37–53.

32. Baker ME. Economic, political and ethnic influences on end-of-life decision-making: a decade in review. J Health Soc Policy 2002;14:27–39.

33. Hopp FP, Duffy SA. Racial variations in end-of-life care. J Am Geriatr Soc 2000;48:658–63.

34. Murphy ST, Palmer JM, Azen S, Frank G, Michel V, Blackhall L. Ethnicity and advance care directives. J Law Med Ethics 1996;24:108–17.

35. Flores G, Law MB, Mayo SJ, Zuckerman B, Abreu M, Medina L, et al. Errors in medical interpretation and their potential clinical consequences in pediatric encounters. Pediatrics 2003;111:6–14.

36. Caplan AL. Twenty years after: the legacy of the Tuskegee syphilis study. In: Teays W, Purdy LM, eds. Bioethics, justice and health care. Belmont, Calif.: Wadsworth-Thomson Learning, 2001:231–5.

37. Smedley BD, Stith AY, Nelson AR, eds. Unequal treatment: confronting racial and ethnic disparities in health care. Washington, D.C.: National Academies Press, 2003.

38. Steinbrook R. Disparities in health care—from politics to policy. N Engl J Med 2004;350:1486–8.

39. Lavizzo-Mourey R, Knickman JR. Racial disparities—the need for research and action. N Engl J Med 2003;349:1379–80.

40. Siminoff LA, Lawrence RH, Arnold RM. Comparison of black and white families' experiences and perceptions regarding organ donation requests. Crit Care Med 2003;31:146–51.

41. McKinley ED, Garrett JM, Evans AT, Danis M. Differences in end-of-life decision making among black and white ambulatory cancer patients. J Gen Intern Med 1996;11:651–6.

42. Tulsky JA, Cassileth BR, Bennett CL. The effect of ethnicity on ICU use and DNR orders in hospitalized AIDS patients. J Clin Ethics 1997;8:150–7.

43. Mebane EW, Oman RF, Kroonen LT, Goldstein MK. The influence of physician race, age, and gender on physician attitudes toward advance care directives and preferences for end-of-life decision-making. J Am Geriatr Soc 1999;47:579–91.

44. Orona LJ, Koenig BA, Davis AJ. Cultural aspects of nondisclosure. Camb Q Healthc Ethics 1994;3:338–46.

45. Morrison RS, Zayas LH, Mulvihill M, Baskin SA, Meier DE. Barriers to completion of healthcare proxy forms: a qualitative analysis of ethnic differences. J Clin Ethics 1998;9:118–26.

46. Moskop JC. Informed consent in the emergency department. Emerg Med Clin North Am 1999;17:327–40.

47. Freedman B. Offering truth. One ethical approach to the uninformed cancer patient. Arch Intern Med 1993;153:572–6.

Amber E. Barnato et al.  **NO**

Racial and Ethnic Differences in Preferences for End-of-Life Treatment

BACKGROUND: Studies using local samples suggest that racial minorities anticipate a greater preference for life-sustaining treatment when faced with a terminal illness. These studies are limited by size, representation, and insufficient exploration of socio-cultural co-variables. . . .

RESULTS: Respondents included 85% non-Hispanic whites, 4.6% Hispanics, 6.3% blacks, and 4.2% "other" race/ethnicity. More blacks (18%) and Hispanics (15%) than whites (8%) want to die in the hospital; more blacks (28%) and Hispanics (21.2%) than whites (15%) want life-prolonging drugs that make them feel worse all the time; fewer blacks (49%) and Hispanics (57%) than whites (74%) want potentially life-shortening palliative drugs, and more blacks (24%, 36%) and Hispanics (22%, 29%) than whites (13%, 21%) want MV for life extension of 1 week or 1 month, respectively. [S]ociodemographic variables, preference for specialists, and an overly optimistic belief in the effectiveness of MV explained some of the greater preferences for life-sustaining drugs and mechanical ventilation among non-whites. Black race remained an independent predictor of concern about receiving too much treatment, preference for dying in a hospital, receiving life-prolonging drugs, MV for 1 week or 1 month's life extension, and a preference not to take potentially life-shortening palliative drugs. Hispanic ethnicity remained an independent predictor of preference for dying in the hospital and against potentially life-shortening palliative drugs.

CONCLUSIONS: Greater preference for intensive treatment near the end of life among minority elders is not explained fully by confounding socio-cultural variables. Still, most Medicare beneficiaries in all race/ethnic groups prefer not to die in the hospital, to receive life-prolonging drugs that make them feel worse all the time, or to receive MV.

Compared to whites, blacks are more likely to die in the hospital and to use intensive care,[1,2] and life-sustaining treatments such as mechanical ventilation (MV), hemodialysis, and feeding tubes.[3] They also incur higher medical care costs in their last 12 months than whites.[4-6] Some, but not all, of these

From *Journal of General Internal Medicine*, vol. 24, no. 6, 2010, pp. 695–701. Copyright © 2010 by Society of General Internal Medicine. Reprinted by permission of Springer Science and Business Media via Rightslink.

differences in end-of-life utilization are due to blacks' living in regions with higher overall end-of-life treatment intensity and spending[7] and their use of higher intensity hospitals.[2,3] Further, some of these differences may be due to minorities' lower uptake of services and strategies, such as hospice[8-11] and advance care plan documents in nursing homes[12] that change the acute care "default" near the end of life.

Some of the differences may be due to systematically different preferences for treatment at the end of life among minorities. Several studies using local samples have found that blacks and Hispanics are more likely to anticipate wanting life-sustaining treatments, even in the context of terminal illness or persistent vegetative state.[13-18] Few of these studies have explored the potential sociocultural confounders of this association. In this study we describe preferences for end-of-life treatment by race/ethnicity in a national sample of Medicare beneficiaries and explore the independent effect of race/ethnicity after controlling for variables hypothesized to impact preference for and use of health services.[19-21]

Methods

Study Population

The study population was a national sample of Medicare beneficiaries. The sampling frame was all community-dwelling Medicare beneficiaries . . . who were age 65 or older on July 1, 2003, . . . and residents of a US Hospital Referral Region (HRR) in 2003 and 2004. . . .

Survey

Development and Administration. We designed the survey instrument to assess beneficiaries' general concerns and preferences for care in the event of a terminal illness. We also collected information on socio-demographics, health status, social networks, and perceptions of quality and access to health care. . . .

Measures

Race and Ethnicity. We categorized self-reported race and ethnicity into mutually exclusive groups of non-Hispanic white, black, Hispanic, or "other," assigning multi-racial or ethic respondents using the hierarchy: black>Hispanic> other (Asian, Native Hawaiian or Pacific Islander, American Indian/Alaskan Indian/Alaskan Native, or Other)>non-Hispanic white. If respondents endorsed a racial category but had missing data for Hispanic ethnicity, we assumed they were non-Hispanic; this included 28 blacks, 100 whites, and 14 "others." Of the 2,847 responents, 2,810 could be categorized into one of these four race/ethnicity groups.

Medicare Beneficiaries End-of-Life Concerns and Preferences. We used responses to five survey questions to create seven dichotomous dependent variables for the current study; two related to concerns and five related to preferences.* When dichotomizing responses, we treated answers other than "yes" or "no" (e.g., "not concerned" or "I don't know") as missing data. The concern variables were: concern about receiving too little medical treatment in the last year of life or receiving too much medical treatment. The preferences variables were: preference for dying in an acute care hospital, for life-prolonging drugs that have side-effects, for palliative drugs with potential for life shortening, and for mechanical ventilation to prolong life. We created a summative "positive attitude toward life prolongation" by summing the more intensive responses (concern about too little medical care, preference for dying in the hospital, for life prolongation, against potentially life-shortening palliation, and for mechanical ventilation).

Covariates. The survey collected extensive information about the beneficiary that could confound the relationship between race/ethnicity and end-of-life medical treatment preferences. Using a behavioral model of health-care utilization,[19–21] we conceptualized these variables as *predisposing* (age, sex, education, financial strain, self-efficacy, preference for specialists, and belief in the effectiveness of mechanical ventilation), *enabling* (living arrangements, social networks), *need* (self-assessed health status and pain), *provider access and utilization* (personal physician, emergency department, and physician visits), *perceptions of their providers* (physicians spends enough time, didn't get tests/treatment desired, quality of care), *health-care environment* (age-sex-race standardized spending in the last 6 months of life among beneficiaries residing in the HRR), and *perceptions of the health-care environment* (amount and quality of care in the community). . . .

Results

. . .

Sample Characteristics

The respondents included 2,105 non-Hispanic whites (74.9%), 113 Hispanics (4.0%), 489 blacks (17.4%), and 103 persons of other race/ethnicity (3.7%). We compare the weighted distribution of sample characteristics to the sampling frame from which it was drawn in Table 1. Compared to the population, our weighted sample had fewer persons age 85+ (9.8% vs 14.7%) and fewer blacks (6.3% vs 8.1%). Hispanic ethnicity data are underreported in the enrollment file[22] and thus not strictly comparable to our survey self-report data.

As expected, the different race/ethnic groups varied considerably in variables known to influence health care use (See Table A2, available online). For example, all non-white minorities reported lower education and greater financial strain, less confidence in their ability to manage their health conditions, and an overly-optimistic view of the effectiveness of MV (specifically, 9.2% of Hispanics and 7.9% of blacks, compared to 3.6% of non-Hispanic whites believed that more than half of patients "requiring a respirator to keep them alive will get back to normal activities"). Non-white minorities were less likely to have a personal doctor, more likely to feel the doctor didn't spend enough

Table 1

Sample Characteristics

Characteristic	Sample weighted mean
Age	75.6
Age 65–69, %	21.4
Age 70–74, %	27.2
Age 75–79, %	23.5
Age 80–84, %	18.1
Age 85+, %	9.8
Male, %	42.5
Non-Hispanic white, %	85.0
Black, %	6.3
Hispanic, %	4.6
Other, %	4.2
Less than HS education, %	21.4

*Imputed from mean US Census ZIP level education

time with them and to report not receiving some medical care they wanted in the last 12 months (nevertheless, their perceptions of their health care quality were similar to those of non-Hispanic whites). Although blacks and Hispanics were more likely to live in hospital referral regions with higher spending for Medicare beneficiaries, they felt that the amount and quality of medical care their community received was lower than others their age.

End-of-Life Concerns and Preferences by Race

We report respondents' concerns and preferences by race, and the correlations among these variables.* The majority of Medicare beneficiaries of all race/ethnic groups say that in the event of a terminal illness with less than a year to live they would want to die at home and would not want to receive life-prolonging drugs with uncomfortable side effects or mechanical ventilation for 1 week's or 1 month's life extension. Fewer blacks (25.6%) than whites (42.1%) were worried about receiving too little medical treatment in the event of a terminal illness (and, conversely a greater proportion were worried about receiving too much treatment: 61.5% vs. 42.8%). However, with respect to particular end-of-life treatments, minorities were more likely to prefer intensive options than whites. Specifically, 17.7% of blacks and 15.2% of Hispanics want to die in a hospital, compared to 8% of non-Hispanic whites. More blacks (28.1%) and Hispanics (21.2%) than whites (15%) would want life-extending drug treatment with uncomfortable side effects. Conversely, fewer blacks (49.3%) and Hispanics (56.6%) than whites (74.2%) would want palliative medications that might be life shortening. Finally more blacks (36.1%, 23.5%) and Hispanics

---

*Additional data tables for this essay are available online at www.dartmouth.edu/~jskinner/documents/BarnatoARacialandEthnic.pdf

(29%, 21.6%) than whites (19.3%, 10.8%) would want to receive ventilator support for 1 month's or 1 week's life extension, respectively.

In . . . models adjusted for variables confounding the relationship between race and preferences for end-of-life medical treatment black race remained a significant predictor of all responses. Only Hispanics' preferences to avoid palliative drugs that might be life shortening and to die in the hospital remained significantly different than non-Hispanic whites. Blacks and Hispanics had more positive attitudes towards life prolongation than non-Hispanic whites, as measured by the summed index of responses.

Several additional findings deserve note (See Table A5, available online). Women of all racial/ethnic groups were less likely to worry about receiving "too little" medical treatment at the end of life and were less likely to want life-prolonging drugs. Those with less than a high school education were less likely to want palliative drugs that might be life shortening. Greater financial strain was associated with worry about receiving too much medical treatment at the end of life, and also with preference for dying in the hospital, for life-prolonging drugs, and avoiding potentially life-shortening palliative drugs. A greater self-efficacy score was associated with a marked decrease in wanting to die in the hospital or to receive mechanical ventilation for 1 week's life extension. Those respondents who preferred specialists over primary care providers were more likely to prefer to die in the hospital, and to receive mechanical ventilation for 1 month's or 1 week's life extension. An overly optimistic belief about the likelihood of return to normal activities after mechanical ventilation for life-support was associated with preference for life-prolonging drugs, against potentially life-shortening palliative drugs, and for mechanical ventilation for 1 month's or 1 week's life extension. Living alone predicted a preference for in-hospital death and against mechanical ventilation for 1 month's life extension. Those who attended church daily were less likely to want potentially life-shortening palliative drugs compared to those who never attend church, as were those with less than weekly personal contact with friends or family. Compared to those in excellent health, those with poorer health were more likely to worry about receiving too much medical treatment at the end of life. Having a condition that often caused pain or discomfort was associated with a greater odds of prefering palliative drugs.

Discussion

The majority of Medicare beneficiaries of all race/ethnic groups say that in the event of a terminal illness with less than a year to live they would want to die at home and would not want to receive life-prolonging drugs with uncomfortable side effects or mechanical ventilation for 1 weeks' or 1 months' life extension. However, there were differences in the distribution of preferences for end-of-life medical treatment by race/ethnicity even after controlling for potentially mediating or confounding demographic and socio-cultural variables. Specifically, black beneficiaries were more likely than Hispanic and non-Hispanic white beneficiaries to prefer life-prolonging drugs and mechanical ventilation; both blacks and Hispanics were more likely than whites to prefer spending their last days in the hospital and to avoid potentially life-shortening palliative drugs.

Although blacks were more likely than whites to want life-sustaining treatments, they also were more worried about receiving too much medical treatment in their last year of life. We wondered if this was a reflection of concern among the majority of black beneficiaries who don't prefer aggressive end-of-life treatment that the higher population prevalence of preferences for life-sustaining treatments among blacks would result in "statistical discrimination"[23,24] by providers that would lead to more medical treatment than most blacks would prefer. Our data did not support this hypothesis, since there were no group-level differences in treatment preferences (for life-prolonging drugs, for palliative drugs, or for mechanical ventilation) among blacks who were and were not worried about receiving "too much" end-of-life treatment. There was a positive correlation between preferences for more intensive end-of-life treatment (preference for death in the hospital, for life-prolonging drugs, and for mechanical ventilation) and concern about "too much" end-of-life treatment among white respondents, but not among black respondents. The correlation among whites is paradoxical—we imagined those who would want more intensive treatment might be worried about receiving too little treatment and vice versa—but perhaps those who want more intensive treatment anticipate the possibility of "overdoing" it? That the correlation was not found among black respondents may reflect insufficient statistical power in the black cohort or point to systematic differences in the interpretation of the question about "too much" treatment by blacks and whites and a flaw in our survey question design. Without race-specific cognitive testing information about this survey item, we cannot interpret this finding; it deserves further exploration.

The concepts of race and ethnicity in the health services literature are imprecise constructs[25] that conflate culture (e.g., beliefs, values, and customs), socioeconomic status, and "racialism" [i.e., "the ways in which we see, value, and behave toward others according to (some notion) of race"].[26,27] For example, Johnson et al. used a combination of socio-cultural variables to completely explain black-white differences in advance directive completion rates and attitudes towards hospice.[28] We sought to approach the explanation of differences in responses to our hypothetical treatment preference questions by using the conceptual framework of the behavioral model of health-care utilization and found several interesting relationships. Among variables hypothesized to predispose individuals to use health services, lower education, financial strain, preference for specialists, and an overly optimistic belief in the effectiveness of mechanical ventilation were each associated with one or more preferences for "more intensive" end-of-life treatment. Among these, the most mutable (and powerful) is the belief in mechanical ventilation, which may be a proxy for belief in health care technology more generally. Over 27% of blacks believed that 50% or more of persons receiving this life-sustaining treatment were returned to their normal activities, compared to 17% of non-Hispanic whites. In reality, 56% of patients who require mechanical ventilation for 48 h or more are dead at 1 year, and almost 60% of the survivors require caregiver assistance at 1 year.[29] This, of course, is in stark contrast to the popular representations of life-sustaining treatments.[30] Even among those with a more clinically realistic estimation of the effectiveness of mechanical ventilation, blacks were twice as likely as Hispanics and non-Hispanic whites to want a ventilator for life extension of 1 month or 1 week.

Among variables hypothesized to enable the use of health-care services, living alone was associated with a preference for dying in the hospital and not wanting mechanical ventilation. Daily church attendance and less than weekly contact with friends and family were associated with a preference against palliative drugs that might be life shortening. In our sample, relative to non-Hispanic whites, Hispanics and those of other race/ethnicity were less likely to live alone, and blacks were more likely. Some studies have implicated low support for in-home care as one factor in the low uptake of the Medicare hospice benefit among blacks.[31] Among terminal cancer patients, those with greater religiousness are more likely to prefer life-sustaining treatments.[32] The relationships between social networks and preferences for life-sustaining treatments have not been previously explored.

Among variables hypothesized to affect need, those in less than excellent health were more likely to worry about receiving too much medical treatment near the end of life, but self-reported general health did not otherwise affect our measures of preference for end-of-life care. Those reporting a condition that frequently caused pain or discomfort were more likely to prefer palliative drugs, even if they might be life shortening.

Among provider variables, having a personal doctor was associated with greater concern about receiving "too much" medical treatment. Although blacks and Hispanics were much more likely than non-Hispanic whites to report that their doctor had never or only sometimes spent enough time with them, that there was medical care, tests, or treatment that they did not receive in the last year, and that they believed their community received care of lesser amount and quality, none of these factors was associated with our measures of end-of-life concerns and preferences. Interestingly, we found no differences by race/ethnicity in perceptions of the quality of *one's own* health care, but significant differences in perceptions of the amount and quality of health care in *one's community*.

Our survey has limitations, including survey and item-non-response, reliance upon a hypothetical scenario, and intentionally over-simplified preference questions.[3] Non-response may limit generalizability. The non-contact rate was much higher among minorities, as was ineligibility due to inability to complete the survey (generally cognitive impairment or severe physical debility). . . .

We created simplified survey questions, which may not predict actual treatment choices or receipt. . . . Additionally, we created artificial dichotomies; for example, we asked about life-prolonging drugs that "make you feel worse all the time" and palliative drugs that "make you feel better, [but] might shorten your life." . . .

Another weakness was the lack of a measure of "trust" in the health-care system, a much vaunted[28] but controversial mechanism for differences in health-care use by race/ethnicity. We hypothesized that beneficiaries' perceptions of the amount and quality of the health care received by their community were a measure of perceived equity that would capture a related construct. . . . Finally, we used a hierarchical approach to assigning race/ ethnicity; specifically, we did not treat Hispanic ethnicity as distinct from race, as is customary, nor did we allow multi-racial categories. So doing simplified our analytic models, but further oversimplifies the constructs of race and ethnicity.

In summary, most Medicare beneficiaries say they would not want drugs with uncomfortable side effects or mechanical ventilation for life extension in the event of a terminal illness. Preference for life-extension, and mechanical ventilation in particular, is associated with an overly optimistic belief in its effectiveness, a misperception that we as providers should seek to rectify because it may have important implications for decision making. From an epidemiologic perspective, our findings reproduce those from smaller regional studies that blacks are more likely than non-Hispanic whites to prefer more intensive treatment near death.[13-18] Despite our efforts to control for a broad array of demographic and socio-cultural variables, these findings may reflect unmeasured confounding since our survey items are imperfect measures of the concepts that we sought to measure, such as experience and perceptions of providers and the health-care system. And, of course, our findings should not be interpreted as permission to generalize; end-of-life treatment decisions always should be customized to individual preferences and goals of care.

References

1. Pritchard RS, Fisher ES, Teno JM, et al. Influence of patient preferences and local health system characteristics on the place of death. SUPPORT Investigators. Study to Understand Prognoses and Preferences for Risks and Outcomes of Treatment [see comments]. J Am Geriatr Soc. 1998; 4610: 1242–50.

2. Barnato AE, Berhane Z, Weissfeld LA, Chang CH, Linde-Zwirble WT, Angus DC. Racial variation in end-of-life intensive care use: a race or hospital effect? Health Serv Res. 2006; in press.

3. Barnato AE, Chang CC, Saynina O, Garber AM. Influence of race on inpatient treatment intensity at the end of life. J Gen Intern Med. 2007; 223: 338–45.

4. Hogan C, Lunney J, Gabel J, Lynn J. Medicare beneficiaries' costs of care in the last year of life. Health Aff. 2001; 204: 188–95.

5. Levinsky NG, Yu W, Ash A, et al. Influence of age on Medicare expenditures and medical care in the last year of life. JAMA. 2001; 28611: 1349–55.

6. Shugarman LR, Campbell DE, Bird CE, Gabel J, Louis TA, Lynn J. Differences in medicare expenditures during the last 3 years of life. J Gen Intern Med. 2004; 192: 127–35.

7. Baicker K, Chandra A, Skinner JS, Wennberg JE. Who You Are And Where You Live: How Race And Geography Affect The Treatment Of Medicare Beneficiaries. Health Aff (Millwood). 2004.

8. Greiner KA, Perera S, Ahluwalia JS. Hospice usage by minorities in the last year of life: results from the National Mortality Followback Survey. J Am Geriatr Soc. 2003; 517: 970–8.

9. Johnson KS, Kuchibhatla M, Tanis D, Tulsky JA. Racial differences in hospice revocation to pursue aggressive care. Arch Intern Med. 2008; 1682: 218–24.

10. Stewart AL, Teno J, Patrick DL, Lynn J. The concept of quality of life of dying persons in the context of health care. Journal of Pain & Symptom Management. 1999; 172: 93–108.

11. Johnson KS, Kuchibhatala M, Sloane RJ, Tanis D, Galanos AN, Tulsky JA. Ethnic differences in the place of death of elderly hospice enrollees. J Am Geriatr Soc. 2005; 5312: 2209–15.

12. Degenholtz HB, Arnold RA, Meisel A, Lave JR. Persistence of racial disparities in advance care plan documents among nursing home residents. J Am Geriatr Soc. 2002; 502: 378–81.

13. Degenholtz HB, Thomas SB, Miller MJ. Race and the intensive care unit: disparities and preferences for end-of-life care. Crit Care Med. 2003; 315 Suppl: S373–8.

14. Diringer MN, Edwards DF, Aiyagari V, Hollingsworth H. Factors associated with withdrawal of mechanical ventilation in a neurology/neurosurgery intensive care unit. Crit Care Med. 2001; 299: 1792–7.

15. Garrett JM, Harris RP, Norburn JK, Patrick DL, Danis M. Life-sustaining treatments during terminal illness: who wants what? J Gen Intern Med. 1993; 87: 361–8.

16. Blackhall LJ, Frank G, Murphy ST, Michel V, Palmer JM, Azen SP. Ethnicity and attitudes towards life sustaining technology. Soc Sci Med. 1999; 4812: 1779–89.

17. Mebane EW, Oman RF, Kroonen LT, Goldstein MK. The influence of physician race, age, and gender on physician attitudes toward advance care directives and preferences for end-of-life decision-making. J Am Geriatr Soc. 1999; 475: 579–91.

18. O'Brien LA, Grisso JA, Maislin G, et al. Nursing home residents' preferences for life-sustaining treatments. Jama. 1995; 27422: 1775–9.

19. Andersen RM. (Center for Health Administration Studies, University of Chicago). Behavioral model of families' use of health services. 1968. Report No.: 25.

20. Andersen RM. Revisiting the behavioral model and access to medical care: does it matter? J Health Soc Behav.. 1995; 361: 1–10.

21. Phillips KA, Morrison KR, Andersen R, Aday LA. Understanding the context of healthcare utilization: assessing environmental and provider-related variables in the behavioral model of utilization. Health Serv Res. 1998; 333 Pt 1: 571–96.

22. Arday SL, Arday DR, Monroe S, Zhang J. HCFA's racial and ethnic data: current accuracy and recent improvements. Health Care Financ Rev. 2000; 214: 107–16.

23. Balsa AI, McGuire TG, Meredith LS. Testing for statistical discrimination in health care. Health Serv Res. 2005; 401: 227–52.

24. Balsa AI, McGuire TG. Statistical discrimination in health care. J Health Econ. 2001; 206: 881–907.

25. LaVeist TA. Beyond dummy variables and sample selection: what health services researchers ought to know about race as a variable. Health Serv Res. 1994; 291: 1–16.

26. Freeman HP. Commentary on the meaning of race in science and society. Cancer Epidemiol Biomarkers Prev. 2003; 123: 232s–36s.

27. Crawley LM. Racial, cultural, and ethnic factors influencing end-of-life care. J Palliat Med. 2005; 8Suppl 1: S58–69.

28. Johnson KS, Kuchibhatla M, Tulsky JA. What Explains Racial Differences in the Use of Advance Directives and Attitudes Toward Hospice Care? J Am Geriatr Soc. 2008.

29. Chelluri L, Im KA, Belle SH, et al. Long-term mortality and quality of life after prolonged mechanical ventilation. Crit Care Med. 2004; 321: 61–9.

30. Diem SJ, Lantos JD, Tulsky JA. Cardiopulmonary resuscitation on television. Miracles and misinformation. N Engl J Med. 1996; 33424: 1578–82.

31. Gordon AK. Deterrents to access and service for blacks and Hispanics: the Medicare Hospice Benefit, healthcare utilization, and cultural barriers. Hosp J. 1995; 102: 65–83.

32. Balboni TA, Vanderwerker LC, Block SD, et al. Religiousness and spiritual support among advanced cancer patients and associations with end-of-life treatment preferences and quality of life. J Clin Oncol. 2007; 255: 555–60.

EXPLORING THE ISSUE

Is Dying Made Better by Culturally Competent End-of-Life Care?

Critical Thinking and Reflection

1. Consider your own cultural and religious background. If you were suffering from the late stages of cancer, who would be involved in decision making from a cultural standpoint? Would you or your family need to consult a rabbi, priest, or other spiritual advisor?
2. In some cultures, women must defer to men or leaders of the community for serious decisions or care at the end of life. In Western societies, health care providers always discuss care options with the patient first. How would you reconcile this if you were the health care provider? How would you show respect for these cultural beliefs.
3. Curlin and colleagues found that physicians from different cultures may not provide options for certain types of end-of-life care because it is against their personal cultural or religious beliefs. What would you tell a family that preferred comfort care only for their elderly mother, but the physician had scheduled a feeding tube placement? How should this be handled?
4. Discuss the cultural approaches and rituals for funeral ceremonies that you have experienced. Share this with other students in the class.

Is There Common Ground?

Years of racial discrimination and limited access to care has left some minority groups distrustful of the medical profession. For end-of-life care, this distrust unfortunately can result families of dying patients demanding everything possible for their loved one at the end of life. Dying in a high-tech environment with numerous uncomfortable procedures may help the family to feel as though they have done "everything," but may not be the most comforting or comfortable environment for the patient. Education on culturally competent approaches to care conversations are now required in the education of health care professionals. Efforts need to be made to ensure that cultural views are respected. Full disclosure of the patient's prognosis should be discussed in a way that family members understand the difference between what the treatment options will actually provide and what they are demanding for care. Not all cultures value autonomy (i.e., patient self-determination) in the way that the American culture values this ideal. Health care professionals must be able to listen to the concerns and issues of other cultures, seek understanding of other points of view, and offer careful guidance as they approach end-of-life discussions. Involving community or spiritual leaders to participate in these conversations can be useful for many cultural groups.

Additional Resources

Barnato, A., Anthony, D. L., Skinner, J., Gallegher, P. M, & Fisher, E. (2010). Racial and ethnic preferences for end of life treatment. *Journal of General Internal Medicine, 24*(6), 695–701.

Curlin, F. A., Nwodim, C., Vance, J., Chin, M. H., & Lantos, J. D. (2008). To die, to sleep: U.S. physicians religious and other objections to physician assisted suicide, terminal sedation, and withdrawal of life support. *American Journal of Hospice and Palliative Care, 25*(2), 112–120. doi:10.1177/1049909107310141

Duffy, S. A., Jackson, F. C., Schim, S. M., Ronis, D., & Fowler, K. E. (2006). Racial/ ethnic preferences, sex preferences, and perceived discrimination related to end-of-life care? *Journal of American Geriatrics Society, 54,* 150–157.

Dzul-Church, V., Cimino, J. W., Adler, S. R., Wong, P., & Anderson, W. G. (2010). "I'm sitting here by myself . . ." Experiences of patients with serious illness at an urban public hospital. *Journal of Palliative Medicine, 13*(6), 695–701.

Gerdner, L., Cha, D., Yang, D., & Tripp-Reimer, T. (2007). The circle of life: End of life and death rituals for Hmong-Americans. *Journal of Gerontological Nursing, 33*(5), 20–29.

Hanchate, A., Kronman, A. C., Young-Xu, Y., Ash, A. S., & Emanuel, E. (2009). Racial and ethnic differences in end of life costs: Why do minorities cost more than whites? *Archives of Internal Medicine, 169*(5), 493–501.

Johnson, K., Kuchibhatla, M., & Tulsky, J. (2010). What explains racial differences in the use of advance directives and attitudes toward hospice care? *Journal of American Geriatrics Society, 56,* 1953–1958.

Searight, H. R. & Gafford, J. (2005). Cultural diversity at the end of life: Issues and guidelines for family physicians. *American Family Physician, 71*(3), 515–522.

Shrank, W. H., Kutner, J. S., Richardson, T., Mularski, R. A., Fischer, S., & Kagawa-Singer, M. (2005). Focus group findings about the influence of culture on communication preferences in end-of-life care. *Journal of General Internal Medicine, 20,* 703–709.

Volandes, A., Paasche-Orlow, M., Gillick, M., Cook, E. F., Shaykevich, S., Abbo, E., et al. (2008). Health literacy not race predicts end-of-life care preferences. *Journal of Palliative Medicine, 11*(5), 754–762.

ISSUE 18

Do Funeral Rituals Help Grief?

YES: Robert Kastenbaum, from "Why Funerals?" *Generations* (vol. 28, no. 2, pp. 5–10, Summer 2004)

NO: Nicholas Köhler, from "We've Been Misled About How to Grieve: Why It May Be Wise to Skip the Months of Journaling and Group Talk We've Been Taught We Need." *Maclean's Magazine* (February 21, 2011)

Learning Outcomes

After reading this issue, you should be able to:

- Gain an understanding of whether and how death rituals help survivors cope with death.
- Describe the difference between the five stages of grieving and the new views on how people grieve and mourn the loss of loved ones.
- Understand the importance of grieving as an important emotional response to the loss of a loved one.
- Identify and debate the benefit or burden of religious affiliation for those coping with death of a loved one.

ISSUE SUMMARY

YES: Robert Kastenbaum, Professor Emeritus of Gerontology and Communications at University of Arizona at Tempe, discusses the historic and current reasons why the rituals of funerals are important to those who mourn.

NO: Nicholas Köhler, a writer/journalist with *Maclean's*, a national news magazine in Canada, discusses inadequacies in Kübler-Ross's five stages of grieving as protective bereavement, and relates newer research by George Bonanno that indicates how individuals have unique grieving processes that include elements of constructive resilience.

$\mathbf{F}$ollowing death of a loved one, family members are faced with dozens of decisions: whether to have a funeral or memorial service, where to locate this service, what rituals or practices to follow related to cultural or religious background, how to manage the financial and legal aspects of closing out an estate of the person who died, and how to manage their own grieving for the loss of the deceased in the midst of all of these decisions (Quillam, 2008). These decisions can be overwhelming if the deceased person was a child, young adult, or young mother or father, and can be very difficult when a frail elderly spouse is handling the affairs. In this issue, we discuss funeral and mourning practices and whether funeral rituals help families with grieving or create additional problems for persons who are in mourning.

Rituals following death vary by cultural group and region. American cultural rituals often include embalming of the body, allowing the body to be open for viewing at a funeral home or place of worship, a memorial or religious service, and a ceremony of lowering the casket to the gravesite for burial. These rituals allow bereaved individuals to celebrate the life of the person who died, mourn his or her death, as well as receive the support of others (Gamino, Easterling, Stirman, et al., 2000). The benefit of having a funeral is not only that it allows a public expression of grief but also allows others to provide support and comfort to survivors (Hayslip, Booher, Scoles, & Guarnaccia, 2007). Some cultural approaches to grieving include loud wailing or sing-song type wailing and weeping as a part of the early mourning and grieving practice. The Hmong population has a period of active mourning, viewing, stroking the body of the dead person, and wailing loudly (Gerdner et al., 2007). This wailing practice as part of mourning is found in other cultures as well: Jewish Yemenite, for example (Juliana & Claassens, 2010), the Highlands of Papua, New Guinea, and in Iranian funeral customs, Serbian, and Bangladesh grieving practices (Wilce, 2009). Indigenous non-Muslim Africans can take up to 2 weeks to bury the body of the deceased, making expensive and elaborate arrangements for the burial while the family gathers (Muga, 2009).

One challenge facing survivors of disaster victims is that of not being able to claim a body, as in the 9-11 Trade Center towers collapse (Kastenbaum, 2004). This robs family members of parts of the ritual that are so important for closure. Other disasters have interrupted grieving rituals as well, such as the inability to provide the usual New Orleans jazz funeral rituals for those that died in Hurricane Katrina. The closure and flooding of the funeral homes and the scattering of survivors interrupted the usual approaches to the burial of the dead (Dass-Brailsford, 2010). Burial rituals that are interrupted by disaster prevent the living from moving ahead with their lives because they unable to conclude their role in allowing the deceased to find peace (Kastenbaum, 2004).

Although funerals may allow families and friends place closure on a person's life, families are particularly vulnerable to be taken advantage of as they grieve. Quillam (2008) writes that the death of a loved one can be disorienting to family members. They can be vulnerable to emotionally laden and expensive decisions when they might otherwise be careful about making costly funeral plans or settling an estate. She identifies that most family members will be left with bills to pay, taxes to file, and estate settlement decisions for which they have no experience and are unlikely to ever do again. With grief clouding these decisions, it is easy for executors of estates to make poor decisions or less than optimal choices (Quillam, 2008). In his article on Kenyan funerals, Muga (2009) discusses the case of a man who came to take out a loan for his aunt's funeral, whose expenses were high because they needed to make arrangements for her to be buried in her ancestral village. The man returned a few months later to take out another loan for the funeral of his own mother, again to transport her back to her ancestral home. These loans were likely to become a huge financial burden to this man, but he could not refuse the obligations of his tribal culture (Muga, 2009).

Some of the first work on grieving, was written in the 1960s when the hospice movement was beginning. In 1969, Dr. Elisabeth Kübler-Ross introduced five stages of grief. These include: Denial stage—trying to avoid the inevitable; Anger stage—frustrated outpouring of bottled-up emotion; Bargaining stage—seeking in vain for a way out; Depression stage—final realization of the inevitable; Acceptance stage—finally finding the way forward. She wrote that grieving had to be experience in a staged and systematic way. Many health care professionals were taught these stages and believed that these transitions must be met for persons to move forward, or they would get "stuck" in the grieving process (Kübler-Ross, 1969).

More recently, researchers have found that grieving occurs in a variety of ways and that there isn't one correct way to grieve. Moules (2010–2011) describes the experience of grief as staying connected to the memory of the person who died while finding ways to say goodbye to his/her physical presence. She provides a therapy approach calling Internalized Other Interviewing, which allows the living person to speak for the person who had died. In essence, this allows a living person with knowledge of how the deceased might speak, answer the interview questions, and in the process work through some of the unfinished business of that relationship and the loss of that person (Moules, 2010–2011). Persons who have more emotional problems tend to do less well in grieving. They may report more anxiety about death and are more likely to experience difficulties with funeral rituals. Alternatively, persons who have a greater satisfaction with life tend to have less problematic grief and less death anxiety (Hayslip et al., 2007).

One researcher who has recently been examining grief and grieving has identified that people are remarkably resilient when it comes to losing a loved one. George Bonanno (2010) examined many mourning rituals and experiences. He looked at what happens when people experience the death of a child or of a parent, and found that people experience many emotions, not just anger and denial, but also joy and relief, allowing them to deal with losses. He argues that grieving goes beyond a feeling of deep sadness. Grieving may involve quietly, internally managing the loss of someone close, or can also involve positive experiences, discussions of good memories, humor, and joy. His research finds that mourning is not a predictable set of stages, but rather a very individualized and sophisticated process (Bonanno, 2010).

In the article for the YES position, Kastenbaum discusses the historic and current reasons why the rituals of funeral are important to those who mourn. He examines the reasons that we have funerals today and how these rituals have changed over time for different groups of people. He reinforces the value of funerals, even for the religiously unaffiliated as an important ritual of passage.

In the opposing view, Köhler discusses inadequacies in Kübler-Ross's five stages of grieving as protective bereavement, and relates newer research by George Bonanno that indicates how individuals have unique grieving processes that include elements of constructive resilience. He argues that people grieve in a variety of ways, with or without rituals.

YES

Robert Kastenbaum

Why Funerals?

We can learn about a society from the questions asked as well as the answers provided. "Funerals are for the living" is a preemptory answer that often presents itself even before a question can be raised. This fast-trigger answer to an unasked question protects us from uncomfortable reflections about our beliefs and assumptions. Crawling through a convenient escape hatch, however, can be inconsistent with our responsibilities as human-service providers. We try to cultivate perspective, a readiness for reflection, and the nerve to cross into difficult territory when the situation so requires.

Coming to the present case, we can be more helpful to people who are facing death-related issues if we are prepared to go beyond the formulaic answer to the question, Why funerals? Echoes from the past are resonating today within a high-tech society that has been trying hard not to listen. Beneath our whiz-bang, cybernetic, palm-pilot daily whirl we still have much in common with those who confronted death long before history found an enduring voice. Our orientation must somehow take into account both the distinctive characteristics of life in the early twenty-first century and our continuing bonds with all who have experienced the loss of loved ones. We begin, then, with a retrospective view and then look at funerals in our own time. For further background we suggest, among other sources, *Handbook of Death and Dying* (Bryant, 2003), *Macmillan Encyclopedia of Death and Dying* (Kastenbaum, 2002), *On Our Way: The Final Passage Through Life and Death* (Kastenbaum, 2004), *At the Hour of Our Death* (Aries, 1981), and *The Sacred Remains: American Attitudes Toward Death* (Laderman, 1996).

The Dead: Vulnerable and Dangerous

Early history speaks to us in the remote and fragmented language of bones, shards, tools, and burial mounds. The archaeological history of life on earth reaches farther back than written records. Bones are still being consulted by forensic investigators (Ubelaker and Scammell, 1992), and remains of eminent citizens of Verona are being exhumed and analyzed more than six hundred years after their owners drew their final breaths (Williams, 2004). Furthermore, ancient documents were often devoted to the perils faced in the journey of the dead. Rituals for guiding and communicating with the dead have been at the core of virtually all world cultures. It has been suggested that the spiritual health of a society can be evaluated by the vigor with which it continues to perform its obligations to the dead. Something crucial to the survival of a society is endangered when the living are unwilling or unable to continue customs and rituals intended to regulate relationships with the dead.

Through the millennia, our ancestors performed rituals both to affirm communal bonds among the living and to secure the goodwill of the resident deities. Ritual performances instructed members in their group responsibilities, celebrated life, encouraged fertility, and offered protection from malevolent forces. In this sense, funerary rites certainly were for the living—but that was only part of the story. Funerals were for the dead, too. An outsider with a sharp pencil and a notebook might insist on separating and classifying societal practices, including the "for the living," and "for the dead." The society itself, though, was more likely to regard all these beliefs and processes as integrated within its worldview. From the insider's perspective it was obvious that the living needed to do right by the dead. Failure to carry through with postmortem obligations could provoke the wrath of the deceased as well as the gods. Moreover, the discontented dead were not only dangerous—they were also vulnerable, needing the help of the living community. Everybody—living and dead—was in it together.

The living had two persuasive reasons for taking good care of their dead: love and fear. Although the details of mourning customs have varied widely, people everywhere have generally sorrowed at the loss of a person dear to them. We would recognize the anguish of newly bereaved people thousands of years ago and they would recognize ours:

- We would both want to feel that our loved one is "all right," even though dead.
- We would not feel ready to sever our ties completely. There seems to be a powerful need for what has become known in recent years as "continuing bonds" (Klass and Walter, 2001).
- And we would want—somehow—to continue to express our love and respect, and to keep something of that person with us.

Today, a widow might not choose to convert her husband's jawbone into a necklace or his skull into a lime-pot, but this worked for the Trobriand Islanders as they preserved and transformed anatomical artifacts to serve as generational hand-me-downs in memory of those who had come before (Barley, 1995). Perhaps the islanders would have made DVDs from the family album had this technology been available—or perhaps the "real thing" was to be preferred in any event. Whatever the particular practice, the living could not rest easy until the departed spirits were likewise settled into their spiritual or symbolic estate.

The vulnerability of the newly dead and their potential for malignant intervention is the side of this story that has been shooshed aside by technologically advanced societies. That the dead have something to fear and that we have something to fear from the dead might be dismissed as outmoded superstition. Nevertheless, by whatever name, fear for and of the dead continues to beset many people even if such fear is less recognized by mainstream society. It is still a powerful force within some ethnic traditions and also an impulse that can break through into the lives of mainstream people when they least expect it.

A Contemporary Example: "Unnatural Deaths" of the Young

The Tohono O'Odham of the American southwest are among the many traditional societies that became outcasts in their own land. A desperate economic situation added to their plight when local employment opportunities fell victim to technological and expansionist change. The most shattering consequence has been the increased frequency of "unnatural deaths" among young males. The official causes of death are (often alcohol-related) suicide, accidents, and homicide. These deaths are disturbing for both personal and cosmic reasons. Those who die before their time are mourned by family and community, who also fear for the future of their hard-pressed society with so many losses among the younger generation. There is another ominous facet to these deaths, however. The young men died before their spirits were prepared for the transition to the next life. This untimely occurrence upsets the natural order of things. It also constitutes a threat to the community because spirits of the deceased like to visit their living family members with a kind and loving attitude. Those who have died "unnaturally" are dangerous visitors.

Kozak (1991) found that

> To counteract this danger, the living erect death-memorials so that the soul of a "bad" death victim will return to the location of their demise, rather than to their previous, worldly existence . . . But the death-memorial is also the location where family and friends of the deceased go to assist the soul to *si' alig weco*. This term means "beyond the eastern horizon," and it is where all O'odham souls reside after death. (pp. 212–13)

Here's the key point: The living can move ahead confidently with their lives only after they have succeeded in helping the newly dead to attain their own kind of peace "beyond the eastern horizon." Funerals and memorials clearly are for the living *and* the dead.

Horrible nightmares have afflicted people in many times and places when they have failed to assist the dead in their passage to the next life. It's the difference between a comforting visit from the spirit of a deceased loved one and the uneasy sense of being haunted. An example of epic proportions occurred during the prime killing years of the Black Death in fourteenth-century North Africa, Asia, and Europe. The dead sometimes outnumbered the living, who, frightened and struggling for their own survival, often had to forgo ritual and dump bodies into large burial pits or crowded shallow graves. Survivor stress included the fear that their own souls had been condemned for the failure to provide the proper rituals and services. It is even possible that the fourteenth century's intensified violence and episodes of mass psychotic behavior owed something to this violation of the implicit contract between the living and the dead (Kastenbaum, 2004).

Ground Zero

The abundant examples in our own time include the repeated television images of "first responders" to the attacks on the World Trade Center on September 11, 2001, as they worked desperately, first to rescue living victims and then to uncover human remains in Ground Zero rubble. Few would have difficulty in understanding the urgent (and, unfortunately, unrewarded) efforts at rescue. The great determination to recover the dead, however, was probably instructive to a public that had become accustomed to a more pragmatic and functionalistic approach. The assumption that "the dead are just dead" was forcefully contradicted. The victims were no longer alive, but they were not yet "safely dead," if the phrase be permitted. Both the victims and their families were in a kind of a limbo—actually, in a *limbic* zone between one identity and another. Rites-of-passage theory (Gennep, 1960) conceives of life as a sequence of many smaller journeys within the larger tour of the total course of existence. The theory often emphasizes the vulnerability of people who have moved from their previous secure status but have not yet reached their next destination or haven.

Both the September 11 victims and the stricken families were trapped in this nowhere zone, and there was no certain endpoint at which this painful situation would be resolved. Families who had lost a member in the September 11 disaster felt they could not really start to go on with their lives until the dead had been "brought home" in some meaningful sense of the term. Funeral and memorial services eventually were held without the bodies when it became clear that the remains would never be recovered and identified. In these and many other instances, the living have expressed their need to do all that should and could be done for the dead. For the living really to get back to life (as best they could) required that the dead also be given the opportunity to move securely to their destination on time's relentless caravan. Such circumstances illustrate how simplistic it would be to insist that funerals were either just for the living or the dead.

The Inconvenient Dead in a Cloud of Confusion

In our times, the "why funerals?" question is sometimes prompted by a feeling that the dead have become an inconvenience. Funerals are merely vestigial rites that drain our precious time, money, and energy. Funerals are usually depressing affairs anyway, not that much help even to the living. We can hardly wait until they are over and then the dead are still dead, so what's been accomplished?

This view does not yet seem to be dominant in North American society but has become increasingly evident since our transformation from an agrarian nation in which most people stayed pretty much in place and the church was a cornerstone of communal life. "Deathways" have moved slowly and reluctantly along with the times as we have become a technologically enhanced land where change of address, job, and partner have become normative. Furthermore, along with other developed nations, we have achieved a significantly longer average life expectancy. Funerals less often become a gathering for sorrowing parents as their young children are laid to rest; more often the mourners are adult children who are paying their respects to a long-lived parent.

There are also signs of generational differences in the importance attached to funerals and memorial services. People still make sentimental journeys to visit family burial places. With disconcerting frequency, however, the remembered neighborhoods of their childhood have been altered beyond recognition or acceptance. Many burial places, whether in churchyards, woodland fields, or town cemeteries, have deteriorated for lack of upkeep, or have even been obliterated by the forces of change. It is understandable that some family members would rather keep their memories than face such sad prospects. The dazzling phenomenon of Americans in motion has dispersed many families who "in the old days" would have been regularly popping into each other's kitchens on a regular basis. Many families do remain emotionally connected and take advantage of up-to-date communication technology. Nevertheless, it is often a physical and financial strain to travel to bedside and funeral. Studies have suggested that older adults tend to find more comfort and meaning in funerals, but it is an open question whether "the new aged" of each generation will continue to find as much value. Even years ago I would often hear from elders that it would be a shame to waste money on "funeral stuff." One of the unforgettable comments came from the resident of a geriatric hospital:

> You come here and everybody thinks you're already dead. Tell the truth: I knew I was near dead before. Every time you walk in a store and wait and nobody sees you . . . Just being old is just almost like being dead. Then, here. Then, dead. Who's going to care? Make a fuss? Not them. Not me.

We can hardly be surprised if people socialized within a gerophobic society should themselves internalize negative attitudes and decide that their deaths as well as their lives are undeserving of attention. Others, though, rally against the ageism and try to secure a dignified and appropriate funeral for themselves. The depressive surrender and the anxious seeking are differential responses to the same underlying concern: that a long life will receive an exit stamp of "Invalid: Discard. Shelf life expired."

Why Funerals Today?

Funerals traditionally have provided both an endpoint and a starting point. The passage from life to death is certified as complete, so the survivors now can turn to their recovery and renewal. The effectiveness of funerals to achieve this bridging purpose can be compromised, however, by some characteristics of our times. For example, many folkways involved intensive family participation in preparing the body and the funeral arrangements (isolated examples still exist, e.g. Bryer, 1977; Crissman, 1994). In general, though, the preparation phase has passed to the funeral industry with the result that family mourners less often have the complete sense of release because of their limited involvement before the funeral. Furthermore, rapid socio-technological change has reduced intergenerational consensus on the value of the funeral process. One cannot assume that multiple-generation families will share priorities and expectations.

Another challenge to the social and spiritual value of funerals has been intensifying in recent years. Garces-Foley (2002–2003) reports an increase in the frequency of "funerals of the unaffiliated." More than a third of the U.S. population do not claim membership in a religious congregation. Religious officials confirm that they are being called upon more often to participate in such funerals in which families request that the religious service be "toned down."

I have noticed a parallel trend that might be called "funerals of the disengaged." People who have outlived—or, over time, drifted away from—their personal support systems are more likely to receive only perfunctory services. Those who would have felt a strong emotional link or at least a powerful sense of obligation have already passed from that person's life. People who have lived essentially solitary lives or become institutional residents have a high probability of exiting this life through the backdoor with minimal attention. Such an exit was a frequent occurrence within institutional settings where many residents seemed to have been forgotten or disregarded by the larger community and the facility itself was locked into a death-avoidance pattern. A funeral process that does not celebrate the life, mourn the passing, or provide symbolic safe passage through the journey of the dead—what else can we expect when the individual has been progressively disvalued through the years?

It is understandable that funerals might be disvalued if they seem to have lost their inner connection to the values and meanings that guide our lives. It is that inner connection that makes a difference between empty ritual and participation in an event that is both universal and deeply personal. To ask "Why funerals?" may sound like a rejection of the whole process. Most often, though, the question expresses a search for renewal of the inner connection between how we live and how we die.

That search is now taking a variety of forms. People who are uncomfortable with the familiar words, symbols, and gestures of mainstream religion are nevertheless finding ways to incorporate spiritual considerations into the funeral process. The "postmodern funeral" (Garces-Foley and Holcomb, in press) may include such elements as a candle-lighting ceremony and improvised memorials, music, and eulogies that are somehow special to the particular people involved. New partnerships are developing between those funeral directors who are open to change and those families who are determined that the funeral process represent their own way of life.

Two very different pathways are among those being explored. Some people are exploring the potentials of virtual funerals and memorials on the Internet—often as a supplement to a more conventional service. Others are turning to "green funerals." These are burials in woodland areas that are intended to return the body to earth in a natural form. There is no embalming to leak chemicals into the ground, and simple, biodegradable materials are used, e.g., willow coffins (Holmes, n.d.; Ross-Bain, n.d.). Funerals are to be removed from the technological-commercial matrix and put in the service of "producing wildlife habitats and forests from green burial sites, where native trees, wild flowers and protected animals are encouraged . . . meadow brown butterfly colonies, grasshoppers, insects, bats, voles and owls to multiply . . . where the mechanical mower does not prey on a regular basis and a self-supporting ecosystem can evolve" (Holmes, n.d.).

The funeral process today is caught up within the broader matrix of social change. Some of the negatives have already been identified. To these must be added that narrow construction of human life that embraces youth and material success but recoils from the specter of loss and limits. Where this attitudinal climate prevails, it is tempting to reject funerals because we are exposed there to the uncomfortable reminders of aging and death. Nevertheless, it remains as true today as ever mat "taking good care of the dead" is a vital part of a society's support for the living. Clea Koff (2004), "The Bone Woman," has demonstrated this fact again as she contributed to the healing process in Rwanda by honoring the remains of the massacre victims.

Yes, funerals can take the form of dysfunctional vestiges if we let them go that way. Another choice is available to us, though. We can recognize that the funeral process offers an opportunity to reach deep into our understanding and values. Perhaps our society today does not offer the clearest and firmest guide to comprehension of life and death. Perhaps it is up to us, then, to review our own beliefs about the meanings of growth and loss, youth and age, life and death—and to listen carefully to the beliefs of those to whom we offer service.

References

Aries, P. 1981. *At the Hour of Our Death*. New York: Knopf.

Barley, N. 1995. *Dancing on the Grave*. London: John Murray.

Bryant, C. D., ed. 2003. *Handbook of Death and Dying*. Thousand Oaks, Calif.: Sage.

Bryer, K. B. 1977. "The Amish Way of Death." *American Psychologist*, 12: 167–74.

Crissman, J. K. 1994. *Death and Dying in Central Appalachia: Changing Attitudes and Practices*. Urbana: University of Illinois Press.

Garces-Foley, K. 2002–2003. "Funerals of the Unaffiliated." *Omega, Journal of Death and Dying* 46: 287–303.

Garces-Foley, K., and Holcomb, J. S. In press. "Contemporary Funerals: Personalizing Tradition." In K. Garces-Foley, ed. *Death and Religion in a Changing World*. New York: M. E. Sharpe.

Gennep, A. van. 1960 (original 1909). *The Rites of Passage*. London: Routledge and Kegan Paul.

Holmes, A. "Willow Coffins." www.druidnetwork.org/qwrites/passing.

Kastenbaum, R., ed. 2002. *Macmillan Encyclopedia of Death and Dying*. New York: Macmillan Reference USA.

Kastenbaum, R. 2004. *On Our Way. The Final Passage Through Life and Death*. Berkeley: University of California Press.

Klass, D., and Walter, T. 2001. "Processes of Grieving: How Bonds Are Continued." In M. S. Stroebe et al., eds., *Handbook of Bereavement Research: Consequence, Coping, and Care*. Washington, D.C.: American Psychological Association.

Koff, C. 2004. *The Bone Woman*. New York: Random House.

Kozak, D. 1991. "Dying Badly: Violent Death and Religious Change Among the Tohono O'Odham." *Omega, Journal of Death and Dying* 23: 207–16.

Laderman, G. 1996. *The Sacred Remains. American Attitudes Toward Death, 1799–1883*. New Haven, Conn.: Yale University Press.

Ross-Bain, I. "Perception of a Green Funeral." www.globalideasbank.org.

Ubelaker, D., and Scammell, H. 1992. *Bones. A Forensic Detective's Casebook*. New York: M. Evans.

Williams, D. 2004. "Exhumations of Long-Dead Nobles Stir Public." *Washingtonpost.com*, Feb. 20.

Nicholas Köhler  **NO**

We've Been Misled About How to Grieve: Why It May Be Wise to Skip the Months of Journaling and Group Talk We've Been Taught We Need

Many years ago, Nancy Moules, a pediatric oncology nurse who specializes in grief, got a call from a family member of one of her clients, a woman in her late 20s whose six-year-old daughter had died of leukemia a month or so earlier. The relative told Moules the woman was carrying an urn full of her daughter's ashes everywhere she went; that if you met her for lunch she'd get a table for three; that, in a nutshell, the family was concerned about how she was coping. Sure enough, when Moules later met the client for lunch, they ate with the ashes at the table. "So, are you wondering why I invited you out?" Moules asked. "Oh no, I know," the woman said. "Somebody phoned you, they're worried about me. They think I'm crazy." Moules probed further: "Do *you* think it's crazy?" she asked. "No," said the woman. "F—k them. This is the last human, physical connection that I have to her and I'll put her down when I'm ready to put her down."

For Moules, who now lectures on grief as a nursing prof at the University of Calgary, the young mother's story helps illustrate the sometimes paradoxical relationship many of us have with the emotions accompanying a loved one's death. "There's all these cultural expectations of grief that are contradictory," she says. "One is, 'Get over it, you should be over it by now!' And the other is, 'What's wrong with you that you aren't continuing to feel it? Didn't you love the person?' And we turn all those judgments inward."

Many of these expectations have, over the past four decades, been set by Elisabeth Kübler-Ross, a Swiss-born psychiatrist who used her interviews with a handful of dying patients in Chicago in the mid-'60s as the basis for a theory of grief that quickly gripped the world's imagination and never let go. *On Death and Dying*, her milestone 1969 book, proposed that a person confronting his or her own death passes through five stages—denial, anger, bargaining, depression and, finally, acceptance. The analysis was backed by no solid research—indeed, as Ruth Davis Konigsberg's new book *The Truth About Grief: The Myth of Its Five Stages and the New Science of Loss* notes, scientific studies around grief remain surprisingly scant even now, and Kübler-Ross hit upon her stages only after getting a book deal and at the end of a bout of writer's block. In an era in which the old customs of black armbands and crepe no longer applied, Kübler-Ross became widely embraced as a grief guru—no matter that her research had always been limited to the dying. Soon an industry had grown up around the funeral business that found it convenient to guide the bereaved through her stages.

Published the year after her death in 2004 and co-written with David Kessler, Kübler-Ross's *On Grief and Grieving* stamped her imprimatur onto a field that she'd largely come to define anyway (better that she remain associated with that than, say, her later interest in contacting the dead via seance). She still does, though academics now pooh-pooh her work: Konigsberg refers to a 2008 Hospice Association of Ontario report that identifies Kübler-Ross as the most recommended resource for bereavement support in that province. Her stages now colour the way we discuss everything from divorce to coming out of the closet to beating addiction.

Yet in *The Truth About Grief*—the title is tongue-in-cheek, as one-size-fits-all models like Kübler-Ross's actually prove incomplete—Konigsberg, a journalist who has worked as an editor at *New York* and *Glamour* magazines, argues stage theory has promoted a view of grief as long and debilitating, when recent research actually suggests people usually accept a loved one's death quickly, experience a few months of pining for the deceased, and are over it all in as little as 6–12 months—a natural evaporation of sadness. Kübler-Ross's stages interrupt that process by casting grief as a "journey" we must "work" through, a notion that heralded a whole industry of "death services" and created standards of grief all of us feel we must now labour to meet. All this served to shift the emphasis away from the deceased and toward those left behind, whose important work it now was to overcome loss. The old mourning rites may be gone, Konigsberg writes, "but they have been replaced by conventions for grief, which are more restrictive in that they dictate not what a person wears or does in public but his or her inner emotional state."

For all that grief work, studies show people who undergo bereavement counselling emerge from grief no more quickly than people who don't—except in the lengthiest cases, where the death of an intimate has likely exposed underlying depression (a condition now often called "complicated grief"). Konigsberg marshals more research suggesting Kübler-Ross's stages don't accurately describe what we typically experience after a death, and argues that adherence to the model does more harm than good in that the doctrine "has actually lengthened the expected duration of grief and made us more judgmental of those who stray from the designated path."

Beamsville, Ont., resident Sandy McBay, whose husband of 35 years, Rick, died suddenly in December of an aortic dissection—"Just in case, I love you," he told her as they awaited the ambulance—found herself as blindsided as anyone despite two decades of work in palliative care and bereavement support. In leading therapy sessions, McBay often encounters a tacit faith in Kübler-Ross. "A lot of people expect they're going to grieve that way," she says. "They are pleasantly surprised, some of them at least, to realize—'Okay, just because I'm not doing it the way I've heard it's supposed to be done doesn't mean I'm doing it wrong.'" Rather than anger or depression, many instead report feelings of yearning. McBay, whose husband was a teacher and choir director, is no different. "I was there when he died, so I know he's not coming back," she says. "But when I am home and looking around and seeing the life that we created together—I look at my 1.3-acre property and go, 'What am I going to do?' Just—him simply not being there."

What to do with such feelings? In fact, the long, agonizing ordeal Kübler-Ross and her disciples have long steeled us for isn't the norm. Here Konigsberg outlines research led by George Bonanno, a psychology prof at Columbia University's Teachers College, that "tracked elderly people whose spouses died of natural causes, and the single largest group— about 45 per cent—showed no signs of shock, despair, anxiety, or intrusive thoughts six months after their loss," Konigsberg writes. "A much smaller group—only about 15 per cent—were still having problems at 18 months." Such numbers belie popular notions that widows and widowers find the second year worse than the first. While Konigsberg takes care not to pathologize those who suffer prolonged turmoil, she argues that what she calls the "grief culture" has stigmatized the more common response of resilience and strength by branding it "cold," even "pathological." Actually, she says, "You probably already have what you need to get through this on your own. If after six months or a year you find you're still having trouble, you should probably seek professional help."

Before that threshold, though, it may be wise to skip the months of disclosure, journaling and group talk that the bereavement services sector, channelling Kübler-Ross, says we need lest our grief fester. ("Telling your story often and in detail is primal to the grieving process," Kübler-Ross tells us. "Grief must be witnessed to be healed.") All that vocalizing may be just the trouble. Reminiscent of the critiques around critical-incident stress debriefing, an intense talk therapy aimed at preventing post-traumatic stress disorder, some studies now say grief can be aggravated by chit-chat. Konigsberg cites another Bonanno study that found bereaved people who did not communicate their "negative emotions" had fewer health complaints than those who did, opening up the tantalizing possibility that tamping down bad feelings "might actually have a protective function."

Not everyone agrees with all this. Mel Borins, a Toronto family physician who lectures doctors on grief, calls complicated grief "underestimated and I think quite common—more than 15 per cent of people get left with unfinished business." And assuming one does tie up those emotional loose ends, what exactly does it feel like to dispense with grief and yet go on remembering the dead? It's a question Konigsberg's book isn't designed to answer, though Kübler-Ross's insistence on "acceptance" cries out for quibbling. Indeed, it's that punishing commitment to recovery that Moules, the Calgary nursing prof, most often sees in those she counsels. "Many people come and say, 'I must be doing this grieving thing wrong, because I still feel something,'" she says, adding: "You will feel that loss for the rest of your life. It won't be as consuming, it won't be as absolutely devastating, as unfathomable as it was. But you never get over it." She recalls the young mother who carted around her daughter's ashes. Several weeks after that lunch, Moules got a call from the woman inviting her to her daughter's inurnment. Finally she was ready to lay the ashes down. But never her daughter.

EXPLORING THE ISSUE

Do Funeral Rituals Help Grief?

Critical Thinking and Reflection

1. Discuss funeral practices that your relatives or family members would expect. What is expected of those attending? Is there food or other gathering that is expected in addition to the actual funeral or memorial service?
2. Consider the situation of families who have lost a loved one, but because of circumstances the body is not available for burial. Do you think this really makes a difference in how the living ones are able to cope or grieve? Why or why not?
3. One of the wishes that many dying patients have is that they wish to leave a legacy, so that they will not be forgotten. Discuss examples from your community of how people have left legacies. Can children leave legacies? How do these practices help survivors to cope with the loss of the person who died?
4. Funeral costs can range from $500 for simple cremation, to thousands of dollars for elaborate large funerals with processions and banquets for those attending. How does planning a funeral at a time when the living ones are grieving make them vulnerable to expensive or unnecessary schemes? Are there laws to protect people from being taken advantage of during these times?
5. Discuss the differences and similarities between religious funeral ceremonies and memorial services for religiously unaffiliated persons who died.

Is There Common Ground?

Funeral rituals generally end with the funeral and burial of the dead. Hunter (2007–2008) acknowledges that these rituals are helpful in providing immediate structure for the bereaved following death. However, grieving extends well beyond the funeral time frame. Rituals that would be most helpful to families would consider the long-term emotional needs and the need for the construction of a new meaning of life after loss, as the person experiences grief (Hunter, 2007–2008). While many recognize the value of private, religious, or other public rituals for mourners, there is newer evidence that people are able to grieve successfully in a variety of different ways (Bonanno, 2010; Koningsberg, 2011).

The frequent discussions and rehashing of a traumatic death with bereavement counselors may not be healthy in moving people on toward a new future as previously thought. Hunter (2007–2008) suggests that the funeral industry provide some guidance to help the bereaved construct a "ritual of remembrance and new meaning." The notion that grieving should be done within a few weeks or months of a loved one's death is unrealistic (Moules, 2010–2011). Many researchers have found that family members or persons who have lost a spouse or a child generally require at least two years to work through a reconstruction processes of making sense of the loss. Bereaved persons need time to find reasons for the loss, and need to understand the benefits of the presence of the deceased in their lives. Bereaved persons need to create a new identity that no longer includes the presence of the person who died, while still embracing the memory of the life that was lost (Hunter, 2007–2008).

References

Bonanno, G. (2010). *The other side of sadness*, New York: Basic Books; First Trade Paper Edition.

Dass-Brailsford, P. (2010). *Ignore the dead, we want the living, from Hurricane Katrina and other disasters*. Thousand Oaks, CA: Sage Publications, Inc.

Gamino, L. A., Easterling, L. W., Stirman, L. S., & Sewell, K. S. (2000). Grief adjustment as influenced by funeral participation and occurrence of adverse funeral events. *OMEGA, 41*(2), 79–92.

Hayslip, B., Booher, S. K., Scoles, M. T., & Guarnaccia, C. A. (2007). Assessing adults difficulty coping with funerals, *OMEGA, 55*(2), 93–115.

Hunter, J. (2007–2008). Bereavement: An incomplete rite of passage. *OMEGA, 56*(2), 153–173.

Juliana, L., Claassens, M. (2010). Calling the keeners: The image of the wailing woman as symbol of survival in a traumatized world. *Journal of Feminist Studies in Religion, 26*(1), 63–77

Kastenbaum, R. (2004). Why funerals? *Generations; 28*(2), 5–10.

Kohler, N. (2011, February 21). We've been misled about how to grieve. *MacLean's Magazine*.

Konigsberg, R. D. (2011, January 24). The good news about grief. *Time*.

Kübler-Ross, E. (1969). *On death and dying*. New York, NY: Touchstone.

Moules, N. (2010–2011). Internal connections and conversations: The internalized other interview in bereavement work, *OMEGA, 62*(2), 187–199.

Muga, W. (2009). The cost of dying is killing! *African Business, 271*(August–September), 59–60.

Wilce, J. M. (2009). *Crying shame: Metaculture, modernity, and the exaggerated death of lament*. Oxford, UK: Wiley-Blackwell. doi:10.1002/9781444306248

Additional Resources

Collins, W. L. & Dolittle, A. (2006). Personal reflections of funeral rituals and spirituality in a Kentucky African American family. *Death Studies, 30*, 957–969.

Do Ka, K. J. & Martin, T. L. (2010*). Grieving beyond gender: Understanding the ways men and women mourn* (Revised Ed.). New York, NY: Routledge. ISBN: 9780415995726

LeBlanc, T. W. (2010). Grief interrupted. *Journal of Palliative Medicine, 13*(4), 469–475. doi:10.1089=jpm.2009.0348

Stow, S. (2010). Agonistic homegoing: Frederick Douglass, Joseph Lowery, and the democratic value of African American public mourning, *American Political Science Review, 104*(4), 681–697. doi:10.1017/S0003055410000481

Contributors to This Volume

EDITORS

WILLIAM J. BUCKLEY, PhD, MA, teaches bioethics and ethics as an assistant professor in the Department of Theology and Religious Studies at Seattle University in Seattle, Washington. He completed his MA in theology and PhD in social ethics at the University of Chicago, where he was a University Fellow and Junior Fellow at the Advanced Institute for Religion. Selected as a Fulbright fellow, he accepted a German Government and University fellowship (Deutscher Akademischer Austauschdienst) to comparatively research shifts in end-of-life decision-making in Europe and the United States. His work has been presented in a variety of forums, including those sponsored by The Society of Christian Ethics, The American Academy of Religion, The Center for Clinical Bioethics at Georgetown University— where he remains an affiliated scholar—and The Catholic Theological Society of America. His early work as a peace volunteer in Northern Ireland has informed much of his subsequent scholarship and writing, including a volume entitled *Kosovo: Contending Voices on Balkan Interventions*, which examined, among others issues, public health and humanitarian intervention in the mid of ethnic conflict.

KAREN S. FELDT, PhD, ARNP, GNP-BC, is an associate professor in the College of Nursing at Seattle University in Seattle, Washington. She holds the Premera Endowed Professorship in Nursing. Over the past 28 years, she has been committed to improving end-of-life care for elders with dementia. Her research has included developing pain assessments for cognitively impaired elders. She recently completed a survey of nurses in the Washington State about their knowledge of the Death with Dignity Act. As a certified gerontological nurse practitioner, she continues to provide primary care to a group of residents in assisted living and adult family homes. She is a fellow in the Gerontological Society of America and is a member of the editorial board of the *Journal of the American Geriatrics Society*. In 2009, she was identified as one of the "100 Distinguished Alumni" of the University of Minnesota School of Nursing for her work with end-of-life care and pain management in older adults.

AUTHORS

DENISE L. ANTHONY, PhD, is an associate professor and past-Chair (2007–2011) in the Department of Sociology at Dartmouth College. She is also the research director of the Institute for Security, Technology, and Society (ISTS) at Dartmouth, and a faculty affiliate at the Center for Health Policy Research at the Dartmouth Institute for Health Policy and Clinical Practice. Dr. Anthony's research interests include collective action and rust, economic sociology, and the sociology of health care. She has studied variation in managed care practices and physician referral behavior. More recently her work examines variation in patient preferences for medical care, the use, and implications of information technology in health care, including compliance with HIPAA requirements, and for the privacy and security of protected health information in health care delivery. Her multidisciplinary research has been published in journals in sociology as well as in health policy and computer science, including among others the *American Sociological Review, Social Science and Medicine, Health Affairs*, and *IEEE Privacy & Security*.

CHARLES BABCOCK, BS, is an editor-at-large for *InformationWeek*, having joined the publication in 2003. He is the former editor-in-chief of *Digital News*, former software editor of Computerworld, and former technology editor of *Interactive Week*. He is a graduate of Syracuse University, where he obtained a bachelor's degree in journalism.

MARIO BARAS, PhD, is a consulting theoretical biostatistician. A retired professor of statistics at The Hadassah Hebrew University, Dr. Baras is a member of the IMPH Admissions Committee, The Hadassah Hebrew University, Braun School of Public Health.

AMBER E. BARNATO, MD, MPH, MS, is an associate professor of medicine, associate professor of Clinical and Translational Science; director, Clinical Scientist Training Program; co-program leader, Doris Duke Clinical Research Fellowship. Dr. Barnato joined the faculty in 2001 after completion of a residency in preventive medicine and a fellowship in health care research and health policy. Her research focuses on the provider and organizational determinants of variation in Medicare beneficiaries' use of intensive care services at the end of life and on racial disparities in end-of-life and other health services utilization.

DORIS BARWICH, MD, is the medical director of palliative care for the Fraser Health Authority in Surrey, British Columbia. She received her medical degree from the University of Manitoba, and her current research focuses on family caregiving and coping in end-of-life cancer care.

MARGARET P. BATTIN, MFA, PhD, is a distinguished professor of philosophy and adjunct professor of internal medicine, Division of Medical Ethics, University of Utah. She has been engaged in research on active euthanasia and assisted suicide in the Netherlands. She is currently at work on a historical sourcebook on ethical issues in suicide, a book on world population growth and reproductive rights, and two multi-authored projects, one on ethics and infectious disease and one on drugs and justice.

AMANDA BENNETT is an executive editor/projects and investigations for Bloomberg News. She was an editor of *The Philadelphia Inquirer* from June 2003 to November 2006, and prior to that was editor of the *Herald-Leader* in Lexington, Kentucky. She also served for 3 years as managing editor/projects for *The Oregonian* in Portland. She is on the board of the Loeb Awards and author of five books.

BENJAMIN BRODY, MD, is a graduate of the University of Pennsylvania. He completed his medical training at the Albert Einstein College of Medicine. In addition to his private practice, Brody is an attending psychiatrist at New York Presbyterian Hospital and an instructor in psychiatry at Weill Cornell Medical College. He is involved in clinical trials for the treatment of major depression and bipolar disorder. He has also written about psychiatry and medical training for the *New England Journal of Medicine* and the *New York Times*.

SHANNON BROWNLEE, MS, is an acting director of the New America Health Policy Program. A nationally known writer and essayist whose work has appeared in the *Atlantic Monthly, New York Times Magazine, The New Republic, Slate, Time, Washington Monthly, Washington Post, Los Angeles Times,* and the *British Medical Journal,* among many other publications, she is best known for her groundbreaking work on avoidable health care, the patchy quality of medical evidence, and the implications for health care policy. Her book, *Overtreated: Why Too Much Medicine is Making Us Sicker and Poorer,* was named the best economics book of 2007 by *New York Times* economics correspondent David Leonhardt. Brownlee's current research and writing focus on issues surrounding delivery system reform, clinical evidence, and health care costs.

HANS-HENRIK BULOW, MD, is a medical consultant and the head of ICU department, MD at Sygehus Nord, Holbæk, Region Sjælland in Copenhagen, Denmark.

NANCY JO BUSH, RN, MN, MA, AOCN, is an assistant clinical professor/lecturer at the University of California, Los Angeles School of Nursing. Her post-master's nurse practitioner degree is from UCLA. Bush is an active member of the ONS Greater Los Angeles Chapter, the Nurse Practitioner ONS Special Interest Group, and serves as an associate editor of the Oncology Nursing Forum. She is a member of the California Association of Nurse Practitioners.

CHRISTOPHER M. CALLAHAN, MD, is the director of the Indiana University Center for Aging Research, as well as an investigator for the Regenstrief Institute, Inc. He is board certified in both internal and geriatric medicine, and focuses his research on improving the care of older adults with late life depression, dementia, and related conditions. Dr. Callahan studies ways to help primary care physicians deliver better care to older adults.

DANIEL CALLAHAN is Senior Research Scholar and President Emeritus of the Hastings Center, a nonpartisan research institution dedicated to bioethics. He is the author of numerous articles and books on bioethical issues.

MICHELE L. CASPER, PhD, is an epidemiologist and acting team leader of the Small Area Analysis Team within the Division for Heart Disease and Stroke Prevention at the Centers for Disease Control and Prevention (CDC). Her research focuses primarily on the geographic, racial, and ethnic disparities in heart disease and stroke.

LI-WEI CHAO, MD, PhD, is an assistant professor of anesthesia/critical care medicine and senior fellow, Leonard Davis Institute of Health Economics. Dr. Chao's research interest focuses on issues and applications of micro-economics to health services research on topics such as HIV/AIDS stigma, funerals, information, quality of life, response shift, vaccine, and drug procurement.

EUN-KYOUNG CHOI, RN, JD, was formerly a Health Law and Ethics Extern at the Charles Warren Fairbanks Center for Medical Ethics at Clarian Health in Indianapolis. She is currently at Hallym University, Chuncheon, Gangwon-do, Korea.

DAVID CRIPPEN, MD, FCCM, is an associate professor of critical care medicine at the University of Pittsburgh Medical Center in Pittsburgh, Pennsylvania. He also holds a secondary appointment as an associate professor in the Department of Emergency Medicine. He is trained in general surgery, emergency medicine, and critical care medicine and a member of the Society for Critical Care Medicine, the European Society for Intensive Care Medicine, and the American College of Emergency Physicians. He is a fellow of the American College of Critical Care Medicine, a diplomate of the American Board of Emergency Medicine, and has European Diploma in Intensive Care Medicine.

DOROTHY J. DUNN, PhD, ARNP, FNP-BC, is on the clinical faculty for the accelerated nursing program in the Christine E. Lynn College of Nursing at Florida Atlantic University. As a board-certified family nurse practitioner, her practice interest is in promoting family health and nurturing well-being of families and persons with memory loss.

ELLIOTT S. FISHER, MD, MPH, is a professor of community and family medicine in the Dartmouth Medical School. His research focuses on the causes, consequences, and implications of variations in health system performance. His current work focuses on advancing the use of patient-reported measures as tools for improvement and accountability, and the development, pilot testing, and evaluation of new models of health care delivery and payment.

GILLIAN FYLES, MD, is a physician at the BC Cancer Agency. She is the medical leader for the Pain & Symptom Management/Palliative Care Program; research leader for the Oncology Palliative Care; and co-medical director and co-investigator for the Kelowna Palliative Response Team.

JENNIFER GAFFORD, PhD, is a psychologist in St. Louis, Missouri. She has been a faculty psychologist at the Forest Park Hospital Family Medicine Residency Program. Dr. Gafford received her doctorate in clinical psychology from Saint Louis University and completed an internship at the University of Vermont Medical Center.

PATRICIA M. GALLAGHER, PhD, is a senior research fellow at the Center for Survey Research, University of Massachusetts, Boston. Her work centers on survey methodology with a particular focus on health-related research. Current projects include collaborating with researchers at The Dartmouth Institute on an NIA-funded study of regional variation in Medicare spending from both the physician and the patient perspectives and developing survey instruments to measure diagnosis-related quality of life in patients, for example, those with limb amputation for ischemia or diagnosed with abdominal aortic aneurysm.

NATHAN E. GOLDSTEIN, MD, is an assistant professor of geriatrics and internal medicine and the director of research at the Hertzberg Palliative Care Institute. Goldstein is a clinician-investigator whose research efforts focus on the ways that clinicians and patients make decisions about the use of advanced technologies at the end of life. He has published extensively on this and other palliative medicine topics. He is the recipient of multiple awards including the American Geriatric Society New Investigator Award, the Hartford Geriatric Health Outcomes Award, and a Mentored Patient-Oriented Research Career Development Award. In addition, he travels throughout the country speaking on a wide array of palliative care topics.

KATRINA HEDBERG, MD, MPH, is the state epidemiologist and administrator of the Office of Disease Prevention and Epidemiology at the Oregon Public Health Division. Dr. Hedberg has been with the Oregon Department of Human Services for the past 20 years, and has worked in a variety of public health programs, including HIV/AIDS, acute and communicable disease, sexually transmitted diseases, injury epidemiology, chronic disease prevention, tuberculosis, and health statistics. Dr. Hedberg is an affiliate associate professor in the Department of Public Health and Preventive Medicine at Oregon Health Sciences University.

CEES M. P. M. HERTOGH is a professor of geriatric ethics in the Department of Nursing Home Medicine and the EMGO, Institute of the Vrije Universiteit Medical Center, Amsterdam. He teaches methodology and ethics of care at the medical faculty and the specialist training course for elderly care physicians. His research focuses on ethical issues in the care and treatment of vulnerable older people using empirical research methods in the use of assistive and surveillance technology; end-of-life decision-making; euthanasia in patients with dementia; advance care planning; and decisional capacity. He is the editor of the *Dutch Journal for Gerontology and Geriatrics* and a member of the Dementia Ethics Steering Committee of Alzheimer Europe and the INTERDEM group on early diagnosis and intervention in dementia.

ROBERT G. HOLLOWAY, MD, MPH, is a professor of neurology and the director of the CTSI Research Education, Training, and Career Development Key Function. Dr. Holloway received his medical degree from the University of Connecticut School of Medicine and Dentistry. He completed his neurology residency, received his master's degree in public health, and completed a fellowship in health services research in the Department of Community and Preventive Medicine at the University of Rochester School of Medicine and Dentistry. Dr. Holloway is board certified in neurology and in hospice and palliative medicine.

DAVID HOPKINS is a data analyst for Oregon Center for Health Statistics, Oregon Health Authority. He is the coauthor on a number of articles pertaining to the issues of death and dying.

ROBERT KASTENBAUM, PhD, is a professor emeritus, Arizona State University. He is the author of many works, including *The Psychology of Death, Death, Society, and Human Experience,* and *Dorian, Graying: Is Youth the Only Thing Worth Having?*

SCOTT Y. H. KIM, MD, PhD, is an associate professor of psychiatry at the University of Michigan. His research interests are in neuropsychiatric illness and decision-making competence research ethics policy and decision science and ethics, and he is a member of the American Board of Psychiatry and Neurology. Kim received his medical degree from Harvard Medical School in 1994 and his PhD from the University of Chicago in 1993.

NICHOLAS KOHLER, PhD, is an adjunct professor of geospatial techniques in the Department of Geography at the University of Oregon, Eugene. Kohler also writes commentary and book reviews for Macleans.CA on Campus.

MELVIN KOHN, PhD, is a William D. and Robin Mayer distinguished professor, School of Arts and Sciences, Johns Hopkins University. Kohn is a past president of the American Sociological Association, the Eastern Sociological Society, and the Sociological Research Association, and a former member of the Executive Committee of the International Sociological Association. He is an honorary foreign member of the Polish Sociological Association, and is or has been a fellow of the American Academy of Arts and Sciences, the American Association for the Advancement of Science, and the Guggenheim Foundation. He has also been a visiting fellow (or the equivalent thereof) of the Institute for Social Research, Oslo, Norway, of the Institute of Advanced Studies of the Australian National University, and of the Japan Society for the Advancement of Science.

KENNETH M. LANGA, MD, PhD, is a professor in the Department of Internal Medicine, a research investigator in the Ann Arbor Veterans Affairs HSR&D Center, a faculty associate at the Institute for Social Research, and the associate director of the Institute of Gerontology at the University of Michigan. He is a coinvestigator for the Health and Retirement Study (HRS), a National Institute on Aging funded longitudinal study of 20,000 adults in the United States (http://hrsonline.isr.umich.edu). He is also a lead investigator for the Aging, Demographics, and Memory Study (ADAMS), a supplemental study to the HRS regarding the risk factors, epidemiology, and outcomes of dementia. Langa graduated from Pritzker School of Medicine, University of Chicago in 1994.

DIDIER LEDOUX, MD, is the head of clinics in the Department of Anesthesiology and General Intensive Care Medicine, Liège University Hospital and an MD postdoctoral fellow at the Coma Science Group, funded by the Belgian National Fund of Scientific Research (FNRS). His areas of expertise include biostatistics, severity of illness assessment, and neuro-intensive care. He is a member of the EU Ethicus Study Group on end-of-life decisions in ICU (*Journal of the American Medical Association*, August 2003).

RICHARD LEMAN, MD, is a medical epidemiologist in the Oregon Department of Human Services, Oregon Health Division.

RONALD A. LINDSAY, JD, is the president and CEO of the Council for Secular Humanism and the Center for Inquiry. Prior to joining CFI in 2006, he practiced law in Washington, DC, for 26 years with the law firm of Seyfarth Shaw LLP. He has taught philosophy courses as an adjunct professor at American University and Georgetown University. Dr. Lindsay has authored numerous articles.

ANNE LIPPERT, MD, is a consultant in the ICU and the Danish Institute of Medical Simulation in the Department of Anesthesiology of the Herlev University Hospital.

WANDA LEIGH MARTIN, RN, MN, is a project coordinator for the Centre on Aging at the University of Victoria. She is active in the Research Committee of the Canadian Association of Nurses in Oncology, and a member of the Canadian Nurses Association and the College of Registered Nurses of British Columbia.

RICHARD A. MULARSKI, MD, MSHS, FCCP, is an academic physician certified in pulmonary, critical care, and palliative medicine. He specializes in obstructive lung disease, dyspnea, palliative care, and end-of-life care. Dr Mularski leads key studies of chronic obstructive pulmonary disease (COPD). Dr. Mularski is a also a clinical assistant professor of medicine at OHSU, a senior scholar at the Center for Ethics in Health Care in Oregon, and a member of the KP Regional Ethics Council. He practices clinical pulmonary and critical care medicine at Kaiser Sunnyside Medical Center.

DAVID ORENTLICHER, JD, is a professor and codirector of the Center for Law and Health at Indiana University Schools of Law and Medicine in Indianapolis. He previously served as the director of the Division of Medical Ethics at the American Medical Association. While there, Dr. Orentlicher led the drafting of the AMA's first patients' bill of rights. And between 2002 and 2008 he served in the Indiana House of Representatives.

JOSÉ A. PAGÁN, PhD, is a professor and the chair of the Department of Health Management and Policy, School of Public Health, University of North Texas Health Science Center at Fort Worth. Dr. Pagán is also an adjunct senior fellow of the Leonard Davis Institute of Health Economics at the University of Pennsylvania. His research work centers on the effects of un-insurance on health care access and quality in local health care markets. He is a member of the National Advisory Committee of the RWJF Health and Society Scholars Program and the RJWF Interdisciplinary Nursing Quality Research Initiative NAC.

ELIZABETH BARNETT PATHAK, PhD, MSPH, is an associate professor in the College of Public Health at the University of Southern Florida. She graduated with an MS in public health in 1990 and a PhD in philosophy in 1993 from University of North Carolina at Chapel Hill. Her training focus has been on epidemiology, and she has published research documents in maternal and child health, mental health, social class disparities, racial/ethnic disparities, geographic patterns of mortality, predictors of the use of percutaneous coronary intervention in ST—elevation myocardial infarction patients, predictors of mortality in myocardial infarction patients, and racial/ethnic disparities in stroke in young adults.

MELINDA PENNER graduated from Concordia University in Seward, Nebraska, with her BS in education, and then earned a BA in theology from Christ College in Irvine, California. She also completed her MA in philosophy of religion and ethics at Talbot School of Theology. She taught middle school in Christian schools until founding Stand to Reason with Greg Koukl and becoming director of operations.

CAROLYN F. PEVEY, PhD, is an associate professor of sociology at Germanna Community College in Fredericksburg, Virginia. Her primary academic interests are religion, gender, and death and society. Dr. Pevey teaches face to face, online, and hybrid Sociology courses. She is involved in the community through her volunteer work at Mary Washington Hospice.

MARYJO PRINCE-PAUL, PhD, APRN, ACHPN, is an associate professor in the School of Nursing at Case Western Reserve University in Cleveland, Ohio. Her research interests lie in palliative care, advanced practice nurse outcomes, relational communication with advanced cancer patients and their loved ones, oncology, and spirituality as a predictor of life completion.

KATHLEEN PUNTILLO, RN, DNS, FAAN, is a professor of physiological nursing and the co-director of the critical care/trauma specialty in the master's program at UCSF School of Nursing. Her research focuses on assessing and treating pain in critically ill and injured patients. Ms. Puntillo emphasizes assessment and treatment of postoperative and procedure-related pain as well as acute pain in ICU and emergency department patients. Her research program has evolved to include symptom management of dying ICU patients.

TIMOTHY E. QUILL, MD, is a professor of medicine, psychiatry, and medical humanities at the University of Rochester School of Medicine and Dentistry. He is also the director of the Center for Ethics, Humanities and Palliative Care, and a board-certified palliative care consultant in Rochester, New York. Quill has published and lectured about the doctor–patient relationship, with focus on end-of-life decision-making and discussing palliative care early. He is the author of *Physician-Assisted Dying: The Case for Palliative Care and Patient Choice, Caring for Patients at the End of Life: Facing an Uncertain Future Together,* and *A Midwife Through the Dying Process: Stories of Healing and Hard Choices at the End of Life.*

STEVEN READER, PhD, is an associate professor of geography at the University of South Florida. He specializes in geographic information systems (GIS), spatial statistics, and medical geography.

SONIA SALARI, PhD, is an associate professor in Human Development & Family Studies and an adjunct associate professor in the Center on Aging and Sociology at University of Utah. She is a sociologist interested primarily in the relationships middle aged and older persons have to informal family based networks as well as their use of formal community-based organizations and services. She focuses on diversity in these relationships, based on characteristics such as race, religion, ethnicity, age, gender, and marital status. Dr. Salari's research findings are used to advise victim's advocates, medical clinicians, policymakers, and community aging service practitioners.

ALLEN G. SANDLER, MD, is an associate professor emeritus of early childhood, speech-language pathology, and special education at Old Dominion University in Norfolk Virginia.

H. RUSSELL SEARIGHT, PhD, MPH, is an associate professor of psychology at Lake Superior State University. He is a past director of behavior medicine at Forest Park Hospital and a clinical associate professor of community and family medicine, Saint Louis University School of Medicine.

MARIA J. SILVEIRA, MD, is an assistant professor of internal medicine at the University of Michigan. Her clinical interest is in palliative care, and she specialized in internal medicine. Silveira graduated from SUNY at Stony Brook in 1996. Her research encompasses palliative care, medical ethics, and GIS health services.

JONATHAN SKINNER, PhD, is a professor of community and family medicine in the Dartmouth Medical School. His research interests are the determinants of health care spending and outcomes among different income groups in the Medicare population. He is currently studying how high- and low-income groups are treated differently for heart attacks and to what extent the better survival outcomes for high-income groups are the consequence of different treatment patterns. He has also studied redistributional effects of the Medicare system and the time-series pattern of catastrophic out-of-pocket expenditures. Related research in economics focuses on why households save and why so many households save virtually nothing for their retirement.

BETH J. SOLDO, PhD, is a distinguished senior scholar, Population Studies Center and adjunct professor, Department of Sociology, University of Pennsylvania.

CHARLES L. SPRUNG, JD, MD, is the director, General Intensive Care Unit and the Institute of Medicine, Ethics and Law at Hadassah Hebrew University Medical Center. He is a professor in the School of Law at the Hebrew

University of Jerusalem, teaching Medicine, Law, and Ethics. Dr. Sprung is the initiator and coordinator of the Annual Intern Basic and Advanced Cardiac Life Support course, as well as the director, Critical Care Fellowship Program at the University of Miami.

KELLI I. STAJDUHAR, RN, PhD, is an associate professor at the University of Victoria, School of Nursing and Center on Aging; an investigator for the Canadian Institutes for Health Research; and a research scholar with the Michael Smith Foundation for Health. Her research interests include palliative and end-of-life care; family caregiving; home care; HIV/AIDS; oncology; vulnerable and marginalized populations; gerontology; health services research; qualitative and quantitative research methods; mixed method study design; collaborative, participatory research.

DANIEL P. SULMASY, OFM, MD, PhD, is a Franciscan friar, internist, and ethicist. He is the Kilbride-Clinton Professor of Medicine and Ethics in the Department of Medicine and Divinity School at the University of Chicago, where he is also the associate director of the MacLean Center for Clinical Medical Ethics in the Department of Medicine. His research interests encompass both theoretical and empirical investigations of the ethics of end-of-life decision-making, ethics education, and spirituality in medicine. He has done extensive work on the role of intention in medical action, especially as it relates to the rule of double effect and the distinction between killing and allowing to die. His empirical studies have explored topics such as decision-making by surrogates on behalf of patients who are nearing death. He is a fellow of the Hastings Center and member of the Board of Advisors of the American Society for Bioethics and Humanities. He serves as the editor-in-chief of the journal *Theoretical Medicine and Bioethics*. His numerous articles have appeared in medical, philosophical, and theological journals.

RODNEY SYME, MD, is the vice-president of Dying with Dignity Victoria, and is a long-time voluntary euthanasia advocate. Rodney Syme has been in medical practice for 45 years, primarily as a urological surgeon. He was the chair of the Victorian Section of the Urological Society of Australasia in 1990–1992, and the chair of the Urology Study Group of the Cancer Council of Victoria in 1992–1994. He has had extensive experience with cancer patients and with people with severe spinal injuries. He has been an advocate for physician-assisted dying for nearly 20 years.

JEAN PAUL TANNER, MD, has been in the Birth Defects Surveillance Program, Department of Community and Family Health, College of Public Health, University of South Florida, Tampa, Florida; the Department of Pediatrics, College of Medicine, University of South Florida, Tampa, Florida; and the Bureau of Environmental Public Health Medicine, Division of Environmental Health, Florida Department of Health, Tallahassee, Florida.

KATHRYN L. TUCKER, JD, is the director of legal affairs for Compassion & Choices, a national nonprofit public interest organization dedicated to improving end-of-life care and expanding and protecting the rights of the terminally ill. Ms. Tucker practiced law with the Seattle-based law firm Perkins Coie prior to moving to Compassion & Choices. She is also an adjunct professor of law at the Lewis & Clark School of Law, teaching in the areas of law, medicine, and ethics, with a focus on the end of life. Ms. Tucker held similar faculty appointments at the University of Washington and Seattle University Schools of Law, for many years.

BEVERLY WARD, PhD, is an associate professor in research at the University of South Florida. She has been the assistant director of the Alabama Transit Association, the transportation director of the Birmingham Office of Senior Citizens Activities, a social worker in the Food Stamp Program of the Department of Human Resources, and the director of special projects with Family and Child Services.

L. S. WASSERMAN, RN, MSN, is an RN formerly with Western State Hospital, Tacoma, Washington.